P9-CKL-846

Hoover Institution Publications 124

A Chinese-English Dictionary of Communist Chinese Terminology

A Chinese-English Dictionary of Communist Chinese Terminology

Dennis J. Doolin

and

Charles P. Ridley

Hoover Institution Press
Stanford University
Stanford, California

The Hoover Institution on War, Revolution and Peace, founded at Stanford University in 1919 by the late President Herbert Hoover, is a center for advanced study and research on public and international affairs in the twentieth century. The views expressed in its publications are entirely those of the authors and do not necessarily reflect the views of the staff, officers, or Board of Overseers of the Hoover Institution.

Hoover Institution Publications 124
International Standard Book Number 0-8179-1241-X
Library of Congress Card Number 70-170210

Printed in the United States of America

Contents

Preface vii
Index of Radicals ix
Dictionary of Communist Chinese Terminology 1

Preface

PURPOSE AND SCOPE

This dictionary is intended for the reader or translator of current Chinese documents and is concerned primarily with words and phrases either coined or given new currency by the Chinese Communist Party and the government of the People's Republic of China. The individual entries furnish, whenever possible, a translation equivalent sanctioned by Communist Chinese usage in official translations prepared by various Chinese governmental organs. In many cases an entry includes not only a translation or equivalent of the term in question, but an elaboration or explanation of the term as well. Thus, for example, following the translation of the term 五反 "the Five-Anti," is a list of the Five-Anti themselves.

The dictionary covers the period from the founding of the Communist movement in the early 1920's to the present. Particular attention has been given to material dating from the establishment of the People's Republic of China in 1949, and within that time-span, emphasis has been given to the language of such movements as the "Great Leap Forward" and the "Great Proletarian Cultural Revolution."

While the basic concern of the dictionary is with political terminology, the entries cover as wide a range of related material as possible. The major types of vocabulary include the following:

1. Political terminology.
2. Chinese governmental organs and public organizations.
3. General philosophical terminology as related to Marxist and Communist ideology.
4. Chinese equivalents for the names of the major newspapers, periodicals, and press organizations of the United States, the Soviet Union, Eastern and Western European nations, Japan, and some other nations.
5. Chinese equivalents of the names of selected countries, cities, and rivers of the world.
6. Chinese equivalents for the names of major world figures.
7. Names of Chinese national minority groups.
8. General vocabulary felt to be of particular assistance to the reader of political documents.

INSTRUCTIONS FOR USE

1. The dictionary is arranged in the order of the traditional 214 radicals. For the convenience of the reader, a separate radical index has also been supplied. The Wade-Giles romanization and the full standard forms of the characters are used throughout.
2. The individual entries are set up with the Chinese characters first, followed by their romanization. Immediately following the romanization, is the body of the entry. This consists of a translation of or an equivalent for the Chinese term, and, where appropriate, an explanation or further elaboration of the term together with cross references as required. Explanatory material, when it occurs, is enclosed in parentheses.

3. The characters included under each radical are listed in order of increasing stroke counts in addition to the number of strokes in the radical itself. The radical and the number of additional strokes are indicated by headings. Thus, radical 9 begins with the compounds of 人 itself. Under each stroke group, the lead characters are arranged alphabetically by Wade-Giles romanization. For example, under the heading "-2 Strokes-" the characters are presented in the order 介 (chièh), 今 (chīn), 仇 (ch'óu), 仁 (jén), 仍 (jéng), and so on.

The second character of each term is arranged by the total number of strokes in that character. The number of strokes in the second character is shown by a superscript to the left of the entry. The superscript is used only to indicate the first of a group of second characters having a given number of strokes. Each character under any given superscript group is further arranged in alphabetical order by romanization. The third and succeeding characters in an entry are also arranged alphabetically. When characters in these positions are identical in pronunciation, they are arranged by radical order.

For example, the first three entries under radical 1 appear as follows:

[2]一二三制 **[í-èrh-sān chìh]**: the one-two-three system (the system whereby cadres spend one day per week studying, two days at meetings, and three days in work)

[3]一小撮 **[ì hsiăo-ts'ò]**: a handful of, a small number of (a contemptuous phrase indicating the small number of people who oppose Communist policy, the Party, or Mao)

一大二公 **[í tà èrh kūng]**: first, big in size; second, public in ownership; both great and public; greater in size and having a higher degree of public ownership (the basic characteristics of the commune)

The first character in all three entries, 一, is of course radical 1. The second character is the first entry, 二, has two strokes. This is indicated by the superscript [2] before the character entry. The second characters in the second and third entries, 小 and 大, respectively, both consist of three strokes, which is similarly indicated by the superscript [3] before the first of these entries. As can be seen, these characters are listed alphabetically, hsiăo (小) preceding tà (大). The romanization is shown in brackets and is followed immediately by the English equivalents. In these three cases, there are also explanations, which are included in parentheses.

ACKNOWLEDGMENT

We would like to express our deep thanks to Dr. Shau Wing Chan of the Department of Asian Languages, Stanford University, for his review of the manuscript of this dictionary and for the many valuable suggestions which he provided.

Index of Radicals

		pg.
1	一	1
2	丨	19
3	丶	26
4	丿	28
5	乙	29
6	亅	29
7	二	30
8	亠	35
9	人 亻	37
10	儿	62

		pg.
11	入	65
12	八	69
13	冂	74
14	冖	75
15	冫	75
16	几	77
17	凵	77
18	刀 刂	79
19	力	87
20	勹	92

		pg.
21	匕	94
22	匚	95
23	匸	95
24	十	96
25	卜	104
26	卩 㔾	105
27	厂	107
28	厶	109
29	又	110
30	口	114

		pg.
31	囗	132
32	土	140
33	士	151
34	夂	152
35	夊	152
36	夕	152
37	大	154
38	女	162
39	子	166
40	宀	168

		pg.			pg.			pg.			pg.
41	寸	179	51	干	197	62	戈	224	73	月	281
42	小	182	52	幺	199	63	户	228	74	曰	284
43	尢 兀 尣	184	53	广	199	64	手 扌	229	75	木	288
44	尸	184	54	廴	202	65	支	257	76	欠	303
45	屮	187	55	廾	203	66	攴 攵	258	77	止	304
46	山	187	56	弋	203	67	文	267	78	歹 歺	307
47	巛 川 巜	188	57	弓	204	68	斗	269	79	殳	309
48	工	189	58	彐 彑	206	69	斤	269	80	毋	310
49	己	192	59	彡	206	70	方	273	81	比	310
50	巾	193	60	彳	207	71	无 旡	275	82	毛	311
			61	心 忄 ⺗	211	72	日	275			

		pg.
83	氏	312
84	气	314
85	水 氵	315
86	火 灬	338
87	爪 爫	348
88	父	349
89	爻	349
90	爿	349
91	片	349
92	牙	350
93	牛 牜	350
94	犬 犭	353
95	玄	356
96	玉 王 ⺩	356
97	瓜	359
98	瓦	359
99	甘	360
100	生	360
101	用	363
102	田	363
103	疋	367
104	疒	367
105	癶	369
106	白	371
107	皮	372
108	皿	373
109	目 罒	374
110	矛	379
111	矢	379
112	石	380
113	示 礻	384
114	禸	387
115	禾	387
116	穴	392
117	立	395
118	竹 ⺮	396
119	米	401
120	糸 糹	404
121	缶	418
122	网 罒 ⺳	418
123	羊	420
124	羽	422
125	老	423
126	而	424

		pg.			pg.			pg.			pg.
127	耒	425	138	艮	441	149	言	464	160	辛	498
128	耳	425	139	色	441	150	谷	478	161	辰	499
129	聿	429	140	艸 艹	442	151	豆	478	162	辵 辶	501
130	肉 月	429	141	虍	451	152	豕	479	163	邑 阝	513
131	臣	433	142	虫	453	153	豸	479	164	酉	515
132	自	433	143	血	454	154	貝	479	165	釆	517
133	至	437	144	行	454	155	赤	486	166	里	517
134	臼	438	145	衣 衤	456	156	走	487	167	金	519
135	舌	439	146	襾	460	157	足	490	168	長 镸	524
136	舛	439	147	見	461	158	身	492	169	門	525
137	舟	440	148	角	463	159	車	493	170	阜 阝	529

		pg.
171	隶	536
172	隹	536
173	雨 ⻗	539
174	青	542
175	非	543
176	面	544
177	革	544
178	韋	546
179	韭	546
180	音	546
181	頁	547
182	風	551
183	飛	552
184	食	552
185	首	554
186	香	554
187	馬	555
188	骨	558
189	高	559
190	髟	560
191	鬥	561
192	鬯	561
193	鬲	561
194	鬼	561
195	魚	562
196	鳥	563
197	鹵	564
198	鹿	564
199	麥	564
200	麻	564
201	黃	565
202	黍	566
203	黑	566
204	黹	568
205	黽	568
206	鼎	568
207	鼓	568
208	鼠	569
209	鼻	569
210	齊	569
211	齒	569
212	龍	569
213	龜	569
214	龠	569

— RADICAL — 1 —

一

2 一二三制 **[í-èrh-sān chìh]**: the one-two-three system (the system whereby cadres spend one day a week studying, two days at meetings, and three days in work)

3 一小撮 **[i-hsiăo-t'sò]**: a handful of, a small number of (a contemptuous phrase indicating the small number of people who oppose Communist policy, the Party, or Mao)

一大二公 **[í tà èrh kūng]**: first, big in size; second, public in ownership; both great and public; greater in size and having a higher degree of public ownership (the basic characteristics of the commune)

4 一切歸公 **[í-ch'ièh kuēi-kūng]**: everything goes to the public (a derogatory phrase indicating the overzealousness of certain cadres in expropriating private property)

一分爲二 **[ì fēn wéi èrh]**: to divide one into two (the Marxist method of dialectical analysis which, in the Chinese interpretation, means that one must look at a person or work from two sides: the good features and the defects, the positive and negative factors–struggle of one against the other brings about progress in a person and uninterrupted development in work)

一夫一妻制 **[ì-fū ì-ch'ī chìh]**: monogamy

一心一意 **[ì-hsīn í-ì]**: one-minded, one-mindedness, wholehearted, to be intent on

一孔之見 **[ì-k'ŭng chīh chièn]**: a peep-hole view, a partial view

一片 **[í-p'ièn]**: one integral whole

一手抓生產，一手抓生活 **[ì-shŏu chuā shēng-ch'ăn, ì-shŏu chuā shēng-huó]**: to grasp production with one hand and to grasp livelihood with the other hand; to give attention both to production and to livelihood

一手扶植 **[ì-shŏu fú-chíh]**: to nurture, to foster single-handedly

一手拿鎗，一手拿鋤 **[ì-shŏu ná ch'iāng, ì-shou ná ch'ú]**: to hold a rifle in one hand and a hoe in the other (a slogan associated with the campaign for training militia in 1958)

一手包辦 **[ì-shŏu pāo-pàn]**: to stage-manage single-handedly

一元化 **[ì-yüán-huà]**: to unite; the principle of simplification

一元論 **[ì-yüán-lùn]**: monism

5 一丘之貉 **[ì-ch'īu chīh hó]**: jackals of the same lair, very much the same

一半農業中等學校 **[í-pàn núng-yèh chūng-tĕng hsüéh-hsiào]**: half-day agricultural secondary school

一本書主義 **[ì-pĕn shū chŭ-ì]**: one book doctrine

一打一拉的政策 **[ì-tă ì-lā te chèng-ts'è]**: policy of striking and stroking alternately, to hit and wheedle by turns

一代 **[í-tài]**: a generation

6 一成不變 **[ì-ch'éng pú-pièn]**: invariable, unalterable, unchangeable, immutable

一好帶四好，四好為一好 **[ì-hăo tài ssù-hăo, ssù-hăo wéi ì-hăo]**: one good brings about four goods, and the four goods lead to one good (i.e., being good in political work assures the attainment of four other goals, and if one is good in the first four goals, one can succeed in implementing plans–the five goods are 1) good in political work; 2) good in three-eight work style; 3) good in enterprise management; 4) good in managing one's livelihood; 5) good in implementing plans)

一向 **[í-hsiàng]**: hitherto, all along, always, consistently, continually

一行 **[ì-hsíng]**: a party, suite, retinue, or entourage

一回合 **[ì-húi-hó]**: a round (as in a round of fighting, etc.)

一共 **[í-kùng]**: all, altogether, wholly, totally, entirely

一再 **[í-tsài]**: repeatedly, time and again, again and again

一次革命論 **[í-tz'ù kó-mìng lùn]**: theory of a single revolution

7 一技之長 **[í-chì chīh ch'áng]**: skilled in some kind of work

一兵多用 **[ì-pīng tō-yùng]**: every soldier capable of many uses

8 一知半解 **[ì-chīh pàn-chiěh]**: half-baked knowledge, scanty knowledge

一事一議 **[í-shìh í-ì]**: discussion of everything that occurs

一定 **[í-tìng]**: certain, positive, definite, determinate; certainly, positively

一定程度 **[í-tìng ch'éng-tù]**: to a certain extent, to a certain degree

一定間隔 **[í-tìng chièn-kó]**: regular interval

一味 **[í-wèi]**: completely, uniformly, persistently

9 一竿子通到底 **[ì-kān-tzu t'ūng tào-tǐ]**: to carry down to the grass roots

一厘錢 **[ì-lí ch'ién]**: one tenth of one cent (the smallest denomination of Chinese currency–the "i-li ch'ien" spirit is that of saving in material worth even the smallest fraction of a cent in production)

一律 **[í-lǜ]**: uniformly, equally, without distinction

一面之詞 **[í-mièn chīh tz'ú]**: one-sided statement

一面倒 **[í-mièn tǎo]**: to lean to one side, to favor one side

一神教 **[ì-shén-chiào]**: monotheism

一神會 **[ì-shén-hùi]**: Unitarian Church

一度 **[í-tù]**: once, at one time, on one occasion

10 一針見血 **[ì-chēn chièn hsüěh]**: to hit the nail on the head, to put one's finger on the weak spot immediately; pertinent argument, cogent argument

一級准尉 **[ì-chí chŭn-wèi]**: Chief Warrant Officer (U.S. Army and Air Force); Commissioned Warrant Officer (U.S. Navy)

一記耳光 **[í-chì ěrh-kuāng]**: to receive a slap, a box on the ears

一紙空文 **[ì-chǐh k'ūng-wén]**: a mere scrap of paper, a scrap of waste paper

一致 **[í-chìh]**: uniform, identical, consistent; unanimity, unity, solidarity

一致性 **[í-chìh-hsìng]**: uniformity, identity, consistency, solidarity

一致行動 **[í-chìh hsíng-tùng]**: concerted action, uniform action

一致意見 **[í-chìh ì-chièn]**: unity of views, harmony of views, consensus, consensus of opinion

一致對外 **[í-chìh tùi-wài]**: unity against the outside (world), unity against foreign (aggression)

一致同意 **[í-chìh t'úng-ì]**: to agree on unanimously

一祝，二唱，三讀 **[í-chù, èrh-ch'àng, sān-tú]**: firstly invoke a blessing, secondly sing, thirdly read (a phrase fixing the formula for public meetings: a meeting should start with a wish for Chairman Mao expressed by twice repeating the slogan "May Chairman Mao live for millions and millions of years," which should be followed by the singing of "Sailing the Seas Depends on the Helmsman," which in turn should be followed by the reading of quotations from Mao)

一脈相承 **[í-mò hsiāng-ch'éng]**: to be imbued with the same spirit, to be a disciple of

一般號召 **[ì-pān hào-chào]**: general directive

一般化領導 **[ì-pān-huà lǐng-tǎo]**: the same general methods of leadership for everything

一般社會人士 **[ì-pān kūng-tsò jén-yüán]**: the rank and file of the working personnel

一般社會人士 **[ì-pān shè-hùi jén-shìh]**: social figures at large

一般與個別相結合 **[ì-pān yǚ kò-piéh hsiāng-chiéh-hó]**: to link the general with the specific

一時 **[ì-shíh]**: passing, for the moment

一時沈寂 **[ī-shíh ch'én-chí]**: momentary lull, respite

一時性 **[ī-shíh-hsìng]**: nonpersistency, temporariness

一套 **[í-t'ào]**: a set, way, the sort of things, the same pattern of behavior

一套大道理 **[í-t'ào tà tào-lǐ]**: high-sounding talk, a lot of high-flown principles

一鬥，二批，三改 **[í-tòu, èrh-p'ī, sān-kǎi]**: one struggle, two criticisms, and three reformations (refers to the resolution concerning the Cultural Revolution passed by the CCP Central Committee on August 8, 1966, in which the purposes of the revolution were set as follows: "At present, our targets are to *struggle* and bring down those power-holders who are travelling on the road to capitalism, to *criticize* the reactionary academic authorities of the bourgeoisie, *criticize* the ideologies of the bourgeoisie and all the exploiting classes, and to *reform* education, *reform* literature, and *reform* all the upper structures that do not harmonize with the socialist economic foundation, thus to be conducive to the consolidation and development of the socialist system."–from Point I of the 16 Points 十六條, q.v.)

一院制 **[í-yüàn-chìh]**: unicameral legislative system, one chamber legislative system

11 一專多能 **[ì-chuān tō-néng]**: one specialty and many skills, mastering many skills while specializing in one

一桿子插到底 **[ì kǎn-tzu ch'ā tào-tǐ]**: to get to the bottom by one pole (to go straight to the bottom of things when investigating problems)

一貫 **[í-kuàn]**: consistent, invariable, uniform, without exception

一掃而空 **[ì-sǎo érh k'ūng]**: to sweep away in a moment, to make a clean sweep of

一視同仁 **[í-shìh t'úng-jén]**: to give equal treatment, to treat equally, without discrimination

一帶二 **[í tài èrh]**: one guides two (the leading of two backward production teams by one advanced one in order to turn the former into advanced teams)

12 一週評論 **[ì-chōu p'íng-lùn]**: review of the week

一棍子打死 **[í kùn-tzu tǎ-ssǔ]**: to kill with one blow, to shatter at one stroke, to deal a fatal blow

一勞永逸 **[ì-láo yǔng-ì]**: with one effort to achieve eternal ease; to set things aright once and for all

一等 **[ì-těng]**: first class

一等兵 **[ì-těng-pīng]**: Lance-Corporal (British Army); Leading Seaman (British Navy)

一等射手 **[ì-těng shè-shǒu]**: sharpshooter

1

一無是處 **[ì wú shìh ch'ù]**: there is not a single merit

13 一意孤行 **[í-ì kū-hsíng]**: to persist in wilfully and arbitrarily, to act in disregard of others' opinions, to act in isolation

一碗水端平 **[i-wăn shŭi tuān-p'íng]**: holding a bowl of water steady (i.e., to be fair to all parties concerned—during the "Unity" campaign following the 9th CCP National Congress, leading cadres of the Revolutionary Committees were asked to treat the revolutionary mass organizations on an equal basis, not favoring one faction at the expense of another)

14 一綫生機 **[í-hsièn shēng-chī]**: a thread of hope or vitality; a last hope

一鼻孔出氣 **[ì pí-k'ŭng ch'ū-ch'ì]**: to breathe through the same nose; i.e., to toe the line of

一團和氣 **[ì-t'uán hó-ch'ì]**: to maintain harmony all around, harmony for the sake of harmony

15 一窮二白 **[ì ch'iúng èrh pái]**: firstly poor and secondly blank, poverty and blankness; i.e., economically poor and culturally blank (a phrase used to indicate that China is not developed economically and is like blank paper on which the new can be written)

一概而論 **[í-kài érh lùn]**: to lump together under one discussion heading

一概排斥 **[í-kài p'ái-ch'ìh]**: to ostracize without discrimination

一輪 **[ì-lún]**: a round (as in a round of fighting), a turn

一輩子 **[í-pèi-tzu]**: a lifetime

17 一環 **[ì-huán]**: a link (as in a chain)

一顆紅心，兩種準備 **[ì-k'ō húng-hsīn, liăng-chŭng chŭn-pèi]**: one red heart; two preparations (i.e., students should be ready either to go on to higher schools or to become farm laborers)

一幫一，一對紅 **[ì pāng ī, í-tùi húng]**: with one assisting another, a couple will become red (i.e., someone who is "red" helps someone who is not so that both will be "red")

一點兩面戰術 **[ì-tiĕn liăng-mièn chàn-shù]**: one-point two-plane tactics (an attack in which an overwhelmingly superior number of troops is used to break through a point in the enemy line, followed by plunges at the flanks and encirclement to cut off the rear)

18 一竅不通 **[í-ch'iào pù-t'ūng]**: to be ignorant of, to know nothing of

19 一邊倒 **[ì-piēn tào]**: to lean to one side, to favor (i.e., to join the communist camp)

20 一觸即發 **[í-ch'ù chí fā]**: touch-and-go, explosive, ready to go off at a touch, at an explosive point

21 一攬子計劃 **[ì lăn-tzu chì-huà]**: a package plan, a package deal

— 1 Stroke —

3 七三佈告 **[ch'ī-sān pù-kào]**: July 3 Notice (on July 3, 1968, the CCP Central Committee, the State Council, the Central Military Commission, and the Central Group in Charge of the Cultural Revolution jointly issued a notice to the "proletarian revolutionaries and the revolutionary broad masses" of Kwangsi Autonomous Region, calling upon them to (a) stop fighting at once; (b) unconditionally return goods they had taken away by force and which were intended for shipment to Vietnam; and (c) unconditionally return weapons and equipment they had stolen from the PLA—the notice was also said to be applicable to other provinces as well)

10 七員 **[ch'ī-yüán]**: the seven personnel (the seven leading cadre members in a production team, including the team chief, the assistant team chief or chiefs, the accountants, the stock controller, the production manager, and the work point recorder)

19 七類份子 **[ch'í-lèi fèn-tzu]**: seven categories of bad elements (i.e., landlords, rich peasants, counterrevolutionaries, Rightists,

bad elements, bourgeois, and black gangsters; the first five are the same as those referred to in the phrase "five categories of bad elements" 五類份子, while the last two were added to the list after the emergence of the Red Guards-black gangsters are CCP cadres and writers who do not conform to Mao's teachings)

丁

丁加奴 **[tīng-chiā-nú]**: Trenganu (Malaya)

丁是丁卯是卯 **[tīng shìh tīng, mǎo shìh mǎo]**: certain, absolute

— 2 Strokes —

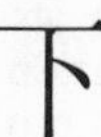

1 下一級 **[hsià ì-chí]**: the next lower level

下一次的 **[hsià í-tzʻù te]**: next, coming, forthcoming

3 下士 **[hsià-shìh]**: Corporal (U.S. Army); Petty Officer 3rd Class (U.S. Navy); Petty Officer 2nd Class (British Navy)

4 下中農 **[hsià-chūng-núng]**: lower middle peasant (**See** 中農)

下水 **[hsià-shüi]**: to launch, to enter the water, to go downstream

下水道 **[hsià-shüi-tào]**: sewer, sewerage, drain

5 下去 **[hsià-chʻü]**: to go down (said of eminent persons who are making inspection tours)

下令取消 **[hsià-lìng chʻü-hsiāo]**: to order an end to, to call off

下半旗 **[hsià pàn-chʻí]**: to fly a flag at half-mast

下台 **[hsià tʻái]**: to step down from the stage, to step down, to leave the scene, to be deprived of office, to lose one's job, to give up office

8 下放 **[hsià-fàng]**: to send down, to send down to lower levels, to send to the countryside from the city

下放幹部 **[hsià-fàng kàn-pù]**: to transfer cadre to lower levels

9 下降 **[hsià-chiàng]**: to drop, to fall, to decline, to decrease; drop, fall, decline, decrease, downtrend, downslide, downturn, reduction; downward

下限 **[hsià-hsièn]**: lower limit

10 下級 **[hsià-chí]**: lower class, subordinates; subordinate, lower, junior

下級軍官 **[hsià-chí chün-kuān]**: junior officers

下級服從上級 **[hsià-chí fú-tsʻúng shàng-chí]**: the lower level subordinates itself to the higher level

下馬觀花 **[hsià-mǎ kuān-huā]**: to get off one's horse and examine the flowers; (i.e., to make a slow, careful inspection)

下班 **[hsià-pān]**: to be off duty, to go off duty

11 下問 **[hsià-wèn]**: to inquire, to consult, to ask a question of a subordinate

下野 **[hsià-yěh]**: to retire from political office, retirement from political office

12 下等 **[hsià-těng]**: low-class, base, inferior, vulgar, unrefined, rude

下等人 **[hsià-těng jén]**: low-class people (a backward cadre's view of the "progressive masses")

下游 **[hsià-yú]**: downstream, lower reaches of a river

下游危險 **[hsià-yú wéi-hsiĕn]**: it is dangerous to fall behind others (**See** 甘居中游)

13 下意識 **[hsià-ì-shìh]**: subconsciousness

下落 **[hsià-lò]**: whereabouts

14 下場 **[hsià-chʻǎng]**: to leave the stage (both in a literal and a figurative sense)

15 下層 **[hsià-ts'éng]**: lower stratum, subordinate level

19 下轎 **[hsià-chiào]**: to get down from a sedan-chair (a demand that high-living Communist Party members unite with and serve the people)

20 下議院 **[hsià-ì-yüàn]**: House of Commons, the Lower House, Chamber of Deputies

三

三 K 黨 **[sān K tăng]**: Ku Klux Klan

2 三七制 **[sān-ch'í chìh]**: the three-seven system (a system used in mountainous regions whereby cadres spend three days in meetings, inspections, etc., and the next seven days in the fields)

三七指示 **[sān-ch'ī chĭh-shìh]**: March 7 Directive (a directive issued on March 7, 1967 by Mao Tse-tung stating that the army should give political and military training in the universities, secondary schools, and higher grades of primary schools, that it should help in the reopening of schools, strengthening organizations, and setting up leading bodies on the principle of the Three-Way Alliance, and that in giving political and military training, it should not exclude teachers and cadres who had made mistakes in the past)

三八作風 **[sān-pā tsò-fēng]**: three-eight working style (three phrases and eight characters written by Mao to describe the working style that officers and men were exhorted to adopt–the three phrases are "correct political direction," "simple and arduous working style," and "flexible strategy and tactics;" the eight characters are 團結 [unity], 緊張 [earnestness], 嚴肅 [seriousness], and 活潑 [activeness])

三八運動 **[sān-pā yǜn-tùng]**: the three-eight movement (**See** 三八作風)

三十年代 **[sān-shíh nién-tài]**: the nineteen thirties (refers specifically to the period 1927–1937)

3 三三制 **[sān-sān chìh]**: the three-three system (a system whereby one-third of the cadres are transferred permanently to lower level offices, one-third are sent on provincial inspection tours, and one-third remain in the provincial offices)

三大紀律, 八項注意 **[sān tà chì-lǜ, pá hsiàng chù-ì]**: The Three Main Rules of Discipline and the Eight Points for Attention (the three rules are: 1) obey orders in all actions; 2) do not take even a needle or a thread from the masses; 3) turn in everything that is captured; the eight points are: 1) speak politely; 2) pay fairly for what you buy; 3) return everything you borrow; 4) pay for anything you damage; 5) do not hit or swear at people; 6) do not damage crops; 7) do not take liberties with women; 8) do not ill-treat captives)

三大任務 **[sān tà jèn-wù]**: the three main tasks (i.e., to grasp revolution, promote production, and promote the preparation for war; a slogan that first appeared in the Chinese press in January 1968 and which was adopted from the earlier slogan 抓革命, 促生產, 促工作, 促戰備, q.v.)

三大革命運動 **[sān tà kó-mìng yǜn-tùng]**: the three great revolutionary movements (i.e., class struggle, struggle for production, and scientific experimentation)

三大觀點 **[sān tà kuān-tiĕn]**: the three great viewpoints (i.e., political viewpoint, production viewpoint, and mass viewpoint)

三大民主 **[sān tà mín-chŭ]**: the three democracies (pertains to the People's Liberation Army during the War of Liberation, 1945–1949: 1) politically, officers and men should feel equal and free to air their views; 2) economically, soldiers should take part in the management of mess halls; 3) militarily, officers and men should follow the principle of helping one another to become red)

三大作風 **[sān tà tí-jén]**: the three big enemies (i.e., imperialism, feudalism, and bureaucratic capitalism)

三大敵人 **[sān tà tsò-fēng]**: the three great work styles (i.e., firm and correct political direction, arduous and plain work style, and agile and mobile strategy and tactics)

4 三支二軍 **[sān-chīh èrh-chūn]**: support three things and carry out two military tasks (after the PLA was called upon to intervene in the Cultural Revolution in January 1967 it was expected to support the leftist masses, support industry, and support agriculture as well as to exercise control over every phase of the people's life and to carry out military training for the Red Guards)

三反 **[sān-fǎn]**: the three anti (anti-corruption, anti-waste, and anti-bureaucratism (*See* 反貪汚)

三反份子 **[sān-fǎn . fèn-tzu]**: three anti elements (during the Cultural Revolution, this term referred to those who were alleged to be anti-Party, anti-Mao Tse-tung's thought, anti-Socialism–crimes attributed to Liu Shao-ch'i and his followers)

三反雙減 **[sān-fǎn shuāng-chiěn]**: the three anti and the double reduction (a policy for the improvement of the conditions of the Tibetans after suppression of the 1960 rebellion–the three anti are: 1) anti-rebellion; 2) anti-corvée; 3) anti-slavery; the double reduction is: 1) reduction in land rent; 2) reduction in interest rate)

三反運動 **[sān-fǎn yǜn-tùng]**: the San Fan movement, the Three Anti movement (a campaign against corruption, waste, and bureaucratism)

三化 **[sān-huà]**: the three changes, the three "-izations" (pertains to the communes, and refers to militarization of organization, martialization of action, and collectivization of life)

三不滿 **[sān pù-mǎn]**: the three dissatisfactions (in educational work: 1) the bad effects of dormitory overcrowding on student health; 2) schools being too far; 3) administrative difficulties because of poor construction plans for school buildings)

三不怕精神 **[sān pú-p'à chīng-shén]**: the three no-fear spirit (athletic trainees should not fear hardship, fatigue, or injury)

5 三民主義 **[sān-mín chǔ-ì]**: the Three Principles of the People (these are the principles enunciated by Sun Yat-sen and include 民族 people's race [nationalism], 民生 people's livelihood [socialism], and 民權 people's rights [democracy])

三包一獎 **[sān-pāo ì-chiǎng]**: three contracts and one reward (a system of fixed targets for output, workdays, and costs, with a part of the extra output as reward)

三平 **[sān-p'íng]**: Tambinh (Vietnam)

三史 **[sān-shǐh]**: the three histories (for peasants, histories of families, villages, and communes; for workers, histories of families, factories or mines, and revolutionary struggles)

三右 **[sān-yù]**: the three rightisms (i.e., rightist opportunism, rightist capitulationism, and rightist splitism)

6 三好 **[sān-hǎo]**: the three goods (in military terms, unification, discipline, and combat)

三好學生 **[sān-hǎo hsüéh-shēng]**: the three-good student (a phrase coined by Mao in September 1955 to indicate that students should exhibit good health, good study, and good work: 身體好, 學習好, 工作好)

三光政策 **[sān-kuāng chèng-ts'è]**: the three-nil policy, the three atrocity policy (a scorched-earth policy of burn all, kill all, loot all)

三光四不留 **[sān-kuāng ssù-pù-líu]**: three emptying and four no-retaining (a phrase from the Cultural Revolution indicating that under the influence of Liu Shao-ch'i the peasants in the People's Communes were encouraged to share everything, eat everything, and use up everything, and to reserve no commune fund, no welfare fund, no food grain, and no production fund–these evil practices were to be eliminated by the "Combat Selfishness and Repudiate Revisionism" campaign)

三老 **[sān-lǎo]**: the three elders (i.e., elderly peasants, elderly Communist Party members, and elderly cadres; those who fought the Kuomintang, rich peasants, and bad social elements of the "old" society)

三老幹部 **[sān-lăo kàn-pù]**: the three old cadres (i.e., "old and sick cadres," "old and good cadres," and "old cadres over the age of 60," who during the Cultural Revolution were regarded as harmless and therefore fit to be included in the Great Revolutionary Alliance and the Three-Way Alliance)

三老四嚴 **[sān-lăo ssù-yén]**: honest in three ways and strict in four aspects (to act as an honest person, speak honest words, and do honest deeds; to be strict in demands on oneself, strict in organization, strict in attitude, and strict in discipline)

三同 **[sān-t'úng]**: the three togethers (to eat, live, and labor together)

三自一包 **[sān-tzù ì-pāo]**: three freedoms and one contract (the three freedoms: 1) extension of plots of land for private production; 2) free markets; 3) increase of private enterprise; the one contract: the allowing of each household to assume a contracted obligation toward the state for producing a fixed quantity of grain)

7 三角洲 **[sān-chiăo-chōu]**: delta

三抓 **[sān-chuā]**: the three grabs in mediation work (1) to grab the case in order to determine the cause of the dispute; 2) to grab the thoughts of the disputants; 3) to grab and make use of the strength and help of relatives, friends, and activists)

三改 **[sān-kăi]**: the three changes (in the austerity program, 1) coarse rice instead of polished rice; 2) congee or thin rice instead of dry cooked rice; 3) bran, not grain, for poultry feed)

三位一體 **[sān-wèi ì-t'ĭ]**: the Trinity (a group in Heilungchiang that was a precursor of the 三結合)

8 三忠於運動 **[sān chūng-yű yǜn-tùng]**: the three loyalties movement (a movement launched in the spring of 1968 urging the masses, and particularly the armed forces, to be "forever loyal to Chairman Mao, forever loyal to Mao Tse-tung's Thought, and forever loyal to Chairman Mao's revolutionary line")

三和一少 **[sān-hó ì-shăo]**: three reconciliations and one reduction (a phrase used by Chou En-lai in a report at the First Session of the 3rd National People's Congress, December 22, 1964, which revealed that in 1959–1962, there were some who wanted to come to a reconciliation with the imperialists, the reactionaries, and the modern revisionists and to reduce aid to other peoples in revolt)

三門幹部 **[sān-mén kān-pù]**: three-door cadres (cadres who have little or no contact with the workers and peasants and who are said to have left the family *doors* only to enter school and university *doors*, and thereafter to have entered the *doors* of government offices–a term from the Cultural Revolution)

三定 **[sān-tìng]**: the three fixings (determination of production, purchase, and sale)

三定一頂 **[sān-tìng ì-tĭng]**: the three fixes and one substitution (a system governing cadre participation in labor that requires them to 1) report to work at fixed hours; 2) labor for a fixed length of time each day; 3) assume fixed responsibilities toward production and to take fixed posts in a productive force; and 4) be able to do the jobs of the ordinary workers so that they can take their places)

9 三查運動 **[sān-ch'á yǜn-tùng]**: three check-ups campaign (during the Cultural Revolution, checking up on die-hard capitalist roaders, renegades and spies of the unreformed landlords, rich peasants, counterrevolutionaries, bad elements, and Rightists in order to eliminate them)

三重 **[sān-ch'úng]**: Mie (Japan)

三軍 **[sān-chün̄]**: the three armed services

三風 **[sān-fēng]**: the three styles (the three bad styles of work: bureaucratism, sectarianism, and subjectivism)

三降一滅 **[sān-hsiáng í-mièh]**: three capitulations and one abolition (a phrase used during the Cultural Revolution by the Mao-

Lin faction to sum up the crimes committed by Liu Shao-ch'i in China's external policies–namely, of capitulating to the imperialists, the Soviet revisionists, and the foreign reactionaries and of seeking to abolish the anti-imperialist struggle of the suppressed people of the world)

三紅 **[sān-húng]**: the Three Reds (the Proletarian Headquarters, the People's Liberation Army, and the Revolutionary Committees–a term from the Cultural Revolution)

三革命化 **[sān kó-mìng-huà]**: the three revolutionizations (to revolutionize enterprises, personnel, and government organs)

三面紅旗 **[sān-mièn húng-ch'í]**: the Three Red Banners (of the General Line of Socialist Construction, the Great Leap Forward, and the People's Communes)

三段論法 **[sān-tuàn lùn-fǎ]**: syllogism

三段式 **[sān-tuàn-shìh]**: triad

10 三級政府委員會 **[sān-chí chèng-fǔ wěi-yüán-hùi]**: three-level government councils (government councils at the village, district, and county levels)

三級所有 **[sān-chí sŏ-yŭ]**: three-level system of ownership (i.e., of the means of production in the communes)

三級所有，隊爲基礎 **[sān-chí sŏ-yŭ, tùi wéi chī-ch'ŭ]**: three-level ownership with the production team as the base–an early stage in the People's Communes (*See* 三級所有)

三家村 **[sān-chiā ts'ūn]**: "The Three-Family Village" (the title of a series of newspaper columns written by Wu Han, Teng T'o, and Liao Mo-sha which were considered subtle attacks against the Communist Party–"The Three-Family Village" became an object of attack during the Cultural Revolution, and was then also referred to as 黑店, "black inn," a primitive roadside hotel operated by gangsters to rob and murder travellers)

三害 **[sān-hài]**: three calamities (a phrase first used in an editorial in the Wen Hui Pao, Shanghai, in reference to "factionalism," "anarchism," and "economism," said to be the weapons employed by Liu Shao-ch'i to obstruct the work of the Revolutionary Committees)

三夏三秋 **[sān-hsià sān-ch'īu]**: the three summers and the three autumns (the three summers are: 1) summer harvesting; 2) summer planting; and 3) summer hoeing; the three autumns are: 1) autumn harvesting; 2) autumn plowing; and 3) autumn sowing)

三個差別 **[sān-kò ch'ā-piéh]**: the three differences (the differences between town and country, worker and peasant, and mental and physical labor)

三流子變工隊 **[sān-líu-tzu pièn-kūng-tùi]**: idlers transformation work squad

三座大山 **[sān-tsò tà-shān]**: the three big mountains (imperialism, feudalism, and bureaucratic capitalism–during the Cultural Revolution the phrase was used to refer to imperialism, modern revisionism, and reactionaries in other countries)

11 三基工作 **[sān-chī kūng-tsò]**: the "three basics" work (基層工作 basic level work, 基礎工作 basic work, and 練基本功 practicing basic tasks)

三强 **[sān–ch'iáng]**: the three strongs (strong in labor force, cattle, and land)

三國協商 **[sān-kuó hsiéh-shāng]**: triple entente

三國協定 **[sān-kuó hsiéh-tìng]**: tripartite agreement

三國協約 **[sān-kuó hsiéh-yüēh]**: triple entente

三猛戰術 **[sān-měng chàn-shù]**: the three-fierce strategy (penetrating advance, fierce blow, and hard pursuit–a tactic used primarily against a retreating enemy)

三參一改 **[sān-ts'ān ì-kǎi]**: three participations and one improvement (a system for improving the operation and management of commercial enterprises in which cadres take part in physical labor, workers and staff in administration, and the masses in supervision)

12 三結合 **[sān chiéh-hó]**: 1) Triple Alliance

(during the Cultural Revolution, an alliance of leading members of revolutionary mass organizations, leading members of local PLA units, and revolutionary leading cadres of Party and Government organizations in setting up provincial organs of power "to ensure thorough victory in the struggle to seize power"); 2) the three combined, three-in-one (coordination between leading cadres, workers, and technical personnel)

三等兵 **[sān-tĕng-pīng]**: Ordinary Seaman (British Navy)

三無兩全論 **[sān-wú liăng-ch'üán lùn]**: the theory of three noes and two alls (the three noes are "no rebels, no conservatives, and no capitalist roaders; the two alls are "all people are leftists," and an "all-people election should be held"–the phrase appears in the Chekiang Daily of December 14, 1968, revealing that there were people who believed that "the struggle between two lines" was over, that everybody should be regarded as a leftist and that an all-people election should be held; this was tantamount to a total annulment of the Cultural Revolution)

13 三過思想 **[sān-kuò ssū-hsiăng]**: the three "passing" concepts, the three concepts of getting by (an attitude on the part of young intellectuals in the fields of science and technology advocating 1) passive attitude toward politics, 2) acquisition of advanced professional skills, and 3) the living of comfortable lives)

三落實 **[sān lò-shíh]**: carrying out work properly in three aspects

14 三對比 **[sān tùi-pĭ]**: three comparisons (whereby the peasants are urged to compare 1) the present with the past, 2) the good features of present life and socialism with the promise of full communism in the future, and 3) the shortcomings of present life and socialism with the promise of full communism in the future)

16 三憶三比 **[sān-ì sān-pĭ]**: three recollections and three comparisons (a phrase that first appeared in the People's Daily on October 26, 1967, indicating that participants in the Studying Group of Mao Tse-tung's Thought are to "remember the bitterness of the old society and contrast it to the sweetness of the new society; remember the nurture and education given them by the Party and compare these with their own contribution to the Party; remember the crimes committed by the 'power-holders' and compare them with the tremendous achievements of the Cultural Revolution")

18 三關 **[sān-kuān]**: the three passes (the three fears of poor peasants who want to join a cooperative: 1) uncertainty whether applications will be accepted; 2) uncertainty whether they can pay the membership fee; and 3) uncertainty, if accepted, whether they will be allowed to hire themselves out as day laborers during slack periods)

19 三寶壟 **[sān-păo-lŭng]**: Semarang (Indonesia)

上

1 上一級 **[shàng-ì-chí]**: the next higher level

上一級黨委 **[shàng-ì-chí tăng-wĕi]**: the next higher Party committee

3 上川鐵路 **[shàng-ch'uān t'iĕh-lù]**: the Shangchuan Railway (the railroad line from 慶寧 [Ch'ingning] to 川沙 [Chuansha])

上士 **[shàng-shìh]**: Sergeant 1st Class (U.S. Army); Petty Officer 1st Class (U.S. Navy); Staff Sergeant (British Army); Flight Sergeant (British Air Force); Chief Petty Officer (British Navy)

4 上中農 **[shàng-chūng-núng]**: upper middle peasant

上升 **[shàng-shēng]**: to rise, to mount, to climb; ascendance, ascendancy, upturn; mounting

5 上台 **[shàng-t'ái]**: to step up onto the stage, to come into power, to assume office, to take office

7 上車 **[shàng-ch'ē]**: to entrain, to entruck

上沃爾特共和國 **[shàng-wò-ĕrh-t'è kùng-hó-kuó]**: Republic of Upper Volta

8 上坡 **[shàng-p'ō]**: upgrade, ascending grade, uphill

上風 **[shàng-fēng]** : upwind, advantage

上限 **[shàng-hsièn]** : upper limit

上南鐵路 **[shàng-nán t'iěh-lù]** : Shangnan Railway (周家渡 Chowkiatu to 周浦 Chowpu)

上映 **[shàng-yìng]** : to show, to be on show; to screen a moving picture

10 上級 **[shàng-chí]** : upper-class, higher authorities, superior grades; superior, of a higher grade

上級機關 **[shàng-chí chī-kuān]** : higher authorities, higher organs

上將 **[shàng-chiàng]** : General (Chinese Army and Air Force); Admiral (Chinese Navy); Colonel General (Soviet Army and Air Force); Air Chief Marshal (British Air Force)

上海人民公社臨時委員會 **[shàng-hǎi jén-mín kūng-shè lín-shíh wěi-yüán-hùi]** : Temporary Committee of the Shanghai People's Commune (an organization formed during the Cultural Revolution in 1967)

上海港務管理局 **[shàng-hǎi kǎng-wù kuǎn-lǐ-chü]** : Shanghai Port Administration

上海市在農村下放工人革命委員會 **[shàng-hǎi-shìh tsài núng-ts'ūn hsià-fàng kūng-jén kó-mìng wěi-yüán-hùi]** : Shanghai City Revolutionary Committee of Workers Sent Down to Villages (Cultural Revolution)

上校 **[shàng-hsiào]** : Colonel (Chinese Army and Air Force); Captain (Navy); Group Captain (British Air Force)

上流 **[shàng-líu]** : upstream, the upper reaches of a stream; upper classes

上流人 **[shàng-líu jén]** : upper class people

上流社會 **[shàng-líu shè-hùi]** : the upper circles of society, rank and fashion

上馬 **[shàng-mǎ]** : to mount a horse; to assume office, to assume authority, to assume power

上班 **[shàng-pān]** : to go on duty, to go to work; first shift

11 上船 **[shàng-ch'uán]** : to board a ship, to embark

上動下不動 **[shàng tùng hsià pú-tùng]** : the top moves but the bottom does not move (method of changing the upper structure while keeping the lower structure unchanged)

上尉 **[shàng-wèi]** : Captain (Chinese Army and Air Force); Lieutenant (Chinese Navy); Senior Lieutenant (Soviet armed forces); Flight Lieutenant (British Air Force)

12 上進心 **[shàng-chìn-hsīn]** : desire to advance

上訴 **[shàng-sù]** : to appeal

上等人 **[shàng-těng jén]** : member of the upper class, an upper class person

上游 **[shàng-yú]** : upstream, the upper reaches of a river

上游冒險 **[shàng-yú mào-hsiěn]** : it is risky to be ahead of others (*See* 甘居中游)

13 上當 **[shàng-tàng]** : to be tricked, to be deceived, to be cheated, to play into someone's hands

14 上演 **[shàng-yěn]** : to stage, to produce, to show

15 上層 **[shàng-ts'éng]** : upper stratum, superstratum, top personnel

上層建築 **[shàng-ts'éng chièn-chú]** : superstructure (both in a literal and a figurative sense; refers also to social and political organizations)

19 上繳 **[shàng-chiǎo]** : to pay in, to turn in

20 上議院 **[shàng-ì-yüàn]** : House of Lords (Great Britain)

上黨課 **[shàng tǎng-k'ò]** : to attend Party classes

— 3 Strokes —

1 不一致 **[pù-í-chìh]** : not in agreement, not

the same, not in concord, at variance, not uniform, not unanimous

不一而足 **[pù-ī érh tsú]**: common; it happens frequently

2 不二價 **[pú-èrh-chià]**: uniform price

不人道 **[pù-jén-tào]**: inhumane; inhumanity

3 不久 **[pù-chĭu]**: soon, shortly, before long

不凡 **[pù-fán]**: unusual, extraordinary

不下於 **[pú-hsià-yǜ]**: not less than

不干涉政策 **[pù-kān-shè chèng-ts′è]**: policy of non-intervention

不干預 **[pù-kān-yǜ]**: non-intervention

不三不四 **[pù-sān pú-ssù]**: neither one thing nor another

不上不下 **[pú-shàng pú-hsià]**: indefinite, inconvenient, to not know what to do

不上算 **[pú-shàng-suàn]**: unprofitable, not worth it; it does not pay

不大可能 **[pú-tà k′ŏ-néng]**: unlikely, improbable, not quite possible

4 不及 **[pù-chí]**: not as good as, not up to

不切實際的 **[pú-ch′ièh shíh-chì te]**: unrealistic, impractical

不切題 **[pú-ch′ièh-t′í]**: not on the subject, beside the mark, alien to the point

不止 **[pù-chĭh]**: not only

不中用的 **[pú-chùng-yùng te]**: useless, unserviceable, not fit for use

不分 **[pù-fēn]**: not distinguish between

不分輕重緩急 **[pù-fēn ch′īng-chùng huăn-chí]**: without regard to the degree of importance or urgency

不分晝夜 **[pù-fēn chòu-yèh]**: day and night, around the clock

不分敵我 **[pù-fēn tí-wŏ]**: not to distinguish between the enemy and ourselves, not to distinguish, without distinction or regard

不日 **[pú-jìh]**: shortly, soon, in a few days

不公開 **[pù-kūng-k′āi]**: private, not made public,

不公開審判 **[pù-kūng-k′āi shĕn-p′àn]**: to hold a hearing behind closed doors, to hear a case *in camera*

不公平的 **[pù-kūng-p′íng te]**: unfair, unjust, inequitable, partial

不毛之地 **[pù-máo chīh tì]**: barren soil, sterile land, arid land

不比任何人差 **[pù-pĭ jén-hó jén ch′à]**: second to no one, not inferior to anyone

不丹 **[pù-tān]**: Bhutan

不丹王國 **[pù-tān wáng-kuó]**: Kingdom of Bhutan

不友好的 **[pù-yŭ-hăo te]**: unfriendly

不予答覆 **[pù-yǚ tá-fù]**: to refrain from answering

5 不正常的 **[pú-chèng-ch′áng te]**: abnormal, unnatural, irregular, aberrant

不正當 **[pú-chèng-tāng]**: improper, unseemly, unjust, immoral, illegitimate, unwarranted, unjustified, devious

不出所料 **[pù-ch′ū sŏ-liào]**: not unexpected, not surprising, what was expected

不去幹 **[pú-ch′ü-kàn]**: to stay away from, to abstain from, to refrain from, to have nothing to do with, to take no part in

不乏 **[pù-fá]**: not lacking, sufficient

不以 ...為.. **[pù-ĭ. . .wéi. . .]**: not to consider as, not to regard as

不以爲意 **[pù-ĭ wéi-ì]**: to leave out of consideration, to pay no heed to

不甘居人後 **[pù-kān chǖ jén-hòu]**: unwilling to be outdone, unwilling to take second place

不甘心 [**pù-kān-hsīn**]: not reconciled to, unwilling

不可戰勝 [**pù-k'ŏ chàn-shèng**]: invincible, unconquerable

不可爭辯的 [**pù-k'ŏ chēng-pièn te**]: indisputable

不可解 [**pù-k'ŏ-chiĕh**]: incomprehensible

不可知論 [**pù-k'ŏ-chīh-lùn**]: agnosticism

不可輕視的 [**pù-k'ŏ ch'īng-shìh te**]: formidable, onerous, arduous, impossible to slight

不可救藥 [**pù-k'ŏ chìu-yào**]: incurable, irremediable, hopeless, incorrigible

不可捉摸 [**pù-k'ŏ chō-mō**]: elusive, evasive

不可缺少的 [**pù-k'ŏ ch'üēh-shăo te**]: indispensable, essential

不可分割 [**pù-k'ŏ fēn-kō**]: indivisible, integral, inseparable, inalienable

不可否認 [**pù-k'ŏ fŏu-jèn**]: undeniable, indisputable, irrefutable

不可想象的 [**pù-k'ŏ hsiăng-hsiàng te**]: inconceivable, unimaginable

不可移易的 [**pù-k'ŏ í-ì te**]: unshakeable, immovable, unalterable, invariable

不可開交 [**pù-k'ŏ k'āi-chiāo**]: endless, unthinkable

不可抗拒的 [**pù-k'ŏ k'àng-chǜ te**]: inviolable, irresistible

不可告人的動機 [**pù-k'ŏ kào-jén te tùng-chī**]: unspeakable, ulterior motives

不可克服的 [**pù-k'ŏ k'ò-fú te**]: insurmountable, insuperable, inconquerable

不可估計的 [**pù-k'ŏ kū-chì te**]: immeasurable, inestimable

不可避免的 [**pù-k'ŏ pì-miĕn te**]: inevitable, unavoidable, inescapable

不可勝數 [**pù-k'ŏ shēng-shŭ**]: innumerable, countless, numberless, incalculable

不可收拾 [**pù-k'ŏ shōu-shíh**]: unmanageable, out of hand

不可思議 [**pù-k'ŏ ssū-ì**]: incomprehensible, inconceivable, unthinkable, mysterious, inscrutable

不可調和的 [**pù-k'ŏ t'iáo-hó te**]: irreconcilable, implacable, uncompromising

不可阻擋的 [**pù-k'ŏ tsŭ-tăng te**]: irresistible, invincible

不可推諉的 [**pù-k'ŏ t'ūi-wĕi te**]: compelling, unavoidable, "unshirkable," something for which the responsibility cannot be delegated

不可動搖的 [**pù-k'ŏ tùng-yáo te**]: unwavering, unfaltering

不可逾越的 [**pù-k'ŏ yü-yüèh te**]: insurmountable, insuperable, unsurpassable

不白之冤 [**pù-pái chīh yüān**]: unjustified accusation, a wrong which has not been righted

不必要的 [**pú-pì-yào te**]: unnecessary, needless, superfluous, inexpedient, undesirable

不平常 [**pù-p'íng-ch'áng**]: remarkable, unique, unusual, extraordinary, rare

不平衡 [**pù-p'íng-héng**]: unbalanced, uneven, out of balance, out of equilibrium

不平等 [**pù-p'íng-tĕng**]: unequal, inequality

不平等條約 [**pù-p'íng-tĕng t'iáo-yüēh**]: the unequal treaties

不打擾 [**pù-tă-jăo**]: to leave alone, to spare the trouble, not to disturb or bother

不外 [**pú-wài**]: none other than, not beyond, nothing more than, merely, only

不由得 [**pù-yú-té**]: unconsciously, unintentionally, involuntarily; cannot help it

不用說 [**pú-yùng shuō**]: it goes without saying, needless to say, to say nothing of

6 不成器 [**pù-ch'éng-ch'ì**]: unfit, good-for-nothing

1

不成文的 **[pù-ch'éng-wén te]**: unwritten, to fail to look well or make any sense

不成問題 **[pù-ch'éng wèn-t'í]**: presents no problem, it is no problem

不合 **[pù-hó]**: disagreement, discord; not in agreement, to have a difference, to be at variance

不合理的 **[pù-hó-lĭ te]**: irrational, unreasonable, inconsistent, absurd

不合時宜的 **[pù-hó shíh-í te]**: inopportune, unseasonable, untimely, ill-timed, inexpedient

不合適 **[pù-hó-shìh]**: unsuitable, unfit; inappropriate

不合算 **[pù-hó-suàn]**: it does not pay; uneconomical

不合作 **[pù-hó-tsò]**: uncooperative

不合作主義 **[pù-hó-tsò chŭ-ì]**: principle of non-cooperation; passive resistance

不行 **[pù-hsíng]**: it will not do, it cannot be done; out of the question, no good

不朽的 **[pù-hsĭu te]**: immortal, undying, imperishable, eternal, perpetual, enduring

不如 **[pù-jú]**: inferior to, not equal to, not up to

不如意 **[pù-jú-ì]**: not to one's liking, dissatisfied, discontented

不考慮 **[pù-k'ăo-lǜ]**: not to consider, not to deliberate, to leave out of account

不列顛 **[pú-lièh-tiēn]**: Britain

不列顛帝國 **[pú-lièh-tiēn tì-kuó]**: British Empire

不再存在的 **[pú-tsài ts'ún-tsài te]**: defunct, no longer existing

不再存在的問題 **[pú-tsài ts'ún-tsài te wèn-t'í]**: a dead issue

7 不見得 **[pú-chièn-té]**: not necessarily so

不見得論 **[pú-chièn-té lùn]**: the theory of "I do not think so" (a phrase referring to the attitude of those who do not believe that the Cultural Revolution is necessary or that the losses due to the Cultural Revolution are "very, very small" and the gains from it "very, very great," an assertion made by Lin Piao–such scepticism was apparently prevalent during November and December 1968)

不住的 **[pú-chù te]**: incessantly, uninterruptedly

不含糊 **[pù-hán-hú]**: clear, unequivocal, unambiguous, explicit, well-defined

不利 **[pú-lì]**: harmful, adverse, injurious, detrimental, prejudicial, disadvantageous

不良 **[pù-liáng]**: bad, evil, unwholesome

不良傾向 **[pù-liáng ch'īng-hsiàng]**: unwholesome trend

不良份子 **[pù-liáng fèn-tzu]**: undesirable element

不良現象 **[pù-liáng hsièn-hsiàng]**: unhealthy phenomena, unhealthy tendencies

5 不良的政施 **[pù-liáng te chèng-shīh]**: maladministration

不妥協的 **[pù-t'ŏ-hsiéh te]**: uncompromising, unyielding, intransigent, unconciliatory

不足 **[pù-tsú]**: insufficient, inadequate; insufficiency, inadequacy, lack, shortage

不言而喻 **[pù-yén érh yǜ]**: obvious, self-evident

8 不承認 **[pù-ch'éng-jèn]**: non-recognition; not to recognize, not to admit

不承認主義 **[pù-ch'éng-jèn chŭ-ì]**: the principle of non-recognition

不承擔義務 **[pù-ch'éng-tān ì-wù]**: not to assume any obligation, to make no commitment, not to commit oneself; uncommitted

不咎既往 **[pú-chìu chì-wăng]**: not to go

into past misdeeds

不注意[**pú-chù-ì**]: to fail to pay attention to, to neglect, be negligent of, ignore, overlook, disregard, be unmindful of; inattention

不忠於[**pù-chūng-yǘ**]: to be disloyal, unfaithful, false, treacherous to

不法[**pù-fă**]: illegal, unlawful

不法行爲[**pù-fă hsíng-wéi**]: illegal activities, lawless behavior

不服上訴[**pù-fú shàng-sù**]: to appeal against, to lodge an appeal

不服從[**pù-fú-ts'úng**]: to disobey; disobedience, non-compliance, insubordination

不和[**pù-hó**]: discord, dissension, disagreement; at odds, at variance, on bad terms

不幸[**pú-hsìng**]: misfortune, bad luck, distress, adversity; unfortunate

不幸事件[**pú-hsìng shìh-chièn**]: unfortunate incident, mishap, accident

不來梅[**pù-lái-méi**]: Bremen

不明智[**pù-míng-chìh**]: ill-advised, unwise, imprudent, injudicious, foolish, stupid

不明確的[**pù-míng-ch'üèh te**]: not clear and correct, obscure, shady

不抵事[**pù-tĭ-shìh**]: unable to do something, incapable of or unsuited to something

不定[**pú-tìng**]: indefinite

不定期[**pú-tìng-ch'í**]: without a fixed date, irregular, non-periodical

不定期貨物船[**pú-tìng-ch'í huò-wù-ch'uán**]: nonscheduled freighter, ocean tramp

不亞於[**pù-yă-yǘ**]: not inferior to

不約而同[**pù-yüēh érh t'úng**]: to be in agreement without prior discussion, to act in concert without previous arrangements

9 不卽不離[**pú-chí pù-lí**]: to maintain a relationship which is neither too close nor too distant, to steer a middle course

不重視[**pú-chŭng-shìh**]: not to attach importance to, to ignore, to neglect, to discount, to be inattentive to, to slight

不負責任的[**pú-fù-tsé-jén te**]: irresponsible, untrustworthy

不相稱[**pù-hsiāng-ch'ēng**]: disproportion, disparity; ill-matched, disproportional, uneven, unequal, incongruous, inconsistent, incompatible

不相容的[**pù-hsiāng-júng te**]: incompatible

不相干[**pù-hsiāng-kān**]: irrelevant to, not pertinent to, not related to, not connected with, inconsequent

不相上下[**pù-hsiāng shàng-hsià**]: of more or less equal strength, without much difference

不信任案[**pú-hsìn-jèn àn**]: motion of no-confidence

不信任投票[**pú-hsìn-jèn t'óu-p'iào**]: vote of no-confidence

不省人事[**pù-hsĭng jén-shìh**]: unconscious, insensible; to faint

不宣而戰[**pù-hsüān érh chàn**]: to conduct an undeclared war

不苟[**pù-kŏu**]: not superficial, not careless, serious, thorough; to work and behave responsibly

不要臉[**pú-yào-liĕn**]: shameless, without self-respect; to have the audacity to

10 不恥下問[**pù-ch'ĭh hsià-wèn**]: not to feel ashamed to ask and learn from people below

不屑[**pú-hsièh**]: not to stoop to, not to condescend to

不容置辯[**pù-júng chìh-pièn**]: indisputable, unequivocal, unimpeachable, undeniable, incontestable, beyond dispute

不倫不類[**pù-lún pú-lèi**]: neither fish nor fowl

不拿槍的敵人 [**pù-ná-ch'iāng te tí-jén**]: enemies not holding guns (refers especially to dissident intellectuals)

不能[**pù-néng**]: unable, incapable of, unqualified, impotent, incompetent, powerless, unfitted

不能接受的[**pù-néng chiēh-shòu te**]: unacceptable

不能相容[**pù-néng hsiāng-júng**]: incompatible, contradictory, discrepant, incongruous, inconsistent, at variance

不能消除的[**pù-néng hsiāo-ch'ú te**]: irremovable, indelible

不能忍受[**pù-néng jĕn-shòu**]: intolerable, insufferable, insupportable, unbearable, unendurable, inadmissible

不能容忍[**pù-néng júng-jĕn**]: intolerable, insufferable, insupportable, unbearable, unendurable, inadmissible

不能工作[**pù-néng kūng-tsò**]: incapacitated, disabled, unable to work

不能理解的[**pù-néng lĭ-chiĕh te**]: incomprehensible, unintelligible, obscure, perplexing, unfathomable, inexplicable

不能設想的[**pù-néng shè-hsiăng te**]: inconceivable, unthinkable

不破不立[**pú-p'ò pú-lì**]: no establishing without destroying; the new does not arise without elimination of the old

不時[**pù-shíh**]: often, frequent, occasionally, from time to time, untimely

不時之需[**pù-shíh chīh hsǖ**]: for emergency use, for later use

不凍港[**pú-tùng-kăng**]: ice-free port

11 不接頭[**pù-chiēh-t'óu**]: to have no contact, to have no clear view

不堅定[**pù-chiēn-tìng**]: to lack resolution, not firm or resolute

不堅定份子[**pù-chiēn-tìng fèn-tzu**]: waverer, wavering element

不情願[**pù-ch'íng-yüàn**]: reluctant, unwilling, indisposed, disinclined, averse; reluctance

不惜[**pù-hsī**]: without regard to, to have no scruple, to be unscrupulous

不惜一切代價 [**pù-hsī í-ch'ièh tài-chià**]: at all costs

不惜工本[**pù-hsī kūng-pĕn**]: to spare neither labor nor money, to spare no expense

不惜犧牲[**pù-hsī hsī-shēng**]: to spare no sacrifice, at all costs

不現實的[**pú-hsièn-shíh te**]: unrealistic, impractical

不夠本[**pú-kòu-pĕn**]: at a loss, less than cost price, under cost price

不規則[**pù-kuēi-tsé**]: irregular

不理[**pù-lĭ**]: to disregard, to ignore, to spurn, to pay no heed to, to pay no attention to, not to bother about

不理會[**pù-lĭ-hùi**]: to disregard, to ignore

不偏心的[**pù-p'iēn-hsīn te**]: impartial, unbiased, equitable, fair

不偏不倚[**pù-p'iēn pù-ĭ**]: without bias and without favor

不速之客[**pú-sù chīh k'ò**]: casual visitor, univited guest; thief, burglar, robber

不得已[**pù-té-ĭ**]: inevitable, unable to avoid, as a last resort

不得人心的[**pù-té-jén-hsīn te**]: unpopular, discredited

不得要領[**pù-té yāo-lĭng**]: to miss the point, to be beside the mark, not to the point

不停[**pù-t'íng**]: without stopping, continual, incessant, uninterrupted, unending

不通[**pù-t'ūng**]: meaningless, illogical, incomprehensible; closed (as a road)

不動產 **[pú-tùng-ch'ǎn]**: real estate, immovable property

不動聲色 **[pú-tùng shēng-sè]**: not to show one's feelings

不動搖 **[pú-tùng-yáo]**: firm, stable; to stand firm

不問青紅皂白 **[pú-wèn ch'īng-húng tsào-pái]**: without asking for the facts

12 不期而遇 **[pù-ch'í érh yǜ]**: to meet by chance, to meet by accident, to run across

不着邊際 **[pù-chó piēn-chì]**: to talk loosely without touching the issue

不絕其自新之路 **[pù-chüéh ch'í tzù-hsīn chīh lù]**: not to deny a person the chance to turn over a new leaf

不發達的 **[pù-fā-tá te]**: underdeveloped

不然的話 **[pù-ján-te-huà]**: or else, if not, otherwise

不開展 **[pù-k'āi-chǎn]**: undeveloped, immature

不敢 **[pù-kǎn]**: to dare not, to be afraid to

不敢正視 **[pù-kǎn chèng-shìh]**: not to dare to face up to

不堪設想 **[pù-k'ān shè-hsiǎng]**: intolerable, unimaginable, inconceivable

不等 **[pù-těng]**: unequal, not to wait

不等組距 **[pù-těng tsǔ-chǜ]**: unequal interval

不測 **[pú-ts'è]**: inconceivable, unexpected, incalculable

不違農時 **[pù-wéi núng-shíh]**: to do farm work in the right season

13 不愛護公共財產 **[pú-ài-hù kūng-kùng ts'ái-ch'ǎn]**: lack of due care for public property

不義之財 **[pú-ì chih ts'ái]**: ill-gotten wealth, money obtained by devious means

不落後於 **[pú-lò-hòu yǘ]**: not to fall behind, to keep up with

不愼 **[pú-shèn]**: careless

不損害 **[pù-sǔn-hài]**: without harm to, without prejudice to

不當 **[pú-tàng]**: unsuitable, inappropriate, incorrect

不道德 **[pú-tào-té]**: immoral

不睬 **[pù-ts'ǎi]**: to pay no regard to, to ignore, to disdain

14 不像樣 **[pú-hsiàng-yàng]**: unbecoming, disgraceful, shameful, degrading, indecent, scandalous, unseemly

不管 **[pù-kuǎn]**: in spite of, irrespective of, regardless of

不滿 **[pù-mǎn]**: to disapprove, to blame, to pass censure on; dissatisfied, discontented, malcontent, critical of; dissatisfaction over

不滿份子 **[pù-mǎn fèn-tzu]**: a dissatisfied element, a malcontent

不團結 **[pù-t'uán-chiéh]**: disunity, disunion, division; to be disunited, to be divided

不對 **[pú-tùi]**: false, incorrect

不對題 **[pú-tùi-t'í]**: beside the mark, not on the subject, not to the point; to go off the subject

15 不魯悉 **[pù-lǔ-hsī]**: Brussels (Belgium)

不論 **[pú-lùn]**: regardless of, irrespective of, no matter, without regard to, without reference to

不適當 **[pú-shìh-tàng]**: unsuitable, improper, unmerited, unfit, inept

不熟練的 **[pù-shóu-lièn te]**: unskilled, inexperienced, raw

16 不懈的 **[pú-hsièh te]**: persistent, tireless, unremitting, persevering, obstinate, unwavering, steady, resolute

不學無術 **[pù-hsüéh wú-shù]**: without learning or training

不遺餘力 **[pù-í yü̆-lì]**: to spare no efforts, to do all one can

不擇手段 **[pù-tsé shŏu-tuàn]**: to resort to all means; by fair means or foul

不錯 **[pú-ts'ò]**: right, good, faultless, free of mistakes

17 不濟 **[pú-chì]**: not up to standard, inadequate, to be of no avail, to be of no help, to be worthless

不瞭解意義 **[pù-liăo-chiĕh ì-ì]**: not to understand the meaning of, to be ignorant of the significance of

不斷 **[pú-tuàn]**: uninterrupted, steady, continuous, continual, unbroken, constant, without interruption

不隱瞞 **[pù-yĭn-mán]**: to keep nothing from, not to conceal

19 不識時務 **[pú-shíh shíh-wù]**: to be ignorant of current affairs

不識擡舉 **[pú-shíh t'ái-chü̆]**: not to know how to appreciate favors

不識字 **[pú-shíh-tzù]**: to be illiterate

不贊成 **[pú-tsàn-ch'éng]**: to disapprove of, to be against

不斷革命論 **[pú-tuàn-kó-mìng lùn]**: the theory of uninterrupted revolution, theory of continual revolution

不斷調整 **[pú-tuàn t'iáo-chĕng]**: continual readjustment

不斷躍進 **[pú-tuàn yüèh-chìn]**: continuous leap forward

不辭 **[pù-tz'ú]**: not to refrain from, to be willing to go so far as to

不辭而別 **[pù-tz'ú érh piéh]**: to leave without announcing departure, to take French leave

21 不顧 **[pú-kù]**: to ignore, disregard, to defy, leave out of account; without regard for, in defiance of

不顧公共利益 **[pú-kù kūng-kùng lì-ì]**: unmindful of the public interest

不顧事實 **[pú-kù shìh-shíh]**: to ignore facts

不顧條件 **[pú-kù t'iáo-chièn]**: to take no account of actual conditions

22 不驕不躁 **[pù-chiāo pú-tsào]**: free from arrogance and rashness, not conceited or rash

不聽 **[pù-t'īng]**: to turn a deaf ear to, impervious to

23 不變基期 **[pú-pièn chī-ch'í]**: fixed base

不變價格 **[pú-pièn chià-kó]**: constant prices

不變資本 **[pú-pièn tzū-pĕn]**: fixed capital

— 4 Strokes —

9 世紀 **[shìh-chì]**: century

世界 **[shìh-chièh]**: world, earth; global, international

世界氣象組織 **[shìh-chièh ch'ì-hsiàng tsŭ-chīh]**: World Meteorological Organization

世界知識 **[shìh-chièh chīh-shìh]**: World Events (semi-monthly periodical)

世界青年聯歡節 **[shìh-chièh ch'īng-nién lién-huān-chiéh]**: World Youth Festival

世界主義 **[shìh-chièh chŭ-ì]**: cosmopolitanism, world-ism

世界範圍的 **[shìh-chièh fàn-wéi te]**: worldwide in scope, of global proportions

世界佛教徒聯誼會 **[shìh-chièh fó-chiào-t'ú lién-ì-hùi]**: The World Fellowship of Buddhists

世界和平理事會 **[shìh-chièh hó-p'íng lĭ-shìh-hùi]**: The World Council of Peace

世界新聞報 **[shìh-chièh hsīn-wén pào]**: News of the World (British Sunday newspaper)

世界科學工作者協會 **[shìh-chièh k'ō-hsüéh kūng-tsò-chě hsiéh-hùi]**: World Federation of Scientific Workers (WFSW)

世界觀 **[shìh-chièh-kuān]**: world view, world outlook

世界工會聯合會 **[shìh-chièh kūng-hùi lién-hó-hùi]**: World Federation of Trade Unions (WFTU)

世界民主青年聯盟 **[shìh-chièh mín-chŭ ch'īng-nién lién-méng]**: World Federation of Democratic Youth (WFDY)

世界霸權 **[shìh-chièh pà-ch'üán]**: world domination, world supremacy

世界報 **[shìh-chièh-pào]**: Die Welt (West German daily newspaper)

世界水平 **[shìh-chièh shŭi-p'íng]**: world standard, world caliber, international level

世界大戰 **[shìh-chièh tà-chàn]**: world war

世界衞生組織 **[shìh-chièh wèi-shēng tsŭ-chīh]**: World Health Organization (WHO)

世界舞台 **[shìh-chièh wŭ-t'ái]**: world arena

世界語 **[shìh-chièh yŭ]**: Esperanto

世界輿論 **[shìh-chièh yǘ-lùn]**: world opinion

世俗的 **[shìh-sú te]**: secular, worldly

— 5 Strokes —

丟 **[tīu]**: to lose, to throw away

[5]丟失 **[tīu-shīh]**: to lose

[8]丟卒保帥 **[tīu-tsú pǎo-shuài]**: to sacrifice a pawn to save the king (often used in the sense of putting blame on junior members to save leading members)

[11]丟掉 **[tīu-tiào]**: to lose, to throw aside, to cast away, to discard, to relinquish

[17]丟臉 **[tīu-liěn]**: to lose face, to be humiliated; disgraceful

— RADICAL 丨 2 —

— 3 Strokes —

[3]中小工廠 **[chūng-hsiăo kūng-ch'ăng]**: medium- and small-sized factories

中小工商業者 **[chūng-hsiăo kūng-shāng-yèh-chě]**: middle and small manufacturers and merchants

中小地主 **[chūng-hsiăo tì-chŭ]**: middle and small landlords

中山大學 **[chūng-shān tà-hsüéh]**: Sun Yat-sen University

中士 **[chūng-shìh]**: Sergeant (U.S. Army); Petty Officer 2nd Class (U.S. Navy); Petty Officer 1st Class (British Navy)

[4]中止 **[chūng-chǐh]**: to discontinue, suspend, interrupt, break off, stop in the middle of; discontinuance in midcourse

中心 **[chūng-hsīn]**: center, core, heart, middle, hub, axis, nucleus; central

中心城市 **[chūng-hsīn ch'éng-shìh]**: metropolitan city, metropolis, key city

中心環節 **[chūng-hsīn huán-chiéh]**: central link, main point, key point

中心問題 **[chūng-hsīn wèn-t'í]**: key problem, pivotal question

[5]中立 **[chūng-lì]**: neutrality; neutral

中立主義 **[chūng-lì chŭ-ì]**: neutralism

2

中立化 **[chūng-lì-huà]** : neutralization

中平 **[chūng-p'íng]** : Trungbinh (Vietnam)

中世紀 **[chūng-shìh-chì]** : the Middle Ages; medieval

中世紀哲學 **[chūng-shìh-chì ché-hsüéh]** : medieval philosophy

中央 **[chūng-yāng]** : 1) center; central. 2) Central Committee of the Chinese Communist Party (abbreviation of 中國共產黨中央委員會)

中央政治局 **[chūng-yāng chèng-chìh chú]** : Central Politburo

中央集權 **[chūng-yāng chí-ch'üán]** : centralization, centralization of authority

中央集權主義 **[chūng-yāng chí-ch'üán chŭ-ì]** : centralism

中央機關 **[chūng-yāng chī-kuān]** : central organs

中央機要交通局 **[chūng-yāng chī-yào chiāo-t'ūng chú]** : Central Confidential Communications Bureau

中央氣象局 **[chūng-yāng ch'ì-hsiàng chú]** : Central Meteorological Bureau

中央氣象科學研究所 **[chūng-yāng ch'ì-hsiàng k'ō-hsüéh yén-chìu-sŏ]** : Central Institute of Meteorological Research

中央局 **[chūng-yāng-chú]** : the Central Committee Bureau

中央人民政府 **[chūng-yāng jén-mín chèng-fŭ]** : Central People's Government

中央日報 **[chūng-yāng jìh-pào]** : Central Daily News (Taiwan daily newspaper)

中央工商行政管理局 **[chūng-yāng kūng-shāng hsíng-chèng kuăn-lĭ-chú]** : Central Industrial and Commercial Administrative Control Bureau

中央國民經濟核算局 **[chūng-yāng kuó-mín chīng-chì hó-suàn-chú]** : Central National Economic Accounting Administration (USSR)

中央手工業管理局 **[chūng-yāng shŏu-kūng-yèh kuăn-lĭ-chú]** : Central Handicraft Industries Control Bureau

中央書記處 **[chūng-yāng shū-chì-ch'ù]** : Central Secretariat

中央條約組織 **[chūng-yāng t'iáo-yüēh tsŭ-chīh]** : Central Treaty Organization (CENTO)

中央統計局(蘇聯部長會議直屬中央統計局) **[chūng-yāng t'ŭng-chì-chú (sū-lién pù-chăng hui-ì chíh-shŭ chūng-yāng t'ŭng-chì-chú)]** : Central Statistical Administration (Council of Ministers, USSR)

中央通訊社 **[chūng-yāng t'ūng-hsün shè]** : Central News Agency (Taiwan)

中央爲主，地方爲輔 **[chūng-yāng wéi chŭ, tì-fāng wéi fŭ]** : the central authorities play the main role while the local authorities play a subsidiary role

中央委員會 **[chūng-yāng wĕi-yüán-hùi]** : Central Committee

中央委員會第二次全體會議 **[chūng-yāng wĕi-yüán-hùi tì-èrh-tz'ù ch'üán-t'ĭ hùi-ì]** : Second Plenum of the Central Committee

6 中共中央 **[chūng-kùng chūng-yāng]** : Central Committee of the Chinese Communist Party (abbreviation of 中國共產黨中央委員會)

中共中央關於反對經濟主義的通知 **[chūng-kùng chūng-yāng kuān-yú făn-tùi chīng-chì chŭ-ì te t'ūng-chīh]** : Circular of the Party Central Concerning Opposition to Economism (January 11, 1967)

中共中央書記處 **[chūng-kùng chūng-yāng shū-chì-ch'ù]** : the Secretariat of the Central Committee of the Communist Party of China

7 中位數 **[chūng-wèi-shù]** : median

8 中非共和國 **[chūng-fēi kùng-hó-kuó]** : Central African Republic

中東通訊社 **[chūng-tūng t'ūng-hsün-shè]** : Middle East News Agency (MENA)

9 中計 **[chùng-chì]**: to play into someone's hands, to fall for someone's tricks

中秋節 **[chūng-ch'īu-chiéh]**: the Mid-Autumn Festival

中型的 **[chūng-hsíng te]**: medium, medium-sized, middle-sized

中型機器製造部 **[chūng-hsíng chī-ch'ì chìh-tsào pù]**: Ministry of Medium Machine Building

中美洲國家組織 **[chūng-mĕi-chōu kuó-chiā tsŭ-chīh]**: Organization of Central American States

中南 **[chūng-nán]**: Central-South (China)

10 中校 **[chūng-hsiào]**: Lieutenant Colonel (Army and Air Force); Commander (Navy); Wing Commander (British Air Force)

11 中產階級 **[chūng-ch'ăn chiēh-chí]**: middle class

中將 **[chūng-chiàng]**: Lieutenant General (Army and Air Force); Vice Admiral (Navy); Air Marshal (British Air Force)

中堅 **[chūng-chiēn]**: center, mainstay, pillar, bulwark, backbone, nucleus

中堅份子 **[chūng-chiēn fèn-tzu]**: backbone elements, those who are the backbone (mainstay) of

中堅力量 **[chūng-chiēn lì-liàng]**: nucleus of (effective) power

中國 **[chūng-kuó]**: China; Chinese, Sino-

中國茶葉出口公司 **[chūng-kuó ch'á-yèh ch'ū-k'ŏu kūng-ssū]**: China National Tea Export Corporation

中國茶葉公司 **[chūng-kuó ch'á-yèh kūng-ssū]**: China National Tea Corporation

中國哲學會 **[chūng-kuó ché-hsüéh hùi]**: China Philosophical Society

中國政治法律學會 **[chūng-kuó chèng-chìh fă-lǜ hsüéh-hùi]**: China Political Law Association

中國機械進口公司 **[chūng-kuó chī-hsièh chìn-k'ŏu kūng-ssū]**: China National Machinery Import Corporation

中國技術進口公司 **[chūng-kuó chì-shù chìn-k'ŏu kūng-ssū]**: China National Technical Import Corporation

中國集郵公司 **[chūng-kuó chí-yú kūng-ssū]**: China Philatelic Corporation

中國交通電工器材公司 **[chūng-kuó chiāo-t'ūng tièn-kūng ch'ì-ts'ái kūng-ssū]**: China National Communications and Electrical Equipment Corporation

中國致公黨 **[chūng-kuó chìh-kūng tăng]**: China Chih Kung Tang (China Devotion to Justice Society–a minor democratic party)

中國進出口公司 **[chūng-kuó chìn-ch'ū-k'ŏu kūng-ssū]**: China National Import and Export Corporation

中國青年報 **[chūng-kuó ch'īng-nién pào]**: The Chinese Youth Journal

中國青年黨 **[chūng-kuó ch'īng-nién tăng]**: The Young China Party (Nationalist China)

中國畜產出口公司 **[chūng-kuó ch'ù-ch'ăn ch'ū-k'ŏu kūng-ssū]**: China National Animal Product Export Corporation

中國畜產公司 **[chūng-kuó ch'ù-ch'ăn kūng-ssū]**: China National Animal Products Corporation

中國防癆協會 **[chūng-kuó fáng-láo hsiéh-hùi]**: China Association foı Preventing Tuberculosis

中國佛教協會 **[chūng-kuó fó-chiào hsiéh-hùi]**: China Buddhist Association

中國福利會 **[chūng-kuó fú-lì-hùi]**: China Welfare Institute

中國新民主主義青年團 **[chūng-kuó hsīn-mín-chŭ chŭ-ì ch'īng-nién-t'uán]**: China New Democratic Youth League

中國新聞工作者聯誼會 **[chūng-kuó hsīn-wén kūng-tsò-chĕ lién-ì-hùi]**: All-China Federation of News Workers

中國新聞社[**chūng-kuó hsīn-wén-shè**]: China News Service (CNS)

中國化工原料公司[**chūng-kuó huà-kūng yüán-liào kūng-ssū**]: China National Chemical Raw Materials Corporation

中國花紗布公司[**chūng-kuó huā-shā-pù kūng-ssū**]: China National Cotton, Yarn, and Cloth Corporation

中國回民文化協會[**chūng-kuó húi-mín wén-huà hsiéh-hùi**]: China Moslem Culture Promotion Association

中國紅十字會[**chūng-kuó húng-shíh-tzù-hùi**]: Red Cross Society of China

中國儀器進口公司[**chūng-kuó í-ch'ì chìn-k'ǒu kūng-ssū**]: China National Instruments Import Corporation

中國醫學科學院[**chūng-kuó ī-hsüéh k'ō-hsüéh-yüàn**]: Chinese Academy of Medical Sciences

中國伊斯蘭教協會[**chūng-kuó ī-ssū-lán-chiào hsiéh-hùi**]: China Islamic Association

中國醫藥公司[**chūng-kuó ī-yào kūng-ssū**]: China National Pharmaceuticals Corporation

中國人民政治協商會議[**chūng-kuó jén-mín chèng-chìh hsiéh-shāng hùi-ì**]: Chinese People's Political Consultative Conference

中國人民解放軍[**chūng-kuó jén-mín chiěh-fàng-chūn**]: Chinese People's Liberation Army (PLA)

中國人民解放軍醫學科學院[**chūng-kuó jén-mín chiěh-fàng-chūn ī-hsüéh k'ō-hsüéh-yüàn**]: Academy of Military Medical Sciences, Chinese People's Liberation Army

中國人民志願軍[**chūng-kuó jén-mín chìh-yüàn-chūn**]: Chinese People's Volunteers (Korean War)

中國人民革命軍事委員會[**chūng-kuó jén-mín kó-mìng chūn-shìh wěi-yüán-hùi**]: Chinese People's Revolutionary Military Council

中國人民保險公司[**chūng-kuó jén-mín pǎo-hsiěn kūng-ssū**]: The People's Insurance Company of China

中國人民保衛世界和平反對美國侵略委員會[**chūng-kuó jén-mín pǎo-wèi shìh-chièh hó-p'íng fǎn-tùi měi-kuó ch'īn-lüèh wěi-yüán-hùi**]: Chinese People's Committee for World Peace and Against American Aggression

中國人民對外文化協會[**chūng-kuó jén-mín tùi-wài wén-huà hsiéh-hùi**]: Chinese People's Association for Cultural Relations with Foreign Countries

中國人民外交學會[**chūng-kuó jén-mín wài-chiāo hsüéh-hùi**]: Chinese People's Institute of Foreign Affairs

中國科技[**chūng-kuó k'ō-chì**]: Scientific and Technical Association of the People's Republic of China (abbreviation of 中華人民共和國科學技術協會)

中國科學技術情報研究所[**chūng-kuó k'ō-hsüéh chì-shù ch'íng-pào yén-chiù-sŏ**]: China Institute of Scientific and Technical Information

中國科學技術大學[**chūng-kuó k'ō-hsüéh chì-shù tà-hsüéh**]: Science and Technology University of China

中國科學院[**chūng-kuó k'ō-hsüéh-yüàn**]: Chinese Academy of Sciences

中國礦產公司[**chūng-kuó k'uàng-ch'ǎn kūng-ssū**]: China National Minerals Corporation

中國國際旅行社[**chūng-kuó kuó-chì lǚ-hsíng shè**]: China International Tourist Service

中國國際貿易促進會[**chūng-kuó kuó-chì mào-ì ts'ù-chìn-hùi**]: China Association for the Promotion of International Trade

中國國民黨革命委員會[**chūng-kuó kuó-mín-tǎng kó-mìng wěi-yüán-hùi**]: The Revolutionary Committee of the Kuomintang

中國工農紅旗軍[**chūng-kuó kūng-núng húng-ch'í-chūn**]: Chinese Red Banner Army of Workers and Peasants (an anti-Mao military organization that was reported to have arisen during the Cultural Revolution)

中國工業品出口公司 [chūng-kuó kūng-yèh-p'ĭn ch'ū-k'ŏu kūng-ssū] : China National Industrial Products Export Corporation

中國共產主義青年團 [chūng-kuó kùng-ch'ăn chŭ-ì ch'īng-nién-t'uán] : Communist Youth League of China

中國共產黨 [chūng-kuó kùng-ch'ăn-tăng] : Chinese Communist Party

中國共產黨中央委員會 [chūng-kuó kùng-ch'ăn-tăng chūng-yāng wĕi-yüán-hùi] : Central Committee of the Chinese Communist Party

中國糧穀油脂出口公司 [chūng-kuó liáng-kŭ yú-chīh ch'ū-k'ŏu kūng-ssū] : China National Cereals, Oils, and Fats Export Corporation

中國糧穀油脂公司 [chūng-kuó liáng-kŭ yú-chīh kūng-ssū] : China National Cereals, Oils, and Fats Corporation

中國糧食公司 [chūng-kuó liáng-shíh kūng-ssū] : China National Grain Corporation

中國聾啞人福利會 [chūng-kuó lúng-yă-jén fú-lì-hùi] : China Welfare Institute for the Deaf and Dumb

中國盲人福利會 [chūng-kuó máng-jén fú-lì-hùi] : China Welfare Institute for the Blind

中國煤業建築器材公司 [chūng-kuó méi-yèh chièn-chú ch'ì-ts'ái kūng-ssū] : China National Coal and Construction Materials Corporation

中國米丘林學會 [chūng-kuó mĭ-ch'īu-lín hsüéh-hùi] : China Michurin Society

中國民主社會黨 [chūng-kuó mín-chŭ shè-hùi-tăng] : Democratic Socialist Party (Taiwan)

中國民主建國會 [chūng-kuó mín-chŭ chièn-kuó-hùi] : China Democratic National Construction Association (a minor democratic party)

中國民主促進會 [chūng-kuó mín-chŭ ts'ù-chìn-hùi] : China Association for the Promotion of Democracy (a minor democratic party)

中國民用航空局 [chūng-kuó mín-yùng háng-k'ūng-chű] : China Civil Aviation Bureau

中國民主同盟會 [chūng-kuó mín-chŭ t'úng-méng-hùi] : China Democratic League (a minor democratic party)

中國木材公司 [chūng-kuó mù-ts'ái kūng-ssū] : China National Lumber Corporation

中國農工民主黨 [chūng-kuó núng-kūng mín-chŭ-tăng] : Chinese Peasants and Workers Democratic Party (a minor democratic party)

中國農業科學院 [chūng-kuó núng-yèh k'ō-hsüéh-yüàn] : Chinese Academy of Agricultural Sciences

中國百貨公司 [chūng-kuó păi-huò kūng-ssū] : China National General Merchandise Corporation

中國保險公司 [chūng-kuó păo-hsiĕn kūng-ssū] : China Insurance Company, Limited

中國食品出口公司 [chūng-kuó shíh-p'ĭn ch'ū-k'ŏu kūng-ssū] : China National Foodstuffs Export Corporation

中國食品公司 [chūng-kuó shíh-p'ĭn kūng-ssū] : China National Foodstuffs Corporation

中國石油公司 [chūng-kuó shíh-yú kūng-ssū] : China National Petroleum Corporation

中國絲綢公司 [chūng-kuó ssū-ch'óu kūng-ssū] : China National Silk Corporation

中國大陸 [chūng-kuō tà-lù] : Chinese mainland, China mainland

中國道教協會 [chūng-kuó tào-chiào hsiéh-hùi] : China Taoist Association

中國電影器材公司 **[chūng-kuó tièn-yǐng ch'ì-ts'ái kūng-ssū]** : China National Motion Picture Supply Corporation

中國電影發行放映公司 **[chūng-kuó tièn-yǐng fā-hsíng fàng-yìng kūng-ssū]** : China National Film Distribution and Exhibition Corporation

中國雜品出口公司 **[chūng-kuó tsá-p'ǐn ch'ū-k'ǒu kūng-ssū]** : China National Sundries Export Corporation

中國作家協會 **[chūng-kuó tsò-chiā hsiéh-hùi]** : China Writers' Association

中國土產出口公司 **[chūng-kuó t'ǔ-ch'ǎn ch'ū-k'ǒu kūng-ssū]** : China National Native Produce Export Corporation

中國土產公司 **[chūng-kuó t'ǔ-ch'ǎn kūng-ssū]** : China National Native Produce Corporation

中國對外貿易運輸公司 **[chūng-kuó tùi-wài mào-ì yǜn-shū kūng-ssū]** : China National Foreign Trade Transportation Corporation

中國通 **[chūng-kuó-t'ūng]** : China hand, China expert

中國文學藝術界聯合會 **[chūng-kuó wén-hsüéh ì-shù-chièh lién-hó-hùi]** : China Federation of Literary and Art Circles

中國文字改革委員會 **[chūng-kuó wén-tzù kǎi-kó wěi-yüán-hùi]** : Committee for the Reform of the Chinese Written Language

中國五金機械公司 **[chūng-kuó wǔ-chīn chī-hsièh kūng-ssū]** : China National Metals and Machinery Corporation

中國五金進口公司 **[chūng-kuó wǔ-chīn chìn-k'ǒu kūng-ssū]** : China National Metals Import Corporation

中國亞洲團結委員會 **[chūng-kuó yà-chōu t'uán-chiéh wěi-yüán-hùi]** : China Committee for Asian Solidarity

中國鹽業公司 **[chūng-kuó yén-yèh kūng-ssū]** : China National Salt Corporation

中國銀行 **[chūng-kuó yín-háng]** : Bank of China

中國運輸機械進口公司 **[chūng-kuó yǜn-shū chī-hsièh chìn-k'ǒu kūng-ssū]** : China National Transport Machinery Import Corporation

中途 **[chūng-t'ú]** : midway, halfway, in mid-course

中尉 **[chūng-wèi]** : 1st Lieutenant (Army and Air Force); Junior Lieutenant (Navy); Lieutenant (Soviet armed services); Lieutenant Junior Grade (U.S. Navy); Flying Officer (British Air Force); Sub-lieutenant (British Navy)

12 中程的 **[chūng-ch'éng te]** : intermediate range, medium range

中間階層份子 **[chūng-chiēn chiēh-ts'éng fèn-tzu]** : people of the middle strata; middle stratum elements

中間份子 **[chūng-chiēn fèn-tzu]** : middle elements, middle-of-the-roaders (those who neither oppose nor actively support Communist policy)

中間人物 **[chūng-chiēn jén-wù]** : middle characters, intermediate characters (those of China's poor, lower, and middle income classes wavering between socialism and capitalism)

中間路綫 **[chūng-chiēn lù-hsièn]** : middle-of-the-road line, neutral line

中間派 **[chūng-chiēn-p'ài]** : middle-of-the-roaders

中間勢力 **[chūng-chiēn shìh-lì]** : middle-of-the-road forces, third forces

中間道路 **[chūng-chiēn tào-lù]** : middle road, middle-of-the-road (a course of wavering between socialism and capitalism characteristic of China's poor, lower, and middle income classes)

中間地帶 **[chūng-chiēn tì-tài]** : the (theory of the) intermediate zone

中間突破 **[chūng-chiēn t'ū-p'ò]** : a break-through in the center

中華全國 [chūng-huá ch'üán-kuó]: All-China (prefix)

中華全國青年聯合會 [chūng-huá ch'üán-kuó ch'īng-nién lién-hó-hùi]: All-China Federation of Youth

中華全國婦女聯合會 [chūng-huá ch'üán-kuó fù-nǚ lién-hó-hùi]: All-China Women's Federation

中華全國合作社聯合總會 [chūng-huá ch'üán-kuó hó-tsò-shè lién-hó tsǔng-hùi]: All-China Federation of Cooperatives

中華全國新聞工作者協會 [chūng-huá ch'üán-kuó hsīn-wén kūng-tsò-chě hsiéh-hùi]: All-China Journalists' Association

中華全國學生聯合會 [chūng-huá ch'üán-kuó hsüéh-shēng lién-hó-hùi]: All-China Students' Federation

中華全國科學技術普及協會 [chūng-huá ch'üán-kuó k'ō-hsüéh chì-shù p'ǔ-chí hsíeh-hùi]: All-China Association for the Dissemination of Scientific and Technical Knowledge

中華全國歸國華僑聯合會 [chūng-huá ch'üán-kuó kuēi-kuó huá-ch'iáo lién-hó-hùi]: All-China Federation of Returned Overseas Chinese

中華全國工商業聯合會 [chūng-huá ch'üán-kuó kūng-shāng-yèh lién-hó-hùi]: All-China Federation of Industry and Commerce

中華全國民主青年聯合會 [chūng-huá ch'üán-kuó mín-chǔ ch'īng-nién lién-hó-hùi]: All-China Federation of Democratic Youth

中華全國民主婦女聯合會 [chūng-huá ch'üán-kuó mín-chǔ fù-nǚ lién-hó-hùi]: All-China Democratic Women's Federation

中華全國世界語協會 [chūng-huá ch'üán-kuó shìh-chièh-yǚ hsiéh-hùi]: All-China World Language Association

中華全國體育總會 [chūng-huá ch'üán-kuó t'ǐ-yǜ tsǔng-hùi]: All-China Athletic Federation

中華全國總工會 [chūng-huá ch'üán-kuó tsǔng-kūng-hùi]: All-China Federation of Trade Unions

中華護士學會 [chūng-huá hù-shìh hsüéh-hùi]: China Nurses Association

中華人民政治協商會議 [chūng-huá jén-mín chèng-chìh hsiéh-shāng-hùi-i]: Chinese People's Political Consultative Conference

中華人民共和國 [chūng-huá jén-mín kùng-hó-kuó]: People's Republic of China

中華人民共和國全國婦女聯合會 [chūng-huá jén-mín kùng-hó-kuó ch'üán-kuó fù-nǚ lién-hó-hùi]: All-China Women's Federation of the People's Republic of China

中華人民共和國全國人民代表大會 [chūng-huá jén-mín kùng-hó-kuó jén-mín tài-piǎo tà-hùi]: National People's Congress of the People's Republic of China

中華人民共和國科學技術協會 [chūng-huá jén-mín-kùng-hó-kuó k'ō-hsüéh chì-shù hsiéh-hùi]: Scientific and Technical Association of the People's Republic of China

中華日報 [chūng-huá jìh-pào]: Chung Hua Jih Pao (Taiwan daily newspaper)

中華民國 [chūng-huá mín-kuó]: Republic of China

中等教育 [chūng-tĕng chiào-yǜ]: secondary education

中等職業學校 [chūng-tĕng chíh-yèh hsüéh-hsiào]: secondary vocational school

中等專業教育 [chūng-tĕng chuān-yèh chiào-yǜ]: secondary vocational education

中等工業學校 [chūng-tĕng kūng-yèh hsüéh-hsiào]: secondary industrial school

中等師範教育 [chūng-tĕng shīh-fàn chiào-yǜ]: secondary normal education

中等資產階級 [chūng-tĕng tzū-ch'ăn chiēh-chí]: middle bourgeoisie

中隊 [chūng-tùi] : a company-sized unit (military)

中游 [chūng-yú] : middle reaches (of a river)

中游思想 [chūng-yú ssū-hsiăng] : middle-of-the-stream thinking (an attitude of being content with mediocrity held by cadres who neither wish to become advanced elements nor dare to remain as backward elements)

13 中意的 [chùng-ì te] : favorite, loved; that meets with one's wishes

中傷 [chùng-shāng] : to vilify, to defame, to malign, to undermine; vilification, defamation

中農 [chūng-núng] : middle peasant (peasants who do not exploit others although they have a fair amount of producer goods)

16 中學 [chūng-hsüéh] : secondary school, middle school, high school

18 中醫 [chūng-ī] : Chinese traditional medicine; Chinese traditional medical doctor

中醫師 [chūng-ī-shīh] : traditional Chinese doctor

中醫研究所 [chūng-ī yén-chìu-sŏ] : Research Institute of Chinese Traditional Medicine

中斷 [chūng-tuàn] : to cut off, to suspend, to disrupt; disruption

19 中獸醫研究所 [chūng-shòu-ī yén-chìu-sŏ] : Institute of Chinese Traditional Veterinary Medicine

中藥研究所 [chūng-yào yén-chìu-sŏ] : Institute of Traditional Drugs

20 中蘇友好同盟互助條約 [chūng-sū yŭ-hăo t'úng-méng hù-chù t'iáo-yüēh] : Sino-Soviet Treaty of Friendship, Alliance, and Mutual Assistance (February 1950)

3 丰山 [fēng-shān] : Pungsan (Korea)

— 6 Strokes —

11 串連 [ch'ùan-lién] : to liaise, to string together, to link together (during the Cultural Revolution, the contracting of revolutionary relationships among Red Guards)

串通 [ch'uàn-t'ūng] : to conspire with, to join with and plot

13 串話 [ch'uàn-huà] : to chatter, to babble, to gossip; idle chatter

— RADICAL 丶 3 —

— 3 Strokes —

4 丹牛皮河 [tān-níu-p'í hó] : Danube River

丹麥 [tān-mài] : Denmark

丹麥王國 [tān-mài wáng-kuó] : Kingdom of Denmark

— 4 Strokes —

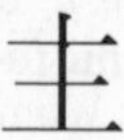

2 主人 [chŭ-jén] : host, master, mistress, owner, proprietor

主人翁 [chŭ-jén-wēng] : master of one's own house, host, owner, hero of a play or novel

主力戰 [chŭ-lì-chàn] : main action

主力艦 **[chŭ-lì-chièn]**: capital ship

主力軍 **[chŭ-lì-chün]**: main force

3 主子 **[chŭ-tzu]**: boss, master, patron, director, ruler, lord

6 主旨演說 **[chŭ-chĭh yĕn-shuō]**: key speech

主任 **[chŭ-jèn]**: director, head (of a department)

7 主角 **[chŭ-chiăo]**: leading character, hero; leading role, title role

8 主和派 **[chŭ-hó-pʻài]**: peace advocating group, advocators of peace, "doves"

主委 **[chŭ-wĕi]**: chairman of a committee

9 主持 **[chŭ-chʻíh]**: to take charge, to preside over, to conduct, to direct

主持正義的 **[chŭ-chʻíh chèng-ì te]**: fair-minded, honest, just, just-minded

主要的 **[chŭ-yào te]**: major, leading, chief, key, decisive, predominant, primary, principal

主要指標 **[chŭ-yào chĭh-piāo]**: major targets

主要環節 **[chŭ-yào huán-chiéh]**: key link, key lever

主要勞動 **[chŭ-yào láo-tùng]**: principal labor, important labor (labor for agricultural production)

主要糧食 **[chŭ-yào liáng-shíh]**: staple food

主要矛盾 **[chŭ-yào máo-tùn]**: principal contradiction

主要標誌 **[chŭ-yào piāo-chìh]**: outstanding feature

主要的區別 **[chŭ-yào te chʻü-piéh]**: essential distinction

10 主席 **[chŭ-hsí]**: chairman, president, master of ceremonies

主席團 **[chŭ-hsí-tʻuán]**: presidium

主流 **[chŭ-líu]**: main current, main trend, main-stream

主流和支流 **[chŭ-líu hó chīh-líu]**: main trend and side issues

11 主張 **[chŭ-chāng]**: to advocate, to uphold, to maintain, to assert, to stand for, advocacy

主教 **[chŭ-chiào]**: bishop, hierarch (Greek Orthodox Church)

主動 **[chŭ-tùng]**: to take action, to take the initiative

主動性 **[chŭ-tùng-hsìng]**: initiative

主動地位 **[chŭ-tùng tì-wèi]**: a position affording initiative

13 主意論 **[chŭ-ì-lùn]**: voluntarism

主義 **[chŭ-ì]**: doctrine, principle

16 主戰論 **[chŭ-chàn-lùn]**: jingoism

主戰派 **[chŭ-chàn-pʻài]**: war clique, war group, "hawks"

主辦 **[chŭ-pàn]**: to sponsor, to be responsible for, to be in charge of, to direct, to undertake, to be the leading spirit in

主導思想 **[chŭ-tăo ssū-hsiăng]**: dominant ideas, dominant ideology

主導原則 **[chŭ-tăo yüán-tsé]**: leading principle, guiding principle

18 主題 **[chŭ-tʻí]**: main theme, thesis, subject

22 主權 **[chŭ-chʻüán]**: sovereignty, sovereign rights

主權實體 **[chŭ-chʻüán shíh-tʻĭ]**: sovereign existence

23 主體 **[chŭ-tʻĭ]**: main body, essential part, mainstay, main subject

25 主觀 **[chŭ-kuān]**: subjectivist, subjective

主觀主義 **[chŭ-kuān chŭ-ì]**: subjectivism

主觀性 **[chŭ-kuān-hsìng]**: subjectivism

主觀認識 [**chŭ-kuān jèn-shíh**]: subjective concepts, subjective views

主觀觀念論 [**chŭ-kuān kuān-nièn-lùn**]: subjective idealism

主觀能動性 [**chŭ-kuān néng-tùng-hsìng**]: subjective initiative

主觀唯心主義 [**chŭ-kuān wéi-hsīn chŭ-ì**]: subjective idealism

主觀願望 [**chŭ-kuān yüàn-wàng**]: subjective wishes, wishful thinking

— RADICAL 丿 4 —

— 1 Stroke —

乃

乃沙立 [**năi-shā-lì**]: Thanarat, Sarit (Thai army officer and statesman)

— 2 Strokes —

久

3 久已 [**chĭu-ĭ**]: for a long time, long since, already

久已向往 [**chĭu-ĭ hsiàng-wăng**]: to look forward for a long time to

10 久留米 [**chĭu-líu-mĭ**]: Kurume (Japan)

12 久等 [**chĭu-tĕng**]: to wait long

13 久經鍛鍊的 [**chĭu-chīng tuàn-lièn te**]: well-steeled, long-tested

— 3 Strokes —

之

之流 [**. . . chīh líu**]: . . . and (his) ilk, . . . and (his) like

10 之流 [**. . . chīh t'ú**]: . . . and (his) ilk, . . . and (his) like

— 4 Strokes —

乍

11 乍得共和國 [**chà-té kùng-hó-kuó**]: Republic of Chad

— 7 Strokes —

乖

5 乖巧 [**kuāi-ch'iăo**]: sly

11 乖張 [**kuāi-chāng**]: perverse

— 9 Strokes —

乘

乘 [**ch'éng**]: to drive, to ride in; to avail of

8 乘其不備 [**ch'éng ch'í pú-pèi**]: to take advantage of a person's lack of preparation

9 乘風破浪 [**ch'éng-fēng p'ò-làng**]: to ride the wind and break the waves

12 乘勝前進 [**ch'éng-shèng ch'ién-chìn**]: to advance in victory (implies that workers and peasants should, on achieving success, continue to strive for further successes)

乘虛而入 [**ch'éng-hsū érh jù**]: to take advantage of a person's weakness, to enter when someone is unprepared

13 乘隙 [**ch'éng-hsì**]: to make use of a loophole, to exploit an opportunity

乘勢 [**ch'éng-shìh**]: to exploit circumstances, to make use of a situation

— RADICAL 乙 5 —

— 1 Stroke —

九

[3]九 三 學 社 **[chiŭ-sān hsüéh-shè]**: Chiu-San Society, September 3rd Society (a minor democratic party)

[6]九 州 **[chiŭ-chōu]**: Kyushu (Japan)

— 2 Strokes —

乞

[7]乞 求 **[ch'ĭ-ch'íu]**: to beg, to entreat, to plead

也

[8]也 門 **[yĕh-mén]**: Yemen

也 門 王 國 **[yĕh-mén wáng-kuó]**: Kingdom of Yemen

— 10 Strokes —

乾

[4]乾 巴 **[kān-pā]**: dry, empty

[7]乾 旱 **[kān-hàn]**: drought; arid

[10]乾 脆 **[kān-ts'ùi]**: direct, straight-forward, simple, without circumlocution

— 13 Strokes —

亂

[3]亂 子 **[luàn-tzu]**: trouble, disturbance

[8]亂 來 一 陣 **[luàn-lái í-chèn]**: to run amuck

[9]亂 紀 **[luàn-chì]**: violation of discipline

[11]亂 殺 **[luàn-shā]**: to kill without discrimination

亂 造 **[luàn-tsào]**: to create capriciously, a capricious creation

[13]亂 搞 **[luàn-kăo]**: to make a mess

亂 碰 **[luàn-p'èng]**: blundering

[15]亂 撞 **[luàn-chuàng]**: headlong

[16]亂 罵 **[luàn-mà]**: verbal garbage, foul abuse, vilification; to curse or revile wildly

— RADICAL 亅 6 —

— 1 Stroke —

了

[8]了 事 **[liăo-shìh]**: to settle a matter

[10]了 望 **[liào-wàng]**: outlook; to observe, to keep a lookout (了 here is used for 瞭)

[13]了 解 **[liăo-chiĕh]**: to understand, to inquire, to realize

— 3 Strokes —

予

[5]予 以 **[yŭ-ĭ]**: to provide, to give

予以檢查 [yü-i chien-ch'á] : to make an inspection

— 7 Strokes —

[6] 事件 [shih-chièn] : event, incident, happening, occurrence, eventuality

事先 [shih-hsiēn] : in advance, prior, beforehand

事在人爲 [shih tsài jén wéi] : man is the determining factor in doing things

[8] 事例 [shih-lì] : instance

事物 [shih-wù] : thing, event

[9] 事故 [shih-kù] : an accident

[11] 事務 [shih-wù] : affair, business, occupation, pursuit

事務主義 [shih-wù chŭ-ì] : routinism, commercialism

事務主義者 [shih-wù chŭ-ì-chĕ] : routineer

[12] 事項 [shih-hsiàng] : item

[13] 事跡 [shih-chī] : past deeds or facts

事業 [shih-yèh] : business, task, undertaking, enterprise

事業用費 [shih-yèh yùng-fèi] : operating expenses

[14] 事實上 [shih-shih-shàng] : actually, in fact, as a matter of fact

事實錯誤 [shih-shih ts'ò-wù] : factual mistake

事端 [shih-tuān] : incident, trouble

[23] 事變 [shih-pièn] : incident

— RADICAL 二 7 —

二

[1] 二一一制 [èrh-ī-ī chih] : the two-one-one system (a system whereby half of the cadres in provincial offices are transferred to lower level offices, one-fourth are sent on provincial inspection tours, and one-fourth remain in the provincial offices–the groups are shifted every three months)

[4] 二中全會 [èrh chūng ch'üán-hùi] : Second Plenum of the Central Committee (abbreviation of 中央委員會第二次全體會議)

二分法 [èrh-fēn-fā] : dichotomy

二心 [èrh-hsīn] : to play a double game, to have two loyalties

二五制 [èrh-wŭ chih] : the two-five system (the system whereby the rural cadres spend two days a week in meetings, inspections, etc., and the remaining five days in the fields)

二元論 [èrh-yüán-lùn] : dualism, dualistic theory

二月逆流 [èrh-yüèh nì-líu] : the February countercurrent (i.e., in February 1967, T'an Chen-lin spoke out against the injustice done to Liu Shao-ch'i, Teng Hsiao-p'ing, and other "power holders" during the course of the Cultural Revolution; this was regarded by the "rebels" as a signal for a counterattack by the disgraced leading cadres)

二月提綱 [èrh-yüèh t'í-kāng] : **The February Outline Report** (an outline report on how to conduct the Cultural Revolution prepared by the "Five-Man Group" (五人小組, q.v.) and approved by the CCP Central Committee on February 12, 1966, which suggested that criticism of Wu Han's controversial play "Hai Jui Dismissed From Office" should not be political but simply academic)

5 二乎 **[èrh-hū]**: doubtful, hesitant

6 二臣 **[èrh-ch'én]**: a double official (a person who accepts a post in a new dynasty which has conquered the dynasty that he has served previously; a derogatory term used by former Kuomintang officials who would not accept posts in the Communist government)

7 二把手 **[èrh-pă-shŏu]**: second fiddle (as in the expression "to play second fiddle")

二把刀 **[èrh-pă-tāo]**: second-in-command; a novice, tyro

9 二重眞理 **[èrh-ch'úng chēn-lĭ]**: two-fold truth

二重性 **[èrh-ch'úng-hsìng]**: dual nature, dual character

二律矛盾 **[èrh-lǜ máo-tùn]**: antinomy

二律背反 **[èrh-lǜ pèi-făn]**: antinomy

10 二級准尉 **[èrh-chí chŭn-wèi]**: Warrant Officer Junior Grade (U.S. Army and Air Force); Warrant Officer (U.S. Navy)

二流子 **[èrh-líu-tzu]**: idler, vagabond, rascal, do-nothing, loafer

11 二連 **[èrh-lién]**: Erhlien (Inner Mongolia Autonomous Region)

12 二等兵 **[èrh-tĕng-pīng]**: Private (British Army); Able Seaman (British Navy)

13 二萬五千里長征 **[èrh-wàn wŭ-ch'iēn lĭ ch'áng-chēng]**: the Long March (of the People's Liberation Army, October 1934 to October 1935)

15 二盤商 **[èrh-p'án-shāng]**: peddling (the reselling of commodities bought from others; a target of the Socialist Education Movement of 1962–1963)

— 2 Strokes —

井

3 井口貞夫 **[chĭng-k'ŏu chēn-fū]**: Iguchi, Sadao (Japanese diplomat)

互

4 互不侵犯 **[hù-pù-ch'īn-fàn]**: mutual nonaggression, nonaggression

互不干涉內政 **[hù-pù-kān-shè nèi-chèng]**: non-interference in each other's internal affairs

7 互助 **[hù-chù]**: mutual assistance, mutual aid

互助組 **[hù-chù-tsŭ]**: mutual aid group

互利 **[hù-lì]**: mutual benefit, mutually profitable, mutually beneficial

9 互相 **[hù-hsiāng]**: mutually

互相銜接步驟 **[hù-hsiāng hsién-chiēh pù-tsòu]**: successive stages

互相依賴 **[hù-hsiāng ī-lài]**: interdependence

互相讓步政策 **[hù-hsiāng jàng-pù chèng-ts'è]**: a give-and-take policy

互相勾結 **[hù-hsiāng kōu-chiéh]**: concerted action

互相諒解 **[hù-hsiāng liàng-chiĕh]**: mutual understanding

互相聯系 **[hù-hsiāng lién-hsì]**: mutual connection, reciprocal relation; interrelated, interconnected, interlocking

互相聯絡 **[hù-hsiāng lién-lò]**: interconnection

互相配合 **[hù-hsiāng p'èi-hó]**: to coordinate with, in coordination

互相尊重主權和領土完整 **[hù-hsiāng tsūn-chùng chŭ-ch'üán hó lĭng-t'ŭ wán-chĕng]**: mutual respect of sovereignty and territorial integrity

互相影響 **[hù-hsiāng yĭng-hsiăng]**: interaction; one influences the other

互派大使 **[hù-pài tà-shĭh]**: exchange of ambassadors

互爲因果 **[hù-wéi yīn-kuŏ]**: reciprocal causation

11 互通 **[hù-t'ūng]** : interconnection

互通有無 **[hù-t'ūng yŭ-wú]** : each making up what the other lacks

12 互換 **[hù-huàn]** : interchange, mutual exchange

互換原則 **[hù-huàn yüán-tsé]** : principal of reciprocity

互惠 **[hù-hùi]** : reciprocity

互惠條約 **[hù-hùi t'iáo-yüēh]** : reciprocal treaty

五

1 五一六指示 **[wŭ-í-lìu chĭh-shìh]** : the May 16 Instructions (a directive issued by Mao Tse-tung on May 16, 1966 in the name of the CCP Central Committee in which he ordered the "Five-Man Group" (五人小組) to be dissolved and established in its place the "Central Group in Charge of the Cultural Revolution" with Ch'en Po-ta at its head and Chiang Ch'ing (Madame Mao) as first deputy)

五一六兵團 **[wŭ-í-lìu pīng-t'uán]** : May 16 Group (an ultra-Leftist group which was said to be particularly opposed to Premier Chou En-lai and the Ministry of Foreign Affairs and allied departments; leaders of this group were alleged to be important lieutenants of Chiang Ch'ing (Madame Mao) during the Cultural Revolution)

2 五七指示 **[wŭ-ch'ī chĭh-shìh]** : the May 7 Instructions (a directive issued by Mao Tse-tung on May 7, 1966 in which he stated that the PLA should be treated as a big school where soldiers, besides learning politics, military affairs, and culture, should also learn to undertake auxiliary agricultural production and run middle and small size factories; that workers, besides working, should also learn military affairs, politics, and culture; that peasants in the people's communes should learn the same as the workers; that students should learn other things besides school work; and that all of them must participate in repudiating bourgeois elements)

五七幹校 **[wŭ-ch'ī kān-hsiào]** : May 7 Cadre Schools (schools established in the country in late 1968 where cadres were sent to do manual work and study Mao's thought–so named because they were founded on the principles embodied in Mao's "May 7 Instructions")

五人小組 **[wŭ-jén hsiăo-tsŭ]** : the Five-Man Group (a group formed in late 1965 to conduct the Cultural Revolution and made up of P'eng Chen, member of the Politburo and Mayor of Peking, Lu Ting-i, Director of the Department of Propaganda, Lo Jui-ch'ing, Chief of the General Staff, Yang Shang-k'un, Alternate Member of the Central Secretariat, and K'ang Sheng, Standing Committee Member of the Politburo–this group was later dissolved for failing to carry out Mao's conception of the Cultural Revolution)

3 五大減少 **[wŭ tà chiĕn-shăo]** : the five big reductions in 1) the purchase and sale of land; 2) the number of families hoarding grain; 3) the employing of hired laborers; 4) the renting of land; and 5) the number of speculators

4 五反 **[wŭ-făn]** : the Five-Anti (1) anti-bribery; 2) anti-evasion and leakage of taxes; 3) anti-theft of state property; 4) anti-skimping on work and cheating on materials; 5) anti-theft of state economic information (*See* 反行賄)

五日報 **[wŭ-jìh-pào]** : reporting at five-day intervals

五四運動 **[wŭ-ssù yün-tùng]** : May Fourth movement (1919)

6 五好戰士 **[wŭ-hăo chàn-shìh]** : five-good soldiers (good in 1) political ideology; 2) military techniques; 3) the "three-eight working style" (*See* 三八作風); 4) carrying out assigned tasks; and 5) physical training)

五好婦女 **[wŭ-hăo fù-nü̆]** : five-good women (good in 1) maintaining good relations with her neighbors; 2) ensuring good health for her family; 3) cleaning; 4) making ends meet; and 5) studies)

五好計劃 **[wŭ-nién chì-huà]** : Five Year Plan

五年試驗，十年推廣 **[wŭ-nién shìh-yèn, shíh-nién t'ūi-kuăng]** : five years to try it, ten years to popularize it (a phrase used in an editorial of December 11, 1965 in the People's Daily to describe the persistence, caution, and patience of the Chinese Communists in the enforcement of the half-work half-study educational system)

五同 **[wŭ-t'úng]** : do five things in each other's company (i.e., in carrying out Mao's ideas of "Educational Revolution," teachers were asked to engage in study, combat, military drill, labor, and recreation together with their students; the phrase first appeared in the People's Daily on December 12, 1967)

7 五角大樓 **[wŭ-chiăo tà-lóu]** : the Pentagon (U.S.A.)

五更歌 **[wŭ-kēng-kō]** : Song of the Five Night-Watches (a folk song adopted by the People's Liberation Army)

五快 **[wŭ-k'uài]** : the five quicks (quick in 1) getting grain to market; 2) dispatching grain from the market; 3) testing quality of grain; 4) weighting grain; and 5) transacting bidding)

五位一體 **[wŭ-wèi ì-t'ĭ]** : five factors in one body, quintiplicity (a term used when the communes were first established to describe the combination of agriculture, industry, commerce, education, and military affairs in the commune organization)

8 五花八門 **[wŭ-huā pā-mén]** : many and manifold, manifold, various

五毒 **[wŭ-tú]** : the five poisons (traditionally, snakes, scorpions, toads, lizards, and centipedes, but used by the Chinese Communist Party to signify the evils of the "five-anti" 五反, q.v.)

9 五風不正 **[wŭ-fēng pú-chèng]** : the five unhealthy tendencies

五星上將 **[wŭ-hsīng shàng-chiàng]** : General of the Army (U.S. Army); General of the Air Force (U.S. Air Force); Fleet Admiral (U.S. Navy)

五保 **[wŭ-păo]** : five guarantees (i.e., food, clothing, fuel, education for children, and burial for the dead)

10 五氣 **[wŭ-ch'ì]** : the five airs (i.e., the five undesirable airs: bureaucratic air, apathetic air, extravagant air, arrogant air, and finicking air)

五個條件 **[wŭ-kò t'iáo-chièn]** : the five conditions (the five conditions for being a proletarian revolutionary successor—as stated by Mao, a proletarian revolutionary successor must be: 1) a true Marxist-Leninist; 2) a revolutionary wholeheartedly in the service of the overwhelming majority of the people of China and the world; 3) a proletarian statesman capable of uniting with the work of the overwhelming majority of the people; a person who will unite not only with those who agree with his own opinions, but one good also at uniting with those of opinions unlike his, and, moreover, one who is good at uniting not only with those who have opposed him but also with those who have been proven by practice to have committed errors; 4) a model implementer of the Party's system of democratic centralism who must learn the leadership method of "gathering the views of the masses and taking the resulting ideas back to the masses," and who must cultivate a democratic work style of being good at listening to the opinions of the masses; 5) one who is modest and cautious and who guards against conceit and impatience, who is rich in the spirit of self-criticism, and who is courageous in correcting the deficiencies and errors in his work)

五個統一 **[wŭ-kò t'ŭng-ī]** : the Five Unifications (unified thinking, unified policies, unified plans, unified command, and unified action—quoted from a speech by Mao in 1962)

11 五彩的 **[wŭ-ts'ăi te]** : colored, multi-colored, of many colors

12 五項原則 **[wŭ-hsiàng yüán-tsé]** : the Five Principles (five principles of peaceful coexistence laid out in an agreement between China and India and signed on April 29, 1954: 1) mutual respect for territory and sovereignty; 2) non-aggression; 3) non-interference in internal affairs of other

states; 4) equality of states and work for mutual benefit; 5) peaceful co-existence)

13 五愛 **[wŭ-ài]**: the Five Loves (i.e., love for the motherland, love for the people, love for labor, love for science, and love for public property)

五過硬 **[wŭ-kuò-yìng]**: tough in five respects (refers to athletes, who should 1) be unwavering in ideology; 2) keep up physical fitness; 3) master athletic skills; 4) never flinch from arduous training; and 5) do their utmost in athletic contests)

五業 **[wŭ-yèh]**: the five occupations (farming, forestry, animal husbandry, side occupations, and fisheries)

14 五滿意 **[wŭ măn-ì]**: the five satisfactions (1) selling surplus grain; 2) buying needed grain; 3) serving customers; 4) obtaining required materials; and 5) buying surplus grain from the state)

19 五類份子 **[wŭ-lèi fèn-tzu]**: five categories of bad elements (i.e., landlords, rich peasants, counterrevolutionaries, Rightists, and bad elements)

— 5 Strokes —

況

5 況且 **[k'uàng-ch'iĕh]**: moreover, furthermore, in addition, besides

— 6 Strokes —

亞

2 亞丁 **[yà-tīng]**: Aden

亞丁城 **[yà-tīng-ch'éng]**: Aden (capital of Aden)

亞丁殖民地 **[yà-tīng chíh-mín-tì]**: Aden Colony

亞丁保護地 **[yà-tīng păo-hù-tì]**: Aden Protectorate

4 亞丹斯密 **[yà-tān ssū-mì]**: Adam Smith (1723–1790)

7 亞利桑那 **[yà-lì-sāng-nà]**: Arizona

亞庇 **[yà-pì]**: Jesselton (also called Api; North Borneo)

8 亞非 **[yà-fēi]**: Asia and Africa; Afro-Asian

亞非人民團結理事會 **[yà-fēi jén-mín t'uán-chiéh lĭ-shìh-huì]**: Afro-Asian People's Solidarity Council

亞非國家 **[yà-fēi kuó-chiā]**: Afro-Asian countries

亞拉佛拉海 **[yà-lā-fó-lā hăi]**: Arafura Sea

亞松森 **[yà-sūng-sēn]**: Asunción (Paraguay)

亞的斯亞貝巴 **[yà-tì-ssū yà-pèi-pā]**: Addis Ababa (Ethiopia)

9 亞洲 **[yà-chōu]**: Asia

亞洲門羅主義 **[yà-chōu mén-ló chŭ-ì]**: Asian Monroe-ism (refers to Japan's attempts at hegemony in Asia before the Second World War)

亞軍 **[yà-chūn]**: runner-up

亞美尼亞 **[yà-mĕi-ní-yà]**: Armenia

亞述 **[yà-shù]**: Assyria

10 亞格拉 **[yà-kó-lā]**: Agra (India)

亞馬孫 **[yà-mă-sūn]**: Amazon

亞馬耶布拉 **[yà-mă-yēh-pù-lā]**: Amarapura (Burma)

11 亞細亞 **[yà-hsì-yà]**: Asia

亞理斯多德 **[yà-lĭ-ssū-tō-té]**: Aristotle

亞速夫海 **[yà-sù-fū hăi]**: Azov Sea

亞得里亞海 **[yà-té-lĭ-yà hăi]**: Adriatic Sea

亞得利亞那堡 **[yà-té-lì-yà-nà-păo]**: Adrianople (Turkey)

12 亞喀巴 **[yà-k'ā-pā]**: Aqaba

14 亞爾及利亞 **[yà-ĕrh-chí-lì-yà]**: Algeria

15 亞熱帶 **[yà-jè-tài]**: subtropics

亞麻紡織廠 **[yà-má fǎng-chīh-ch'ǎng]**: linen textile mill

亞麻材料廠 **[yà-má ts'ál-liào-ch'ǎng]**: flax mill

16 亞歷山大城 **[yà-lì-shān-tà ch'éng]**: Alexandria (Egypt)

亞曆山大羅夫斯克 **[yà-lì-shān-tà-ló-fū-ssū-k'ò]**: Aleksandrovsk

— RADICAL 亠 8 —

— 1 Stroke —

亡

11 亡國 **[wáng-kuó]**: to destroy a country or state

亡國奴 **[wáng-kuó-nú]**: people without a country, colonial slaves, slaves of a foreign power

— 4 Strokes —

交 ... 辦理 **[chiāo. . . pàn-lǐ]**: to leave (put). . . into the hands of. . . for handling or transaction

3 交叉 **[chiāo-ch'ā]**: to crisscross, to intersect; point of intersection

交叉火網 **[chiāo-ch'ā huǒ-wǎng]**: cross-fire, net of cross-fire

交叉射擊 **[chiāo-ch'ā shè-chī]**: cross-fire

交叉作業 **[chiāo-ch'ā tsò-yèh]**: to change jobs; alternating work

交工 **[chiāo-kūng]**: to hand over a job (that has been finished)

4 交心 **[chiāo-hsīn]**: to make a clean breast of

交互 **[chiāo-hù]**: mutual

交互作用 **[chiāo-hù tsò-yùng]**: reciprocal action, reciprocal effect

交手 **[chiāo-shǒu]**: to fight (with one another)

交友 **[chiāo-yǔ]**: to become friends, to make friends (with someone)

5 交付 **[chiāo-fù]**: to deliver, to pay, to hand over

交代 **[chiāo-tài]**: to hand over, to explain, to forward to, to inform

交代政策 **[chiāo-tài chèng-ts'è]**: to explain policy (to one's successor)

6 交好 **[chiāo-hǎo]**: to make friends; friendship

8 交易 **[chiāo-ì]**: business transaction, commerce, interchange

交易稅 **[chiāo-ì shùi]**: business tax

交易所 **[chiāo-ì-sǒ]**: stock exchange

9 交界 **[chiāo-chièh]**: boundary; bordering

交卸 **[chiāo-hsièh]**: to hand over an office

交派 **[chiāo-p'ài]**: to order, to command, to issue an order through a superior

10 交流 **[chiāo-líu]**: exchange, interflow, confluence

交流經驗 **[chiāo-líu chīng-yèn]**: to exchange experiences

交納 **[chiāo-nà]**: to pay (tax)

交涉 **[chiāo-shè]**: to negotiate, to deal with, to discuss terms, to confer; negotiation

11 交接 **[chiāo-chiēh]**: to have contact, to come into contact, to join

交趾支那 **[chiāo-chǐh chīh-nà]**: Cochin China

交情 **[chiāo-ch'íng]**: friendship

交貨 **[chiāo-huò]**: to deliver goods or merchandise; delivery, consignment

交通 **[chiāo-t'ūng]**: transportation, communications, traffic; to be in contact, to communicate

交通車 **[chiāo-t'ūng ch'ē]**: transport vehicles

交通警察 **[chiāo-t'ūng chǐng-ch'á]**: traffic police

6 交通警察部隊 **[chiāo-t'ūng chǐng-ch'á pù-tuì]**: traffic police corps

交通壕 **[chiāo-t'ūng háo]**: connecting trench

交通工具 **[chiāo-t'ūng kūng-chù]**: vehicles, means of transportation

交通工具部 **[chiāo-t'ūng kūng-tsò pù]**: Communications Work Department

交通部 **[chiāo-t'ūng pù]**: Ministry of Communications

交通設備工業部 **[chiāo-t'ūng shè-pèi kūng-yèh pù]**: Ministry of Communications Equipment Industries

交通網 **[chiāo-t'ūng wǎng]**: transportation network

12 交換 **[chiāo-huàn]**: to alternate with, to take turns, to exchange

交換價值 **[chiāo-huàn chià-chíh]**: exchange value

交換意見 **[chiāo-huàn ì-chièn]**: to exchange views, to compare notes

交給 **[chiāo-kěi]**: to hand over to, to turn over to, to delegate, to furnish, to deliver

交割 **[chiāo-kō]**: to finish, to have finished, to relieve; delivery

交替 **[chiāo-t'ì]**: to alternate, to relieve, to replace; in alternation, by turns

13 交會 **[chiāo-huì]**: intersection, convergence

交會點 **[chiāo-huì-tiěn]**: focal point

交道 **[chiāo-tào]**: intercourse; to have something to do with someone

14 交際 **[chiāo-chì]**: social intercourse, contacts, relations

15 交誼 **[chiāo-í]**: friendship

交稿 **[chiāo-kǎo]**: to hand in copy (to a printer)

交談 **[chiāo-t'án]**: to converse with

16 交戰 **[chiāo-chàn]**: to fight with, to be at war with, to join battle

交戰狀態 **[chiāo-chàn chuàng-t'ài]**: state of war

交戰國 **[chiāo-chàn kuó]**: belligerent, belligerent power, belligerent nation

交錯 **[chiāo-ts'ò]**: to overlap, to interlace, to cross, to intersect, to intertwine

17 交還 **[chiāo-huán]**: to restore, to give back, to return

交點 **[chiāo-tiěn]**: point of contact, point of intersection, crossing point

亦

3 亦工亦農 **[ì kūng ì núng]**: workers as well as peasants

7 亦步亦趨 **[ì pù ì ch'ū]**: to dance to someone's tune

— 6 Strokes —

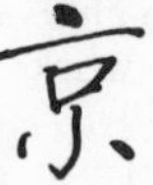

京 **[chīng]**: Peking (abbreviation for 北京)

9 京城 **[chīng-ch'éng]**: Seoul (Korea)

12 京都 **[chīng-tū]**: Kyoto (Japan)

15 京劇 **[chīng-chù]**: Peking opera

享

6 享年 **[hsiăng-nién]** : to die at the age of

8 享受 **[hsiăng-shòu]** : to enjoy

享受權利 **[hsiăng-shòu ch'üán-lì]** : to enjoy rights, to enjoy privileges

15 享樂 **[hsiăng-lè]** : enjoyment

享樂主義 **[hsiăng-lè chŭ-ì]** : hedonism, self-indulgence

— 7 Strokes —

9 亮相 **[liàng-hsiàng]** : to brighten one's countenance (i.e., to come forward and clarify one's position–said of leading cadres)

亭'

3 亭子 **[t'íng-tzu]** : arbor, pavilion, garret

— RADICAL 人 9 —

2 人人爲我，我爲人人 **[jén-jén wèi wŏ, wŏ wèi jén-jén]** : all for one and one for all (literally, everyone for me and I for everyone)

人力連 **[jén-lì-lién]** : labor company (People's Liberation Army)

人力, 物力, 財力 **[jén-lì, wù-lì, ts'ái-lì]** : manpower, material and financial resources

3 人口 **[jén-k'ŏu]** : population

人口稠密 **[jén-k'ŏu ch'óu-mì]** : populous, crowded, dense, densely populated, densely inhabited

人士 **[jén-shìh]** : people, personages, circles, sources, quarters

人大 **[jén-tà]** : National People's Congress (abbreviation of: 人民代表大會); China People's University (abbreviation of: 人民大學)

4 人心所向 **[jén-hsīn sŏ-hsiàng]** : where the feelings of the people point; popular support

人不犯我，我不犯人；人若犯我，我必犯人 **[jén pú-fàn wŏ, wŏ pú-fàn jén; jén jò fàn wŏ, wŏ pì fàn jén]** : "We will not attack unless we are attacked; if we are attacked, we will certainly attack"

人手 **[jén-shŏu]** : hand, workers, personnel

人文主義 **[jén-wén chŭ-ì]** : humanism

5 人民 **[jén-mín]** : 1. the people; popular, public. 2. Le Peuple (French periodical)

人民陣綫 **[jén-mín chèn-hsièn]** : popular front

人民政治協商會議 **[jén-mín chèng-chìh hsiéh-shāng hùi-ì]** : People's Political Consultative Conference

人民政協 **[jén-mín chèng-hsiéh]** : People's Political Consultative Conference (abbreviation of 人民政治協商會議)

人民解放戰爭 **[jén-mín chiĕh-fàng chàn-chēng]** : People's War of Liberation

人民解放軍 **[jén-mín chiĕh-fàng chūn]** : People's Liberation Army

人民檢察 **[jén-mín chiĕn-ch'á]** : People's Prosecutor

人民監察委員會 **[jén-mín chiēn-ch'á wěi-yüán-hùi]** : People's Supervisory Committee

人民鑑定員 **[jén-mín chièn-tìng-yüán]** : People's Assessors

人民志願軍 **[jén-mín chìh-yüàn chūn]** : People's Volunteers

人民法院 **[jén-mín fă-yüàn]** : People's Court

人民性 **[jén-mín-hsìng]** : popular nature

人民畫報 **[jén-mín huà-pào]** : China (People's) Pictorial (Chinese Communist monthly periodical)

人民議會 **[jén-mín ì-hùi]** : People's Chamber (East Germany); People's Assembly (Albania)

人民日報 **[jén-mín jìh-pào]** : 1. the People's Daily (Chinese daily newspaper); 2. Harian Rakjat (Indonesian daily newspaper)

人民功臣 **[jén-mín kūng-ch'én]** : people's hero

人民公社 **[jén-mín kūng-shè]** : people's commune

人民公敵 **[jén-mín kūng-tí]** : public enemy, common enemy of the people

人民民主制度 **[jén-mín mín-chŭ chìh-tù]** : people's democracy (democratic system)

人民民主專政 **[jén-mín mín-chŭ chuān-chèng]** : people's democratic dictatorship

人民民主自治 **[jén-mín mín-chŭ tzù-chìh]** : people's democratic self-government

人民內部矛盾 **[jén-mín nèi-pù máo-tùn]** : contradictions among the people

人民報 **[jén-mín-pào]** : Il Popolo (Italian daily newspaper)

人民陪審制 **[jén-mín p'éi-shĕn chìh]** : people's jury system

人民幣 **[jén-mín-pì]** : people's currency, the *renminbi*

人民票 **[jén-mín-p'iào]** : people's currency banknote

人民社會黨 **[jén-mín shè-hùi tăng]** : Praja Socialist Party (India)

人民大會堂 **[jén-mín tà-hùi t'áng]** : Great Hall of the People

人民代表大會 **[jén-mín tài-piăo tà-hùi]** : People's Congress

人民敵人 **[jén-mín tí-jén]** : people's enemy (people's enemies include bureaucratic capitalists, feudal landlords, counter-revolutionaries, and criminals)

人民財產 **[jén-mín ts'ái-ch'ăn]** : public property, the people's property

人民委員會 **[jén-mín wĕi-yüán-hùi]** : people's committee, people's council

人民院 **[jén-mín-yüàn]** : Lok Sabha (House of the People, India)

人本主義 **[jén-pĕn chŭ-ì]** : humanism

人生觀 **[jén-shēng-kuān]** : view of life, philosophy of life

7 人身攻擊 **[jén-shēn kūng-chī]** : personal abuse, attacks concerning personal matters, attack *ad hominem*

人身自由 **[jén-shēn tzù-yú]** : freedom of the person, personal freedom

8 人性 **[jén-hsìng]** : human nature

人性論 **[jén-hsìng-lùn]** : theory of human nature, the advocacy of human nature (considered to be a bourgeois, revisionist strain of thought)

人事檔案 **[jén-shìh tàng-àn]** : personnel dossier

人物 **[jén-wù]** : figure, personality, personage, character

9 人爲 **[jén-wéi]** : man-made, artificial

10 人浮於事 **[jén fú yǘ shìh]** : there are more men than vacant positions

人海戰術 **[jén-hăi chàn-shù]** : "human-sea" military tactics

人浬 **[jén-lĭ]** : passenger-nautical miles

人格 [jén-kó] : personality, character, stature

人馬 [jén-mǎ] : men and horses, military personnel, troops

人剝削人 [jén pō-hsüeh jén] : exploitation of man by man

人財兩旺 [jén ts'ái liǎng wàng] : men and finance both prosper (a slogan used in the land reform to portray the advantages of the movement)

人員 [jén-yüán] : personnel, staff, members (of an administration)

11 人情 [jén-ch'íng] : human feelings, favor, kindness, sympathy

人情的 [jén-ch'íng te] : humanistic

人情味 [jén-ch'íng-wèi] : flavor of human feelings, sense of humanity

人造的 [jén-tsào te] : artificial, synthetic, man-made

人造纖維 [jén-tsào hsiēn-wéi] : synthetic fiber

人造纖維廠 [jén-tsào hsiēn-wéi ch'ǎng] : artificial fiber plant

人造石油 [jén-tsào shíh-yú] : synthetic petroleum

人造地球衞星 [jén-tsào tì-ch'íu wèi-hsīng] : man-made earth satellite

人造衛星 [jén-tsào wèi-hsīng] : artificial satellite, man-made satellite

12 人間奇跡 [jén-chiēn ch'í-chì] : miracles in the mundane world (i.e., those which the thought of Mao can accomplish)

人道主義 [jén-tào chǔ-ì] : humanism

人道報 [jén-tào pào] : L'Humanité (French daily newspaper)

14 人種 [jén-chǔng] : race

人種主義 [jén-chǔng chǔ-ì] : nationalism, racism

15 人質 [jén-chìh] : hostage

19 人證 [jén-chèng] : testimony (of a witness)

人類 [jén-lèi] : mankind, humanity, the human race, the human species

人類中心說 [jén-lèi chūng-hsīn shuō] : anthropocentrism

人類學 [jén-lèi-hsüéh] : anthropology

人類本性 [jén-lèi pěn-hsìng] : human nature

人類大同 [jén-lèi tà-t'úng] : universal harmony, brotherhood of man

22 人權 [jén-ch'üán] : human rights, rights of the individual

— 2 Strokes —

5 介乎 [chièh-hú] : in between

11 介紹 [chièh-shào] : to recommend, to introduce, to present; recommendation

13 介意 [chièh-ì] : to mind, to care about, to regard with attention, to heed

4 今天說來 [chīn-t'iēn shuō-lái] : speaking (of something) in terms of today

9 今後 [chīn-hòu] : henceforth, from now on

仇

9 仇恨 [ch'óu-hèn] : hatred, animosity, enmity

11 仇視 [ch'óu-shìh] : to be hostile to, to hate, to regard as an enemy

15 仇敵 [ch'óu-tí] : enemy

3 仁川 [jén-ch'uān] : Inchon (Korea)

9 仁政 **[jén-chèng]**: benevolent government

13 仁義道德 **[jén-ì tào-té]**: humanity, righteousness, and morality

仍

12 仍然 **[jéng-ján]**: yet, as ever, as yet, still

仍然是 **[jéng-ján shìh]**: still; to remain

什

12 什普奇 **[shíh-p'ŭ-ch'í]**: Shipki (Tibet)

— 3 Strokes —

仗

13 仗義執言 **[chàng-ì chíh-yén]**: to speak boldly in defense of justice

仗勢欺人 **[chàng-shìh ch'ī-jén]**: to abuse one's power and bully the people

付

3 付之一笑 **[fù-chīh í-hsiào]**: to laugh off, to afford to laugh at

5 付出 **[fù-ch'ū]**: to pay, to pay out, to remit

8 付表決 **[fù piăo-chüéh]**: to put to a vote

16 付諸實施 **[fù-chū shíh-shīh]**: to put into practice, to carry into effect

仙

5 仙台 **[hsiēn-t'ái]**: Sendai (Japan)

14 仙境 **[hsiēn-chìng]**: fairyland

以

3 以一當十，以十當百 **[ĭ ī tāng-shíh, ĭ shíh tāng păi]**: to pit one against ten and ten against one hundred

以工代賑 **[ĭ kūng tài chèn]**: to give work instead of direct relief; method of relief through production

以大吃小 **[ĭ tà ch'īh hsiăo]**: to eat the little by use of the large (i.e., to use a large body of troops to defeat a smaller body of troops)

5 以功臣自居的情緒 **[ĭ kūng-ch'én tzù-chü te ch'íng-hsü]**: with the air of a self-styled hero

6 以色列 **[ĭ-sè-lièh]**: Israel

以色列共和國 **[ĭ-sè-lièh kùng-hó-kuó]**: Republic of Israel

以此 **[ĭ tz'ŭ]**: with this, by this

7 以身作則 **[ĭ shēn tsò tsé]**: to set an example with one's own conduct

8 以毒攻毒 **[ĭ tú kūng tú]**: to administer poison as an antidote to poison

以物易物 **[ĭ wù ì wù]**: to barter, to exchange one commodity for another

9 以紅帶專 **[ĭ húng tài chuān]**: redness must guide expertness (i.e., loyalty to the Party must come before professional expertness)

以便於 **[ĭ-pièn-yű]**: in order to, with a view to, to facilitate

以爲 **[ĭ-wéi]**: to regard as, to consider, to believe, to presume

以怨報德 **[ĭ yüàn pào té]**: to return evil for good, to repay good with evil

11 以貨易貨 **[ĭ huò ì huò]**: to barter, to exchange one commodity for another

12 以逸待勞 **[ĭ ì tài láo]**: to wait at one's ease for the fatigued enemy

13 以農村包圍城市 **[ĭ núng-ts'ūn pāo-wéi ch'éng-shìh]**: to encircle cities with rural areas

以農爲主，以副養農 **[ĭ núng wéi chŭ, ĭ fù yăng núng]**: to regard agriculture as the main factor and let subsidiary production nurture agriculture (i.e., production of food grains is the main task of farmers, while subsidiary production of vegetables, pigs, etc., generates capital for the former)

以農爲榮，以農爲樂 **[ǐ núng wéi júng, ǐ núng wéi lè]**: to look upon agriculture as glory and joy

以農業爲基礎，以工業爲主導 **[ǐ núng-yèh wéi chī-ch'ǔ, ǐ kūng-yèh wéi chǔ-tǎo]**: with agriculture as the foundation and industry as the dominant factor (in the national economy)

以資 **[ǐ-tzū]**: in order to, by means of which one may

以資彌補 **[ǐ tzū mí-pǔ]**: in order to make up a shortage

15 以德報怨 **[ǐ té pào yüàn]**: to return good for evil

16 以戰止戰 **[ǐ chàn chǐh chàn]**: to end war by means of war

以戰養戰 **[ǐ chàn yǎng chàn]**: to sustain war by war

17 以點帶面 **[ǐ tiěn tài mièn]**: to let one unit guide a whole area (i.e., to have one advanced unit help backward units)

18 以豐補歉 **[ǐ fēng pǔ ch'ièn]**: to make up for poor harvests during years of rich harvests, to make up for dearth with abundance

以糧爲綱 **[ǐ liáng wéi kāng]**: with food grain as the key policy; to place primary emphasis on the production of foodstuffs

以糧爲綱，多種經營 **[ǐ liáng wéi kāng, tō-chǔng chīng-yíng]**: diversified economy with foodstuffs as the key link

20 以鬥爭求團結 **[ǐ tòu-chēng ch'íu t'uán-chiéh]**: to attain unity through struggle

令

2 令人 **[lìng-jén]**: to cause one (to feel, etc.)

令人震驚的 **[lìng-jén chèn-chīng te]**: shocking, frightening

令人興奮的 **[lìng-jén hsīng-fèn te]**: rousing, exciting

令人失望的 **[lìng-jén shīh-wàng te]**: disappointing, discouraging

令人厭倦的 **[lìng-jén yèn-chüàn te]**: tiresome, boring, tedious, jaded

他

20 他羅帽 **[t'ā-ló-mào]**: Tarokmaw (Burma)

代

5 代用品 **[tài-yùng-p'ǐn]**: substitute, substitute goods

6 代行 **[tài-hsíng]**: to act for another person (in an official capacity)

7 代言人 **[tài-yén-jén]**: spokesman

8 代表 **[tài-piǎo]**: to represent; representative, delegate, deputy

代表人物 **[tài-piǎo jén-wù]**: representatives

代表大會 **[tài-piǎo tà-hùi]**: congress, conference, meeting of representatives

代表團 **[tài-piǎo-t'uán]**: delegation, mission, deputation

代表資格審查委員會 **[tài-piǎo tzū-kó shěn-ch'á wěi-yüán-hùi]**: Credentials Committee

11 代理 **[tài-lǐ]**: to act for, to act as, to act for another

代理人 **[tài-lǐ-jén]**: agent

12 代勞 **[tài-láo]**: to do something for another

14 代號 **[tài-hào]**: number, figure

15 代價 **[tài-chià]**: price, cost

代銷 **[tài-hsiāo]**: to act as a commission agent, to sell as an agent, to distribute for the state on a commission basis

代銷人 [tài-hsiāo-jén]: retail distributor, commission agent of the state

16 代辦 [tài-pàn]: deputy, agent, chargé d'affaires; to act in place of

20 代議制 [tài-ì-chìh]: parliamentary system

仔

11 仔細 [tzǔ-hsì]: cautious, careful, prudent, scrupulous, meticulous, punctilious

— 4 Strokes —

伎

10 伎倆 [chì-liǎng]: astute, cunning; ability, skill

企

13 企業 [ch'ì-yèh]: undertaking, enterprise

企業家 [ch'ì-yèh-chiā]: entrepreneur, industrialist

企業獎勵基金 [ch'ì-yèh chiǎng-lì chī-chīn]: director's funds (funds allocated by the government to enterprises for meritorious work)

14 企圖 [ch'ì-t'ú]: to attempt, to try, to venture; attempt, try, venture, endeavor

件

3 件工 [chièn-kūng]: piecework, pieceworker

仲

10 仲家 [chùng-chiā]: Chung-chia (minority nationality)

12 仲裁 [chùng-ts'ái]: arbitration

仲裁人 [chùng-ts'ái-jén]: arbitrator

份

3 份子 [fèn-tzu]: element, component, member

仿

10 仿效 [fǎng-hsiào]: to follow the example of, to copy, to model after

12 仿單 [fǎng-tān]: directions, instructions for use, commercial handbills

13 仿照 [fǎng-chào]: to imitate, to copy, according to

伏

6 伏地 [fú-tì]: local, on the spot

13 伏罪 [fú-tsùi]: to admit guilt, to accept punishment

14 伏爾加 [fú-ěrh-chiā]: Volga

17 伏擊 [fú-chī]: to attack from ambush

19 伏羅希洛夫 [fú-ló-hsī-lò-fū]: Voroshilov, Klimentiy Efremovich (Russian officer and statesman); Voroshilov, Nikolsk

休

10 休息 [hsīu-hsí]: to rest; recreation, rest, repose, relaxation

休息時間 [hsīu-hsí shíh-chiēn]: interval, intermission, recess, break, pause

11 休戚 [hsīu-ch'ì]: joy and sorrow, good fortune and ill

休戚相關 [hsīu-ch'ì hsiāng-kuān]: feeling of solidarity

休戚與共 [hsīu-ch'ì yü-kùng]: sharing the common good and bad fortune, sharing the common joy and sorrow

休假 **[hsīu-chià]**: to go on vacation, to have a holiday; holiday, furlough, leave

12 休閑地 **[hsīu-hsién-tì]**: fallow land

13 休會 **[hsīu-hùi]**: to adjourn; adjournment, recess

15 休養所 **[hsīu-yăng-sŏ]**: rest home, sanitarium

休養地 **[hsīu-yăng-tì]**: resort, health resort

16 休戰 **[hsīu-chàn]**: truce, armistice, cease-fire, cessation of hostilities

休整 **[hsīu-chĕng]**: rest and consolidation

18 休謨 **[hsīu-mó]**: David Hume (1711–1776)

伙

4 伙友 **[hŭo-yŭ]**: partner

6 伙同 **[hŭo-t'úng]**: together

7 伙伴 **[hŭo-pàn]**: partner, friend, mate, comrade, companion

9 伙計 **[hŭo-chì]**: assistant, apprentice, clerk (in a store), waiter

14 伙種 **[hŭo-chùng]**: to cultivate jointly

伊

3 伊川 **[ī-ch'uān]**: Ichon (Korea); Ichuan (China)

4 伊比利亞 **[ī-pĭ-lì-yà]**: Iberia

5 伊比河 **[ī-pĭ hó]**: Elbe River

7 伊利湖 **[ī-lì hú]**: Lake Erie

伊利諾斯 **[ī-lì-nò-ssū]**: Illinois

8 伊拉克 **[ī-lā-k'ò]**: Iraq

伊拉克共和國 **[ī-lā-k'ò kùng-hó-kuó]**: Republic of Iraq

9 伊洛瓦底江 **[ī-lò-wă-tì chiāng]**: Irrawaddy River

10 伊格納提夫 **[ī-kó-nà-t'í-fū]**: Ignatov, Nikalai (Russian statesman)

伊朗 **[ī-lăng]**: Iran (Persia)

伊朗王國 **[ī-lăng wáng-kuó]**: Kingdom of Iran (Persia)

12 伊斯蘭教 **[ī-ssū-lán chiào]**: Islam

伊斯坦布爾 **[ī-ssū-t'ăn-pù-ĕrh]**: Istanbul (Turkey)

13 伊勢灣 **[ī-shìh wān]**: Ise Bay (Japan)

伊葉 **[ī-yèh]**: Ye (Burma)

14 伊爾庫次克 **[ī-ĕrh-k'ù-tz'ù-k'ò]**: Irkutsk (Soviet Union)

16 伊壁鳩魯 **[ī-pì-chīu-lŭ]**: Epicurus (341 B.C. to 270 B.C.)

21 伊蘭國 **[ī-lán kuó]**: Iran

7 任何 **[jèn-hó]**: any

8 任其自流 **[jèn ch'í tzù-líu]**: to let things run their own course

任命 **[jèn-mìng]**: to appoint, to commission, to assign, to nominate; nomination

11 任務 **[jèn-wù]**: assignment, role, duty, job, mission

12 任期 **[jèn-ch'í]**: term of office, tenure of office, duration of service, period of appointment

13 任意 **[jèn-ì]**: at will, according to one's feelings; arbitrary, unrestrained, unbridled

任意擺佈 **[jèn-ì păi-pù]**: to manipulate as one likes

16 任憑 **[jèn-p'íng]**: despite, in spite of, regardless of, to leave a course of action or a decision up to a person

仰

6 仰光 **[yǎng-kuāng]** : Rangoon (Burma)

8 仰承鼻息 **[yǎng-ch'éng pí-hsí]** : to bend to someone's every whim, to be at someone's beck and call

— 5 Strokes —

佔

3 佔上風 **[chàn shàng-fēng]** : to gain the upper hand, to have the advantage

6 佔先 **[chàn-hsiēn]** : to assume precedence, to assume leadership

佔有 **[chàn-yǔ]** : to possess, to occupy, to have, to hold; possession

佔有者 **[chàn-yǔ-chě]** : possessor, holder

佔有權 **[chàn-yǔ-ch'üán]** : rights of possession

7 佔住地位 **[chàn-chù tì-wèi]** : to stand firm, to hold one's own

佔便宜 **[chàn p'ién-í]** : to take advantage of, to gain advantage over, to have the advantage of, to turn to one's profit

12 佔統治地位 **[chàn t'ǔng-chìh tì-wèi]** : to assume a predominant position

14 佔領 **[chàn-lǐng]** : to occupy, to take, to seize, to take possession of

佔領制度 **[chàn-lǐng chìh-tù]** : occupation regime

佔領軍 **[chàn-lǐng-chǖn]** : army or troops of occupation

佔領地區 **[chàn-lǐng tì-ch'ǖ]** : occupied area

16 佔優勢 **[chàn yū-shìh]** : to enjoy superiority, to be superior to, to get the advantage of; preponderance, dominance; predominant

伽

7 伽利略 **[chiā-lì-lüèh]** : Galileo

住

6 住宅 **[chù-chái]** : dwelling, house, residence, living quarters, housing

住宅建築 **[chù-chái chièn-chù]** : housing construction

住宅區 **[chù-chái-ch'ǖ]** : residential area

佛

10 佛朗哥 **[fó-lǎng-kō]** : Franco, Francisco

11 佛教 **[fó-chiào]** : Buddhism

14 佛爾加 **[fó-ěrh-chiā]** : Volga River

佛爾泰 **[fó-ěrh-t'ài]** : Voltaire (1694–1778)

佛蒙特 **[fó-méng-t'è]** : Vermont

20 佛羅里達 **[fó-ló-lǐ-tá]** : Florida

佛羅里斯海 **[fó-ló-lǐ-ssū hǎi]** : Flores Sea

佛羅倫薩 **[fó-ló-lún-sà]** : Florence

佧

7 佧佤 **[k'ā-wǎ]** : Kawa (a minority nationality in Yunnan)

估

9 估計 **[kū-chì]** : to estimate, to gauge

估計過高 **[kū-chì kuò-kāo]** : to overrate, to overestimate

估計過低 **[kū-chì kuò-tī]** : to underrate, to underestimate

估計錯誤 **[kū-chì ts'ò-wù]** : to miscalculate; miscalculation, wrong estimate

12 估量 **[kū-liàng]** : to evaluate, to calculate

14 估摸 **[kū-mō]** : to appraise, brief estimate

15 估價 **[kū-chià]** : to appraise, to evaluate, to assess, to grade; appraisal, evaluation, assessment

伶

伶 **[líng]** : Ling (a minority nationality)

你

6 你死我活的鬥爭 **[nǐ-ssŭ wŏ-huó te tòu-chēng]** : life-and-death struggle

伴

16 伴隨 **[pàn-súi]** : to accompany, to follow

伯

2 伯力 **[pó-lì]** : Khabarovsk

7 伯利兹 **[pó-lì-tzū]** : Belize (British Honduras)

伯利恒 **[pó-lì-héng]** : Bethlehem

8 伯林 **[pó-lín]** : Berlin

伯明罕 **[pó-míng-hăn]** : Birmingham

9 伯南布哥 **[pó-nán-pù-kō]** : Pernambuco

10 伯恩斯坦主義 **[pó-ēn-ssū-t'ăn chŭ-ì]** : Bernsteinism

12 伯斯 **[pó-ssū]** : Perth

14 伯爾尼 **[pó-ĕrh-ní]** : Bern (Switzerland)

18 伯爵 **[pó-chüéh]** : count (continental Europe); earl (England)

佈

7 佈告 **[pù-kào]** : notice, ordinance, edict

8 佈依 **[pù-ī]** : Pu-i (a minority nationality)

12 佈景 **[pù-chĭng]** : scenery, stage setting

3 佘山觀象台 **[shé-shān kuān-hsiàng-t'ái]** : Zose Observatory

伸

2 伸入 **[shēn-jù]** : to make one's way into

4 伸手派 **[shēn-shŏu-p'ài]** : the hat-in-hand group, panhandlers (those who rely on government for support)

17 伸縮性 **[shēn-sō-hsìng]** : flexibility, elasticity

似

5 似乎 **[ssù-hū]** : to look like, to appear, to seem, to have the appearance of

9 似是而非 **[ssù-shìh érh fēi]** : spurious, counterfeit, imitation

10 似狼的 **[ssù-láng te]** : wolfish

但

9 但是 **[tàn-shìh]** : but, yet, however, nevertheless, nonetheless

10 但書 **[tàn-shū]** : proviso

19 但願 **[tàn-yüàn]**: only to hope, only to wish, to be only too glad to

低

3 低工資職工 **[tī kūng-tzū chíh-kūng]**: low-paid workers

7 低估 **[tī-kū]**: to underestimate, to underrate, to minimize

低利息 **[tī lì-hsí]**: low interest

低利貸款 **[tī-lì tài-k'uǎn]**: low interest loan

8 低拉瓦 **[tī-lā-wǎ]**: Thelawa (Burma)

10 低級的 **[tī-chí te]**: primary, low-grade, elementary

低級趣味 **[tī-chí ch'ǜ-wèi]**: bad taste

11 低產作物 **[tī-ch'ǎn tsò-wù]**: low-yield crop

15 低潮 **[tī-ch'áo]**: ebb tide, low tide (in a figurative sense, of a revolutionary movement)

16 低頭 **[tī-t'óu]**: to bow the head (used to refer to the landlords' and bourgeoisie's bowing to the will of the workers and peasants)

低頭認錯 **[tī-t'óu jèn-ts'ò]**: to confess one's mistake by lowering one's head

17 低聲下氣 **[tī-shēng hsià-ch'ì]**: to be meek and submissive by subduing one's voice

佃

4 佃戶 **[tièn-hù]**: tenant

10 佃租 **[tièn-tsū]**: tenancy, rent

12 佃富農 **[tièn-fù-núng]**: a well-to-do tenant peasant (i.e., a well-to-do peasant who does not own his own land)

13 佃農 **[tièn-núng]**: tenant farmer, tenant

佐

5 佐世保 **[tsŏ-shìh-pǎo]**: Sasebo (Japan)

12 佐賀 **[tsŏ-hò]**: Saga (Japan)

作

2 作人的原則 **[tsò-jén te yüán-tsé]**: the principles of being a man

5 作用 **[tsò-yùng]**: function

7 作見證 **[tsò chièn-chèng]**: to bear witness, to be a witness, to give evidence, to give testimony (as a witness)

作坊 **[tsò-fāng]**: workshop

8 作物 **[tsò-wù]**: crop

作物育種栽培研究所 **[tsò-wù yǜ-chǔng tsāi-p'éi yén-chìu-sŏ]**: Institute of Crop Seed Cultivation

9 作者 **[tsò-chě]**: author, writer

作風 **[tsò-fēng]**: style, working style, style of work

作風不純 **[tsò-fēng pù-ch'ún]**: impurity in style of work

作品 **[tsò-p'ǐn]**: work, composition

作威作福 **[tsò-wēi tsò-fú]**: to abuse one's power tyrannically and ride roughshod over the people

10 作家協會 **[tsŏ-chiā hsiéh-hùi]**: Writers' Union

12 作惡多端 **[tsò-ò tō-tuān]**: to commit all kinds of evil; guilty of every conceivable atrocity

16 作戰區域 **[tsò-chàn ch'ǖ-yǜ]**: theater of battle, war zone

作戰效能 **[tsò-chàn hsiào-néng]**: fighting efficiency, combat efficiency

作戰命令 [**tsò-chàn mìng-lìng**]: combat order

作戰不利 [**tsò-chàn pú-lì**]: to sustain reverses in fighting

作戰部隊 [**tsò-chàn pù-tùi**]: combat troops

20 作孽 [**tsò-nièh**]: evil-doing, to do evil

伺

16 伺機 [**ssù-chī**]: to await a chance, to wait for an opening, to bide one's time

位

8 位居 [**wèi-chū**]: to rank, to have a position

位於 [**wèi-yú**]: to be located, to be situated, to be placed, to be at a point

— 6 Strokes —

佳

7 佳作 [**chiā-tsò**]: a brilliant piece of work

14 佳節 [**chiā-chiéh**]: festival, beautiful festival

佳境 [**chiā-chìng**]: a favorable situation, a favorable position; a beautiful region

侈

15 侈談 [**ch'ǐh-t'án**]: to boast, to brag; extravagant talk

19 侈靡 [**ch'ǐh-mǐ**]: wasteful extravagance

依

2 依人定量 [**ī-jén tìng-liàng**]: to fix an allocation according to the individual

6 依次 [**ī-tz'ù**]: consecutive, successive, to follow the order, in order of, in turn, by turns

8 依法 [**ī-fǎ**]: according to law, legally

依附 [**ī-fù**]: to adhere, to follow, to hang onto the coattails of

11 依率計征 [**ī-lǜ chì-chēng**]: taxation in accordance with fixed rates

13 依照 [**ī-chào**]: according to, in accordance with, in terms of, in conformance with

15 依靠 [**ī-k'ào**]: to rely on, to depend on; dependence; dependent upon

16 依據 [**ī-chǜ**]: according to, in accordance with, in terms of, in conformance with

依賴 [**ī-lài**]: to rely on, to depend on; dependence; dependent upon

供

2 供人利用 [**kūng-jén lì-yùng**]: to serve as a lackey, to be a cat's paw

4 供不應求 [**kūng pú-yìng ch'íu**]: supply short of demand, supply failing to meet demand, supply behind demand

7 供求 [**kūng-ch'íu**]: supply and demand

11 供產銷 [**kūng-ch'ǎn-hsiāo**]: supply, production, and marketing

12 供給 [**kūng-chǐ**]: to supply, to furnish, to provide

供給制 [**kūng-chǐ chìh**]: supply system, free supply system, free board and lodging system (a system whereby government employees are given free board and lodging together with a small amount of cash for miscellaneous expenses)

供給量 [**kūng-chǐ liàng**]: supply quota

供給資金 [**kūng-chǐ tzū-chīn**]: supply financing

15 供銷 **[kūng-hsiāo]**: supply and distribution, supply and sales, marketing

供銷合作社 **[kūng-hsiāo hó-tsò-shè]**: supply and marketing cooperative

供銷合同 **[kūng-hsiāo hó-t'úng]**: supply and marketing agreement

供銷部 **[kūng-hsiāo-pù]**: retail department, shop

供銷生產小組 **[kūng-hsiāo shēng-ch'ǎn hsiǎo-tsǔ]**: supply and marketing production team

供銷生產社 **[kūng-hsiāo shēng-ch'ǎn-shè]**: supply and marketing producer cooperative

供養 **[kūng-yǎng]**: to provide for, to support, to nourish

17 供應 **[kūng-yìng]**: to supply, to provide, to furnish

供應站 **[kūng-yìng-chàn]**: supply station

18 供瞻仰 **[kūng-chān-yǎng]**: to lie in state

來

8 來往 **[lái-wǎng]**: coming and going, intercourse, social relations, relationship, transaction, round trip

來往文件 **[lái-wǎng wén-chièn]**: correspondence, communications

13 來源 **[lái-yüán]**: source, spring, origin

14 來賓 **[lái-pīn]**: guest

例

3 例子 **[lì-tzu]**: example, instance, case in point

5 例外 **[lì-wài]**: exception

6 例行公事 **[lì-hsíng kūng-shìh]**: routine, regular procedure, regular course of official duties

例如 **[lì-jú]**: for example, for instance, such as

19 例證 **[lì-chèng]**: to exemplify, to illustrate by example; example, illustration, evidence

佩

2 佩刀式噴氣機 **[p'èi-tāo-shìh p'ēn-ch'ì-chī]**: sabre jet

使

5 使用 **[shǐh-yùng]**: to use, to employ, to exercise, to apply

8 使命 **[shǐh-mìng]**: mission

9 使勁 **[shǐh-chìn]**: to exert force; forcefully, vigorously

使信服 **[shǐh hsìn-fú]**: to convince a person

15 使節 **[shǐh-chiéh]**: envoy, diplomatic agent

侍

10 侍候 **[shìh-hòu]**: to serve, to wait upon, to look after

11 侍從 **[shìh-ts'úng]**: aide, lieutenant, attaché, secretary, subordinate, member of one's entourage

17 侍應員 **[shìh-yìng-yüán]**: waiter, attendant

侗

侗 **[t'ùng]**: T'ung (a minority nationality)

10 侗家 **[t'ùng-chiā]**: T'ung-chia (a minority group in the border region of Kueichow, Hunan, and Kwangsi)

— 7 Strokes —

侵

2 侵入 **[ch'īn-jù]**: to invade, to intrude, to trespass; invasion, intrusion, penetration

6 侵犯 **[ch'īn-fàn]**: to encroach upon, to infringe upon, to intrude, to violate; encroachment, infringement, intrusion, violation

7 侵佔 **[ch'īn-chàn]**: to occupy illegally

侵呑 **[ch'īn-t'ūn]**: to embezzle, to squeeze; embezzlement, illegal appropriation

10 侵埃戰爭 **[ch'īn-āi chàn-chēng]**: War of Aggression Against Egypt

11 侵略 **[ch'īn-lüèh]**: to invade, to aggress against; aggression, invasion; aggressive

侵略戰爭 **[ch'īn-lüèh chàn-chēng]**: aggressive war

侵略者 **[ch'īn-lüèh-chě]**: aggressor, invader

侵略成性的 **[ch'īn-lüèh ch'éng-hsìng te]**: aggressive by nature

侵略主義 **[ch'īn-lüèh chǔ-ì]**: jingoism

12 侵朝戰爭 **[ch'īn-ch'áo chàn-chèng]**: War of Aggression Against Korea

19 侵攏 **[ch'īn-lǔng]**: to invade and harass

22 侵襲 **[ch'īn-hsí]**: to encroach upon; encroachment

俅

2 俅人 **[ch'íu-jén]**: Jujen (a minority nationality)

俘

13 俘虜 **[fú-lǔ]**: to capture; captive, prisoner of war

17 俘獲 **[fú-huò]**: to capture, to be taken prisoner

侯

18 侯爵 **[hóu-chüéh]**: marquess

信

3 信口胡說 **[hsìn-k'ǒu hú-shuō]**: to jabber, to babble, to talk nonsense; sheer nonsense

4 信心 **[hsìn-hsīn]**: confidence, conviction, faith, belief; confident

5 信用合作社 **[hsìn-yùng hó-tsò-shè]**: credit cooperative

信用部 **[hsìn-yùng-pù]**: credit department

6 信任 **[hsìn-jèn]**: to trust, to count on; confidence, faith, credit

信任投票 **[hsìn-jèn t'óu-p'iào]**: vote of confidence

信守諾言 **[hsìn-shǒu nò-yén]**: to keep one's word

信仰 **[hsìn-yǎng]**: faith, belief, religion, worship

信仰自由 **[hsìn-yǎng tzù-yú]**: freedom of religious belief

8 信念 **[hsìn-nièn]**: belief, faith, creed

10 信息論 **[hsìn-hsí-lùn]**: cybernetics, information theory

信條 **[hsìn-t'iáo]**: credo, creed, article of faith

信徒 **[hsìn-t'ú]**: believer, worshipper, adherent, disciple, follower, convert, devotee

12 信貸資金 **[hsìn-tài tzū-chīn]**: credit funds, funds for extending credits

13 信號 **[hsìn-hào]**: signal

俚

14 俚語 [lĭ-yŭ] : slang

俄

6 俄亥俄 [ó-hài-ó] : Ohio

7 俄克拉何馬 [ó-k'ò-lā-hó-mă] : Oklahoma

9 俄帝 [ó-tì] : Russian imperialism

11 俄勒崗 [ó-lè-kāng] : Oregon

16 俄羅斯 [ó-ló-ssū] : Russia

保

保 [păo] : 1. Paoting (abbreviation for 保定), 2. a member of the Chinese Communist Party (used in the People's Liberation Army); 3. crop protection (prevention of insect pests and plant diseases–an element of the 八字憲法, q.v.)

2 保人 [păo-jén] : guarantor

保丁 [păo-tīng] : security guards

3 保大 [păo-tà] : Bao Dai (Vietnamese statesman)

4 保不住 [paŏ-pú-chù] : unable to protect or answer for, cannot be vouched for

5 保加利亞 [păo-chiā-lì-yà] : Bulgaria

保加利亞人民共和國 [păo-chiā-lì-yà jén-mín kùng-hó-kuó] : People's Republic of Bulgaria

保加利亞人民共和國國民議會 [păo-chiā-lì-yà jén-mín kùng-hó-kuó kuó-mín ì-hùi] : National Assembly of the People's Republic of Bulgaria

保加利亞通訊社 [păo-chiā-lì-yà t'ūng-hsǜn-shè] : Bulgarian Telegraph Agency (BTA)

保甲 [păo-chiă] : the pao-chia system

6 保安 [păo-ān] : 1. Pao-an (a minority nationality in Kansu); 2. security

保安部隊 [păo-ān pù-tùi] : peace preservation corps

保安措施 [păo-ān ts'ò-shīh] : security precautions, security measures

保吃 [păo-ch'īh] : to guarantee food (one of the 五保, q.v.)

保全 [păo-ch'üán] : to preserve intact; preservation

保全工 [păo-ch'üán-kūng] : mechanic

保守 [păo-shŏu] : to protect, to guard, to save, to preserve; conservative

保守主義 [păo-shŏu-chŭ-ì] : conservatism

保守派 [păo-shŏu-p'ài] : conservatives

保守思想 [păo-shŏu ssū-hsiăng] : conservative ideas, conservative thinking, conservative ideology

保守黨 [păo-shŏu-tăng] : conservative party

保存 [păo-ts'ún] : to preserve, to retain, to protect

保字號 [păo-tzù-hào] : Pao Tzu Hao (the name of a secret society that was known to exist in 1967 in Shantung and Shansi provinces among overthrown Party Committee people)

8 保育 [păo-yǜ] : to raise, to rear, to care for

保育工作 [păo-yǜ kūng-tsò] : child welfare

保育事業 [păo-yǜ shìh-yèh] : child care, child welfare

9 保持 [păo-ch'íh] : to remain, to retain, to maintain, to perpetuate, to preserve; preservation

保持政權 [păo-ch'íh chèng-ch'üán] : to maintain power

保持艱苦備鬥作風 [păo-ch'íh chiēn-k'ŭ pèi-tòu tsò-fēng] : to keep to a spirit of plain living and hard work

保持警惕[**pǎo-ch'íh chǐng-t'ì**]: to keep watch, to maintain vigilance

保持革命幹勁 [**pǎo-ch'íh kó-mìng kàn-chìn**]: to keep up one's revolutionary enthusiasm

保持控制[**pǎo-ch'íh k'ùng-chìh**]: to retain one's hold on

保持冷靜的頭腦 [**pǎo-ch'íh lěng-chìng te t'óu-nǎo**]: to keep a cool head, to keep cool

保持優勢[**pǎo-ch'íh yū-shìh**]: to maintain one's lead or superiority

保持原樣[**pǎo-ch'íh yüán-yàng**]: to keep intact, to leave intact the original appearance

保穿 [**pǎo-ch'uān**]: to guarantee clothing (one of the 五保, q.v.)

保皇黨 [**pǎo-huáng-tǎng**]: royalists (during the Cultural Revolution, those supporting Liu Shao-ch'i and Teng Hsiao-p'ing)

保皇黨人[**pǎo-huáng-tǎng jén**]: royalist

10 保留 [**pǎo-líu**]: to retain, to reserve, to keep, to keep back; reserve, reservations (i.e., in the sense of "to answer with reservations")

保送 [**pǎo-sùng**]: to recommend for advanced training or education

11 保教 [**pǎo-chiào**]: to guarantee education for children (one of the 五保, q.v.)

保健站 [**pǎo-chièn-chàn**]: health station, health center

保健工作[**pǎo-chièn kūng-tsò**]: public health work

保健事業[**pǎo-chièn shìh-yèh**]: health service

保健室 [**pǎo-chièn-shìh**]: health office

保健綱 [**pǎo-chièn-wǎng**]: health protection network

保密 [**pǎo-mì**]: to keep secret

13 保葬 [**pǎo-tsàng**]: to guarantee burial for the dead (one of the 五保, q.v.)

14 保障 [**pǎo-chàng**]: to guarantee, to safeguard; protection, safeguard

保障生活[**pǎo-chàng shēng-huó**]: to ensure livelihood

保管 [**pǎo-kuǎn**]: to guarantee, to certify, to be responsible for

15 保衛 [**pǎo-wèi**]: to defend, to protect, to guard, to safeguard, to secure

保養 [**pǎo-yǎng**]: to nourish, to maintain; maintenance

16 保險 [**pǎo-hsiěn**]: to insure; insurance

保險費 [**pǎo-hsiěn-fèi**]: insurance premium

保險公司 [**pǎo-hsiěn kūng-ssū**]: insurance company, underwriter

保燒 [**pǎo-shāo**]: to guarantee fuel (one of the 五保, q.v.)

19 保證 [**pǎo-chèng**]: to guarantee; guarantee

保證人 [**pǎo-chèng-jén**]: guarantor

保證書 [**pǎo-chèng-shū**]: guarantee, affidavit, deed of security

保羅一世 [**pǎo-ló í-shìh**]: King Paul (King of Greece)

保鏢 [**pǎo-piāo**]: bodyguard, guard, armed escort

20 保釋 [**pǎo-shìh**]: to bail (out of prison); bail

21 保護 [**pǎo-hù**]: to protect, to shield, to shelter, to safeguard, to defend

保護和發展[**pǎo-hù hó fā-chǎn**]: to protect and foster

保護人[**pǎo-hù-jén**]: guardian, protector

保護關稅[**pǎo-hù kuān-shùi**]: protective tariff

保護國 [**pǎo-hù-kuó**]: protectorate

保護勝利果實 [**pǎo-hù shèng-lì kuǒ-shíh**]: protect the fruits of victory (a slogan used during the land reform of the early 1950s)

保鏢 **[pǎo-p'iào]** : an armed guard

便

6 便衣 **[pièn-ī]** : plain clothes; not in uniform

便衣警察 **[pièn-ī chǐng-ch'á]** : plainclothes man, plainclothes policeman

7 便利 **[pièn-lì]** : to facilitate; convenience, facilities; convenient

8 便宜行事 **[pièn-í hsíng-shìh]** : to act according to the circumstances

13 便當 **[pièn-tāng]** : pleasant, convenient, appropriate, handy

俗

2 俗人 **[sú-jén]** : layman

13 俗話 **[sú-huà]** : common saying, proverb, colloquial speech

促

5 促生 **[ts'ù-shēng]** : to precipitate, to cause

6 促成 **[ts'ù-ch'éng]** : to precipitate, to prompt, to cause to happen

8 促使 **[ts'ù-shǐh]** : to bring about

10 促退派 **[ts'ù-t'ùi-p'ài]** : factions promoting retrogression, retrogressive elements, backward elements

12 促進 **[ts'ù-chìn]** : to further, to stimulate, to enhance, to accelerate, to give impetus to

促進派 **[ts'ù-chìn-p'ài]** : promoters of progress

侮

10 侮辱 **[wǔ-jù]** : to insult, to affront, to outrage, to humiliate, to dishonor; insult, affront, disagrace

— 8 Strokes —

倡

16 倡辦 **[ch'àng-pàn]** : to begin, to lead, to introduce, to promote, to found

倡導 **[ch'àng-tǎo]** : to advocate, to initiate, to lead

20 倡議 **[ch'àng-ì]** : to advocate, to propose, to introduce, to promote, to suggest; initiative

借

3 借口 **[chièh-k'ǒu]** : pretext, excuse, subterfuge, cover, cloak

7 借助 **[chièh-chù]** : to depend on

12 借款 **[chièh-k'uǎn]** : to lend money; to take a loan; loan

22 借鑒 **[chièh-chièn]** : to draw lessons from, to take something as an example, to profit from the experiences of others

值

11 值得 **[chíh-té]** : to merit, to deserve; worthwhile, worthy of

倬

14 倬爾羅斯 **[chó-ěrh-ló-ssū]** : Choros (a minority nationality)

俱

15 俱樂部 **[chǜ-lè-pù]** : club

候

7 候車室 **[hòu-ch'ē-shìh]** : waiting room (in a train or bus depot)

[13] 候補[hòu-pŭ]: alternate, deputy

候補委員[hòu-pŭ wĕi-yüán]: alternate member

[16] 候選人[hòu-hsüăn-jén]: candidate (in an election)

候選資格[hòu-hsüăn tzū-kó]: candidacy qualifications

倖

[7] 倖免[hsìng-miĕn]: a lucky escape

修

[3] 修女[hsīu-nǚ]: nun, sister (Roman Catholic)

[5] 修正案[hsīu-chèng-àn]: amendment

修正主義[hsīu-chèng chŭ-ì]: revisionism (any modification of Marxist-Leninist theory or the method of carrying it out)

修正主義者[hsīu-chèng chŭ-ì chĕ]: revisionist

[6] 修好[hsīu-hăo]: to foster friendly relations; rapprochement, reconciliation; to complete a repair

[7] 修改[hsīu-kăi]: to modify, to revise, to correct; amendment, modification, correction

[9] 修建[hsīu-chièn]: to erect, to construct, to repair

修訂[hsīu-tìng]: to revise, to amend

[11] 修理[hsīu-lĭ]: to repair, to mend; repairing, overhauling

[12] 修復[hsīu-fù]: to repair, to restore

[15] 修養[hsīu-yăng]: to cultivate; cultivation, self-discipline; self-cultivation–(an abbreviation of Liu Shao-ch'i's work How to Be a Good Communist [論共產黨員的修養]

[16] 修濬[hsīu-chǜn]: to dredge

個

[2] 個人經歷[kò-jén chīng-lì]: personal history, personal experience

個人主義[kò-jén chŭ-ì]: individualism (as opposed to collectivism)

個人主義思想[kò-jén chŭ-ì ssū-hsiăng]: individualist thinking

個人主義野心家[kò-jén chŭ-ì yĕh-hsīn-chiā]: individualist careerist

個人崇拜[kò-jén ch'úng-pài]: personality cult

個人消費[kò-jén hsiāo-fèi]: private consumption

個人迷信[kò-jén mí-hsìn]: cult of the individual

個人包辦[kò-jén pāo-pàn]: one individual monopolizing the conduct of affairs

個人所有制[kò-jén sŏ-yŭ-chìh]: individual private ownership, personal ownership

個人第一[kò-jén tì-ī]: the individual coming first, putting the individual in first place

個人英雄主義 [kò-jén yīng-hsíung chŭ-ì]: individualist heroism

[7] 個別[kò-piéh]: isolated, separate, individual

[8] 個性解放[kò-hsìng chiĕh-fàng]: emancipation of man's individual personality

[23] 個體[kò-t'ĭ]: individual (as opposed to collective, 集體)

個體指數[kò-t'ĭ chĭh-shù]: individual index

個體經濟[kò-t'ĭ chīng-chì]: individual economy

個體小農業[kò-t'ĭ hsiăo-núng-yèh]: individual small-scale agriculture

個體勞動者[kò-t'ĭ láo-tùng chĕ]: individual laborer, laborer working on his own

個體農民[kò-t'ǐ núng-mín]: individual peasant

個體手工業[kò-t'ǐ shǒu-kūng-yèh]: individual handicraft industry

俫

俫[lài]: Lai (a minority nationality)

倮

12 倮黑[lǒ-hēi]: Lohei (a minority nationality)

倫

11 倫理[lún-lǐ]: moral principles; ethical

倫理學[lún-lǐ-hsüéh]: ethics

12 倫敦[lún-tūn]: London

倍

倍[pèi]: times; -fold (suffix)

5 倍加[pèi-chiā]: twofold

15 倍增[pèi-tsēng]: to redouble, to multiply

16 倍諾斯愛勒[pèi-nò-ssū-ài-lè]: Buenos Aires (Argentina)

俾

12 俾斯麥群島[pì-ssū-mài ch'ǘn-tǎo]: Bismarck Islands

13 俾路芝[pì-lù-chīh]: Baluchistan

併

併[pìng]: to merge; together; even, equal

6 併成[pìng-ch'éng]: to merge, to fuse, to combine, to amalgamate, to unify, to integrate into, to incorporate into

7 併社[pìng-shè]: to merge smaller cooperatives into bigger ones

併吞[pìng-t'ūn]: to swallow, to absorb, to annex

倒

4 倒戈[tào-kō]: to mutiny, to defect

倒戈投敵[tào-kō t'óu-tí]: to turn traitor, to be a turncoat

6 倒向[tǎo-hsiàng]: to swing to, to move to

倒行逆施[tào-hsíng nì-shīh]: perverted action; to attempt to go against the tide of history, to turn things upside down

10 倒流[tào-líu]: to flow upstream, to go backwards

倒退[tào-t'ùi]: to withdraw, to retreat, to go backward; regression, retrogression

11 倒帳[tào-chàng]: to go bankrupt, to close shop; bankrupt

倒閉[tǎo-pì]: to close down, to go into bankruptcy; bankruptcy

12 倒換[tǎo-huàn]: to exchange, to replace

倒過來[tào-kuò-lái]: to reverse, to turn over, to invert; reverse, inversion; on the contrary

13 倒塌[tǎo-t'ā]: to collapse

14 倒臺[tǎo-t'ái]: downfall, bankruptcy

18 倒轉[tào-chuǎn]: to turn back; to turn the tables on

倉

3 倉口[ts'āng-k'óu]: ship's hatch

8 倉房 **[ts'āng-fáng]** : granary

9 倉促 **[ts'āng-ts'ù]** : hastily, in a hurry

10 倉庫 **[ts'āng-k'ù]** : storehouse, warehouse, depot, storage

— 9 Strokes —

假

假 **[chiǎ]** : feigned, false, pseudo-, counterfeit, sham, bogus; to be untrue

4 假仁假義 **[chiǎ-jén chiǎ-ì]** : false kindness and righteousness, hypocrisy

假日 **[chià-jìh]** : holiday

假公濟私 **[chiǎ-kūng chì-ssū]** : to promote one's private interests under the guise of serving the public, to satisfy private ends by utilizing public means

假手於 **[chiǎ-shǒu yǘ]** : at the hands of, through the hands of; to make use of, to entrust to the care of

5 假令 **[chiǎ-lìng]** : if, in case, assuming

6 假充 **[chiǎ-ch'ūng]** : to pose as somebody, to pretend to be

假如 **[chiǎ-jú]** : if, supposing, provided that

假死 **[chiǎ-ssǔ]** : pretended death

假托 **[chiǎ-t'ō]** : excuse, pretext; under the pretext of

7 假扮 **[chiǎ-pàn]** : to disguise oneself (as)

假言判斷 **[chiǎ-yén p'àn-tuàn]** : hypothetical judgment

8 假使 **[chiǎ-shǐh]** : assuming that, supposing if

假定 **[chiǎ-tìng]** : to presume; hypothesis, postulate

9 假紅旗 **[chiǎ húng-ch'í]** : false red banner (raised by Anti-Mao elements during the Cultural Revolution)

假冒 **[chiǎ-mào]** : to pass oneself off falsely, to pass something false off as genuine

假面具 **[chiǎ-mièn-chǜ]** : mask

10 假借 **[chiǎ-chièh]** : to borrow; implied meaning

11 假設 **[chiǎ-shè]** : hypothesis, assumption

假造 **[chiǎ-tsào]** : to forge, to falsify; forged

假做 **[chiǎ-tsò]** : to fabricate, to make up

12 假期 **[chià-ch'í]** : vacation

13 假裝 **[chiǎ-chuāng]** : to disguise, to pretend, to feign; disguise, sham, camouflage

假象 **[chiǎ-hsiàng]** : false appearance, semblance, illusion; pseudomorphous

假想 **[chiǎ-hsiǎng]** : assumption, hypothesis; hypothetical

假想敵 **[chiǎ-hsiǎng tí]** : hypothetical enemy

假話 **[chiǎ-huà]** : lie, untruth, falsehood

假意 **[chiǎ-ì]** : dishonest opinion, insincerity

15 假模假樣 **[chiǎ-mō chiǎ-yàng]** : affected, artificial

20 假釋 **[chiǎ-shìh]** : to parole, to release on parole; parole, conditional release

偵

9 偵查 **[chēn-ch'á]** : investigation, to investigate

11 偵探 **[chēn-t'àn]** : to spy, to detect; detective, spy; espionage, detection

14 偵察 **[chēn-ch'á]** : to detect, to inspect; reconnaissance

偵察機 **[chēn-ch'á-chī]** : reconnaissance plane

偵察轟炸機 **[chēn-ch'á hūng-chà-chī]** : reconnaissance bomber

健

6 健全 **[chièn-ch'üán]** : healthy, sound

7 健壯 **[chièn-chuàng]** : healthy and strong

健身操 **[chièn-shēn-ts'āo]** : calisthenics

健忘 **[chièn-wàng]** : to have a poor memory, forgetful

10 健康 **[chièn-k'āng]** : health, healthy

健康水平 **[chièn-k'āng shŭi-p'íng]** : health standards

11 健將 **[chièn-chiàng]** : master, champion (in sports)

偶

6 偶因論 **[ŏu-yīn-lùn]** : occasionalism

12 偶然 **[ŏu-ján]** : accidentally, casually, incidentally, occasionally, by chance

偶然現象 **[ŏu-ján hsièn-hsiàng]** : accidental phenomenon, fortuitous phenomenon, fluke

偶然性 **[ŏu-ján-hsìng]** : fortuity, contingency

偶然事件 **[ŏu-ján shìh-chièn]** : accident, incident

15 偶像 **[ŏu-hsiàng]** : idol

偶像崇拜 **[ŏu-hsiàng ch'úng-pài]** : idolatry

偏

偏 **[p'iēn]** : P'ien (a minority nationality)

6 偏向 **[p'iēn-hsiàng]** : deviation

7 偏見 **[p'iēn-chièn]** : fixed idea, bias, one-sided view, prejudice

8 偏於 **[p'iēn-yǘ]** : to have a bias towards, to be inclined to, to tend to, to lean to

9 偏信 **[p'iēn-hsìn]** : to believe in one side only

10 偏差 **[p'iēn-ch'ā]** : deviation, deflection, variation, partial difference

11 偏斜 **[p'iēn-hsiéh]** : to deflect from

13 偏愛 **[p'iēn-ài]** : to be partial to, to have a partiality for, undue partiality

15 偏廢 **[p'iēn-fèi]** : to do one thing to the neglect of another

22 偏聽 **[p'iēn-t'īng]** : to listen to one side only

11 傣國 **[t'ài-kuó]** : Thailand

停

4 停止 **[t'íng-chĭh]** : to stop, to halt, to discontinue, to cease; stop, halt, discontinuance

7 停步 **[t'íng-pù]** : to halt, to stop moving

停步不前 **[t'íng-pù pù-ch'ién]** : to mark time, to stay

8 停泊時間 **[t'íng-pó shíh-chiēn]** : layover time

13 停頓 **[t'íng-tùn]** : to tie up, to halt, to stop business, to cease progress; standstill, stalemate, impasse

14 停滯 **[t'íng-ch'ìh]** : to obstruct, to delay, to tie up; standstill, stalemate, impasse, stagnation; stagnant

16 停戰 **[t'íng-chàn]** : armistice, truce, ceasefire, cessation of hostilities

18 停職 **[t'íng-chíh]** : to suspend from a post

偷

2 偷入 **[t'ōu-jù]** : to sneak in, to steal in

[3] 偷工 [t'ōu-kūng]: to skimp on work, to do shoddy work (a target of the 五反, q.v.)

偷工減料 [t'ōu-kūng chiĕn-liào]: to do shoddy work and use inferior materials, to cheat on labor and materials, to cheat on government contracts (a target of the 五反, q.v.)

[10] 偷梁換柱 [t'ōu-liáng huàn-chù]: to steal beams and pillars (and put rotten timber in their place); fraudulent, deceiving

[12] 偷稅 [t'ōu-shùi]: tax evasion (a target of the 五反, q.v.)

偷稅漏稅 [t'ōu-shùi lòu-shùi]: tax evasion (*See* 偷稅)

[14] 偷漏 [t'ōu-lòu]: to smuggle

偷漏稅 [t'ōu-lòu-shùi]: tax evasion

[22] 偷竊 [t'ōu-ch'ièh]: to steal, to pilfer; theft, robbery, larceny

側

[6] 側耳 [ts'è-ĕrh]: to listen, to listen closely

[9] 側重 [ts'è-chùng]: one-sided, prejudiced, to attach special importance to something

側面 [ts'è-mièn]: side, profile, side-view

[17] 側擊 [ts'è-chī]: to make a flank attack; flank attack

側翼 [ts'è-ì]: flank

做

[6] 做好 [tsò-hăo]: to do a good job; to get through with

做好人的工作 [tsò-hăo jén te kūng-tsò]: to do a good job of the work of dealing with men

偉

[3] 偉大 [wĕi-tà]: great

— 10 Strokes —

傑

[5] 傑出 [chiéh-ch'ū]: prominent, distinguished, eminent

[7] 傑沙縣 [chiéh-shā hsièn]: Katha District (Burma)

傑作 [chiéh-tsò]: masterpiece, masterstroke

傅

[7] 傅利葉 [fù-lì-yèh]: Fourier, Charles (1772–1837)

傀

[17] 傀儡 [k'uĕi-lĕi]: puppet

備

[6] 備件 [pèi-chièn]: spare parts

備而不用 [pèi érh pú-yùng]: to prepare for any event

備考 [pèi-k'ăo]: appendix for reference

[7] 備忘錄 [pèi-wàng-lù]: memorandum, note, aide-memoire

[8] 備取 [pèi-ch'ŭ]: to accept as reserve more than the full number

[9] 備查 [pèi-ch'á]: for later reference, for examination

[10] 備案 [pèi-àn]: to keep on record, to register, to enter on the records; registration

16 備戰 **[pèi-chàn]**: to prepare for war; war preparations

備辦 **[pèi-pàn]**: to procure, to prepare for action, to supply

傘

7 傘兵 **[săn-pīng]**: paratrooper, parachutist, parachute troops

傜

傜 **[yáo]**: Yao (a minority nationality)

— 11 Strokes —

傲

傲 **[ào]**: conceited, proud, haughty, arrogant

14 傲慢 **[ào-màn]**: arrogance, overbearance, haughtiness, contempt; arrogant, overbearing, haughty, contemptuous, supercilious

債

10 債務 **[chài-wù]**: debt, obligation, liability

債務人 **[chài-wù-jén]**: debtor

12 債款支出 **[chài-k'uan chīh-ch'ū]**: expenditure for loan payments

債款收入 **[chài-k'uăn shōu-jù]**: revenue from loans

22 債權人 **[chài-ch'üán-jén]**: creditor

僅

6 僅次於 **[chĭn-tz'ù-yǘ]**: next only to, second only to

13 僅僅 **[chĭn-chĭn]**: only, merely, just, alone

傾

6 傾向 **[ch'īng-hsiàng]**: tendency, trend, inclination; to be inclined to, to tend to

傾向性 **[ch'īng-hsiàng-hsìng]**: tendentiousness

8 傾軋 **[ch'īng-yà]**: strife, struggle, discord, internecine dissension

15 傾銷 **[ch'īng-hsiāo]**: to dump; dumping (of goods on the market)

22 傾聽意見 **[ch'īng-t'īng ì-chièn]**: to pay heed to the opinion of, to listen carefully to the views of

傳

3 傳下 **[ch'uán-hsià]**: to hand down

5 傳布 **[ch'uán-pù]**: to spread, to disseminate; dissemination

傳世 **[ch'uán-shìh]**: to transmit from one generation to another

傳代 **[ch'uán-tài]**: to transmit from one generation to another

9 傳染病 **[ch'uán-jăn-pìng]**: infectious disease, contagious disease

10 傳眞 **[ch'uán-chēn]**: faithful portrait, facsimile

傳眞電報機 **[ch'uán-chēn tièn-pào-chī]**: phototelegraph

傳家法寶 **[ch'uán-chiā fă-păo]**: heirloom

11 傳教士 **[ch'uán-chiào-shìh]**: missionary

傳情 **[ch'uán-ch'íng]**: to hint, to indicate, to communicate one's feelings, to disclose one's inclinations

傳票 **[ch'uán-p'iào]**: court summons, summons

傳授 [ch'uán-shòu] : to pass on, to impart to

12 傳喚 [ch'uán-huàn] : to summon; summons

傳單 [ch'uán-tān] : leaflet, propaganda sheet

傳統 [ch'uán-t'ǔng] : tradition, heritage; traditional

13 傳達 [ch'uán-tá] : to convey, to transmit, to relay

14 傳種 [ch'uán-chǔng] : to transplant, to propagate

傳說 [ch'uán-shuō] : legend, rumor, traditional account

傳遞 [ch'uán-tì] : to pass on, to transmit, to hand over

傳聞 [ch'uán-wén] : news transmitted orally, hearsay

15 傳播 [ch'uán-pō] : to disseminate, to spread

16 傳導帶 [ch'uán-tǎo-tài] : transmission belt

傈

13 傈僳 [lì-sù] : Lisu (a minority nationality)

傷

傷 [shāng] : to wound, to injure, to hurt, to harm, to maim; wound, injury

3 傷亡 [shāng-wáng] : casualty, dead and wounded

4 傷心 [shāng-hsīn] : to grieve, to lament, to feel deeply about; suffering, lament; heartbroken

10 傷害 [shāng-hài] : to wound, to hurt, to harm, to injure, to damage; injury, harm, damage

傷員 [shāng-yüán] : wounded personnel, wounded soldiers

催

11 催淚彈 [ts'ūi-lèi-tàn] : tear gas bomb

催淚毒氣 [ts'ūi-lèi tú-ch'ì] : tear gas

傭

8 傭金 [yùng-chīn] : commission, brokerage

— 12 Strokes —

僥

10 僥倖成功 [chiǎo-hsìng ch'éng-kūng] : easy success through good luck

僥倖取勝 [chiǎo-hsìng ch'ǚ-shèng] : to defeat someone by a narrow margin, to inflict a narrow defeat

僑

9 僑胞 [ch'iáo-pāo] : overseas compatriots

11 僑務報 [ch'iáo-wù-pào] : Overseas Chinese Affairs (a monthly Chinese periodical)

僮

僮 [chuàng] : Chuang (a minority nationality)

像

像 [hsiàng] : statue; appearance, resemblance, image; like, similar

15 像樣 [hsiàng-yàng] : decent looking, becoming, seemly, handsome, proper

僱

13 僱傭軍 **[kù-yūng-chūn]**: mercenaries, hirelings (a term used during the Korean War to indicate United Nations' forces other than those of the United States and the Republic of Korea)

僚

21 僚屬 **[liáo-shŭ]**: subordinates, entourage, staff, associates

僰

僰 **[pó]**: Po (a minority nationality)

僕

11 僕從 **[p'ú-ts'úng]**: lackey, servant, retainer, flunkey, dependent, vassal

僧

9 僧俗 **[sēng-sú]**: monks and laymen, ecclesiastical and secular (people)

僞

7 僞君子 **[wĕi-chūn-tzŭ]**: hypocrite

9 僞軍 **[wĕi-chūn]**: puppet army

11 僞國大 **[wĕi-kuó-tà]**: the bogus National Assembly

僞造 **[wĕi-tsào]**: forgery, invention; made-up, sham, false, fraudulent, spurious, counterfeit, trumped up; to fabricate

12 僞智論 **[wĕi-chìh-lùn]**: Gnosticism

僞善 **[wĕi-shàn]**: hypocrisy; hypocritical

僞善者 **[wĕi-shàn-chĕ]**: hypocrite

14 僞裝 **[wĕi-chuāng]**: to disguise, to make believe; camouflage, disguise; under the mask of, under the cloak of

16 僞選 **[wĕi-hsüăn]**: false election, fake election

— 13 Strokes —

傻

3 傻子 **[shă-tzu]**: fool, idiot, simpleton

5 價目 **[chià-mù]**: price

價本 **[chià-pĕn]**: purchase price, cost

10 價値 **[chià-chíh]**: worth, value

價値法律 **[chià-chíh fă-lǜ]**: the law of value

價値規律 **[chià-chíh kuēi-lǜ]**: the law of value

價格 **[chià-kó]**: price

價格政策 **[chià-kó chèng-ts'è]**: price policy

15 價碼 **[chià-mă]**: list price, price, price tag

16 價錢 **[chià-ch'ién]**: price

僵

7 僵局 **[chiāng-chú]**: deadlock, stalemate, impasse

8 僵事 **[chiāng-shìh]**: deadlock, insoluble matter

9 僵持 **[chiāng-ch'íh]**: to insist on one's own opinion

12 僵硬 [chiāng-yìng] : inflexible, stubborn, petrified

僥

10 僥倖 [chiǎo-hsìng] : fortunately, luckily

儉

9 儉省 [chiěn-shěng] : frugality; frugal

16 儉樸 [chiěn-p'ǔ] : frugal and modest

億

13 億萬富翁 [ì-wàn fù-wēng] : multi-millionaire

儀

5 儀仗隊 [í-chàng-tùi] : guard of honor

6 儀式 [í-shìh] : ceremony, function, rite, ritual

16 儀器 [í-ch'ì] : instrument, apparatus

儂

2 儂人 [núng-jén] : Nung-Jen (a minority nationality)

僻

15 僻論 [p'ì-lùn] : paradox

— 15 Strokes —

償

13 償債 [ch'áng-chài] : to repay debts

17 償還 [ch'áng-huán] : to repay, to refund, to pay back, to restore, to return

19 償願 [ch'áng-yüàn] : to fulfill a vow, to redeem a promise, to fulfill a wish

優

5 優生學 [yū-shēng-hsüéh] : eugenics

6 優先 [yū-hsiēn] : priority, precedence, preference

優先權 [yū-hsiēn-ch'üán] : preferential right, priority

優先發展 [yū-hsiēn fā-chǎn] : to give priority to the development of. . .

7 優秀 [yū-hsiù] : outstanding, brilliant, excellent

優秀幹部 [yū-hsìu kàn-pù] : outstanding cadre

優秀工作者 [yū-hsìu kūng-tsò-chě] : outstanding worker

優良 [yū-liáng] : excellent, superior, choice

優良傳統 [yū-liáng ch'uán-t'ǔng] : excellent tradition, fine tradition

優良品種 [yū-liáng p'ǐn-chǔng] : good seed strains, good stock

優良作風 [yū-liáng tsò-fēng] : excellent working style

9 優待 [yū-tài] : preferential treatment, special favor, special care for

12 優勝者 [yū-shèng-chě] : winner, champion

優勝獎 [yū-shèng-chiǎng] : winning prize

優越性 [yū-yüèh-hsìng] : superiority, supremacy, prowess

13 優勢 [yū-shìh] : superiority, advantage, supremacy

15 優質鋼 [yū-chíh-kāng] : quality steel

17 優點 **[yū-tiĕn]**: merit, strong point, virtue, excellence

— 16 Strokes —

儲

6 儲存 **[ch'ú-ts'ún]**: to store, to put away, to accumulate; accumulation

8 儲金 **[ch'ú-chīn]**: savings

12 儲備 **[ch'ú-pèi]**: reserve, stockpile, stock

14 儲蓄 **[ch'ú-hsǜ]**: to save; deposits, savings

— RADICAL 儿 10 —

— 2 Strokes —

11 允許 **[yŭn-hsŭ]**: to permit, to allow, to consent, to promise; permission, consent

元

3 元山 **[yüán-shān]**: Wonsan (Korea)

4 元月 **[yüán-yüèh]**: January, the first month of the lunar calendar

5 元旦 **[yüán-tàn]**: New Year's Day

6 元年 **[yüán-nién]**: first year of a reign

9 元首 **[yüán-shŏu]**: chief of state, chief executive, ruler, head of a state

元帥 **[yüán-shuài]**: Marshal (Chinese and Soviet Armies); Field Marshal (British Army); Admiral of the Fleet (British Navy)

10 元素 **[yüán-sù]**: element

— 3 Strokes —

7 兄弟 **[hsiūng-tì]**: brothers; fraternal

兄弟之邦 **[hsiūng-tì chīh pāng]**: fraternal states

兄弟關係 **[hsiūng-tì kuān-hsì]**: brotherhood, fraternal relations

兄弟國家 **[hsiūng-tì kuó-chiā]**: fraternal countries

兄弟似的 **[hsiūng-tì-shìh te]**: fraternal, brotherly

兄弟黨 **[hsiūng-tì-tăng]**: fraternal parties

8 兄長 **[hsiūng-chăng]**: elder brother; the Soviet Union

— 4 Strokes —

4 充分 **[ch'ūng-fèn]**: full, adequate, ample, sufficient, complete, to the fullest

充公 **[ch'ūng-kūng]**: to confiscate; confiscation

5 充斥 **[ch'ūng-ch'ìh]**: to fill; overfull

6 充耳不聞 **[ch'ūng-ĕrh pù-wén]**: to fill the ears without hearing; heedlessness

7 充足 **[ch'ūng-tsú]**: full, sufficient, enough

8 充其量 **[ch'ūng ch'í-liàng]**: at the best, at the maximum

12 充裕 **[ch'ūng-yǜ]**: abundance; abundant

13 充當 **[ch'ūng-tāng]**: to serve as, to fill an office

14 充滿 **[ch'ūng-mǎn]**: full, to be filled, crowded; to fill

充實 **[ch'ūng-shíh]**: to substantiate, to strengthen; abundant, overflowing

先

4 先天的 **[hsiēn-t'iēn te]**: inborn, innate, congenital, hereditary, a priori

5 先令 **[hsiēn-lìng]**: shilling

7 先見之明 **[hsiēn-chièn chīh míng]**: foresight, prescience, prevision, prophetic vision

先決條件 **[hsiēn-chüéh t'iáo-chièn]**: precondition, prerequisite

8 先例 **[hsiēn-lì]**: precedent

先於 **[hsiēn-yǘ]**: preliminary to, prior to, previous to; to precede

9 先前的 **[hsiēn-ch'ién te]**: previous, prior, preceding, former, earlier

先後 **[hsiēn-hòu]**: successive, in succession, one after the other

10 先破後立 **[hsiēn-p'ò hòu-lì]**: destroy first and then establish (a phrase in use during the Cultural Revolution)

12 先進 **[hsiēn-chìn]**: progressive, advanced; those who have gone before

先進集體 **[hsiēn-chìn chí-t'ǐ]**: outstanding collective, advanced collective

先進遷就落後 **[hsiēn-chìn ch'iēn-chìu lò-hòu]**: to restrain the advanced to keep pace with the backward

先進經驗 **[hsiēn-chìn chīng-yèn]**: advanced experience (the experience acquired by a worker who has advanced in production technique and production)

先進區域 **[hsiēn-chìn ch'ū-yǜ]**: advanced areas

先進份子 **[hsiēn-chìn fèn-tzu]**: advanced element

先進工作者 **[hsiēn-chìn kūng-tsò-chě]**: advanced worker, outstanding worker

先進工作方法 **[hsiēn-chìn kūng-tsò fāng-fǎ]**: advanced working method

先進水平 **[hsiēn-chìn shǔi-p'íng]**: advanced level

先發制人 **[hsiēn-fā chìh-jén]**: to make the first move to restrain other people; to make the first move to get control

先發制人之戰 **[hsiēn-fā chìh-jén chīh chàn]**: preventive war

15 先鋒 **[hsiēn-fēng]**: vanguard

先鋒主義 **[hsiēn-fēng chǔ-ì]**: vanguardism

先鋒作用 **[hsiēn-fēng tsò-yùng]**: role of the vanguard

先鋒隊 **[hsiēn-fēng-tùi]**: vanguard unit

16 先頭部隊 **[hsiēn-t'óu pù-tùi]**: advanced unit, advanced detachment, spearhead, attacking echelon

21 先驅 **[hsiēn-ch'ū]**: forerunner, harbinger, vanguard, pioneer

先驅論壇報 **[hsiēn-ch'ū lùn-t'án pào]**: New York Herald Tribune

23 先驗的 **[hsiēn-yèn te]**: transcendental

光

6 光州 **[kuāng-chōu]**: Kwangju (Korea)

光年 **[kuāng-nién]**: light year

7 光芒 **[kuāng-máng]**: light flash, shaft of light, radiance

光芒萬丈 **[kuāng-máng wàn-chàng]**: blazing brightly ahead, gloriously shining, to be forever glorious

8 光明 **[kuāng-míng]**: bright, shining, magnificent; glory, light

光明正大[**kuāng-míng chèng-tà**]: lustrous and upright

光明前途[**kuāng-míng ch'ién-t'ú**]: bright future, promising future, glorious prospect

光明日報[**kuāng-míng jìh-pào**]: Kwang-ming Daily (Chinese Communist daily newspaper)

光明磊落[**kuāng-míng lĕi-lò**]: lustrously and distinctly; clear and distinct

9 光亮[**kuāng-liàng**]: bright, shining

11 光彩[**kuāng-ts'ăi**]: honor, luster; magnificent, brilliant

12 光景[**kuāng-chĭng**]: circumstances, situation, time, conditions

光復[**kuāng-fù**]: restoration; to restore

14 光榮[**kuāng-júng**]: glory, honor, splendor, magnificence; splendid, magnificent

光榮榜[**kuāng-júng-păng**]: honor roll, board of honor

15 光線[**kuāng-hsièn**]: ray, beam, light

光輝[**kuāng-hūi**]: splendor, grandeur, gloriousness; brilliant, magnificent, illustrious, bright, radiant, grand, majestic

光輝照耀下[**kuāng-hūi chào-yào hsià**]: under the shining light of . . ., under the guiding light of . . .

16 光學[**kuāng-hsüéh**]: optics

光學精密機械儀器研究所[**kuāng-hsüéh chīng-mì chī-hsièh í-ch'ì yén-chìu-sŏ**]: Optics and Precision Instruments Institute

光頭[**kuāng-t'óu**]: bald, bareheaded

光澤[**kuāng-tsé**]: luster; lustrous

17 光臨[**kuāng-lín**]: to arrive; honorable presence (your presence)

— 5 Strokes —

克

4 克什美彷[**k'ò-shíh-mĕi-lè**]: Kashmir

7 克里米[**k'ò-lĭ-mĭ**]: Crimea

克里姆林宮[**k'ò-lĭ-mŭ-lín-kūng**]: Kremlin

8 克制[**k'ò-chìh**]: to restrain, to check, to curb, to control, to bridle; restraint, check

克服[**k'ò-fú**]: to overcome, to conquer, to master, to subjugate, to subdue, to defeat

克拉地峽[**k'ò-lā tì-hsiá**]: Kra Isthmus

10 克倫[**k'ò-lún**]: krone; crown (unit of currency)

12 克萊[**k'ò-lái**]: Clay, General Lucius

克勞什維茲[**k'ò-láo-shíh-wéi-tzū**]: Clausewitz, Karl von (1780-1831)

13 克勤克儉[**k'ò-ch'ín k'ò-chiĕn**]: to be diligent and frugal; industriousness and frugality

克魯曉夫[**k'ò-lŭ-hsiăo-fú**]: Khruschchev, Nikita

克魯泡特金[**k'ò-lŭ-p'ào-t'è-chīn**]: Kropotkin

克虜伯[**k'ò-lŭ-pó**]: Krupp

11 兌現[**tùi-hsièn**]: to realize, to make good; to convert into cash

12 兌換[**tùi-huàn**]: to convert, to exchange; exchange, convertibility

兌換率[**tùi-huàn-lǜ**]: rate of exchange

— 6 Strokes —

兒

9 兒科研究所 **[érh-k'ō yén-chìu-sŏ]**: Pediatrics Institute

12 兒童團 **[érh-t'úng-t'uán]**: Young Pioneers

免

免 **[miĕn]**: to spare, to excuse from, to avoid, to keep from doing

6 免刑 **[miĕn-hsíng]**: to be exempt from criminal punishment

9 免疫 **[miĕn-ì]**: immunity from disease

10 免除 **[miĕn-ch'ú]**: to avoid, to exempt from, to remove, to discharge, to release, to free, to absolve from; exemption

12 免費 **[miĕn-fèi]**: free of expense, free of charge

免費醫療 **[miĕn-fèi ī-liáo]**: free health services, free medical treatment

14 免罪 **[miĕn-tsùi]**: to absolve, to acquit, to set free, to be cleared of guilt

18 免職 **[miĕn-chíh]**: to relieve from a post, to dismiss from office; dismissed, released from office

— 10 Strokes —

11 兜售 **[tōu-shòu]**: to peddle, to hawk, to sell

— 18 Strokes —

競

17 競賽 **[chìng-sài]**: to race, to compete; emulation, competition

— RADICAL 入 11 —

入

3 入口 **[jù-k'ŏu]**: entrance; import

6 入伍 **[jù-wŭ]**: to enlist, to enroll, to join

12 入場 **[jù-ch'ăng]**: entrance, admission, admittance

入超 **[jù-ch'āo]**: adverse trade balance, trade deficit, import excess

14 入境簽證 **[jù-chìng ch'iēn-chèng]**: entry visa

— 2 Strokes —

5 內外夾攻 **[nèi-wài chiā-kūng]**: to be under fire from within and without; to attack internally and externally

內外物資交流 **[nèi-wài wù-tzū chiāo-líu]**: exchange of commodities between home and abroad

6 內行 **[nèi-háng]**: expert; skillful

內地 **[nèi-tì]**: inland, interior, hinterland; China proper

內地水運部 **[nèi-tì shŭi-yǜn pù]** : Ministry of Inland Water Transport

內在的 **[nèi-tsài te]** : immanent, inherent

8 內河運輸 **[nèi-hó yǜn-shū]** : inland waterway transportation

內科 **[nèi-k'ō]** : internal medicine

內科研究所 **[nèi-k'ō yén-chìu-sŏ]** : Internal Medicine Institute

內定的 **[nèi-tìng te]** : designated

9 內政 **[nèi-chèng]** : internal affairs, internal administration

10 內訌 **[nèi-hùng]** : internal dissension, strife or conflict

內容 **[nèi-júng]** : content, internal substance

內容貧乏 **[nèi-júng p'ín-fá]** : scanty, poor, empty or meager in content or substance

11 內部 **[nèi-pù]** : internal

內部積累 **[nèi-pù chī-lĕi]** : internal accumulation

內部紛爭 **[nèi-pù fēn-chēng]** : internal strife

內部矛盾 **[nèi-pù máo-tùn]** : internal contradiction, inner contradiction

內部資金 **[nèi-pù tzū-chīn]** : internal capital

內務勞動部 **[nèi-wù láo-tùng pù]** : internal labor department

內務部 **[nèi-wù-pù]** : Ministry of Internal Affairs

14 內閣 **[nèi-kó]** : cabinet

內閣改組 **[nèi-kó kăi-tsŭ]** : cabinet reorganization, cabinet reshuffle

內蒙 **[nèi-mĕng]** : Inner Mongolia

內幕 **[nèi-mù]** : inside story; behind the scenes

16 內戰 **[nèi-chàn]** : civil war

19 內羅畢 **[nèi-ló-pì]** : Nairobi (Kenya)

— 4 Strokes —

全

2 全力的 **[ch'üán-lì te]** : full force, all-out

4 全心全意 **[ch'üán-hsīn ch'üán-ì]** : wholehearted, with heart and soul

全日制的 **[ch'üán-jìh-chìh te]** : full-time

全日制學校 **[ch'üán-jìh-chìh hsüéh-hsiào]** : full-time school, full day school

全文 **[ch'üán-wén]** : full text

5 全民 **[ch'üán-mín]** : whole people, entire people, whole population, nation-wide

全民皆兵 **[ch'üán-mín chiēh-pīng]** : all the people are soldiers, all citizens are soldiers

全民競賽運動 **[ch'üán-mín chìng-sài yǜn-tùng]** : nation-wide emulation movement

全民性運動 **[ch'üán-mín-hsìng yǜn-tùng]** : a nation-wide movement, all-out drive

全民搞工業運動 **[ch'üán-mín kăo kūng-yèh yǜn-tùng]** : "all the people run industry" movement

全民辦工業 **[ch'üán-mín pàn kūng-yèh]** : development of industry by the whole people

全民表決 **[ch'üán-mín piăo-chüéh]** : plebiscite, referendum

全民所有制 **[ch'üán-mín sŏ-yŭ-chìh]** : ownership by all the people

全世界無產者聯合起來 **[ch'üán shìh-chièh wú-ch'ăn-chĕ lién-hó-ch'ĭ-lái]** : Workers of the world, unite!; Proletarians of the world, unite!

7 全局觀點 **[ch'üán-chǘ kuān-tiĕn]** : an overall viewpoint (i.e., a viewpoint whereby one works hard at one's assigned task while keeping the interests of the whole in view)

8 全非青年大會 **[ch'üán-fēi ch'īng-nién tà-hùi]** : All African Youth Conference

全非人民大會常設機構[**ch'üán-fēi jén-mín tà-hùi ch'áng-shè chī-kòu**]: Permanent Organization of the All African People's Conference

9 全負荷[**ch'üán-fù-hò**]: full load, capacity load

全面[**ch'üán-mièn**]: comprehensive, full, total, full-scale, complete, all-out, all-around, all embracing

全面戰爭[**ch'üán-mièn chàn-chēng**]: full-scale war, all-out war, total war

全面計劃[**ch'üán-mièn chì-huà**]: overall planning

全面發展[**ch'üán-mièn fā-chǎn**]: all-around development

全面內戰[**ch'üán-mièn nèi-chàn**]: total civil war, country-wide civil war

全面大躍進[**ch'üán-mièn tà-yüèh-chìn**]: all-around big leap forward

全面總結[**ch'üán-mièn tsǔng-chiéh**]: comprehensive summing up

10 全級總體[**ch'üán-chí tsǔng-t'ǐ**]: total population, entire population

全能的[**ch'üán-néng te**]: omnipotent, all-capable

11 全副武裝[**ch'üán-fù wǔ-chuāng**]: fully armed, armed to the teeth

全國[**ch'üán-kuó**]: nation-wide; All China

全國一盤棋[**ch'üán-kuò ì-p'án ch'í**]: the whole country is like one chess game (this statement means that the interests of the whole country should be taken into consideration in planning the economic development of a region or an industry)

全國人口調查[**ch'üán-kuó jén-k'ǒu tiào-ch'á**]: nation-wide census

全國人民代表大會[**ch'üán-kuó jén-mín tài-piǎo tà-hùi**]: National People's Congress

全國人民代表大會常務委員會[**ch'üán-kuó jén-mín tài-piǎo tà-hùi ch'áng-wù wěi-yüán-hùi**]: Standing Committee of the National People's Congress

全國性的[**ch'üán-kuó-hsìng te**]: pertaining to the country as a whole, national

全國工農榮復轉退革命軍人捍衞毛澤東思想紅旗軍上海革命造反總部[**ch'üán-kuó kūng-núng júng-fù chǔan-t'ùi kó-mìng chūn-jén hàn-wèi Máo Tsé-tūng ssū-hsiǎng húng-ch'í-chūn shàng-hǎi kó-mìng tsào-fǎn tsǔng-pù**]: The Shanghai Revolutionary Rebels General Bureau of the All-China Workers, Peasants, Meritorious, Demobilized, or Transferred Revolutionary Soldiers' Red Flag Army for the Protection of the Thoughts of Mao Tse-tung (a "counterrevolutionary" group during the Cultural Revolution)

全國工農榮復轉退革命軍人捍衞毛澤東思想紅旗軍上海第一縱隊革命造反總部 [**ch'üán-kuó kūng-núng júng-fù chǔan-t'ùi kó-mìng chūn-jén hàn-wèi Máo Tsé-tūng ssū-hsiǎng húng-ch'í-chūn shàng-hǎi tì-ī tsùng-tùi kó-mìng tsào-fǎn tsǔng-pù**]: The Shanghai First Troop Revolutionary Rebels General Department of the All-China Workers, Peasants, Meritorious, Demobilized, and Transferred Revolutionary Soldiers' Red Flag Army for the Protection of the Thoughts of Mao Tse-tung (a "counterrevolutionary" group during the Cultural Revolution)

全國代表大會[**ch'üán-kuó tài-piǎo tà-hùi**]: All-China Party Congress

全國自然科學專門協會聯合會[**ch'üán-kuó tzù-ján k'ō-hsüéh chuān-mén hsiéh-hùi lién-hó-hùi**]: All-China Federation of Natural Science Societies

12 全勞動力的[**ch'üán láo-tùng-lì te**]: able-bodied, with full working capacity

全集[**ch'üán-chí**]: complete works

全然[**ch'üán-ján**]: wholly, fully, completely, totally, in entirety

13 全新[**ch'üán-hsīn**]: brand-new, altogether new

14 全綫[**ch'üán-hsièn**]: entire front

全綫進攻 [ch'üán-hsièn chìn-kūng]: to attack all along the entire front

全綫出擊 [ch'üán-hsièn ch'ū-chī]: to launch attacks on the entire front

15 全盤 [ch'üán-p'án]: overall, complete, entire

全盤西化 [ch'üán-p'án hsī-huà]: wholesale westernization

22 全權 [ch'üán-ch'üán]: full powers, plenary powers; plenipotentiary, fully accredited

全權證書 [ch'üán-ch'üán chèng-shū]: full powers, plenipotentiary credentials

全權公使 [ch'üán-ch'üán kūng-shǐh]: minister plenipotentiary, envoy with full powers

全權大使 [ch'üán-ch'üán tà-shǐh]: ambassador plenipotentiary

全權代表 [ch'üán-ch'üán tài-piǎo]: a plenipotentiary

全權代表團 [ch'üán-ch'üán tài-piǎo-t'uán]: delegation with full powers

23 全體 [ch'üán-t'ǐ]: all, entire, whole, total, en bloc, en masse; plenary

全體會議 [ch'üán-t'ǐ hùi-ì]: plenary meeting, plenary session

— 6 Strokes —

2 兩刀論法 [liǎng-tāo lùn-fǎ]: dilemma

4 兩手 [liǎng-shǒu]: two tactics

6 兩利用 [liǎng lì-yùng]: the two utilizations (in mediation work: 1) utilize spare time to settle disputes at the village level; 2) utilize market days for the mediation committee to carry on work at the market town level)

8 兩放 [liǎng-fàng]: the two releases (i.e., the decentralization of personnel and capital)

9 兩相情願 [liǎng-hsiāng ch'íng-yüàn]: mutual consent, mutual willingness

兩重 [liǎng-ch'úng]: dual

兩重性 [liǎng-ch'úng-hsìng]: dual nature

兩面性 [liǎng-mièn-hsìng]: two sidedness, dual character, two-faced

兩面派 [liǎng-mièn-p'ài]: double-dealers, two-faced clique (during the Cultural Revolution refers to anti-Maoist groups)

兩面三刀 [liǎng-mièn sān-tāo]: two-faced and three-sworded (during the Cultural Revolution, refers to treacherous anti-Maoists)

兩面手 [liǎng-mièn shǒu]: two-sided hands, double faced, double-faced tactics, duplicity

兩面手法 [liǎng-mièn shǒu-fǎ]: two-faced method, double dealing

兩面外交 [liǎng-mièn wài-chiāo]: two-sided diplomacy

10 兩個階級 [liǎng-kò chiēh-chí]: the two classes (i.e., the proletariat and the bourgeoisie)

兩倍 [liǎng-pèi]: double, twofold, twice as much

兩院制 [liǎng-yüàn-chìh]: two-chamber system

11 兩條道路 [liǎng-t'iáo tào-lù]: the two roads (i.e., socialism and capitalism)

兩條道路的鬥爭 [liǎng-t'iáo tào-lù te tòu-chēng]: the struggle between the two roads (the struggle between socialism and capitalism)

兩條腿走路 [liǎng-t'iáo t'ǔi tsǒu-lù]: walking on two legs (Mao's policy of combining the modern with the primitive to increase production)

兩參，一改，三結合 [liǎng-ts'ān, ì-kǎi, sān-chiéh-hó]: two participations, one change, three combinations (i.e., workers participate in planning and management, administrative personnel participate in production; change of all outmoded rules and regulations; combination of the efforts of leading cadre, workers, and technicians)

12 兩極 **[liăng-chí]**: two extremes

14 兩種意識形態 **[liăng-chŭng ì-shìh hsíng-t'ài]**: the two ideologies (the proletarian and bourgeois ideologies)

16 兩憶三察 **[liăng-ì sān-ch'á]**: the two recollections and three investigations (recollection of class suffering and national suffering, and investigation of one's standpoint, will to fight, and work)

兩頭冒尖 **[liăng-t'óu mào-chiēn]**: double-ended prominence (the two ends are technical achievement and ideological backwardness; politics must be put in command if technical achievement is to benefit the proletariat)

20 兩黨制 **[liăng-tăng-chìh]**: two-party system

兩黨的 **[liăng-tăng te]**: bipartisan

— RADICAL 八 12 —

1 八一 **[pā-ī]**: August 1 (anniversary of the founding of the Chinese Red Army in 1927)

八一建軍節 **[pā-ī chièn-chūn chiéh]**: Army Day (August 1)

八一三事件 **[pā-ī-sān shìh-chièn]**: Incident of August 13 (1937, Shanghai)

6 八字方針 **[pá-tzù fāng-chēn]**: the eight character policy (i.e., adjustment, consolidation, reinforcement, elevation—a slogan in use in the aftermath of the Great Leap Forward)

八字憲法 **[pá-tzù hsièn-fă]**: Eight Point Charter (eight characters that constituted a code for agricultural development: 1) 水 irrigation, 2) 肥 fertilizer; 3) 土 soil improvement; 4) 種 good seed strains; 5) 密 close planting; 6) 保 crop protection (prevention of insect pests and plant diseases); 7) 工 technical innovation; 8) 管 good management)

8 八股 **[pā-kŭ]**: stereotyped writing, jargon (literally, "eight-legged," a reference to the essay form used in the former civil service examinations)

9 八面玲瓏 **[pá-mièn líng-lúng]**: clever in dealing with people, "slippery as an eel"

11 八國聯軍 **[pā-kuó lién-chūn]**: the Eight Nation United Army (the allied army in the Boxer Rebellion)

12 八項注意 **[pá-hsiàng chŭ-ì]**: The Eight Points for Attention (*See* 三大紀律)

13 八路軍 **[pá-lù-chūn]**: Eighth Route Army

15 八幡 **[pā-fān]**: Yawata (Japan)

— 2 Strokes —

公 **[kūng]**: public, the common good (as opposed to 私: private, selfish)

4 公方 **[kūng-fāng]**: government side (government representative attached to enterprises partially owned by the government); square meter

公文 **[kūng-wén]**: official document, official papers

公元 **[kūng-yüán]**: A.D.

5 公正 **[kūng-chèng]**: fairminded, equitable, unbiased

公民 **[kūng-mín]**: citizen, national

公民權 **[kūng-mín-ch'üán]**: civil rights, rights of citizenship

公民投票 **[kūng-mín t'óu-p'iào]**: referendum, plebiscite

公平 **[kūng-p'íng]**: fair, fair-minded, just, impartial, equitable, unbiased

公平合理[kūng-p'íng hó-lǐ]: fair and reasonable

公佈[kūng-pù]: to make public, to announce, to publicize

公司[kūng-ssū]: company, firm, corporation

公用事業[kūng-yùng shìh-yèh]: public utilities, public utility services

6 公安[kūng-ān]: public security

公安軍司令部[kūng-ān-chün ssū-lìng-pù]: public security force headquarters

公安部[kūng-ān-pù]: Ministry of Public Security

公共積累[kūng-kùng chī-lěi]: public accumulation, accumulated public funds

公共食堂[kūng-kùng shíh-t'áng]: canteen, public service canteen, community dining hall

公共財產[kūng-kùng ts'ái-ch'ǎn]: public property

公共衞生[kūng-kùng wèi-shēng]: public health

公式[kūng-shìh]: formula

公式主義[kūng-shìh chǔ-ì]: formulism; formulistic (refers to the methods of officials who act according to fixed programs without taking the actual and current situation into consideration)

公式化[kūng-shìh-huà]: to formularize, to formulate; formulation

公地[kūng-tì]: public land

公有[kūng-yǔ]: public ownership; publicly owned

公有制[kūng-yǔ-chìh]: public ownership system

公有化[kūng-yǔ-huà]: socialization

公有財產[kūng-yǔ ts'ái-ch'ǎn]: common property

7 公告[kūng-kào]: official announcement, official communique

公社[kūng-shè]: commune

公社化[kūng-shè-huà]: to convert to communes; communalization

公私兼顧[kūng-ssū chiēn-kù]: to give concurrent consideration to public and private interests

公私合營[kūng-ssū hó-yíng]: state-private, operated jointly by state and private interests

公私合營企業[kūng-ssū hó-yíng ch'ì-yèh]: state-private enterprise, joint state and private enterprise, joint state and privately operated enterprise

公私關係[kūng-ssū kuān-hsì]: relation between the government and private enterprise

公私兩利[kūng-ssū liǎng-lì]: both public and individual interests are benefited

8 公制[kūng-chìh]: the metric system

公股[kūng-kǔ]: government capital in semi-government-owned enterprise

公使[kūng-shǐh]: envoy, minister

公事[kūng-shìh]: official business

公使館[kūng-shǐh-kuǎn]: legation

公物[kūng-wù]: government property

9 公約[kūng-yüēh]: treaty, pact, convention

10 公差[kūng-ch'ā]: tolerance, arithmetical ratio

公海[kūng-hǎi]: the open sea, international waters

公益[kūng-ì]: public welfare, public interest

公益金[kūng-ì-chīn]: public welfare fund; common fund set aside for welfare

11 公娼制[kūng-ch'āng-chìh]: public prostitution system

公衆[kūng-chùng]: public

公衆輿論[kūng-chùng yǘ-lùn]: public opinion

公理[kūng-lǐ]: axiom, general principle

公理會[kūng-lǐ-hùi]: Congregational Church

公堂[kūng-t'áng]: court, courtroom

公務員[kūng-wù-yüán]: government employee, government functionary, civil servant

12 公費[kūng-fèi]: public expenses, government expenditure

公費醫療[kūng-fèi ī-liáo]: free medical treatment, free medical service

公然[kūng-ján]: openly, overtly, publicly

公開[kūng-k'āi]: open, open to the public, overt

公開信[kūng-k'āi-hsìn]: open letter, public letter

公報[kūng-pào]: official report, public bulletin, official communique

公報私仇[kūng-pào ssū-ch'óu]: to revenge personal grievances in the name of the public

公訴[kūng-sù]: public prosecution

13 公債[kūng-chài]: state loan, government bond

公路[kūng-lù]: highway

公路網[kūng-lù-wǎng]: highway network

公園[kūng-yüán]: park

14 公認[kūng-jèn]: to approve officially, to recognize publicly; to be established, known or acknowledged officially

15 公論報[kūng-lùn-pào]: Kung Lun Pao (a Taiwan daily newspaper)

公署[kūng-shǔ]: government office

公德[kūng-té]: public morality (in Article 42 of the Common Program, this term refers specifically to the "Five Loves" 五愛, q.v.)

公敵[kūng-tí]: public enemy

公養猪[kūng-yǎng-chū]: pigs raised collectively

16 公積金[kūng-chī-chīn]: common reserve fund, public reserve fund, accumulation fund

公曆[kūng-lì]: Gregorian calendar

公噸[kūng-tùn]: metric ton

17 公營企業[kūng-yíng ch'ǐ-yèh]: public enterprise

18 公職[kūng-chíh]: public duty

公爵[kūng-chüéh]: duke

公斷[kūng-tuàn]: to judge publicly, to arbitrate; arbitration, a just decision

19 公證[kūng-chèng]: notorization

公證人[kūng-chèng-jén]: notary public

公糧[kūng-liáng]: agricultural tax in kind, public tax contribution in kind (grain)

20 公議[kūng-ì]: public discussion, public deliberation

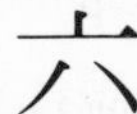

15 六論[lìu-lùn]: the six theories (i.e., "the theory of the withering away of the classes," "the theory of docile tools," "the theory of joining the Party in order to become an official," "the theory of the backwardness of the masses," "the theory of peace within the Party," and "the theory of merging public and private interests"—theories alleged to have been originated by Liu Shao-ch'i; an editorial in the Red Flag of October 15, 1968 asserted that these theories amounted to the nullification of the proletarian dictatorship)

— 4 Strokes —

共

5 共犯 **[kùng-fàn]**: to commit a crime together; accomplice

共甘苦 **[kùng-kān-k'ǔ]**: to share joys and sorrows

6 共同 **[kùng-t'úng]**: common, joint

共同防禦公約 **[kùng-t'úng fáng-yǜ kūng-yüēh]**: joint defense pact

共同奮鬥 **[kùng-t'úng fèn-tòu]**: to unite in a common struggle

共同綱領 **[kùng-t'úng kāng-lǐng]**: The Common Program (1949)

共同努力 **[kùng-t'úng nǔ-lì]**: to make joint efforts, to join in an endeavor

共同市場 **[kùng-t'úng shìh-ch'ǎng]**: common market

共同體 **[kùng-t'úng-t'ǐ]**: community

共同存在 **[kùng-t'úng ts'ún-tsài]**: to coexist; coexistence

共同通信社 **[kùng-t'úng t'ūng-hsìn-shè]**: Kyodo News Agency (Japan)

共存 **[kùng-ts'ún]**: to coexist; coexistence

共有 **[kùng-yǔ]**: to possess in common

8 共青團 **[kùng-ch'īng-t'uán]**: Communist Youth League

共青團眞理報 **[kùng-ch'īng-t'uán chēn-lǐ-pào]**: Komsomolskaya Pravda (Russian daily newspaper)

共和 **[kùng-hó]**: republican

共和國 **[kùng-hó-kuó]**: republic

共性 **[kùng-hsìng]**: common characteristic

共命運 **[kùng-mìng-yǜn]**: to share the same fate, common fate

共事 **[kùng-shìh]**: to work together, to be colleagues

11 共產主義 **[kùng-ch'ǎn chǔ-ì]**: communism

共產主義精神 **[kùng-ch'ǎn chǔ-ì chīng-shén]**: communist spirit

共產主義覺悟 **[kùng-ch'ǎn chǔ-ì chüéh-wù]**: communist consciousness

共產主義風格 **[kùng-ch'ǎn chǔ-ì fēng-kó]**: communist style

共產主義學校 **[kùng-ch'ǎn chǔ-ì hsüéh-hsiào]**: communism school (a type of school run by labor unions)

共產主義道德 **[kùng-ch'ǎn chǔ-ì tào-té]**: communist ethics

共產國際 **[kùng-ch'ǎn kuó-chì]**: Communist International

共產黨 **[kùng-ch'ǎn-tǎng]**: Communist Party

共產黨宣言 **[kùng-ch'ǎn-tǎng hsüān-yén]**: The Communist Manifesto

共產黨人 **[kùng-ch'ǎn-tǎng-jén]**: Kommunist (Russian periodical)

共產黨工人黨情報局 **[kùng-ch'ǎn-tǎng kūng-jén-tǎng ch'íng-pào-chǘ]**: Information Bureau of the Communist and Worker Parties

共處 **[kùng-ch'ǔ]**: to coexist; coexistence

14 共鳴 **[kùng-míng]**: to echo; an echo

16 共謀 **[kùng-móu]**: to conspire with, to intrigue with; in complicity with, in collusion with

— 5 Strokes —

兵

2 兵力 **[pīng-lì]**: military force, military strength

3 兵工廠 **[pīng-kūng-ch'ǎng]**: armory, ordinance factory, arsenal

7 兵役 **[pīng-ì]** : military service

兵役委員會 **[pīng-ì wĕi-yüán-hùi]** : Commission for Military Conscription

8 兵法 **[pīng-fă]** : military tactics

10 兵庫 **[pīng-k'ù]** : armory

12 兵痞 **[pīng-p'ĭ]** : irregulars

14 兵種 **[pīng-chŭng]** : branch of military service, arm

兵團 **[pīng-t'uán]** : army, army group

17 兵營 **[pīng-yíng]** : barracks

23 兵變 **[pīng-pièn]** : military uprising, mutiny

— 6 Strokes —

其

6 其因河 **[ch'í-yīn-hó]** : Gyang River (Burma)

14 其實 **[ch'í-shíh]** : indeed, in reality, in truth, in fact, as a matter of fact

具

6 具有 **[chǜ-yŭ]** : to have; there is

12 具結 **[chǜ-chiéh]** : to make a written statement of guarantee

具備 **[chǜ-pèi]** : to be equipped with

具備一切條件 **[chǜ-pèi í-ch'ièh t'iáo-chièn]** : there is every requisite

23 具體 **[chǜ-t'ĭ]** : concrete, specific, actual

具體現實 **[chǜ-t'ĭ hsièn-shíh]** : concrete reality

具體同一性 **[chǜ-t'ĭ t'úng-ī-hsìng]** : concrete identity

典

9 典型 **[tiĕn-hsíng]** : model; typical, representative

典型化 **[tiĕn-hsíng-huà]** : typification, standardization

典故 **[tiĕn-kù]** : classical allusion, quotation, classical source

典要 **[tiĕn-yào]** : classical, authoritative, time-honored

15 典範 **[tiĕn-fàn]** : model, example, sample, pattern

17 典禮局 **[tiĕn-lĭ-chǘ]** : Bureau of Ceremonies

— 8 Strokes —

兼

6 兼任 **[chiēn-jèn]** : to hold concurrent posts, to serve concurrently in more than one position

8 兼併 **[chiēn-pìng]** : to annex, to incorporate, to unite

兼併主義者 **[chiēn-pìng chŭ-ì-chĕ]** : annexationist

12 兼程開往 **[chiēn-ch'éng k'āi-wàng]** : to go by double stages; to go at double speed

16 兼辦 **[chiēn-pàn]** : to administer simultaneously

18 兼職 **[chiēn-chíh]** : to hold more than one position at the same time; concurrent position

21 兼顧 **[chiēn-kù]** : to attend to two or more matters at the same time

— 14 Strokes —

冀 **[chì]** : Hopeh Province (abbreviation)

— RADICAL 冂 13 —

— 3 Strokes —

册

3 册子 **[ts'è-tzu]**: register, volume

6 册次 **[ts'è-tz'ù]**: volume

15 册數 **[ts'è-shù]**: number of volumes

— 4 Strokes —

1 再一次 **[tsài í-tz'ù]**: once more, again, once again

3 再三 **[tsài-sān]**: repeatedly, over and over, again and again

再三再四地 **[tsài-sān tsài-ssù tì]**: time and again

4 再分組 **[tsài-fēn-tsŭ]**: secondary classification; to subdivide further into groups

5 再犯 **[tsài-fàn]**: to repeat an offense, to violate again

再生 **[tsài-shēng]**: reincarnation, rebirth; to be reborn or regenerated

6 再次 **[tsài-tz'ù]**: anew, again, once more

再次聲明 **[tsài-tz'ù shēng-míng]**: restatement, to state again

8 再版 **[tsài-păn]**: second edition, reprint; to reprint

12 再發生 **[tsài-fā-shēng]**: to recur, to happen again; recurrence

再開始 **[tsài-k'āi-shĭh]**: to resume, to renew, to begin again; resumption, renewal

13 再補滿 **[tsài pŭ-măn]**: to replenish

— 7 Strokes —

5 冒犯 **[mào-fàn]**: to offend, to affront, to provoke, to give offense

6 冒尖 **[mào-chiēn]**: outstanding, prominent, extraordinary

冒充 **[mào-ch'ūng]**: to palm off, to pass off as, to pretend to be

9 冒昧 **[mào-mèi]**: to take the liberty of, to have the boldness to; brashness; reckless

12 冒着 **[mào-che]**: to brave, to defy; in the teeth of, in spite of

冒進 **[mào-chìn]**: to advance recklessly; reckless advance, adventurist progress (i.e., progress in a reckless manner)

冒牌的 **[mào-p'ái te]**: spurious, counterfeit, false, bogus

16 冒險 **[mào-hsiĕn]**: to venture, to run risks, to brave danger

冒險政策 **[mào-hsiĕn chèng-ts'è]**: adventurist policy

冒險主義 **[mào-hsiĕn chŭ-ì]**: adventurism

— RADICAL 冖 14 —

— 6 Strokes —

冠

9 冠 軍 [**kuàn-chǖn**] : champion; first place

— 8 Strokes —

冢

4 冢 中 枯 骨 [**chŭng-chūng k'ū-kŭ**] : rotting bone in a tomb, an absolutely useless person

冥

4 冥 王 星 [**míng-wáng-hsīng**] : the planet Pluto

— RADICAL 冫 15 —

—3 Strokes —

冬

10 冬 耕 [**tūng-kēng**] : winter ploughing or tilling

冬 眠 [**tūng-mién**] : to hibernate; hibernation

16 冬 學 [**tūng-hsüéh**] : winter school (school for peasants with primary emphasis on ideological education and on reading and writing)

— 4 Strokes —

決

8 決 定 性 [**chüéh-tìng-hsìng**] : decisive nature

決 定 論 [**chǘeh-tìng-lùn**] : determinism

20 決 議 [**chüéh-ì**] : resolution

冲

9 冲 突 [**ch'ūng-t'ù**] : clash, conflict, collision

10 冲 破 [**ch'ūng-p'ò**] : to break down, to break through

11 冲 動 [**ch'ūng-tùng**] : to shake; germinating power, excited

12 冲 陷 [**ch'ūng-hsièn**] : to make an inroad, to attack and defeat

15 冲 撞 [**ch'ūng-chuàng**] : to strike, to push, to give offense

冲 鋒 [**ch'ūng-fēng**] : to push forward, to make a bold advance, to charge

16 冲 激 [**ch'ūng-chī**] : to excite

冲 積 [**ch'ūng-chī**] : deposit, sedimentation; alluvial

19 冲 繩 [**ch'ūng-shéng**] : Okinawa

— 5 Strokes —

冷

10 冷 笑 [**lĕng-hsiào**] : cold smile, cynical leer, sneer

11 冷 淡 [**lĕng-tàn**] : indifference, apathy, unconcern; indifferent, apathetic, half-hearted, lukewarm, dull (in trade)

13 冷 落 [**lĕng-lò**] : quiet and deserted

14 冷酷 **[lěng-k'ù]** : grim, merciless, harsh, callous, stern, cynical

16 冷戰 **[lěng-chàn]** : cold war

冶

8 冶金 **[yěh-chīn]** : metallurgy; metallurgical

冶金工業 **[yěh-chīn kūng-yèh]** : metallurgical industry

冶金工業部 **[yěh-chīn kūng-yèh pù]** : Ministry of Metallurgical Industry

冶金陶瓷研究所 **[yěh-chīn t'áo-tz'ú yén-chìu-sŏ]** : Institute of Metallurgy and Ceramics

13 冶煉 **[yěh-lièn]** : to smelt

冶煉廠 **[yěh-lièn-ch'ăng]** : smelting plant

冶煉爐 **[yěh-lièn-lú]** : smelting furnace

— 8 Strokes —

9 凈重 **[chìng-chùng]** : net weight

13 凈載重 **[chìng-tsài-chùng]** : net weight of load

准

10 准將 **[chŭn-chiàng]** : Brigadier General (U.S. Army and Air Force); Commodore (U.S. Navy); Brigadier (British Army); Air Commodore (British Air Force)

11 准許 **[chŭn-hsŭ]** : to permit, to allow, to consent to, to approve of, to sanction; permission, approval

准尉 **[chŭn-wèi]** : Warrant Officer

凍

12 凍結 **[tùng-chiéh]** : frozen hard, blocked; to freeze

凍結資金 **[tùng-chiéh tzū-chīn]** : frozen capital; to freeze capital

— 14 Strokes —

8 凝固汽油彈 **[níng-kù ch'ì-yú-tàn]** : napalm bomb

14 凝聚 **[níng-chǜ]** : to stick together, to cohere, to coagulate; cohesion, consolidation, cementation, coherence, coagulation

— RADICAL 几 16 —

几

4 凡內亞共和國 [chī-nèi-yà kùng-hó-kuó]: Republic of Guinea

— 1 Stroke —

凡

14 凡爾登 [fán-ěrh-tēng] : Verdun (France)

凡爾塞 [fán-ěrh-sài] : Versailles (France)

— 10 Strokes —

凱

6 凱因斯 [k'ǎi-yīn-ssū] : Keynes, J. M. (British economist, 1883–1946)

凱因斯主義 [k'ǎi-yīn-ssū chǔ-ì]: Keynesism

14 凱歌 [k'ǎi-kō] : song of victory

— RADICAL 凵 17 —

— 2 Strokes —

4 凶手 [hsiūng-shǒu] : murderer, assassin

10 凶耗 [hsiūng-hào] : bad tidings

12 凶惡 [hsiūng-ò]: cruel, savage, brutal, barbarous, evil, vicious, inhuman

14 凶焰 [hsiūng-yèn] : rage and ferocity

15 凶暴 [hsiūng-pào]: vindictive, malignant, implacable, ruthless

— 3 Strokes —

2 出人意外 [ch'ū jén-ì wài] : it is unexpected that, out of (people's) expectation, as a great surprise

出入 [ch'ū-jù]: to enter and leave; discrepancy

出力 [ch'ū-lì]: to expend energy, to exert effort

3 出口 [ch'ū-k'ǒu]: to export; exports, exportation, exit

4 出毛病 [ch'ū máo-pìng]: to become defective, to break down, to go wrong

出世 [ch'ū-shìh] : to be born; birth

5 出主意 [ch'ū chǔ-ì]: to give an opinion, to make a decision, to offer a suggestion

出出氣 [ch'ū-ch'ū ch'ì]: to blow off steam, to give vent to

出乎 [ch'ū-hū] : to proceed from, out of

出乎意外 [ch'ū-hū ì-wài] : unexpectedly

出乎能力之外 [ch'ū-hū néng-lì chīh wài] : beyond the capacity of

6 出色的 [ch'ū-sè te] : remarkable, splendid, grand, exceptional, wonderful, noteworthy

出自 [ch'ū tzù] : to arise from, to stem from

7 出岔子 [ch'ū ch'à-tzu] : to meet with an accident

出兵 [ch'ū-pīng] : to send out troops

出身 [ch'ū-shēn] : to come of, to be born of; social or personal origin

8 出奇 [ch'ū-ch'í] : strange, marvelous, wonderful, unusual

出奇制勝 [ch'ū-ch'í chìh-shèng] : to achieve a victory through unusual tactics

出其不意 [ch'ū ch'í-pú-ì] : to take one unawares, to be taken unawares, to take one by surprise

出來 [ch'ū-lái] : to come out, to emerge

出版 [ch'ū-pǎn] : to publish, to print

出版人 [ch'ū-pǎn-jén] : publisher

出版社 [ch'ū-pǎn-shè] : publishing house

出版總署 [ch'ū-pǎn tsǔng-shǔ] : Bureau of Publication

出版自由 [ch'ū-pǎn tzù-yú] : freedom of the press, freedom of publication

出版物 [ch'ū-pǎn-wù] : publication

出事 [ch'ū-shìh] : to give rise to an accident

出於 [ch'ū-yú] : to proceed from

出於自願 [ch'ū-yú tzù-yüàn] : on a voluntary basis, of one's own accord

9 出風頭 [ch'ū fēng-t'óu] : to cut a smart figure, to show off

出席 [ch'ū-hsí] : to attend (as a meeting)

出席宴會 [ch'ū-hsí yèn-hùi] : to attend a banquet, to be a guest at a banquet

出活 [ch'ū-huó] : to manufacture, to produce

出面 [ch'ū-mièn] : to appear (as when speaking for others); to initiate (on behalf of others and one's self)

出品 [ch'ū-p'ǐn] : product

出洋 [ch'ū-yáng] : to go abroad

10 出差 [ch'ū-ch'āi] : to send abroad, to go on an official trip

出氣 [ch'ū-ch'ì] : to vent one's anger, to blow off steam

出納部 [ch'ū-nà-pù] : Paymaster General's Office

出租 [ch'ū-tsū] : to rent out

11 出產 [ch'ū-ch'ǎn] : to produce, to manufacture; products

出現 [ch'ū-hsièn] : to appear, to come out, to come into existence, to arise, to come to light; appearance, occurrence, presence

出售 [ch'ū-shòu] : to sell; sale

出動 [ch'ū-tùng] : to set in motion, to set out

12 出超 [ch'ū-ch'āo] : export surplus, favorable balance of trade

出發 [ch'ū-fā] : to set out, to depart, to begin (as a journey)

出發點 [ch'ū-fā-tiěn] : starting point, point of departure

13 出路 [ch'ū-lù] : exit, doorway, way out, outlet

14 出勤 [ch'ū-ch'ín] : to report for work; work attendance

出勤率 [ch'ū-ch'ín-lǜ] : rate of attendance

出滿勤 [ch'ū mǎn-ch'ín] : full attendance (i.e., full attendance in field work by farmers)

出榜 **[ch'ū-pǎng]**: to announce examination results, to publish a list of successful candidates in an examination

15 出價 **[ch'ū-chià]**: to bid, to offer a price

出賣 **[ch'ū-mài]**: to betray, to sell out; betrayal; to sell; for sale

16 出頭 **[ch'ū-t'óu]**: to come to the fore, to take over leadership, to distinguish oneself, to put oneself forward

17 出擊 **[ch'ū-chī]**: to launch an attack

— 6 Strokes —

函

11 函授 **[hán-shòu]**: to teach through correspondence

函授學校 **[hán-shòu hsüéh-hsiào]**: correspondence school

函授科 **[hán-shòu k'ō]**: correspondence course

17 函購 **[hán-kòu]**: to order by mail, to purchase by mail

函館 **[hán-kuǎn]**: Hakodate (Japan)

— RADICAL 刀 18 —

— 2 Strokes —

切

4 切切 **[ch'ièh-ch'ièh]**: urgently, earnestly

切切此命 **[ch'ièh-ch'ièh tz'ǔ-lìng]**: this order is to be strictly obeyed

切切此布 **[ch'ièh-ch'ièh tz'ǔ-pù]**: this proclamation is hereby issued in all earnestness

切中要害 **[ch'ièh-chùng yào-hài]**: pertinent, fit, proper, relevant; to hit, to hit the nail on the head

6 切合 **[ch'ièh-hó]**: to fit in well with

切合時宜 **[ch'ièh-hó shíh-í]**: timely, well timed, at the right time; opportune

7 切身 **[ch'ièh-shēn]**: vital, serious, genuine, one's own

11 切望 **[ch'ièh-wàng]**: to hope eagerly for, to be desirous of

15 切實 **[ch'ièh-shíh]**: practical, practicable, effective, feasible; sincere, genuine

18 切題 **[ch'ièh-t'í]**: to be to the point, to be on the subject; pertinent, appropriate

切斷 **[ch'iēh-tuàn]**: to cut, to cut off, to sever, to split, to break apart, to disjoin

分

3 分工 **[fēn-kūng]**: division of labor

分工合作 **[fēn-kūng hó-tsò]**: division of work and responsibility, division of labor and sharing of responsibility, proper division of labor and coordination

分寸 **[fēn-ts'ùn]**: discreet, appropriate

分子 **[fēn-tzǔ]**: molecule

分子輻射 **[fēn-tzǔ fú-shè]**: molecular radiation

4 分支部委員會 **[fēn-chīh-pù wěi-yüán-hùi]**: Party Sub-Branch Committee

分化 **[fēn-huà]**: to split up, to disintegrate, to divide; (political) ferment, dissension, polarization

分內 [**fèn-nèi**] : obligation; within one's area of obligation; part of one's duty

分水嶺 [**fēn-shŭi-lĭng**] : watershed

5 分外 [**fèn-wài**] : beyond one's duty, outside one's area of obligation; special, extraordinary; exceptionally, unusually

7 分局 [**fēn-chǘ**] : branch office; sub-bureau

分批分期 [**fēn-p'ī fēn-ch'í**] : by groups and stages, group by group, at different times

分別 [**fēn-piéh**] : to part, to differentiate

分別地 [**fēn-piéh tì**] : respectively

分別對待 [**fēn-piéh tùi-tài**] : to deal with separately; to deal with each case on its own merits

分佈 [**fēn-pù**] : to distribute, to scatter, to spread

分社 [**fēn-shè**] : branch commune

8 分歧 [**fēn-ch'í**] : to be divided over, to disagree with; divergence, diversity, difference, discord, disparity; divergent

分析 [**fēn-hsī**] : to analyze; analysis; analytical

分析修勻 [**fēn-hsī hsīu-yǘn**] : analytical smoothing; curve fitting

分析判斷 [**fēn-hsī p'àn-tuàn**] : analytic judgment

分析表 [**fēn-hsī-piăo**] : analytical table or chart

分析態度 [**fēn-hsī t'ài-tù**] : analytical approach, analytical attitude

分明 [**fēn-míng**] : to clarify, to differentiate clearly; clear, obvious

分享 [**fēn-hsiăng**] : to share enjoyment, to have a share in enjoyment

9 分界綫 [**fēn-chièh-hsièn**] : demarcation line, dividing line, line of demarcation

分洪 [**fēn-húng**] : to channel off flood waters, to mitigate a flood

分紅 [**fēn-húng**] : to distribute dividends, to distribute profits

分派 [**fēn-p'ài**] : to form factions, to form parties

分神 [**fēn-shén**] : to pay attention to (something)

10 分級管理 [**fēn-chí kuăn-lĭ**] : level to level administration, administration by different levels

分家 [**fēn-chiā**] : to divide the property of a family; to split an organization

分班 [**fēn-pān**] : to divide into groups, to divide into classes

分配 [**fēn-p'èi**] : to distribute, to assign, to apportion, to allot; portion, allocation, distribution, apportionment

分配制度 [**fēn-p'èi chìh-tù**] : distribution system

分配曲綫 [**fēn-p'èi ch'ǖ-hsièn**] : distribution curve

分配到戶 [**fēn-p'èi tào-hù**] : household distribution, to supply directly to each household

分庭抗禮 [**fēn-t'íng k'àng-lĭ**] : to treat equally, to have equal standing

11 分清 [**fēn-ch'īng**] : to distinguish clearly, to differentiate clearly

分清界綫 [**fēn-ch'īng chièh-hsièn**] : to differentiate boundaries clearly, to draw a sharp line of demarcation

分清是非 [**fēn-ch'īng shìh-fēi**] : to distinguish clearly between right and wrong

分清大是大非 [**fēn-ch'īng tà-shìh tà-fēi**] : to distinguish clearly between right and wrong on vital questions

分清敵我 [**fēn-ch'īng tí-wŏ**] : to draw a clearcut line between the enemy and ourselves

分崩離析 [**fēn-pēng lí-hsī**] : to disintegrate (internally), to fall apart; divergence and disintegration

分設並存[fēn-shè pìng-ts'ún]: to be established separately and coexist

分組討論[fēn-tsŭ t'ăo-lùn]: to hold group discussions

分野[fēn-yĕh]: division, field, sphere, scope, realm

12 分期[fēn-ch'í]: by stages, by time periods

分期付款[fēn-ch'í fù-k'uăn]: to pay by installment, installment payment

分開[fēn-k'āi]: to divide, to separate; separation

分割[fēn-kō]: to divide up, to partition; partition

分裂[fēn-lièh]: to disrupt, to split up, to cause dissension; disruption, disunity, division, fission

分裂主義[fēn-lièh chŭ-ì]: separatism, secessionism (in the sense of disruption of the international communist movement)

分裂主義者[fēn-lièh chŭ-ì chĕ]: separatist, secessionist

分散[fēn-sàn]: to scatter, to disperse, to decentralize; decentralization; decentralized, scattered, dispersed

分散經營[fēn-sàn chīng-yíng]: decentralized management

分散主義[fēn-sàn chŭ-ì]: decentralization, fragmentationism, departmentalism, excessive decentralization

分散兵力[fēn-sàn pīng-lì]: dispersal of military strength or troops

分散的資金[fēn-sàn te tzū-chīn]: non-centralized funds, scattered funds

分等[fēn-tĕng]: grading

分等級[fēn tĕng-chí]: to divide into grades or levels

分等論價[fēn-tĕng lùn-chià]: to grade commodities and fix prices according to quality

分隊[fēn-tùi]: unit (this term is used loosely to refer to a company-size or smaller unit)

13 分解[fēn-chiĕh]: to decompose, to dissolve

分發[fēn-fā]: to send out, to send away, to distribute, to hand out

分會[fēn-hùi]: auxiliary organization, branch association

14 分遣隊[fēn-ch'iĕn-tùi]: contingent, detachment, detail

分署[fēn-shŭ]: branch office

15 分廠[fēn-ch'ăng]: branch plant, branch factory

分銷[fēn-hsiāo]: to sell in retail; retail sale, retail business

分層[fēn-ts'éng]: to divide into levels or layers

16 分辨[fēn-pièn]: to distinguish, to differentiate

分擔[fēn-tān]: to distribute, to share (work or burden)

分頭[fēn-t'óu]: to go different ways

17 分類[fēn-lèi]: to classify, to sort out, to catalogue; classification

分類數字[fēn-lèi shù-tzù]: break-down figures

19 分離[fēn-lí]: to leave, to separate, to isolate; dissociation

21 分辯[fēn-pièn]: to clarify, to explain

分贓[fēn-tsāng]: to share the plunder, to divide the spoils

— 3 Strokes —

刊

8 刊物[k'ān-wù]: journal, periodical, publication

12 刊登[k'ān-tēng]: to publish

13 刊載 **[k'ān-tsǎi]** : to carry, to print, to publish, to feature

— 4 Strokes —

刑

8 刑法 **[hsíng-fǎ]** : criminal code

刑事 **[hsíng-shìh]** : criminal case

刑事案 **[hsíng-shìh àn]** : criminal case

刑事審判庭 **[hsíng-shìh shěn-p'àn-t'íng]** : criminal court

10 刑訊逼供 **[hsíng-hsǜn pī-kùng]** : to extort confession by torture

列

2 列入 **[lièh-jù]** : to include, to list

4 列支敦士登公國 **[lièh-chīh-tūn-shìh-tēng kūng-kuó]** : Principality of Liechtenstein

10 列席 **[lièh-hsí]** : to sit in a meeting as an observer

列席代表 **[lièh-hsí tài-piǎo]** : delegate without power to vote

10 列島 **[lièh-tǎo]** : island group, archipelago

12 列强 **[lièh-ch'iáng]** : the great powers

14 列寧 **[lièh-níng]** : Lenin (1870–1924)

列寧主義 **[lièh-níng chǔ-ì]** : Leninism

17 列舉 **[lièh-chǚ]** : to list, to enumerate, to specify, to cite item by item

划

3 划子 **[huá-tzu]** : rowboat

11 划船 **[huá ch'uán]** : to row a boat

— 5 Strokes —

劫

9 劫持 **[chiéh-ch'íh]** : to abduct, to sieze, to hold under duress, to force

12 劫富濟貧 **[chiéh-fù chì-p'ín]** : to rob the rich to help the poor

初

4 初中 **[ch'ū-chūng]** : junior secondary school

5 初犯 **[ch'ū-fàn]** : first offense; first offender

6 初次登台 **[ch'ū-tz'ù tēng-t'ái]** : debut, first public appearance, first formal entrance into society

7 初步 **[ch'ū-pù]** : the first step; preliminary, rudimentary, initial, primary

初步加工 **[ch'ū-pù chiā-kūng]** : preliminary processing

初步分析 **[ch'ū-pù fēn-hsī]** : preliminary analysis

初步打擊 **[ch'ū-pù tǎ-chī]** : initial blow

10 初級 **[ch'ū-chí]** : elementary grade; elementary

初級社 **[ch'ū-chí-shè]** : elementary cooperative, initial cooperative

初級市場 **[ch'ū-chí shìh-ch'ǎng]** : basic level market

12 初等 **[ch'ū-těng]** : elementary grade, beginning grade

15 初稾 **[ch'ū-kǎo]** : first draft

利

3 利己主義 **[lì-chǐ chǔ-ì]** : egoism, egotism

利已主義者[lì-chǐ chǔ-ì chě] : egotist

4 利比里亞[lì-pǐ-lǐ-yà] : Liberia

利比里亞共和國[lì-pǐ-lǐ-yà kùng-hó-kuó] : Republic of Liberia

利比亞[lì-pǐ-yà] : Libya

利比亞聯合王國[lì-pǐ-yà lién-hó wáng-kuó] : United Kingdom of Libya

5 利他主義[lì-t'ā chǔ-ì] : altruism

利用[lì-yùng] : to make use of, to exploit; utilization

利用系數[lì-yùng hsì-shù] : utilization coefficient, capacity factor

利用，限制，和改造[lì-yùng, hsièn-chìh, hó kǎi-tsào] : utilization, restriction, and transformation (policy)

利用率[lì-yùng-lǜ] : utilization rate, operation rate

7 利伯維爾[lì-pó-wéi-ěrh] : Libreville (Gabon)

10 利害[lì-hài] : advantage and disadvantage, interest; serious, severe, injurious

利害衝突[lì-hài ch'ūng-t'ù] : clash of interests, conflict of interests

利害相關[lì-hài hsiāng-kuān] : to be vitally involved, interested

利馬[lì-mǎ] : Lima (Peru)

利息[lì-hsí] : interest, dividend

利益[lì-ì] : benefit, advantage, gain, profit

利原[lì-yüán] : Iwon (Korea)

11 利處[lì-ch'ù] : advantage

利率[lì-lǜ] : interest rate

12 利雅得[lì-yǎ-té] : Riyadh (Saudi Arabia)

13 利奧波德維爾[lì-ào-pō-té-wéi-ěrh] : Leopoldville (Congo)

15 利潤[lì-jùn] : profit

判

6 判決[p'àn-chüéh] : to sentence, to pronounce sentence, to convict; verdict, court sentence

判刑[p'àn-hsíng] : to impose a criminal sentence

11 判處[p'àn-ch'ǔ] : to sentence

13 判罪[p'àn-tsùi] : to sentence

18 判斷[p'àn-tuàn] : to judge, to evaluate, to estimate, to interpret; judgment

别

6 别有用心[piéh-yǔ yùng-hsīn] : to have ulterior motives or purpose; calculated

8 别府[piéh-fǔ] : Beppu (Japan)

别的[piéh-te] : another, other

11 别處[piéh-ch'ù] : elsewhere

23 别體[piéh-t'ǐ] : modification, different reading or style (penmanship)

5 删去[shān-ch'ǜ] : to delete, to cut, to strike out, to write off, to erase, to cancel, to obliterate

7 删改[shān-kǎi] : to revise, to correct

— 6 Strokes —

制

4 制止[chìh-chǐh] : to curb, to restrain, to control, to hold back

6 制成[chìh-ch'éng] : to enact into (law)

8 制服[chìh-fú] : 1. uniform; 2. to conquer, to defeat, to overthrow, to overpower

制空權[chìh-k'ūng-ch'üán] : air control, air supremacy

制定[chìh-tìng] : to formulate, to enact

制度[chìh-tù] : system

9 制訂[chìh-tìng] : to draw up, to map out, to formulate

12 制裁[chìh-ts'ái] : to punish, to censure, to impose sanctions against, to restrain, to control; sanction

刻

4 刻不容緩的[k'ò-pù-júng-huǎn te] : imminent, pressing, most urgent

9 刻苦[k'ò-k'ǔ] : painstaking, hard-working, industrious, strenuous; to take pains over

17 刻薄[k'ò-pó] : cutting, pointed, sarcastic, sharp, harsh

刮

6 刮地皮[kuā tì-p'í] : to exploit the people, to seek one's own benefit in public office at the expense of the people

到

1 到一定時候[tào í-tìng shíh-hòu] : in due time, at a certain time, in due course

5 到目前為止[tào mù-ch'ién wéi chǐh] : as yet, up to now, by now, to date

6 到任[tào-jèn] : to assume an office

8 到底[tào-tǐ] : after all, to the end, to the bottom, finally

12 到達[tào-tá] : to arrive at, to reach, to come to

刺

刺[tz'ù] : to stab, to bayonet, to thrust

2 刺刀[tz'ù-tāo] : bayonet, dagger

11 刺探[tz'ù-t'àn] : to probe, to detect

16 刺激[tz'ù-chī] : to stimulate, to spur, to excite, to provoke; stimulus; provocative

— 7 Strokes —

前

前[ch'ién] : former, previous, ex-

8 前所未有的[ch'ién-sŏ-wèi-yǔ te] : unprecedented, unexampled, unparalleled

9 前者[ch'ién-chě] : the former

前述[ch'ién-shù] : the above-mentioned

前奏[ch'ién-tsòu] : prelude

10 前哨[ch'ién-shào] : outpost

11 前途[ch'ién-t'ú] : prospects, future

12 前進[ch'ién-chìn] : to advance, to move forward, to make headway, to push ahead, to make progress

前進報[ch'ién-chìn-pào] : Avanti (Italian daily newspaper)

前提[ch'ién-t'í] : prerequisite, premise (logical)

14 前綫[ch'ién-hsièn] : front

削

10 削弱[hsüeh-jò] : to diminish, to curtail, to weaken; decreased, enfeebled, depleted

12 削減[hsüeh-chiĕn] : to curtail, to cut, to cut down, to retrench; cut, curtailment

— 8 Strokes —

剗

5 剗平 **[ch'ǎn-p'íng]**: to level, to level to the ground

9 剗削 **[ch'ǎn-hsiāo]**: to level, to smooth off, to plane

剛

8 剛果共和國 **[kāng-kuǒ kùng-hó-kuó]**: Republic of Congo

12 剛愎 **[kāng-pì]**: obstinate, stubborn

15 剛毅 **[kāng-ì]**: constant, firm, steady, determined

剝

9 剝削 **[pō-hsüeh]**: to exploit, to extort; exploitation; exploitative

剝削者 **[pō-hsüeh-chě]**: exploiter

剝削階級 **[pō-hsüeh chiēh-chí]**: exploiting class

剝削方式 **[pō-hsüeh fāng-shìh]**: form of exploitation

剝削思想 **[pō-hsüeh ssū-hsiǎng]**: exploiting outlook

14 剝奪 **[pō-tó]**: to rob of, to snatch from, to be stripped of; deprivation

15 剝食 **[pō-shíh]**: corrosion, decomposition, disintegration

剖

12 剖開 **[p'ǒu-k'āi]**: to dissect, to cut, to cut open, to carve, to break up

— 9 Strokes —

剪

2 剪刀差 **[chiěn-tāo-ch'ā]**: disparity (i.e., in prices between industrial goods and agricultural produce)

10 剪除 **[chiěn-ch'ú]**: to root out, to destroy, to exterminate

剪草除根 **[chiěn-ts'ǎo ch'ú-kēn]**: to uproot, to eradicate

11 剪彩 **[chiěn-ts'ǎi]**: to cut the ribbon (at opening ceremonies)

12 剪報 **[chiěn-pào]**: clipping, press cutting; to clip from a newspaper

16 剪輯 **[chiěn-chí]**: cutting, clipping, montage

副

副 **[fù]**: vice- (as in vice-chairman, etc.); associate, secondary, minor, subsidiary

4 副手 **[fù-shǒu]**: assistant

5 副主任 **[fù-chǔ-jèn]**: deputy director

副本 **[fù-pěn]**: copy, transcript

7 副系主任 **[fù-hsì-chǔ-jèn]**: vice-department head, associate chairman of a department

副作用 **[fù-tsò-yùng]**: side-effect, secondary effect, undesirable effects

8 副官 **[fù-kuān]**: aide, adjutant, aide-de-camp

9 副食品 **[fù-shíh-p'ǐn]**: non-staple food, subsidiary foodstuffs (i.e., meat and vegetables, rice being considered as the principal food)

11 副產品 **[fù-ch'ǎn-p'ǐn]**: by-product, subsidiary product

副產物 **[fù-ch'ǎn-wù]**: by-product

副教授 **[fù-chiào-shòu]**: associate professor

副國務卿 [**fù-kuó-wù-ch'īng**]: Under-Secretary of State (U.S.A.)

副國務卿幫辦 [**fù-kuó-wù-ch'īng pāng-pàn**]: Deputy Under-Secretary of State (U.S.A.)

副部長 [**fù-pù-chăng**]: Vice Minister, Deputy Minister

13 副業 [**fù-yèh**]: secondary occupation, side-occupation, sideline

副業作物 [**fù-yèh tsò-wù**]: subsidiary crop

副業運輸隊 [**fù-yèh yǜn-shū tùi**]: part-time transport team

16 副縣長 [**fù-hsièn-chăng**]: county vice-governor

— 10 Strokes —

創

5 創立 [**ch'uàng-lì**]: to establish, to set up, to originate

7 創見 [**ch'uàng-chièn**]: something unprecedented, a unique interpretation

9 創紀錄 [**ch'uàng chì-lù**]: to set a record, to establish a record

11 創設 [**ch'uàng-shè**]: to create

創造 [**ch'uàng-tsào**]: to create; creation

創造經驗 [**ch'uàng-tsào chīng-yèn**]: to create experience

創造性 [**ch'uàng-tsào-hsìng**]: creativity, creativeness

創造性達爾文主義 [**ch'uàng-tsào-hsìng tá-ĕrh-wén chŭ-ì**]: creative Darwinism

創造力 [**ch'uàng-tsào-lì**]: creative energy, creative ability

13 創新紀錄 [**ch'uàng hsīn chì-lù**]: to set a new record, to create a new record

創傷 [**ch'uāng-shāng**]: wound, injury, damage

17 創舉 [**ch'uàng-chŭ**]: a new creation

創獲 [**ch'uàng-huò**]: to discover; invention, work success

割

10 割草機 [**kō-ts'ăo-chī**]: mower, hay mower

11 割捨 [**kō-shĕ**]: to give up, to leave

12 割裂 [**kō-lièh**]: to split

13 割煤 [**kō-méi**]: to mine coal; coal extraction

16 割據 [**kō-chǜ**]: carve out and occupy (an area)

18 割斷 [**kō-tuàn**]: to cut off, to sever

24 割讓 [**kō-jàng**]: to cede

3 剩下 [**shèng-hsià**]: to remain, to be left over

15 剩餘 [**shèng-yü**]: surplus, remainder

剩餘價值 [**shèng-yǘ chià-chíh**]: surplus value

剩餘勞動 [**shèng-yü láo-tùng**]: surplus labor

剩餘勞動力 [**shèng-yǘ láo-tùng-lì**]: surplus labor force

— 11 Strokes —

11 剷掉 [**ch'ăn-tiào**]: to uproot, to remove, to extirpate

— 12 Strokes —

劃

1 劃一 [**huà-ī**]: to unify, to standardize; uniform

2 劃入 **[huà-jù]**: to include, to include in the calculation

4 劃分 **[huà-fēn]**: to carve out, to draw a line, to classify, to differentiate; differentiation, classification

劃分階級成份 **[huà-fēn chiēh-chí ch'éng-fèn]**: to determine class status, to differentiate class status; class differentiation

5 劃出 **[huà-ch'ū]**: to separate, to exclude, to set aside

6 劃成分 **[huà ch'éng-fèn]**: to determine status

8 劃定 **[huà-tìng]**: to fix, to delimit

9 劃界 **[huà-chièh]**: to delimit the boundary

10 劃時代 **[huà-shíh-tài]**: epoch-making, epoch-marking, opening a new era

11 劃淸 **[huà-ch'īng]**: to draw a sharp line, to distinguish clearly

劃淸界綫 **[huà-ch'īng chièh-hsièn]**: to draw clearly a dividing line, to draw a clear line

13 劃階級 **[huà chiēh-chí]**: to determine class status

18 劃歸 **[huà-kuēi]**: to hand over, to leave, to transfer, to transmit

— 13 Strokes —

劍

8 劍拔弩張 **[chièn-pá nŭ-chāng]**: with the sword drawn and the bow stretched, a tense atmosphere (as in preparation for war), saber-rattling

16 劍橋大學 **[chièn-ch'iáo tà-hsüéh]**: Cambridge University

劇

5 劇本原稿 **[chǜ-pĕn yüán-kăo]**: original manuscript of a drama or play

7 劇作家 **[chǜ-tsò-chiā]**: playwright, dramatist

10 劇烈 **[chǜ-lièh]**: bitter, intensive, sharp, keen, acute, violent, fierce, drastic

劇院 **[chǜ-yüàn]**: theater

14 劇團 **[chǜ-t'uán]**: theatrical group, theatrical troupe

劊

3 劊子手 **[k'uài-tzu-shŏu]**: executioner

— RADICAL 力 19 —

力

7 力求 **[lì-ch'íu]**: to strive for, to make every effort to achieve

8 力爭 **[lì-chēng]**: to struggle hard

力爭上游 **[lì-chēng shàng-yú]**: to strive for the upper reaches of a stream, to aim high

12 力量 **[lì-liàng]**: strength, force, power, might

力量對比 **[lì-liàng tùi-pĭ]**: ratio of force, ratio of power, relative strength

14 力圖 **[lì-t'ú]**: to strive for, to make every effort to achieve

16 力學 **[lì-hsüéh]**: dynamics: to study or learn diligently

力學研究所 **[lì-hsüéh yén-chìu-sŏ]**: Institute of Dynamics

— 3 Strokes —

加

2 加入 **[chiā-jù]**: to enter into, to join, to participate

3 加工[**chiā-kūng**]: to process; processing, refining, finishing

加工品[**chiā-kūng-p'ǐn**]: finished goods, processed goods

加工訂貨[**chiā-kūng tìng-huò**]: to process and manufacture goods; orders placed by the state with private enterprises for manufacturing and processing

加上[**chiā-shàng**]: to add to, to join, to attach, to annex; plus, with

5 加布里島[**chiā-pù-lǐ tǎo**]: Capri

7 加快[**chiā-k'uài**]: to accelerate, to speed up, to step up, to quicken, to hasten

加利福尼亞[**chiā-lì-fú-ní-yà**]: California

加里寧[**chiā-lǐ-níng**]: Kalinin

8 加固[**chiā-kù**]: to strengthen, to reinforce

加拉加斯[**chiā-lā-chiā-ssū**]: Caracas (Venezuela)

加來[**chiā-lái**]: Calais

加油[**chiā-yú**]: to add fuel, to refuel, to lubricate; to make more of an effort, to try harder, to put more muscle into

加油站[**chiā-yú-chàn**]: oil station, service station, filling station

9 加勁[**chiā-chìn**]: to make a greater effort

10 加納共和國[**chiā-nà kùng-hó-kuó**]: Republic of Ghana

加拿大[**chiā-ná-tà**]: Canada

加拿大自治領[**chiā-ná-tà tzù-chìh-lǐng**]: Dominion of Canada

加班[**chiā-pān**]: overtime work, extra shift, extra schedule

加倍[**chiā-pèi**]: to double, to multiply; twice as much as

加特爾[**chiā-t'è-ěrh**]: cartel

11 加强[**chiā-ch'iáng**]: to reinforce, to strengthen, to intensify

加勒比海[**chiā-lè-pǐ hǎi**]: Caribbean Sea

加隆河[**chiā-lúng hó**]: Garonne River

加冕[**chiā-miěn**]: coronation

加深[**chiā-shēn**]: to deepen, to intensify, to aggravate, to accent

加速[**chiā-sù**]: to accelerate

加得加特海[**chiā-té-chiā-t'è hǎi**]: Kattegat

加添[**chiā-t'iēn**]: to add, to supplement

12 加斯特羅[**chiā-ssū-t'è-ló**]: Castro, Fidel

加雅[**chiā-yǎ**]: Gaya

13 加盟共和國[**chiā-méng kùng-hó-kuó**]: a union republic

加農炮[**chiā-núng p'ào**]: cannon

14 加緊[**chiā-chǐn**]: to intensify, to step up, to aggravate, to heighten

加爾各答[**chiā-ěrh-kò-tá**]: Calcutta

加爾文會[**chiā-ěrh-wén hùi**]: Calvinist Church

15 加劇[**chiā-chì**]: to intensify, to speed up, to aggravate, to heighten

加寬[**chiā-k'uān**]: to widen

加蓬共和國[**chiā-p'éng kùng-hó-kuó**]: Republic of Gabon

加德滿都[**chiā-té-mǎn-tū**]: Katmandu (Nepal)

加增[**chiā-tsēng**]: to increase

16 加薪[**chiā-hsīn**]: to increase salary

17 加薩[**chiā-sà**]: Gaza

19 加羅林群島[**chiā-ló-lín ch'ǘn-tǎo**]: Caroline Islands

功

4 功夫 **[kūng-fū]**: time, capability, training

5 功用 **[kūng-yùng]**: effect

6 功臣 **[kūng-ch′én]**: a meritorious official; hero (a peasant, worker, or soldier honored for meritorious performance)

7 功利主義 **[kūng-lì chŭ-ì]**: utilitarianism

10 功能 **[kūng-néng]**: function, effect, effectiveness, capability

11 功率 **[kūng-lǜ]**: efficiency, capacity

12 功勛 **[kūng-hsūn]**: merit, feat, meritorious achievement

功勞 **[kūng-láo]**: meritorious deed, exploit, achievement

13 功過 **[kūng-kuò]**: merits and faults

17 功績 **[kūng-chī]**: meritorious deed, meritorious service, distinguished service, feat, accomplishment, merit, achievement

— 4 Strokes —

8 劣於 **[lièh-yǘ]**: inferior to, worse than

10 劣根性 **[lièh-kēn-hsìng]**: the evil inherent in man

11 劣紳 **[lièh-shēn]**: bad gentry

12 劣等 **[lièh-tĕng]**: inferiority; inferior

— 5 Strokes —

4 助手 **[chù-shŏu]**: assistant, aid, helper

10 助弱抑强 **[chù-jò ì-ch′iáng]**: to fight for the weak against the strong

11 助教 **[chù-chiào]**: assistant instructor, teaching assistant

助理 **[chù-lĭ]**: assistant

2 努力 **[nŭ-lì]**: to exert, to strive; effort

5 努瓦克肖特 **[nŭ-wă-k′ò-hsiào-t′è]**: Nouakchott (Mauritania)

— 7 Strokes —

8 勇往直前 **[yŭng-wăng chíh-ch′ién]**: to go ahead boldly

12 勇敢 **[yŭng-kăn]**: bravery, boldness, courage; brave, bold, courageous

16 勁頭 **[chìn-t′óu]**: vigor, zip

勉

12 勉强 **[miĕn-ch′iăng]**: to force oneself to, to compel, to constrain; reluctant, unwilling, disinclined

17 勉勵 **[miĕn-lì]**: to urge, to incite

勃

6 勃列日涅夫 **[pó-lièh-jìh-nièh-fú]**: Brezhnev, Leonid (Soviet statesman)

10 勃起 **[pó-ch′ĭ]**: to swell up, to rise, to become large and powerful

11 勃朗峯 **[pó-lǎng fēng]** : Mont Blanc

16 勃興 **[pó-hsīng]** : to thrive

— 8 Strokes —

務

12 務虛 **[wù-hsǖ]** : to discuss matters from the angle of politics and principles

14 務實 **[wù-shíh]** : to discuss concrete matters

— 9 Strokes —

勘

12 勘測 **[k'ān-ts'è]** : to survey

14 勘察 **[k'ān-ch'á]** : to prospect, to survey

勒

10 勒索 **[lè-sǒ]** : to extort, to exact from, to wring from, to compel to give; extortion

動

2 動力 **[tùng-lì]** : motive force, motivating force, driving force, momentum, impetus

動力學 **[tùng-lì-hsüéh]** : dynamics, kinetics; dynamic

動力來源 **[tùng-lì lái-yüán]** : power resources

動力研究所 **[tùng-lì yén-chìu-sŏ]** : Institute of Dynamics

4 動心 **[tùng-hsīn]** : to move, to shake, to touch the heart; pathetic

動手 **[tùng-shǒu]** : to start work, to take in hand

5 動用 **[tùng-yùng]** : to use, to put into use

6 動向 **[tùng-hsiàng]** : tendency, move

7 動身 **[tùng-shēn]** : to set out, to get under way

動作 **[tùng-tsò]** : to act; action, performance, behavior

8 動物學 **[tùng-wù-hsüéh]** : zoology

動物研究所 **[tùng-wù yén-chìu-sŏ]** : Institute of Zoology

10 動能 **[tùng-néng]** : motive force

動員 **[tùng-yüán]** : to mobilize; mobilization

11 動產 **[tùng-ch'ǎn]** : movable property

動氣 **[tùng-ch'ì]** : to become excited, to become angry

動情 **[tùng-ch'íng]** : to excite the emotions, to arouse passions

13 動搖 **[tùng-yáo]** : to vacillate, to move back and forth; wavering, vacillation; unstable

動搖派 **[tùng-yáo-p'ài]** : waverers

動搖不定的兩面性 **[tùng-yáo pú-tìng te liǎng-mièn-hsìng]** : two-sided wavering

14 動態 **[tùng-t'ài]** : change, movement, situation, circumstances

16 動機 **[tùng-chī]** : motive, cause, occasion

動盪 **[tùng-tàng]** : turbulent

動盪不定 **[tùng-tàng pú-tìng]** : in flux

動盪不穩 **[tùng-tàng pù-wěn]** : shaky and unstable

— 10 Strokes —

勛

11 勛章 **[hsǖn-chāng]** : decoration, medal

勞

3 勞工後備部 **[láo-kūng hòu-pèi pù]** : Ministry of Labor Reserves

6 勞艾德 **[láo-ài-té]**: Lloyd, Selwyn (British statesman)

7 勞役 **[láo-ì]**: hard labor

勞役隊 **[láo-ì-tùi]**: forced labor corps

9 勞苦 **[láo-k'ŭ]**: toil, pains

勞保 **[láo-păo]**: labor insurance (abbreviation of 勞動保險)

勞保條例 **[láo-păo t'iáo-lì]**: labor insurance regulations

11 勞動者 **[láo-tùng-chĕ]**: worker, laborer, the working people

勞動紀律 **[láo-tùng chì-lǜ]**: labor discipline

勞動强度 **[láo-tùng ch'iáng-tù]**: intensity of labor, degree of strength in labor (the amount of physical strength exerted or required to do a job)

勞動節 **[láo-tùng-chiéh]**: Labor Day, May Day, International Labor Day

勞動競賽 **[láo-tùng chìng-sài]**: labor emulation, emulation drive

勞動分工 **[láo-tùng fēn-kūng]**: division of labor

勞動效率 **[láo-tùng hsiào-lǜ]**: labor efficiency

勞動合作 **[láo-tùng hó-tsò]**: labor cooperation

勞動新聞 **[láo-tùng hsīn-wén]**: Nodong Sinmun (Korean newspaper)

勞動化 **[láo-tùng-huà]**: to "laborize," to "proletarianize" (used in reference to students sent to farms)

勞動改造 **[láo-tùng kăi-tsào]**: labor reform, correction through labor, to reform through labor

勞動觀點 **[láo-tùng kuān-tiĕn]**: labor viewpoint (i.e., an attitude of respect for manual labor; one of the 四大觀點, q.v.)

勞動力 **[láo-tùng-lì]**: labor force, labor power

勞動力缺乏 **[láo-tùng-lì ch'üēh-fá]**: labor shortage

勞動力的分配 **[láo-tùng-lì te fēn-p'èi]**: allocation of labor power

勞動力的調配 **[láo-tùng-lì te tiào-p'èi]**: allocation of labor force

勞動力模範 **[láo-tùng mó-fàn]**: labor hero, model worker

勞動保險 **[láo-tùng păo-hsiĕn]**: labor insurance

勞動保險基金 **[láo-tùng păo-hsiĕn chī-chīn]**: labor insurance fund

勞動保險金 **[láo-tùng păo-hsiĕn chīn]**: labor insurance fund

勞動保險條例 **[láo-tùng păo-hsiĕn t'iáo-lì]**: labor insurance law

勞動報 **[láo-tùng-pào]**: Trud (Russian daily newspaper)

勞動報酬 **[láo-tùng pào-ch'óu]**: payment for labor, remuneration for labor

勞動部 **[láo-tùng-pù]**: Ministry of Labor

勞動生產率 **[láo-tùng shēng-ch'ăn-lǜ]**: productivity of labor, labor productivity

勞動生產定額 **[láo-tùng shēng-ch'ăn tìng-ó]**: labor production quota

勞動手段 **[láo-tùng shŏu-tuàn]**: means of labor

12 勞逸結合 **[láo-ì chiéh-hó]**: integration of labor and rest

13 勞資關係 **[láo-tzū kuān-hsì]**: labor-capital relationship

勞資兩利 **[láo-tzū liăng-lì]**: of benefit to both labor and capital

15 勞模 **[láo-mó]**: model worker (abbreviation of 勞動模範)

勞衛制 **[láo-wèi chìh]**: labor and defense training system (a program of physical training having as its objective preparation for labor and defense)

勞衞制奬章 **[láo-wèi-chìh chiăng-chāng]**: labor and defense medal

勝

6 勝任 **[shēng-jèn]**: competent, well qualified, competent to carry out the duties of an office

7 勝利 **[shèng-lì]**: to win, to triumph; victory, triumph, success

13 勝過 **[shèng-kuò]**: to surpass, to outdo, to eclipse, to get the better of

— 11 Strokes —

勤

3 勤工儉學 **[ch'ín-kūng chiĕn-hsüéh]**: to study while one works, the practice of working while studying

9 勤勉 **[ch'ín-miĕn]**: industrious, assiduous, devoted, diligent, zealous

11 勤務 **[ch'ín-wù]**: fatigue duty, labor, duty, service

勤務員 **[ch'ín-wù-yüán]**: orderly

15 勤儉 **[ch'ín-chiĕn]**: hard work and thrift, industry and thrift, diligent and thrifty

勤儉建國 **[ch'ín-chiĕn chièn-kuó]**: to carry out national construction through hard work and thrift

勤儉辦社 **[ch'ín-chiĕn pàn-shè]**: to run the communes industriously and economically

2 勢力 **[shìh-lì]**: influence, power

勢力範圍 **[shìh-lì fàn-wéi]**: sphere of influence

4 勢不可擋 **[shìh pù-k'ŏ-tăng]**: irresistible trend

勢不兩立 **[shìh pù-liăng-lì]**: antagonistic, irreconcilable, hostile, on bad terms

5 勢必 **[shìh-pì]**: necessarily, inevitably

7 勢均力敵 **[shìh-chūn lì-tí]**: balance of power, balance of forces

16 勢頭 **[shìh-t'óu]**: power, might, force, influence, momentum, state of affairs, condition, situation

— 18 Strokes —

勸

7 勸告 **[ch'üàn-kaò]**: to advise, to urge, to counsel, to persuade; advice

8 勸阻 **[ch'üàn-tsŭ]**: to dissuade, to discourage from, to remonstrate

— RADICAL 勹 20 —

— 2 Strokes —

勾

4 勾引 **[kōu-yĭn]**: to lead astray, to seduce, to involve

7 勾串 **[kōu-ch'uàn]**: to have secret contacts

10 勾除 **[kōu-ch'ú]**: to cross out, to strike out

11 勾通 **[kōu-t'ūng]**: to join in a plot, to ally oneself secretly

12 勾結 **[kōu-chiéh]**: to be in league with, to have secret contacts, to enter into collusion with; complicity with

13 勾搭 **[kōu-tā]**: to ally oneself, to make a

secret alliance, to involve, to mislead, to lead astray

勾當 **[kōu-tāng]**: plot, conspiracy, business, affair, secret dealing

15 勾銷 **[kōu-hsiāo]**: to cancel, to undo, to eliminate, to annul, to abrogate, to abolish, to rescind; cancellation, annulment, abrogation

勾輪廓 **[kōu lún-k'uò]**: to outline, to sketch; outline, sketch

— 3 Strokes —

包 **[pāo]**: Paotow (Inner Mongolia) (used as abbreviation)

3 包干制 **[pāo-kān-chìh]**: system of free public care

包工 **[pāo-kūng]**: to contract for, to take on work

包工制 **[pāo-kūng-chìh]**: contract labor system, piece-work system (a system of fixed responsibility for a specified job)

包工包料 **[pāo-kūng pāo-liào]**: to contract for labor and material

7 包含 **[pāo-hán]**: to contain, to imply

包身工 **[pāo-shēn kūng]**: slave laborer

8 包庇 **[pāo-p'ì]**: to shield, to cover up, to screen, to harbor

包括 **[pāo-k'uò]**: to contain, to include, to comprise, to consist of, to embrace, to cover

10 包格貝 **[pāo-kó-pèi]**: Bourguiba, Habib Ben Ali (Tunisian statesman)

包租的 **[pāo-tsū te]**: chartered

11 包產合同 **[pāo-ch'ǎn hó-t'úng]**: contract for fixed output (a contract between a production team and a production brigade in which the team guarantees to fulfil a fixed target of output)

包產到戶 **[pāo-ch'ǎn tào-hù]**: household contract production, production contract for each household (i.e., production on land farmed out to individual households, which undertake to produce a fixed output for a fixed amount of costs and a fixed number of work points)

包袱 **[pāo-fú]**: a pack, a burden

12 包飯 **[pāo-fàn]**: to provide board, to make arrangements for one's meals

包圍 **[pāo-wéi]**: to surround, to encircle, to encompass, to hem in

包圍攻擊 **[pāo-wéi kūng-chī]**: encircling attack

14 包管 **[pāo-kuǎn]**: to guarantee, to be responsible for

包爾斯 **[pāo-ěrh-ssū]**: Bowles, Chester (American statesman)

16 包辦 **[pāo-pàn]**: to undertake, to take over completely

包辦管理 **[pāo-pàn kuǎn-li]**: exclusive control

包辦代替 **[pāo-pàn tài-t'ì]**: to monopolize all activities, to take everything into one's own hands

19 包羅無遺 **[pāo-ló wú-í]**: all-inclusive

21 包蘭鐵路 **[pāo-lán t'iěh-lù]**: Paotow-Lanchow Railroad

— 4 Strokes —

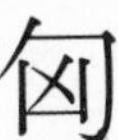

4 匈牙利 **[hsiūng-yá-lì]**: Hungary

匈牙利人民共和國 **[hsiūng-yá-lì jén-mín kùng-hó-kuó]**: People's Republic of Hungary

匈牙利人民共和國國民議會 **[hsiūng-yá-lì jén-mín kùng-hó-kuó kuó-mín ì-huì]**: National Assembly of the People's Republic of Hungary

匈牙利通訊社 **[hsiūng-yá-lì t'ūng-hsǜn-shè]** : Magyar Tavirati Iroda: The Hungarian Telegraph Agency (MTI)

8 匈京 **[hsiūng-chīng]** : Budapest (Hungary)

11 匈國 **[hsiūng-kuó]** : Hungary

— RADICAL 匕 21 —

— 2 Strokes —

化

3 化干戈爲玉帛 **[huà kān-kō wéi yǜ-pó]** : to stop war and make alliance

化工 **[huà-kūng]** : chemical industry, chemical technology, chemical engineering

化工冶金研究所 **[huà-kūng yĕh-chīn yén-chìu-sŏ]** : Institute of Chemical Engineering and Metallurgy

6 化合物 **[huà-hó-wù]** : chemical compound

化名 **[huà-míng]** : to change one's name, pseudonym

7 化身 **[huà-shēn]** : personification, embodiment, incarnation

8 化肥 **[huà-féi]** : chemical fertilizer

9 化爲烏有 **[huà-wéi wū-yŭ]** : to bring to naught, to disappear, to vanish

10 化除 **[huà-ch'ú]** : to eliminate, to adjust

12 化粧 **[huà-chuāng]** : make-up dressing up, painted up

13 化裝 **[huà-chuāng]** : to disguise; disguise, disguised, masked, veiled, cloaked

16 化整爲零 **[huà-chĕng wéi-líng]** : to break up the whole into parts

化險爲夷 **[huà-hsiĕn wéi í]** : to change rough places into smooth places, to convert danger into safety

化學 **[huà-hsüéh]** : chemistry; chemical

化學肥料 **[huà-hsüéh féi-liào]** : chemical fertilizers

化學纖維廠 **[huà-hsüéh hsiēn-wéi ch'ăng]** : chemical fiber plant

化學工業部 **[huà-hsüéh kūng-yèh pù]** : Ministry of Chemical Industry

化學武器 **[huà-hsüéh wŭ-ch'ì]** : chemical weapons

化學研究所 **[huà-hsüéh yén-chìu-sŏ]** : Institute of Chemistry

21 化鐵爐 **[huà-t'iĕh-lú]** : smelting furnace

— 3 Strokes —

北

3 北大 **[pĕi-tà]** : National Peking University

北大西洋公約 **[pĕi-tà-hsī-yáng kūng-yüēh]** : North Atlantic Treaty

北大西洋公約組織 **[pĕi-tà-hsī-yáng kūng-yüēh tsŭ-chīh]** : North Atlantic Treaty Organization (NATO)

北大年 **[pĕi-tà-nién]** : Patani (Thailand)

4 北方海運管理局 **[pĕi-fāng hăi-yǜn kuăn-lĭ-chǘ]** : Northern Regional Sea Transport Administration

5 北寧 **[pĕi-níng]** : Bacninh (Vietnam)

北半球 **[pĕi-pàn-ch'íu]** : northern hemisphere

6 北安普敦 **[pĕi-ān-p'ŭ-tūn]** : Northampton

北伐 **[pĕi-fá]** : The Northern Expedition (1926–1928)

北光 **[pĕi-kuāng]** : Bacquang (Vietnam)

7 北角 **[pĕi-chiăo]** : North Cape (Norway)

8 北京紅色造反團 **[pĕi-chīng húng-sè tsào-făn-t'uán]** : Peking Red Rebel Group

北京天文台 **[pĕi-chīng t'iēn-wén-t'ai]** : Peking Observatory

北明翰 **[pĕi-míng-hàn]** : Birmingham

9 北南 **[pĕi-nán]** : Bacnam (Vietnam)

北洋 **[pĕi-yáng]** : North Sea; Gulf of Chihli

10 北海道 **[pĕi-hăi-tào]** : Hokkaido (Japan)

11 北婆羅洲 **[pĕi p'ó-ló-chōu]** : North Borneo

12 北極 **[pĕi-chí]** : North Pole

北極圈 **[pĕi-chí-ch'üān]** : The Arctic Circle

北溫帶 **[pĕi-wēn-tài]** : North Temperate Zone

13 北達科他 **[pĕi tá-k'ō-t'ā]** : North Dakota (U.S.A.)

15 北遼 **[pĕi-liáo]** : Baclieu (Vietnam)

北歐理事會 **[pĕi-ōu lĭ-shìh-hùi]** : Nordic Council

20 北羅得西亞 **[pĕi ló-té-hsī-yà]** : Northern Rhodesia

— RADICAL 匚 22 —

— 2 Strokes —

匹

10 匹兹堡 **[p'ĭ-tzū-păo]** : Pittsburgh

— 4 Strokes —

匠

2 匠人 **[chiàng-jén]** : craftsman

4 匠心 **[chiàng-hsīn]** : inventive genius

10 匠師 **[chiàng-shīh]** : master craftsman

11 匠氣 **[chiàng-ch'ì]** : craftsman-like (commonplace, without artistic inspiration, without creative inclination)

— 8 Strokes —

匪

匪 **[fĕi]** : bandit

10 匪幫 **[fĕi-pāng]** : a gang of bandits, bandits, gang

匪特 **[fĕi-t'è]** : bandit agent, spy

— 11 Strokes —

滙

6 滙合 **[hùi-hó]** : to converge

11 滙理東方銀行 **[hùi-lĭ tūng-fāng yín-háng]** : Indo China Bank

18 滙豐銀行 **[hùi-fēng yín-háng]** : Hongkong and Shanghai Banking Corporation

— RADICAL 匸 23 —

— 9 Strokes —

區

區 **[ch'ū]** : administrative area, ward, zone

2 區人民代表大會 **[ch'ū jén-mín tài-piăo tà-hùi]** : Ward People's Congress

2 區人民委員會 [ch'ǖ jén-mín wěi-yüán-hùi] : Ward People's Council

7 區別 [ch'ǖ-piéh] : to distinguish, to discriminate; difference, distinction, discrimination, dissimilarity, disparity

8 區長 [ch'ǖ-chăng] : ward chief, district chief

區委 [ch'ǖ-wěi] : district party committee, district committee

11 區域聯盟 [ch'ǖ-yǜ lién-méng] : regional alliance

區域自治 [ch'ǖ-yǜ tzù-chìh] : regional autonomy

20 區黨委 [ch'ǖ-tăng-wěi] : area party committee

匿

6 匿名 [nì-míng] : anonymous

— RADICAL 十 24 —

3 十大牢事原則 [shíh tà láo-shìh yüán-tsé] : the ten major principles of operation

十大關係 [shíh tà kuān-hsì] : the ten great relationships (as stated by Mao in April 1956: 1) industry and agriculture, heavy, and light industry; 2) coastal and inland industries; 3) economic construction and national defense; 4) the state, the cooperatives, and individuals; 5) central and local authorities; 6) the Han Chinese people and the national minorities; 7) Party and non-Party people; 8) revolution and counter-revolution; 9) right and wrong inside and outside the Party; 10) international relations)

十大增加 [shíh tà tsēng-chiā] : the ten big increases (i.e., 1) the number of agricultural producers' cooperatives and mutual aid teams; 2) the number of business cooperatives; 3) the number of credit cooperatives; 4) in the understanding of socialism by cadres and peasants; 5) the number of activist elements; 6) in fervor in agricultural production; 7) number of mules and horses; 8) in heavy agricultural implements and large carts; 9) number of tile-roofed houses; 10) number of people wearing new clothes)

十之八九 [shíh-chīh-pā-chĭu] : in all probability, with every chance to, eight or nine times out of ten

十分 [shíh-fēn] : fully, completely, wholly, perfectly, extremely

十分指標，十二分措施 [shíh-fēn chĭh-piāo, shíh-èrh-fēn ts'ò-shīh] : to fix targets in a forward-looking way and take measures that will more than guarantee their fulfilment

十六條 [shíh-lìu t'iáo] : the Sixteen Points (the 16 points adopted by the 11th Plenum of Central Committee of the Chinese Communist Party on August 8, 1966 for the purpose of regulating the activities of the Red Guard; the full text of the 16 Points is as follows:

DECISION OF THE CENTRAL COMMITTEE OF THE CHINESE COMMUNIST PARTY CONCERNING THE GREAT PROLETARIAN CULTURAL REVOLUTION

1) A New Stage in the Socialist Revolution The great proletarian cultural revolution now unfolding is a great revolution that touches people to their very souls and constitutes a new stage in the development of the socialist revolution in our country, a deeper and more extensive stage.

At the Tenth Plenary Session of the Eighth Central Committee of the Party, Comrade Mao Tse-tung said: To overthrow a political power, it is always necessary, first of all, to create public opinion, to do work in the ideological sphere. This is true for the revolutionary class as well as for the counterrevolutionary class. This thesis of Comrade Mao Tse-tung's has been proved entirely correct in practice.

Although the bourgeoisie has been overthrown, it is still trying to use the old ideas, culture, customs and habits of the exploiting classes to corrupt the masses, capture their minds and endeavour to stage a come-back. The proletariat must do just the opposite: it must meet head-on every challenge of the bourgeoisie in the ideological field and use the new ideas, culture, customs and habits of the proletariat to change the mental outlook of the whole of society. At present, our objective is to struggle against and crush those persons in authority who are taking the capitalist road, to criticize and repudiate the reactionary bourgeois academic "authorities" and the ideology of the bourgeoisie and all other exploiting classes and to transform education, literature and art and all other parts of the superstructure that do not correspond to the socialist economic base, so as to facilitate the consolidation and development of the socialist system.

2) The Main Current and the Zigzags The masses of the workers, peasants, soldiers, revolutionary intellectuals and revolutionary cadres form the main force in this great cultural revolution. Large numbers of revolutionary young people, previously unknown, have become courageous and daring pathbreakers. They are vigorous in action and intelligent. Through the media of big-character posters and great debates, they argue things out, expose and criticize thoroughly, and launch resolute attacks on the open and hidden representatives of the bourgeoisie. In such a great revolutionary movement, it is hardly avoidable that they should show shortcomings of one kind or another, but their main revolutionary orientation has been correct from the beginning. This is the main current in the great proletarian cultural revolution. It is the main direction along which the great proletarian cultural revolution continues to advance.

Since the cultural revolution is a revolution, it inevitably meets with resistance. This resistance comes chiefly from those in authority who have wormed their way into the Party and are taking the capitalist road. It also comes from the old force of habit in society. At present, this resistance is still fairly strong and stubborn. However, the great proletarian cultural revolution is, after all, an irresistible general trend. There is abundant evidence that such resistance will crumble fast once the masses become fully aroused.

Because the resistance is fairly strong, there will be reversals and even repeated reversals in this struggle. There is no harm in this. It tempers the proletariat and other working people, and especially the younger generation, teaches them lessons and gives them experience, and helps them to understand that the revolutionary road is a zigzag one, and not plain sailing.

3) Put Daring Above Everything Else and Boldly Arouse the Masses The outcome of this great cultural revolution will be determined by whether the Party leadership does or does not dare boldly to arouse the masses.

Currently, there are four different situations with regard to the leadership being given to the movement of cultural revolution by Party organizations at various levels:

1) There is the situation in which the persons in charge of Party organizations stand in the van of the movement and dare to arouse the masses boldly. They put daring above everything else, they are dauntless communist fighters—and good pupils of Chairman Mao. They advocate the big-character posters and great debates. They encourage the masses to expose every kind of ghost and monster and also to criticize the shortcomings and errors in the work of the persons in charge. This correct kind of leadership is the result of putting proletarian politics in the forefront and Mao Tse-tung's thought in the lead.

(2) In many units, the persons in charge have a very poor understanding of the task of leadership in this great struggle, their leadership is far from being conscientious and effective, and they accordingly find themselves incompetent and in a weak position. They put fear above everything else, stick to out-moded ways and regulations, and are unwilling to break away from conventional practices and move ahead. They have been taken unawares by the new order of things, the revolutionary order of the masses, with the result that their leadership lags behind the situation, lags behind the masses.

(3) In some units, the persons in charge, who

made mistakes of one kind or another in the past, are even more prone to put fear above everything else, being afraid that the masses will catch them out. Actually, if they make serious self-criticism and accept the criticism of the masses, the Party and the masses will make allowances for their mistakes. But if the persons in charge don't, they will continue to make mistakes and become obstacles to the mass movement.

(4) Some units are controlled by those who have wormed their way into the Party and are taking the capitalist road. Such persons in authority are extremely afraid of being exposed by the masses and therefore seek every possible pretext to suppress the mass movement. They resort to such tactics as shifting the targets for attack and turning black into white in an attempt to lead the movement astray. When they find themselves very isolated and no longer able to carry on as before, they resort still more to intrigues, stabbing people in the back, spreading rumours, and blurring the distinction between revolution and counter-revolution as much as they can, all for the purpose of attacking the revolutionaries.

What the Central Committee of the Party demands of the Party committees at all levels is that they persevere in giving correct leadership, put daring above everything else, boldly arouse the masses, change the state of weakness and incompetence where it exists, encourage those comrades who have made mistakes but are willing to correct them to cast off their mental burdens and join in the struggle, and dismiss from their leading posts all those in authority who are taking the capitalist road and so make possible the recapture of the leadership for the proletarian revolutionaries.

4) Let the Masses Educate Themselves in the Movement In the great proletarian cultural revolution, the only method is for the masses to liberate themselves, and any method of doing things on their behalf must not be used.

Trust the masses, rely on them and respect their initiative. Cast out fear. Don't be afraid of disorder. Chairman Mao has often told us that revolution cannot be so very refined, so gentle, so temperate, kind, courteous, restrained and magnanimous. Let the masses educate themselves in this great revolutionary movement and learn to distinguish between right and wrong and between correct and incorrect ways of doing things.

Make the fullest use of big-character posters and great debates to argue matters out, so that the classes can clarify the correct views, criticize the wrong views and expose all the ghosts and monsters. In this way the masses will be able to raise their political consciousness in the course of the struggle, enhance their abilities and talents, distinguish right from wrong and draw a clear line between the enemy and ourselves.

5) Firmly Apply the Class Line of the Party Who are our enemies? Who are our friends? This is a question of the first importance for the revolution and it is likewise a question of the first importance for the great cultural revolution.

Party leadership should be good at discovering the Left and developing and strengthening the ranks of the Left, and should firmly rely on the revolutionary Left. During the movement this is the only way to isolate thoroughly the most reactionary Rightists, win over the middle and unite with the great majority so that by the end of the movement we shall achieve the unity of more than 95 per cent of the cadres and more than 95 per cent of the masses.

Concentrate all forces to strike at the handful of ultra-reactionary bourgeois Rightists and counter-revolutionary revisionists, and expose and criticize to the full their crimes against the Party, against socialism and against Mao Tse-tung's thought so as to isolate them to the maximum.

The main target of the present movement is those within the Party who are in authority and are taking the capitalist road.

Care should be taken to distinguish strictly between the anti-Party, anti-socialist Rightists and those who support the Party and socialism but have said or done something wrong or have written some bad articles or other works.

Care should be taken to distinguish strictly between the reactionary bourgeois scholar despots and "authorities" on the one hand and people who have the ordinary bourgeois academic ideas on the other.

6) Correct Handling of Contradictions Among the People A strict distinction must be made between the two different types of contradictions: those among the people and those between ourselves and the enemy. Contradictions among the people must not be made into contradictions between ourselves and the enemy; nor must contradictions between ourselves and the enemy be regarded as those among the people.

It is normal for the masses to hold different views. Contention between different views is unavoidable, necessary and beneficial. In the course of normal and full debate, the masses will affirm what is right, correct what is wrong and gradually reach unanimity.

The method to be used in debates is to present the facts, reason things out, and persuade through reasoning. Any method of forcing a minority holding different views to submit is impermissible. The minority should be protected, because sometimes the truth is with the minority. Even if the minority is wrong, they should still be allowed to argue their case and reserve their views.

When there is a debate, it should be conducted by reasoning, not by coercion or force.

In the course of debate, every revolutionary should be good at thinking things out for himself and should develop the communist spirit of daring to think, daring to speak and daring to act. On the premise that they have the same main orientation, revolutionary comrades should, for the sake of strengthening unity, avoid endless debate over side issues.

7) Be on Guard Against Those Who Brand the Revolutionary Masses as "Counter-Revolutionaries" In certain schools, units, and work teams of the cultural revolution, some of the persons in charge have organized counter-attacks against the masses who put up big-character posters against them. These people have even advanced such slogans as: opposition to the leaders of a unit or a work team means opposition to the Party's Central Committee, means opposition to the Party and socialism, means counter-revolution. In this way it is inevitable that their blows will fall on some really revolutionary activists. This is an error on matters of orientation, an error of line, and is absolutely impermissible.

A number of persons who suffer from serious ideological errors, and particularly some of the anti-Party and anti-socialist Rightists, are taking advantage of certain shortcomings and mistakes in the mass movement to spread rumours and gossip, and engage in agitation, deliberately branding some of the masses as "counter-revolutionaries." It is necessary to beware of such "pick-pockets" and expose their tricks in good time.

In the course of the movement, with the exception of cases of active counter-revolutionaries where there is clear evidence of crimes such as murder, arson, poisoning, sabotage or theft of state secrets, which should be handled in accordance with the law, no measures should be taken against students at universities, colleges, middle schools and primary schools because of problems that arise in the movement. To prevent the struggle from being diverted from its main objective, it is not allowed, whatever the pretext, to incite the masses to struggle against each other or the students to do likewise. Even proven Rightists should be dealt with on the merits of each case at a later stage of the movement.

8) The Question of Cadres The cadres fall roughly into the following four categories:

(1) good;

(2) comparatively good;

(3) those who have made serious mistakes but have not become anti-Party, anti-socialist Rightists;

(4) the small number of anti-Party, anti-socialist Rightists.

In ordinary situations, the first two categories (good and comparatively good) are the great majority.

The anti-Party, anti-socialist Rightists must be fully exposed, hit hard, pulled down and completely discredited and their influence eliminated. At the same time, they should be given a way out so that they can turn over a new leaf.

9) Cultural Revolutionary Groups, Committees and Congresses Many new things have begun to emerge in the great proletarian cultural revolution. The cultural revolutionary groups, committees and other organizational forms created by the masses in many schools and units are something new and of great historic importance.

These cultural revolutionary groups, committees and congresses are excellent new forms of organization whereby under the leadership of the Communist Party the masses are educating themselves. They are an excellent bridge to keep our Party in close contact with the masses. They are organs of power of the proletarian cultural revolution.

The struggle of the proletariat against the old ideas, culture, customs and habits left over from all the exploiting classes over thousands of years will necessarily take a very, very long time. Therefore, the cultural revolutionary groups, committees and congresses should not be temporary organizations but permanent, standing mass organizations. They are suitable not only for colleges, schools and government and other organizations, but generally also for factories, mines, other enterprises, urban districts and villages.

It is necessary to institute a system of general elections, like that of the Paris Commune, for electing members to the cultural revolutionary groups and committees and delegates to the cultural revolutionary congresses. The lists of candidates should be put forward by the revolutionary masses after full discussion, and the elections should be held after the masses have discussed the lists over and over again.

The masses are entitled at any time to criticize members of the cultural revolutionary groups and committees and delegates elected to the cultural revolutionary congresses. If these members or delegates prove incompetent, they can be replaced through election or recalled by the masses after discussion.

The cultural revolutionary groups, committees and congresses in colleges and schools should consist mainly of representatives of the revolutionary students. At the same time, they should have a certain number of representatives of the revolutionary teaching staff and workers.

10) Educational Reform In the great proletarian cultural revolution a most important task is to transform the old educational system and the old principles and methods of teaching.

In this great cultural revolution, the phenomenon of our schools being dominated by bourgeois intellectuals must be completely changed.

In every kind of school we must apply thoroughly the policy advanced by Comrade Mao Tse-tung, of education serving proletarian politics and education being combined with productive labour, so as to enable those receiving an education to develop morally, intellectually and physically and to become labourers with socialist consciousness and culture.

The period of schooling should be shortened. Courses should be fewer and better. The teaching material should be thoroughly transformed, in some cases beginning with simplifying complicated material. While their main task is to study, students should also learn other things. That is to say, in addition to their studies they should also learn industrial work, farming and military affairs, and take part in the struggles of the cultural revolution as they occur to criticize the bourgeoisie.

11) The Question of Criticizing by Name in the Press In the course of the mass movement of the cultural revolution, the criticism of bourgeois and feudal ideology should be well combined with the dissemination of the proletarian world outlook and of Marxism-Leninism, Mao Tse-tung's thought.

Criticism should be organized of typical bourgeois representatives who have wormed their way into the Party and typical reactionary bourgeois academic "authorities," and this should include criticism of various kinds of reactionary views in philosophy, history, political economy and education, in works and theories of literature and art, in theories of natural science, and in other fields.

Criticism of anyone by name in the press should be decided after discussion by the Party committee at the same level, and in some cases submitted to the Party committee at a higher level for approval.

12) Policy Towards Scientists, Technicians and Ordinary Members of Working Staffs As regards scientists, technicians and ordinary members of working staffs, as long as they are patriotic, work energetically, are not against the Party and socialism, and maintain no illicit relations with any foreign country, we should in the present movement continue to apply the policy of "unity, criticism, unity." Special care should be taken of those scientists and scientific and technical personnel who have made contributions. Efforts should be made to help them gradually transform their world outlook and their style of work.

13) The Question of Arrangements for Integration with the Socialist Education Movement in City and Countryside. The cultural and educational units and leading organs of the Party and government in the large and medium cities are the points of concentration of the present proletarian cultural revolution.

The great cultural revolution has enriched the socialist education movement in both city and countryside and raised it to a higher level. Efforts should be made to conduct these two movements in close combination. Arrangements to this effect may be made by various regions and departments in the light of the specific conditions.

The socialist education movement now going on in the countryside and in enterprises in the cities should not be upset where the original arrangements are appropriate and the movement is going well, but should continue in accordance with the original arrangements. However, the questions that are arising in the present great proletarian cultural revolution should be put to the masses for discussion at a proper time, so as to further foster vigorously proletarian ideology and eradicate bourgeois ideology.

In some places, the great proletarian cultural revolution is being used as the focus in order to add momentum to the socialist education movement and clean things up in the fields of politics, ideology, organization and economy. This may be done where the local Party committee thinks it appropriate.

14) Take Firm Hold of the Revolution and Stimulate Production The aim of the great proletarian cultural revolution is to revolutionize people's ideology and as a consequence to achieve greater, faster, better and more economical results in all fields of work. If the masses are fully aroused and proper arrangements are made, it is possible to carry on both the cultural revolution and production without one hampering the other, while guaranteeing high quality in all our work.

The great proletarian cultural revolution is a powerful motive force for the development of the social productive forces in our country. Any idea of counterposing the great cultural revolution against the development of production is incorrect.

15) The Armed Forces In the armed forces, the cultural revolution and the socialist education movement should be carried out in accordance with the instructions of the Military Commission of the Central Committee and the General Political Department of the People's Liberation Army.

16) Mao Tse-tung's Thought is the Guide for Action in the Great Proletarian Cultural Revolution In the great proletarian cultural revolution, it is imperative to hold aloft the great red banner of Mao Tse-tung's thought and put proletarian politics in command. The movement for the creative study and application of Chairman Mao Tse-tung's works should be carried forward among the masses of the workers, peasants and soldiers, the cadres and the intellectuals, and Mao Tse-tung's thought should be taken as the guide for action in the cultural revolution.

In this complex great cultural revolution, Party committees at all levels must study and apply Chairman Mao's works all the more conscientiously and in a creative way. In particular, they must study over and over again Chairman Mao's writings on the cultural revolution and on the Party's methods of leadership, such as On New Democracy, Talks at the Yenan Forum on Literature and Art, On the Correct Handling of Contradictions Among the People, Speech at the Chinese Communist Party's National Conference on Propaganda Work, Some Questions Concerning Methods of Leadership and Methods of Work of Party Committees.

Party committees at all levels must abide by the directions given by Chairman Mao over the years, namely that they should thoroughly apply the mass line of "from the masses and to the masses" and that they should be pupils before they become teachers. They should try to avoid being one-sided or narrow. They should foster materialist dialectics and oppose metaphysics and scholasticism.

The great proletarian cultural revolution is bound to achieve brilliant victory under the leadership of the Central Committee of the Party headed by Comrade Mao Tse-tung.

十月革命 **[shíh-yüèh kó-mìng]** : the October Revolution (1917)

6 十全十美 **[shíh-ch'üán shíh-měi]** : perfect, wonderful, in perfect order

十字街頭 **[shíh-tzù chiēh-t'óu]** : Carrefour (French periodical); crossroads

十字軍 **[shíh-tzù-chūn]** : crusaders

十字路 **[shíh-tzù-lù]** : crossroads

12 十進幣制 **[shíh-chìn pì-chìh]** : decimal currency system; decimal coinage

15 十億 **[shíh-ì]** : one billion

— 1 Stroke —

千 **[ch'iēn]** : thousand, kilo-

4 千方百計 **[ch'iēn-fāng pǎi-chì]** : by all sorts of means, in a thousand and one ways, using every strategem, by a multitude of schemes

千夫所指 **[ch'iēn-fū sŏ-chǐh]** : to be universally condemned

6 千百年 **[ch'iēn-pǎi-nién]** : centuries, thousands of years, for millennia

8 千周 **[ch'iēn-chōu]** : kilocycle

10 千島群島 **[ch'iēn-tǎo ch'ǘn-tao]** : Kurile Islands

12 千鈞重負 **[ch'iēn-chūn chùng-fù]** : crushing burden

千絲萬縷的關係 **[ch'iēn-ssū wǎn-lǚ te kuān-hsì]** : a relationship tied up with a thousand threads and ten thousand fibers (i.e., the close relationship between counter-revolutionaries and their followers)

13 千葉 **[ch'iēn-yèh]** : Chiba (Japan)

15 千篇一律 **[ch'iēn-p'iēn í-lǜ]** : a set form for all cases; to apply a set rule to everything; stereotyped, indiscriminate

23 千變萬化 **[ch'iēn-pièn wǎn-huà]** : kaleidoscopic, protean, endlessly changing

— 2 Strokes —

10 升級 **[shēng-chí]** : promotion, upgrade, promote

升起 **[shēng-ch'ǐ]** : to fly, to raise, to hoist, to run up

14 升旗典禮 **[shēng-ch'í tiěn-lǐ]** : flag-raising ceremony

— 3 Strokes —

半 **[pàn]** : semi-, half

3 半工半讀 **[pàn-kūng pàn-tú]** : part-work and part-study

4 半心半意 **[pàn-hsīn pàn-ì]** : half-hearted, lukewarm

半月 **[pàn-yüèh]** : fortnightly

半月刊 **[pàn-yüèh-k'ān]** : fortnightly (periodical)

5 半生 **[pàn-shēng]** : immature, half-ripe

6 半吊子 **[pàn tiào-tzu]** : half-educated, phony

半自耕農 **[pàn tzù-kēng núng]** : semi-tenant peasant

半自動化 **[pàn tzù-tùng-huà]** : semi-automation, semi-automatic

半年報 **[pàn-nién pào]** : semi-annual reporting

7 半社會主義性質的 **[pàn-shè-hùi chǔ-ì hsìng-chíh te]** : semi-socialist

8 半官方 **[pàn-kuān-fāng]** : semi-official

9 半封建 **[pàn-fēng-chièn]** : semi-feudal

10 半島 **[pàn-tǎo]** : peninsula

11 半球 **[pàn-ch'íu]** : hemisphere

半脫產 **[pàn-t'ō-ch'ǎn]** : half-day off from work

半脫離生產 **[pàn-t'ō-lí shēng-ch'ǎn]** : partially engaged in production, partially removed from production

12 半殖民地 **[pàn-chíh-mín-tì]** : semi-colonial, semi-colony

半勞動力 **[pàn-láo-tùng-lì]** : people who can fulfill only half the quota of work

14 半旗 **[pàn-ch'í]** : half-mast

15 半價 **[pàn-chià]** : half price

16 半機械化 **[pàn-chī-hsièh-huà]** : semi-mechanization; semi-mechanized

半導體 **[pàn-tǎo-t'ǐ]** : semi-conductor

19 半邊天 **[pàn-piēn-t'iēn]** : the other half of the sky (i.e., workers' families)

— 6 Strokes —

12 卓越 **[chō-yüèh]** : outstanding, distinguished, superior

協

6 協同一致 **[hsiéh-t'úng í-chìh]** : coordination; to bring into line; concerted, combined; to take combined action

協同作戰 **[hsiéh-t'úng tsò-chàn]** : combined action in war

7 協助 **[hsiéh-chù]** : to assist, to aid, to help; assistance, aid, help

協作 **[hsiéh-tsò]** : coordination, coordination and cooperation

8 協定 **[hsiéh-tìng]** : agreement, convention

12 協商 **[hsiéh-shāng]** : to consult, to confer, to discuss, to negotiate; negotiation, conference, consultation

13 協會 **[hsiéh-hùi]** : association

15 協調 **[hsiéh-t'iáo]** : to coordinate; coordination, synchronization, agreement, accord, concord, harmony

協調事宜行政委員會 **[hsiéh-t'iáo shìh-í hsíng-chèng wěi-yüán-hùi]** : Administrative Committee on Coordination (United Nations)

20 協議 **[hsiéh-ì]** : agreement, accord, concord

卑

11 卑視地 **[pēi-shìh ti]** : condescendingly, contemptuously, disdainfully

14 卑鄙 **[pēi-pǐ]** : slight, mean, humble; despicable, base, dirty, foul, contemptible, beneath contempt

卑鄙手段 **[pēi-pǐ shǒu-tuàn]** : contemptible measure, unscrupulous measure

— 7 Strokes —

南

4 南方日報 **[nán-fāng jìh-pào]** : Nanfang Daily, Nam Fong Yat Bo (Canton daily newspaper)

南方晚報 **[nán-fāng wǎn-pào]** : Nanfang Evening Post (Singapore Chinese language newspaper)

南日 **[nán jìh]** : Nam Il (North Korean political leader)

5 南卡羅來納 **[nán k'ǎ-ló-lái-nà]** : South Carolina

6 南回歸綫 **[nán-húi-kuēi-hsièn]** : Tropic of Capricorn

8 南昌起義 **[nán-ch'āng ch'ĭ-ì]**: Nanchang Uprising (August 1, 1927; led by Chou En-lai and Chu Teh in command of 30,000 troops)

南非 **[nán-fēi]**: South Africa

南泥灣精神 **[nán-ní-wān chīng-shén]**: the Spirit of Nanniwan (the dauntless spirit of the Eighth Route Army in facing hardships during land reclamation in Nanniwan, Shensi; thus, a dauntless spirit in tackling arduous tasks)

9 南洋商報 **[nán-yáng shāng-pào]**: Nan Yang Siang Pau (Singapore Chinese language newspaper)

10 南海 **[nán-hăi]**: South China Sea

11 南望 **[nán-wàng]**: Rembang

12 南朝鮮 **[nán ch'áo-hsiĕn]**: South Korea

南華晚報 **[nán-huá wăn-pào]**: Nan Hua Wan Pao (Hong Kong newspaper)

南開 **[nán-k'āi]**: Namhkai (Burma); Nankai (China)

南斯拉夫 **[nán-ssū-lā-fū]**: Yugoslavia

南斯拉夫共產主義者聯盟 **[nán-ssū-lā-fū kùng-ch'ăn chŭ-ì chĕ lién-méng]**: League of Communists of Yugoslavia

南斯拉夫通訊社 **[nán-ssū-lā-fū t'ūng-hsùn-shè]**: Tanjug (Telegrafeka Agencija Nova Jugoslavija: Yugoslav News Agency)

南越 **[nán-yüèh]**: South Vietnam

16 南錫 **[nán-hsí]**: Nancy (France)

20 南羅得西亞 **[nán ló-té-hsī-yà]**: Southern Rhodesia

— 10 Strokes —

博

3 博士 **[pó-shìh]**: doctor, scholar, Ph.D.

博士昵 **[pó-shìh-ní]**: Bosnia

博大 **[pó-tà]**: all-embracing

8 博物會 **[pó-wù-hùi]**: fair, exhibition

博物館 **[pó-wù-kuăn]**: museum

11 博得 **[pó-té]**: to gain, to achieve, to arrive at

博得信任 **[pó-té hsìn-jèn]**: to win confidence

12 博斯普魯斯海峽 **[pó-ssū-p'ŭ-lŭ-ssū hăi-hsiá]**: Bosporus Strait

13 博愛 **[pó-ài]**: universal love, brotherhood, fraternity

14 博聞 **[pó-wén]**: wide knowledge; well read

20 博羅敦湖 **[pó-ló-tūn hú]**: Lake Balaton

21 博覽會 **[pó-lăn-hùi]**: fair, exhibit, exhibition

— 11 Strokes —

準

12 準備金 **[chŭn-pèi-chīn]**: reserve fund

準備條件 **[chŭn-pèi t'iáo-chièn]**: to prepare the conditions, to prepare the ground for

— RADICAL 卜 25 —

— 3 Strokes —

9 占星術 **[chān-hsīng-shù]**: astrology

3 卡山 **[k'ă-shān]**: Kashan (Iran)

4 卡介苗 **[k'ă-chièh miáo]**: B.C.G. vaccine

卡內基 [k'ă-nèi-chī]: Carnegie (American financier)

5 卡寧半島 [k'ă-nìng pàn-tăo]: Kanin

卡瓦 [k'ă-wă]: Kawa (minority nationality)

7 卡車 [k'ă-ch'ē]: truck

卡利庫特 [k'ă-lì-k'ù-t'è]: Calicut (India)

卡沙弗布 [k'ă-shā-fú-pù]: Kasavubu, Joseph (statesman of Republic of Congo)

9 卡查林斯克 [k'ă-chā-lín-ssū-k'ò]: Kazalinsk

10 卡宴 [k'ă-yèn]: Cayenne (French Guiana)

12 卡斯特羅 [k'ă-ssū-t'è-ló]: Castro, Fidel

卡達爾 [k'ă-tá-ĕrh]: Kadar, Janos (Hungarian political leader)

13 卡塔爾 [k'ă-t'ă-ĕrh]: Qatar

卡塔爾酋長國 [k'ă-tă-ĕrh ch'iú-chăng-kuó]: Sheikdom of Qatar

14 卡爾卡塔 [k'ă-ĕrh-k'ă-t'ă]: Calcutta (India)

卡賓槍 [k'ă-pīn ch'iāng]: carbine

15 卡德爾 [k'ă-té-ĕrh]: Kardelj, Edvard

18 卡薩佛 [k'ă-sà-fó]: Kasavubu, Joseph (statesman of Republic of Congo)

卡薩布蘭卡非洲憲章 [k'ă-sà-pù-lán-k'ă fēi-chōu hsièn-chāng]: African Charter of Casablanca

— RADICAL 卩 26 —

— 4 Strokes —

危

6 危地馬拉 [wéi-tì-mă-lā]: Guatemala

危地馬拉城 [wéi-tì-mă-lā ch'éng]: Ciudad Guatemala

危地馬拉共和國 [wéi-tì-mă-lā kùng-hó-kuó]: Republic of Guatemala

7 危言聳聽 [wéi-yén sŭng-t'īng]: sensationalism; sensational

9 危急 [wéi-chí]: emergency, emergent, urgent

10 危害 [wéi-hài]: to endanger, to injure, to hurt, to maltreat, to cause harm to

16 危機 [wéi-chī]: crisis

危險 [wéi-hsiĕn]: danger, peril, risk, jeopardy; dangerous, perilous, precarious, critical, hazardous

印

5 印尼 [yìn-ní]: Indonesia (abbreviation of 印度尼西亞)

7 印把子 [yìn pà-tzu]: the handle of the seal

8 印花 [yìn-huā]: revenue stamps

印花布 [yìn-huā-pù]: printed cloth

印花稅 [yìn-huā-shùi]: revenue tax, revenue duty

印刷品 [yìn-shuā-p'ĭn]: printed matter

9 印染廠 [yìn-jăn ch'ăng]: printing and dyeing plant

印度 [yìn-tù]: India

印度新聞處 [yìn-tù hsīn-wén-ch'ù]: Indian Information Service (IIS)

印度快報 [yìn-tù k'uài-pào]: India Express

印度共和國 [yìn-tù kùng-hó-kuó]: Republic of India

印度尼西亞 [yìn-tù-ní-hsī-yà]: Indonesia

印度尼西亞新聞社 [yìn-tù-ní-hsī-yà hsīn-wén-shè] : Persbiro Indonesia Agency (PIA–a news agency)

印度尼西亞共和國 [yìn-tù-ní-hsī-yà kùng-hó-kuó] : Republic of Indonesia

印度尼西亞國民黨 [yìn-tù-ní-hsī-yà kúo-mín-tăng] : Indonesian Nationalist Party

印度尼西亞民族通訊社 [yìn-tù-ní-hsī-yà mín-tsú t'ūng-hsùn-shè] : Indonesian National Press (INP)

印度尼西亞通訊社 [yìn-tù-ní-hsī-yà t'ūng-hsùn-shè] : Indonesian News Agency

印度報業托辣斯 [yìn-tù pào-yèh t'ō-là-ssū] : Press Trust of India (PTI–a news agency)

印度時報 [yìn-tù shíh-pào] : The Times of India (Indian daily newspaper)

印度斯坦旗報 [yìn-tù-ssū-t'ăn ch'í-pào] : Hindustan Standard (Indian daily newspaper)

印度斯坦時報 [yìn-tù-ssū-t'ăn shíh-pào] : Hindustan Times (Indian daily newspaper)

12 印象 [yìn-hsiàng] : to impress; impression, mental image

— 6 Strokes —

卷

卷 [chüàn] : volume, book

卸

3 卸下 [hsièh-hsià] : to unload

6 卸任 [hsièh-jèn] : to retire from office, to resign from office

8 卸肩 [hsièh-chīen] : to rest the shoulders, to put down a burden, to lay down a responsibility

— 7 Strokes —

即

4 即日 [chí-jìh] : on the same day, on this day

7 即位 [chí-wèi] : to ascend the throne

8 即刻 [chí-k'ò] : right now, immediately, this instant

即使 [chí-shĭh] : even though, if, even if, although, even

9 即便 [chí-pièn] : at this time, then, forthwith

即是 [chí-shìh] : namely, that is, that is to say, i.e.

10 即席而作 [chí-hsí érh tsò] : to improvise, to extemporize; unrehearsed, spontaneous, unpremeditated, on the spur of the moment

即時 [chí-shíh] : just now, now, immediately, this moment

11 即將到來的 [chí-chiāng tào-lái te] : forthcoming, coming, pending, approaching, impending, imminent, to be in sight

即速 [chí-sù] : quickly, as fast as possible

— 10 Strokes —

鄉

鄉 [hsiāng] : hsiang, township, village

7 鄉村 [hsiāng-ts'ūn] : the countryside, villages; rural

— RADICAL 厂 27 —

— 2 Strokes —

厄

5 厄瓜多爾 [ò-kuā-tō-ĕrh] : Ecuador

厄瓜多爾共和國 [ò-kuā-tō-ĕrh kùng-hó-kuó] : Republic of Ecuador

13 厄運 [ò-yǜn] : bad luck

14 厄爾巴島 [ò-ĕrh-pā tăo] : Elba Island

— 7 Strokes —

厚

4 厚今薄古 [hòu-chīn pó-kŭ] : to lay more stress on the present than on the past, to emphasize the new and deemphasize the old

7 厚利 [hòu-lì] : big profit

13 厚意 [hòu-ì] : good intentions, kindness

厚道 [hòu-tào] : magnanimous, kindly; kindness, considerateness

18 厚顏無恥 [hòu-yén wú-ch'ĭh] : brazen-faced, shameless, cynical, brazen

— 8 Strokes —

原

3 原子 [yüán-tzŭ] : atom

原子戰爭 [yüán-tzŭ chàn-chēng] : atomic war

原子擊破器 [yüán-tzŭ chī-p'ò-ch'ì] : capacitron

原子基地 [yüán-tzŭ chī-tì] : atomic base

原子氫複合炸彈 [yüán-tzŭ ch'īng fù-hó chà-tàn] : combined atomic-hydrogen bomb

原子訛詐政策 [yüán-tzŭ ó-chà chèng-ts'è] : policy of atomic blackmail

原子反應堆 [yüán-tzŭ făn-yīng-tūi] : atomic reactor, atomic pile

原子輻射影響科學會 [yüán-tzŭ fú-shè yĭng-hsiăng k'ō-hsüéh-hùi] : Scientific Committee on Effects of Atomic Radiation (United Nations)

原子核 [yüán-tzŭ-hó] : atomic nucleus, nuclear

原子核委員會 [yüán-tzŭ-hó wĕi-yüán-hùi] : Nuclear Commission

原子核物理學 [yüán-tzŭ-hó wù-lĭ-hsüéh] : nuclear physics

原子感應加速運動器 [yüán-tzŭ kăn-yìng chiā-sù yǜn-tùng ch'ì] : betatron

原子論 [yüán-tzŭ-lùn] : atomic theory; atomism

原子論者 [yüán-tzŭ-lùn chĕ] : atomist

原子能 [yüán-tzŭ-néng] : atomic energy, nuclear energy

原子能發電站 [yüán-tzŭ-néng fā-tièn-chàn] : atomic power station, nuclear power station

原子能研究所 [yüán-tzŭ-néng yén-chìu-sŏ] : Institute of Atomic Energy

原子射綫 [yüán-tzŭ shè-hsièn] : atomic ray

原子時代 [yüán-tzŭ shíh-tài] : atomic age

原子彈 [yüán-tzŭ-tàn] : atomic bomb, atom bomb

原子彈頭 [yüán-tzŭ tàn-t'óu] : atomic warhead

原子外交 [yüán-tzŭ wài-chiāo] : atomic diplomacy

原子武器 [yüán-tzŭ wŭ-ch'ì] : atomic weapon

4 原木 [yüán-mù]: timber

原文 [yüán-wén]: text, original text, original

原文如此 [yüán-wén jú-tz'ŭ]: sic, thus

5 原主 [yüán-chŭ]: original proprietor, original owner

原本原樣的事實 [yüán-pĕn yüán-yàng te shìh-shíh]: crude fact, naked truth

原平 [yüán-p'íng]: Nguyenbinh (Vietnam)

6 原任 [yüán-jèn]: original incumbent; to hold the former post

原因 [yüán-yīn]: cause, reason, grounds, occasion, motive, rationale

7 原形 [yüán-hsíng]: true shape, true colors, original form, real appearance

原形畢露 [yüán-hsíng pì-lù]: to show one's true colors

原告 [yüán-kào]: plaintiff, accuser, appellant, claimant, complainant

8 原始 [yüán-shĭh]: primitive, primeval, primordial

原始記錄 [yüán-shĭh chì-lù]: primary accounting

原始主義 [yüán-shĭh chŭ-ì]: primitivism

原始人 [yüán-shĭh-jén]: primitive man

原始人類學 [yüán-shĭh-jén-lèi-hsüéh]: agriology

原始森林 [yüán-shĭh sēn-lín]: virgin forest, primeval forest

原始社會 [yüán-shĭh shè-hùi]: primitive society

原定 [yüán-tìng]: originally decided, originally fixed as, originally scheduled

原油 [yüán-yú]: crude oil

9 原封不動 [yüán-fēng pú-tùng]: to preserve intact; untouched

原型 [yüán-hsíng]: prototype, mould

原則 [yüán-tsé]: principle, axiom, fundamental principle, tenet

10 原料 [yüán-liào]: raw materials, materiel

11 原動力 [yüán-tùng-lì]: prime power, motive force, driving force, impetus

原理 [yüán-lĭ]: principle, axiom, theory, tenet

15 原稿 [yüán-kăo]: manuscript, original copy, rough copy

原諒 [yüán-liàng]: to excuse; to be lenient; excuse, pardon

原樣 [yüán-yàng]: original form

原樣照抄 [yüán-yàng chào-ch'āo]: to copy mechanically

18 原職 [yüán-chíh]: former post, original appointment

20 原籍 [yüán-chí]: native place, native home, domicile of origin

— 10 Strokes —

厦

厦 [hsià]: Amoy (abbreviation of 厦門); a mansion

— 12 Strokes —

厭

4 厭世觀 [yèn-shìh-kuān]: pessimism

11 厭倦 [yèn-chüàn]: to be tired, fatigued, exhausted

12 厭惡 [yèn-wù]: to detest, to dislike, to be tired of, to have an aversion for; antipathy, disgust; reluctant

— 15 Strokes —

厲

6 厲行 [lì-hsíng]: to enforce strictly, to carry

out strictly

厲行節約 **[lì-hsíng chiéh-yüēh]**: to practice economy, to make a sustained effort to practice strict economy

[10] 厲害 **[lì-hài]**: strong-handed, iron-handed, violent, harsh, severe, rigorous

— RADICAL 厶 28 —

— 3 Strokes —

[11] 去掉 **[ch'ǜ-tiào]**: to do away with, to get rid of, to remove, to discard, to relinquish, to give up

— 9 Strokes —

[5] 參加 **[ts'ān-chiā]**: to participate in, to take part in, to join, to attend

參加者 **[ts'ān-chiā-chě]**: participant

[7] 參考 **[ts'ān-k'ǎo]**: to consult, to refer to; reference

參考資料 **[ts'ān-k'ǎo tzū-liào]**: reference data, reference material

[8] 參事 **[ts'ān-shìh]**: consultant, counselor

[9] 參政 **[ts'ān-chèng]**: to participate in government; to be politically active

參軍 **[ts'ān-chūn]**: to enter military service

參革 **[ts'ān-kó]**: to impeach and deprive of rank, to accuse and downgrade

[13] 參照 **[ts'ān-chào]**: to compare, to refer, to confer; in the light of

參與 **[ts'ān-yǔ]**: to share in, to participate in, to have a hand in, to assist

[15] 參謀 **[ts'ān-móu]**: to consult; staff, staff officer

參謀長 **[ts'ān-móu-chǎng]**: chief-of-staff

參謀軍士 **[ts'ān-móu chūn-shìh]**: Staff Sergeant (U.S. Airforce)

參謀總長 **[ts'ān-móu tsǔng-chǎng]**: Chief of the General Staff

[19] 參贊 **[ts'ān-tsàn]**: embassy counselor

[20] 參議會 **[ts'ān-ì-hùi]**: assembly, council

參議院 **[ts'ān-ì-yüàn]**: Senate (U.S.A.); Chamber of Lords (German Democratic Republic); House of Councillors (Japan); Bundesrat (West Germany); Council of the Republic (France)

[24] 參觀 **[ts'ān-kuān]**: to observe, to look over

— RADICAL 又 29 —

又

又 **[yù]**: and, also, again, in addition to, more, moreover, further

9 又紅又專 **[yù-húng yù-chuān]**: both red and expert (i.e., both politically and professionally qualified; unquestioningly loyal to the Party and professionally competent)

14 又團結，又鬥爭 **[yù t'uán-chiéh, yù tòu-chēng]**: both unity and struggle, simultaneously to unite with and wage struggle against

又團結，又鬥爭，以鬥爭之手段，達團結之目的 **[yù t'uán-chiéh, yù tòu-chēng, ĭ tòu-chēng chīh shŏu-tuàn, tá t'uán-chiéh chīh mù-tì]**: unity, struggle, unity through struggle

— 2 Strokes —

6 及早 **[chí-tsăo]**: early, prompt, at an early date, to make an early start

10 及格 **[chí-kó]**: to pass an examination, to meet the standard

及時 **[chí-shíh]**: timely, opportune; duly

12 及期 **[chí-ch'í]**: within the deadline

反 **[făn]**: 1) counter-, anti-; 2) to oppose, to turn over, to retreat, to rebel, to turn back; 3) abbreviation for "reactionaries"; 4) abbreviation for "counterrevolutionaries"

2 反人民 **[făn jén-mín]**: anti-popular; to turn against the people

3 反三右 **[făn sān-yù]**: opposition to the three rightisms (i.e., opposition to rightist opportunism, rightist capitulationism, and rightist splittism, which were the content of the anti-rightist campaign launched in early 1968)

5 反正 **[făn-chèng]**: in any case

反比例 **[făn-pĭ-lì]**: inverse ratio, inverse proportion

反右傾 **[făn-yù-ch'īng]**: to oppose right deviation, to fight against right deviation

反右派鬥爭 **[făn yù-p'ài tòu-chēng]**: anti-rightist struggle

6 反而 **[făn-érh]**: on the contrary

反行賄，反偸稅漏稅，反盜竊國家資財，反偸工減料，反盜竊國家經濟情報 **[făn hsíng-hùi, făn t'ōu-shùi lòu-shùi, făn tào-ch'ièh kuó-chiā tzū-ts'ái, făn t'ōu-kūng chiĕn-liào, făn tào-ch'ièh kuó-chiā chīng-chì ch'íng-pào]**: anti-bribery, anti-tax evasion, anti-theft of government property, anti-skimping on work and cheating on materials, anti-theft of state economic information (the 五反)

反攻 **[făn-kūng]**: counterattack; to counterattack

反共 **[făn-kùng]**: anti-communism

7 反抗 **[făn-k'àng]**: to resist, to defy, to stand against, to oppose; resistance, defiance, opposition

反作用 **[făn tsò-yùng]**: counterreaction, opposite effect

8 反官僚主義 **[făn kuān-liáo chŭ-ì]**: anti-bureaucratism (one of the 三反)

反坦克砲 **[făn-t'ăn-k'ò-p'ào]**: anti-tank gun

9 反建議 **[făn-chièn-ì]**: counter-proposal

反軍國主義 **[făn-chūn-kuó chŭ-ì]**: anti-militarism

反封建 **[făn-fēng-chièn]**: anti-feudalism, anti-feudal

反限制 **[fǎn-hsièn-chìh]**: opposition to restriction

反省 **[fǎn-hsǐng]**: repentance, reflection, introspection, self-examination

反省自己 **[fǎn-hsǐng tzù-chǐ]**: self-examination, introspection, to examine oneself, to introspect

反革命 **[fǎn-kó-mìng]**: counterrevolution, anti-revolution

反革命份子 **[fǎn-kó-mìng fèn-tzu]**: counterrevolutionary elements, anti-revolutionary elements

反面 **[fǎn-mièn]**: negative aspect, negative side; negative

反面教育 **[fǎn-mièn chiào-yǜ]**: negative education (teaching by negative example to show the undesirable consequences that follow when bad habits are not corrected)

反面教員 **[fǎn-mièn chiāo-yüán]**: teacher by negative example

反面人物 **[fǎn-mièn jén-wù]**: villainous character, negative personality

反叛 **[fǎn-p'àn]**: to rebel; rebellion, revolt, insurrection, insurgence, uprising

反叛者 **[fǎn-p'àn-chě]**: rebel, insurgent

反帝 **[fǎn-tì]**: anti-imperialism

反映 **[fǎn-yìng]**: to reflect; reflection

反映論 **[fǎn-yìng-lùn]**: theory of reflection

10 反弱爲强 **[fǎn-jò wéi ch'iáng]**: to turn weakness into strength

反躬自省 **[fǎn-kūng tzù-hsǐng]**: to examine oneself by self-inspection

反浪費 **[fǎn làng-fèi]**: anti-waste (one of the 三反)

反馬克思主義 **[fǎn-mǎ-k'ò-ssū chǔ-ì]**: anti-Marxism, anti-Marxist

反射 **[fǎn-shè]**: to reflect

11 反常 **[fǎn-ch'áng]**: abnormal

反常心理 **[fǎn-ch'áng hsīn-lǐ]**: abnormal mentality or psychology

反理性主義 **[fǎn-lǐ-hsìng chǔ-ì]**: anti-rationalism

反貪汚，反浪費，反官僚主義 **[fǎn t'ān-wū fǎn làng-fèi, fǎn kuān-liáo chǔ-ì]**: anti-corruption, anti-waste, and anti-bureacratism (the 三反)

反貪汚浪費 **[fǎn t'ān-wū làng-fèi]**: against corruption and waste

反盜竊國家經濟情報 **[fǎn tào-ch'ièh kuó-chiā chīng-chì ch'íng-pào]**: anti-theft of state economic information (one of the 五反)

反盜竊國家資財 **[fǎn tào-ch'ièh kuó-chiā tzū-ts'ái]**: anti-theft of government property (one of the 五反)

反偸工減料 **[fǎn t'ōu-kūng chiěn-liào]**: anti-skimping on work and cheating on materials (one of the 五反)

反偸稅漏稅 **[fǎn t'ōu-shùi lòu-shùi]**: anti-tax evasion (one of the 五反)

反動 **[fǎn-tùng]**: reaction; reactionary

反動集團 **[fǎn-tùng chí-t'uán]**: reactionary group, reactionary bloc, reactionary clique

反動行爲 **[fǎn-tùng hsíng-wéi]**: reactionary behavior or activities

反動派 **[fǎn-tùng-p'ài]**: reactionary clique

反動堡壘 **[fǎn-tùng pǎo-lěi]**: reactionary fortress (during the Cultural Revolution, a term used to designate a stronghold of Mao's opponents)

反動地方武裝 **[fǎn-tùng tì-fāng wǔ-chuāng]**: reactionary local armed bandits

反動統治 **[fǎn-tùng t'ǔng-chìh]**: reactionary rule

12 反間 **[fǎn-chièn]**: to sow discontent

29

反殖民主義 **[fǎn-chíh-mín chǔ-ì]**: anti-colonialism

反圍攻 **[fǎn-wéi-kūng]**: counter-encirclement

反猶太主義 **[fǎn-yú-t'ài chǔ-ì]**: anti-semitism

13 反話 **[fǎn-huà]**: irony

反感 **[fǎn-kǎn]**: resentment, repugnance, dislike, distaste, aversion

反過來 **[fǎn-kuò-lái]**: vice-versa, to turn something around, in turn, in return

14 反對 **[fǎn-tùi]**: to object to, to combat, to counter, to oppose

反對核武器國際會議 **[fǎn-tùi hó-wǔ-ch'ì kuó-chì hùi-ì]**: International Convention Against Atomic Arms

反對派 **[fǎn-tùi-p'ài]**: opposition faction

反對黨 **[fǎn-tùi-tǎng]**: opposition party

反對黨八股 **[fǎn-tùi tǎng pā-kǔ]**: to oppose Party jargon

反駁 **[fǎn-pó]**: to refute, to rebut, to disprove, to reply to a charge

反語 **[fǎn-yǚ]**: irony

17 反擊 **[fǎn-chī]**: to counter-attack, to rebuff, to repel, to repulse, to retaliate, to hit back at

反應 **[fǎn-yìng]**: response, reaction

反應不一 **[fǎn-yìng pù-ī]**: mixed reaction, diverse reactions

18 反覆 **[fǎn-fù]**: repeated, time and again, over and over

反覆無常 **[fǎn-fù wú-ch'áng]**: capricious, fickle

反題 **[fǎn-t'í]**: antithesis

20 反黨 **[fǎn-tǎng]**: anti-Party

反黨集團 **[fǎn-tǎng chí-t'uán]**: anti-Party bloc

反黨老手 **[fǎn-tǎng lǎo-shǒu]**: old hand in opposing the Party (during the Cultural Revolution, refers to such discredited intellectuals as Chou Yang and Hsia Yen)

21 反響 **[fǎn-hsiǎng]**: to echo, to reverberate; echo, reaction

友

6 友好 **[yǔ-hǎo]**: friendly, cordial, amicable; good will, friendship

友好訪問 **[yǔ-hǎo fǎng-wèn]**: friendly visit

友好協會 **[yǔ-hǎo hsiéh-hùi]**: friendship association

友好關係 **[yǔ-hǎo kuān-hsì]**: friendly relations, ties of friendship

友好團結 **[yǔ-hǎo t'uán-chiéh]**: friendship and unity

友好往來 **[yǔ-hǎo wǎng-lái]**: friendly intercourse

9 友軍 **[yǔ-chǖn]**: friendly troops

11 友情 **[yǔ-ch'íng]**: friendship, cordial feelings

15 友誼 **[yǔ-í]**: friendship, cordial feelings

— 6 Strokes —

取

4 取之不盡的 **[ch'ǚ-chīh-pú-chìn te]**: inexhaustible, abounding in, unexhausted

5 取巧[ch'ŭ-ch'iăo]: to manipulate, to take advantage of a situation, to handle skilfully; skilful management

6 取決於[ch'ŭ-chüéh yǘ]: to depend on, to be contingent on, to hinge on, to be decided by

取而代之[ch'ŭ-érh-tài-chīh]: to take someone's place, to replace

8 取長補短[ch'ŭ-ch'áng pŭ-tuăn]: to overcome one's weaknesses by acquiring the strong points of others

10 取消[ch'ŭ-hsiāo]: to revoke, to rescind, to cancel, to nullify, to abrogate; annulment, nullification, cancellation

取消主義[ch'ŭ-hsiāo chŭ-ì]: liquidationism

取消資格[ch'ŭ-hsiāo tzū-kó]: to deprive someone of his status; annulment of status

11 取得[ch'ŭ-té]: to get, to obtain, to acquire, to secure, to seize, to win

12 取款[ch'ŭ-k'uăn]: to draw money, to draw on account

15 取締[ch'ŭ-tì]: to repress, to control, to suppress, to ban, to prohibit, to outlaw, to interdict, to forbid; prohibition

受

8 受制於[shòu-chìh yǘ]: to be restrained by

受法律制裁[shòu fă-lǜ chìh-ts'ái]: to be restricted by law

受命[shòu-mìng]: to receive a mandate, to be charged with, to be given the duty of, to be ordered to

受到[shòu-tào]: to suffer, to sustain, to receive, to be inflicted with

10 受害者[shòu-hài-chĕ]: victim

受益[shòu-ì]: to benefit by, to benefit from

12 受惑的少年們[shòu-huò te shào-nién-mén]: beguiled teenagers

13 受傷[shòu-shāng]: to receive an injury, to be injured, to be wounded

15 受審[shòu-shĕn]: to stand trial, to face trial

19 受難者[shòu-nàn-chĕ]: victim

5 叔本華[shú-pĕn-huá]: Schopenhauer, Arthur (1783–1860)

— 7 Strokes —

7 敘利亞[hsǜ-lì-yà]: Syria

叛

10 叛匪[p'àn-fĕi]: rebel bandit, rebels

叛逆[p'àn-nì]: to revolt against

叛徒[p'àn-t'ú]: rebel, traitor, turncoat, mutineer, renegade

13 叛亂[p'àn-luàn]: revolt, insurrection, rebellion, mutiny, putsch, uprising, riot, disorders

20 叛黨[p'àn-tăng]: to turn traitor to the Party

— 14 Strokes —

12 睿智[jùi-chìh]: intuitive wisdom, intelligence

— RADICAL 口 30 —

口

3 口口聲聲說 [**k'ǒu-k'ǒu shēng-shēng shuō**]: to say glibly, to speak glibly

5 口令 [**k'ǒu-lìng**]: password, word of command, verbal order

8 口服 [**k'ǒu-fú**]: to give verbal submission

口供 [**k'ǒu-kùng**]: confession, deposition, testimony

9 口是心非 [**k'ǒu-shìh hsīn-fēi**]: to be a hypocrite, to say one thing but mean another; hypocrisy, lip service

10 口徑 [**k'ǒu-chìng**]: caliber, bore

13 口號 [**k'ǒu-hào**]: watchword, slogan, catchword

口號化 [**k'ǒu-hào-huà**]: "sloganization"

口試 [**k'ǒu-shìh**]: oral test, oral examination

16 口頭 [**k'ǒu-t'óu**]: oral

口頭上的 [**k'ǒu-t'óu-shàng te**]: verbal, spoken, oral

口頭上掛着 [**k'ǒu-t'óu-shàng kuà-chě**]: to pay lip service to

口頭採訪法 [**k'ǒu-t'óu ts'ǎi-fǎng fǎ**]: oral interview method

— 2 Strokes —

召

6 召回 [**chào-húi**]: to recall; recall

12 召集 [**chào-chí**]: to call, to hold, to convoke, to assemble, to gather, to summon, to convene; convocation

召開 [**chào-k'āi**]: to convene

叫

8 叫屈 [**chiào-ch'ǖ**]: to complain about injustice

叫花子 [**chiào-huā-tzu**]: beggar

9 叫苦 [**chiào-k'ǔ**]: to complain about one's grievances or suffering

叫苦連天 [**chiào-k'ǔ lién-t'iēn**]: to ventilate endless grievances, to "gripe"

10 叫陣 [**chiào-chèn**]: to incite to battle

叫做 [**chiào-tsò**]: to name, to designate as, to brand as, to be known as

12 叫喊 [**chiào-hǎn**]: to shout

15 叫賣 [**chiào-mài**]: to put up for sale, to peddle by hawking

16 叫醒 [**chiào-hsǐng**]: to awaken by a call

20 叫嚷 [**chiào-jǎng**]: to clamor, to shout, to yell; outcry, uproar, clamor, shout

21 叫囂 [**chiào-hsiāo**]: to clamor, to make a din, to bluster; clamor, outburst, outcry, ballyhoo

只

11 只專不紅 [**chǐh-chuān pù-húng**]: merely expert, not red (i.e., only technically proficient but not ideologically correct)

叱

5 叱斥 [**ch'ìh-ch'ìh**]: to blame, to reproach, to curse, to revile

6 叱咤風雲 [**ch'ìh-chà fēng-yǖn**]: to order about the winds and the clouds; to possess unlimited power

16 叱罵 [ch'ìh-mà] : to blame, to reproach, to curse, to revile

可

4 可以 [k'ŏ-ĭ] : can, may; very well, that will do; possible

可以證明 [k'ŏ-ĭ chèng-míng] : demonstrable, verifiable, able to stand the proof

可以接受的 [k'ŏ-ĭ chiēh-shòu te] : acceptable, agreeable, welcome

可以想像的 [k'ŏ-ĭ hsiăng-hsiàng te] : conceivable, thinkable, imaginable

可以理解的 [k'ŏ-ĭ lĭ-chiĕh te] : understandable, comprehensible, intelligible

可以允許的 [k'ŏ-ĭ yŭn-hsŭ te] : permissible

6 可行的 [k'ŏ-hsíng te] : feasible, practicable, workable, achievable

7 可見的 [k'ŏ-chièn te] : visible, perceptible, perceivable, discernible,

可兌換的 [k'ŏ tùi-huàn te] : convertible, exchangeable

8 可乘之機 [k'ŏ ch'éng chīh chī] : an opportunity that can be taken advantage of

可怕的 [k'ŏ-p'à te] : terrible, fearful, dreadful, formidable, sinister, frightening

10 可恥的 [k'ŏ-ch'ĭh te] : humiliating, shameful, disgraceful, ignominious, detestable

可恥的人 [k'ŏ-ch'ĭh te jén] : despicable person

可笑的 [k'ŏ-hsiào te] : ridiculous, absurd, ludicrous, nonsensical, laughable

可耕地 [k'ŏ-kēng-tì] : arable land

可倫比亞 [k'ŏ-lún-pĭ-yà] : Columbia

可倫坡 [k'ŏ-lún-p'ō] : Colombo

可能 [k'ŏ-néng] : likely, probable, possible

可能性 [k'ŏ-néng-hsìng] : possibility, potentiality

11 可得到的 [k'ŏ té-tào te] : available, obtainable, accessible, attainable

可採用的 [k'ŏ ts'ăi-yùng te] : applicable, adoptable

12 可貴 [k'ŏ-kuèi] : admirable, valuable, precious, estimable, worthy

可惡的 [k'ŏ-wù te] : abominable, wicked, evil, mischievous, hateful, obnoxious, abhorrent, loathesome, disgusting

13 可敬的 [k'ŏ-chìng te] : honorable, respectable, esteemed, revered, venerable

14 可疑的 [k'ŏ-í te] : suspicious, questionable, unreliable, dubious

可厭的 [k'ŏ-yèn te] : repulsive, detestable, ugly, hateful, disgusting, offensive, obnoxious

15 可靠的 [k'ŏ-k'ào te] : reliable, trustworthy, dependable

可適用的 [k'ŏ shìh-yùng te] : applicable, fit, suitable

17 可應用的 [k'ŏ yìng-yùng te] : applicable

23 可驚的 [k'ŏ-chīng te] : amazing, wonderful, astonishing, shocking, surprising, phenomenal

25 可觀的 [k'ŏ-kuān te] : appreciable, considerable

古

2 古 [kŭ] : ancient, antique; antiquity

4 古今 [kŭ-chīn] : then and now, old and new, for all times

古今中外 [kŭ-chīn chūng-wài] : for all times and for all countries

古巴[**kŭ-pā**]: Cuba

古巴共和國[**kŭ-pā kùng-hó-kuó**]: Republic of Cuba

古文[**kŭ-wén**]: classical literature, ancient language

古文字學[**kŭ-wén-tzù-hsüéh**]: paleography

5 古生代[**kŭ-shēng-tài**]: Paleozoic

古生物研究所[**kŭ-shēng-wù yén-chìu-sŏ**]: Institute of Paleontology

古代的[**kŭ-tài te**]: ancient

古來[**kŭ-lái**]: since long ago, since the old days

8 古典[**kŭ-tiĕn**]: classics, classical, classical allusion

古典主義[**kŭ-tiĕn chŭ-ì**]: classicism

古宗[**kŭ-tsūng**]: Kutsung (minority nationality)

9 古風[**kŭ-fēng**]: tradition, primitive ways, customs of former days

古爲今用[**kŭ wèi chīn yùng**]: application of old traditions for modern purposes

10 古晉[**kŭ-chìn**]: Kuching (Sarawak)

14 古爾族[**kŭ-ĕrh tsú**]: the Kurds

古銅[**kŭ-t'úng**]: ancient bronzes

19 古蹟[**kŭ-chī**]: ancient remains, ancient relics and ruins

21 古蘭經[**kŭ-lán chīng**]: the Koran

叻

11 叻埠[**lì-fù**]: Singapore

另

1 另一方面[**lìng ì-fāng-mièn**]: on the other hand

史

4 史巴克[**shĭh-pā-k'ò**]: Spaak, Paul-Henri (Belgian statesman)

史太林[**shĭh-t'ài-lín**]: Stalin

5 史汀生主義[**shĭh-t'īng-shēng chŭ-ì**]: Stimson-ism, the Stimson doctrine (non-recognition of Japanese gains in China)

史册[**shĭh-ts'è**]: history book

11 史密斯[**shĭh-mì-ssū**]: Smith

13 史詩[**shĭh-shīh**]: epic poem, epic

史塔生[**shĭh-t'ă-shēng**]: Stassen, Harold (American statesman)

史蒂文生[**shĭh-tì-wén-shēng**]: Stevenson, Adlai (American statesman)

14 史維尼克[**shĭh-wéi-ní-k'ò**]: Shvernik, Nikolai (Russian statesman)

司

5 司令長官[**ssū-lìng chăng-kuān**]: commanding officer

司令部[**ssū-lìng-pù**]: headquarters

司令員[**ssū-lìng-yüán**]: commander, commanding officer

8 司長[**ssū-chăng**]: director, branch chief, director of a division of a ministry

司法[**ssū-fă**]: judicial

司法部[**ssū-fă-pù**]: Ministry of Justice

司法委員會[**ssū-fă wĕi-yüán-hùi**]: Judicial Committee

13 司號員[**ssū-hào-yüán**]: bugler

台

台[**t'ái**]: Taiwan (abbreviation of 台灣)

5 台白 [t'ái-pái] : stage dialogue

9 台柱 [t'ái-chù] : mainstay, pillar of support; star, head man

台風 [t'ái-fēng] : typhoon

26 台灣民主自治同盟 [t'ái-wān mín-chŭ tzù-chìh t'úng-méng] : Taiwan Democratic Self-Government League

右

右 [yù] : 1. right, the right hand side, the foregoing; 2. rightist (abbreviation)

9 右派份子 [yù-p'ài fèn-tzu] : rightist

13 右傾 [yù-ch'īng] : right deviation, rightist tendency

右傾機會主義 [yù-ch'īng chī-hùi chŭ-ì] : right opportunism

右傾機會主義份子 [yù-ch'īng chī-hùi chŭ-ì fèn-tzu] : right opportunist, right deviationist

右傾機會主義路綫 [yù-ch'īng chī-hùi chŭ-ì lù-hsièn] : right opportunist line

右傾情緒 [yù-ch'īng ch'íng-hsǜ] : right deviationist sentiments

右傾主義 [yù-ch'īng chŭ-ì] : right deviationism

右傾份子 [yù-ch'īng fèn-tzu] : right deviationist (i.e., one who believes that Chinese Communist Party policy is too radical or impracticable)

右傾保守主義 [yù-ch'īng păo-shŏu chŭ-ì] : right deviationist conservatism

右傾保守思想 [yù-ch'īng păo-shŏu ssū-hsiăng] : right conservative ideas

右傾思想 [yù-ch'īng ssū-hsiăng] : rightist ideas, rightist way of thinking

右傾錯誤 [yù-ch'īng ts'ò-wù] : right deviationist mistakes

17 右翼 [yù-ì] : right wing

右翼份子 [yù-ì fèn-tzu] : right-winger

— 3 Strokes —

吉

吉 [chí] : Kirin Province (abbreviation of 吉林)

4 吉仁尼邦 [chí-jén-ní pāng] : Karenni State (Burma)

吉仁邦 [chí-jén pāng] : Karen State (Burma)

5 吉布提 [chí-pù-t'í] : Djibouti (French Somalie)

6 吉兆 [chí-chào] : a good sign, an auspicious omen

7 吉利 [chí-lì] : auspicious, auspiciousness

8 吉林 [chí-lín] : Kirin

11 吉祥 [chí-hsiáng] : good fortune, luck; lucky

吉連丹 [chí-lién-tān] : Kelantan (Malaya)

12 吉隆 [chí-lúng] : Kirong (Tibet)

吉隆坡 [chí-lúng-p'ō] : Kuala Lumpur (Malaya)

13 吉普車 [chí-p'ŭ-ch'ē] : jeep

吉塞朗島 [chí-sài-lăng tăo] : Kisseraing Island

21 吉蘭丹 [chí-lán-tān] : Kelantan (Malaya)

吃

1 吃一虧，長一智 [ch'īh ì-k'uēi, chăng í-chìh] : to grow in wisdom through suffering misfortune, to learn the hard way, to live and learn

2 吃力 [ch'īh-lì] : to require effort, difficult

4 吃不消 [ch'īh-pù-hsiāo] : to be unable to endure

8 吃苦 [ch'īh-k'ŭ] : to suffer hardship

[9] 吃勁[ch'īh-chìn]: to require great strength, to necessitate a great effort

吃垮[ch'īh-k'uă]: to suffer a collapse

[11] 吃軟不吃硬[ch'īh-juăn pù-ch'īh yìng]: to accept the soft but not the hard (i.e., to be amenable to friendly persuasion but not to compulsion)

吃透兩頭[ch'īh-t'òu liăng-t'óu]: to digest thoroughly both ends (i.e., to come to a thorough understanding of Party policy on the upper level and of actual conditions of an enterprise on the lower level; to link the Party line with local needs; to link theory with practice)

[12] 吃喝[ch'īh-hō]: to eat and drink, to live profligately

吃閒飯[ch'īh hsién-fàn]: to eat without working, to be a parasite or idler

[14] 吃緊[ch'īh-chĭn]: pressing urgent, tense

[15] 吃醋[ch'īh-ts'ù]: to drink vinegar, to envy, to be jealous

[17] 吃虧[ch'īh-k'uēi]: to suffer loss, to get the worst of, to be wronged

[23] 吃驚[ch'īh-chīng]: to be frightened, to be surprised

合

[5] 合乎[hó-hū]: to meet, to conform to

合乎規律[hó-hū kuēi-lǜ]: in conformity with law, according to law

[6] 合成纖維[hó-ch'éng hsiēn-wéi]: synthetic fiber

合成品[hó-ch'éng-p'ĭn]: synthetic product

合成油類[hó-ch'éng yú-lèi]: synthetic oils

合同[hó-t'úng]: contract, agreement

[7] 合作[hó-tsò]: to cooperate with, to work together; cooperation

合作化[hó-tsò-huà]: "cooperativization"

合作化運動[hó-tsò-huà yǜn-tùng]: the co-operative movement

合作股分基金[hó-tsò kŭ-fèn chī-chīn]: cooperation foundation fund

合作社[hó-tsò-shè]: a cooperative, co-op

合作社企業[hó-tsò-shè ch'ì-yèh]: cooperative-run enterprise

合作社營工業[hó-tsò-shè yíng kūng-yèh]: cooperative-operated industry

合作事務部[hó-tsò-shìh-wù-pù]: Bureau of Cooperatives

[8] 合金[hó-chīn]:alloy

合金鋼[hó-chīn-kāng]: alloy steel

合金優制鋼[hó-chīn yū-chìh kāng]: high-grade alloy steel

合法[hó-fă]: legal, legitimate, lawful, rightful, de jure

合法主義[hó-fă chŭ-ì]: legalism

合法化[hó-fă-huà]: legalization

合法馬克思主義[hó-fă mă-k'ò-ssū chŭ-ì]: legal Marxism

合並[hó-pìng]: to merge with, to fuse with, to affiliate with, to incorporate, to annex; merger, fusion, annexation

[9] 合計[hó-chì]: to total, to amount to, to add up; total, gross amount

合約[hó-yüēh]: contract

[10] 合併[hó-pìng]: to merge into, to incorporate with, to unite with, to amalgamate, to blend; merger, union

合格[hó-kó]: to qualify, to meet requirements; qualified, competent, up to the mark

[11] 合理[hó-lĭ]: rational, reasonable, proper, just, fair

合理發揮[hó-lĭ fā-hūi]: to give proper scope to

合理負擔[hó-lĭ fù-tān]: reasonable distribution of burden

合理化[hó-lǐ-huà]: to rationalize; rationalization

合理化建議[hó-lǐ-huà chièn-ì]: rationalization proposal

合理庫存[hó-lǐ k'ù-ts'ún]: reasonable inventories

合理密植[hó-lǐ mì-chíh]: reasonably close planting—a modification of "close planting," which proved disastrous (*See* 八字憲法)

合理使用勞動力[hó-lǐ shǐh-yùng láo-tùng-lì]: rational utilization of labor power

12 合衆國際社[hó-chùng kuó-chì-shè]: United Press International (UPI)

合圍[hó-wéi]: to besiege, to encircle; encirclement

13 合資[hó-tzū]: joint capital

15 合適的[hó-shìh te]: suitable, appropriate, proper, desirable, fit, becoming

17 合營[hó-yíng]: joint operation, jointly operated, partnership

合營企業[hó-yíng ch'ì-yèh]: joint enterprise

向

3 向下[hsiàng-hsià]: downward

向山區進軍[hsiàng shān-ch'ū chìn-chūn]: march to mountainous areas (a slogan current in 1957 to interest people into going to mountainous regions to reclaim wasteland)

向上[hsiàng-shàng]: upward

4 向日葵[hsiàng-jìh-k'uéi]: sunflower

8 向往[hsiàng-wǎng]: to long for, to desire, to wish

9 向前推進[hsiàng-ch'ién t'ūi-chìn]: to push forward, to promote

向科學進軍[hsiàng k'ō-hsüéh chìn-chūn]: to march forward to science

12 向着[hsiàng-ché]: to turn toward, to be facing

4 各方面[kò fāng-mièn]: in various fields, in various aspects, in various fields of

6 各安生業[kò ān shēng-yèh]: each person follows his usual pursuits

各行其是[kò hsíng ch'í-shìh]: each person does what he thinks is right; each person goes his own way

各自[kò-tzù]: respective, respectively

各自爲政[kò-tzù wéi-chèng]: each goes his own way

7 各別[kò-piéh]: separate, respective, individual, one's own

9 各界[kò-chièh]: every walk of life, all spheres, various circles, various quarters

10 各級[kò-chí]: various levels, all levels, different levels

各個擊破[kò-kò chī-p'ò]: to knock things or persons down one by one, to smash the enemy one by one

11 各執一辭[kò-chíh ì-tz'ú]: to cling to one's own interpretation

各國政府海事協商組織[kò-kuó chèng-fǔ hǎi-shìh hsiéh-shāng tsǔ-chīh]: Inter-Governmental Maritime Consultative Organization

各國議會聯盟[kò-kuó ì-hùi lién-méng]: Inter-Parliamentary Union (IPU)

各得其所[kò té ch'í-sǒ]: each takes its proper place

12 各階層[kò chiēh-ts'éng]: various levels, all walks of life, people of all strata, all strata

13 各該行業[kò-kāi háng-yèh]: various branches of industry

14 各盡所能，按勞分配 **[kò chìn sŏ néng, àn láo fēn-p'èi]**: "From each according to his ability and to each according to his work"

各盡所能，按勞付酬 **[kò chìn sŏ néng, àn láo fù-ch'óu]**: "From each according to his ability and to each according to his work"

各盡所能，按需分配 **[kò chìn sŏ néng, àn hsū fēn-p'èi]**: "From each according to his ability and to each according to his needs"

各盡所能，各取所需 **[kò chìn sŏ néng, kò ch'ŭ sŏ hsū]**: "From each according to his ability and to each according to his needs"

各種 **[kò-chŭng]**: all kinds of, all varieties

各種各樣 **[kò-chŭng kò-yàng]**: all kinds, all varieties

名

2 名人 **[míng-jén]**: leading lights, notables, celebrities, famous persons

5 名古屋 **[míng-kŭ-wū]**: Nagoya (Japan)

7 名利 **[míng-lì]**: fame and profit, fame and material gains

11 名副其實 **[míng fù ch'í shíh]**: to have the name correspond with the fact, in the true sense of the term, worthy of the name, veritable

12 名單 **[míng-tān]**: roster

名爲 **[míng-wéi]**: to name, to call, to be called, to be named or entitled

13 名義 **[míng-ì]**: name, title, in the name of; nominal

名義上 **[míng-ì-shàng]**: nominally, in name

14 名稱 **[míng-ch'ēng]**: title, designation, name, nomenclature

18 名額 **[míng-ó]**: quota

21 名譽 **[míng-yù]**: honor, reputation, name; honorary

名譽會員 **[míng-yù hùi-yüán]**: honorary member

名譽掃地 **[míng-yù săo-tì]**: to be discredited, to come to dishonor, to lose all standing; dishonored reputation

11 吊船 **[tiào-ch'uán]**: lifeboat

16 吊橋 **[tiào-ch'iáo]**: suspension bridge

18 吊鎖 **[tiào-sŏ]**: padlock

吐

9 吐故納新 **[t'u-kù nà-hsīn]**: to get rid of the stale and take in the fresh (a physiological analogy used by Mao Tse-tung to explain that a proletarian political party must constantly cleanse itself and take in new blood in order to maintain its vigor)

吐苦水 **[t'ù k'ŭ-shŭi]**: to spit bitter water (i.e., to air personal or family grievances, usually in a public meeting–a slogan used in the land reform to arouse class hatred)

吐怨氣 **[t'ŭ yüàn-ch'ì]**: to vent one's grievances, to air one's grievances

21 吐露 **[t'ŭ-lù]**: to disclose, to confide to

1 同一性 **[t'úng-í-hsìng]**: identity

同一律 **[t'úng-í-lü]**: principle of identity

3 同工同酬 **[t'úng-kūng t'úng-ch'óu]**: equal pay for equal work

4 同仇 **[t'úng-ch'óu]**: common enemy

同仇敵愾 **[t'úng-ch'óu tí-k'ài]**: to have a common enmity and hatred

同心協力 [t'úng-hsīn hsiéh-lì] : united effort, with concerted effort

同心同德 [t'úng-hsīn t'úng-té] : with one heart and one mind

同化 [t'úng-huà] : to assimilate; assimilation

5 同甘共苦 [t'úng-kān kùng-k'ŭ] : to share joys and sorrows

6 同舟共濟 [t'úng-chōu kùng-chì] : in the same boat, through thick or thin

7 同志 [t'úng-chìh] : comrade

同志式的 [t'úng-chìh-shìh te] : comradely, of comradeship

同步 [t'úng-pù] : synchronous

同步加速器 [t'úng-pù chiā-sù-ch'ì] : synchrotron

同步前進 [t'úng-pù ch'ién-chìn] : to keep pace in marching forward, to keep the same pace in advancing

同步迴旋加速器 [t'úng-pù húi-hsüán chià-sù-ch'ì] : synchrocyclotron

同步穩相加速器 [t'úng-pù wĕn-hsiāng chiā-sù-ch'ì] : synchrophasotron, proton synchrotron

同位素 [t'úng-wèi-sù] : isotope

同位素應用委員會 [t'úng-wèi-sù yìng-yùng wĕi-yüán-hùi]: Committee on Application of Isotopes

同胞 [t'úng-pāo] : compatriot, fellow countryman, fellow citizen

10 同流合汚 [t'úng-líu hó-wū] : to join in evil doings

同時 [t'úng-shíh] : simultaneous, concurrent, at the same time

同時並舉 [t'úng-shíh pìng-chü] : to develop simultaneously; simultaneous development

同格 [t'úng-kó] : coordination

11 同情 [t'úng-ch'íng] : to sympathize, to commiserate; sympathy, compassion

同情者 [t'úng-ch'íng-chĕ] : sympathizer

12 同等 [t'úng-tĕng] : same class or rank; equal, equivalent, on a level with

13 同鄉 [t'úng-hsiāng] : fellow townsman, fellow villager, a person from the same province, city, or county

同意 [t'úng-ì] : to agree, to approve, to assent, to consent, to acquiesce in; endorsement

同路人 [t'úng-lù-jén] : fellow traveler

同盟 [t'úng-méng] : ally, alliance, union; to ally with

同盟軍 [t'úng-méng-chün] : allied forces

同盟國最高委員會 [t'úng-méng-kuó tsùi-kāo wĕi-yüán-hùi] : Allied High Commission

14 同語反復 [t'úng-yü făn-fù] : tautology, redundancy

16 同謀 [t'úng-móu] : to plot together; accomplice

18 同歸於盡 [t'úng kuēi yü chìn] : to perish together, to end in common ruin

吁

15 吁請 [yü-ch'ĭng] : to appeal, to petition; appeal, petition

— 4 Strokes —

13 吵鬧的 [ch'ăo-nào te] : tumultuous, noisy

呈

6 呈交 [ch'éng-chiāo] : to submit, to present

10 呈核 [ch'éng-hó] : to submit for considera-

tion, to submit for approval

呈遞國書 **[ch'éng-tì kuó-shū]**: to present credentials

11 呈現 **[ch'éng-hsièn]**: to disclose, manifest

12 呈報 **[ch'éng-pào]**: to present a report, to submit a report

吹

4 吹牛 **[ch'ūi-níu]**: to boast, to brag

吹牛的人 **[ch'ūi-níu te jén]**: boaster, braggart

14 吹噓 **[ch'ūi-hsū]**: to advertise, to ballyhoo, to crack oneself up to be

君

3 君子國 **[chūn-tzŭ-kuó]**: "Land of Gentlemen"

5 君主政體 **[chūn-chŭ chèng-t'ĭ]**: monarchical form of government, monarchy

君主立憲 **[chūn-chŭ lì-hsièn]**: constitutional monarchy

吩

8 吩咐 **[fēn-fù]**: to leave instructions, to order, to command, to give an order; instruction, order, command

否

7 否決 **[fŏu-chüéh]**: to veto, to decide against, to reject

否決權 **[fŏu-chüéh-ch'üán]**: veto, veto power

8 否定 **[fŏu-tìng]**: to deny, to negate; negation; negative

否定成績 **[fŏu-tìng ch'éng-chī]**: to negate the achievements of, to deny the achievements of

9 否則 **[fŏu-tsé]**: otherwise, or else, lest

14 否認 **[fŏu-jèn]**: to deny, to disclaim, to disavow, to repudiate

7 含沙射影 **[hán-shā shè-yĭng]**: insinuation

11 含混 **[hán-hŭn]**: indistinct, ambiguous, unclear

13 含義 **[hán-ì]**: connotation

15 含糊其詞 **[hán-hú ch'í-tz'ú]**: to talk in vague terms, to be ambiguous, to slur over a matter; uncertain, obscure, vague

吸

4 吸引 **[hsī-yĭn]**: to attract, to appeal to

吸引進 **[hsī-yĭn-chìn]**: to be drawn into

吸引力 **[hsī-yĭn-lì]**: attraction, appeal, power of attraction

6 吸血鬼 **[hsī-hsiĕh-kuĕi]**: leech, vampire, bloodsucker (during the Cultural Revolution, a term to describe anti-Mao elements)

吸收 **[hsī-shōu]**: to absorb, to draw, to admit, to be admitted

7 吸住 **[hsī-chù]**: to grip, to grip hold of, to attract

8 吸取 **[hsī-ch'ŭ]**: to absorb, to draw

12 吸乾 **[hsī-kān]**: to suck dry

告

5 告白 **[kào-pái]**: advertisement, announcement, notice

告示 **[kào-shìh]**: notification, notice, bulletin, proclamation

6 告老 **[kào-lăo]**: to retire, to pension off

7 告別[kào-piéh]: to take leave, to bid farewell

8 告知[kào-chīh]: to make known, to inform

告狀[kào-chuàng]: to sue, to prosecute, to bring an action against, to indict

9 告急[kào-chí]: to ask for help in an emergency

11 告假[kào-chià]: to ask for a leave of absence

12 告發[kào-fā]: to denounce, to accuse, to inform on someone

告訴[kào-sù]: to tell, to inform, to convey, to make known

14 告誡[kào-chièh]: to caution, to warn, to admonish, to reprimand

19 告辭[kào-tz'ú]: to take leave of, to bid farewell

呂

7 呂宋[lǚ-sùng]: Luzon (Philippines)

吧

9 吧城[pā-ch'éng]: Batavia

吞

7 呑沒[t'ūn-mò]: to swallow up, to devour, to gobble up, to embezzle

呑呑吐吐[t'ūn-t'ūn t'ŭ-t'ŭ]: to mutter and mumble, to mince words; vague, ambiguous, noncommittal

10 呑併[t'ūn-pìng]: to annex; annexation

吳

吳[wú]: Kure (Japan)

7 吳努[wú-nŭ]: U Nu (Burmese statesman and political figure)

10 吳庭艷[wú t'íng-yèn]: Ngo Dinh Diem (Vietnamese political figure)

12 吳溫貌[wú wēn mào]: U Win Maung (Burmese statesman)

— 5 Strokes —

周

5 周刊[chōu-k'ān]: weekly (i.e., periodical)

11 周旋[chōu-hsüán]: to treat politely, to be courteous to

周密，廣泛的調查[chōu-mì, kuăng-fàn te tiào-ch'á]: a comprehensive survey, a minute investigation, a careful inquiry

12 周期[chōu-ch'í]: period; periodic

周期性的[chōu-ch'í-hsìng te]: periodic, cyclical

周報[chōu-pào]: weekly

周圍[chōu-wéi]: circumference, contour, periphery

18 周轉[chōu-chuăn]: turnover

周轉資金[chōu-chuăn tzū-chīn]: revolving fund

呪

16 呪罵[chòu-mà]: to curse, to abuse, to swear at

呵

11 呵責[hō-tsé]: to abuse, to dress down, to indulge in insulting speech

和

5 和平[hó-p'íng]: peace; peaceful, pacific

和平倡議[hó-p'íng ch'àng-ì]: peace proposal, peace initiative

和平陣營[hó-p'íng chèn-yíng]: peace camp

和平獎金[hó-p'íng chiăng-chīn]: peace prize

和平建國方針 [hó-p'íng chièn-kuó fāng-chēn]: policy of peace and national construction

和平支柱[hó-p'íng chīh-chù]: mainstay of peace

和平競賽[hó-p'íng chìng-sài]: peaceful competition

和平主義[hó-p'íng chŭ-ì]: pacifism

和平中立政策 [hó-p'íng chūng-lì chèng-ts'è]: policy of peace and neutrality

和平分田[hó-p'íng fēn-t'ién]: just distribution of land

和平相處[hó-p'íng hsiāng-ch'ŭ]: to live at peace with, to live together in peace

和平協商[hó-p'íng hsiéh-shāng]: peaceful negotiations

和平宣言[hó-p'íng hsüān-yén]: Peace Manifesto

和平鴿[hó-p'íng kō]: dove of peace

和平共處[hó-p'íng kùng-ch'ŭ]: to live together peacefully; peaceful coexistence

和平共處五項原則 [hó-p'íng kùng-ch'ŭ wŭ-hsiàng yüán-tsé]: the five principles of peaceful coexistence

和平攻勢[hó-p'íng kūng-shìh]: peace offensive

和平公約[hó-p'íng kūng-yüēh]: peace treaty, peace covenant

和平過渡的辦法[hó-p'íng kuò-tù te pàn-fă]: peaceful means of transition

和平利用原子能[hó-p'íng lì-yùng yüán-tzŭ-néng]: peaceful use of atomic energy

和平民主運動 [hó-p'íng mín-chŭ yǜn-tùng]: movement of peace and democracy

和平堡壘[hó-p'íng păo-lĕi]: bulwark of peace

和平談判[hó-p'íng t'án-p'àn]: peace negotiations

和平抵抗[hó-p'íng tĭ-k'àng]: civil disobedience

和平調子[hó-p'íng tiào-tzu]: peace tune

和平演變[hó-p'íng yĕn-pièn]: peaceful evolution, peaceful transformation (during the Cultural Revolution indicated a retrogression to capitalism)

6 和好[hó-hăo]: to come to agreement; reconciled

8 和尚[hó-shàng]: Buddhist monk, bonze

和事佬[hó-shìh-lăo]: peace-maker

9 和風細雨[hó-fēng hsì-yŭ]: a gentle breeze and a light rain, in a gentle fashion

和約[hó-yüēh]: peace treaty, peace pact

12 和稀泥[hùo hsī-ní]: mixing thin mud (a slang expression of North China used during the Cultural Revolution by the "revolutionary masses" to criticize the way in which the Great Revolutionary Alliance and the Three-Way Alliance (三結合, q.v.) were being formed, with the implication that the alliances contained counter-revolutionaries and bad elements as well as revolutionaries)

13 和解[hó-chiĕh]: to settle a quarrel, to settle differences, to reconcile; conciliation, amicable settlement, settlement by mediation; conciliatory

和解精神[hó-chiĕh chīng-shén]: conciliatory spirit

和睦[hó-mù]: harmonious, amicable, amiable, friendly, cordial

14 和歌山[hó-kō-shān]: Wakayama (Japan)

15 和緩[hó-huăn]: to ease, to lessen, to relax, to soften, to tone down

和盤托出[hó-p'án t'ō-ch'ū]: to tell everything, to make a full account or confession

16 和諧[hó-hsiéh]: to agree, to live in harmony; in harmony, harmonious

17 和聲 **[hó-shēng]** : harmony

20 和議 **[hó-ì]** : peace negotiations

呼

6 呼吁 **[hū-yǜ]** : to call for, to urge, to appeal to

8 呼拉爾 **[hū-lā-ĕrh]** : Hural (Mongolia)

12 呼喊 **[hū-hǎn]** : to call, to shout, to cry out

13 呼號 **[hū-hào]** : call signal

17 呼聲 **[hū-shēng]** : voice, outcry, cry, shout

命

4 命中 **[mìng-chùng]** : to hit, to score a hit; direct hit

5 命令 **[mìng-lìng]** : command, order

命令主義 **[mìng-lìng chǔ-ì]** : authoritarianism, commandism

8 命定 **[mìng-tìng]** : to be fated to, to be doomed to

10 命脈 **[mìng-mài]** : life, pulse, the life of something

13 命運 **[mìng-yǜn]** : fate, destiny

18 命題 **[mìng-t'í]** : proposition

呢

12 呢絨 **[ní-júng]** : woolen textiles

咆

10 咆哮 **[p'áo-hsiāo]** : to bluster, to growl; bluster, growl

— 6 Strokes —

哀

8 哀的美敦書 **[āi-tì-mĕi-tūn shū]** : ultimatum

哈

哈 **[hā]** : Harbin (abbreviation of 哈爾濱)

4 哈巴羅夫斯克 **[hā-pā-ló-fū-ssū-k'ò]** : Khabarovsk

哈巴那 **[hā-pā-nà]** : Havana (Cuba)

5 哈尼 **[hā-ní]** : Hani (minority nationality)

哈瓦那 **[hā-wă-nà]** : Havana (Cuba)

哈瓦斯 **[hā-wă-ssū]** : Havas (French news service)

7 哈佛 **[hā-fó]** : Harvard (University)

哈佛爾 **[hā-fó-ĕrh]** : Le Havre

哈里曼 **[hā-lǐ-mán]** : Harriman, Averell (American statesman)

10 哈馬舍爾德 **[hā-mă-shè-ĕrh-té]** : Hammarskjold, Dag

14 哈爾科夫 **[hā-ĕrh-k'ō-fū]** : Kharkov

18 哈薩克 **[hā-sà-k'ò]** : Kazakhs (minority nationality); Kazakhstan

哄

7 哄弄 **[hŭng-nùng]** : to fool, to cheat, to swindle

11 哄動 **[hūng-tùng]** : to create a rumpus, to arouse attention, to astonish

19 哄騙 **[hŭng-p'ièn]** : to deceive, to cheat, to trick, to delude

品

14 品種 [p'ĭn-chŭng] : variety, species, kind

15 品質 [p'ĭn-chíh] : quality, character

咨

4 咨文 [tzū-wén] : an official memorandum, communication or despatch between equals

— 7 Strokes —

哲

15 哲學 [ché-hsüéh] : philosophy

哲學家 [ché-hsüéh-chiā] : philosopher

哲學思想 [ché-hsüéh ssū-hsiăng] : philosophical thinking

哲學研究所 [ché-hsüéh yén-chìu-sŏ] : Institute of Philosophy

哥

2 哥丁根 [kō-tīng-kēn] : Goettingen (Germany)

5 哥本哈根 [kō-pĕn-hā-kēn] : Copenhagen (Denmark)

10 哥倫比亞 [kō-lún-pĭ-yà] : Columbia

哥倫比亞共和國 [kō-lún-pĭ-yà kùng-hó-kuó] : Republic of Columbia

哥倫坡 [kō-lún-p'ō] : Colombo (Ceylon)

哥倫布 [kō-lún-pù] : Columbus

12 哥斯達黎加 [kō-ssū-tá lí-chiā] : Costa Rica

哥斯達黎加共和國 [kō-ssū-tá lí-chiā kùng-hó-kuó] : Republic of Costa Rica

16 哥穆爾卡 [kō-mù-ĕrh-k'ă] : Gomulka, Wladyslaw (Polish political leader)

18 哥薩克 [kō-sà-k'ò] : Cossack

哺

8 哺育 [pŭ-yǜ] : to nourish, to rear, to bring up; nourishment, rearing

哨

7 哨兵 [shào-pīng] : sentry, sentinel, guard

唆

8 唆使 [sō-shĭh] : to instigate

唆使 .... 反對 [sō-shĭh . . . făn-tùi] : to play one against the other

— 8 Strokes —

10 唱高調 [ch'àng kāo-tiào] : to talk big, to have a big mouth but nothing behind it

啓

12 啓發 [ch'ĭ-fā] : to enlighten, to inspire, to awaken, to arouse, to elicit, to prompt; enlightenment, inspiration

14 啓蒙 [ch'ĭ-méng] : enlightenment

啓蒙時期 [ch'ĭ-méng shíh-ch'í] : period of enlightenment

啓蒙運動 [ch'ĭ-méng yǜn-tùng] : enlightenment campaign

唬

8 唬事 [hŭ-shìh] : to intimidate, to frighten

商

2 商人 [shāng-jén] : merchant, businessman, trader

8 商店[shāng-tièn]: shop, store, business establishment

9 商品[shāng-p'ǐn]: commodity, goods, merchandise

商品價格[shāng-p'ǐn chià-kó]: commodity price

商品性生產[shāng-p'ǐn-hsìng shēng-ch'ǎn]: production for exchange

商品糧[shāng-p'ǐn-liáng]: commercial food grain

商品零售額[shāng-p'ǐn líng-shòu ó]: retail turnover of commodities

商品流轉[shāng-p'ǐn líu-chuǎn]: commodity turnover

商品流轉費用[shāng-p'ǐn líu-chuǎn fèi-yùng]: cost of commodity turnover, charges for commodity turnover

商品流轉額[shāng-p'ǐn lín-chuǎn ó]: volume of commodity turnover, volume of commodity circulation

商品流通[shāng-p'ǐn líu-t ūng]: commodity circulation

商品流通環節[shāng-p'ǐn líu-t'ūng huán-chiéh]: commodity circulation; transaction

商品率[shāng-p'ǐn-lü]: marketed rate, marketed proportion

商品排隊[shāng-p'ǐn p'ái-tùi]: arrangement of commodities

商品生產[shāng-p'ǐn shēng-ch'ǎn]: commodity production

商約[shāng-yüēh]: commercial treaty

10 商務專員[shāng-wù chuān-yüán]: commercial attaché

商務參贊[shāng-wù ts'ān-tsàn]: commercial counsellor

11 商船通航[shāng-ch'uán t'ūng-háng]: commercial navigation

12 商量[shāng-liáng]: to consult, to confer

13 商會[shāng-hùi]: chamber of commerce

商業[shāng-yèh]: commerce, trade, business

商業界人士[shāng-yèh-chièh jén-shìh]: commercial circles

商業部[shāng-yèh pù]: Ministry of Commerce

商業稅[shāng-yèh shùi]: business tax, tax on commerce

售

7 售完[shòu-wán]: sold out

11 售票處[shòu-p'iào-ch'ù]: box office

唾

12 唾棄[t'ò-ch'ì]: to repudiate, to cast aside, to cast off, to renounce

唯

1 唯一[wéi-ī]: sole, only, single, solitary, lone, unique, exclusive

3 唯川[wéi-ch'uān]: Duyxuyen (Vietnam)

4 唯心主義[wéi-hsīn chǔ-ì]: idealism

唯心主義者[wéi-hsīn chǔ-ì chě]: idealist

唯心論[wéi-hsīn-lùn]: idealism

6 唯成份論[wéi-ch'éng-fèn-lùn]: taking account of class origin only

唯名論[wéi-míng-lùn]: nominalism

7 唯利是圖[wéi lì shìh t'ú]: to engage solely in unscrupulous profiteering, to work exclusively for profit; profit grabbing, profit seeking

唯我獨革，唯我獨左[wéi wǒ tú-kó, wéi-wǒ tú-tsǒ]: "I alone am revolutionary, I alone am a Leftist" (during the forming of the Great Revolutionary Alliance, a phrase used by a "Chieftain" of a faction in claiming that he alone was revolutionary and leftist and that he or his faction should be considered as the nucleus of the alliance and allocated more seats on the committee)

唯我論 **[wéi-wŏ-lùn]** : solipsism

8 唯命是從 **[wéi mìng shìh ts'úng]** : to be at someone's beck and call

唯武器論 **[wéi-wŭ-ch'ì-lùn]** : the theory that weapons decide everything

唯物主義 **[wéi-wù chŭ-ì]** : materialism

唯物主義者 **[wéi-wù chŭ-ì chĕ]** : materialist

唯物論 **[wéi-wù-lùn]** : materialism; materialist (adj.)

唯物辯證法 **[wéi-wù pièn-chèng-fă]** : materialistic dialectics

9 唯美主義 **[wéi-mĕi chŭ-ì]** : the doctrine of art for art's sake

11 唯理論 **[wéi-lĭ-lùn]** : rationalism

唯唯諾諾的人 **[wĕi-wĕi nò-nò te jén]** : yes-man

20 唯覺論 **[wéi-chüéh-lùn]** : sensualism

24 唯靈論 **[wéi-líng-lùn]** : spiritualism

問

10 問候 **[wèn-hòu]** : to ask about, to send greetings, to give regards to

18 問題 **[wèn-t'í]** : question, problem, issue, question at issue, subject of inquiry

問題的關鍵 **[wèn-t'í te kuān-chièn]** : the key to a question, the key to the solution of a question

問題的實質 **[wèn-t'í te shíh-chíh]** : essence of a problem, actual point at issue

啞

8 啞的 **[yă te]** : dumb, mute

15 啞劇 **[yă-chǜ]** : pantomime, dumb show

— 9 Strokes —

喬

8 喬治敦 **[ch'iáo-chìh-tūn]** : Georgetown (British Guiana)

喝

11 喝彩 **[hò-ts'ăi]** : to applaud, to acclaim, to hail; applause, ovation, acclaim

喉

6 喉舌 **[hóu-shé]** : mouthpiece, spokesman, speaker

15 喜劇 **[hsĭ-chǜ]** : comedy

22 喜歡 **[hsĭ-huān]** : to love, to enjoy, to delight in, to be pleased with, to take pleasure in, to be fond of

15 喧嘩 **[hsüān-huā]** : noise, clamor, tumult, roar, uproar

喚

10 喚起 **[huàn-ch'ĭ]** : to arouse

喚起注意 **[huàn-ch'ĭ chù-ì]** : to call attention to, to draw attention to

喚起民衆 **[huàn-ch'ĭ mín-chùng]** : to arouse the masses

16 喚醒 **[huàn-hsĭng]** : to arouse, to excite

喀

3 喀土穆 [k'à-t'ŭ-mù] : Khartoum (Sudan)

4 喀什米爾 [k'à-shíh-mĭ-ĕrh] : Kashmir

喀巴羅夫克 [k'à-pā-ló-fū-k'ò] : Khabarovsk

5 喀布爾 [k'à-pù-ĕrh] : Kabul (Afghanistan)

8 喀拉海 [k'à-lā hăi] : Kara Sea

11 喀麥隆共和國 [k'à-mài-lúng kùng-hó-kuó] : Republic of Cameroon

喀得加得峽 [k'à-té-chiā-té hsiá] : Kattegat

12 喀鍁邦 [k'à-ch'īn pāng] : Kachin State (Burma)

喀喇蚩時報 [k'à-lă-ch'īh shíh-pào] : Times of Karachi

喀喇地 [k'à-lă-tì] : Karachi; Kurrachi

喇

14 喇嘛 [lă-ma] : lama (priest of Tibetan Buddhism)

喇嘛廟 [lă-ma-miào] : lamasery

喪

5 喪失 [sàng-shīh] : to lose

10 喪氣 [sàng-ch'ì] : downcast, dejected, depressed, melancholy, discouraged, in low spirits

20 喪鐘 [sāng-chūng] : death knell

善

5 善本 [shàn-pĕn] : rare edition

8 善於 [shàn-yű] : skilled in, proficient at, accomplished in

9 善後 [shàn-hòu] : rehabilitation, reconstruction

12 善惡 [shàn-ò] : good and evil

13 善意 [shàn-ì] : good will, good intentions; well-intentioned, well-meant

單

1 單一 [tān-ī] : simple, uncomplicated

單一化 [tān-í-huà] : simplification

單一兵種 [tān-ī pīng-chŭng] : a force of a single arm (i.e., military branch)

4 單方面的 [tān-fāng-mièn te] : one-sided, unilateral

7 單利息 [tān-lì-hsí] : simple interest

單位 [tān-wèi] : unit

10 單純 [tān-ch'ún] : pure, unmixed, unadulterated, simple, sole

單純技術觀點 [tān-ch'ún chì-shù kuān-tiĕn] : a purely technical viewpoint (i.e., one that does not take politics into consideration)

單純軍事觀點 [tān-ch'ún chūn-shìh kuān-tiĕn] : a purely military viewpoint

單純任務觀點 [tān-ch'ún jèn-wù kuān-tiĕn] : a purely task-oriented viewpoint, a purely job-oriented viewpoint

單純業務觀點 [tān-ch'ún yèh-wù kuān-tiĕn] : a purely business viewpoint

13 單幹 [tān-kàn] : to work on one's own; to do something single handedly or by oneself alone

單幹風 [tān-kàn-fēng] : spirit of independence, the spirit of individual enterprise (a target of the Socialist Education movement of 1962–1963, it includes household contract production, abstaining from collective work, doing odd jobs outside of the commune, peddling, reclaiming unused land for private use, etc.)

單幹戶[tān-kàn-hù]: independent farmer, independent household

單幹農戶[tān-kàn núng-hù]: individual peasant household

單幹包[tān-kàn-pāo]: individual enterprise contracting; to enter into contract for household contract production (*See* 包產到戶)

單幹思想[tān-kàn ssū-hsiăng]: independent thought, the concept of independence, the concept of going it alone

15 單價[tān-chià]: list price, unit price

單調[tān-tiào]: monotonous

16 單獨[tān-tú]: lone, sole, individual, single, separate, singlehanded, unique

— 10 Strokes —

8 嗔怪[ch'ēn-kuài]: to rebuke, to reprimand, to blame

嗜

6 嗜好[shìh-hào]: delight, taste, appetite, bent, liking, love for, hobby, weakness for; to be fond of

嗜血的[shìh-hsiěh te]: bloodthirsty

— 11 Strokes —

13 嘗試[ch'áng-shìh]: to attempt, to make a try

嘉

11 嘉許[chiā-hsŭ]: to admire, to praise, to give recognition

14 嘉獎[chiā-chiăng]: to praise, to reward

嘉賓[chiā-pīn]: an honored guest

— 12 Strokes —

嘲

7 嘲弄[ch'áo-nùng]: to mock at; mockery, joke

10 嘲笑[ch'áo-hsiào]: to ridicule, to scoff at; jeer

嘰

8 嘰咕[chī-kū]: to grumble, to mumble

嘩

12 嘩然[huá-ján]: clamorously, noisily; clamor, noisy laughter

嘎

7 嘎里古達[kā-lĭ-kŭ-tá]: Calcutta (India)

嘴

3 嘴上說說[tsŭi-shàng shuō-shuō]: to pay lip service

4 嘴巴子[tsŭi-pà-tzu]: cheeks, a blow on the face

7 嘴快心直[tsŭi-k'uài hsīn-chíh]: plain spoken and straight forward

14 嘴緊[tsŭi-chĭn]: tight-lipped

17 嘴臉[tsŭi-liĕn]: face

— 13 Strokes —

器

7 器材[ch'ì-ts'ái]: equipment, materials and equipment

器材場[ch'ì-ts'ái-ch'ăng] : depot

器材儲備[ch'ì-ts'ái ch'ú-pèi] : stock of equipment, stockpiling of equipment and materials

噶

10 噶倫堡[kā-lún-pǎo] : Kalimpong

13 噶廈[kā-shà] : Kashag (an organ of the Tibetan government)

噴

10 噴氣發動機[p'ēn-ch'ì fā-tùng-chī] : jet engine

噴氣轟炸機[p'ēn-ch'ì hūng-chà-chī] : jet bomber

噴氣式戰鬥機 [p'ēn-ch'ì-shìh chàn-tòu-chī] : jet fighter

噴氣式直升飛機[p'ēn-ch'ì-shìh chíh-shēng fēi-chī] : jet helicopter

噴氣式飛機[p'ēn-ch'ì-shìh fēi-chī] : jet airplane

18 噴霧器[p'ēn-wù-ch'ì] : sprayer, atomizer

噸

4 噸公里[tūn kūng-lǐ] : ton-kilometers

7 噸位[tūn-wèi] : tonnage

10 噸浬[tūn-lǐ] : ton-nautical miles

— 14 Strokes —

嚇

10 嚇殺[hsià-shā] : to be killed by fright, to be frightened to death

嚇倒[hsià-tǎo] : to be intimidated, to be overwhelmed, to be deterred, to be daunted

11 嚇唬 [hsià-hǔ] : to frighten, to scare, to alarm, to terrify, to startle, to intimidate, to cow

12 嚇跑 [hsià-p'ǎo] : to frighten away, to be frightened off, to run away in fear

— 17 Strokes —

嚴 [yén] : severe, stern

5 嚴正[yén-chèng] : solemn, stern, severe, serious, grave

9 嚴重[yén-chùng] : serious, severe, stern, crucial, critical, grave

10 嚴格[yén-kó] : strictness, exactness; strict, exact, scrupulous

11 嚴密[yén-mì] : strict, close, compact

13 嚴禁逼供信[yén-chìn pī-kūng-hsìn] : it is strictly forbidden to extort confessions and accept such confessions (one of Mao's "latest instructions" as quoted by a People's Daily editorial of January 1, 1969)

14 嚴酷[yén-k'ù] : stern, ruthless, pitiless, merciless, harsh

嚴肅[yén-sù] : serious, solemn, seriousness, solemnity (also two of the eight characters of the 三八作風, q.v.)

嚴肅性[yén-sù-hsìng] : strictness, solemnity

15 嚴厲[yén-lì] : harsh, severe, rigid, stern, stringent, inflexible, relentless

— 18 Strokes —

囂

11 囂張[hsiāo-chāng] : to rage, to storm about; blatant, clamorous

— 21 Strokes —

囑

8 囑咐[chǔ-fù] : to enjoin, to order, to tell to do

— RADICAL 囗 31 —

— 2 Strokes —

13 囚禁 **[ch'íu-chìn]**: to imprison, to put in prison; imprisonment

四

3 四大 **[ssù-tà]**: four greats (i.e., great contending, great blooming, big character posters, and great debate–the four methods for carrying out "struggle by reasoning")

四大家族 **[ssù tà chiā-tsú]**: the four big families (i.e., of Chiang Kai-shek, T.V. Soong, H. H. Kung, and the brothers Ch'en Li-fu and Ch'en Kuo-fu

四大觀點 **[ssù tà kuān-tiĕn]**: the four great viewpoints (i.e., class viewpoint, labor viewpoint, mass viewpoint, viewpoint of dialectical materialism)

四大自由 **[ssù-tà tzù-yú]**: four great freedoms (i.e., the freedom to engage in usury, to hire labor, to sell land, and to run private enterprises–a slogan alleged to have been advanced by Liu Shao-ch'i during the land reform period)

四大文件 **[ssù tà wén-chièn]**: the Four Great Documents (by Mao: 1) Talks at the Yenan Forum on Literature and Art [May 1942]; 2) On the Correct Handling of Contradictions Among the People [February 1957]; 3) speech at the national CCP Propaganda Work Conference [March 1957]; 4) On the New Democracy [January 1940])

4 四分五裂 **[ssù-fēn wŭ-lièh]**: to disintegrate, to go to pieces, to be split up; disintegration, split, disunity; divided and at odds

四化 **[ssù-huà]**: 1. the four "-izations" (i.e., organization militarized, work martialized, life collectivized, and management democratized); 2. the four transformations (in agriculture: mechanization 機械化, electrification 電氣化, irrigation 水利化, and chemicalization 化學化)

四不 **[ssù-pù]**: the four do-nots (in order to achieve the "Great Revolutionary Alliance," the people were asked not to say or do anything, hold any meeting, or put out any slogan or big character poster that would be unfavorable to the formation of the "Great Revolutionary Alliance")

6 四好 **[ssù-hăo]**: the four goods (i.e., good in political and ideological work, good in carrying out "three-good" (三好, q.v.) activities, good in perfecting organizational life, and good in maintaining ties with the masses)

四好連隊 **[ssù-hăo lién-tùi]**: the four-good company (a company of the People's Liberation Army that was good in the 四好)

四同 **[ssù-t'úng]**: the four togethers (to eat, live, work, and consult together)

四同幹部 **[ssù-t'úng kàn-pù]**: four together cadre (a cadre who eats, lives, works, and consults with the masses)

四快一慢戰法 **[ssù-k'uài í-màn chàn-fă]**: the four fast, one slow tactic (i.e., fast in approaching and pursuing the enemy, in exploiting success in battle, and in preparing to encircle the enemy; slow in the general attack, which is prepared deliberately and carefully)

8 四周 **[ssù-chōu]**: in the vicinity of, around, all round

四注意 **[ssù chù-ì]**: the four pay attentions (i.e., prevent children from wasting food, use miscellaneous cereals in place of rice as a staple food, give up feasts, and learn the correct technique of rice husking)

四固定 **[ssù kù-tìng]**: the four fixed (the fixed use of manpower, land, farm tools, and draft animals, which are assigned to the production teams for their permanent use)

9 四面包抄法 **[ssù-mièn pāo-ch'āo fă]**: the technique of total encirclement (a four-sided tactical technique to envelop the enemy)

10 四害 **[ssù-hài]**: the four pests (i.e., flies, mosquitoes, rats, and sparrows, which were

the object of a campaign begun in 1956; sparrows were later replaced by bedbugs)

四個一切 **[ssù-ko í-ch'ièh]**: the four everythings (i.e., to think of Chairman Mao in everything, to obey Chairman Mao in everything, to follow closely Chairman Mao in everything, and everything for Chairman Mao)

四個一樣 **[ssù-kò í-yàng]**: the four thesames (i.e., everyone is to work hard and efficiently day or night, in good or bad weather, with or without supervision, and regardless of whether results are to be examined)

四個第一 **[ssù-kò tì-ī]**: the four firsts (enunciated by Lin Piao in 1960: the human factor first, political work first, ideological work first, and living ideas first)

四員 **[ssù-yüán]**: the four personnel: the four leading administrative personnel in a production team (**See** 七員)

11 四現代化 **[ssù hsièn-tài-huà]**: the four modernizations (i.e., in agriculture, industry, national defense, and science and technology)

四國 **[ssù-kuó]**: Shikoku (Japan)

四組一隊戰法 **[ssù-tsǔ í-tùi chàn-fǎ]**: the four elements in one unit tactic (a tactical movement involving a special combat team consisting of a firepower element, a demolition element, assault infantry, and supporting elements)

12 四淸運動 **[ssù-ch'īng yǜn-tùng]**: the Four Cleanings Campaign (in which masses and lower level cadres were called upon to give a clean account of their political and ideological stand, family background, and financial situation; it is believed to have originated from a report by Chou En-lai in December 1964 to the Third National People's Congress)

13 四新 **[ssù-hsīn]**: the four news (i.e., of the Cultural Revolution: new thought 新思想, new culture 新文化, new customs 新風俗, and new habits 新習慣)

15 四增 **[ssù-tsēng]**: the four increases (in educational work: in basic construction costs, in the burden on the masses, in the size of the school's administrative staff, and in operating costs)

18 四舊 **[ssù-chìu]**: the four olds (i.e., the targets of the Red Guard during the Cultural Revolution: old thought 舊思想, old culture 舊文化, old customs 舊風俗, and old habits 舊習慣)

19 四類份子 **[ssù-lèi fèn-tzu]**: the four bad elements, the four categories of bad elements (i.e., landlords, rich peasants, counterrevolutionaries, and local bad elements such as thieves and criminals)

— 3 Strokes —

回 **[húi]**: Moslems

4 回升 **[húi-shēng]**: to improve, to pick up, to recover; pickup

回手 **[húi-shǒu]**: to counter, to retaliate

5 回民 **[húi-mín]**: the Moslem nationality

回生 **[húi-shēng]**: to return to life; regeneration, feed-back

6 回合 **[húi-hó]**: encounter, round (as in boxing)

回扣 **[húi-k'òu]**: kickback, rebate

回收 **[húi-shōu]**: to collect

8 回到 **[húi-tào]**: to go back to, to return to

9 回紇 **[húi-hó]**: Uighurs

回拜 **[húi-pài]**: to make a return visit

回音 **[húi-yīn]**: echo, response, reply

11 回教 **[húi-chiào]**: Islam

回教堂 **[húi-chiào-t'áng]**: mosque

回教徒 **[húi-chiào-t'ú]**: Moslem

回執 **[húi-chíh]**: receipt

回族 **[húi-tsú]**: the Hui people (a minority nationality)

12 回報 **[húi-pào]**: to bring a reply, to revenge oneself

回答 **[húi-tá]**: to reply, to answer, to respond; response, answer

13 回敬 **[húi-chìng]**: to reciprocate the courtesy, to return the courtesy

回想 **[húi-hsiǎng]**: to recall, to remember, to remind, to call to mind, to review, to look back upon

16 回憶錄 **[húi-ì-lù]**: memoirs

回憶對比 **[húi-ì tùi-pǐ]**: to recollect and to contrast (i.e., to recollect past suffering and to contrast it with the present happiness)

回曆 **[húi-lì]**: Islamic calendar

回頭 **[húi-t′óu]**: to turn the head, to repent, to reform

回頭是岸 **[húi-t′óu shìh àn]**: to repent and find salvation, to turn from evil ways

17 回擊 **[húi-chī]**: to resist, to repel, to repulse; counterattack, rebuff

回聲 **[húi-shēng]**: to resound; echo, reverberation, resonance

18 回歸線 **[húi-kuēi hsièn]**: Tropic of Cancer

21 回鶻 **[húi-hú]**: Uighur

因

4 因公 **[yīn-kūng]**: on duty, in line of duty, on public business, on government service

6 因地制宜 **[yīn-tì chìh-í]**: adaptation to local conditions, to adapt working methods to local conditions, in a manner suitable to a particular case

因此 **[yīn-tz′ŭ]**: therefore, thus, accordingly, for this reason, consequently

8 因果 **[yīn-kuŏ]**: cause and effect

因果性 **[yīn-kuŏ-hsìng]**: causality

因果觀 **[yīn-kuŏ-kuān]**: causal point of view

因果論 **[yīn-kuŏ-lùn]**: theory of causation

因果論者 **[yīn-kuŏ-lùn-chě]**: champion of the theory of causation

因果報應 **[yīn-kuŏ pào-yìng]**: karma, retributive justice

10 因時制宜 **[yīn-shíh chìh-í]**: in a manner suitable to a particular time

因素 **[yīn-sù]**: factor, element

12 因循 **[yīn-hsün]**: to follow (the course of least resistance); meek, mild, conservative, opposed to change, perfunctory

— 4 Strokes —

6 困守 **[k′ùn-shŏu]**: to be hemmed in, beseiged, surrounded

9 困苦 **[k′ùn-k′ŭ]**: tribulation, distress; distressing

12 困惑 **[k′ùn-huò]**: to trouble, to bewilder, to perplex, to puzzle, to be vexed at; troublesome

19 困難 **[k′ùn-nán]**: trouble, difficulty, embarrassment; to be embarrassed, to be harassed, to be in difficult straits

16 囤積 **[t′ún-chī]**: to store up, to buy up, to hoard up

囤積居奇 **[t′ún-chī chü-ch′í]**: hoarding and speculation

— 5 Strokes —

6 固守 **[kù-shŏu]**: to keep to, to maintain, to hold one's ground; entrenchment

固有 **[kù-yŭ]**: intrinsic, inherent, innate, inborn

8 固定 **[kù-tìng]**: to fix, to fasten, to attach; fixed, immovable, firm, stationary

固定設備 **[kù-tìng shè-pèi]**: fixed equipment

固定資產 **[kù-tìng tzū-ch'ǎn]**: fixed assets

11 固執 **[kù-chíh]**: to cling to; stubborn, obstinate, persistent

23 固體 **[kù-t'ǐ]**: solid body, solid

固體燃料 **[kù-t'ǐ ján-liào]**: solid fuel

固體作燃料的 **[kù-t'ǐ tsò ján-liào te]**: solid-fueled

— 8 Strokes —

3 圈子 **[ch'üān-tzu]**: circle, group

10 圈套 **[ch'üān-t'ào]**: trap, plot, pitfall, snare, net

4 國父 **[kuó-fù]**: father of his country, founder of a country; Sun Yat-sen (1866–1925)

國內 **[kuó-nèi]**: domestic, local, home, internal

國內戰爭 **[kuó-nèi chàn-chēng]**: civil war

國內和平協定 **[kuó-nèi hó-p'íng hsiéh-tìng]**: Agreement on Internal Peace

國內外 **[kuó-nèi-wài]**: at home and abroad, domestic and foreign

國手 **[kuó-shǒu]**: an expert, a national champion

國王 **[kuó-wáng]**: king, shah (Iran), rajah (India), caliph (Arabia)

5 國民經濟 **[kuó-mín chīng-chì]**: national economy

國民經濟各部門 **[kuó-mín chīng-chì kò pù-mén]**: the various sectors of the national economy

國民議會 **[kuó-mín ì-hùi]**: National Assembly (for most countries); Sjem (Poland)

國民收入 **[kuó-mín shōu-jù]**: national income

國民大會 **[kuó-mín tà-hùi]**: National Assembly (Nationalist China)

國外貿易部 **[kuó-wài mào-ì pù]**: Ministry of Foreign Trade

6 國交 **[kuó-chiāo]**: diplomatic relations

國有 **[kuó-yǔ]**: state-owned

國有化 **[kuó-yǔ-huà]**: to nationalize; nationalization

國有農場部 **[kuó-yǔ núng-ch'ǎng pù]**: Ministry of State Farms

7 國防 **[kuó-fáng]**: national defense

國防軍 **[kuó-fáng-chün]**: national defense army

國防部 **[kuó-fáng-pù]**: Ministry of National Defense (China); Department of Defense

國防委員會 **[kuó-fáng wěi-yüán-hùi]**: National Defense Commission

國防文學 **[kuó-fáng wén-hsüéh]**: National Defense Literature (a slogan coined by Chou Yang in the 1930s and labeled in the mid-1960s as a "capitalist slogan")

8 國法 **[kuó-fǎ]**: national law

國事訪問 **[kuó-shìh fǎng-wèn]**: state visit

9 國計民生 **[kuó-chì mín-shēng]**: national economy and people's livelihood

國界 **[kuó-chièh]**: national boundary

10 國家 **[kuó-chiā]**: state, nation, country

國家安全部 **[kuó-chiā ān-ch'üán pù]**: Ministry of State Security

國家機器 **[kuó-chiā chī-ch'ì]**: state apparatus, state machinery

國家計劃委員會 **[kuó-chiā chì-huà wĕi-yüán-hùi]** : State Planning Commission

國家機構 **[kuó-chiā chī-kòu]** : government organ

國家機關 **[kuó-chiā chī-kuān]** : state organ, state apparatus

國家機關工作人員 **[kuó-chiā chī-kuān kūng-tsò jén-yüán]** : state functionary, personnel of state organs, members of state administration, civil service personnel

國家計量局 **[kuó-chiā chì-liáng chǘ]** : National Bureau of Weights and Measures

國家機密 **[kuó-chiā chī-mì]** : state secrets

國家基本建設委員會 **[kuó-chiā chī-pĕn chièn-shè wĕi-yüán-hùi]** : State Capital Construction Commission

國家建築委員會 **[kuó-chiā chièn-chú wĕi-yüán-hùi]** : State Committee for Building

國家建設委員會 **[kuó-chiā chièn-shè wĕi-yüán-hùi]** : State Construction Commission

國家制度 **[kuó-chiā chìh-tù]** : state institutions, state system

國家津貼 **[kuó-chiā chīn-tiēh]** : state subsidies

國家經濟委員會 **[kuó-chiā chīng-chì wĕi-yüán-hùi]** : State Economic Commission

國家主權 **[kuó-chiā chŭ-ch'üán]** : state sovereignty

國家儲備金 **[kuó-chiā ch'ú-pèi-chīn]** : state reserve funds

國家權力 **[kuó-chiā ch'üán-lì]** : state power, state sovereignty

國家決算 **[kuó-chiā chüéh-suàn]** : final account of state revenue and expenditure, final state budget

國家消亡 **[kuó-chiā hsiāo-wáng]** : withering away of the state apparatus

國家管制部 **[kuó-chiā kuăn-chìh pù]** : Ministry of State Control

國家壟斷資本主義 **[kuó-chiā lŭng-tuàn tzū-pĕn chŭ-ì]** : state-monopoly capitalism

國家保險部 **[kuó-chiā păo-hsiĕn pù]** : Ministry of State Insurance

國家報表 **[kuó-chiā pào-piăo]** : overall state reporting

國家設計委員會 **[kuó-chiā shè-chì wĕi-yüán-hùi]** : State Planning Commission

國家收入 **[kuó-chiā shōu-jù]** : state revenue

國家收購機關 **[kuó-chiā shōu-kòu chī-kuān]** : state purchasing organs

國家大事 **[kuó-chiā tà-shìh]** : the affairs of the nation, affairs of state

國家檔案局 **[kuó-chiā tàng-àn chǘ]** : Bureau of State Archives

國家投資 **[kuó-chiā t'óu-tzū]** : state investment

國家財政撥款 **[kuó-chiā ts'ái-chèng pō-k'uăn]** : state financial allocations

國家測繪總局 **[kuó-chiā ts'è-hùi tsŭng-chǘ]** : State Bureau of Surveying and Cartography

國家統計局 **[kuó-chiā t'ŭng-chì chǘ]** : State Statistical Bureau

國家統計委員會 **[kuó-chiā t'ŭng-chì wĕi-yüán-hùi]** : Council for State Statistical Affairs (USSR)

國家資本主義 **[kuó-chiā tzū-pĕn chŭ-ì]** : state capitalism

國家豫算 **[kuó-chiā yǜ-suàn]** : state budget, national budget

國家豫算收入 **[kuó-chiā yǜ-suàn shōu-jù]** : budgetary revenue

國恥 **[kuó-ch'ĭh]** : national disgrace

國庫 **[kuó-k'ù]** : national treasury, state treasury

國庫部 **[kuó-k'ù pù]** : Ministry of Treasury

國庫預算部 **[kuó-k'ù yǜ-suàn pù]** : Ministry of the Treasury and Budget

國書[kuó-shū]: credentials, letter of credence

國宴[kuó-yèn]: state dinner

國產[kuó-ch'ǎn]: domestic products, local products

11 國情咨文[kuó-ch'íng tzū-wén]: State of the Union Message (U.S.A.)

國貨[kuó-huò]: domestic products, local products

國務卿[kuó-wù-ch'īng]: Secretary of State (U.S.A.)

國務院[kuó-wù-yüàn]: State Council

國務院機關事務管理局[kuó-wù-yüàn chī-kuān shìh-wù kuǎn-lǐ-chǘ]: Agency Affairs Control Bureau of the State Council

國務院專家工作局[kuó-wù-yüàn chuān-chiā kūng-tsò chǘ]: Specialists Work Bureau of the State Council

國務院法制局[kuó-wù-yüàn fǎ-chìh chǘ]: Law Bureau of the State Council

國務院人事局[kuó-wù-yüàn jén-shìh chǘ]: Personnel Bureau of the State Council

國務院祕書廳[kuó-wù-yüàn mì-shū-t'īng]: Secretariate of the State Council

國務院參事室[kuó-wù-yüàn ts'ān-shìh shìh]: Office of Councilors of the State Council

國務院宗教事務局[kuó-wù-yüàn tsūng-chiào shìh-wù chǘ]: Religious Affairs Bureau of the State Council

國務院外國專家局[kuó-wù-yüàn wài-kuó chuān-chiā chǘ]: Bureau of Foreign Experts of the State Council

12 國都[kuó-tū]: national capital

13 國會[kuó-hùi]: Congress (U.S.A.); National Diet (Japan); National Assembly (Democratic Republic of Vietnam)

國葬[kuó-tsàng]: state funeral

14 國際[kuó-chì]: international

國際奧林匹克委員會[kuó-chì ào-lín-p'ĭ-k'ò wěi-yüán-hùi]: International Olympic Committee (IOC)

國際爭端[kuó-chì chēng-tuān]: international dispute

國際機構[kuó-chì chī-kòu]: international agency or organ

國際金融公司[kuó-chì chīn-júng kūng-ssū]: International Finance Corporation (IFC)

國際主義[kuó-chì chǔ-ì]: internationalism

國際局勢[kuó-chì chǘ-shìh]: international situation

國際準則[kuó-chì chǔn-tsé]: standards of international law

國際法[kuó-chì fǎ]: international law

國際法協會[kuó-chì fǎ hsiéh-hùi]: International Law Association (ILA)

國際法委員會[kuó-chì fǎ wěi-yüán-hùi]: International Law Commission (United Nations)

國際法院[kuó-chì fǎ-yüàn]: International Court of Justice

國際復興建設銀行[kuó-chì fù-hsìng chièn-shè yín-háng]: International Bank for Reconstruction and Development

國際航空運輸協會[kuó-chì háng-k'ūng yǜn-shū hsiéh-hùi]: International Air Transport Association (IATA)

國際和平獎金[kuó-chì hó-p'íng chiǎng-chīn]: international peace prize

國際合作[kuó-chì hó-tsò]: cooperation among nations, international cooperation

國際合作社聯盟[kuó-chì hó-tsò-shè lién-méng]: International Cooperative Alliance (ICA)

國際新聞[kuó-chì hsīn-wén]: international news, international news coverage

國際新聞工作者協會[kuó-chì hsīn-wén kūng-tsò-chě hsiéh-hùi]: International

Organization of Journalists (IOJ)

國際新聞社[kuó-chì hsīn-wén-shè]: International News Service (INS)

國際化[kuó-chì-huà]: to internationalize; internationalization

國際學生聯合會[kuó-chì hsüéh-shēng lién-hó-hùi]: International Union of Students (IUS)

國際紅十字大會[kuó-chì húng-shíh-tzù tà-hùi]: International Red Cross Conference

國際貨幣基金[kuó-chì huò-pì chī-chīn]: International Monetary Fund

國際人權公約[kuó-chì jén-ch'üán kūng-yüēh]: International Agreement on Human Rights

國際歌[kuó-chì-kō]: the Internationale

國際管制[kuó-chì kuǎn-chìh]: international control

國際關係[kuó-chì kuān-hsì]: international relations

國際關係研究所[kuó-chì kuān-hsì yén-chìu-sǒ]: Institute of International Relations

國際慣例[kuó-chì kuàn-lì]: international practice, international convention

國際廣播組織[kuó-chì kuǎng-pō tsǔ-chīh]: International Broadcasting Organization (IBO)

國際共管[kuó-chì kùng-kuǎn]: condominium

國際勞工組織[kuó-chì láo-kūng tsǔ-chīh]: International Labor Organization (ILO)

國際勞動節[kuó-chì láo-tùng chiéh]: International Labor Day, Labor Day, May Day

國際禮節[kuó-chì lǐ-chiéh]: international convention, international propriety, comity of nations

國際聯絡部[kuó-chì lién-lò pù]: International Liaison Department

國際貿易[kuó-chì mào-ì]: international trade, world trade

國際貿易促進會[kuó-chì mào-ì ts'ù-chìn-hùi]: Association for the Promotion of International Trade

國際民主婦女聯合會[kuó-chì mín-chǔ fù-nǚ lién-hó-hùi]: Women's International Democratic Federation

國際民用航空組織[kuó-chì mín-yùng háng-k'ūng tsǔ-chīh]: International Civil Aviation Organization (ICA0)

國際商會[kuó-chì shāng-hùi]: International Chamber of Commerce (ICC)

國際事務[kuó-chì shìh-wù]: international affairs or matters

國際書店[kuó-chì shū-tièn]: Guozi Shudian (International Bookstore)

國際水平[kuó-chì shǔi-p'íng]: world level, the world standard

國際地球物理年[kuó-chì tì-ch'íu wù-lǐ-nién]: International Geophysical Year

國際地位[kuó-chì tì-wèi]: international position, international prestige

國際電訊同盟[kuó-chi tièn-hsün t'úng-méng]: International Telecommunication Union (ITU)

國際托管制度[kuó-chì t'ō-kuǎn chìh-tù]: international trusteeship system

國際威信[kuó-chì wēi-hsìn]: international prestige

國際舞台[kuó-chì wǔ-t'ái]: the international scene, the international stage

國際原子能機構[kuó-chì yüán-tzǔ-néng chī-kòu]: International Atomic Energy Agency

國旗[kuó-ch'í]: national flag

國境[kuó-chìng]: national boundary, frontier

國歌[kuó-kō]: national anthem

國粹 [kuó-ts'ùi]: national essence, national heritage

國粹主義 [kuó-ts'ùi chŭ-ì]: the doctrine of national purity, the doctrine that "everything Chinese is best"

國語 [kuó-yŭ]: the national language

15 國慶節 [kuó-ch'ìng chiéh]: National Day

國慶日 [kuó-ch'ìng jìh]: National Day (1. October 1, the anniversary of the founding of the People's Republic of China in 1949; 2. October 10, the anniversary of the Wuchang Uprising in 1912, celebrated in the Republic of China)

國慶觀禮 [kuó-ch'ìng kuān-lĭ]: review of the National Day parade

國賓 [kuó-pīn]: state guest

17 國徽 [kuó-hūi]: state emblem, national emblem, national insignia

國營 [kuó-yíng]: state-operated

國營企業 [kuó-yíng ch'ì-yèh]: state enterprise, state-owned enterprise

國營經濟 [kuó-yíng chīng-chì]: state operated economy, state economy

國營農場 [kuó-yíng núng-ch'ăng]: state farm

國營商業部門 [kuó-yíng shāng-yèh pù-mén]: state trading departments

19 國難 [kuó-nàn]: national disaster

20 國籍 [kuó-chí]: nationality

23 國體 [kuó-t'ĭ]: form of government, national structure

— 9 Strokes —

7 圍攻 [wéi-kūng]: to besiege; siege, encirclement campaign

12 圍堰 [wéi-yèn]: cofferdam

13 圍剿 [wéi-chiăo]: encirclement and suppression

18 圍繞 [wéi-jào]: to surround, to encircle, to beset, to confine, to circumscribe

— 10 Strokes —

圓 [yüán]: Yuan (unit of Chinese currency); Yen (unit of Japanese currency); dollar

4 圓心 [yüán-hsīn]: center of a circle

7 圓形 [yüán-hsíng]: circle, circular shape, round shape; circular

圓形劇場 [yüán-hsíng chù-ch'ăng]: amphitheater

9 圓柱 [yüán-chù]: round column, pillar

10 圓桌 [yüán-chō]: Round Table (British periodical)

圓桌會議 [yüán-chō hùi-ì]: round-table conference

12 圓圈 [yüán-ch'üān]: circle, ring, hoop, loop

14 圓滿 [yüán-măn]: complete, perfect, absolute, consummate

圓滿結束 [yüán-măn chiéh-shù]: to round off, to conclude satisfactorily

15 圓潤 [yüán-jùn]: smooth, suave, polished

圓熟 [yüán-shóu]: mature, mellow, ripe, deft, adroit, practiced

19 園藝 [yüán-ì]: gardening, horticulture

園藝學 [yüán-ì-hsüéh]: horticulture

— 11 Strokes —

8 圖表 **[t'ú-piăo]**: chart, illustration, blue print, graph, diagram; graphic

10 圖案 **[t'ú-àn]**: design, pattern

11 圖淸靜 **[t'ú ch'īng-chìng]**: to want to avoid complications

團 **[t'uán]**: regiment, corps; Youth Corps (abbreviation of 青年團)

12 團結 **[t'uán-chiéh]**: to unite, to rally; unity, solidarity (also two of the eight characters of the 三八作風, q.v.)

團結會 **[t'uán-chiéh-hùi]**: unification meeting (for the purpose of uniting the cadres and the peasants)

團結一致 **[t'uán-chiéh í-chìh]**: to unite as one; monolithic solidarity, monolithic unity

團結報 **[t'uán-chiéh pào]**: L'Unità (Italian daily newspaper)

團結、批評、團結 **[t'uán-chiéh-p'ī-p'íng-t'uán-chiéh]**: unity-criticism-unity (a method of conducting ideological struggles within the Party: the criticism of dissidents from the standpoint of a desire for unity)

團結、鬥爭、團結 **[t'uán-chiéh-tòu-chēng-t'uán-chiéh]**: unity-struggle-unity (i.e., in reference to Party policy toward its opponents)

23 團體 **[t'uán-t'ĭ]**: body, public body, group, organization

— RADICAL 土 32 —

土

土 **[t'ŭ]**: Monguors (minority nationality); "soil improvement" (one of the eight characters of the 八字憲法, q.v.)

4 土方 **[t'ŭ-fāng]**: earthwork

土化肥 **[t'ŭ-huà-féi]**: indigenous chemical fertilizer, chemical fertilizer produced by indigenous methods

土木建築研究所 **[t'ŭ-mù chièn-chú yén-chìu-sŏ]**: Institute of Civil and Architectural Engineering

土木工程 **[t'ŭ-mù kūng-ch'éng]**: civil engineering

5 土包子 **[t'ŭ-pāo-tzu]**: boor, bumpkin, clodhopper, hick, rube

土布 **[t'ŭ-pù]**: native cloth

土生的 **[t'ŭ-shēng te]**: indigenous, native, innate

土瓦 **[t'ŭ-wă]**: Tavoy (Burma)

6 土耳其 **[t'ŭ-ĕrh-ch'í]**: Turkey

土耳其共和國 **[t'ŭ-ĕrh-ch'í kùng-hó-kuó]**: Republic of Turkey

土地證 **[t'ŭ-tì-chèng]**: land certificate

土地法 **[t'ŭ-tì-fă]**: land law

土地小私有者 **[t'ŭ-tì hsiăo-ssū-yŭ chĕ]**: small holder of land

土地入股 **[t'ŭ-tì jù-kŭ]**: the pooling of land in the form of shares

土地改革 **[t'ŭ-tì kăi-kó]**: land reform, agrarian reform

土地改革法 **[t'ŭ-tì kăi-kó fă]**: Land Reform Law

土地革命 **[t'ŭ-tì kó-mìng]**: agrarian revolution

土地報酬 **[t'ŭ-tì pào-ch'óu]**: dividends on land shares

土地所有制 **[t'ŭ-tì sŏ-yŭ-chìh]**: system of land ownership

土地私有制 [t'ŭ-tì ssū-yŭ-chìh]: system of private ownership of land

7 土改 [t'ŭ-kăi]: land reform (abbreviation of 土地改革)

8 土法 [t'ŭ-fă]: native ways, old methods

9 土星 [t'ŭ-hsīng]: Saturn

土洋結合 [t'ŭ-yáng chiéh-hó]: integration of indigenous and foreign ways (i.e., as in industry)

土洋並舉 [t'ŭ-yáng pìng-chŭ]: using both indigenous and foreign ways (a slogan from the Great Leap Forward)

10 土匪 [t'ŭ-fĕi]: local bandit, brigand, outlaw, highwayman

土高爐 [t'ŭ-kāo-lú]: indigenous blast furnaces

土特產 [t'ŭ-t'è-ch'ăn]: native special products, local special products (i.e., the well-known or special products of a particular locality)

11 土產 [t'ŭ-ch'ăn]: native products, local products

13 土話 [t'ŭ-huà]: dialect

14 土爾扈特 [t'ŭ-ĕrh-hù-t'è]: Torguts (minority nationality)

土豪 [t'ŭ-háo]: rural despot, local bully, village boss

土豪劣紳 [t'ŭ-háo lièh-shēn]: local bullies and bad gentry

16 土辦法 [t'ŭ-pàn-fă]: indigenous methods, native methods

20 土壤 [t'ŭ-jăng]: soil

土壤肥料研究所 [t'ŭ-jăng féi-liào yén-chìu-sŏ]: Soil and Fertilizer Institute

土壤改良 [t'ŭ-jăng kăi-liáng]: soil improvement

土壤流失 [t'ŭ-jăng líu-shīh]: soil erosion

土壤研究所 [t'ŭ-jăng yén-chìu-sŏ]: Institute of Pedology

21 土鐵 [t'ŭ-t'ieh]: pig iron produced by indigenous methods

— 3 Strokes —

圭

8 圭亞那 [kuēi-yà-nà]: Guiana

地

地 [tì]: land, earth, soil, ground, place, position; landlord (abbreviation of 地主, one of the 四類份子, q.v.)

2 地力 [tì-lì]: productivity of the soil

3 地下 [tì-hsià]: underground, illegal, clandestine, secret

地下工作 [tì-hsià kūng-tsò]: underground work, illegal work

地下黨 [tì-hsià tăng]: underground party, illegal party

地下資源 [tì-hsià tzū-yüán]: underground resources, hidden resources

地下鐵道 [tì-hsià t'iĕh-tào]: underground railroad, subway

4 地中海 [tì-chūng hăi]: Mediterranean Sea

地方 [tì-fāng]: region, area, locality, point; local

地方主義 [tì-fāng chŭ-ì]: localism

地方分權 [tì-fāng fēn-ch'üán]: decentralization

地方工業 [tì-fāng kūng-yèh]: local industry

地方工業部 [tì-fāng kūng-yèh pù]: Ministry of Local Industry

地方國營企業 [tì-fāng kuó-yíng ch'ì-yèh]: locally administered state enterprise, local state-operated enterprise

地方國營農場 [tì-fāng kuó-yíng núng-ch'ăng]: local state-operated farm

地方民族主義 [**tì-fāng mín-tsú chŭ-ì**]: local nationalism

地方當局 [**tì-fāng tāng-chǘ**]: local authorities

地方自治 [**tì-fāng tzù-chìh**]: local autonomy, local self-government

地方政權 [**tì-fāng chèng-ch'üán**]: local organ of state power, local regime

地方武裝 [**tì-fāng wŭ-chuāng**]: regional armed forces

地少人多 [**tì-shăo jén-tō**]: a large population over a small area of land

5 地主 [**tì-chŭ**]: landlord (one of the 四類份子)

地主階級 [**tì-chŭ chiēh-chí**]: landlord class

7 地形 [**tì-hsíng**]: physical contour, terrain, topographical make-up; topographical

地形圖 [**tì-hsíng-t'ú**]: topographical map

地步 [**tì-pù**]: stage, condition, situation

地位 [**tì-wèi**]: position, rank, standing, status, place, site

8 地拉那 [**tì-lā-nà**]: Tirana (Albania)

地委 [**tì-wĕi**]: "prefectural" Party Committee

9 地契 [**tì-ch'ì**]: land contract, land-owning contract

地面情報接收站 [**tì-mièn ch'íng-pào chiēh-shōu chàn**]: terrestrial reception point

地面遙測站 [**tì-mièn yáo-ts'è chàn**]: terrestrial telemetric station

10 地峽 [**tì-hsiá**]: isthmus

地財 [**tì-ts'ái**]: hidden wealth (property)

11 地基 [**tì-chī**]: foundation

地球中心說 [**tì-ch'íu chūng-hsīn shuō**]: geocentrism

地球衞星 [**tì-ch'íu wèi-hsīng**]: earth satellite

地球物理學 [**tì-ch'íu wù-lĭ hsüéh**]: geophysics

地球物理探礦研究所 [**tì-ch'íu wù-lĭ t'àn-k'uàng yén-chìu-sŏ**]: Institute of Geophysics Prospecting

地球物理研究所 [**tì-ch'íu wù-lĭ yén-chìu-sŏ**]: Geophysics Institute

地區 [**tì-ch'ǖ**]: district, local district, area

地理學 [**tì-lĭ-hsüéh**]: geography

地理研究所 [**tì-lĭ yén-chìu-sŏ**]: Geography Institute

地帶 [**tì-tài**]: zone, area

12 地軸 [**tì-chóu**]: the earth's axis

地富反壞右 [**tì fù făn huài yù**]: landlords, rich peasants, counterrevolutionaries, bad elements, and rightists

地痞流氓 [**tì-p'ĭ líu-máng**]: riffraff, rabble, rascal, rowdy, hoodlum, ruffian

地痞無產階級 [**tì-p'ĭ wú-ch'ăn chiēh-chí**]: propertyless local rowdies

13 地勢 [**tì-shìh**]: terrain, physical features, topography

14 地對空導彈 [**tì-tùi-k'ūng tăo-tàn**]: ground-to-air missile

地對地導彈 [**tì-tùi-tì tăo-tàn**]: ground-to-ground missile

15 地震 [**tì-chèn**]: earthquake

地震學 [**tì-chèn-hsüéh**]: seismology

地震觀測站 [**tì-chèn kuān-ts'è-chàn**]: seismographic observatory

地質學 [**tì-chíh-hsüéh**]: geology

地質力學研究所 [**tì-chíh lì-hsüéh yén-chìu-sŏ**]: Geomechanics Institute

地質部 [**tì-chíh pù**]: Ministry of Geology

地質測量部 [**tì-chíh ts'è-liáng pù**]: Ministry of Geological Survey

地質圖書館 [**tì-chíh t'ú-shū-kuăn**]: Geological Library (of the Ministry of Geology)

地質研究所[tì-chíh yén-chìu-sŏ] : Geology Institute

地廣人稀 [tì-kuăng jén-hsī] : a sparse population over a large area of land

地盤 [tì-p'án] : territory, area of operation

16 地學部 [tì-hsüéh pù] : department of earth sciences

在

1 在一個時期內 [tsài í-kò shíh-ch'í nèi] : for a period, for a time, during a certain period

在一定程度上 [tsài í-tìng ch'éng-tù shàng] : to a certain degree

5 在可能條件下 [tsài k'ŏ-néng t'iáo-chièn hsià] : as far as conditions permit, as far as possible

8 在考慮中 [tsài k'ăo-lǜ chūng] : under contemplation, under consideration

在…招牌下[tsài . . . chāo-p'ái hsià] : under the guise of, under the name of

在延安文藝座談會上的講話 [tsài yén-ān wén-ì tsò-t'án-hùi shàng te chiăng-huà] : in the Talks at the Yenan Forum on Literature and Art (Mao)

在於 [tsài-yǘ] : to lie in, to rest with, to depend on

10 在案 [tsài-àn] : on record

在座 [tsài-tsò] : to be present, present

11 在望 [tsài-wàng] : in sight, within sight, within reach

在野 [tsài-yĕh] : to be out of power

在野者 [tsài-yĕh-chĕ] : those out of power, those out of office

在野黨 [tsài-yĕh-tăng] : the party out of office, opposition party

12 在朝 [tsài-ch'áo] : to be in power

在朝者 [tsài-ch'áo-chĕ] : those in office, members of the government

在朝黨 [tsài-ch'áo-tăng] : the ruling party, the party in power

在場 [tsài-ch'ăng] : present, on the scene, in the presence of

在傍 [tsài-p'áng] : alongside, beside

13 在意 [tsài-ì] : to mind, to care about, to pay heed to, to notice, to bear in mind

20 在黨的總路綫光輝照耀下 [tsài tăng te tsŭng-lù-hsièn kuāng-hūi chào-yào hsià] : under the beacon light of the Party's general line, guided by the beacon light of the Party's general line

— 4 Strokes —

均

16 均衡 [chūn-héng] : balance, equilibrium

坊

坊 [fāng] : subdivision of a city, neighborhood, ward; workshop, store

坎

10 坎拿大[k'ăn-ná-tà] : Canada

坑

13 坑道[k'ēng-tào] : gallery, trench passage, tunnel

坑道戰[k'ēng-tào-chàn] : tunnel warfare, underground warfare

坑道工事[k'ēng-tào kūng-shìh] : tunnel fortifications

坐

5 坐失時機[tsò-shīh shíh-chī] : to allow an opportunity to slip past

6 坐地籌糧[tsò-tì ch'óu-liáng]: locally requisitioned rations

— 5 Strokes —

垂

3 垂亡的命運[ch'úi-wáng te mìng-yǜn]: doom

6 垂死 [ch'úi-ssŭ]: moribund, decaying, dying

垂死掙扎[ch'úi-ssŭ chēng-chā]: last-ditch struggle, last struggle, death struggle

坤

10 坤俸 [k'ūn-fèng]: Kompong (Indochina)

垃

7 垃圾[lè-sè]: waste, garbage, rubbish, trash, debris

垃圾堆[lè-sè-tūi]: garbage heap, trash heap

坦

5 坦白 [t'ăn-pái]: to confess; confession

坦白從寬，抗拒從嚴[t'ăn-pái ts'úng-k'uān, k'àng-chǜ ts'úng-yén]: leniency toward those who confess their crimes, but severe punishment to those who resist

7 坦克 [t'ăn-k'ò]: tank

11 坦率 [t'ăn-shuài]: frank, straightforward, candid, open, outspoken

16 坦噶尼喀[t'ăn-kō-ní-k'à]: Tanganyika

— 6 Strokes —

城

5 城市 [ch'éng-shìh]: city, municipality, town; urban, municipal

城市建設[ch'éng-shìh chièn-shè]: municipal construction

城市區 [ch'éng-shìh ch'ǖ]: urban area

城市小資產階級[ch'éng-shìh hsiăo-tzū-ch'ăn chiēh-chí]: urban petty bourgeoisie

城市規劃[ch'éng-shìh kuēi-huà]: city planning

城市工作部[ch'éng-shìh kūng-tsò pù]: urban work department

城市公用事業 [ch'éng-shìh kūng-yùng shìh-yèh]: municipal public utilities

城市貧民[ch'éng-shìh p'ín-mín]: the city poor, the urban poor

9 城郊[ch'éng-chiāo]: suburb

13 城鄉[ch'éng-hsiāng]: city and country; urban and rural

城鄉差異[ch'éng-hsiāng ch'ā-ì]: the differences between city and village

城鄉交流[ch'éng-hsiāng chiāo-líu]: exchange (of goods) between city and village, urban-rural circulation

城鄉兼顧[ch'éng-shìh chiēn-kù]: concern for both city and village

城鄉互助[ch'éng-hsiāng hù-chù]: mutual aid between cities and villages, urban-rural mutual aid

城鄉私人資本主義[ch'éng-hsiāng ssū-jén tzū-pĕn chŭ-ì]: urban and rural private capitalism

城鄉對立[ch'éng-hsiāng tùi-lì]: antagonism between town and country

城鄉物資交流[ch'éng-hsiāng wù-tzū chiāo-líu]: exchange of goods between the city and countryside

5 垮台[k'uă-t'ái]: to collapse, to fall, to fail,

to fall down, to be overthrown; collapse, breakdown, downfall, failure

— 7 Strokes —

埃

[4] 埃及 **[āi-chí]**: Egypt

[8] 埃佛拉斯峰 **[āi-fó-lā-ssū fēng]**: Mt. Everest

[13] 埃塞俄比亞 **[āi-sè-ó-pǐ-yà]**: Ethiopia

埃塞俄比亞帝國 **[āi-sè-ó-pǐ-yà tì-kuó]**: Kingdom of Ethiopia

埋

[6] 埋伏 **[mái-fú]**: to lie in waiting for, to ambush, to lay an ambush for; ambush

埋伏以待 **[mái-fú ǐ-tài]**: to waylay, to lie in ambush waiting for

埋怨 **[mán-yüàn]**: to bear a grudge against, to blame, to brood over a grievance, to complain about, to grumble about

[13] 埋葬 **[mái-tsàng]**: to bury

[16] 埋頭 **[mái-t'óu]**: to devote oneself to, to occupy oneself with; to be engrossed in, immersed in

— 8 Strokes —

基

[5] 基本 **[chī-pěn]**: foundation, basis, base; basic, fundamental

基本建設 **[chī-pěn chièn-shè]**: basic construction, capital construction (as used by Chou En-lai, refers to thoroughgoing changes in the political, economic, ideological, and organizational fields)

基本建設區 **[chī-pěn chièn-shè ch'ǖ]**: capital construction area

基本群衆 **[chī-pěn ch'ǖn-chùng]**: basic sections of the masses

基本好轉 **[chī-pěn hǎo-chuǎn]**: fundamental turn for the better

基本粒子 **[chī-pěn lì-tzǔ]**: fundamental particle

基本上 **[chī-pěn-shàng]**: in the main, on the whole, by and large, mainly, basically, fundamentally

基本單位 **[chī-pěn tān-wèi]**: basic unit

基本特點 **[chī-pěn t'è-tiěn]**: essential features

基本點 **[chī-pěn-tiěn]**: basis, fundamental point

基本投資 **[chī-pěn t'óu-tzū]**: capital investment

基本原理 **[chī-pěn yüán-lǐ]**: fundamental principle, basic principle, rudiments

[6] 基年 **[chī-nién]**: base year

基地 **[chī-tì]**: base (i.e., military)

基托 **[chī-t'ō]**: Quito (Ecuador)

[8] 基金 **[chī-chīn]**: fund, foundation, reserve fund

基金會 **[chī-chīn-hùi]**: foundation (i.e., a philanthropic organization)

基於 **[chī-yǘ]**: to be based upon

[9] 基建 **[chī-chièn]**: capital construction

[12] 基期 **[chī-ch'í]**: base period, base

[13] 基準 **[chī-chǔn]**: postulate, guideline, basic standard

基幹民兵 **[chī-kàn mín-pīng]**: basic unit of the militia, backbone militia

基督教 **[chī-tū-chiào]**: Christianity

基督教科學箴言報 **[chī-tū-chiào k'ō-hsüéh chēn-yén pào]**: Christian Science Monitor (U.S. daily newspaper)

基督教科學會 **[chī-tū-chiào k'ō-hsüéh hùi]**: Christian Science Church

基督教民主聯盟 **[chī-tū-chiào mín-chŭ lién-méng]**: Christian Democratic Union (East Germany)

14 基綫 **[chī-hsièn]**: base line

基數 **[chī-shù]**: base, base quantity, base number

15 基層 **[chī-ts'éng]**: basic level, foundation, basic unit, basic level unit, primary unit, grass roots, grass roots level

基層政權 **[chī-ts'éng chèng-ch'üán]**: basic unit of state power

基層選舉 **[chī-ts'éng hsüăn-chŭ]**: elections at the lowest level, basic level elections

基層公社 **[chī-ts'éng kūng-shè]**: basic level commune

基層單位 **[chī-ts'éng tān-wèi]**: primary unit, basic level unit

基層黨組織 **[chī-ts'éng tăng tsŭ-chīh]**: primary Party organization

基層組織 **[chī-ts'éng tsŭ-chīh]**: basic level organization

18 基礎 **[chī-ch'ŭ]**: basis, base, foundation, groundwork

基礎資料 **[chī-ch'ŭ tzū-liào]**: basic data

5 埼玉 **[ch'í-yù]**: Saitama (Japan)

堅

6 堅守 **[chiēn-shŏu]**: to hold fast, to defend stubbornly

7 堅決 **[chiēn-chüéh]**: resolute, determined, persistent, firm, steadfast, tenacious; resolution, perseverance

堅決，徹底，乾淨，全部地消滅敵人 **[chiēn-chüéh, ch'è-tĭ, kān-chìng, ch'üán-pù tì hsiāo-mièh tí-jén]**: to annihilate the enemy resolutely, thoroughly, wholly, and completely

堅決性 **[chiēn-chüéh-hsìng]**: decisiveness, resoluteness, determination

堅決地放，大膽地放，徹底地放 **[chiēn-chüéh tì fàng, tà-tăn tì fàng, ch'è-tĭ tì fàng]**: to let the masses air their views resolutely, boldly, and thoroughly

堅忍 **[chiēn-jĕn]**: persistent, enduring

堅忍不拔的 **[chiēn-jĕn pù-pá te]**: firm and indomitable

堅牢 **[chiēn-láo]**: solid, firm, secure; firmly, securely

8 堅固 **[chiēn-kù]**: strong, solid, firm, steady; to make secure

堅定 **[chiēn-tìng]**: firm, resolute, unswerving, fixed, undeviating, steadfast, steady

堅定性 **[chiēn-tìng-hsìng]**: firmness, steadfastness, resoluteness, staunchness, perseverance

堅定不移 **[chiēn-tìng pù-í]**: firm and steadfast, unswerving, undeviating, invariable, resolute and firm

9 堅貞 **[chiēn-chēn]**: faithful, chaste

堅貞不屈 **[chiēn-chēn pù-ch'ū]**: to stand firm; faithful, chaste, unshakable

堅持 **[chiēn-ch'íh]**: to persist in, to persevere in, to adhere firmly to, to stand firm, to insist on; persistent, insistent, persevering

堅持眞理，修正錯誤 **[chiēn-ch'íh chēn-lĭ, hsīu-chèng ts'ò-wù]**: to hold fast to the truth and to correct mistakes

堅持不渝 **[chiēn-ch'íh pù-yú]**: persistent, persevering, consistent, unremitting

堅信 **[chiēn-hsìn]**: to believe firmly; firm conviction, firm belief

堅苦[chiēn-k′ŭ]: to hold through, to stick it out; hard-working

10 堅强[chiēn-ch′iáng]: unbending, of strong character

堅强堡壘[chiēn-ch′iáng pǎo-lěi]: stout bulwark, strong bastion

12 堅硬[chiēn-yìng]: hard, unbreakable, solid, firm

15 堅毅[chiēn-ì]: firmly determined, persevering

堅實[chiēn-shíh]: solid, firm, strong, hard, durable

堅實可靠的[chiēn-shíh k′ŏ-k′ào te]: substantial and dependable, solid, stout, staunch

16 堅壁[chiēn-pì]: to fortify a position

堅壁淸野[chiēn-pì ch′īng-yěh]: to strengthen the bulwarks and leave no provisions outside, to fortify and evacuate a region

執

6 執行[chíh-hsíng]: to perform, to implement, to carry out, to put into effect, to execute, to realize; performance, implementation, execution

執行者[chíh-hsíng-chě]: executor

執行機關[chíh-hsíng chī-kuān]: executive organ

執行主席[chíh-hsíng chŭ-hsí]: presiding chairman

執行委員會[chíh-hsíng wěi-yüán-hùi]: executive council, executive committee

8 執拗[chíh-ào]: to cling to, to stick to, to adhere to; obstinacy, stubbornness; obstinate, stubborn

9 執政[chíh-chèng]: to be in power, to rule

執政黨[chíh-chèng tǎng]: the ruling party, party in power, the government party

執政的地位[chíh-chèng te tì-wèi]: ruling position

10 執迷不悟[chíh-mí pú-wù]: to persist in error, to refuse to come to one's senses

堪

11 堪培拉[k′ān-p′éi-lā]: Canberra (Australia)

14 堪察地[k′ān-ch′á-tì]: Kamchatka

17 堪薩斯[k′ān-sà-ssū]: Kansas

培

12 培植[p′éi-chíh]: to cultivate and train, to nurture

15 培養[p′éi-yǎng]: to bring up, to foster, to nurture, to cultivate, to train

培養典型[p′éi-yǎng tiěn-hsíng]: to foster exemplary experience (i.e., to encourage and cultivate advanced experience)

堂

9 堂皇[t′áng-huáng]: majesty, dignity, grandeur, stateliness, magnificence, splendor; splendid, majestic

堆

10 堆垜[tūi-tò]: to pile up, to accumulate

12 堆棧[tūi-chàn]: warehouse, silo

16 堆積[tūi-chī]: to pile up, to store up

— 9 Strokes —

報

2 報人協會 **[pào-jén hsiéh-hùi]**: press association

4 報仇 **[pào-ch'óu]**: to avenge a grievance, to take revenge; revenge

5 報刊事務處 **[pào-k'ān shìh-wù-ch'ù]**: Office of Newspaper and Publication Affairs

6 報名 **[pào-míng]**: to register, to enroll

7 報告 **[pào-kào]**: to report, to announce, to give an account of, to inform; a report

報告季 **[pào-kào chì]**: current quarter, reported quarter

報告期 **[pào-kào ch'í]**: current period, reported period

報告年 **[pào-kào nién]**: current year, reported year

報告文學 **[pào-kào wén-hsüéh]**: reportorial literature

報告月 **[pào-kào yüèh]**: current month, reported month

8 報到 **[pào-tào]**: to report on duty, to announce one's presence

9 報界 **[pào-chièh]**: the press, press circles

報信 **[pào-hsìn]**: to report, to spread news

11 報案 **[pào-àn]**: to report a case (to the police)

報紙 **[pào-chǐh]**: journal, newspaper, daily, the press

12 報復 **[pào-fù]**: to take revenge on, to get even with, to retaliate, to avenge; revenge, reprisal, retaliation; retaliatory

報復主義 **[pào-fù chǔ-ì]**: revenge-ism, doctrine of revenge

報喪 **[pào-sāng]**: to announce a death; obituary

報答 **[pào-tá]**: to reciprocate, to return, to repay, to compensate

報道 **[pào-tào]**: to report to, to inform

13 報酬 **[pào-ch'óu]**: to compensate, to reward, to remunerate; emolument, reward, return, compensation, remuneration

15 報請 **[pào-ch'ǐng]**: to submit to

報請批準 **[pào-ch'ǐng p'ī-chǔn]**: to submit for approval

報銷 **[pào-hsiāo]**: to submit accounts, to send in accounts

堡

堡 **[pǎo]**: village, town, fortified castle

18 堡壘 **[pǎo-lěi]**: fortress, citadel, bulwark, bastion, stronghold, rampart (during the Cultural Revolution, referred to the intransigent power of those opposing Mao)

堡壘戶 **[pǎo-lěi hù]**: bulwark families (i.e., pro-Communist households)

堤

堤 **[tī]**: dike

8 堤岸 **[tī-àn]**: embankment, dike

12 堤堰 **[tī-yèn]**: dike

堵

7 堵住 **[tǔ-chù]**: to block up, to stop up, to stop

堵住嘴 **[tǔ-chù tsǔi]**: to gag, to muzzle, to suppress

13 堵塞 **[tǔ-sāi]**: to stop up, to block

堵塞道路 **[tǔ-sāi tào-lù]**: to block the way

14 堵截 **[tǔ-chiéh]**: to interrupt, to block

堰

11 堰堤 **[yèn-tī]** : dam

— 10 Strokes —

塊

塊 **[k′uài]** : piece, bit, block, lump, fraction, portion, part

塞

4 塞內加爾共和國 **[sè-nèi-chiā-ĕrh kùng-hó-kuó]** : Republic of Senegal

塞文山脈 **[sè-wén shān-mài]** : Cevennes (France)

5 塞瓦斯托波爾 **[sè-wă-ssū-t′ō-pō-ĕrh]** : Sevastopol (Soviet Union)

7 塞住 **[sāi-chù]** : to stop up, to close up, to seal, to obstruct, to barricade

8 塞拉西一世 **[sè-lā-hsī í-shìh]** : Haile Selassie I (Emperor of Ethiopia)

塞拉勒窩內 **[sè-lā lō-wō-nèi]** : Sierra Leone

10 塞納河 **[sè-nà hó]** : Seine River

塞班島 **[sài-pān tăo]** : Saipan Island

塞浦路斯共和國 **[sè-p′ŭ-lù-ssū kùng-hó-kuó]** : Republic of Cyprus

13 塞當 **[sè-tāng]** : Sedan

14 塞爾維亞 **[sè-ĕrh-wéi-yà]** : Serbia

20 塞羅爾島 **[sè-ló-ĕrh tăo]** : Sellore Island (Burma)

塑

10 塑料廠 **[sù-liào ch′ăng]** : plastics plant

15 塑膠 **[sù-chiāo]** : plastic

塔

3 塔士墾 **[t′ă-shìh-k′ĕn]** : Tashkent

6 塔吉克 **[t′ă-chí-k′ò]** :Tajiks (minority nationality)

塔伊玆 **[t′ă-ī-tzū]** : Ta'izz (Yemen)

7 塔那那利佛 **[t′ă-nà-nà-lì-fó]** : Tananarive (Malgache Republic)

12 塔斯社 **[t′ă-ssū shè]** : Telegraph Agency of the Soviet Union (TASS)

13 塔塔爾 **[t′ă-t′ă-ĕrh]** : Tatars

14 塔爾沙漠 **[t′ă-ĕrh shā-mò]** : Thar Desert

塡

5 塡平 **[t′ién-p′íng]** : to fill up, to level

塡平鴻溝 **[t′ién-p′íng húng-kōu]** : to fill in the gap, to close the gap between

13 塡塞 **[t′ién-sāi]** : to fill in, to fill up

塗

10 塗脂抹粉 **[t′ú-chīh mò-fĕn]** : to rouge and powder, to paint the face, to embellish, to gloss over, to whitewash

11 塗掉 **[t′ú-tiào]** : to strike out, to cross out, to eliminate

23 塗髒 **[t′ú-tsāng]** : to smear, to daub, to smirch, to soil, to dirty, to make filthy

— 11 Strokes —

場

6 場合 **[ch′ăng-hó]** : occasion, circumstances, situation

8 場所 **[ch′ăng-sŏ]** : place, location

塵

5 塵世 [ch'én-shìh] : the mundane world

10 塵埃 [ch'én-āi] : dust, dirt

墊

3 墊上運動 [tièn-shàng yùn-tùng] : calisthenics

5 墊平 [tièn-p'íng] : to level

11 墊款 [tièn-k'uăn] : to advance money

12 墊補 [tièn-pŭ] : to replace

16 墊錢 [tièn-ch'ién] : to advance money

— 12 Strokes —

2 墜入 [chùi-jù] : to fall into, to ensnare into

墨

6 墨西哥 [mò-hsī-kō] : Mexico

墨西哥城 [mò-hsī-kō ch'éng] : Mexico City

墨西哥合衆國 [mò-hsī-kō hó-chùng-kuó] : United States of Mexico

墨守成規 [mò-shŏu ch'éng-kuēi] : to adhere conservatively to established rules, to get into a rut; established practices

8 墨兒本 [mò-érh-pĕn] : Melbourne (Australia)

10 墨索里尼 [mò-sŏ-lĭ-ní] : Mussolini, Benito (1883–1945)

14 墨維理 [mò-wéi-lĭ] : Couve de Murville, Maurice (French statesman)

墮

13 墮落 [tò-lò] : to deteriorate, to fall, to sink low

墮落蛻化 [tò-lò t'ùi-huà] : demoralization and degeneration

增

5 增加 [tsēng-chiā] : to increase, to enlarge, to multiply, to intensify, to grow; growth

增加一倍 [tsēng-chiā í-pèi] : to double

增加兩倍 [tsēng-chiā liăng-pèi] : to treble

增加三倍 [tsēng-chiā sān-pēi] : to quadruple

增刊 [tsēng-k'ān] : supplement

6 增光 [tsēng-kuāng] : to add glory, to add luster

7 增刪 [tsēng-shān] : to add and delete, to emend, to revise; addition and deletion, emendation, revision

11 增產 [tsēng-ch'ăn] : to increase production

增產節約 [tsēng-ch'ăn chiéh-yüēh] : to increase production and practice economy

增產節約運動 [tsēng-ch'ăn chiéh-yüēh yün-tùng] : movement for increasing production and practicing economy

12 增進 [tsēng-chìn] : to increase, to develop, to improve, to promote, to advance, to enhance

增援 [tsēng-yüán] : to reinforce; reinforcement

增援部隊 [tsēng-yüán pù-tùi] : reinforcement troops

— 13 Strokes —

墾

10 墾荒 [k'ĕn-huāng] : to reclaim wasteland, to open up virgin soil

壁

3 壁上觀 [pì-shàng kuān] : to watch idly or indifferently

5 壁立 [pì-lì] : to stand upright

9 壁虱 [pì-shīh] : bedbug

12 壁畫 [pì-huà] : mural painting

壁報 [pì-pào] : wall newspaper

18 壁壘 [pì-lĕi] : barrier (i.e., as a tariff barrier), breastwork

— 14 Strokes —

壕

13 壕溝 [háo-kōu] : ditch, gutter, channel

壓

2 壓力 [yā-lì] : pressure

8 壓制 [yā-chìh] : to suppress, to repress; suppression; repression

9 壓迫 [yā-p'ò] : to oppress, to trample on; oppression, coercion

10 壓倒 [yā-tǎo] : to overwhelm, to overpower, to subjugate; overwhelming

15 壓價出售 [yā-chià ch'ū-shòu] : to sell at reduced prices, to sell for a lower price

17 壓縮 [yā-sō] : to curtail, to cut down, to compress, to reduce

— 16 Strokes —

壞

壞 [huài] : out of order; to ruin, to spoil; bad, spoiled, morally bad; undesirable element (abbreviation of 壞份子, one of the 四類份子, q.v.)

2 壞了 [huài-le] : to be out of order, to have gone wrong, broken down

4 壞份子 [huài fèn-tzu] : bad element (one of the 四類份子, q.v.)

壞心眼 [huài hsīn-yĕn]: bad intention, malicious intention

7 壞良心 [huài liáng-hsīn] : a bad conscience

8 壞事 [huài-shìh] : wrongdoing, a bad thing, sinful act; mischief, evil, wickedness

壞東西 [huài tūng-hsī] : a crook, rascal; bad or undesirable things

11 壞蛋 [huài-tàn] : a bad egg, crook, rascal

壟

18 壟斷 [lǔng-tuàn] : to monopolize; monopoly

壟斷價格 [lǔng-tuàn chià-kó] : monopoly price, monopoly-priced

壟斷市場 [lǔng-tuàn shìh-ch'áng] : to monopolize the market, to corner the market

壟斷資本主義 [lǔng-tuàn tzū-pĕn chǔ-ì] : monopolistic capitalism

— 21 Strokes —

壩

壩 [pà] : dike

— RADICAL 士 33 —

士

7 士兵 [shìh-pīng] : rank and file, enlisted personnel, enlisted man; Private (U.S. Army); Airman (U.S. Air Force); Seaman (U.S. Navy); Aircraftman (British Air Force)

士兵幹部 [shìh-pīng kàn-pù] : enlisted cadre

10 士氣 [shìh-ch'ì] : morale, fighting spirit, martial spirit

士氣沮喪[shih-ch'i chü-sàng] : low morale, loss of morale, demoralized

士氣旺盛[shih-ch'i wàng-shèng] : good morale, high morale

— 4 Strokes —

壯

2 壯丁[chuàng-tīng] : able-bodied man, draftee, recruit, conscript

3 壯大[chuàng-tà] : strong, robust; to strengthen, to grow strong

17 壯膽[chuàng-tăn] : to strengthen one's courage

— RADICAL 夂 34 —

— RADICAL 夊 35 —

— 7 Strokes —

夏

5 夏令營[hsià-lìng-yíng] : summer camp, summer playground

6 夏收[hsià-shōu] : summer harvest

9 夏洛特阿馬利[hsià-lò-t'è à-mă-lì] : Charlotte Amalie (Virgin Islands, U.S.)

16 夏默孝[hsià-mò-hsiào] : Hammarskjold, Dag

— RADICAL 夕 36 —

— 2 Strokes —

外

6 外交[wài-chiāo] : diplomacy, foreign affairs; diplomatic

外交部[wài-chiāo-pù] : Ministry of Foreign Affairs

外交部長[wài-chiāo-pù-chăng] : Minister of Foreign Affairs; Minister for External Affairs (India, Canada); Secretary of Foreign Affairs (Phillipines, Mexico)

外交使節[wài-chiāo shih-chiéh] : diplomatic envoy

外交使團[wài-chiāo shih-t'uán] : diplomatic corps, diplomatic mission

外交事務[wài-chiāo shih-wù] : foreign affairs

外交大臣[wài-chiāo tà-ch'én] : Secretary of Foreign Affairs (England)

外交途徑[wài-chiāo t'ú-chìng] : diplomatic channel, diplomatic means

外行[wài-háng] : layman, amateur, someone outside the profession

8 外來幹部[wài-lái kàn-pù] : cadre from other areas

外來干涉[wài-lái kān-shè] : outside interference

外表[wài-piăo] : outward appearance, outward show, surface, exterior; outside, outward, external

外事辦公室[wài-shih pàn-kūng-shih] : Staff Office for Foreign Affairs

9 外科[wài-k'ō] : surgery, department of surgery

外科研究所[wài-k'ō yén-chìu-sŏ]: Surgery Institute

10 外流人口[wài-líu jén-k'ŏu]: population that drifts outside (i.e., villagers who drifted to the cities during the economic crises following the Great Leap Forward)

11 外部[wài-pù]: external, exterior, outer, outward; Ministry of Foreign Affairs (abbreviation of 外交部)

外務相[wài-wù-hsiàng]: Minister of Foreign Affairs (Korea, Japan)

12 外强中乾[wài-ch'iáng chūng-kān]: strong without but feeble (dried up) within, outwardly strong but inwardly weak

外援[wài-yüán]: foreign aid

13 外債[wài-chài]: foreign loan or debt, loans from foreign countries

外傾性格者[wài-ch'īng hsìng-kó-chĕ]: extrovert

外匯[wài-hùi]: foreign exchange

14 外貌[wài-mào]: external appearance, outward appearance, exterior aspect

外賓[wài-pīn]: foreign guests

15 外層空間[wài-ts'éng k'ūng-chiēn]: outer space

— 3 Strokes —

3 多才多藝的[tō-ts'ái tō-ì te]: talented, versatile, gifted in many ways

4 多中心論[tō-chūng-hsīn lùn]: polycentrism; the theory of many centers (a phrase first discovered in an editorial in the People's Daily of August 5, 1968, in which it was stated that "polycentrism" is a sort of bourgeois "mountain-top-ism" (山頭主義, q.v.) and that Chairman Mao's headquarters was the only center in the country)

多心[tō-hsīn]: suspicious, fickle

多元論[tō-yüán-lùn]: pluralism

5 多民族的國家[tō-mín-tsú te kuó-chiā]: multi-national state

多半[tō-pàn]: majority; mostly, most

6 多米尼加[tō-mĭ-ní-chiā]: Dominican Republic

多米尼加共和國[tō-mĭ-ní-chiā kùng-hó-kuó]: Dominican Republic

多多少少[tō-tō shăo-shăo]: to some extent, more or less

多次[tō-tz'ù]: again and again, time and again, repeatedly, often

7 多快好省[tō k'uài hăo shĕng]: more, faster, better, and more economically (i.e., to achieve greater, faster, better, and more economical results)

多兵種合成軍隊[tō pīng-chŭng hó-ch'éng chūn-tùi]: combined force of different military branches

8 多事[tō-shìh]: officious, interfering, meddling, busy

9 多哈[tō-hā]: Dohar (Qatar)

多科性工學院[tō-k'ō-hsìng kūng-hsüéh-yüàn]: polytechnic college

多面手[tō-mièn-shŏu]: versatile person, a well-rounded person; having many skills

10 多級[tō-chí]: multi-stage

多級火箭[tō-chí hŭo-chièn]: multi-stage rocket

多哥共和國[tō-kō kùng-hó-kuó]: Republic of Togo

11 多倫多星報[tō-lún-tō hsīng-pào]: Toronto Daily Star (Canadian daily newspaper)

13 多瑙河[tō-năo-hó]: Danube River

14 多種經營[tō-chŭng chīng-yíng]: diversified management

多種多樣[tō-chŭng tō-yàng]: multiform, diversified, diverse, various

多數[tō-shù]: majority

多維爾海峽 **[tō-wéi-ĕrh hăi-hsiá]**: Dover Straits

15 多樣性 **[tō-yàng-hsìng]**: diversity

多餘 **[tō-yǘ]**: remnant, surplus; superfluous, redundant, excessive

多餘人 **[tō-yǘ-jén]**: the superfluous man

多餘人員 **[tō-yǘ jén-yüán]**: excess personnel

19 多邊 **[tō-piēn]**: multi-lateral

多邊協定 **[tō-piēn hsiéh-tìng]**: a multi-lateral treaty, a multi-lateral agreement

多邊形 **[tō-piēn-hsíng]**: polygon, polygonal

20 多黨制度 **[tō-tăng chìh-tù]**: multi-party system

— 5 Strokes —

夜

5 夜以繼日 **[yèh ĭ chì-jìh]**: day and night

10 夜校 **[yèh-hsiào]**: evening school

夜班 **[yèh-pān]**: night shift

— 8 Strokes —

夠

5 夠本 **[kòu-pĕn]**: to break even with the capital invested

8 夠受 **[kòu-shòu]**: unbearable, intolerable

夠味 **[kòu-wèi]**: adequately flavored, up to standard

13 夠資格的 **[kòu-tzū-kó te]**: eligible, qualified, competent

— 11 Strokes —

夢

13 夢想 **[mèng-hsiăng]**: to dream, to fancy; dream, fancy, illusion

22 夢囈 **[mèng-ì]**: to rave, to utter in a frenzy; delirious raving, humbug

— RADICAL 大 37 —

大

大 **[tà]**: big, great, large; Dairen (abbreviation of 大連)

2 大人民呼拉爾 **[tà jén-mín hū-lā-ĕrh]**: Great People's Hural (People's Republic of Mongolia)

大人物 **[tà jén-wù]**: big shot, VIP, personage

大力 **[tà-lì]**: strenuous effort, great effort, great force; powerful, vigorous, strong, energetic

3 大小强弱 **[tà-hsiăo ch'iáng-jò]**: size and strength

大工業 **[tà kūng-yèh]**: large industry, heavy industry

大大的 **[tà-tà te]**: great, big, large, considerable, greatly, considerably

4 大中華日報 **[tà chūng-huá jìh-pào]**: Great China Press (Philippine Chinese language newspaper)

大分 **[tà-fēn]**: Oita (Japan)

大公報 **[tà kūng pào]**: Ta Kung Pao (Chinese daily newspaper)

大公無私 **[tà-kūng wú-ssū]**: selfless, just and fair

大不列顛 **[tà pù-lièh-tiēn]**: Great Britain

大不列顛及北愛爾蘭聯合王國 **[tà pù-lièh-tiēn chí pĕi ài-ĕrh-lán lién-hó wáng-kuó]**: United Kingdom of Great Britain and Northern Ireland)

大手大脚 **[tà-shŏu tà-chiăo]**: crude, raw, in a rough way

大王 **[tà-wáng]**: king, magnate, boss

大元帥 **[tà yüán-shuài]**: supreme marshal, grand marshal, field marshal, generalissimo

5 大民主 **[tà mín-chŭ]**: Great Democracy (during the Cultural Revolution, the permitting of the masses to use the media of free airing of views, big character posters, and extensive exchange of revolutionary experience to criticize and supervise the Party and leading government institutions and leaders at all levels; the term first appeared in Lin Piao's speech to the Red Guards in Peking on November 3, 1966)

大民族主義 **[tà mín-tsú chŭ-ì]**: chauvinism, greater nationalism (refers to the arrogant attitude of some Han Chinese cadres toward minority peoples)

大本營 **[tà pĕn-yíng]**: headquarters

6 大臣 **[tà-ch'én]**: minister, secretary

大企業主 **[tà ch'ì-yèh chŭ]**: owners of large private enterprises

大吃大喝 **[tà-ch'īh tà-hō]**: extravagant eating and drinking, overeating and overdrinking, excessive feasting

大好形勢 **[tà-hăo hsíng-shìh]**: exceedingly favorable situation

大好時機 **[tà-hăo shíh-chī]**: an exceedingly favorable time, just the time for, high time

大西洋 **[tà-hsī-yáng]**: Atlantic Ocean, Atlantic

大西洋憲章 **[tà-hsī-yáng hsièn-chāng]**: Atlantic Charter

大西洋公約 **[tà-hsī-yáng kūng-yüēh]**: Atlantic Pact

大伊斯蘭主義 **[tà ī-ssū-lán chŭ-ì]**: Great Islamism

大名鼎鼎的 **[tà-míng tĭng-tĭng te]**: famous, well-known, celebrated

大牟田 **[tà-móu-t'ién]**: Omuta (Japan)

大多數 **[tà tō-shù]**: the great majority

大同 **[tà-t'úng]**: great unity, great commonwealth, universal concord, one world

大同書 **[tà-t'úng shū]**: The Book of the Great Unity (a book by K'ang Yu-wei completed in 1902 and published posthumously in 1935 on his utopian vision of a one-world philosophy)

大字報 **[tà-tzù-pào]**: big character poster, big character bulletin (a wall newspaper written in large characters; widely used during the 1957 "anti-rightist" campaign, the 1958 commune movement, and the 1966 Cultural Revolution)

大字標題 **[tà-tzù piāo-t'í]**: banner headline, streamer, banner line

大宇宙 **[tà yŭ-chòu]**: macrocosm

7 大局 **[tà-chǘ]**: general situation

大快人心 **[tà-k'uài jén-hsīn]**: to the satisfaction of the masses

大阪 **[tà-păn]**: Osaka (Japan)

大批 **[tà-p'ī]**: a great batch of, a large group of, a large quantity of

大批生產 **[tà-p'ī shēng-ch'ăn]**: mass production

大兵團作戰 **[tà pīng-t'uán tsò-chàn]**: to wage a war by mobilizing vast groups of people

大災難 **[tà tsāi-nàn]**: great catastrophe, disaster or calamity

大材小用 **[tà-ts'ái hsiăo-yùng]**: large material for small uses, waste of talents, improper use of material; to use a talented man in an inferior capacity

大尾巴會 **[tà wĕi-pā hùi]**: "big tail" meeting

8 大邱 **[tà-ch'īu]**: Taegu (Korea)

大使 **[tà-shĭh]**: ambassador

大使館 **[tà-shĭh-kuăn]**: embassy

大使館隨員[tà-shǐh-kuăn súi-yüán]: embassy attaché

大事記[tà shǐh-chì]: chronicle of great events

大事宣揚[tà-shǐh hsüān-yáng]: to give wide publicity to

大事攻擊[tà-shǐh kūng-chī]: all-out attack

9 大前提[tà ch'ién-t'í]: major premise, prerequisite

大津[tà-chīn]: Otsu (Japan)

大型[tà-hsíng]: large type, heavy

大型記錄片[tà-hsíng chì-lù-p'ièn]: documentary film

大型運輸機[tà-hsíng yǜn-shū-chī]: heavy transport plane

大面積增產運動[tà mièn-chī tsēng-ch'ăn yǜn-tùng]: the movement for high yields on large tracts of land

大牲畜[tà shēng-ch'ù]: big livestock (i.e., cattle and horses)

大施[tà-shīh]: Daithi (Vietnam)

大是大非[tà-shǐh tà-fēi]: major right and major wrong, basic dispute

大是大非問題[tà-shǐh tà-fēi wèn-t'í]: question of principle, major question of right and wrong

大洋洲[tà-yáng-chōu]: Oceania

大英銀行[tà-yīng yín-háng]: Bank of England

大約[tà-yüēh]: in broad outline, approximately more or less; generally, roughly, probably

10 大家知道[tà-chīa chīh-tào]: everybody knows, it is a matter of common knowledge

大將[tà-chiàng]: Senior General (Chinese Army and Air Force); Senior Admiral (Chinese Navy); General of the Army (Soviet Army); team star; superman type

大致上[tà-chìh-shàng]: on the whole, in broad outline, more or less; generally, mainly, roughly

大校[tà-hsiào]: Senior Colonel (Chinese Army and Air Force); Senior Captain (Chinese Navy)

大宮[tà-kūng]: Omiya (Japan)

大馬士革[tà-mă-shǐh-kó]: Damascus (Syria)

大砲[tà-p'ào]: gun, artillery, cannon

大烟[tà-yēn]: opium

11 大張旗鼓[tà-chāng ch'í-kŭ]: on a grand scale

大衆[tà-chùng]: people, population, mass; popular

大衆化[tà-chùng-huà]: to popularize; popularization

大衆語[tà-chùng-yŭ]: the language of the masses

大規模[tà-kuēi-mó]: large scale, grand scale, massive, widespread

大國[tà-kuó]: great power, big power, leading power

大國主義[tà-kuó chŭ-ì]: chauvinism, great power chauvinism

大國民議會[tà kuó-mín ì-hùi]: Grand National Assembly (Rumania)

大國首腦會議[tà-kuó shŏu-năo hùi-ì]: conference of the heads of government of the great powers

大連[tà-lién]: Dairen

大陸[tà-lù]: continent, mainland (refers usually to mainland China)

大陸雜誌[tà-lù tsá-chìh]: The Continent Magazine (Taiwan periodical)

大麻[tà-má]: hemp

大麥[tà-mài]: barley

大敗 **[tà-pài]**: fiasco, great defeat, big failure; to defeat thoroughly; to be defeated thoroughly

大部分 **[tà pù-fēn]**: the greater part, the main part, a large proportion; mostly, mainly

大赦 **[tà-shè]**: general amnesty, general pardon

大尉 **[tà-wèi]**: Senior Captain (Chinese Army and Air Force); Senior Lieutenant (Chinese Navy); Captain (Soviet Army and Air Force); Lieutenant Captain (Soviet Navy)

12 大集體，小自由 **[tà chí-t'ǐ, hsiǎo-tzù-yú]**: big collective and small freedom (i.e., the individual can enjoy his freedom only within the framework of the collective; 小自由 refers to small private plots within the collective)

大量 **[tà-liàng]**: a great deal, in great number, in vast quantity; mass, large quantity, liberal minded, broad-minded

大量現象 **[tà-liàng hsièn-hsiàng]**: mass phenomenon

大量生產 **[tà-liàng shēng-ch'ǎn]**: mass production

大勝 **[tà-shèng]**: great victory; to be impressively victorious; to triumph impressively over

大堤 **[tà-tī]**: main dike, levee

大隊 **[tà-tùi]**: battalion

13 大較場 **[tà-chiào ch'ǎng]**: Ta-chiao Ch'ang (Nanking Airfield)

大話 **[tà-huà]**: boasting, boast, exaggeration

大會 **[tà-hùi]**: congress, general meeting

大幹特幹 **[tà-kàn t'è-kàn]**: to work vigorously and with all of one's energy

大搞群衆運動 **[tà kǎo ch'ǘn-chùng yǜn-tùng]**: to start a full scale mass movement, to organize an extensive mass movement

大勢 **[tà-shìh]**: general situation, general course of events

大勢已定 **[tà-shìh ǐ-tìng]**: the general situation or course of events has been fixed, settled or decided

大勢所趨 **[tà-shìh sǒ-ch'ǖ]**: the general trend or course of development

大肆 **[tà-ssù]**: ruthlessly, without restraint, excessively

大肆攻擊 **[tà-ssù kūng-chī]**: to launch unbridled attacks against

大肆汚蔑 **[tà-ssù wū-mièh]**: to slander violently, to slander indiscriminately

大罪狀 **[tà tsùi-chuàng]**: serious indictment

大資產階級 **[tà tzū-ch'ǎn chiēh-chí]**: big bourgeoisie

大資本家 **[tà tzū-pěn-chiā]**: big capitalist, monopoly capitalist, monopolist, magnate

14 大寨 **[tà-chài]**: Tachai (district of Shansi Province)

大寨精神 **[tà-chài chīng-shén]**: the Tachai spirit (a revolutionary spirit of hard work and self-reliance exhibited by the Tachai Production Brigade in its outstanding success in wasteland reclamation and agricultural development in the poverty stricken Tachai district of Shansi Province)

大寨式 **[tà-chài-shìh]**: Tachai-type, à la Tachai

大漢族主義 **[tà hàn-tsú chǔ-ì]**: Han chauvinism

大綱 **[tà-kāng]**: program, outline

大鳴、大放、大爭、大辯、貼大字報 **[tà-míng, tà-fàng, tà-chēng, tà-pièn, t'iēh tà-tzù-pào]**: to air one's views, contend and debate to the fullest extent, and publicize one's views in big character posters (大字報, q.v.)

15 大慶 **[tà-ch'ìng]**: Ta-ch'ing (a large oil field in North China)

大慶精神 **[tà-ch'ìng chīng-shén]**: the Ta-ch'ing spirit (the hard working spirit of the workers of the Ta-ch'ing oil field)

大興水利[**tà-hsīng shŭi-lì**]: large-scale building of water conservancy projects

大興土木[**tà-hsīng t'ŭ-mù**]: large-scale building of installations

大選[**tà-hsüăn**]: general election

大概[**tà-kài**]: probably, in all probability, presumably

大潰敗[**tà k'uèi-pài**]: disastrous rout, severe defeat

大練兵[**tà lièn-pīng**]: to train troops on a grand scale; mass training

大鳴大放[**tà-míng tà-fàng**]: free expression of opinion; free, unlimited criticism of defects in ideology or work style

大踏步[**tà t'à-pù**]: giant stride, long step; to stride

大談特談[**tà-t'án t'è-t'án**]: to talk at length

16 大戰[**tà-chàn**]: full scale war, general engagement

大戰畧部署[**tà chàn-lüèh pù-shŭ**]: great strategic plan (i.e., Mao's plan for spreading Maoist control over the entire country; to bring about unity and the formation of revolutionary committees on a nation-wide scale)

大學[**tà-hsüéh**]: university; The Great Learning (one of the four books of the Confucian canon)

大學大比[**tà-hsüéh tà-pĭ**]: to learn and emulate energetically

大學夜校部[**tà-hsüéh yèh-hsiào pù**]: university night department

大錯[**tà-ts'ò**]: great blunder, gross mistake

17 大舉進攻[**tà-chŭ chìn-kūng**]: to attack in great force; a large scale attack

大糞[**tà-fèn**]: manure

大韓[**tà-hán**]: Korea

大韓民國[**tà-hán mín-kuó**]: Republic of Korea

大聯合[**tà lién-hó**]: great coordination, grand union

大聲疾呼[**tà-shēng chí-hū**]: to raise a hue and cry, to shout at the top of one's voice

大聲辱罵[**tà-shēng jŭ-mà**]: to insult loudly

大膽[**tà-tăn**]: boldness; bold, daring, fearless, brave

大膽地放[**tà-tăn tì fàng**]: (*See* 堅決地放)

18 大雜會[**tà-tsá-hùi**]: big mixed meeting

大藏省[**tà-tsàng-shĕng**]: Ministry of Finance (Japan)

20 大艦[**tà-lán**]: Dalam (Vietnam)

21 大躍進[**tà-yüèh-chìn**]: Great Leap Forward

22 大權在握[**tà-ch'üán tsài-wò**]: to hold immeasurable power in one's hands

大變動[**tà pièn-tùng**]: a great, momentous, profound or violent change or upheaval, cataclysm

大廳[**tà-t'īng**]: hall, assembly room

23 大壩[**tà-pà**]: dam

大體[**tà-t'ĭ**]: the main principle, morality; in general, on the whole

大體相同[**tà-t'ĭ hsiāng-t'úng**]: in general very much the same, very similar on the whole

大體上[**tà-t'ĭ-shàng**]: on the whole, mainly, in broad outline, more or less, generally

— 1 Stroke —

3 太上皇[**t'ài-shàng-huáng**]: father of the emperor, overlord

太子港[**t'ài-tzŭ kăng**]: Port-au-Prince (Haiti)

太子派 [t'ài-tzŭ p'ài] : Sun Fo Clique

5 太古 [t'ài-kŭ] : antiquity; Tagu (Burma)

太平 [t'ài-p'íng] : peace; Taiping (regime); Perak (Malaya)

太平洋 [t'ài-p'íng-yáng] : Pacific Ocean

太平洋憲章 [t'ài-p'íng-yáng hsièn-chāng] : Pacific Charter

太平洋學會 [t'ài-p'íng-yáng hsüéh-hùi] : Institute of Pacific Relations

太平洋公約 [t'ài-p'íng-yáng kūng-yüēh] : Pacific Pact

6 太伊 [t'ài-ī] : Thai; Thailand

8 太空人 [t'ài-k'ūng-jén] : astronaut

10 太原 [t'ài-yüán] : Thainguyen (Vietnam); Taiyuan (China)

12 太陽 [t'ài-yáng] : sun (a symbol for Mao, particularly during the Cultural Revolution)

天

3 天下 [t'iēn-hsià] : the world

天下第一號 [t'iēn-hsià tì-í hào] : the world's number-one (war criminal, etc.)

天才 [t'iēn-ts'ái] : genius, talent, gift; talented, gifted

4 天王星 [t'iēn-wáng-hsīng] : Uranus

天文學 [t'iēn-wén-hsüéh] : astronomy

天文館 [t'iēn-wén-kuăn] : planetarium

天文台 [t'iēn-wén-t'ái] : observatory

5 天主教 [t'iēn-chŭ-chiào] : Catholicism, Roman Catholicism

天主教民主黨 [t'iēn-chŭ-chiào mín-chŭ tăng] : Christian Democratic Party (Italy)

天外還有天 [t'iēn-wài hái yŭ t'iēn] : there is sky beyond the sky (a phrase urging the peasants to prepare for the future, as in harvests, and to discourage complacency)

6 天安門廣場 [t'iēn-ān-mén kuăng-ch'ăng] : Tienanmen Square

7 天災 [t'iēn-tsāi] : natural calamity, natural disaster

8 天性 [t'iēn-hsìng] : innate nature, inborn quality

天花 [t'iēn-huā] : smallpox

9 天皇 [t'iēn-huáng] : Emperor (Japan)

10 天眞 [t'iēn-chēn] : innocent, artless, simple, unaffected

11 天堂 [t'iēn-t'áng] : paradise, heaven, the heavenly kingdom

12 天象儀 [t'iēn-hsiàng-í] : planetarium, armillary sphere

天然氣 [t'iēn-ján ch'ì] : natural gas

天然材料 [t'iēn-ján ts'ái-liào] : natural materials

天然資源 [t'iēn-ján tzū-yüán] : natural resources

13 天經地義 [t'iēn-chīng tì-ì] : unalterable principles

15 天賦 [t'iēn-fù] : heaven endowed

20 天壤之別 [t'iēn-jăng chīh piéh] : worlds apart, poles apart

23 天體 [t'iēn-t'ĭ] : heavenly body, celestial body

天體力學 [t'iēn-t'ĭ lì-hsüéh] : celestial mechanics

— 2 Strokes —

失

5 失去 [shīh-ch'ù] : to lose, to be deprived of, to be denied

失去時效 [shīh-ch'ù shíh-hsiào] : to be no longer valid

7 失言 **[shīh-yén]**: to misstate, to make a gaffe; slip of the tongue

8 失事 **[shīh-shìh]**: accident, mishap

9 失約 **[shīh-yüēh]**: to break one's promise, to fail to keep an appointment

11 失敗 **[shīh-pài]**: to fail, to be defeated; defeat, failure; abortive

失敗主義 **[shīh-pài chŭ-ì]**: defeatism

失望 **[shīh-wàng]**: to give up hope, to be disappointed; disappointment, hopelessness, despair

13 失業 **[shīh-yèh]**: unemployment; unemployed, out of work

失業者 **[shīh-yèh-chě]**: the unemployed

14 失實的 **[shīh-shíh te]**: false, untrue, erroneous, fallacious, incorrect, misleading

失算 **[shīh-suàn]**: miscalculation

15 失調 **[shīh-t'iáo]**: ailment, maladjustment, disproportion, out of proportion

失踪 **[shīh-tsūng]**: missing, without traces

18 失職 **[shīh-chíh]**: dereliction of duty, neglect of duty

24 失靈 **[shīh-líng]**: to malfunction; malfunction; to be a dud

— 3 Strokes —

夸

3 夸大 **[k'uā-tà]**: to exaggerate, to brag, to boast

20 夸耀 **[k'uā-yüèh]**: to boast, to brag

— 4 Strokes —

6 夾攻 **[chiā-kūng]**: to attack from both sides, to hem in; pincers attack, converging attack

7 夾注 **[chiā-chù]**: notation, comment

10 夾帶 **[chiā-tài]**: to smuggle, to cheat on an examination by smuggling notes into the examination hall (literally, to carry in the girdle)

12 夾着尾巴 **[chiā-che wěi-pā]**: to put one's tail between one's legs

17 夾擊 **[chiā-chī]**: to attack the enemy on both flanks

— 5 Strokes —

5 奇功 **[ch'í-kūng]**: distinguished merit, meritorious service

8 奇怪 **[ch'í-kuài]**: strange, curious, astonishing, incredible, amazing

9 奇計 **[ch'í-chì]**: clever strategy, ingenious plan

10 奇迹 **[ch'í-chī]**: wonder, miracle

13 奇零 **[chī-líng]**: surplus, fraction

奇遇 **[ch'í-yǜ]**: strange adventure

14 奇數 **[chī-shù]**: odd number

22 奇襲白虎團 **[ch'í-hsí pái-hŭ-t'uán]**: Raid on the White Tiger Regiment (name of a play)

奉

3 奉上 **[fèng-shàng]**: to offer, to proffer, to present a gift to a superior

4 奉公守法 **[fèng-kūng shŏu-fă]**: to be just and respect the laws

奉天 **[fèng-t'iēn]**: old name for Liaoning (遼寧) Province

6 奉行 **[fèng-hsíng]**: to pursue, to follow, to act according to orders

奉托 **[fèng-t'ō]**: to ask someone to do something, to entrust something to someone

8 奉承 **[fèng-ch'éng]**: to fawn on, to court favor, to bow and scrape, to toady

奉命 **[fèng-mìng]**: to receive orders

奈

7 奈良 **[nài-liáng]**: Nara (Japan)

奄

9 奄美大島 **[yēn-měi tà-tǎo]**: Amami Oshima (Japan)

— 6 Strokes —

奔

5 奔寧山脈 **[pēn-níng shān-mò]**: Pennine Mountains

6 奔忙 **[pēn-máng]**: to take pains, to strive; busy, hasty, ambitious

7 奔放 **[pēn-fàng]**: to bolt (as a horse), to run riot (as imagination)

10 奔逃 **[pēn-t'áo]**: to flee, to escape, to run away from

16 奔頭 **[pèn-t'óu]**: to have good prospects

17 奔薩 **[pēn-sà]**: Penza (USSR)

— 7 Strokes —

奚

13 奚落 **[hsī-lò]**: to make a fool of, to rail at; a cold reception

套

3 套上 **[t'ào-shàng]**: to put on, to fit (one thing over another)

套上絞索 **[t'ào-shàng chiǎo-sǒ]**: to put a noose around one's neck

— 9 Strokes —

奢

8 奢侈 **[shē-ch'ǐh]**: wasteful, extravagant, luxurious

奢侈浪費 **[shē-ch'ǐh làng-fèi]**: luxury and waste

奢侈品 **[shē-ch'ǐh-p'ǐn]**: luxury good(s)

奠

8 奠定 **[tièn-tìng]**: to lay (as groundwork), to secure (as foundations), to make firm, to establish, to put on a firm basis

11 奠基人 **[tièn-chī-jén]**: founder, creator, originator

— 10 Strokes —

6 奥列克明斯克 **[ào-lièh-k'ò-míng-ssū-k'ò]**: Olekminsk

奥地利 **[ào-tì-lì]**: Austria

奥地利共和國 **[ào-tì-lì kùng-hó-kuó]**: Republic of Austria

7 奥克蘭 **[ào-k'ò-lán]**: Auckland (New Zealand)

奥克內群島 **[ào-k'ò-nèi ch'ǘn-tǎo]**: Orkney Islands

8 奥林匹克運動會 **[ào-lín-p'ǐ-k'ò yǜn-tùng hùi]**: Olympic Games

10 奥格斯堡 **[ào-kó-ssū-pǎo]**: Augsburg (Bavaria)

12 奥斯陸 **[ào-ssū-lù]**: Oslo (Norway)

— 11 Strokes —

獎

[8] 獎金 [chiăng-chīn]: bonus, premium, reward, prize, prize money

獎狀 [chiăng-chuàng]: written citation, certificate of merit

[9] 獎品 [chiăng-p'ĭn]: prize, award, reward

[11] 獎章 [chiăng-chāng]: decoration, medal

[14] 獎旗 [chiăng-ch'í]: pennant, victor's pennant

[15] 獎勵 [chiăng-lì]: to praise and encourage; praise and encouragement

獎勵基金 [chiăng-lì chī-chīn]: premium funds

獎勵制度 [chiăng-lì chìh-tù]: system of rewards, award system

獎勵金 [chiăng-lì-chīn]: bounty

獎勵工資制 [chiăng-lì kūng-tzū chìh]: incentive wage system

獎賞 [chiăng-shăng]: reward, award

奪

[5] 奪去 [tó-ch'ü]: to take from, to deprive of, to appropriate, to grab

奪目 [tó-mù]: to blind, to dazzle

[6] 奪回 [tó-húi]: to retake, to recapture, to recover

[8] 奪取 [tó-ch'ŭ]: to usurp, to seize, to capture, to carry off

[11] 奪得政權 [tó-té chèng-ch'üán]: to come to power

[15] 奪標 [tó-piāo]: to win a prize, to win a decoration, to win an award

[22] 奪權 [tó-ch'üán]: to seize power; seizure of power

— 13 Strokes —

奮

[2] 奮力 [fèn-lì]: to make every effort, to strain

[9] 奮勇 [fèn-yŭng]: courageous, intrepid

[10] 奮勉 [fèn-miĕn]: to spur on, to incite

[13] 奮發 [fèn-fā]: to become enthusiastic, to burst forth

[24] 奮鬥 [fèn-tòu]: to struggle; struggle, strife

— RADICAL 女 38 —

女

[3] 女工 [nŭ-kūng]: female worker, working women; woman's work

[4] 女王 [nŭ-wáng]: queen

女王陛下 [nŭ-wáng pì-hsià]: Her Majesty

[5] 女主角 [nŭ chŭ-chiăo]: leading lady, heroine

[9] 女飛行員 [nŭ fēi-hsíng-yüán]: aviatress, aviatrix

女皇 [nŭ-huáng]: empress

女皇陛下 [nŭ-huáng pì-hsià]: Her Imperial Majesty

[14] 女演員 [nŭ yĕn-yüán]: actress

— 2 Strokes —

奴

[3] 奴工營 **[nú-kūng-yíng]** : slave labor camp

奴才 **[nú-ts'ái]** : slave, servant, vassal, lackey, underling, hireling

[4] 奴化思想 **[nú-huà ssū-hsiăng]** : slave ideology, slavish thought

[7] 奴役 **[nú-ì]** : to subjugate, to enslave, to subject, to reduce to slavery; slavery, enslavement

奴役性商約 **[nú-ì-hsìng shāng-yüēh]** : commercial treaty of an enslaving nature

[16] 奴隸 **[nú-lì]** : slave, serf, bondsman; slavery, bondage

奴隸主 **[nú-lì chŭ]** : slave owner

奴隸主義 **[nú-lì chŭ-ì]** : slavery, the doctrine of slavery

[18] 奴顏婢膝 **[nú-yén pì-hsī]** : servility, subservience, fawning, obsequiousness; cringing, grovelling

— 3 Strokes —

奸

[9] 奸商 **[chiēn-shāng]** : dishonest merchant

[11] 奸細 **[chiēn-hsì]** : spy, informer

奸淫 **[chiēn-yín]** : treacherous, lecherous

奸淫擄掠 **[chiēn-yín lŏ-lüèh]** : to rape and plunder, to loot

奸淫燒殺 **[chiēn-yín shāo-shā]** : to engage in rape, arson, and murder

[12] 奸詐 **[chiēn-chà]** : insidious, tricky, cunning

奸雄 **[chiēn-hsiúng]** : a master of treachery, a master of deceit

[13] 奸滑 **[chiēn-huá]** : tricky, deceptive, faithless

奸賊 **[chiēn-tséi]** : traitor, scoundrel

[16] 奸險 **[chiēn-hsiĕn]** : insidious

[20] 奸黨 **[chiēn-tăng]** : treacherous clique, traitor party

好

[3] 好大喜功 **[hào-tà hsĭ-kūng]** : to crave after greatness and success

[4] 好心好意 **[hăo-hsīn hăo-ì]** : sincere and well-intentioned, kind-hearted, with good intentions

好手 **[hăo-shŏu]** : efficient, skilled; an adept, clever or skillful worker

[5] 好比 **[hăo-pĭ]** : comparable; may be compared to

[8] 好奇的 **[hào-ch'í te]** : curious, inquisitive

[12] 好萊塢 **[hăo-lái-wù]** : Hollywood

好評 **[hăo-p'íng]** : good opinion, favorable criticism, praise, approbation, commendation

[13] 好感 **[hăo-kăn]** : favorable impression

[16] 好戰 **[hào-chàn]** : bellicose, warlike, militant

好戰份子 **[hào-chàn fèn-tzu]** : bellicose elements, "hawks"

[18] 好轉 **[hăo-chuăn]** : to recover, to become better; recovery, a turn for the better

[21] 好辯 **[hào-pièn]** : quarrelsome, contentious, disputatious

如

[5] 如出一轍 **[jú ch'ū ì-ch'è]** : to originate as though from the same source; one and the same, equivalent, identical

[9] 如果 **[jú-kuŏ]** : if, in case, in the event of, provided that, on condition that

如果不 **[jú-kuŏ pù]**: unless, if not, except that, if otherwise

12 如期 **[jú-ch'í]**: punctually, on time, at a set time, on schedule

13 如意 **[jú-ì]**: smooth going, as one likes, according to one's wishes

妄

6 妄自菲薄 **[wàng-tzù fĕi-pó]**: to underestimate one's achievements; sense of inferiority, inferiority complex

妄自尊大 **[wàng-tzù tsūn-tà]**: to have enormous conceit, to boast oneself; sense of superiority, swelled head; arrogant, haughty, self-opinionated

13 妄想 **[wàng-hsiăng]**: to have vain hopes, to dream wildly of; illusion, wild thought

14 妄圖翻天 **[wàng-t'ú fān-t'iēn]**: to attempt wildly to revolt

— 4 Strokes —

妨

10 妨害 **[fáng-hài]**: to jeopardize, to hinder, to disturb, to damage, to harm, to impair; hindrance, harm, impairment

19 妨礙 **[fáng-ài]**: to hinder, to obstruct, to block, to bar, to impede, to hamper; obstacle, obstruction, hindrance

妨礙物 **[fáng-ài-wù]**: deterrent

妙

9 妙計 **[miào-chì]**: ingenious plan, clever device, skillful trick

15 妙論 **[miào-lùn]**: an ingenious argument, fine reasoning

妥

8 妥協 **[t'ŏ-hsiéh]**: to compromise; compromise

妥協份子 **[t'ŏ-hsiéh fèn-tzu]**: compromisers

12 妥善 **[t'ŏ-shàn]**: good, proper; well, properly; satisfactory

妥善安排 **[t'ŏ-shàn ān-p'ái]**: well-thought out arrangement, judicious preparation

13 妥當 **[t'ŏ-tāng]**: properly, well, satisfactorily done

妖

9 妖風 **[yāo-fēng]**: demonic wind (i.e., during the Cultural Revolution, an anti-Maoist force or trend)

— 5 Strokes —

姑

10 姑媳 **[kū-hsí]**: to spoil, to appease; appeasement, indulgence

姆

4 姆巴巴納 **[mŭ-pā-pā-nà]**: Mbabane (Swaziland)

始

11 始終 **[shĭh-chūng]**: from first to last, all along, constantly, consistently, from beginning to end

4 委內瑞拉 **[wĕi-nèi-jùi-lā]**: Venezuela

委內瑞拉共和國 **[wĕi-nèi-jùi-lā kùng-hó-kuó]** : Republic of Venezuela

6 委曲求全 **[wĕi-ch'ū ch'íu-ch'üán]** : to yield too far, to make too many concessions in trying to achieve one's purpose

委任 **[wĕi-jèn]** : to appoint, to commission, to commit; appointment, commission

委任書 **[wĕi-jèn-shū]** : letter of appointment

委托 **[wĕi-t'ō]** : to entrust, to commission, to delegate, to depute

8 委屈 **[wĕi-ch'ū]** : grievance

9 委派 **[wĕi-p'ài]** : to accredit, to assign, to delegate, to depute

10 委員長 **[wĕi-yüán-chăng]** : Chairman (Korea)

委員會 **[wĕi-yüán-hùi]** : committee, commission, council, board, panel

11 委婉 **[wĕi-wăn]** : polite, skillful, suave, polished, urbane

— 6 Strokes —

14 姿態 **[tzū-t'ài]** : attitude, appearance, gesture, posture, carriage, deportment

威

2 威力 **[wēi-lì]** : might, power, strength, force, vigor, majesty, intimidation

9 威風 **[wēi-fēng]** : dignity, pomp, majesty, grandeur; majestic, imposing, magnificent

威風掃地 **[wēi-fēng săo-tì]** : to make a clean sweep of someone's prestige; with one's prestige in the dust

威信 **[wēi-hsìn]** : prestige, high repute, credit

威信下降 **[wēi-hsìn hsià-chiàng]** : to cause a loss of prestige; decline of prestige

10 威脅 **[wēi-hsiéh]** : to threaten, to menace, to intimidate, to coerce; threat, menace, intimidation, coercion

威脅利誘 **[wēi-hsiéh lì-yù]** : coercion and bribery

13 威廉斯塔特 **[wēi-lién-ssū-t'ă-t'è]** : Willemstad (Netherlands Antilles)

15 威震全國 **[wēi-chèn ch'üán-kuó]** : to win resounding fame throughout the country

威震世界 **[wēi-chèn shìh-chièh]** : world-shaking prestige

21 威懾力量 **[wēi-shè lì-liàng]** : deterrent power

24 威靈敦 **[wēi-líng-tūn]** : Wellington

— 7 Strokes —

娛

15 娛樂 **[yǘ-lè]** : recreation, amusement, entertainment, pleasure, fun

— 8 Strokes —

婦

3 婦女工作委員會 **[fù-nǚ kūng-tsò wĕi-yüán-hùi]** : Women's Work Committee

婦女節 **[fù-nǚ chiéh]** : Women's Day (March 8)

5 婦幼保健站 **[fù-yù păo-chièn chàn]** : maternity and infant welfare station

8 婦委 **[fù-wĕi]** : women's commission

17 婦濟會 **[fù-chì-hùi]** : women's relief association

婚

8 婚事[hūn-shìh] : marriage

9 婚姻法[hūn-yīn fǎ] : marriage law

18 婚禮[hūn-lǐ] : wedding

婆

20 婆羅洲[p'ó-ló chōu] : Borneo

— 10 Strokes —

嫉

7 嫉妒[chì-tù] : to be jealous, to envy; jealousy, envy

嫌

12 嫌惡[hsién-wù] : to dislike, to hate, to detest; dislike, distaste, aversion, antipathy

14 嫌疑[hsién-í] : to suspect; suspect

嫌疑犯[hsién-í-fàn] : suspect, a suspected criminal

— 12 Strokes —

嬌

10 嬌氣[chiāo-ch'ì] : spoiled, over-delicate attitude, finicky air

11 嬌羞[chiāo-hsīu] : timid, bashful

12 嬌貴[chiāo-kuèi] : refined, delicate, dainty, highborn

— RADICAL 子 39 —

子

4 子午綫[tzŭ-wŭ-hsièn] : meridian

7 子弟小學[tzŭ-tì hsiăo-hsüéh] : dependent's elementary school (i.e., a school for dependents of workers for a company)

15 子彈[tzŭ-tàn] : bullet, shell, cartridge, projectile

18 子爵[tzŭ-chüéh] : viscount

— 1 Stroke —

孔

15 孔德[k'ŭng-té] : Comte, Auguste

— 3 Strokes —

存

4 存心[ts'ún-hsīn] : to intend, to have the intention, to set the mind on; intention, state of mind

存心爲惡[ts'úng-hsīn wéi-ò] : premeditated malice, malice aforethought

6 存在[ts'ún-tsài] : being, existence; to exist

存在決定意識[ts'ún-tsài chüéh-tìng ì-shìh] : man's (social) being determines his consciousness

10 存案[ts'ún-àn] : to put in the files, to keep in the files

11 存貨[ts'ún-huò] : stock, stockpile, reserve, goods in store

字

9 字面上兜圈子[tzù-mièn-shàng tōu-ch'üān-tzu] : involved phraseology, garlands of words, embellishments

11 字眼[tzù-yĕn] : wording, phraseology, term

— 4 Strokes —

孚

11 孚衆望 **[fú chùng-wàng]** : to enjoy the love and confidence of the masses

孜

7 孜別克 **[tzū-piéh-k'ò]** : Tzu-Pieh-K'o (a minority nationality)

孜孜不倦 **[tzū-tzū pú-chüàn]** : assiduous and never tired, indefatigable, untiring, diligent, assiduous

— 5 Strokes —

5 季刊 **[chì-k'ān]** : quarterly (magazine)

9 季度 **[chì-tù]** : quarter

10 季候風 **[chì-hòu fēng]** : monsoon

12 季報 **[chì-pào]** : quarterly reporting

13 季節 **[chì-chiéh]** : season, time

季節性 **[chì-chiéh-hsìng]** : seasonal; seasonal nature

季節工 **[chì-chiéh kūng]** : seasonal labor, seasonal laborer

孤

2 孤丁 **[kū-tīng]** : a person left alone

5 孤立 **[kū-lì]** : to isolate; isolation; isolated

孤立主義 **[kū-lì chŭ-ì]** : isolationism

9 孤軍作戰 **[kū-chūn tsò-chàn]** : to carry on a struggle single-handed

孟

4 孟什維克 **[mèng-shíh-wéi-k'ò]** : Menshevik

5 孟加拉 **[mèng-chiā-lā]** : Bengal (India)

9 孟席斯 **[mèng-hsí-ssū]** : Menzies, Robert (Australian statesman)

12 孟買 **[mèng-măi]** : Bombay (India)

孟買紀事報 **[mèng-măi chì-shìh pào]** : Bombay Chronicle (Indian daily newspaper)

孟都亞 **[mèng-tū-yà]** : Mantua (Italy)

15 孟德斯 **[mèng-té-ssū]** : Menderes, Adnan (Turkish political leader)

孟德斯鳩 **[mèng-té-ssū-chīu]** : Montesquieu

— 9 Strokes —

孱

19 孱軀 **[ch'án-ch'ū]** : feeble body

— 13 Strokes —

學…的話 **[hsüéh . . . te huà]** : to parrot someone's words, to repeat what someone else says

3 學大寨 **[hsüéh tà-chài]** : to learn from Tachai (*See* 大寨精神)

學王傑 **[hsüéh wáng chiéh]** : to learn from Wang Chieh (*See* 王傑)

5 學以致用 **[hsüéh ĭ chìh yùng]** : to learn in order to put to use

學生 **[hsüéh-shēng]** : pupil, learner, novice

學用會 **[hsüéh-yùng hùi]** : learning and application meeting (i.e., a meeting devoted to learning and application of the works and thought of Mao)

6 學先進 **[hsüéh hsiēn-chìn]** : to learn from the advanced (*See* 比學趕幫)

7 學究 **[hsüéh-chīu]** : pedant

學步邯鄲 **[hsüéh-pù hán-tān]** : to imitate others slavishly and lose one's own originality

學位 **[hsüéh-wèi]** : academic degree

8 學制改革 **[hsüéh-chìh kăi-kó]** : reform of the school system

學到手 **[hsüéh tào shŏu]** : to learn to hand (i.e., to learn a skill thoroughly and practically)

9 學者 **[hsüéh-chĕ]** : scholar, learned man (a term used in a pejorative sense during the Cultural Revolution)

學者權威 **[hsüéh-chĕ ch'üán-wēi]** : scholars and authorities

學科 **[hsüéh-k'ō]** : subject

學派 **[hsüéh-p'ài]** : school of thought, school, academic school

10 學校 **[hsüéh-hsiào]** : school

學校辦工廠，工廠辦學校 **[hsüéh-hsiào pàn kūng-ch'ăng, kūng-ch'ăng pàn hsüéh-hsiào]** : establishment of factories by schools and the setting up of schools by factories

學徒 **[hsüéh-t'ú]** : apprentice

學院 **[hsüéh-yüàn]** : academy, college, school, institute

11 學習 **[hsüéh-hsí]** : to study, to learn (particularly in a political sense); Study (a semi-monthly Chinese periodical)

學習雷鋒運動 **[hsüéh-hsí léi fēng yùn-tùng]** : the learn from Lei Feng movement (*See* 雷鋒)

學理 **[hsüéh-lĭ]** : theory

學部常務委員會 **[hsüéh-pù ch'áng-wù wĕi-yüán-hùi]** : departmental standing committee

學術 **[hsüéh-shù]** : learning, art; academic

學術界 **[hsüéh-shù chièh]** : academic circles

學術性質 **[hsüéh-shù hsìng-chíh]** : of an academic nature

學術上的 **[hsüéh-shù-shàng te]** : academic

學術委員會 **[hsüéh-shù wĕi-yüán-hùi]** : academic committee (of an institute, laboratory, etc.)

12 學期 **[hsüéh-ch'í]** : semester, term

學費 **[hsüéh-fèi]** : tuition, school fees

13 學會 **[hsüéh-hùi]** : scholarly association, learned society

14 學說 **[hsüéh-shuō]** : doctrine, theory

學銜 **[hsüéh-hsién]** : academic title

19 學識造詣 **[hsüéh-shìh tsào-ì]** : scholarly attainments

— 14 Strokes —

孺

3 孺子牛 **[jú-tzŭ níu]** : children's ox (based on a quotation from Lu Hsun and indicating that a revolutionary is as obedient as an ox in serving the people while he calmly withstands the enemy)

— RADICAL 宀 40 —

— 2 Strokes —

8 宂長 **[jŭng-ch'áng]** : tediously long, interminable, long drawn out, verbose

— 3 Strokes —

安

3 安大略湖 **[ān-tà-lüèh hú]** : Lake Ontario

安山口[ān shān-k'ǒu]: An Pass (Burma)

4 安分[ān-fèn]: to be content, to be satisfied, to be happy with one's job

5 安加拉河[ān-chiā-lā hó]: Angara River

安卡拉[ān-k'ǎ-lā]: Ankara (Turkey)

安民告示[ān-mín kào-shìh]: notice to reassure the public

6 安全[ān-ch'üán]: safety; safe

安全人員[ān-ch'üán jén-yüán]: safety personnel

安全理事會[ān-ch'üán lǐ-shìh-hùi]: Security Council (United Nations)

安全生產[ān-ch'üán shēng-ch'ǎn]: safety in production

安多拉[ān-tō-lā]: Andorra

7 安那其主義[ān-nà-ch'í chǔ-ì]: anarchism

8 安和[ān-hó]: Anhoa (Vietnam)

安定社會秩序[ān-tìng shè-hùi chìh-hsǜ]: to maintain social order, to establish social order

安東[ān-tūng]: Andong (Korea)

安于現狀，故步自封[ān yǘ hsièn-chuàng, kù-pù tzù-fēng]: satisfaction with things as they are and inertia in moving forward

安于已得名譽[ān yǘ ǐ té míng-yǜ]: to rest on one's laurels

安於現狀[ān yǘ hsièn-chuàng]: to be satisfied with the present state of affairs, to be satisfied with things as they are

安於落後[ān yǘ lò-hòu]: to be content with being backward, to be content with staying behind

10 安家落戶[ān-chiā lò-hù]: to be happy with one's lot in life

安哥拉[ān-kō-lā]: Angola

安特衞普[ān-t'è-wèi-p'ǔ]: Antwerp (Belgium)

11 安曼[ān-mán]: Amman (Jordan)

安排[ān-p'ái]: to arrange, to fix up, to organize; arrangement, placement

安排生活[ān-p'ái shēng-huó]: to arrange one's livelihood

安莎通訊社[ān-shā t'ūng-hsǜn-shè]: Ansa News Agency: Agenzia Nazionale Stampa Associata (Italian News Agency)

12 安道耳[ān-tào-ěrh]: Andorra

安道耳共和國[ān-tào-ěrh kùng-hó-kuó]: Republic of Andorra

13 安置[ān-chìh]: to place (as, to place a person in a state farm)

安塔拉通訊社[ān-t'ǎ-lā t'ūng-hsǜn-shè]: Indonesian National News Agency (ANTARA)

15 安德羅斯島[ān-té-ló-ssū tǎo]: Andros Island

安德衞普[ān-té-wèi-p'ǔ]: Antwerp (Belgium)

安慰語[ān-wèi yǔ]: soothing or consoling remark

宅

8 宅邸[chái-tǐ]: residence, dwelling, domicile

守

8 守法[shǒu-fǎ]: law-abiding; to be law-abiding

9 守紀律[shǒu chì-lǜ]: to uphold discipline, to keep discipline

守軍[shǒu-chūn]: defense troops, defender

守信[shǒu-hsìn]: to keep one's word, to live

up to one's word, to keep faith

12 守備 [**shǒu-pèi**] : to defend; on garrison duty

守備隊 [**shǒu-pèi-tùi**] : garrison

13 守勢 [**shǒu-shìh**] : defensive operation; defensive

15 守衞 [**shǒu-wèi**] : to guard, to defend, to keep a watch over

宇

7 宇努 [**yǔ nǔ**] : U Nu (Burmese statesman)

8 宇宙 [**yǔ-chòu**] : universe, cosmos; cosmic, cosmological

宇宙飛船 [**yǔ-chòu fēi-ch'uán**] : space ship

宇宙飛行 [**yǔ-chòu fēi-hsíng**] : space flight

宇宙飛行站 [**yǔ-chòu fēi-hsíng-chàn**] : space station

宇宙飛行員 [**yǔ-chòu fēi-hsíng-yüán**] : cosmonaut, astronaut

宇宙火箭 [**yǔ-chòu hǔo-chièn**] : space rocket

宇宙觀 [**yǔ-chòu-kuān**] : cosmological view, world outlook

宇宙空間 [**yǔ-chòu k'ūng-chiēn**] : cosmic space, outer space

宇宙論 [**yǔ-chòu-lùn**] : cosmology

宇宙射綫 [**yǔ-chòu shè-hsièn**] : cosmic radiation

宇宙始原論 [**yǔ-chòu shǐh-yüán lùn**] : cosmogony

— 4 Strokes —

宏

3 宏大 [**húng-tà**] : large, vast, spacious

11 宏偉 [**húng-wěi**] : splendid, solemn, grand, spectacular, ceremonial

完

6 完成 [**wán-ch'éng**] : to fulfill, to complete, to finish; fulfillment, completion

完全 [**wán-ch'üán**] : whole, full, perfect, entire, complete

完全一致 [**wán-ch'üán í-chìh**] : in full accord, entirely at one

完全脫離現實 [**wán-ch'üán t'ō-lí hsièn-shíh**] : to lose all touch with reality

11 完蛋 [**wán-tàn**] : all up, finished, to come to an end

12 完備 [**wán-pèi**] : perfect, faultless, elaborate, complete

完善 [**wán-shàn**] : perfect, excellent

16 完整 [**wán-chěng**] : integrated, entire, whole, intact; integrity

完整的社會主義工業體系 [**wán-chěng te shè-hùi chǔ-ì kūng-yèh t'ǐ-hsì**] : well-integrated system of socialist industry

— 5 Strokes —

10 宜耕荒地 [**í-kēng huāng-tì**] : reclaimable wasteland

4 官巴 [**kuān-pā**] : Quanba (Vietnam)

5 官司 [**kuān-ssū**] : lawsuit

6 官吏 [**kuān-lì**] : an official

7 官兵 [**kuān-pīng**] : officers and men

官佐 [**kuān-tsǒ**] : noncommissioned officer

10 官員 [**kuān-yüán**] : official

11 官氣 [**kuān-ch'ì**] : bureaucratic behavior, bureaucratic airs

12 官腔 **[kuān-ch'iāng]**: bureaucratic way of talking, bureacratic behavior

官階 **[kuān-chiēh]**: official rank

13 官話 **[kuān-huà]**: Mandarin, standard language

14 官銜 **[kuān-hsién]**: official title, official rank

官僚 **[kuān-liáo]**: bureaucrat

官僚主義 **[kuān-liáo chŭ-ì]**: bureaucratism (one of the targets of the 三反, q.v.: the attitude of officials who remain in their offices without making on-the-spot inspections and who put on airs in dealing with people)

官僚主義作風 **[kuān-liáo chŭ-ì tsò-fēng]**: bureaucratic practices

官僚買辦資產階級 **[kuān-liáo măi-pàn tzū-ch'ăn chiēh-chí]**: bureaucrat-comprador bourgeoisie

官僚資產階級 **[kuān-liáo tzū-ch'ăn chiēh-chí]**: bureaucrat-capitalist class

官僚資本主義 **[kuān-liáo tzū-pĕn chŭ-ì]**: bureaucratic capitalism (the running of private enterprises while holding government posts)

15 官價 **[kuān-chià]**: official price, official rate

官樣文章 **[kuān-yàng wén-chāng]**: red tape, routine bureaucratic automatism

18 官職 **[kuān-chíh]**: public office, public function

25 官廳水庫 **[kuān-t'īng shŭi-k'ù]**: Kuan-t'ing Reservoir (Hopeh Province)

定

7 定言判斷 **[tìng-yén p'àn-tuàn]**: categorical judgment

8 定金 **[tìng-chīn]**: deposit, advance payment

定命論 **[tìng-mìng-lùn]**: determinism

定於 **[tìng-yŭ́]**: to be scheduled or planned for, to be timed for

9 定律 **[tìng-lǜ]**: law

10 定案 **[tìng-àn]**: judgment, decision in a case

定息 **[tìng-hsí]**: fixed interest, fixed rate of interest

定時炸彈 **[tìng-shíh chà-tàn]**: time bomb

定員 **[tìng-yüán]**: fixed number of staff

定員制度 **[tìng-yüán chìh-tù]**: personnel norm system

11 定產 **[tìng-ch'ăn]**: fixed production, fixed output volume

定基指數 **[tìng-chī chĭh-shù]**: base index

定規 **[tìng-kuēi]**: set pattern, set rule or regulation

定理 **[tìng-lĭ]**: theorem

12 定期 **[tìng-ch'í]**: a fixed period; to set a time or date; periodic, regular, at regular intervals

定期存款 **[tìng-ch'í ts'ún-k'uăn]**: fixed deposit

定量 **[tìng-liàng]**: a fixed quantity, quota

定量供應 **[tìng-liàng kūng-yìng]**: fixed supply

定評 **[tìng-p'íng]**: definitive evaluation, ultimate judgment

13 定義 **[tìng-ì]**: definition

定罪 **[tìng-tsùi]**: to convict; conviction

14 定論 **[tìng-lùn]**: to come to a decision, to reach a decision; decision, conclusion

15 定廠辦校 **[tìng-ch'ăng pàn-hsiào]**: certain schools are to be run by certain factories (schools in urban areas are to be run by factories on the following principles: (a) a factory near a school will run that school; (b) secondary schools are to be run by big factories; and (c) primary schools are to be run by medium and small-sized factories–a phrase from the Cultural Revolution)

定價 **[tìng-chià]**: to fix the price; fixed price

定稿[tìng-kǎo]: a writing in final form

16 定錢[tìng-ch'ién]: deposit money, down payment

18 定額[tìng-ó]: a fixed number, quota, standard, allotment, norm, planned target figure

定額管理[tìng-ó kuǎn-lǐ]: norm control (i.e., control of production by a system of norms)

定額工作[tìng-ó kūng-tsò]: norm work (i.e., work based on a norm)

宗

5 宗主權[tsūng-chǔ-ch'üán]: suzerainty

宗主國[tsūng-chǔ-kuó]: suzerain

6 宗旨[tsūng-chǐh]: aim, intention, object, purpose

10 宗派[tsūng-p'ài]: sect, faction, clique, group

宗派主義[tsūng-p'ài chǔ-ì]: sectarianism, cliquism, sectism, factionalism

宗派主義傾向[tsūng-p'ài chǔ-ì ch'īng-hsiàng]: sectarian tendency

宗派分裂活動[tsūng-p'ài fēn-lièh huó-tùng]: factional splitting

11 宗教[tsūng-chiào]: religion; religious

宗教信仰自由[tsūng-chiào hsìn-yǎng tzù-yú]: freedom of religious belief, freedom of worship

宗教派別[tsūng-chiào p'ài-piéh]: religious sects or denominations

宗教寺院[tsūng-chiào ssù-yüàn]: religious establishment

宗族[tsūng-tsú]: clan

宗族關係[tsūng-tsú kuān-hsì]: family clan relationships

— 6 Strokes —

宣

5 宣布[hsüān-pù]: to proclaim, to announce, to declare

宣布戒嚴[hsüān-pù chièh-yén]: to proclaim martial law

宣布爲非法[hsüān-pù wéi fēi-fǎ]: to declare as illegal, to outlaw

7 宣告[hsüān-kào]: to proclaim, to pronounce

宣告中外[hsüān-kào chūng-wài]: to proclaim to the nation and the world

宣判[hsüān-p'àn]: to pass sentence, to pass judgment, to give a decision in a case

宣言[hsüān-yén]: manifesto, proclamation, declaration, pronouncement

12 宣揚[hsüān-yáng]: to publish, to declare, to proclaim, to advertise

13 宣傳[hsüān-ch'uán]: to propagandize, to propagate, to publicize, to spread; propaganda

宣傳場所[hsüān-ch'uán ch'ǎng-sǒ]: places of propaganda

宣傳家[hsüān-ch'uán-chiā]: expert in publicity, propagandist

宣傳工具[hsüān-ch'uán kūng-chǜ]: instruments of publicity, means of publicity, media of publicity

宣傳部[hsüān-ch'uán pù]: propaganda department

宣傳對象[hsüān-ch'uán tùi-hsiàng]: objects of propaganda, audience for propaganda, those at whom propaganda is aimed

14 宣稱[hsüān-ch'ēng]: to declare

宣誓就職[hsüān-shìh chìu-chíh]: to be

sworn into office

宣誓就職典禮**[hsüān-shìh chìu-chíh tiĕn-lĭ]**: swearing-in ceremony

16 宣戰**[hsüān-chàn]**: to declare war; declaration of war

22 宣讀**[hsüān-tú]**: to read out, to read aloud

宦

8 宦官**[huàn-kuān]**: eunuch

客

2 客人**[k'ò-jén]**: guest, visitor

7 客車**[k'ò-ch'ē]**: passenger train, coach, bus, passenger car

12 客隊**[k'ò-tùi]**: visiting team, guest team

13 客滿**[k'ò-măn]**: full of or packed with guests, a full house

客運**[k'ò-yǜn]**: passenger service, passenger transportation

16 客機**[k'ò-chī]**: passenger plane, air liner for passengers

25 客觀**[k'ò-kuān]**: objective

客觀眞理**[k'ò-kuān chēn-lĭ]**: objective truth

客觀現實**[k'ò-kuān hsièn-shíh]**: objective reality

客觀觀念論**[k'ò-kuān kuān-nièn lùn]**: objective idealism

客觀規律**[k'ò-kuān kuēi-lǜ]**: objective laws

客觀必然性**[k'ò-kuān pì-ján-hsìng]**: objective necessity

— 7 Strokes —

5 家用**[chiā-yùng]**: domestic expenditures, household expenditures

6 家伙**[chiā-huŏ]**: element, tool, fellow, man, boy

7 家私**[chiā-ssū]**: family property; domestic affair

8 家長制**[chiā-chăng chìh]**: patriarchy, matriarchy; patriarchal, matriarchal

家長式統治**[chiā-chăng-shìh t'ŭng-chìh]**: to rule arbitrarily, to rule like a patriarch; patriarchal type rule

家長作風**[chiā-chăng tsò-fēng]**: patriarchal behavior

10 家家戶戶**[chiā-chiā hù-hù]**: each household

家畜**[chiā-ch'ù]**: domestic animals

家庭**[chiā-t'íng]**: family, home; domestic, household

家庭教育**[chiā-t'íng chiào-yǜ]**: domestic education, family education

家庭出身**[chiā-t'íng ch'ū-shēn]**: family origin

家庭婦女**[chiā-t'íng fù-nǚ]**: housewife

家庭副業**[chiā-t'íng fù-yèh]**: subsidiary household industry

家庭副業生產 **[chiā-t'íng fù-yèh shēng-ch'ăn]**: domestic side-occupations

家庭開支**[chiā-t'íng k'āi-chīh]**: family expenditure

家庭補助**[chiā-t'íng pŭ-chù]**: family grant, family subsidy

家庭收支調查 **[chiā-t'íng shōu-chīh tiào-**

ch′á] : family expenditure survey

家庭手工業[**chiā-t′íng shǒu-kūng-yèh**]: domestic handicrafts

家財[**chiā-ts′ái**]: family property, family holdings

11 家產[**chiā-ch′ǎn**]: family possession, family property

家常便飯[**chiā-ch′áng pièn-fàn**]: simple fare, ordinary meal; commonplace

家族主義[**chiā-tsú chǔ-ì**]: clan system, clannishness

家務[**chiā-wù**]: household affairs; household (noun and adjective)

家務勞動[**chiā-wù láo-tùng**]: household work

家務勞動社會化[**chiā-wù láo-tùng shè-hùi-huà**]: socialization of household work

12 家禽[**chiā-ch′ín**]: domestic fowl

家鄉[**chiā-hsiāng**]: home, home town, home village

家喻戶曉[**chiā-yü hù-hsiǎo**]: to make known to every family; generally known

13 家當[**chiā-tāng**]: family property, family estate

家道[**chiā-tào**]: family condition, financial situation of the family

14 家境[**chiā-chìng**]: family condition, financial situation of the family

17 家醜外揚[**chiā-ch′ǒu wài-yáng**]: to publicize family shame; to wash one's dirty linen in public

19 家譜[**chiā-p′ǔ**]: genealogical register, family history

21 家屬[**chiā-shǔ**]: family dependents

害

2 害人蟲[**hài-jén ch′úng**]: injurious vermin (during the Cultural Revolution, an epithet for anti-Mao elements)

11 害羞的[**hài-hsīu te**]: bashful, coy, shy, shamefaced, timid, diffident

宵

13 宵禁[**hsiāo-chìn**]: curfew

容

7 容忍[**júng-jěn**]: to bear, to endure, to tolerate

8 容易[**júng-ì**]: easy, facile; readily, easily

11 容許[**júng-hsü**]: to allow, to permit, to give permission to

12 容量[**júng-liàng**]: capacity

16 容積[**júng-chī**]: volume, contents, bulk

宮

宮[**kūng**]: palace

3 宮山[**kūng-shān**]: Cungson (Vietnam)

9 宮城[**kūng-ch′éng**]: Miyagi (Japan)

宮庭[**kūng-t′íng**]: royal court

宮庭政變[**kūng-t′íng chèng-pièn**]: Palace Revolt (during the Cultural Revolution, the term for the P'eng Chen case in inner Party circles)

11 宮崎[**kūng-ch′í**]: Miyazaki (Japan)

宰

10 宰殺[**tsǎi-shā**]: to slaughter, to kill

12 宰割[**tsǎi-kō**]: to cut up, to carve, to butcher

宴

13 宴會 **[yèn-hùi]**: banquet, reception, feast, dinner party

— 8 Strokes —

16 寂靜主義 **[chí-chìng chŭ-ì]**: quietism

2 寄人籬下 **[chì-jén lí-hsià]**: to sponge on others, to depend on other people, to live under subjugation, to be under someone's thumb

5 寄以希望 **[chì-ĭ hsī-wàng]**: to put one's hopes on

寄生 **[chì-shēng]**: to be a parasite, to live off; parasitic

寄生蟲 **[chì-shēng-ch'úng]**: parasite, parasitic worms (during the Cultural Revolution, an epithet for anti-Mao elements)

寄生蟲病研究所 **[chì-shēng-ch'úng-pìng yén-chìu-sŏ]**: Parasitology Institute

寄生生活 **[chì-shēng shēng-huó]**: parasitism, parasitical life

6 寄存 **[chì-ts'ún]**: to deposit

11 寄售 **[chì-shòu]**: to consign, to sell on commission

寄宿學校 **[chì-sù hsüéh-hsiào]**: boarding school

寄宿舍 **[chì-sù-shè]**: dormitory

寄宿生 **[chì-sù-shēng]**: boarding student

15 寄賣 **[chì-mài]**: to sell on consignment, to entrust sale to

20 寄籍 **[chì-chí]**: temporary residence; to live in a place temporarily

密

密 **[mì]**: close, dense, thick, secret; "close planting" (one of the eight characters of the 八字憲法, q.v.)

3 密士失必河 **[mì-shìh-shīh-pì hó]**: Mississippi River

4 密切 **[mì-ch'ièh]**: close, intimate

7 密告者 **[mì-kào-chĕ]**: informer

9 密約 **[mì-yüēh]**: secret treaty, secret agreement

10 密特威 **[mì-t'è-wēi]**: Midway

11 密執安 **[mì-chíh-ān]**: Michigan

密商 **[mì-shāng]**: to hold secret talks, to discuss privately

12 密植 **[mì-chíh]**: close planting, serried row planting

15 密碼 **[mì-mă]**: code, cipher, cipher group code

密碼電報 **[mì-mă tièn-pào]**: code telegram, cipher telegram

16 密諾爾島 **[mì-nò-ĕrh tăo]**: Minorca Island

20 密蘇里 **[mì-sū-lĭ]**: Missouri

宿

8 宿命論 **[sù-mìng-lùn]**: fatalism

宿舍 **[sù-shè]**: dormitory, hostel, apartments, residence compound

寓

7 寓言 **[yǜ-yén]**: fable

13 寓意 **[yǜ-ì]**: allegory, implication

冤

6 冤有頭，債有主 [yüān yŭ t'óu, chài yŭ chŭ]: every wrong has its cause, every debt has its debtor

8 冤屈 [yüān-ch'ü]: to wrong; grievance, injustice, wrong, false charge

冤枉 [yüān-wăng]: to wrong; grievance, injustice, wrong, false charge

10 冤家 [yüān-chiā]: enemy, foe, opponent, adversary, antagonist, rival

— 9 Strokes —

富 [fù]: to enrich; wealth; wealthy; rich peasant (one of the 四類份子, q.v.)

3 富山 [fù-shān]: Toyama (Japan)

6 富安 [fù-ān]: Phuyen (Vietnam)

7 富足 [fù-tsú]: rich and self-sufficient

10 富海 [fù-hăi]: Phuhai (Vietnam)

富馬親王 [fù-mă ch'īn-wáng]: Prince Souvanna Phouma (Laotian political leader)

12 富强 [fù-ch'iáng]: mighty and prosperous

富裕 [fù-yǜ]: well-off, well-to-do, prosperous

富裕者 [fù-yǜ-chĕ]: the well-to-do, the rich, the prosperous

富裕中農 [fù-yǜ chūng-núng]: well-to-do middle peasants

富裕農民 [fù-yǜ núng-mín]: well-to-do peasants, well-off peasants

13 富溪 [fù-hsī]: Phukhe (Vietnam)

富農 [fù-núng]: rich peasant

富農經濟 [fù-núng chīng-chì]: rich peasant economy

14 富壽 [fù-shòu]: Phutho (Vietnam)

20 富礦 [fù-k'uàng]: high grade ore

寒

4 寒心的 [hán-hsīn te]: to be afraid, to be in trepidation

10 寒流 [hán-líu]: cold wave

11 寒帶 [hán-tài]: frigid zone

15 寒潮 [hán-ch'áo]: cold wave

— 11 Strokes —

察 [ch'á]: Chahar Province (abbreviation of 察哈爾)

11 察勘 [ch'a-k'ān]: to examine

7 寡言 [kuă-yén]: taciturn

16 寡頭 [kuă-t'óu]: oligarch, magnate, boss

寡頭政治 [kuă-t'óu chèng-chìh]: oligarchy

18 寡斷 [kuă-tuàn]: indecision

寧

寧 [níng]: Nanking (abbreviation for 南京); Ningsia (abbreviation of 寧夏)

5 寧尼 [níng-ní]: Ning-Ni (minority nationality)

寧平 [níng-p'íng]: Ninh Binh (Vietnam)

8 寧和 [níng-hó]: Ninhhoa (Vietnam)

19 寧願 [níng-yüàn]: to prefer, to have rather, to choose rather

實

2 實力 **[shíh-lì]**: actual strength, real strength or power

實力地位政策 **[shíh-lì tì-wèi chèng-ts'è]**: policy of positions of actual strength

5 實力主義 **[shíh-yùng chŭ-ì]**: pragmatism

6 實行 **[shíh-hsíng]**: to put into effect, to conduct, to practice, to pursue, to exercise

實地 **[shíh-tì]**: on the spot, practical, actual

實在 **[shíh-tsài]**: real, really

實在論 **[shíh-tsài-lùn]**: realism

8 實事求是 **[shíh-shìh ch'íu-shìh]**: to seek truth from facts; realistic, practical and realistic

實物 **[shíh-wù]**: substance, solid matter, goods in kind

實物交換 **[shíh-wù chiāo-huàn]**: to barter, barter

實物稅 **[shíh-wù-shùi]**: taxes in kind, taxation in kind

9 實施 **[shíh-shīh]**: to enforce, to put into operation, to put into effect, to implement, to put into practice

實施綱要 **[shíh-shīh kāng-yào]**: general program for implementation

11 實習 **[shíh-hsí]**: to practice; field demonstration, on-the-job training, practical course

實習生 **[shíh-hsí-shēng]**: apprentice, trainee, probationer, learner

實現 **[shíh-hsièn]**: to realize, to come about, to make real, to carry out, to implement, to materialize; realization, implementation

13 實幹 **[shíh-kàn]**: to work perseveringly

實幹，苦幹的精神 **[shíh-kàn, k'ŭ-kàn te chīng-shén]**: a spirit of perseverance and energy in work (i.e., a good, solid style of work that displays energy, perseverance, and ingenuity)

14 實際 **[shíh-chì]**: practical, actual, real; actuality, reality

實際產量 **[shíh-chì ch'ăn-liàng]**: actual, output, physical output

實際情况 **[shíh-chì ch'íng-k'uàng]**: actual conditions

實際意義 **[shíh-chì ì-ì]**: practical significance

實際可行 **[shíh-chì k'ŏ-hsíng]**: practicable and feasible

實際工資 **[shíh-chì kūng-tzū]**: real wage

實際上 **[shíh-chì-shàng]**: practically, virtually, in actual fact, as a matter of fact

實際生活 **[shíh-chì shēng-huó]**: everyday reality, experience in life

實際生活鍛鍊 **[shíh-chì shēng-huó tuàn-lièn]**: to be tempered in the thick of life, to be tempered by experience in life

實際事物 **[shíh-chì shìh-wù]**: reality, actuality, practical matters

實際收入 **[shíh-chì shōu-jù]**: real income

實際問題 **[shíh-chì wèn-t'í]**: actual problem, practical problem

15 實踐 **[shíh-chièn]**: to put into practice; practice; practical

實踐論 **[shíh-chièn-lùn]**: On Practice (Mao)

實踐的考驗 **[shíh-chièn te k'ăo-yèn]**: the test of practice

實質 **[shíh-chíh]**: substance, essence, nature

實質上 **[shíh-chíh-shàng]**: in substance, in essence, materially, virtually

實彈射擊 **[shíh-tàn shè-chī]**: firing with live ammunition

18 實職 **[shíh-chíh]**: actual position

19 實證主義[shíh-chèng chŭ-ì]: pragmatism

22 實權 [shíh-ch'üán]: actual power

23 實體[shíh-t'ĭ]: substance

24 實驗[shí-yèn]: to test, to carry out an experiment; experimentation, test, experiment; experimental

實驗農場[shíh-yèn núng-ch'ăng]: experimental farm

實驗生物研究所[shíh-yèn shēng-wù yén-chìu-sŏ]: Institute of Experimental Biology

實驗室[shíh-yèn-shìh]: laboratory

— 12 Strokes —

寫

10 寫眞實[hsiĕh chēn-shíh]: writing the truth

寬

3 寬大[k'uān-tà]: leniency, magnanimity, moderation, clemency; lenient, magnanimous

寬大政策[k'uān-tà chèng-ts'è]: policy of leniency

寬大處理[k'uān-tà ch'ŭ-lĭ]: to settle or dispose leniently

5 寬打窄用[k'uān-tă chăi-yùng]: to budget liberally and spend sparingly

9 寬待[k'uān-tài]: to treat leniently

10 寬容[k'uān-júng]: to tolerate

寬恕[k'uān-shù]: to pardon, to forgive; clemency, forgiveness

14 寬銀幕電影[k'uān yín-mù tièn-yĭng]: wide screen film, cinemascope

15 寬廣[k'uān-kuăng]: extensive, vast

17 寬闊[k'uān-k'uò]: spacious, immense, vast

審

7 審判 [shĕn-p'àn]: to try, to judge, to put on trial; trial; judicial

審判權 [shĕn-p'àn-ch'üán]: judicial authority

審判員 [shĕn-p'àn-yüán]: judicial official, judge

9 審查[shĕn-ch'á]: to investigate, to examine, to inspect; examination, investigation, inspection

審計[shĕn-chì]: auditing

審計制度[shĕn-chì chìh-tù]: auditing system

審計員[shĕn-chì-yüán]: auditor

10 審核[shĕn-hó]: to review, judicial inquiry

審訊[shĕn-hsǜn]: trial

20 審議[shĕn-ì]: to review and consider

— 13 Strokes —

寰

6 寰宇[huán-yŭ]: the universe, the cosmos

10 寰海[huán-hăi]: the world

11 寰球[húan-ch'íu]: the world

— 16 Strokes —

9 寶城[păo-ch'éng]: Posong (Korea)

10 寶庫[păo-k'ù]: treasury

寶座[păo-tsò]: throne

12 寶貴[păo-kuèi]: precious, valuable

13 寶塔[păo-t'ă]: pagoda

— RADICAL 寸 41 —

寸

[3] 寸土必爭[ts'ùn-t'ŭ pì-chēng]: to fight for every inch of land, to dispute every inch of ground

[22] 寸權必奪，寸利必得[ts'ùn-ch'üán pì tó, ts'ùn-lì pì té]: to try to seize every ounce of power and every ounce of gain

— 6 Strokes —

封

[9] 封建[fēng-chièn]: feudal

封建制度[fēng-chièn chìh-tù]: feudalism

封建主義[fēng-chièn chŭ-ì]: feudalism

封建割據[fēng-chièn kō-chǜ]: feudal separatism

封建殘餘[fēng-chièn ts'án-yǘ]: feudal remnant

封建餘孽[fēng-tièn yǘ-nièh]: feudal dregs

[11] 封閉[fēng-pì]: to seal up; closure

[18] 封鎖[fēng-sŏ]: to seal off, to blockade; blockade

封鎖交通[fēng-sŏ chiāo-t'ūng]: to cordon off; a cordon

封鎖禁運[fēng-sŏ chìn-yǜn]: blockade and embargo

封鎖新聞[fēng-sŏ hsīn-wén]: news blackout

— 7 Strokes —

射

[4] 射手[shè-shŏu]: gunner, marksman

[12] 射程[shè-ch'éng]: range, amplitude

[17] 射擊場[shè-chī-ch'ăng]: firing range, target range

射擊術[shè-chī-shù]: gunnery, marksmanship

— 8 Strokes —

將

[1] 將一軍[chiāng ì chǖn]: to checkmate, to challenge; checkmate, challenge

[5] 將功贖罪[chiāng-kūng shú-tsùi]: to make amends for one's crimes by good deeds

[8] 將近[chiāng-chìn]: on the verge of, near, impending

[9] 將計就計[chiāng-chì chìu-chì]: to meet an adversary with his own strategy

將軍[chiàng-chǖn]: general, admiral, commander

將帥[chiàng-shuài]: commander-in-chief

[14] 將領[chiàng-lĭng]: commander

專

[2] 專人分工負責[chuān-jén fēn-kūng fù-tsé]: division of labor and fixed responsibility

[4] 專心[chuān-hsīn]: devotion; wholehearted

專心致志於[chuān-hsīn chìh-chìh yǘ]: to devote oneself to, to commit oneself to, to be intent on

專心於[chuān-hsīn yǘ]: to devote oneself to, to commit oneself to

專文[chuān-wén]: special article, feature, feature article

5 專用綫[**chuān-yùng hsièn**]: special rail lines

6 專有[**chuān-yŭ**]: to possess exclusively, to monopolize; sole, single, peculiar, special, particular, exclusive

8 專長[**chuān-ch'áng**]: to be adept in, to excel in, to be a specialist in; proficient, expert

專制政治[**chuān-chìh chèng-chìh**]: autocracy

專門[**chuān-mén**]: technical, specialized

專門技能[**chuān-mén chì-néng**]: specialized technical ability, technical know-how

專門化[**chuān-mén-huà**]: specialization

9 專政[**chuān-chèng**]: dictatorship, autocracy, despotism

專修科[**chuān-hsīu-k'ō**]: special course

專科學校[**chuān-k'ō hsüéh-hsiào**]: school with special courses of study

10 專案[**chuān-àn**]: special course

專家[**chuān-chiā**]: expert, specialist

專家路線[**chuān-chiā lù-hsièn**]: the expert line (the tendency of experts in a field to emphasize elegance or grandeur in their designs at the expense of money, materials, and time)

11 專區[**chuān-ch'ū**]: special region, administrative region

專務人民法院[**chuān-wù jén-mín fă-yüàn**]: special people's court

13 專業[**chuān-yèh**]: specialty, special work, special course; professional, vocational

專業教育[**chuān-yèh chiào-yù**]: vocational education

專業知識[**chuān-yèh chīh-shìh**]: professional knowledge

專業分工[**chuān-yèh fēn-kūng**]: specialization and division of labor

專業學校[**chuān-yèh hsüéh-hsiào**]: vocational school

專業化[**chuān-yèh-huà**]: specialization

專業人員[**chuān-yèh jén-yüán**]: professional staff, professional personnel, professional men

專業生產會議[**chuān-yèh shēng-ch'ăn hùi-ì**]: production meeting concerned with specialized trades, conference on specialized trades

專業隊伍[**chuān-yèh tùi-wŭ**]: specialized personnel

專業運輸隊[**chuān-yèh yùn-shū tùi**]: full-time transport team

14 專署[**chuān-shŭ**]: prefectural commissioner's office

15 專論[**chuān-lùn**]: monograph, treatise on a special subject

專賣[**chuān-mài**]: to have a monopoly in, to be the exclusive sellers of; monopoly

專賣業[**chuān-mài-yèh**]: monopoly trade

16 專橫[**chuān-hèng**]: to take the law into one's own hands; despotic, arbitrary

18 專斷[**chuān-tuàn**]: to decide arbitrarily; arbitrary decision; arbitrary

21 專欄[**chuān-lán**]: newspaper column

專欄作家[**chuān-lán tsò-chiā**]: columnist

— 9 Strokes —

7 尋找[**hsún-chăo**]: to look for, to search for, to hunt for

尋找出路[**hsún-chăo ch'ū-lù**]: to find a way out

9 尊重[**tsūn-chùng**]: to respect, to honor, to esteem; dignity, respect, honor

— 11 Strokes —

對

4 對方 **[tùi-fāng]**: the other side, the opposite side

對牛彈琴 **[tùi níu t'án-ch'ín]**: to play music to an ox, to preach to deaf ears, to talk over people's heads, to cast pearls before swine

對比 **[tùi-pǐ]**: balance; contrasting, corresponding

5 對立 **[tùi-lì]**: to oppose; opposition; antagonistic

對立而又統一 **[tùi-lì érh yù t'ŭng-ī]**: both contradictory and in unity

對立關係 **[tùi-lì kuān-hsì]**: antagonistic relations

對立面 **[tùi-lì-mièn]**: opposites, opposite side

對立統一法則 **[tùi-lì t'ŭng-ī fă-tsé]**: the law of the unity of opposites

對付 **[tùi-fù]**: to cope with, to deal with, to encounter, to see to

對白 **[tùi-pái]**: dialogue

對外政策 **[tùi-wài chèng-ts'è]**: foreign policy, external policy

對外關係 **[tùi-wài kuān-hsì]**: foreign relations, external relations

對外擴張 **[tùi-wài k'uò-chāng]**: external expansion

對外貿易 **[tùi-wài mào-ì]**: foreign trade

對外貿易部 **[tùi-wài mào-ì pù]**: Ministry of Foreign Trade

對外貿易逆差 **[tùi-wài mào-ì nì-ch'ā]**: trade deficit, unfavorable balance of trade

對外文化聯絡局 **[tùi-wài wén-huà lién-lò chǘ]**: Foreign Cultural Liaison Bureau

對外文化聯絡委員會 **[tùi-wài wén-huà lién-lò wĕi-yüán-hùi]**: Commission for Cultural Relations with Foreign Countries

7 對抗 **[tùi-k'àng]**: to oppose, to counter, to resist; antagonism antagonistic, rival

對抗性 **[tùi-k'àng-hsìng]**: antagonism

9 對面 **[tùi-mièn]**: opposite

對待 **[tùi-tài]**: to treat, to deal with

10 對流層 **[tùi-líu ts'éng]**: troposphere

對馬 **[tùi-mă]**: Tsushima (Japan)

12 對象 **[tùi-hsiàng]**: target, object

對換 **[tùi-huàn]**: to barter, to exchange

對答 **[tùi-tá]**: to reply, to answer

對策 **[tùi-ts'è]**: countermeasure

13 對照 **[tùi-chào]**: to contrast with, to compare with; control (in a scientific experiment)

14 對稱 **[tùi-ch'èn]**: symmetry; symmetric

— 13 Strokes —

導

4 導火綫 **[tăo-huŏ-hsièn]**: fuse, cause of unrest

10 導致 **[tăo-chìh]**: to cause, to lead to, to result in

導師 **[tăo-shīh]**: tutor, guide, mentor, guardian (during the Cultural Revolution, an epithet for Mao), advisor

14 導語 **[tăo-yü]**: a lead (as in a news story)

15 導彈 **[tăo-tàn]**: missile, guided missile

23 導體 **[tăo-t'ĭ]**: conductor (physical)

— RADICAL 小 42 —

小

3 小口徑的 **[hsiăo k'ŏu-chìng te]**: small-bore, small-caliber

小土群 **[hsiăo t'ŭ-ch'ǘn]**: small indigenous groups (during the Great Leap Forward, small mass-run enterprises using indigenous production methods)

小土爐 **[hsiăo t'ŭ-lú]**: small indigenous blast furnace

小土地出租者 **[hsiăo t'ŭ-tì ch'ū-tsū-chĕ]**: small landleaser

4 小丑 **[hsiăo-ch'ŏu]**: clown, comedian

小心的 **[hsiăo-hsīn te]**: prudent, cautious, careful, discreet, watchful, wary, guarded

5 小生產 **[hsiăo shēng-ch'ăn]**: small production, small-scale production

小生產者 **[hsiăo shēng-ch'ăn-chĕ]**: small producer

小生意 **[hsiăo shēng-ì]**: petty trading

小册子 **[hsiăo ts'è-tzu]**: tract, pamphlet, manual, booklet, brochure

6 小米 **[hsiăo-mĭ]**: millet

小米加步槍 **[hsiăo-mĭ chiā pù-ch'iāng]**: millet plus rifles

小自由 **[hsiăo tzù-yú]**: little freedoms (refers to private plots within the collective and the freedom to cultivate one's private plot and reclaimed land as well as to engage in private business and sell one's produce on the free market)

小宇宙 **[hsiăo yŭ-chòu]**: microcosm

8 小亞細亞 **[hsiăo yà-hsì-yà]**: Asia Minor

9 小前提 **[hsiăo ch'ién-t'í]**: minor premise

小型 **[hsiăo-hsíng]**: small, small-sized

小型農具 **[hsiăo-hsíng núng-chù]**: small farm tools

小洋群 **[hsiăo yáng-ch'ǘn]**: small foreign groups (during the Great Leap Forward, small mass-run enterprises using foreign production methods)

小洋爐 **[hsiăo yáng-lú]**: small, modern blast furnace

10 小高爐 **[hsiăo kāo-lú]**: small blast furnace

小倉 **[hsiăo-ts'āng]**: Kokura (Japan)

11 小將 **[hsiăo-chiàng]**: Little Generals (i.e., the Red Guard–a euphemistic term)

小笠原諸島 **[hsiăo-lì-yüán chū-tăo]**: Bonin Islands (Japan)

小麥 **[hsiăo-mài]**: wheat

小商小販 **[hsiăo-shāng hsiăo-fàn]**: small traders and peddlers

小商人 **[hsiăo shāng-jén]**: petty trader

小商品 **[hsiăo shāng-p'ĭn]**: petty commodities

小偸 **[hsiăo-t'ōu]**: petty thief, pilferer

小組 **[hsiăo-tsŭ]**: section, small group, team, circle, cell

小組會 **[hsiăo-tsŭ-hùi]**: group meeting

小組委員會 **[hsiăo-tsŭ wĕi-yüán-hùi]**: subcommittee

12 小圈子 **[hsiăo ch'üān-tzu]**: a small circle

小隊 **[hsiăo-tùi]**: squad

13 小意思 **[hsiăo ì-ssù]**: a mere trifle, nothing important, a slight token of regard

小農經濟 **[hsiăo-núng chīng-chì]**: small peasant economy

小資產階級 **[hsiăo tzū-ch'ăn chiēh-chí]**: petty bourgeoisie

小資產階級知識份子[hsiăo tzū-ch'ăn chiēh-chí chīh-shìh fèn-tzu]: petty bourgeois intellectual

小業主[hsiăo yèh-chŭ]: small proprietor

15 小廣播[hsiăo kuăng-pō]: to spread rumors; gossip, hearsay, loose talk

小標題[hsiăo piāo-t'í]: sub-heading

小團體主義[hsiăo t'uán-t'ĭ chŭ-ì]: cliquism

16 小學教育[hsiăo-hsüéh chiào-yǜ]: primary education

小學校[hsiăo hsüéh-hsiào]: primary school

小鋼炮[hsiăo kāng-p'ào]: light artillery

17 小聰明[hsiăo ts'ūng-míng]: sharp-witted but petty-minded, to have the intelligence of a small-minded person; small-minded; small-mindedness

18 小轉爐[hsiăo chuăn-lú]: small converter

小額[hsiăo-ó]: small amount

小題大做[hsiăo-t'í tà-tsò]: to make a fuss over nothing, to make a mountain out of a molehill

— 1 Stroke —

6 少而精[shăo èrh chīng]: little but well

少先隊[shào-hsiēn-tùi]: Pioneers

少先隊輔導員[shào-hsiēn-tùi fŭ-tăo-yüán]: Pioneer counsellor

少年[shào-nién]: youngster, teenager, youth; young, juvenile

少年中國晨報[shào-nién chūng-kuó ch'én-pào]: Young China Morning Post (Chinese language newspaper, San Francisco)

少年兒童俱樂部[shào-nién érh-t'úng chǜ-lò-pù]: children's club

少年先鋒眞理報[shào-nién hsiēn-fēng chēn-lĭ pào]: Pionerskaya Pravda (Russian daily newspaper)

少年先鋒宮[shào-nién hsiēn-fēng kūng]: Palace of the Young Pioneers

少年先鋒隊[shào-nién hsiēn-fēng tùi]: Young Pioneers

少年先鋒隊員[shào-nién hsiēn-fēng tùi-yüán]: member of Young Pioneers

少年宮[shào-nién kūng]: Palace of Youth

少年共產國際[shào-nién kùng-ch'ăn kuó-chì]: Young Communist International

少有[shăo-yŭ]: rare, exceptional, unusual, unique, seldom found, seldom seen, seldom heard

8 少壯派[shào-chuàng p'ài]: young guard (i.e., as opposed to "old guard")

10 少將[shào-chiàng]: Major General (Chinese Army and Air Force); Rear Admiral (Chinese Navy); Air Vice-Marshal (British Air Force)

少校[shào-hsiào]: Major (Chinese Army and Air Force); Lieutenant Commander (Chinese Navy); Squadron Leader (British Navy)

11 少尉[shào-wèi]: Lieutenant (Chinese Army and Air Force); Ensign (Chinese Navy); Junior Lieutenant (Russian armed services); Pilot Officer (British Air Force); Acting Sub-lieutenant (British Navy)

13 少爺兵[shào-yéh-pīng]: young gentleman soldiers, American soldiers (a derogatory term used particularly during the Korean War)

15 少數[shăo-shù]: minority, a handful of, few, a limited number of

少數服從多數[shăo-shù fú-ts'úng tō-shù]: the minority (must) obey the majority

少數民族[shăo-shù mín-tsú]: minority nationalities, national minorities

少數民族語言研究所[shăo-shù mín-tsú

yŭ-yén yén-chìu-sŏ]: Institute of National Minority Languages

— 3 Strokes —

尖

8 尖刻[chiēn-k'ò]: sharp, sarcastic

14 尖端[chiēn-tuān]: tip, pinnacle, peak, point, summit, zenith; top, top level, most advanced, pioneering

尖端產品[chiēn-tuān ch'ăn-p'ĭn]: top product

尖端科學[chiēn-tuan k'ō-hsüéh]: top level sciences, pinnacle of science, acme of science

15 尖銳[chiēn-jùi]: acute, sharp, keen, pointed

尖銳化[chiēn-jùi-huà]: to sharpen, to become sharp, to become acute

— RADICAL 尢兀尣 43 —

— 8 Strokes —

就

6 就地[chìu-tì]: on the spot

就地取材[chìu-tì ch'ŭ-ts'ái]: to use local materials

就地審判[chìu-tì shĕn-p'àn]: on-the-spot trial

8 就近[chìu-chìn]: at close quarters, nearby, in the neighborhood

9 就要到來的[chìu-yào tào-lái te]: imminent, forthcoming, coming, impending

10 就座[chìu-tsò]: to take one's seat

13 就業[chìu-yèh]: employment

18 就職[chìu-chíh]: to take office, to swear in, to induct

就職典禮[chìu-chíh tiĕn-lĭ]: inauguration, installation ceremony

就職演說[chìu-chíh yĕn-shuō]: inauguration speech, investiture speech

— RADICAL 尸 44 —

— 1 Stroke —

尺

8 尺度[ch'ĭh-tù]: measurement, measuring stick

尹

12 尹普善[yĭn p'ŭ-shàn]: Yoon Bosun (South Korean statesman)

— 2 Strokes —

尼

4 尼日爾共和國[ní-jìh-ĕrh kùng-hó-kuó]: Republic of Niger

尼日利亞[ní-jìh-lì-yà]: Nigeria

尼日利亞聯邦[ní-jìh-lì-yà lién-pāng]: Federation of Nigeria

5 尼加拉瓜[ní-chiā-lā-kuā]: Nicaragua

尼加拉瓜共和國 [ní-chiā-lā-kuā kùng-hó-kuó] : Republic of Nicaragua

尼古拉耶夫 [ní-kŭ-lā-yéh-fū] : Nikolaev

尼古拉耶夫斯克 [ní-kŭ-lā-yéh-fū-ssū-k'ò] : Nikolaievsk

7 尼克森 [ní-k'ò-sēn] : Nixon, Richard M.

尼克遜 [ní-kò-hsùn] : Nixon, Richard M. (used in Hong Kong)

尼克松 [ní-k'ò-sūng] : Nixon, Richard M. (used on mainland)

8 尼姑 [ní-kū] : nun, Buddhist nun

尼泊爾 [ní-pó-ĕrh] : Nepal

尼泊爾王國 [ní-pó-ĕrh wáng-kuó] : Kingdom of Nepal

尼亞美 [ní-yà-mĕi] : Niamey (Republic of Niger)

尼亞薩蘭 [ní-yà-sà-lán] : Nyasaland

9 尼科西亞 [ní-k'ō-hsī-yà] : Nicosia (Cyprus)

10 尼兹瓦 [ní-tzū-wă] : Nizwa (Oman)

14 尼赫魯 [ní-hò-lŭ] : Nehru, Jawaharlal (Indian statesman)

16 尼龍 [ní-lúng] : nylon

— 4 Strokes —

局

5 局外人 [chǘ-wài jén] : outsider

9 局面 [chǘ-mièn] : situation, condition, phase, aspect

11 局部 [chǘ-pù] : partial, local

局部协定 [chǘ-pù hsiéh-tìng] : local agreement

局部立場 [chǘ-pù lì-ch'ăng] : partial stand

局部利益 [chǘ-pù lì-ì] : local interests, partial interests

局部偏差 [chǘ-pù p'iēn-ch'ā] : partial deviations

局部錯誤 [chǘ-pù ts'ò-wù] : to be mistaken in part; partially in error, local mistake

13 局勢 [chǘ-chìh] : situation, state of affairs, circumstances, conditions

尾

4 尾巴主義 [wĕi-pā chŭ-ì] : tailism (refers to "rightist henchmen" who only follow their leaders)

16 尾隨 [wĕi-súi] : to trail after, to tail after, to follow in the wake of

— 5 Strokes —

居

4 居止 [chū-chĭh] : Cuchi (Vietnam)

居心 [chū-hsīn] : attitude, motive, intention

5 居功 [chū-kūng] : to claim credit

居民 [chū-mín] : inhabitant, resident

居民集團 [chū-mín chí-t'uán] : population group

居民點 [chū-mín tiĕn] : residential quarters, housing estate

居民委員會 [chū-mín wĕi-yüán-hùi] : neighborhood committee

6 居合 [chū-hó] : Cuhap (Vietnam)

7 居住之處 [chū-chù chīh ch'ù] : place of residence, lodging, domicile, dwelling, abode

居住條件 [chū-chù t'iáo-chièn] : housing conditions

8 居奇 **[chǖ-ch'í]**: to hoard for a price rise

居於少數 **[chǖ-yǘ shăo-shù]**: to constitute a minority

10 居留 **[chǖ-líu]**: to reside, to remain, to stay; residence

11 居第一位 **[chǖ tì-í wèi]**: to rank first, to stand first; to be in first place

12 居間人 **[chǖ-chiēn-jén]**: intermediary

居虛位者 **[chǖ-hsǖ-wèi-chĕ]**: figurehead, nominal head

居然 **[chǖ-ján]**: after all, easily, simply, really, regularly, uneventfully, contrary to expectations

屈

8 屈服 **[ch'ǖ-fú]**: to render into submission; to submit to, to yield to, to give way; submission, subservience

10 屈辱 **[ch'ǖ-jŭ]**: humiliation, disgrace, dishonor, shame

11 屈從 **[ch'ǖ-ts'úng]**: to submit to, to yield to, to give way; submission, subservience

— 6 Strokes —

屍

9 屍首 **[shīh-shŏu]**: corpse, remains, dead body

— 7 Strokes —

展

5 展出 **[chăn-ch'ū]**: to exhibit, to be on display, to put on display, to be on show; exhibition, exposition

11 展望 **[chăn-wàng]**: to look at, prospect, outlook, perspective, vista; Look (American periodical)

12 展期 **[chăn-ch'í]**: to postpone, to put off, to defer, to delay, to retard, to extend a time limit

展開 **[chăn-k'āi]**: to open, to unfold, to launch, to inaugurate, to develop, to start, to begin

21 展覽 **[chăn-lăn]**: to exhibit, to be on display, to put on display; exhibition, exposition

展覽館 **[chăn-lăn-kuăn]**: exhibition hall

展覽館分館 **[chăn-lăn-kuăn fēn-kuăn]**: pavilion in an exhibition hall

— 8 Strokes —

屛

5 屛斥 **[pĭng-ch'ìh]**: to ward off, to chase away, to rebuke

11 屛棄 **[pĭng-ch'ì]**: to reject, to desert, to abandon

— 9 Strokes —

屠

2 屠刀 **[t'ú-tāo]**: butcher's knife, killer's sword

10 屠殺 **[t'ú-shā]**: to massacre, to slaughter; slaughter, massacre

— 11 Strokes —

6 屢次 **[lǚ-tz'ù]**: over and over, again and again, time and again, repeatedly

— 12 Strokes —

履

6 履行 **[lǚ-hsíng]**: to carry out, to implement, to discharge; implementation, performance, carrying out

層

6 層次 **[ts'éng-tz'ù]** : sequence, order, rank

層次重叠 **[ts'éng-tz'ù ch'úng-tiéh]** : overlapping (i.e., as of organizational structure)

12 層報 **[ts'éng-pào]** : to give a report in stages

— 18 Strokes —

屬

屬 **[shŭ]** : genus, genre

8 屬性 **[shŭ-hsìng]** : attributive, an attribute

屬於 **[shŭ-yǘ]** : to belong to, to be affiliated with, to be associated with

11 屬國 **[shŭ-kuó]** : vassal state, dependency

— RADICAL 屮 45 —

— RADICAL 山 46 —

山

3 山口 **[shān-k'ŏu]** : Yamaguchi (Japan)

7 山形 **[shān-hsíng]** : Yamagata (Japan)

山谷水庫 **[shān-kŭ shŭi-k'ù]** : gorge-type reservoir

9 山炮 **[shān-p'ào]** : mountain gun, pack howitzer

10 山脈 **[shān-mài]** : mountain range

11 山區 **[shān-ch'ǖ]** : mountain region, mountainous area, upland region

山崩 **[shān-pēng]** : landslide, avalanche

山野重炮 **[shān-yĕh chùng-p'ào]** : heavy mountain and field guns

16 山頭 **[shān-t'óu]** : mountaintop; Shantou (minority nationality)

山頭主義 **[shān-t'óu chŭ-ì]** : mountaintopism, isolationist deviation (i.e., the undesirable attitude of certain cadres who regard the areas or organizations under their control as their personal "kingdoms")

18 山額主義 **[shān-ó chŭ-ì]** : Sangerism

— 4 Strokes —

3 岔子 **[ch'à-tzu]** : accident, setback

13 岔道 **[ch'à-tào]** : crossroads

17 岔錯 **[ch'à-ts'ò]** : mistake

岐

8 岐阜 **[ch'í-fù]** : Gifu (Japan)

— 5 Strokes —

岸

9 岸信介 **[àn hsìn-chièh]** : Kishi, Nobusuke (Japanese statesman)

岡

3 岡山 **[kāng-shān]** : Okayama (Japan)

4 岡比亞 **[kāng-pĭ-yà]** : Gambia

岩

4 岩手 **[yén-shŏu]** : Iwate (Japan)

— 8 Strokes —

崇

9 崇美 **[ch'úng-mĕi]** : to glorify America, to worship America

崇拜 **[ch'úng-pài]** : to venerate, to worship

崇拜權威 **[ch'úng-pài ch'üán-wēi]** : cult of authority

10 崇高 **[ch'úng-kāo]** : lofty, high, solemn, elevated, exalted

崗

7 崗位 **[kāng-wèi]** : post, sentry post

崩

崩 **[pēng]** : to collapse, to fall into ruin; to shoot dead; the death of an emperor

15 崩潰 **[pēng-k'uèi]** : to disintegrate, to go to pieces, to break up, to give way; breakdown, collapse, disintegration, demise

— 11 Strokes —

嶄

13 嶄新 **[chăn-hsīn]** : up-to-date, brand-new, renovated, modern

— 18 Strokes —

巍

巍然屹立 **[wēi-ján ch'ì-lì]** : to stand majestically, to stand firmly

— RADICAL 巛 川 巜 47 —

川

川 **[ch'uān]** : Szechuan Province (abbreviation for 四川)

4 川木 **[ch'uān-mù]** : Xuyenmoc (Vietnam)

11 川崎 **[ch'uān-ch'í]** : Kawasaki (Japan)

13 川資 **[ch'uān-tzū]** : fare, travel expenses

— 3 Strokes —

州

8 州長 **[chōu-chăng]** : governor

州長地位 **[chōu-chăng tì-wèi]** : position of governor, governorship

— 4 Strokes —

9 巡洋艦 **[hsún-yáng-chièn]** : cruiser

10 巡迴法庭 **[hsún-húi fă-t'íng]** : circuit court

12 巡視 **[hsún-shìh]** : inspection tour, patrol

巡視團 **[hsún-shìh-t'uán]** : inspection team

巡游 **[hsún-yú]** : to tour; parade

23 巡邏 **[hsún-ló]** : to patrol, patrol

— RADICAL 工 48 —

工

工 **[kūng]**: work, duty, workman, a job; technical innovation (one of the eight characters of the 八字憲法 q.v.)

2 工人技術學校 **[kūng-jén chì-shù hsüéh-hsiào]**: workers' technical school

工人階級 **[kūng-jén chiēh-chí]**: working class, proletariat

工人日報 **[kūng-jén jìh-pào]**: Worker's Daily (Chinese daily newspaper); Daily Worker (British daily newspaper)

工人貴族 **[kūng-jén kuèi-tsú]**: labor aristocracy

工人業餘文化學校 **[kūng-jén yèh-yű wén-huà hsüéh-hsiào]**: workers' spare time literacy school

4 工分 **[kūng-fēn]**: work point, work credit

5 工本 **[kūng-pěn]**: operating costs

6 工地 **[kūng-tì]**: construction site, work site

7 工坊 **[kūng-fāng]**: workshop

工序 **[kūng-hsǜ]**: working processes, operation sequence

工兵團 **[kūng-pīng-t'uán]**: engineer corps

工作 **[kūng-tsò]**: to work; work, task

工作戰鬥化 **[kūng-tsò chàn-tòu-huà]**: martialization of action (one of the 三化, q.v.)

工作效率 **[kūng-tsò hsiào-lǜ]**: working efficiency

工作人員 **[kūng-tsò jén-yüán]**: staff, working personnel

工作日 **[kūng-tsò jìh]**: working day

工作量 **[kūng-tsò liàng]**: amount of work

工作表 **[kūng-tsò piǎo]**: working table, work sheet

工作作風 **[kūng-tsò tsò-fēng]**: working style

工作組 **[kūng-tsò tsǔ]**: work team

工作隊 **[kūng-tsò tùi]**: working team, work unit

8 工長 **[kūng-chăng]**: foreman

工具 **[kūng-chǜ]**: tool, implement, cat's paw

工具改革 **[kūng-chǜ kǎi-kó]**: reform of tools, improvement of tools

工事 **[kūng-shìh]**: fortification

工委 **[kūng-wěi]**: work committee, labor commission

9 工科 **[kūng-k'ō]**: technology, technical subject

10 工徒 **[kūng-t'ú]**: apprentice

11 工票 **[kūng-p'iào]**: work coupon

工商界 **[kūng-shāng chièh]**: industrial and business circles

工商戶 **[kūng-shāng hù]**: industrial and commercial establishment

工商日報 **[kūng-shāng jìh-pào]**: Kung Shang Jih Pao (Hong Kong daily newspaper)

工商聯 **[kūng-shāng-lién]**: Federation of Industry and Commerce (abbreviation of 工商業聯合會)

工商部 **[kūng-shāng pù]**: Ministry of Industry and Trade

工商業 [kūng-shāng-yèh] : industry and commerce

工商業者 [kūng-shāng-yèh-chě] : industrialists and business men, industrialists and traders, industrialists and merchants

工商業家 [kūng-shāng-yèh-chiā] : industrialist and merchant

工商業聯合會 [kūng-shāng-yèh lién-hó-hùi] : Federation of Industry and Commerce

工務部 [kūng-wù pù] : Ministry of Public Works

12 工程 [kūng-ch'éng] : construction project, works, project

工程項目 [kūng-ch'éng hsiàng-mù] : construction items

工程師 [kūng-ch'éng-shīh] : engineer

工間操 [kūng-chiēn ts'āo] : calisthenics during work break

工棚 [kūng-p'éng] : workers' housing (i.e., temporary worker housing at a construction site)

13 工會 [kūng-hùi] : trade union, labor union

工會會員 [kūng-hùi hùi-yüán] : union member

工會工作者 [kūng-hùi kūng-tsò-chě] : unionist, union official

工會運動工作委員會 [kūng-hùi yùn-tùng kūng-tsò wěi-yüán-hùi] : Trade Union Movement Work Committee

工農出身 [kūng-núng ch'ū-shēn] : of peasant and worker origin

工農革命政府 [kūng-núng kó-mìng chèng-fǔ] : workers' and peasants' revolutionary government

工農聯盟 [kūng-núng lién-méng] : alliance of workers and peasants

工農兵 [kūng núng pīng] : workers, peasants, and soldiers

工農兵學商 [kūng núng pīng hsüéh shāng] : workers, peasants, soldiers, intellectuals, and businessmen

工農商學兵相結合 [kūng núng shāng hsüéh pīng hsiāng chiéh-hó] : to combine industry, agriculture, trade, education, and military affairs

工農速成初等學校 [kūng núng sù-ch'éng ch'ū-těng hsüéh-hsiào] : workers' and peasants' accelerated elementary school

工農速成中學 [kūng-núng sù-ch'éng chūng-hsüéh] : workers' and peasants' accelerated middle school

工農業結合 [kūng-núng-yèh chiéh-hó] : integration of industry and agriculture

工農業並舉的方針 [kūng-núng-yèh pìng-chǚ te fāng-chēn] : the policy of simultaneously developing industry and agriculture

工農業總產值 [kūng-núng-yèh tsǔng-ch'ăn-chíh] : gross output value of industry and agriculture

工農業餘教育 [kūng-núng yèh-yű chiào-yǜ] : spare-time education for workers and peasants

工傷事故 [kūng-shāng shìh-kù] : work accident

工賊 [kūng-tséi] : strikebreaker, scab

工資 [kūng-tzū] : wages, pay, salary

工資基金 [kūng-tzū chī-chīn] : wage fund

工資制和供給制相結合 [kūng-tzū-chìh hó kūng-chì-chìh hsiāng chiéh hó] : combining the wage system with the (government) supply system (a system under which cadres receive their pay partly in cash and partly in kind)

工資制度 [kūng-tzū chìh-tù] : wages system

工資分 [kūng-tzū fēn] : wage unit

工資等級 [kūng-tzū těng-chí] : wage grade

工業 [kūng-yèh] : industry; industrial

工業基地 [kūng-yèh chī-tì] : industrial

center

工業化 [kūng-yèh-huà]: to industrialize; industrialization

工業抗旱 [kūng-yèh k'àng-hàn]: struggle against raw material shortage; industrial combat against drought

工業革命 [kūng-yèh kó-mìng]: industrial revolution

工業工作部 [kūng-yèh kūng-tsò pù]: industrial work department

工業壟斷 [kūng-yèh lŭng-tuàn]: industrial monopoly

工業品 [kūng-yèh-p'ĭn]: industrial product

工業生產 [kūng-yèh shēng-ch'ăn]: industrial production

工業的合理布局 [kūng-yèh te hó-lĭ pù-chǘ]: rational geographical distribution of industry

工業總產值 [kūng-yèh tsŭng-ch'ăn-chíh]: gross value of industrial output

工業原料 [kūng-yèh yüán-liào]: industrial raw material

工業原料作物 [kūng-yèh yüán-liào tsò-wù]: industrial crops

14 工種 [kūng-chŭng]: work category, kind of work

工團 [kūng-t'uán]: syndicate

工團主義 [kūng-t'uán chŭ-ì]: syndicalism

15 工廠 [kūng-ch'ăng]: factory, plant, mill

16 工錢 [kūng-ch'ién]: wages

工頭 [kūng-t'óu]: foreman

17 工聯 [kūng-lién]: labor union

工聯主義 [kūng-lién chŭ-ì]: syndicalism

20 工齡 [kūng-líng]: seniority, length of time employed

工藝 [kūng-ì]: technology

工藝規程 [kūng-ì kuēi-ch'éng]: technological regulations, technological process

— 2 Strokes —

巧

7 巧妙 [ch'iăo-miào]: ingenuity, subtlety; ingenious, cunning, skillful, subtle

13 巧幹 [ch'iăo-kàn]: to work resourcefully

巨

3 巨大 [chǜ-tà]: tremendous, vast, immense, huge, gigantic, enormous

9 巨型 [chǜ-hsíng]: huge, heavy, giant

12 巨港 [chǜ-kăng]: Palembang

16 巨頭 [chǜ-t'óu]: magnate, boss, king

17 巨濟島 [chǜ-chì tăo]: Koje Island (Korea)

18 巨額 [chǜ-ó]: big amount

左

5 左右手 [tsŏ-yù-shŏu]: right-hand man, valuable assistant

左右搖擺 [tsŏ-yù yáo-păi]: to vacillate, now to the left and now to the right

9 左派 [tsŏ-p'ài]: leftist, left-wing (i.e., those whose thinking conforms to the thought of Mao Tse-tung)

左派幼稚病 [tsŏ-p'ài yù-chìh-pìng]: Left-Wing Communism, An Infantile Disorder (Lenin, 1920)

11 左袒 [tsŏ-t'ăn]: to take sides, to give improper protection to

13 左傾機會主義 [tsŏ-ch'īng chī-hùi chŭ-ì]: left opportunism

左傾份子 [tsŏ-ch'īng fèn-tzu]: left deviationist (i.e., one who thinks the party is too conservative)

左傾空談主義 **[tsŏ-ch'īng k'ūng-t'án chŭ-ì]**: leftist phrase-mongering

左傾路綫 **[tsŏ-ch'īng lù-hsièn]**: left deviationist line

左傾冒險主義 **[tsŏ-ch'īng mào-hsiĕn chŭ-ì]**: left adventurism

左傾幼稚病 **[tsŏ-ch'īng yù-chìh-pìng]**: left-wing infantile disorder

左道旁門 **[tsŏ-tào p'áng-mén]**: heretical doctrines

15 左輪手槍 **[tsŏ-lún shŏu-ch'iāng]**: revolver

17 左翼 **[tsŏ-ì]**: left wing

左翼份子 **[tsŏ-ì fèn-tzu]**: left winger

左翼作家 **[tsŏ-ì tsò-chiā]**: left-wing writer

— 7 Strokes —

差

7 差別 **[ch'ā-piéh]**: difference, distinction, diversity, dissimilarity, discrepancy, differential

8 差事 **[ch'āi-shìh]**: official position, office, post, official business

14 差遣 **[ch'āi-ch'iĕn]**: to send, to dispatch

15 差價 **[ch'ā-chià]**: cost differential, price difference

差數 **[ch'ā-shù]**: balance, difference, margin

16 差錯 **[ch'ā-ts'ò]**: accident, mistake, error

18 差額 **[ch'ā-ó]**: margin, balance, difference

— RADICAL 己 49 —

7 己見 **[chĭ-chièn]**: personal opinion, personal view

— 1 Stroke —

巴

2 巴力斯坦 **[pā-lì-ssū-t'ăn]**: Palestine

4 巴比倫 **[pā-pĭ-lún]**: Babylon

5 巴古寧 **[pā-kŭ-níng]**: Bakunin, Mikhail (1814–1876)

巴古寧主義 **[pā-k'ū-níng chŭ-ì]**: Bakunism, anarchism

巴布厄爾曼特峽 **[pā-pù-ò-ĕrh-màn-t'è hsiá]**: Bab el Mandeb

巴布亞 **[pā-pù-yà]**: Papua

6 巴伐利亞 **[pā-fá-lì-yà]**: Bavaria

巴西 **[pā-hsī]**: Brazil

巴伊亞 **[pā-ī-yà]**: Bahia (Brazil)

巴西合衆共和國 **[pā-hsī hó-chùng kùng-hó-kuó]**: United States of Brazil

巴地 **[pā-tì]**: Baria (Vietnam)

7 巴利 **[pā-lì]**: Pale (Burma); Bari (Italy)

巴里群島 **[pā-lĭ ch'ǘn-tăo]**: Parry Islands

8 巴拉圭 **[pā-lā-kuēi]**: Paraguay

巴拉圭共和國 **[pā-lā-kuēi kùng-hó-kuó]**: Republic of Paraguay

巴林酋長國 **[pā-lín ch'iú-chăng-kuó]**: Sheikdom of Bahrein

9 巴哈運動 **[pā-hā yǜn-tùng]**: Bahaism

10 巴格達 **[pā-kó-tá]**: Baghdad (Iraq)

巴格達條約組織 **[pā-kó-tá t'iáo-yüēh tsŭ-chīh]**: The Baghdad Treaty Organization, The Baghdad Pact

巴馬科 **[pā-mă-k'ō]**: Bamako (Republic of

Mali)

巴拿馬 **[pā-ná-mă]** : Panama

巴拿馬城 **[pā-ná-mă ch'éng]** : Panama City (Panama)

巴拿馬共和國 **[pā-ná-mă kùng-hó-kuó]** : Republic of Panama

巴庫 **[pā-k'ù]** : Baku

11 巴基斯坦 **[pā-chī-ssū-t'ăn]** : Pakistan

巴基斯坦伊斯蘭共和國 **[pā-chī-ssū-t'ăn ī-ssū-lán kùng-hó-kuó]** : Islamic Republic of Pakistan

巴基斯坦時報 **[pā-chī-ssū-t'ăn shíh-pào]** : Pakistan Times

巴勒斯坦 **[pā-lè-ssū-t'ăn]** : Palestine

巴勒維 **[pā-lē-wéi]** : Pahlavi, Mohamed-Reza (Emperor of Iran from 1941)

12 巴結 **[pā-chiēh]** : to flatter, to toady to, to curry favor with, to fawn on; sycophancy

巴港 **[pā-kăng]** : Palembang (Indonesia)

巴斯峽 **[pā-ssū hsiá]** : Bass Strait (Australia)

巴斯特爾 **[pā-ssū t'è-ĕrh]** : Basse-Terre (Guadeloupe and Dependencies)

巴敦群島 **[pā-tūn ch'ün-tăo]** : Batan Islands (Philippines)

13 巴塞羅那 **[pā-sài-ló-nà]** : Barcelona (Spain)

巴瑟斯特 **[pā-sè-ssū-t'è]** : Bathurst (Gambia)

巴達維亞 **[pā-tá-wéi-yà]** : Batavia

巴塔哥尼亞 **[pā-t'ă-kō-ní-yà]** : Patagonia

14 巴爾哈什湖 **[pā-ĕrh-hā-shíh hú]** : Lake Balkhash

巴爾西克 **[pā-ĕrh-hsí-k'ò]** : Baltic

巴爾干 **[pā-ĕrh-kàn]** : Balkan

巴爾的摩太陽報 **[pā-ĕrh-tì-mō t'ài-yáng pào]** : Baltimore Sun (American daily newspaper)

15 巴黎 **[pā-lí]** : Paris (France)

巴黎和會 **[pā-lí hó-hùi]** : Versailles Conference

巴黎公社 **[pā-lí kūng-shè]** : Paris Commune

巴黎公社式選舉 **[pā-lí kūng-shè-shìh hsüăn-chŭ]** : Paris Commune elections (in the 16 point decision (六十條, q.v.) of the Central Committee of the CCP in August 1966, it was stated that revolutionary groups, committees, and congresses were to be elected on similar lines to the system of the Paris Commune (1871), a statement that was interpreted by Chou En-lai to mean elections on a mass scale with 95 percent participation of the masses and to which he was opposed on the grounds that left-wing forces in China were not yet in the majority)

巴鄰旁 **[pā-lín-p'áng]** : Palembang (Indonesia)

20 巴蘇陀蘭 **[pā-sū-t'ó-lán]** : Basutoland

— RADICAL 巾 50 —

— 2 Strokes —

布

4 布丹 **[pù-tān]** : Bhutan

5 布加利 **[pù-chiā-lì]** : Bulgaria

布加勒斯特 **[pù-chiā-lò-ssū-t'è]** : Bucharest

6 布防 **[pù-fáng]** : to arrange defensive positions

布西曼 **[pù-hsī-màn]** : Bushmen

7 布告 **[pù-kào]** : announcement

布利維亞 **[pù-lì-wéi-yà]** : Bolivia

布里雅特蒙古 **[pù-lĭ-yă-t'è mĕng-kŭ]**: Buriat Mongols (minority nationality)

布利揚斯克 **[pù-lì-yáng-ssū-k'ò]**: Bryansk (USSR)

布里斯托爾峽 **[pù-lĭ-ssū-t'ō-ĕrh hsiá]**: Bristol Channel

8 布宜諾斯艾利斯 **[pù-í-nò-ssū aì-lì-ssū]**: Buenos Aires (Argentina)

布拉柴維爾 **[pù-lā-ch'ái-wéi-ĕrh]**: Brazzaville (Congo)

布拉格 **[pù-lā-kó]**: Prague (Czechoslovakia)

9 布哈爾 **[pù-hā-ĕrh]**: Bukhara (Uzbek S.S.R.)

10 布朗 **[pù-lăng]**: Pulang (minority nationality)

布朗基主義 **[pù-lăng-chī chŭ-ì]**: Boulangerism

布納 **[pù-nà]**: Buna (New Guinea)

11 布國 **[pù-kuó]**: Prussia

12 布隆迪王國 **[pù-lúng-tí wáng-kuó]**: Kingdom of Burundi

布達佩斯 **[pù-tá-p'èi-ssū]**: Budapest (Hungary)

13 布置 **[pù-chìh]**: to plan, to arrange, to decorate

布路嘎里亞 **[pù-lù-kā-lĭ-yà]**: Bulgaria

14 布爾加寧 **[pù-ĕrh-chiā-níng]**: Bulganin, Nikolai (Russian statesman)

布爾什維主義 **[pù-ĕrh-shíh-wéi chŭ-ì]**: Bolshevism

布爾什維克 **[pù-ĕrh-shíh-wéi-k'ò]**: Bolshevik

15 布魯塞爾 **[pù-lŭ-sài-ĕrh]**: Brussels (Belgium)

21 布蘭登堡 **[pù-lán-tēng păo]**: Brandenburg

市

市 **[shìh]**: city, municipality

市人民代表大會 **[shìh jén-mín tài-piăo tà-hùi]**: municipal people's congress

市人民委員會 **[shìh jén-mín wĕi-yüán-hùi]**: municipal people's council

3 市川 **[shìh-ch'uān]**: Ichikawa (Japan)

5 市民 **[shìh-mín]**: townspeople

8 市長 **[shìh-chăng]**: mayor

9 市政官員 **[shìh-chèng kuān-yüán]**: municipal official

12 市場 **[shìh-ch'ăng]**: market

15 市價 **[shìh-chià]**: market price

市儈 **[shìh-k'uài]**: broker, opportunist, Philistine

市儈主義 **[shìh-k'uài chŭ-ì]**: Philistinism

— 4 Strokes —

7 希伯來 **[hsī-pó-lái]**: Hebrew

11 希望 **[hsī-wàng]**: to aspire, to hope; aspiration, prospect, hope

19 希臘 **[hsī-là]**: Greece

希臘王國 **[hsī-là wáng-kuó]**: Kingdom of Greece

希臘猶太哲學 **[hsī-là yú-t'ài ché-hsüéh]**: Graeco-Judaic philosophy

帕

8 帕拉馬里博 **[p'à-lā-mă-lĭ-pó]**: Paramaribo (Netherlands Guiana)

— 6 Strokes —

8 帝制 **[tì-chìh]**: monarchy, monarchical system

11 帝國主義[tì-kuó chŭ-ì] : imperialism

帝國主義陣營[tì-kuó chŭ-ì chèn-yíng] : the imperialist camp

帝國主義侵略集團[tì-kuó chŭ-ì ch'īn-lüèh chí-t'uán] : the aggressive imperialist bloc

帝國主義列强[tì-kuó chŭ-ì lièh-ch'iáng] : the big imperialist powers

— 7 Strokes —

席

7 席位[hsí-wèi] : seat, place

席位主義[hsí-wèi chŭ-ì] : "seat-ism" (during the Cultural Revolution, refers to fights among cadres of various factions for seats and chairmanships of the Great Revolutionary Alliance and the Three-Way Alliance)

8 席卷[hsí-chüăn] : to sweep over, to engulf, to conquer, to overrun

師

師[shīh] : division, teacher

8 師長[shīh-chăng] : division commander

10 師徒關係[shīh-t'ú kuān-hsì] : master-apprentice relationship

11 師部[shīh-pù] : division headquarters

12 師傅[shīh-fù] : teacher, tutor, expert, master workman

師傅帶徒弟方式[shīh-fù tài t'ú-tì fāng-shìh] : apprenticeship system, the master-apprentice system

15 師範學校[shīh-fàn hsüéh-hsiào] : normal school, teacher training school

師範大學[shīh-fàn tà-hsüéh] : National Normal University (Peking)

— 8 Strokes —

帳

5 帳目[chàng-mù] : account, details of accounts, items of account

帳目不清[chàng-mù pù-ch'īng] : accounts not in order

17 帳篷[chàng-p'éng] : tent, tabernacle

19 帳簿[chàng-pù] : account book

常

3 常久[ch'áng-chiŭ] : long, protracted, enduring

6 常任理事[ch'áng-jèn lĭ-shìh] : member of the executive committee, member of the standing committee

8 常法[ch'áng-fă] : ordinary law, an established rule

常事[ch'áng-shìh] : commonplace occurrence, everyday occurrence

常委會[ch'áng-wĕi-hùi] : standing committee (abbreviation of 常務委員會)

11 常常[ch'áng-ch'áng] : always, constantly, frequently

常規[ch'áng-kuēi] : common custom, ordinary rule, common usages; conventional

常設[ch'áng-shè] : permanent, standing

常務委員[ch'áng-wù wĕi-yüán] : member of a standing committee

常務委員會[ch'áng-wù wĕi-yüán-hùi] : standing committee

12 常備軍[ch'áng-pèi-chūn] : standing troops, standing army

13 常會[ch'áng-hùi] : regular meeting

常態[ch'áng-t'ài] : normal pace, normal behavior, normal conditions

15 常談 [ch'áng-t'án]: common talk, platitude

19 常識 [ch'áng-shìh]: common knowledge, common sense, general knowledge

帶

4 帶手 [tài-shǒu]: to do at the same time

帶水 [tài-shǔi]: to pilot; pilot

帶引 [tài-yǐn]: to lead, to guide

8 帶來 [tài-lái]: to carry, to bear, to transport, to load, to convey

9 帶勁 [tài-chìn]: infused with vigor

帶信 [tài-hsìn]: to inform, to transmit a message, to carry letters

10 帶徒弟 [tài t'ú-tì]: to train an apprentice

11 帶累 [tài-lèi]: to implicate, to involve

帶動 [tài-tùng]: to drive, to propel

12 帶着 [tài-che]: to carry, to bear, to transport, to convey

13 帶落後 [tài lò-hòu]: to bring forward the backward, to bring up those who lag behind

16 帶頭 [tài-t'óu]: to lead, to guide, to direct, to conduct, to take the initiative, to take the lead

帶頭作用 [tài-t'óu tsò-yùng]: forward role

— 9 Strokes —

幅

9 幅度 [fú-tù]: extent

— 10 Strokes —

幌

3 幌子 [huǎng-tzu]: shop sign; pretext, guise, cover, cloak, smoke screen

— 11 Strokes —

幕

幕 [mù]: screen, curtain, scene, veil

8 幕後 [mù-hòu]: behind the scenes

幕後人物 [mù-hòu jén-wù]: wire-puller, those directing behind the scenes

幕後操縱 [mù-hòu ts'āo-tsùng]: wire-pulling; to pull strings behind the scenes

— 12 Strokes —

8 幣制 [pì-chìh]: monetary system, currency system

— 14 Strokes —

幫

3 幫工 [pāng-kūng]: hired man; to use human and animal labor together

6 幫兇 [pāng-hsiūng]: accomplice, henchman, accessory, cat's-paw

幫忙 [pāng-máng]: to help, to support, to assist; help, assistance

7 幫助 [pāng-chù]: to help, to support, to assist; assistance, help

10 幫倒忙 [pāng tǎo-máng]: to do a disservice

12 幫腔 [pāng-ch'iāng]: to follow, to imitate, to sing in unison

幫閑 [pāng-hsién]: toady

13 幫會 [pāng-hùi]: association, group, clique, secret society

— RADICAL 干 51 —

干

5 干犯[kān-fàn]: to transgress, to violate; violation

6 干休[kān-hsīu]: to settle, to terminate a dispute

10 干脆[kān-ts'ùi]: direct, unequivocal, crisp, blunt, frank

11 干涉[kān-shè]: to intervene, to meddle with, to interfere with, to pry into; intervention, interference

13 干預[kān-yǜ]: to interfere in, to intervene, to intrude in; intervention, interference

— 2 Strokes —

平

平[p'íng]: Peking (abbreviation of 北平)

4 平反[p'íng-fǎn]: to reverse a decision; exoneration, rehabilitation

平分[p'íng-fēn]: to divide equally; equal distribution

平心靜氣[p'íng-hsīn chìng-ch'ì]: coolheaded, unflustered, calm

5 平民[p'íng-mín]: civilian, commoner, common people; plebeian

6 平行[p'íng-hsíng]: parallel, on an equal footing, of equal rank

平行論[p'íng-hsíng-lùn]: parallelism

7 平局[p'íng-chǘ]: a draw, a tie, tie score

平均[p'íng-chūn]: mean, average, on the average

平均主義[p'íng-chūn chǔ-ì]: equalitarianism, egalitarianism

平均地權[p'íng-chūn tì-ch'üan]: equalization of land ownership

8 平易近人[p'íng-ì chìn-jén]: plain and affable, amicable, well-disposed, without ceremony

9 平面圖[p'íng-mièn t'ú]: plane chart, plane view drawing, plane figure

10 平息[p'íng-hsī]: to quell, to put down, to stamp out, to placate, to subdue

平射炮[p'íng-shè-p'ào]: cannon, anti-tank gun

平時[p'íng-shíh]: ordinarily, at ordinary times, as a rule, in peace time, peace time, ordinary conditions

平時兵力[p'íng-shíh pīng-lì]: peace-time strength

平原[p'íng-yüán]: plain

11 平淡[p'íng-tàn]: commonplace, uninteresting, flat, pointless, dull, unimaginative

12 平等互惠通商友好條約[p'íng-těng hù-hùi t'ūng-shāng yǔ-hǎo t'íao-yüēh]: treaty of trade and friendship on the basis of equality and reciprocity

平等互利[p'íng-těng hù-lì]: reciprocity based on equality, equality and mutual benefit

平等關係[p'íng-těng kuān-hsì]: relations on an equal basis

平等待人[p'íng-těng tài-jén]: equal treatment, to treat others on an equal footing

平等待遇[p'íng-těng tài-yǜ]: equal treatment

平等地位[p'íng-těng tì-wèi]: equal standing

13 平溪[p'íng-hsī]: Binhkhe (Vietnam)

16 平靜[p'íng-chìng]: tranquility; calm, quiet, peaceful, tranquil

平衡 [p'íng-héng] : balance, equilibrium; to balance; balanced, evened out

平衡狀態 [p'íng-héng chuàng-t'ài] : state of equilibrium

平衡財政收支 [p'íng-héng ts'ái-chèng shōu-chīh] : to balance revenue and expenditure

平衡預算 [p'íng-héng yǜ-suàn] : to balance a budget; balanced budget

平澤 [p'íng-tsé] : Pyongtaek (Korea)

20 平壤 [p'íng-jăng] : Pyongyang (Korea)

平爐 [p'íng-lú] : open-hearth furnace

— 3 Strokes —

年

9 年度 [nién-tù] : annual, yearly

11 年產量 [nién ch'ăn-liàng] : annual production, annual output

年產能力 [nién-ch'ăn néng-lì] : annual production capacity

12 年景 [nién-chĭng] : annual harvest or crops, state of the annual harvest

年報 [nién-pào] : annual reporting

13 年會 [nién-hùi] : annual conference, annual meeting

22 年鑒 [nién-chièn] : annals, year book

— 5 Strokes —

7 幸災樂禍 [hsìng-tsāi lò-huò] : to take pleasure in the calamity of others, to be glad when other people are in difficulties

13 幸福 [hsìng-fú] : welfare, happiness, well-being, blessing, fortune; Fortune (American monthly periodical)

幸福院 [hsìng-fú-yüàn] : happy home, old-age home

17 幸虧 [hsìng-k'uēi] : fortunately, happily, thanks to

幷

幷 [pìng] : T'aiyuan (abbreviation for 太原)

6 幷行 [pìng-hsíng] : parallel

8 幷肩 [pìng-chiēn] : shoulder to shoulder, side by side, abreast

11 幷排 [pìng-p'ái] : alongside

15 幷駕齊驅 [pìng-chià ch'í-ch'ū] : to keep pace with

17 幷擧 [pìng-chŭ] : to promote simultaneously, to develop simultaneously; simultaneous development of

— 10 Strokes —

幹

10 幹起來 [kàn-ch'ĭ-lái] : to fall to (work)

幹流 [kàn-líu] : a river and its main tributaries, river course

11 幹部 [kàn-pù] : cadre, activist, functionary

幹部下放 [kàn-pù hsià-fàng] : to send cadres from higher to lower organs, cadres sent to lower-level units (a slogan originated in 1956-57)

14 幹綫 [kàn-hsièn] : trunk line, main line

15 幹練 [kàn-lièn] : capable and experienced

— RADICAL 幺 52 —

— 1 Stroke —

幻

13 幻想 [**huàn-hsiăng**] : to imagine; illusion, fantasy, mirage, wishful thinking; imaginative

14 幻像 [**huàn-hsiàng**] : phantom, fantasy

幻夢 [**huàn-mèng**] : pipe dream, illusion

15 幻影 [**huàn-yĭng**] : illusion, phantom

16 幻燈 [**huàn-tēng**] : projector

20 幻覺 [**huàn-chüéh**] : hallucination, vision

— 2 Strokes —

幼

8 幼兒 [**yù-érh**] : baby, infant, child

幼兒教育 [**yù-érh chiào-yǜ**] : children's education

幼兒園 [**yù-érh-yüán**] : kindergarten

幼芽 [**yù-yá**] : sprout, young shoot, offshoot

13 幼稚 [**yù-chìh**] : childish, infantile, naive, puerile, juvenile

幼稚病 [**yù-chìh-pìng**] : infantile disorder

— 6 Strokes —

幽

16 幽默 [**yū-mò**] : humor; humorous

24 幽靈 [**yū-líng**] : ghost, spirit, apparition

— 9 Strokes —

幾

2 幾十個 [**chĭ shíh-kò**] : scores of, tens of, dozens of

幾十年 [**chĭ shíh-nién**] : decades, tens of years, dozens of years

4 幾內亞共和國 [**chĭ-nèi-yà kùng-hó-kuó**] : Republic of Guinea

5 幾乎不 [**chī-hú pù**] : hardly, scarcely, barely

6 幾年辛苦，萬年幸福 [**chĭ-nién hsīn-k'ŭ, wàn-nién hsìng-fú**] : hard work for a few years, happiness for thousands of years

7 幾何圖 [**chĭ-hó-t'ú**] : diagram, chart

— RADICAL 广 53 —

— 4 Strokes —

庋

18 庋藏 [**chĭ-ts'áng**] : to preserve, to store up, to keep

序

7 序言 [**hsǜ-yén**] : introduction, preface, foreword, preamble, prelude

庇

[21] 庇護[pì-hù]: to protect, to shield, to shelter, to harbor, to take under one's protection

— 5 Strokes —

府

[13] 府葵[fu-k'uéi]: Phuqui (Vietnam)

庚

[3] 庚子年[kēng-tzŭ nién]: 1900; the Boxer year, the year of the Boxer outbreak (庚子 are the characters for the cyclical year 1900)

庚子賠款[kēng-tzŭ p'éi-k'uăn]: the Boxer indemnity

底

[4] 底片[tĭ-p'ièn]: photographic plate, negative

[7] 底那[tĭ-nà]: dinar (unit of currency)

[8] 底拉那[tĭ-lā-nà]: Tirana (Albania)

[10] 底格里斯河[tĭ-kó-lĭ-ssū hó]: Tigris River

底特律[tĭ-t'è-lü]: Detroit

[15] 底稾[tĭ-kǎo]: draft, manuscript

店

[8] 店東[tièn-tūng]: owner, proprietor

[14] 店夥[tièn-huŏ]: shop employee, clerk

— 6 Strokes —

度

[12] 度量[tù-liàng]: mass, capacity, measure; capacity of mind, generosity

[14] 度數[tù-shù]: percentage, degree

— 7 Strokes —

庫

[6] 庫存物資[k'ù-ts'ún wù-tzū]: stockpiled material, reserve of materials

[9] 庫頁[k'ù-yèh]: Sakhalin

[10] 庫庫諾爾[k'ù-k'ù-nò-ĕrh]: Kokonor

[14] 庫爾干[k'ù-ĕrh-kān]: Kurgan

庭

[8] 庭長[tíng-chăng]: director, superintendent

座

[5] 座右銘[tsò-yù-míng]: motto, maxim

[15] 座談[tsò-t'án]: forum, discussion

座談會[tsò-t'án-hùi]: forum, symposium, discussion meeting, round table discussion

— 8 Strokes —

康

康[k'āng]: Sikang Province (abbreviation of 西康)

[9] 康拜因收割機[k'āng-pài-yīn shōu-kō-chī]: combine (harvester)

[15] 康德[k'āng-té]: Kant, Immanuel

庸

[9] 庸俗[yūng-sú]: vulgar, Philistine, boorish, common, coarse

庸俗化[yūng-sú-huà]: to vulgarize; vulgarization, Philistinism

庸俗社會學[yūng-sú shè-hùi-hsüéh]: vulgar sociology

— 10 Strokes —

廈

8 廈門 **[hsià-mén]** : Amoy, Hsiamen

廉

15 廉價 **[lién-chià]** : cheap, inexpensive, low-priced

廉潔 **[lién-chiéh]** : honesty, integrity, moral soundness, purity, uprightness, probity, rectitude

— 12 Strokes —

廠

4 廠內報表 **[ch'ăng-nèi pào-piăo]** : intra-plant reporting

6 廠地 **[ch'ăng-tì]** : factory site

7 廠址 **[ch'ăng-chĭh]** : factory location

8 廠長 **[ch'ăng-chăng]** : factory director, factory chief

廠房 **[ch'ăng-fáng]** : factory building

廠房設備 **[ch'ăng-fáng shè-pèi]** : plant equipment

9 廠前區 **[ch'ăng ch'ién-ch'ǖ]** : factory frontage (the area in front of a factory, including the gate, the watchman's shed, parking spaces, administration building, and other structures)

20 廠齡 **[ch'ăng-líng]** : seniority in a plant, number of years of service in a plant

廢

2 廢人 **[fèi-jén]** : disabled person, invalid

6 廢弛 **[fèi-shĭh]** : careless, lax; to neglect; negligence

8 廢物利用 **[fèi-wù lì-yùng]** : utilization of cast-off things, recycling

9 廢品 **[fèi-p'ĭn]** : rejected product, reject

10 廢紙 **[fèi-chĭh]** : waste paper, scraps of paper

廢除 **[fèi-ch'ú]** : to abrogate, to revoke, to repeal, to cancel, to discard; abrogation, revocation, cancellation, annulment

廢料 **[fèi-liào]** : waste material

12 廢棄 **[fèi-ch'ì]** : to abolish, to abrogate, to revoke, to repeal, to annul, to cancel, to discard; abolition, abrogation, revocation, annulment, cancellation

16 廢鋼 **[fèi-kāng]** : scrap steel

17 廢黜 **[fèi-ch'ū]** : to dismiss (from office); dismissal

21 廢鐵 **[fèi-t'iĕh]** : scrap iron

廣

3 廣大 **[kuăng-tà]** : broad, large, vast, inclusive

4 廣化 **[kuăng-huà]** : Quanghoa (Vietnam)

6 廣州公社 **[kuăng-chōu kūng-shè]** : the Canton Commune

7 廣告 **[kuăng-kào]** : poster, notice, advertisement

廣告畫 **[kuăng-kào-huà]** : poster

8 廣泛 **[kuăng-fàn]** : broad, wide, comprehensive, extensive

9 廣南 **[kuăng-nán]** : Quangnam (Vietnam)

10 廣島 **[kuăng-tăo]** : Hiroshima (Japan)

12 廣開言路 **[kuăng-k'āi yén-lù]** : to open the way for words, to encourage the masses to voice their opinions

13 廣義 **[kuăng-ì]** : in a broad sense

廣博 **[kuăng-pó]** : extensive

14 廣場 **[kuăng-ch'ăng]** : plaza, square

15 廣播 **[kuăng-pō]** : to broadcast, to carry (as a

program); radio broadcast

廣播節目[kuǎng-pō chiéh-mù]: broadcasting program

廣播裝置[kuǎng-pō chuāng-chìh]: broadcasting installations

廣播事業局[kuǎng-pō shìh-yèh chú]: Broadcast Affairs Bureau

廣播電臺[kuǎng-pō tièn-t'ái]: broadcasting station

廣播網[kuǎng-pō wǎng]: radio broadcast network

廣播演說[kuǎng-pō yěn-shuō]: radio speech, broadcast speech

廟

6 廟宇[miào-yǔ]: temple

— 22 Strokes —

廳

廳[t'īng]: office, bureau, department (department in a provincial government)

8 廳長[t'īng-chǎng]: department chief, provincial commissioner

— RADICAL 廴 54 —

— 5 Strokes —

延

8 延長[yén-ch'áng]: to prolong, to draw out, to protract, to lengthen; prolongation; prolonged, protracted

12 延期[yén-ch'í]: to postpone, to put off, to defer, to delay, to prolong

17 延擱[yén-kō]: to delay, to procrastinate, to be dilatory

延擱時間[yén-kō shíh-chiēn]: to play for time, to use delaying tactics, to waste time

— 6 Strokes —

建

5 建立[chièn-lì]: to establish, to set up, to install

建立功勳[chièn-lì kūng-hsūn]: to be meritorious, to do something praiseworthy

6 建交[chièn-chiāo]: to establish diplomatic relations

8 建制[chièn-chìh]: to establish a rule or system

9 建軍[chièn-chūn]: to found an army; the founding of an army

建軍節[chièn-chūn chiéh]: Army Day (the anniversary on August 1 of the founding of the People's Liberation Army by Mao on August 1, 1927)

11 建國[chièn-kuó]: the founding of the country (with special reference to the founding of the People's Republic of China on October 1, 1949)

建設[chièn-shè]: to build, to construct, to reconstruct; construction, reconstruction, building, development,

建設項目[chièn-shè hsiàng-mù]: construction items

建設性的[chièn-shè-hsìng te]: of a constructive nature

建設部[chièn-shè pù]: Ministry of Reconstruction

建造[chièn-tsào]: to make, to build, to construct

15 建廠 **[chièn-ch'ăng]**: to found a factory, to erect a factory

16 建築 **[chièn-chú]**: to construct, to build; construction, architecture; architectural

建築學 **[chièn-chú-hsüéh]**: architecture

建築工廠化 **[chièn-chú kūng-ch'ăng-huà]**: assembly line method in construction, construction of prefabricated buildings

建築工程部 **[chièn-chú kūng-ch'éng pù]**: Ministry of Construction and Engineering, Ministry of Building

建築工地 **[chièn-chú kūng-tì]**: building site, construction site

建築師 **[chièn-chú shīh]**: architect

建築材料 **[chièn-chú ts'ái-liào]**: building materials

建築材料工業部 **[chièn-chú ts'ái-liào kūng-yèh pù]**: Ministry of Building Materials Industry

建築物 **[chièn-chú-wù]**: building structure, edifice

建樹 **[chièn-shù]**: to erect, to set up

20 建議 **[chièn-ì]**: to suggest, to propose; suggestion, recommendation, proposal, bid, offer

建黨 **[chièn-tăng]**: to found a party, the founding of a party

— RADICAL 廾 55 —

— 4 Strokes —

弄

弄 **[nùng]**: to handle, to do, to act, to play with

6 弄死 **[nùng-ssŭ]**: to kill, to do away with someone

11 弄清 **[nùng-ch'īng]**: to clarify, to clear up

16 弄錯 **[nùng-ts'ò]**: to make a mistake, to err, to be at fault

— 11 Strokes —

弊

弊 **[pì]**: fraudulence, corrupt practices

10 弊病 **[pì-pìng]**: abuses, corrupt practices

14 弊端 **[pì-tuān]**: abuses, corrupt practices

— RADICAL 弋 56 —

— 3 Strokes —

式

15 式樣 **[shìh-yàng]**: type, fashion, style

— RADICAL 弓 57 —

— 1 Stroke —

引

2 引入 [yĭn-jù]: to draw into, to introduce, to lead in, to bring in

引入歧途 [yĭn-jù ch'í-t'ú]: to mislead, to lead astray, to deceive

4 引水壩 [yĭn-shŭi-pà]: diversion dam

引水隧道 [yĭn-shŭi sùi-tào]: water conduit

5 引出 [yĭn-ch'ū]: to draw out, to draw forth, to derive, to elicit, to educe

引用 [yĭn-yùng]: to quote, to cite; quotation, citation

引用語 [yĭn-yùng-yŭ]: quotation, citation

6 引向 [yĭn-hsiàng]: to lead to

7 引言 [yĭn-yén]: introduction, foreword, preface

10 引起 [yĭn-ch'ĭ]: to arouse, to give rise to, to invoke, to prompt, to bring about, to provoke, to cause, to arise, to lead to

引起爭論的 [yĭn-ch'ĭ chēng-lùn te]: controversial, polemical, disputatious, contentious

引起警惕 [yĭn-ch'ĭ chĭng-t'ì]: to put one on one's guard, to call for vigilance

引起作用 [yĭn-ch'ĭ tsò-yùng]: to serve the function of . . .

12 引進 [yĭn-chìn]: to draw into, to bring in, to entice into

引渡 [yĭn-tù]: to extradite; extradition

13 引經據典 [yĭn-chīng chǜ-tiĕn]: to quote authoritative works, to quote from the classics

14 引誘 [yĭn-yù]: to lure, to entice, to tempt, to seduce, to bewitch, to wheedle, to coax

16 引導 [yĭn-tăo]: to guide, to usher, to show one the way

19 引證 [yĭn-chèng]: to quote, to cite; quotation, citation

— 2 Strokes —

弗

7 弗里敦 [fú-lĭ-tūn]: Freetown (Sierra Leone)

— 4 Strokes —

弟

5 弟兄們 [tì-hsiūng-mén]: brothers, comrades

— 7 Strokes —

弱

6 弱肉强食 [jò-jòu ch'iáng-shíh]: jungle law, the law of the jungle, survival of the fittest

17 弱點 [jò-tiĕn]: weakness, weak point, vulnerable spot, deficiency

— 8 Strokes —

張

4 張牙舞爪 [chāng-yá wŭ-chăo]: to bare one's fangs and show one's claws, to indulge in saber-rattling

9 張皇失措 [chāng-huáng shīh-ts'ò]: to be frightened and at a loss what to do, to be frightened to death

10 張家口 [chāng-chiā-k'ŏu]: Changchiak'ou, Kalgan (Chahar)

强

3 强大 [ch'iáng-tà]: powerful, strong, mighty, stalwart

4 强化 [ch'iáng-huà]: to strengthen

5 强加 **[ch'iăng-chiā]**: to impose upon, to force on, to coerce into

强生 **[ch'iáng-shēng]**: Johnson, Lyndon

6 强行 **[ch'iăng-hsíng]**: to enforce, to do by force

强有力的 **[ch'iáng-yŭ-lì te]**: vigorous, robust, powerful, forceful

7 强求 **[ch'iăng-ch'íu]**: to make unreasonable demands, to make forcible demands

强求一律 **[ch'iăng-ch'íu í-lǜ]**: to unify by force; forcibly unified

8 强制 **[ch'iăng-chìh]**: to compel, to force; compulsory, forcible, forced, coercive

强制勞動 **[ch'iăng-chìh láo-tùng]**: forced labor

强制兵役 **[ch'iăng-chìh pīng-ì]**: forced conscription, compulsory conscription

强制手段 **[ch'iăng-chìh shŏu-tuàn]**: high-handed action, compulsory measures

强取豪奪 **[ch'iăng-ch'ü háo-tó]**: to seize by force; rapacity; rapacious, ravenous, voracious

强迫 **[ch'iăng-p'ò]**: to compel, to force; coercion; compulsory, coercive

强迫命令 **[ch'iăng-p'ò mìng-lìng]**: to force one's orders on; coercion and commandism, arbitrary orders

强度 **[ch'iáng-tù]**: intensity

10 强烈 **[ch'iáng-lièh]**: strong, sharp, violent, lively, ardent

11 强健的 **[ch'iáng-chièn te]**: physically fit; strong and healthy

强盛 **[ch'iáng-shèng]**: powerful and flourishing

12 强盜 **[ch'iáng-tào]**: bandit, robber

强盜行爲 **[ch'iáng-tào hsíng-wéi]**: piratical act

强盜邏輯 **[ch'iáng-tào ló-chí]**: gangster logic, gun law, law of the jungle

强渡 **[ch'iăng-tù]**: forced passage of a river

14 强奪 **[ch'iăng-tó]**: to usurp, to rob, to seize, to take by force

15 强敵 **[ch'iáng-tí]**: formidable enemy, powerful enemy

强調 **[ch'iáng-tiào]**: to emphasize, to stress, to accent, to underline; emphasis

22 强權 **[ch'iáng-ch'üán]**: force, power, brute force

强權政治 **[ch'iáng-ch'üán chèng-chìh]**: power politics

— 12 Strokes —

彈

3 彈子 **[tàn-tzu]**: bullet

7 彈坑 **[tàn-k'ēng]**: shell crater

12 彈殼 **[tàn-k'ó]**: shell casing

13 彈道 **[tàn-tào]**: bullet trajectory, trajectory of a projectile; ballistic

彈道導彈 **[tàn-tào tăo-tàn]**: ballistic missile

15 彈膛 **[tàn-t'áng]**: cartridge chamber

16 彈頭 **[tàn-t'óu]**: war-head

18 彈藥 **[tàn-yào]**: gunpowder, ammunition

彈藥筒 **[tàn-yào-t'ŭng]**: cartridge

— 14 Strokes —

彌

13 彌補 **[mí-pŭ]**: to make up for, to make good, to compensate for, to fill up

— 19 Strokes —

13 彎路 **[wān-lù]**: roundabout way, tortuous road

— RADICAL ヨ彑彐 58 —

— 8 Strokes —

彗

[9] 彗星 [**huì-hsīng**] : comet

— 10 Strokes —

彙

[12] 彙集 [**huì-chí**] : to gather, to collect

彙報 [**huì-pào**] : to report on, to make a comprehensive report; comprehensive report

[17] 彙總 [**huì-tsŭng**] : processing of raw data; to sum up

彙總技術 [**huì-tsŭng chì-shù**] : data processing technique

— 13 Strokes —

彝

彝 [**í**] : Yi (minority nationality)

— RADICAL 彡 59 —

— 4 Strokes —

形

[6] 形而上學 [**hsíng-érh-shàng-hsüéh**] : metaphysics; metaphysical

形式 [**hsíng-shìh**] : shape, form; formal, formalistic

形式主義 [**hsíng-shìh chŭ-ì**] : formalism

形式和內容 [**hsíng-shìh hó nèi-júng**] : form and content

形式邏輯 [**hsíng-shìh ló-chí**] : formal logic

[7] 形成 [**hsíng-ch'éng**] : to form, to take shape; formation

形形色色 [**hsíng-hsíng sè-sè**] : every shape and hue, every description, every kind, every variety

形容 [**hsíng-júng**] : to describe, to express; description, expression

[12] 形象 [**hsíng-hsiàng**] : image

形象地說 [**hsíng-hsiàng tì shuō**] : figuratively speaking, metaphorically speaking, symbolically speaking

[13] 形勢 [**hsíng-shìh**] : conditions, circumstances, state of affairs, posture, aspect, outline, configuration; topological, relief

形勢倒轉 [**hsíng-shìh tào-chuăn**] : to turn the tables on; the tide turns

形勢地圖 [**hsíng-shìh tì-t'ú**] : relief map

[14] 形態 [**hsíng-t'ài**] : form, configuration, Gestalt

— 9 Strokes —

彭

[8] 彭奇 [**p'éng-ch'í**] : Bunche, Ralph (American statesman)

— 12 Strokes —

影

[3] 影子內閣 [**yĭng-tzu nèi-kó**] : shadow cabinet

[4] 影片 [**yĭng-p'ièn**] : film

[21] 影響 [**yĭng-hsiăng**] : to influence, to affect; influence, effect, impact, repercussion

— RADICAL 彳 60 —

— 5 Strokes —

征

8 征服 [chēng-fú] : to conquer, to vanquish, to subdue, to overcome, to overthrow, to compel submission by force

彼

11 彼得格勒 [pǐ-té-kó-lè] : Petrograd

17 彼薩 [pǐ-sà] : Pisa

— 6 Strokes —

後

2 後人 [hòu-jén] : descendants

4 後方 [hòu-fāng] : rear echelon, rear, back

後方勤務 [hòu-fāng ch'ín-wù] : rear echelon services

後天的 [hòu-t'iēn te] : a posteriori

5 後世 [hòu-shìh] : future generations, later generations

後代 [hòu-tài] : succeeding generations, younger generation, posterity, offspring

7 後言 [hòu-yén] : postscript

8 後果 [hòu-kuǒ] : effect, result, aftermath, consequence

後來 [hòu-lái] : afterwards, subsequently, thereafter, thereupon, subsequent

9 後者 [hòu-chě] : the latter

10 後悔 [hòu-hŭi] : to regret

12 後備軍 [hòu-pèi-chün] : reserve army, reserve troops

後援 [hòu-yüán] : reinforcement

13 後勤 [hòu-ch'ín] : rear echelon services, logistics service

後路 [hòu-lù] : back road, rear of an army, route of retreat

後補 [hòu-pŭ] : alternate

15 後輩 [hòu-pèi] : younger generation

16 後衞 [hòu-wèi] : rear guard

20 後繼的 [hòu-chì te] : successors, descendants; subsequent, following, posterior, succeeding

徇

7 徇私 [hsǜn-ssū] : to practice favoritism; favoritism, nepotism

律

10 律師 [lǜ-shīh] : lawyer, attorney, advocate

待

12 待遇 [tài-yü] : treatment, wages, salary

17 待避 [tài-pì] : to seek shelter

— 7 Strokes —

徐 [hsǘ] : Hsuchow (abbreviation for 徐州)

10 徐家匯觀象台 [hsǘ-chiā-hùi kuān-hsiàng-t'ái] : Zikawei Observatory

徒

6 徒刑 [t'ú-hsíng] : imprisonment

12 徒費唇舌 [t'ú-fèi ch'ún-shé] : to waste one's breath

徒勞[t'ú-láo] : to labor in vain; futile

徒勞無益[t'ú-láo wú-ì] : to no purpose, to come to naught, of no avail, in vain, futile

— 8 Strokes —

徘

9 徘徊[p'ái-húi] : to loiter, to walk irresolutely, to walk to and fro, irresolute

徘徊歧路[p'ái-húi ch'í-lù] : to walk irresolutely at the crossroads

得

2 得人心的[té-jén-hsīn te] : popular, beloved and supported by the people

4 得不償失[té pù-ch'áng-shīh] : to lose more than one gains, a Pyrrhic victory

5 得出[té-ch'ū] : to get, to gain, to produce, to obtain, to acquire, to derive

得以[té-ǐ] : to manage to, to contrive to, to bring about, to succeed

得失[té-shīh] : profit and loss, success and failure, gain and loss

得失相當[té-shīh hsiāng-tāng] : to break even

得用[té-yùng] : useful

8 得空[té-k'ùng] : to have leisure

得到[té-tào] : to get, to acquire, to obtain, to achieve, to attain

得到成功[té-tào ch'éng-kūng] : to achieve success

得到教訓[té-tào chiào-hsün] : to draw lessons from

得到優勢[té-tào yū-shìh] : to gain the upper hand

10 得逞[té-ch'ěng] : to realize, to achieve, to succeed, to be fulfilled, to come to pass

11 得第一[té tì-ī] : to win the first place

12 得勝[té-shèng] : to win

13 得過且過[té kuò ch'iěh kuò] : to let things drift

得意[té-ì] : to have one's way; elated

得意忘形[té-ì wàng-hsíng] : elated to the degree of forgetting one's form; excessively complacent or self-satisfied

得勢[té-shìh] : to be in power

得罪[té-tsùi] : to offend, to displease, to anger

從

1 從一開始[ts'úng-ī k'āi-shǐh] : from the very beginning

3 從下到上[ts'úng hsià tào shàng] : from the bottom to top

從上到下[ts'úng shàng tào hsià] : from top to bottom

4 從公社來，回公社去 [ts'úng kūng-shè lái, húi kūng-shè ch'ǜ] : coming from the communes and returning to the communes (refers generally to the training of commune members in outside schools and returning them to the communes to practice their skills)

5 從犯[ts'úng-fàn] : accessory (to a crime)

8 從長期來看[ts'úng ch'áng-ch'í lái k'àn] : from the long term viewpoint, in the long run

從來[ts'úng-lái] : all along

從事[ts'úng-shìh] : to embark on, to devote oneself to

9 從前一直是[ts'úng-ch'ién ì-chíh shìh] : all along in the past it was. . .

從軍[ts'úng-chūn] : to enlist; enlistment

10 從容[ts'ūng-júng] : at ease, calm

從容考慮[ts'ūng-júng k'ăo-lǜ]: to consider in an unhurried manner, to deliberate in a leisurely manner

從根本上來說 [ts'úng kēn-pĕn-shang lái-shuō]: fundamentally speaking, basically speaking

13 從群眾中來，到群眾中去 [ts'úng ch'ǘn-chùng-chūng lái, tào ch'ǘn-chùng-chūng ch'ǜ]: from the masses, to the masses; coming from the masses and going back to the masses; to have its cause in the masses and take effect among the masses; to gather and sum up the views of the masses and take the resulting ideas back to the masses

從新 [ts'úng-hsīn]: anew, over again

14 從實際出發[ts'úng shíh-chì ch'ū-fā]: to proceed from the actual situation

15 從寬 [ts'úng-k'uān]: leniently

16 從頭到尾[ts'úng t'óu tào wĕi]: from first to last, from beginning to end, throughout

21 從屬 [ts'úng-shŭ]: to be subordinated to

從屬關係[ts'úng-shŭ kuān-hsì]: subordinate relationship

— 9 Strokes —

復

4 復仇[fù-ch'óu]: to revenge, to avenge; revenge, vengeance

復仇主義[fù-ch'óu chŭ-ì]: revanchism

復仇主義者[fù-ch'óu chŭ-ì chĕ]: revanchist

5 復古[fù-kŭ]: to revive old customs

復旦大學[fù-tàn tà-hsüéh]: Futan University, Aurora University

9 復查[fù-ch'á]: to recheck, to check up

10 復員[fù-yüán]: to demobilize, to deactivate; demobilized

復員軍人[fù-yüán chǖn-jén]: demobilized serviceman, ex-serviceman

13 復辟[fù-pì]: to restore a monarchy, to return an emperor to power, to stage a comeback; a restoration

15 復興[fù-hsīng]: reconstruction, renaissance, regeneration, revival

18 復職[fù-chíh]: to reinstate; reinstatement

復舊[fù-chìu]: to restore the former state of affairs

20 復議[fù-ì]: to submit to reconsideration; reconsideration

循

7 循序漸進[hsǘn-hsǜ chièn-chìn]: to follow in proper sequence and make steady progress

17 循環[hsǘn-huán]: to circulate, to revolve; circulation

循環不息[hsǘn-huán pù-hsī]: to revolve ceaselessly

— 10 Strokes —

微

3 微小[wēi-hsiăo]: minute, small, tiny

微小的差數[wēi-hsiăo te ch'ā-shù]: narrow margin

微小的多數[wēi-hsiăo te tō-shù]: narrow majority

4 微不足道[wēi pù-tsú tào]: insignificant, negligible, trifling

5 微生物研究所 [wēi-shēng-wù yén-chìu-sŏ]: Institute of Microbiology

7 微妙[wēi-miào]: delicacy; delicate, subtle, ethereal, fine, minute

10 微弱[wēi-jò]: slim, thin, feeble

— 12 Strokes —

徹

8 徹底[**ch'è-tǐ**]: thorough, utter, exhaustive, thorough-going, complete

徹底腐化[**ch'è-tǐ fǔ-huà**]: rotten to the core

徹底消滅[**ch'è-tǐ hsiāo-mièh**]: to uproot, utterly destroy

徹底改變[**ch'è-tǐ kǎi-pièn**]: radical change

徹底破產[**ch'è-tǐ p'ò-ch'ǎn**]: complete bankruptcy

徹底掃盲[**ch'è-tǐ sǎo-máng**]: to make a thorough sweep of illiteracy

徹底地放[**ch'è-tǐ ti fàng**]: *See* 堅決地放

16 徹頭徹尾[**ch'è-t'óu ch'è-wěi**]: out-and-out, utter, through and through

徵

5 徵用[**chēng-yùng**]: expropriation, requisition

6 徵收[**chēng-shōu**]: to levy, to levy and collect, to impose a duty on

徵收額[**chēng-shōu-ó**]: income from taxes

7 徵求[**chēng-ch'íu**]: to canvass, to seek, to solicit, to ask for, to request

徵兵[**chēng-pīng**]: conscription, draft

12 徵集[**chēng-chí**]: to collect, to gather, to muster; collection

徵稅[**chēng-shùi**]: to levy taxes; tax collection, taxation

13 徵詢[**chēng-hsǘn**]: to consult, to ask advice of, to probe

17 徵購[**chēng-kòu**]: to requisition, to procure; requisition, procurement

19 徵糧[**chēng-liáng**]: grain levy, grain collection (i.e., collection of the agricultural tax in kind by the state)

德

3 德才兼備[**té ts'ái chiēn pèi**]: having both virtue and talent, to combine talent with character, equal stress on integrity and ability

5 德瓦[**té-wǎ**]: Maharajadhiraja Mahendra Bir Bikram Shah Deva (King of Nepal, born 1920, died 1972)

7 德里[**té-lǐ**]: Delhi

8 德波林學派[**té-pō-lín hsüéh-p'ài**]: Deborin school

德育[**té-yǜ**]: moral education, ethical training

德育心理[**té-yǜ hsīn-lǐ**]: the psychology of moral education

9 德政[**té-chèng**]: good government

德勃雷[**té-pò-léi**]: Debré Michel (French statesman)

10 德島[**té-tǎo**]: Tokushima (Japan)

11 德國[**té-kuó**]: Germany

德累斯頓[**té-lèi-ssū-tùn**]: Dresden

12 德黑蘭[**té-hēi-lán**]: Teheran (Iran)

德普[**té-p'ǔ**]: Ducpho (Vietnam)

13 德意志[**té-ì-chìh**]: Germany

德意志新聞社[**té-ì-chìh hsīn-wén-shè**]: Deutsche Presse-Agentur: DPA (West German news agency)

德意志聯邦共和國[**té-ì-chìh lién-pāng kùng-hó-kuó**]: Federal Republic of Germany

德意志民主共和國[**té-ì-chìh mín-chǔ kùng-hó-kuó**]: Democratic Republic of Germany, German Democratic Republic

德意志民主共和國人民議院[**té-ì-chìh**

mín-chŭ kùng-hó-kuó jén-mín ì-yüàn]: People's Chamber of the German Democratic Republic

德意志通訊社 **[té-ì-chìh t'ūng-hsǜn-shè]**: Allgemeiner Deutscher Nachrichtendienst: ADN (East German news agency)

14 德慶 **[té-ch'ìng]**: Dechen (Tibet)

18 德謨克里特 **[té-mò-k'ò-lĭ-t'è]**: Democritus (460 B.C.–350 B.C.)

21 德蘭斯瓦尼亞 **[té-lán-ssū-wă-ní-yà]**: Transylvania

— 14 Strokes —

徽

11 徽章 **[hūi-chāng]**: insignia, badge, emblem, medal

14 徽號 **[hūi-hào]**: honorary title

— RADICAL 心 61 —

心

4 心中無數 **[hsīn-chūng wú shù]**: not to have the numbers in one's mind (i.e., not to have a grasp of a situation and thus not know what to do)

心中有鬼 **[hsīn-chūng yŭ kuĕi]**: to have ulterior motives, to have ulterior designs

心中有數 **[hsīn-chūng yŭ shù]**: to have the numbers in one's mind (i.e., to have a grasp of a situation and to know what to do)

5 心目中 **[hsīn-mù chūng]**: in one's eyes, in one's mind

6 心安理得 **[hsīn-ān lĭ-té]**: to have an easy conscience

心交給黨 **[hsīn chiāo-kĕi tăng]**: to give one's heart to the Party

心地光明 **[hsīn-tì kuāng-míng]**: pure-hearted

8 心事 **[hsīn-shìh]**: cares, worries, concern, things that weigh on the mind

10 心胸開闊 **[hsīn-hsiūng k'āi-k'uò]**: broad-minded

11 心情 **[hsīn-ch'íng]**: mood, feelings, state of mind

心情舒暢 **[hsīn-ch'íng shū-ch'àng]**: to have one's mind at ease; ease of mind; cheerful

心軟的 **[hsīn-juăn te]**: soft-hearted, exorable, ready to give in

心理戰爭 **[hsīn-lĭ chàn-chēng]**: psychological warfare

心理學 **[hsīn-lĭ-hsüéh]**: psychology

心理不正常 **[hsīn-lĭ pú-chèng-ch'áng]**: mentally abnormal

心理上的 **[hsīn-lĭ-shàng te]**: psychological, mental

心理動搖 **[hsīn-lĭ tùng-yáo]**: a wavering state of mind

心理研究所 **[hsīn-lĭ yén-chìu-sŏ]**: Institute of Psychology

心得 **[hsīn-té]**: attainment, understanding or achievement from intense study

12 心虛 **[hsīn-hsū]**: nervous, afraid of being found out

心勞日拙 **[hsīn-láo jìh-chō]**: to get nothing for one's pains, to go on a wild goose chase

13 心照不宣 **[hsīn-chào pù-hsüān]**: tacit agreement

心腹話 **[hsīn-fù huà]**: confidential remarks

23 心驚膽戰 **[hsīn-chīng tăn-chàn]**: panic-stricken, trembling with fear

— 1 Stroke —

必

4 必不可免[**pì pù-k'ŏ-miĕn**]: inevitable, necessary, unavoidable

必不可少[**pì pù-k'ŏ-shăo**]: indispensable, essential

5 必由之路[**pì yú chīh lù**]: the road that must be taken

8 必定會[**pì-tìng hùi**]: bound to, necessarily, likely

9 必修[**pì-hsīu**]: required to study

必修科[**pì-hsīu k'ō**]: required course, required subject

必修課[**pì-hsīu k'ò**]: required course, compulsory course

必要[**pì-yào**]: it is necessary to; necessary, imperative, essential, indispensable, required

必要條件[**pì-yào t'iáo-chièn**]: essential condition, requisite condition

12 必然[**pì-ján**]: certain, inevitable

必然性[**pì-ján-hsìng**]: necessity, certainty

必然會[**pì-ján hùi**]: to be bound to, to be certain to, will certainly

必然判斷[**pì-ján p'àn-tuàn**]: apodictic judgment

必然的結果[**pì-ján te chiéh-kuŏ**]: corollary, natural result, inevitable result, inevitable consequence

14 必需[**pì-hsǖ**]: obligatory, essential, required, necessary, imperative, indispensable

必需品[**pì-hsǖ-p'ĭn**]: necessities, essential articles of consumption

— 3 Strokes —

7 忌妒[**chì-tù**]: to envy, to be jealous of

9 忌恨[**chì-hèn**]: to hate, to begrudge, to hold a grudge against; hatred, grudge

15 忌憚[**chì-tàn**]: to fear, to be afraid of; fear

17 忌諱[**chì-hùi**]: taboo, superstitious avoidance of things tabooed; to avoid things that are taboo

志

5 志司[**chìh-ssū**]: Headquarters of the Chinese People's Volunteers (abbreviation of 中國人民志願軍司令部)

10 志氣[**chìh-ch'ì**]: morale

19 志願[**chìh-yüàn**]: voluntary, of one's own free will; aspiration

志願者[**chìh-yüàn-chĕ**]: volunteer

志願軍[**chìh-yüàn-chǖn**]: volunteer force

8 忍受[**jĕn-shòu**]: to endure, to suffer, to bear with, to put up with

8 忙於[**máng-yǘ**]: to be busy with, occupied

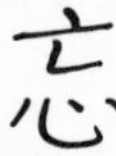

5 忘本思想[**wàng-pĕn ssū-hsiăng**]: ingratitude, thought which forgets the source of good (also implies the forgetting of the basic precepts of socialism)

7 忘形[**wàng-hsíng**]: to forget one's form, to let oneself go, not to control oneself; unconventional

忘我[**wàng-wŏ**]: selfless

忘我勞動[**wàng-wŏ láo-tùng**]: selfless labor (a slogan of 1958)

10 忘恩負義[**wàng-ēn fù-ì**]: devoid of all gratitude

— 4 Strokes —

忠

4 忠心 **[chūng-hsīn]**: allegiance, loyalty, faithfulness, devotion; loyal, faithful

6 忠字牌 **[chūng-tzù p'ái]**: a loyalty tablet; a tablet bearing the character "loyalty" (the display of the "loyalty tablet," which was intended to take the place of the traditional ancestral tablet, became obligatory around September 1968)

8 忠於 **[chūng-yǘ]**: to be true to, to be loyal to, to be faithful to

14 忠誠 **[chūng-ch'éng]**: faithful and sincere; loyalty and sincerity

忠實 **[chūng-shíh]**: loyal and honest; loyalty and honesty

忽

11 忽略 **[hū-lüèh]**: to ignore, to neglect, to overlook; careless, forgetful, remiss; carelessness, negligence

12 忽視 **[hū-shìh]**: to disregard, to neglect, to overlook

忽視成份 **[hū-shìh ch'éng-fèn]**: to take no account of class origin

快

7 快車 **[k'uài-ch'ē]**: express train

快完蛋 **[k'uài wán-tàn]**: to be on one's last legs, to have one's days numbered, soon to be doomed

11 快速 **[k'uài-sù]**: quick, swift, fast

快速切削 **[k'uài-sù ch'iēh-hsiāo]**: fast cutting

快速艦 **[k'uài-sù-chièn]**: frigate

快速報表 **[k'uài-sù pào-piǎo]**: rapid reporting, periodic reporting, scheduled reports

快速電子計算機 **[k'uài-sù tièn-tzu chì-suàn-chī]**: high-speed electronic computer

快速軋鋼法 **[k'uài-sù yà-kāng fǎ]**: high-speed rolling method

快要 **[k'uài-yào]**: on the verge of, on the point of, just about to

12 快報 **[k'uài-pào]**: L'Express (French periodical)

15 快樂 **[k'uài-lè]**: happiness, joy; gay, happy, joyful

快樂主義 **[k'uài-lè chǔ-ì]**: hedonism

— 5 Strokes —

急

4 急公好義 **[chí-kūng hào-ì]**: to concern oneself with the public welfare, zealous for the public interests

5 急功近利 **[chí-kūng chìn-lì]**: quick success and instant benefits

6 急行軍 **[chí-hsíng chūn]**: forced march

8 急性病 **[chí-hsìng pìng]**: rashness, acute disease

急於 **[chí-yǘ]**: to be anxious to, to be impatient, in a hurry, eager to

急於求成 **[chí-yǘ ch'íu-ch'éng]**: to be impatient for success

急迫 **[chí-p'ò]**: urgent

急促 **[chí-ts'ù]**: hasty, in great haste

10 急症 **[chí-chèng]**: acute illness

急起直追 **[chí-ch'ǐ chíh-chūi]**: to forge ahead and catch up with full strength, to forge ahead at full strength

11 急救 **[chí-chìu]**: to render first aid; first aid

急速 **[chí-sù]**: rapid

13 急電 **[chí-tièn]**: urgent telegram, urgent cable

14 急需[chí-hsü]: urgently needed, to need something badly

15 急劇[chí-chù]: drastic, acute, sudden

急劇變化[chí-chü pièn-huà]: sudden change, precipitate change, sharp change

急劇增加[chí-chü tsēng-chiā]: sharp growth, steep increase

19 急難[chí-nán]: acute danger, great emergency

20 急躁[chí-tsào]: hasty

急躁冒進[chí-tsào mào-chìn]: to advance recklessly and in haste; reckless and hasty advance

怯

5 怯尼亞[ch'ièh-ní-yà]: Kenya

17 怯懦[ch'ièh-nò]: cowardice; cowardly

性

9 性急的[hsìng-chí te]: impetuous, hasty, quick-tempered, impatient, excitable

10 性格[hsìng-kó]: personality, temperament, character, disposition, nature

性能[hsìng-néng]: innate ability, function

15 性質[hsìng-chíh]: temperament, disposition, nature, quality

怙

12 怙惡不悛[hù-ò pù-ch'üān]: incorrigible

怪

8 怪事[kuài-shìh]: strange occurrence

怪物[kuài-wù]: monstrosity, apparition, monster

15 怪僻[kuài-p'ì]: eccentric

怒

怒[nù]: Nu (minority nationality)

7 怒吼[nù-hǒu]: an angry roar

怕

怕[p'à]: to fear, to be afraid of

8 怕沾邊[p'à chān-piēn]: afraid of being tainted (i.e., the fear of workers of being accused of associating with capitalists)

思

8 思明[ssū-míng]: Amoy

11 思惟[ssū-wéi]: thinking, thought

13 思想[ssū-hsiǎng]: thought, thinking, idea, ideology,

思想戰綫[ssū-hsiǎng chàn-hsièn]: ideological front

思想障礙[ssū-hsiǎng chàng-ài]: ideological stumbling block, ideological hindrance, ideological impediment, ideological obstruction

思想僵化[ssū-hsiǎng chiāng-huà]: mental stagnation, to be rigid in one's thinking

思想解放[ssū-hsiǎng chiěh-fàng]: ideological emancipation, emancipation of the mind

思想健康[ssū-hsiǎng chièn-k'āng]: ideological healthiness, ideological soundness

思想見面[ssū-hsiǎng chièn-mièn]: meeting of minds, frank exchange of views

思想準備[ssū-hsiǎng chǔn-pèi]: mental preparation, mental groundwork

思想方法上[ssū-hsiǎng fāng-fǎ-shàng]: in method of thinking

思想修養[ssū-hsiǎng hsīu-yǎng]: ideological cultivation

思想混亂[**ssū-hsiang hùn-luàn**]: ideologically confused

思想一致[**ssū-hsiang í-chìh**]: ideological uniformity

思想認識[**ssū-hsiang jèn-shìh**]: ideological understanding

思想認識問題[**ssū-hsiang jèn-shìh wèn-t'í**]: problems of ideological understanding

思想改造[**ssū-hsiang kǎi-tsào**]: ideological remolding, thought reform

思想蓋子[**ssū-hsiang kài-tzu**]: ideological lid (i.e., anything that hampers thought reform)

思想感情[**ssū-hsiang kǎn-ch'íng**]: ideas and sentiments, thoughts and feelings, minds and hearts

思想革命家[**ssū-hsiang kó-mìng-chiā**]: ideological revolutionary

思想懶漢[**ssū-hsiang lǎn-hàn**]: lazy-bones in thinking (i.e., one who does not think deeply)

思想落後於實際[**ssū-hsiang lò-hòu yű shíh-chì**]: ideas lagging behind actual events

思想落戶[**ssū-hsiang lò-hù**]: to let an idea settle deeply into one's mind

思想包袱[**ssū-hsiang pāo-fú**]: a load on one's thought (i.e., ideas and concepts of the old society that make one hesitant to accept communism or to follow communist policies)

思想不純[**ssū-hsiang pù-ch'ún**]: impurity in ideology

思想動向[**ssū-hsiang tùng-hsiàng**]: ideological trend, ideological tendency, ideological drift

15 思潮[**ssū-ch'áo**]: current of thought, trend of thought, mental tendencies

16 思辨哲學[**ssū-pièn ché-hsüéh**]: speculative philosophy

20 思議[**ssū-ì**]: to conceive of

怠

3 怠工[**tài-kūng**]: sabotage, loafing on the job, dragging out work

怠工者[**tài-kūng-chě**]: saboteur, slow-down striker

怨

7 怨言[**yüàn-yén**]: spiteful words, grumbling complaints, grumbling, complaining, reproach

8 怨命[**yüàn-mìng**]: to lay the blame on fate, to blame one's lot on fate

9 怨恨[**yüàn-hèn**]: to hate, to resent, to bear a grudge against; hatred, enmity, resentment

— 6 Strokes —

恰

5 恰瓜臘馬斯[**ch'ià-kuā-là-mǎ-ssū**]: Chaguaramas (Federation of West Indies)

6 恰如其分[**ch'ià-jú ch'í-fèn**]: well-measured, to a proper extent, in appropriate measure, well-chosen

9 恰恰[**ch'ià-ch'ià**]: pertinent, fitting, proper, precisely, exactly

恰恰相反[**ch'ià-ch'ià hsiāng-fǎn**]: just the opposite, on the contrary

13 恰當[**ch'ià-tāng**]: pertinent, fitting, appropriate, precisely, exactly

恥

10 恥辱[**ch'ǐh-jù**]: humiliation, disgrace, shame

恩

2 恩人[**ēn-jén**]: benefactor

7 恩克努瑪[ēn-k'ò-nŭ-mă]: Nkrumah, Kwame (Ghana statesman)

8 恩典[ēn-tiĕn]: benevolence, kindness

10 恩格斯[ēn-kó-ssū]: Engels, Friedrich (1820–1895)

11 恩情[ēn-ch'íng]: graciousness, grace, kindness, affection, love

15 恩賜[ēn-tz'ù]: mercy, grace, favor, grant, bestowal, the granting of special favors

恩賜觀點[ēn-tz'ù kuān-tiĕn]: favor-granting viewpoint (i.e., the attitude on the part of officials, rural cadre, and commune members that sums of money appropriated to communes are favors)

恨

恨[hèn]: to hate, to detest, to abominate, to abhor, to loathe; hatred, hate, enmity, animosity, antipathy, abhorrence

2 恨入骨髓[hèn jù kŭ-sŭi]: to hate to the marrow, to hate intensely

8 恨事[hèn-shìh]: a regrettable thing, a disappointing matter, a matter of regret

恒

3 恒久[héng-chĭu]: long, steady, constant, long-lasting, durable

4 恒心[héng-hsīn]: persistence, constancy, perseverance, steadiness of mind; constant in purpose

7 恒言[héng-yén]: proverb, saying

8 恒河[héng-hó]: the Ganges River (India)

恒例[héng-lì]: traditional rule, custom

9 恒風[héng-fēng]: prevailing wind

11 恒情[héng-ch'íng]: natural feeling, general propensity

14 恒態[héng-t'ài]: constant condition, normal attitude

息

10 息息相關[hsí-hsí hsiāng-kuān]: to be linked with each other closely

恢

12 恢復[hūi-fú]: to revive, to recover, to restore, to rehabilitate, to recuperate; restoration, revival, resumption, renewal, recuperation, rehabilitation

恭

13 恭敬[kūng-chìng]: to honor, to respect; honor, respect; respectful

恐

8 恐怖主義[k'ŭng-pù chŭ-ì]: terrorism

13 恐慌[k'ŭng-huāng]: alarm, fear, dread, panic, horror, consternation; panic-stricken

17 恐嚇[k'ŭng-hò]: to frighten, to alarm, to scare, to startle, to terrify, to horrify, to intimidate; bluff

恐嚇信[k'ŭng-hò hsìn]: threatening letter (refers to an anonymous letter written to Lu Yü-wen, a member of the Revolutionary Committee of the Kuomintang, in which he was warned that he would be punished by the people if he continued to make pro-communist statements)

悖

12 悖逆[pèi-nì]: rebellious, obstinate, refractory

18 悖謬[pèi-mìu]: false, perverse and erroneous

恫

17 恫嚇[tùng-hò]: to menace, to threaten, to intimidate

恣

13 恣意 **[tzŭ-ì]**: to act recklessly, to do as one likes

— 7 Strokes —

9 患者 **[huàn-chĕ]**: a person suffering from a calamity or an illness

10 患病 **[huàn-pìng]**: to fall ill, to become sick

11 患得患失 **[huàn-té huàn-shīh]**: to worry about personal gains and losses

19 患難 **[huàn-nàn]**: disaster, calamity, adversity, misfortune, predicament

患難之交 **[huàn-nàn chīh chiāo]**: friends in adversity, friends in need

悔

7 悔改 **[hŭi-kăi]**: to repent, to reform

9 悔恨 **[hŭi-hèn]**: to regret; repentance, penitence

10 悔悟 **[hŭi-wù]**: to awaken from sin and repent, to awake to a sense of wrongdoing and repent, to regret mistakes

13 悔過 **[hŭi-kuò]**: to repent, to acknowledge errors

悔過自新 **[hŭi-kuò tzù-hsīn]**: to repent and turn over a new leaf

悍

12 悍然 **[hàn-ján]**: brazenly, crudely, barbarously, wantonly, flagrantly, high-handedly

悟

8 悟性 **[wù-hsìng]**: intelligence, understanding

悠

3 悠久 **[yū-chĭu]**: old, long, long-standing, enduring, long-lived

— 8 Strokes —

情

7 情況 **[ch′íng-k′uàng]**: conditions, circumstances, state of affairs, event, case, fact, instance

9 情面 **[ch′íng-mièn]**: personal consideration, face saving, partiality; sentimental, partial

12 情報 **[ch′íng-pào]**: information, intelligence

情報部 **[ch′íng-pào pù]**: Ministry of Information

15 情節 **[ch′íng-chiéh]**: circumstances of a case

情緒 **[ch′íng-hsü]**: sentiment, disposition, mood, temper, feelings, emotion

惠

24 惠靈頓 **[hùi-líng-tùn]**: Wellington (New Zealand)

12 惑衆 **[huò-chùng]**: to delude the people, to stir up and mislead the masses

14 惑亂人心 **[huò-luàn jén-hsīn]**: to mislead the masses

惡

4 惡化 **[ò-huà]**: to deteriorate, to worsen; worsening, deteriorating

6 惡劣的 **[ò-lièh te]**: evil, bad, ill (i.e., as in ill effect)

8 惡性的 **[ò-hsìng te]**: malignant, evil

9 惡毒[ò-tú] : wicked, malicious, malevolent, vicious, pernicious

11 惡習[ò-hsí] : bad habits

13 惡感[ò-kăn] : antipathy

21 惡魔主義[ò-mó chŭ-ì] : decadence, "decadentism," "Baudelaire-ism"

惡霸[ò-pà] : local despot, local tyrant, bully

惡霸反革命份子[ò-pà făn-kó-mìng fèn-tzu] : counterrevolutionary local tyrants

惡霸地主[ò-pà tì-chŭ] : tyrannical landlord, despotic landlord

悲

15 悲劇[pēi-chǜ] : tragedy, tragic

24 悲觀[pēi-kuān] : pessimism, pessimistic

悲觀慶世[pēi-kuān ch'ìng-shìh] : pessimism and misanthropy

悲觀主義[pēi-kuān chŭ-ì] : pessimism

悼

10 悼念[tào-nièn] : to mourn for

19 悼辭[tào-tz'ú] : memorial speech

惋

9 惋惜[wăn-hsī] : to regret, to be sorry, to deplore, to lament; regrettable, lamentable

— 9 Strokes —

2 愛人[ài-jén] : lover, spouse

愛丁堡[ài-tīng-păo] : Edinburgh (Scotland)

5 愛世語[ài-shìh yŭ] : Esperanto

6 愛好[ài-hào] : to like, to treasure, to take a liking to, to have a fancy for

愛好正義的人民[ài-hào chèng-ì te jén-mín] : just-minded people

愛西屋皮亞[ài-hsī-wū-p'í-yà] : Ethiopia

愛因斯坦[ài-yīn-ssū-t'ăn] : Einstein, Albert

7 愛克斯光[ài-k'ò-ssū kuāng] : X-rays

愛沙尼亞[ài-shā-ní-yà] : Estonia

愛社如家[ài shè jú chiā] : to love the commune as one's family, to cherish as warm a regard for the people's commune as for one's family

8 愛知[ài-chīh] : Aichi (Japan)

9 愛面子[ài mièn-tzu] : keen on face saving

10 愛烏罕[ài-wū-hăn] : Afghanistan

11 愛國主義[ài-kuó chŭ-ì] : patriotism

愛國主義還是賣國主義[ài-kuó chŭ-ì hái-shih mài-kuó chŭ-ì] : "Patriotism or Betrayal" (an article by Ch'i Pen-yü 戚本禹 on April 1, 1967 in the People's Daily attacking Liu Shao-ch'i on the basis of the latter's praise of the film 清宮祕史, q.v.)

愛國增產運動[ài-kuó tsēng-ch'ăn yŭn-tùng] : patriotic production campaign

愛國衛生運動[ài-kuó wèi-shēng yŭn-tùng] : patriotic public health campaign, patriotic campaign for better sanitation

12 愛琴海[ài-ch'ín hăi] : Aegean Sea

13 愛奧尼亞海[ài-ào-ní-yà hăi] : Ionian Sea

愛達荷[ài-tá-hó] : Idaho

14 愛爾蘭[ài-ĕrh-lán] : Ireland

愛爾蘭海[ài-ĕrh-lán hăi] : Irish Sea

愛爾蘭共和國[ài-ĕrh-lán kùng-hó-kuó] : Republic of Ireland

15 愛黎[ài-lí] : Aili (minority nationality)

17 愛戴[ài-tài] : to revere, to love, to honor, to cherish, to respect

[21] 愛護公共財物[ài-hù kūng-kùng ts'ái-wù]: concern for public property

愁

[9] 愁思[ch'óu-ssū]: depressed thoughts, anxious thoughts

[12] 愁悶的[ch'óu-mèn te]: gloomy, melancholy, dejected, depressed, dismal, dreary

惶

[12] 惶惶無主[huáng-huáng wú-chŭ]: to be panicky and not know what to do

意

[3] 意大利[ì-tà-lì]: Italy

意大利日報[ì-tà-lì jìh-pào]: Il Giornale d'Italia (Italian daily newspaper)

意大利共和國[ì-tà-lì kùng-hó-kuó]: Republic of Italy

[5] 意外[ì-wài]: unexpected, fortuitous, unanticipated

意外之財[ì-wài chīh ts'ái]: wealth on which one has no claim, windfall

[6] 意向[ì-hsiàng]: intention, object

[7] 意志[ì-chìh]: will, purpose

意志自由[ì-chìh tzù-yú]: freedom of the will

意見[ì-chièn]: opinion, idea, suggestion, thought, view

意見分歧[ì-chièn fēn-ch'í]: difference in opinion, dissension, discord, disagreement; dissident

意見一致[ì-chièn í-chìh]: unity of views, meeting of minds, agreement; to agree

[8] 意味[ì-wèi]: to signify, to purport, to convey the idea, to imply

意味深長的[ì-wèi shēn-ch'áng te]: significant, expressive, of profound significance

[10] 意氣風發[ì-ch'ì fēng-fā]: boundless enthusiasm

[13] 意義[ì-ì]: significance, sense, meaning, purport, effect

[19] 意識[ì-shíh]: consciousness

意識形態[ì-shíh hsíng-t'ài]: ideology; ideological

意願[ì-yüàn]: desire, wish

惹

惹[jĕ]: to irritate, to vex, to offend, to nettle

[8] 惹事[jĕ-shìh]: to stir up trouble

惹事份子[jĕ-shìh fèn-tzu]: agent provocateur, trouble-maker, provoker

[10] 惹起[jĕ-ch'ĭ]: to incite, to provoke, to anger, to irritate

感

[4] 感化[kăn-huà]: to move, to have an effect on, to influence, to convert, to improve

[8] 感性[kăn-hsìng]: emotional, perceptual, sensory, sensual

感性知識[kăn-hsìng chīh-shíh]: perceptual knowledge

感性的形象[kăn-hsìng te hsíng-hsiàng]: affective image

感官[kăn-kuān]: sensory organs

感受[kăn-shòu]: to suffer, affected by, impressed with

感到[kăn-tào]: to sense, to feel, to perceive, to have the impression that

感到冒犯[kăn-tào mào-fàn]: to be offended

[9] 感染[kăn-jăn]: infused with, imbued with, tinged with, stained with

11 感情[kǎn-ch'íng]: sentiment, emotion, feeling, affection

感動[kǎn-tùng]: to impress, to touch, to move, to move emotionally

13 感想 [kǎn-hsiǎng]: impression, feeling, opinion

感傷主義[kǎn-shāng chǔ-ì]: sensationalism

17 感謝 [kǎn-hsièh]: to appreciate; gratitude, appreciation; grateful

感應 [kǎn-yìng]: reaction, influence, induction, sympathy

20 感覺[kǎn-chüéh]: feelings, sensations, impressions, sense, sensibility; sensory

感覺主義[kǎn-chüéh chǔ-ì]: "Marinetti-ism," "feeling-ism"

惱

9 惱怒[nǎo-nù]: anger; galling

想

4 想不到[hsiǎng-pú-tào]: unforeseen, unexpected, unanticipated, unthought of

7 想見[hsiǎng-chièn]: to visualize

8 想法[hsiǎng-fǎ]: idea, conception, notion, view, opinion, way of looking at a thing

想到[hsiǎng-tào]: to think of, to have an idea that

13 想當然[hsiǎng tāng-ján]: to assume, to jump to a conclusion without proof

14 想像[hsiǎng-hsiàng]:to imagine, to visualize, to fancy; imagination

想像不到的[hsiǎng-hsiàng pú-tào te]: unthinkable, inconceivable

惰

8 惰性[tò-hsìng]: inertia, laziness

慈

12 慈悲[tz'ú-pēi]: sympathy, compassion, love; compassionate, kind

愚

4 愚公精神[yǘ-kūng chīng-shén]: the Yü Kung spirit (recommended to Party members by Mao at the Seventh National Party Congress of June 11, 1945; refers to a Chinese fable in which Yü Kung (The Simple Peasant Who Moved the Mountain) determined to level two mountains in front of his house, saying that if he couldn't finish the job in his lifetime, then his sons and grandsons would continue the task until it was completed)

愚公移山[yǘ-kūng í-shān]: How Yü Kung Removed the Mountains; The Simple Peasant Who Moved the Mountain (Mao, June 11, 1945; one of the 老三篇, q.v.)

5 愚民政策[yǘ-mín chèng-ts'è]: policy of hoodwinking the people

愚民主義[yǘ-mín chǔ-ì]: obscurantism

9 愚昧[yǘ-mèi]: ignorance, incomprehension; ignorant, uneducated

21 愚蠢[yǘ-ch'ǔn]: foolish, stupid, clumsy, blunt-witted, muddle-headed

愉

7 愉快[yǘ-k'uài]: pleasure, joy, delight; happy, joyful, delightful, agreeable

— 10 Strokes —

慌

6 慌忙[huāng-máng]: hastily, hurriedly

11 慌張[huāng-chāng]: confusion, bewilderment; flustered, upset, in a hurry, helter-skelter

13 慌亂[huāng-luàn]: hurried, confused, chao-

tic, in disorder, in tumult, in chaos

慎

9 慎重 [shèn-chùng]: prudent, discreet, cautious

態

8 態度 [t'ài-tù]: attitude, behavior, demeanor, standpoint, posture

慈

12 慈善 [tz'ú-shàn]: charity, philanthropy

慈善家 [tz'ú-shàn-chiā]: philanthropist

— 11 Strokes —

慶

5 慶功會 [ch'ìng-kūng-hùi]: commendation meeting, success celebration meeting (a meeting held to celebrate new achievements by those who have taken part in a job)

6 慶州 [ch'ìng-chōu]: Kyongju (Korea)

9 慶祝 [ch'ìng-chù]: to celebrate, to honor, to mark, to commemorate, to congratulate; commemoration, congratulations, celebration; congratulatory

12 慶賀 [ch'ìng-hò]: to celebrate, to observe, to commemorate, to congratulate; celebration, commemoration, congratulations; congratulatory

慷

14 慷慨 [k'āng-k'ǎi]: generous, liberal, bountiful, hospitable

慣

8 慣例 [kuàn-lì]: usage, convention, usual practice; routine, conventional

慣於 [kuàn-yǘ]: to be accustomed to, to be used to

10 慣匪 [kuàn-fěi]: habitual bandits, bandits with long records

11 慣習 [kuàn-hsí]: habit, custom; habitual

慢

8 慢性 [màn-hsìng]: chronic

慕

5 慕尼黑 [mù-ní-hēi]: Munich

慫

15 慫慂 [sǔng-yǔng]: to abet, to incite, to instigate, to encourage, to promote, to back

慘

9 慘重的 [ts'ǎn-chùng te]: disastrous, calamitous, ruinous, catastrophic, tragic, dire

11 慘敗 [ts'ǎn-pài]: serious defeat

慰

11 慰問 [wèi-wèn]: to console, to send one's regards to; consolation, sincere regards

慰問信 [wèi-wèn-hsìn]: letter of condolence, consolatory letter

憂

13 憂傷 [yū-shāng]: grief, sorrow, distress, affliction, sadness, anguish, unhappiness; mournful, sad, grieved

15 憂慮 [yū-lǜ]: concern, anxiety, worry, solicitude

— 12 Strokes —

憤

9 憤恨[**fèn-hèn**]: anger, wrath, indignation, irritation, hatred, enmity, dislike, displeasure

憤怒[**fèn-nù**]: anger, wrath, indignation, irritation, hatred, enmity, dislike, displeasure

14 憤慨[**fèn-k'ăi**]: anger, wrath, indignation, irritation, hatred, enmity, dislike, displeasure

16 憤激[**fèn-chī**]: exasperation

憲

7 憲兵[**hsièn-pīng**]: military police, gendarme

憲兵部隊[**hsièn-pīng pù-tùi**]: gendarmerie

8 憲法[**hsièn-fă**]: constitution

憲法法院[**hsièn-fă fă-yüàn**]: constitutional court

憲法草案[**hsièn-fă ts'ăo-àn**]: draft constitution

11 憲章[**hsièn-chāng**]: charter

憑

11 憑票付款[**p'íng-p'iào fù-k'uăn**]: draft payable to bearer

16 憑據[**p'íng-chǜ**]: guarantee, proof, evidence

18 憑藉[**p'íng-chièh**]: to resort to, to have recourse to, to draw on

憎

12 憎惡[**tsēng-wù**]: to hate, to detest, to abominate; animosity, antipathy, hatred, repugnance; abhorrent, odious, repulsive, offensive

— 13 Strokes —

懊

10 懊悔[**ào-hŭi**]: to regret, to reproach oneself

12 懊惱[**ào-năo**]: annoyed, angry, vexed

憶

9 憶苦思甜[**ì-k'ŭ ssū-t'ién**]: to remember bitterness and think of sweetness (i.e., to think of the contrast between the "old" and the "new" societies)

懇

7 懇求[**k'ĕn-ch'íu**]: to pray, to entreat, to beseech, to implore, to petition; plea, supplication

懂

9 懂政治的[**tŭng chèng-chìh te**]: politically conscious

應

4 應允[**yìng-yŭn**]: to comply with, to agree to, to assent to, to acquiesce; acquiescence

5 應付[**yìng-fù**]: to cope with, to deal with, to meet, to contend with

應用[**yīng-yùng**]: to apply; application; applied

應用眞菌研究所[**yīng-yùng chēn-chǜn yén-chìu-sŏ**]: Institute of Applied Mycology

應用化學研究所[**yīng-yùng huà-hsüéh yén-chìu-sŏ**]: Institute of Applied Chemistry

應用物理研究所[**yīng-yùng wù-lĭ yén-chìu-sŏ**]: Institute of Applied Physics

8 應屆畢業生 [yìng-chièh pì-yèh-shēng]: graduates of this term (i.e., students about to graduate in the coming term or year)

11 應得 [yīng-té]: to deserve, to be worthy of, to merit; due, proper, entitled to

13 應酬 [yìng-ch'óu]: to entertain, to receive; social intercourse, social function

16 應戰 [yìng-chàn]: to accept a challenge, to accept battle

17 應聲蟲 [yìng-shēng ch'úng]: echoer, parrot, yes-man

— 14 Strokes —

懦

10 懦弱性 [nò-jò-hsìng]: spinelessness, weakness, feebleness

— 15 Strokes —

懲

8 懲治 [ch'éng-chìh]: to punish; punishment

14 懲罰 [ch'éng-fá]: to reprimand and fine; to punish; punishment

懲罰性的 [ch'éng-fá-hsìng te]: punitive

16 懲辦 [ch'éng-pàn]: to punish, to deal with severely

懲辦主義 [ch'éng-pàn chǔ-ì]: punitivism (i.e., the punishment of Party members for having bourgeois ideas by leading cadre, a method considered to be contrary to those of persuasion and education)

懲辦和寬大相結合 [ch'éng-pàn hó k'uān-tà hsiāng chiéh-hó]: combining punishment with leniency (i.e., a policy of severe punishment to those who resist pleading guilty to their crimes and one of leniency to those who confess)

— 16 Strokes —

懸

6 懸而未決的 [hsüán érh wèi chüéh te]: outstanding, pending, remaining, left over, not yet decided

8 懸念 [hsüán-nièn]: suspense; anxious, worried

10 懸案 [hsüán-àn]: pending case, undecided case, outstanding issue, an issue pending decision

懸殊 [hsüán-shū]: disparity, unevenness, great distance between, distant

11 懸掛 [hsüán-kuà]: to hang; hanging

15 懸賞 [hsüán-shǎng]: to offer a reward, to post a reward, to set a price (on someone's head)

懷

5 懷古 [huái-kǔ]: to think of the past, to cherish thoughts of the past

懷孕 [huái-yùn]: to conceive, to become pregnant; conception, pregnancy

8 懷念 [huái-nièn]: to long for, to yearn for, to have a nostalgia for, to remember

懷抱 [huái-pào]: to harbor, to cherish, to entertain

9 懷恨 [huái-hèn]: to nurse a grudge, to cherish enmity

懷胎 [huái-t'āi]: to be pregnant; pregnancy

12 懷着 [huái-che]: to have, to cherish, to embrace, to have something in mind

懷着好意 [huái-che hǎo-ì]: well-disposed, fair-minded, bona fide, kind-hearted, well-intentioned

懷着鬼胎 [huái-che kuěi-t'āi]: with evil in one's heart

懷着惡意[huái-che ò-ì]: malicious, malevolent, malign, with ill will, ill-disposed, ill-intentioned, evil minded, with bad intent

懷鄉[huái-hsiāng]: homesickness; homesick

13 懷想[huái-hsiăng]: to long for

14 懷疑[huái-í]: to suspect, to distrust; scepticism, doubt; sceptical, doubtful, distrustful

懷疑論[huái-í-lùn]: scepticism

懷疑論派[huái-í-lùn p'ài]: sceptics

18 懷舊[huái-chìu]: to think back to the past, to think of old friends

12 懶惰[lăn-tò]: laziness; lazy, indolent

— RADICAL 戈成 62 —

戈

12 戈登[kō-tēng]: C. G. Gordon (1833-1885; British military officer who led the Ever Victorious Army under Li Hung-chang during the Taiping Rebellion)

15 戈德堡[kō-té-păo]: Goldberg, Arthur (American statesman)

16 戈壁[kō-pì]: Gobi Desert

— 2 Strokes —

成

2 成人[ch'éng-jén]: adult

成人教育[ch'éng-jén chiào-yù]: adult education

4 成分[ch'éng-fèn]: elements, constituents, ingredients, component part, factor

成比例的[ch'éng pĭ-lì te]: proportionate

成文法[ch'éng-wén-fă]: statute, written law

5 成功[ch'éng-kūng]: to succeed, to achieve, to accomplish; success, accomplishment, achievement

成立[ch'éng-lì]: to found, to set up, to establish, to form

成本[ch'éng-pĕn]: cost, production costs

6 成份[ch'éng-fèn]: sector, personal background, class characteristics

成份不純[ch'éng-fèn pù-ch'ún]: impurity in class composition

成名[ch'éng-míng]: to make a name for oneself, to achieve fame

7 成見[ch'éng-chièn]: preconceived idea, preoccupation, bias

8 成果[ch'éng-kuŏ]: result, effect, fruit

成例[ch'éng-lì]: a precedent

成事[ch'éng-shìh]: to succeed in doing something, to accomplish something; finished business

9 成品[ch'éng-p'ĭn]: product, finished product

成爲[ch'éng-wéi]: to become, to grow into, to turn into

成爲泡影[ch'éng-wéi p'ào-yĭng]: to become a bubble, to end in naught, to come to nothing

成爲事實[ch'éng-wéi shìh-shíh]: to materialize

10 成效[ch'éng-hsiào]: effect, success, positive result

成倍[ch'éng-pèi]: to increase several times, an increase of several fold

成套設備[ch'éng-t'ào shè-pèi]: complete set of equipment

成員[ch'éng-yüán]: member, constituent member (i.e., member of a team or party)

成員國[ch'éng-yüán-kuó]: member state, member country

12 成就[ch'éng-chìu]: accomplishment, achievement, attainment

14 成語[ch'éng-yǔ]: phrase, idiom, set expression

15 成熟[ch'éng-shóu]: to mature; ripeness, maturity; mature, ripe

17 成績[ch'éng-chī]: achievement, success, attainment

— 3 Strokes —

4 戒心[chièh-hsīn]: to be alert to, to be on one's guard, on the alert, on the watch against; alertness, vigilant

12 戒備[chièh-pèi]: to be alert, to take precautions

20 戒嚴[chièh-yén]: to proclaim martial law, to be under martial law; martial law, a state of siege

22 戒驕戒躁[chièh-chiāo chièh-tsào]: to shun complacency and impetuosity, to guard against conceit and impatience, to guard against pride and haste

— 4 Strokes —

3 我也是一個[wǒ yěh shìh í-kò]: I for one, I too, I also

或

6 或多或少地[huò-tō huò-shǎo tì]: to a greater or lesser degree

9 或者[huò-chě]: perhaps, probably, likely

或是[huò-shìh]: perhaps, probably so, likely

11 或許[huò-hsǔ]: perhaps, possibly

12 或然率[huò-ján lǜ]: probability

— 9 Strokes —

戡

13 戡亂[k'ān-luàn]: to suppress a riot, to suppress an insurrection, to put down a rebellion

— 10 Strokes —

截

4 截止[chiéh-chǐh]: to intercept, to cut off, to stop

7 截住[chiéh-chù]: to block, to hold back, to cut off

8 截長補短[chiéh-ch'áng pǔ-tuǎn]: to cut off from the long to supply the deficiency of the short, to make up for one's shortcomings by means of one's merits

9 截面[chiéh-mièn]: cross-section

10 截留[chiéh-líu]: to detain, to hold back, to refuse to hand over, to retain goods or money for local use when it should have been forwarded

17 截擊[chiéh-chī]: to intercept

截擊機[chiéh-chī-chī]: interceptor, interceptor plane

截獲[chiéh-huò]: to catch, to capture, to intercept

18 截斷[chiéh-tuàn]: to divide, to sever, to cut in two

20 截攔[chiéh-lán]: to cut off, to block, to hold up, to block one's way

— 12 Strokes —

3 戰上海[chàn shàng-hǎi]: Fight Shanghai (a

Red Guard newspaper during the Cultural Revolution)

戰士 **[chàn-shìh]**: soldier, combatant, fighter, enlisted man

4 戰火 **[chàn-huŏ]**: conflagration of war, torch of war

戰友 **[chàn-yŭ]**: comrade-in-arms, ally

5 戰犯 **[chàn-fàn]**: war criminal

7 戰車 **[chàn-ch'ē]**: tank

戰役 **[chàn-ì]**: battle, campaign

戰役部置 **[chàn-ì pù-chìh]**: disposition of troops for a campaign

戰役的持久戰 **[chàn-ì te ch'íh-chĭu chàn]**: protracted campaign

戰役的速決戰 **[chàn-ì te sù-chüéh chàn]**: campaign of quick solution

戰利品 **[chàn-lì-p'ĭn]**: spoils, booty, prizes of war

8 戰爭 **[chàn-chēng]**: war, warfare, hostilities, fighting

戰爭機器 **[chàn-chēng chī-ch'ì]**: apparatus of war

戰爭叫囂 **[chàn-chēng chiào-hsiāo]**: war cries, saber-rattling, clamor for war

戰爭景氣 **[chàn-chēng chĭng-ch'ì]**: war boom, war prosperity

戰爭狀態 **[chàn-chēng chuàng-t'ài]**: state of war

戰爭準備者 **[chàn-chēng chŭn-pèi chĕ]**: war plotter

戰爭全局 **[chàn-chēng ch'üán-chǘ]**: whole military situation, overall military situation

戰爭販子 **[chàn-chēng fàn-tzu]**: warmonger

戰爭火炕 **[chàn-chēng huŏ-k'àng]**: fiery furnace of war

戰爭狂 **[chàn-chēng k'uáng]**: war hysteria

戰爭狂人 **[chàn-chēng k'uáng-jén]**: war maniac

戰爭邊緣政策 **[chàn-chēng piēn-yüán chèng-ts'è]**: brink-of-war policy, "brinksmanship"

戰爭災難 **[chàn-chēng tsāi-nàn]**: the horrors of war

戰爭溫床 **[chàn-chēng wēn-ch'uáng]**: hotbed of war

戰果 **[chàn-kuŏ]**: fruits of battle, spoils of battle

9 戰俘 **[chàn-fú]**: prisoner of war, captive

戰後的 **[chàn-hòu te]**: postwar

10 戰時 **[chàn-shíh]**: wartime, in time of war

11 戰區 **[chàn-ch'ǖ]**: war zone, theater of operations

戰略 **[chàn-lüèh]**: strategy; strategic

戰略家 **[chàn-lüèh-chiā]**: strategist

戰略進攻 **[chàn-lüèh chìn-kūng]**: strategic offensive

戰略轉移 **[chàn-lüèh chuăn-í]**: strategic shift

戰略追擊 **[chàn-lüèh chūi-chī]**: strategic pursuit

戰略反攻 **[chàn-lüèh făn-kūng]**: strategic counteroffensive

戰略方針 **[chàn-lüèh fāng-chēn]**: strategy

戰略防禦 **[chàn-lüèh fáng-yǜ]**: strategic defensive

戰略性機動 **[chàn-lüèh-hsìng chī-tùng]**: strategic maneuver

戰略轟炸 **[chàn-lüèh hūng-chà]**: strategic bombardment

戰略意義 **[chàn-lüèh ì-ì]**: strategic importance

戰略上藐視困難，戰術上重視困難

[chàn-lüèh-shàng miǎo-shǐh k'ùn-nán, chàn-shù-shàng chùng-shǐh k'ùn-nán]: to scorn difficulties strategically while paying full attention to them tactically

戰略上藐視敵人，戰術上重視敵人 **[chàn-lüèh-shàng miǎo-shǐh tí-jén, chàn-shù-shàng chùng-shǐh tí-jén]**: to slight the enemy strategically while taking full account of him tactically (a frequently quoted statement by Mao Tse-tung meaning that the Chinese Communists should never fear to match their strength with that of the enemy; also applied to the overcoming of difficulties that may arise in fulfilling daily work or assigned tasks)

戰略的持久戰 **[chàn-lüèh te ch'íh-chiǔ-chàn]**: strategic protracted war

戰略的速決戰 **[chàn-lüèh te sù-chüéh-chàn]**: strategic war of quick solution

戰略退却 **[chàn-lüèh t'ùi-ch'üèh]**: strategic retreat

戰略物資 **[chàn-lüèh wù-tzū]**: strategic materials

戰略原料 **[chàn-lüèh yüán-liào]**: strategic raw materials

戰敗 **[chàn-pài]**: to lose a battle, to be defeated

戰敗國 **[chàn-pài-kuó]**: defeated country, vanquished country

戰術 **[chàn-shù]**: tactics

12 戰場 **[chàn-ch'ǎng]**: battlefield

戰勝 **[chàn-shèng]**: to be victorious, to overcome, to conquer, to defeat, to vanquish; victory

戰無不勝 **[chàn wú pú-shèng]**: ever-triumphant, ever-victorious, invincible

戰無不勝，攻無不克 **[chàn wú pú-shèng, kūng wú pú-k'ò]**: "There is no battle that we cannot win, and no fortress that we cannot storm"

戰無不勝的毛澤東思想 **[chàn wú pú-shèng te máo tsé-tūng ssū-hsiǎng]**: the invincible thought of Mao Tse-tung

14 戰綫 **[chàn-hsièn]**: battle line, front

17 戰壕 **[chàn-háo]**: trench

戰壕裡的眞實 **[chàn-háo lǐ te chēn-shíh]**: the truth of the trenches

20 戰鬥 **[chàn-tòu]**: combat, battle, fighting, conflict, encounter, struggle

戰鬥性的 **[chàn-tòu-hsìng te]**: militant

戰鬥任務 **[chàn-tòu jèn-wù]**: combat duty, combat mission, a militant task (i.e., work to be done in a hurry)

戰鬥口號 **[chàn-tòu k'ǒu-hào]**: battle cry

戰鬥力 **[chàn-tòu-lì]**: combat effectiveness, fighting capacity, fighting strength

戰鬥報 **[chàn-tòu pào]**: Borba (Yugoslav daily newspaper); Combat (French daily newspaper)

戰鬥隊 **[chàn-tòu-tùi]**: a fighting force

戰鬥英雄 **[chàn-tòu yīng-hsiúng]**: combat hero

戰鬥員 **[chàn-tòu-yüán]**: fighters, soldiers

— 13 Strokes —

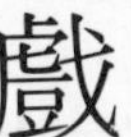

7 戲弄 **[hsì-nùng]**: to make fun of, to tease, to make a fool of, to make jokes at the expense of; banter, hoax

8 戲法 **[hsì-fǎ]**: trick, machination, sharp practice

10 戲院 **[hsì-yüàn]**: theater

13 戲裝 **[hsì-chuāng]**: theater costumes

15 戲劇 **[hsì-chǜ]**: drama, play

戲劇家 **[hsì-chǜ-chiā]**: stage artist

戲劇節目 **[hsì-chǜ chiéh-mù]**: repertoire, repertory

戲劇性[**hsì-chü-hsìng**]: theatrical, theatricalism; dramatic

戲劇報[**hsì-chü pào**]: Theatre (Chinese Communist monthly publication)

— 14 Strokes —

戳

9 戳穿[**ch'ō-ch'uān**]: to lay bare, to expose, to perforate, to pierce

戴

10 戴高樂[**tài-kāo-lè**]: De Gaulle, Charles (French statesman)

— RADICAL 户 63 —

戶

戶[**hù**]: household, family, house

3 戶口[**hù-k'ǒu**]: population, domicile, household registry, residential permit

戶口簿[**hù-k'ǒu pù**]: family register, house register (i.e., list of house tenants or inhabitants)

戶口冊[**hù-k'ǒu ts'è**]: register

20 戶籍[**hù-chí**]: population record, list of inhabitants

— 4 Strokes —

房

6 房地產稅[**fáng-tì-ch'ǎn shùi**]: land and building taxes

8 房舍[**fáng-shè**]: residence, premises

10 房租[**fáng-tsū**]: rent

11 房產[**fáng-ch'ǎn**]: real estate

房產稅[**fáng-ch'ǎn shùi**]: building tax, tax on urban buildings

所

6 所向披靡[**sŏ-hsiàng p'ī-mǐ**]: ever triumphant, ever victorious, mowing down the enemy, to rout all opponents

所有制[**sŏ-yǔ-chìh**]: ownership, proprietorship

所有主[**sŏ-yǔ-chǔ**]: owner, possessor, holder, proprietor

所有權[**sŏ-yǔ-ch'üán**]: ownership, title, claim, right of ownership

11 所得[**sŏ-té**]: income, earnings, wages

所得稅[**sŏ-té-shùi**]: income tax

12 所爲[**sŏ-wéi**]: actions, behavior

所爲[**sŏ-wèi**]: the reason for

16 所謂[**sŏ-wèi**]: so-called, alleged

19 所羅門群島[**sŏ-ló-mén ch'ǘn-tǎo**]: Solomon Islands

— 5 Strokes —

5 扁平[**piěn-p'íng**]: flat, level, flat and even

— 6 Strokes —

扇

7 扇形 **[shàn-hsíng]** : sector, section, quadrant; fan-shaped

扇形地區 **[shàn-hsíng tì-ch'ǖ]** : sector

扇形推進 **[shàn-hsíng t'ūi-chìn]** : fan-shaped propagation

— 7 Strokes —

11 扈從 **[hù-ts'úng]** : entourage, retinue

— RADICAL 手 64 —

才 **[ts'ái]** : talent, ability, skill

10 才能 **[ts'ái-néng]** : talent, capability, ability; talented, resourceful, able, capable, gifted

13 才幹 **[ts'ái-kàn]** : talent, capability, ability; talented, resourceful, able, capable, gifted

3 手工 **[shǒu-kūng]** : manual labor, handicraft; manual

手工彙總 **[shǒu-kūng hùi-tsǔng]** : manual processing

手工藝 **[shǒu-kūng-ì]** : handicraft, craftmanship

手工業 **[shǒu-kūng-yèh]** : handicraft industry, handicrafts

手工業主 **[shǒu-kūng-yèh chǔ]** : master handicraftsman

手工業合作化 **[shǒu-kūng-yèh hó-tsò-huà]** : organization of cooperation in handicrafts

手工業生產合作社 **[shǒu-kūng-yèh shēng-ch'ǎn hó-tsò-shè]** : handicraft producers' co-operatives

5 手册 **[shǒu-ts'è]** : handbook

8 手法 **[shǒu-fǎ]** : maneuver, tactics

9 手段 **[shǒu-tuàn]** : measure, strategem, means, method

12 手提機關槍 **[shǒu-t'í chī-kuān-ch'iāng]** : tommy gun, Thompson sub-machine gun, sub-machine gun

手腕 **[shǒu-wàn]** : skill, trick, maneuvering, tactics, strategem, finesse, cunning

14 手槍 **[shǒu-ch'iāng]** : pistol, revolver

手銬 **[shǒu-k'ào]** : manacles, handcuffs

手榴彈 **[shǒu-líu-tàn]** : grenade, hand-grenade

19 手藝工人 **[shǒu-ì kūng-jén]** : handicraft laborers

手邊 **[shǒu-piēn]** : on hand, at hand, in one's hand

21 手續 **[shǒu-hsǜ]** : formalities, procedure

— 1 Stroke —

扎

4 扎什曲宗 **[chā-shíh-ch'ǖ tsūng]** : Tashi-cho Dzong (summer capital of Bhutan)

10 扎根 **[chā-kēn]** : to take root, to strike root

— 2 Strokes —

打

[3] 打下基礎[tă-hsià chī-ch'ŭ]: to lay the foundation for, to prepare the ground for

打上[tă-shàng]: to make, to get, to obtain

打上烙印[tă-shàng lào-yìn]: to be stamped with a brand (i.e., as of "imperialist aggression")

[4] 打手[tă-shŏu]: bully, thug, hatchetman

打手式[tă shŏu-shìh]: to gesticulate; sign language

[5] 打仗[tă-chàng]: to make war, to fight

打主意[tă chú-ì]: to think of a plan, to plan, to decide

打包[tă-pāo]: to pack

[6] 打成一片[tă-ch'éng í-p'ièn]: to merge with, to be at one with, to unite as one, to work side by side

打交道[tă chiāo-tào]: to deal with, to negotiate, to treat, to handle, to have intercourse with, to associate with

打回老家去，就地鬧革命[tă-húi lăo-chiā ch'ǜ chìu-tì nào kó-mìng]: to be sent back home to work the revolution there (an order of January 18, 1967 during the Cultural Revolution to Chekiang youth in Shanghai)

[8] 打官話[tă kuān-huà]: to speak in a bureaucratic way, to talk official language

打官司[tă kuān-ssū]: to go to law, to sue, to engage in litigation

[9] 打政治仗[tă chèng-chìh chàng]: to fight political battles, to create a favorable impression among the masses

打架[tă-chià]: to fight, to quarrel

打垮[tă-k'uă]: to break down, to crush, to smash, to defeat

[10] 打消[tă-hsiāo]: to destroy, to cancel, to abolish

打馬虎眼[tă mă-hŭ-yĕn]: to exploit the carelessness of others, to deceive, to trick

打埋伏[tă mái-fú]: to ambush, to conceal oneself, to have something in reserve, to keep booty without reporting to the proper authorities

打破[tă-p'ò]: to break, to damage, to break down, to smash, to find a way out of

打破常規[tă-p'ò ch'áng-kuēi]: to shatter normal standards, to break with precedent

打破舊框框[tă-p'ò chìu k'uàng-k'uang]: to smash old frames (i.e., old frames refer to standards and records set in the past)

打倒[tă-tăo]: to knock down, to overthrow, to bring about the downfall of, down with!

打砸搶抄抓[tă tsá ch'iăng ch'āo chuā]: beating, smashing, looting, house-raiding and kidnapping (the five acts of violence that the Red Guards were warned not to commit during the Cultural Revolution)

打草站[tă-ts'ăo chàn]: haying station

[11] 打通[tă-t'ūng]: to pierce, to penetrate, to knock through, to make a hole in

打通心[tă-t'ūng hsīn]: to arouse the thought of the masses

打通思想[tă-t'ūng ssū-hsiăng]: to bring someone around to a correct attitude, to break through a mental block

打掩護[tă yĕn-hù]: to cover, to camouflage

[12] 打着....旗幟[tă-che .... ch'í-chìh]: to raise the flag of, in the name of, to be under the flag of

打着紅旗反紅旗[tă-che húng-ch'í făn húng-ch'í]: to raise red flags to oppose the Red Flag (i.e., to "don the cloak of Marxism-Leninism and the thought of Mao Tse-tung to oppose Marxism-Leninism and the thought of Mao Tse-tung")

打進[tă-chìn]: to make one's way into

打發[tă-fā]: to send, to dispatch

打開[tă-k'āi]: to open up, to lead the way, to make a beginning, to take the initiative

打開缺口[tă-k'āi ch'üēh-k'ŏu]: to make a breach, to drive a wedge

打靶[tă-pă]: to fire, to shoot; target shooting

打短[tă-tuăn]: to work for a daily wage, to work on a daily basis, to work on a temporary job

打游擊[tă yú-chī]: to fight guerrilla warfare

13 打場[tă-ch'áng]: to thresh, to thresh grain

打雷，不下雨[tă-léi, pú-hsià-yü̆]: thunder without rain (i.e., merely to go through the motions of purging bad elements)

打落水狗[tă lò-shŭi kŏu]: to hit a dog that has fallen into the water, to throw stones at a dog that has fallen into the water, to kick a man when he is down (implies that there should be no fair play for an enemy)

打靶場[tă-pă-ch'ăng]: shooting range, rifle range, practice range

打圓場[tă yüán-ch'ăng]: to make a compromise

14 打鬧[tă-nào]: to create a disturbance, to fight

打漂亮戰[tă p'iào-liàng chàn]: to fight a smart battle (i.e., the completion of a task efficiently and economically)

打算[tă-suàn]: to plan, to aim at, to intend, to have in view, to propose

15 打嘴巴[tă tsŭi-pā]: to cuff, to give a cuff, to slap in the face

16 打頭[tă-t'óu]: to be at the head, to be the leader

打錯算盤[tă-ts'ò suàn-p'án]: to miscalculate

17 打擊[tă-chī]: to strike, to hit, to beat, to knock; blow, hit

打擊一大片，保護一小撮[tă-chī í tà-p'ièn, păo-hù ì hsiăo-ts'ò]: to hit hard at many to protect a handful (during the Cultural Revolution, a slogan devised by reactionary leading cadres for the purpose of inciting the masses to attack cadres indiscriminately in order to protect their own interests)

打擊力量[tă-chī lì-liàng]: striking force

打擊面[tă-chī mièn]: scope of attack, area of attack

打擊歪風[tă-chī wāi-fēng]: to combat unhealthy tendencies, to eliminate improper social trends

打點[tă-tiĕn]: to arrange, to arrange beforehand

18 打糧食[tă liáng-shíh]: to harvest

打斷[tă-tuàn]: to intercept, to break off, to discontinue, to cut short

21 打殲滅戰[tă chiēn-mièh chàn]: to fight an extermination battle, to fight a war of annihilation (i.e., concentration of forces in order to complete a job thoroughly and effectively)

22 打聽[tă-t'īng]: to ask, to question, to investigate, to inquire into

23 打壩[tă-pà]: to build a dike, to erect a dam

— 3 Strokes —

扣

8 扣押[k'òu-yā]: to detain, to intern, to hold

10 扣留[k'òu-líu]: to detain, to intern, to hold

12 扣帽子[k'òu mào-tzu]: to fasten on a hat; to label, to put labels on; name-calling; to accuse someone of a fault (particularly, to accuse someone of being a reactionary, rightist, etc.)

托

8 托兒所 **[t'ō-érh-sŏ]** : nursery

9 托洛茨基 **[t'ō-lò-tz'ú-chī]** : Trotsky, L. D. (1877–1940)

托洛茨基主義 **[t'ō-lò-tz'ú-chī chŭ-ì]** : Trotskyism

10 托馬斯 **[t'ō-mă-ssū]** : St. Thomas Aquinas

14 托管 **[t'ō-kuăn]** : to put under trusteeship; trusteeship

托管人 **[t'ō-kuăn-jén]** : trustee

托管地 **[t'ō-kuăn-tì]** : trust territory, mandated territory

19 托辭 **[t'ō-tz'ú]** : pretext, excuse, subterfuge, alibi

— 4 Strokes —

找 **[chăo]** : to look for, to search for, to hunt for

5 找出 **[chăo-ch'ū]** : to find out, to discover, to bring to light

8 找到 **[chăo-tào]** : to find out, to discover, to bring to light

找到出路 **[chăo-tào ch'ū-lù]** : to find a way out, to find one's way

10 找差距 **[chăo ch'ā-chǜ]** : to find disparities (i.e., the realization by the backward of disparities in their ideology, knowledge, skills, or achievements so that they can increase their efforts to learn from and emulate the advanced)

18 找竅門 **[chăo ch'iào-mén]** : to find the secret of success, to find better techniques, to get the knack

抄

5 抄本 **[ch'āo-pĕn]** : copy, manuscript copy of a book, copy-book

9 抄家 **[ch'āo-chiā]** : to confiscate property

13 抄路 **[ch'āo-lù]** : to take a short cut

15 抄寫 **[ch'āo-hsiĕh]** : to copy, to transcribe

22 抄襲 **[ch'āo-hsí]** : to plagiarize, to copy, to make a surprise attack

折

6 折扣 **[ché-k'òu]** : discount

10 折衷主義 **[ché-chūng chŭ-ì]** : eclecticism (according to the Maoist view, compromise between the two extremes of the proletarian revolutionary line and the bourgeois counterrevolutionary line, a course considered to be taking the side of the enemy)

折衷方案 **[ché-chūng fāng-àn]** : compromise, middle way

折衷學派 **[ché-chūng hsüéh-p'ài]** : eclectic school

折射 **[ché-shè]** : refraction

14 折實價 **[ché-shíh chià]** : net price

折實公債 **[ché-shíh kūng-chài]** : parity bond

折實單位 **[ché-shíh tān-wèi]** : parity unit

15 折價 **[ché-chià]** : to give a discount

16 折磨 **[ché-mó]** : to afflict, to torture, to harass, to disturb, to torment, to undergo an ordeal, to be tortured by; suffering, distress, torment, ordeal

18 折舊費 **[ché-chìu fèi]** : depreciation funds

扯

6 扯舌頭 **[ch'ĕ shé-t'óu]** : to make mischief

14 扯腿 **[ch'ĕ-t'ŭi]** : to obstruct, to hinder

15 扯談 **[ch'ĕ-t'án]** : to blab, to gossip, to talk nonsense, to talk rubbish

16 扯謊[ch'ĕ-huăng]: to lie

8 承受[ch'éng-shòu]: to receive, to inherit, to accept

13 承當[ch'éng-tāng]: to take over, to be responsible for, to undertake for and abide by the consequences

14 承認[ch'éng-jèn]: to acknowledge, to admit, to concede, to recognize; recognition, admission

承管[ch'éng-kuăn]: to administer, to be responsible for

16 承擔[ch'éng-tān]: to assume, to bear, to undertake; assumption

承擔義務[ch'éng-tān ì-wù]: to undertake an obligation, to commit oneself to, to accept the responsibility for

承擔不起[ch'éng-tān pù-ch'ĭ]: ill afford to

技

3 技工[chì-kūng]: mechanic, technical worker, skilled worker

技士[chì-shìh]: technician

5 技巧[chì-ch'iăo]: ingenious, skillful

10 技倆[chì-liăng]: tactics, maneuver, trick, artifice, cheating device, crafty practice

技能[chì-néng]: skill, technical proficiency, craftsmanship

技師[chì-shīh]: technician, artisan, expert, engineer

11 技術[chì-shù]: art, skill, technique, expertness, technology; technical

技術裝備[chì-shù chuāng-pèi]: technical installation

技術軍士[chì-shù chūn-shìh]: Technical Sergeant (U.S. Air Force)

技術協助局[chì-shù hsiéh-chù chǘ]: Technical Assistance Board (United Nations)

技術人員[chì-shù jén-yüán]: technician, technical expert

技術改革[chì-shù kăi-kó]: technical transformation, technical improvement, technical innovation

技術革新[chì-shù kó-hsīn]: technical innovation

技術科學部[chì-shù k'ō-hsüéh pù]: Department of Technical Sciences

技術革命[chì-shù kó-mìng]: technical revolution, technological revolution (i.e., the general use of modern machinery in industry and agriculture)

技術工人[chì-shù kūng-jén]: skilled worker, craftsman, worker with technical skill

技術力量[chì-shù lì-liàng]: technical strength

技術標準[chì-shù piāo-chŭn]: technical standard

技術兵種[chì-shù pīng-chŭng]: technical arms branches of the armed forces

技術定額[chì-shù tìng-ó]: technical norm, technical target

技術操作規程 [chì-shù ts'āo-tsò kūei-ch'éng]: technical operations

技術作物[chì-shù tsò-wù]: industrial crops

技術推廣站[chì-shù t'ūi-kuăng chàn]: agro-technical station

技術資料[chì-shù tzū-liào]: technical data

技術員 [chì-shù-yüán]: technician

19 技藝 [chì-ì]: feat, skill, act, stunt

抓

抓 [chuā]: to grip, to clutch, to grab, to seize, to pay close attention to

5 抓生產 [chuā shēng-ch'ăn]: to grasp produc-

tion, to give attention to production

6 抓好兩頭 **[chuā-hăo liăng-t'óu]**: to grasp both ends well (i.e., to come to a thorough understanding of Party policy on the upper level and of the actual conditions of an enterprise on the lower level, that is to link the Party line with local needs and to link theory with practice)

7 抓住 **[chuā-chù]**: to seize, to grasp, to get hold of

8 抓兩頭帶中間 **[chuā liăng-t'óu tài chūng-chiēn]**: to keep watch over the most advanced and the most backward (i.e., the two ends) so as to bring along the majority in between

9 抓重點 **[chuā chùng-tiĕn]**: to grasp the essential point

抓革命促生產 **[chuā kó-mìng ts'ù shēng-chăn]**: to take hold of revolution and promote production, to grasp revolution and promote production (the 14th point of the 十六條, q.v.)

抓革命促生產第一綫指揮 **[chuā kó-mìng ts'ù shēng-ch'ăn tì-í-hsìen chĭh-hūi]**: Seize Revolution Promote Production First Line Command (a low level army-supported organization for spring plowing in 1967)

抓革命，促生產，促工作，促戰備 **[chuā kó-mìng, ts'ù shēng-ch'ăn, ts'ù kūng-tsò, ts'ù chàn-pèi]**: to grasp revolution, promote production, promote work, and promote the preparation for war (the phrases "promote work" and "promote the preparation for war" were added to the original slogan "to grasp revolution and promote production" in October 1967 after the campaign for the "Great Revolutionary Alliance" was launched)

14 抓緊 **[chuā-chĭn]**: to grasp firmly, to grasp tightly

抓緊解決 **[chuā-chĭn chiĕh-chüéh]**: to make every effort to solve, to make every effort to tackle

抓緊領導 **[chuā-chĭn lĭng-tăo]**: to give firm leadership to

扶

7 扶助 **[fú-chù]**: to assist, to help, to support

扶助工農 **[fú-chù kūng-núng]**: to give assistance to the peasants and workers

9 扶持 **[fú-ch'íh]**: to support, to help, to assist

12 扶植 **[fú-chíh]**: to foster, to build up, to sponsor, to bolster up, to support and maintain

15 扶養 **[fú-yăng]**: to nourish, to bring up, to care for

抑

8 抑制 **[ì-chìh]**: to refrain from, to stifle, to curb, to restrain from

抗

2 抗丁 **[k'àng-tīng]**: to resist pressganging

3 抗大 **[k'àng-tà]**: abbreviation of 抗日大學, q.v.

4 抗日 **[k'àng-jìh]**: War of Resistance Against Japan (1937–1945)

抗日戰爭 **[k'àng-jìh chàn-chēng]**: War of Resistance Against Japan

抗日大學 **[k'àng-jìh tà-hsüéh]**: Resist-Japan University (operated in Yenan by the Chinese communists during the Sino-Japanese War, 1937–1945)

7 抗旱作物 **[k'àng-hàn tsò-wù]**: drought resistant crop

8 抗拒 **[k'àng-chü]**: to defy, to resist, to oppose, to withstand, to act in defiance of

9 抗美援朝 **[k'àng-mĕi yüán-ch'áo]**: Resist America, Aid Korea; Resist U.S. Aggression and Aid Korea (a slogan in use during the Korean War)

[12] 抗菌素[k'àng-chùn-sù] : antibiotics

抗菌素研究所[k'àng-chùn-sù yén-chiù-sŏ] : Antibiotics Institute

[13] 抗毒素[k'àng-tú-sù] : antitoxin

[16] 抗戰[k'àng-chàn] : War of Resistance Against Japan (abbreviation of 抗日戰爭)

抗戰人員[k'àng-chàn jén-yüán] : resistance fighter, resistance personnel

[17] 抗擊[k'àng-chī] : to resist and pin down

[18] 抗糧[k'àng-liáng] : to resist the grain levy

[20] 抗議[k'àng-ì] : to protest, to challenge; protest

扭

[18] 扭轉[nĭu-chuăn] : to turn, to turn away from, to divert, to head away from

扼

[6] 扼守[ò-shŏu] : to hold, to occupy

[9] 扼要[ò-yào] : to occupy a strategical position, to hold a key position; important, essential, necessary, vital

扼要地[ò-yào tì] : briefly, concisely, summarily, succinctly, tersely

[10] 扼殺[ò-shā] : to smother, to strangle, to suffocate, to suppress, to deaden, to stifle, to choke

把

[6] 把式[pă-shìh] : expert, master of a trade

[9] 把持[pă-ch'íh] : to control, to maintain exclusive control, to retain one's grip on

把風[pă-fēng] : to keep watch; look-out, scout

[10] 把家庭關[pă chiā-t'íng kuān] : to guard the family pass (i.e., to guard against the corrosive influence of exploiting families)

[12] 把握[pă-wò] : to take hold of, to seize; authority for taking action, safeguard, security, guarantee

[17] 把戲[pă-hsì] : to juggle, to perform tricks (i.e., as in juggling with ideas or policy); juggling, trick

[19] 把關[pă-kuān] : to hold the pass, to guard a pass (an old military term now applied to struggle against bourgeois ideology)

扮

[7] 扮作[pàn-tsò] : to dress up, to pretend to be; in the guise of

[14] 扮演 ... 角色[pàn-yĕn . . . chiăo-sè] : to play a role in, to play the part of

拋

[10] 拋射[p'āo-shè] : to project

拋射體[p'āo-shè-t'ĭ] : projectile

拋射筒[p'āo-shè-t'ŭng] : missile-projector

[11] 拋售[p'āo-shòu] : to undersell, to dump; sacrifice sale

[12] 拋棄[p'āo-ch'ì] : to reject, to cast aside, to abandon, to repudiate, to throw away

[17] 拋錨[p'āo-máo] : to cast anchor, to drop anchor, to be out of gear, to break down

批

批[p'ī] : batch, lot, delivery, group, occasion

[7] 批判主義[p'ī-p'àn chŭ-ì] : criticism, critique-ism, Kant-ism

批判性的[p'ī-p'àn-hsìng te] : critical

批判掉 [p'ī-p'àn-tiào] : to criticize away, to repudiate

10 批準 [p'ī-chŭn] : to sanction, to endorse, to authorize, to ratify, to approve; ratification

11 批深，批透，批倒，批臭 [p'ī-shēn p'ī-t'òu, p'ī-tăo, p'ī-ch'òu] : to criticize profoundly and thoroughly and to criticize until (our enemies) collapse and stink (from Cultural Revolution, illustrating Mao's insistence that "reasoning" must be used instead of "violence")

12 批發 [p'ī-fā] : to wholesale; wholesale (as both noun and adjective)

批發站 [p'ī-fā chàn] : wholesale station

批發商 [p'ī-fā shāng] : wholesale merchant

批評 [p'ī-p'íng] : to criticize; criticism

14 批駁 [p'ī-pó] : to rebut, to disapprove, to reject

抒

11 抒情詩 [shū-ch'íng shīh] : lyric poetry

投

2 投入 [t'óu-jù] : to throw into, to fall into, to enter on

投入生產 [t'óu-jù shēng-ch'ăn] : to put into operation, to start production, to go into production

6 投合 [t'óu-hó] : to fit, to meet, to appeal to, to be suitable to

投合口味 [t'óu-hó k'ŏu-wèi] : to cater to the taste of

9 投降 [t'óu-hsiáng] : to capitulate, to surrender, to yield, to give in; capitulation

投降主義 [t'óu-hsiáng chŭ-ì] : capitulationism (a policy Liu Shao-Ch'i was accused of following during the war against Japan when he asked the CCP to abandon its leadership of the national united front to the Kuomintang)

投降主義思想 [t'óu-hsiáng chŭ-ì ssū-hsiăng] : capitulationist ideas

投降派 [t'óu-hsiáng p'ài] : capitulators, capitulators' clique

10 投案 [t'óu-àn] : to appear before a court

投案自首 [t'óu-àn tzù-shŏu] : to surrender oneself to justice

11 投票 [t'óu-p'iào] : to vote, to ballot, to cast a ballot; vote, ballot, poll

投票處 [t'óu-p'iào ch'ù] : polls, polling booth, voting booth

13 投誠 [t'óu-ch'éng] : to surrender; surrender

投資 [t'óu-tzū] : to invest, to subscribe capital

投資的比例 [t'óu-tzū te pĭ-lì] : ratio of investment

15 投靠 [t'óu-k'ào] : to enter the service of, to go over completely to; subservience, dependence, servility

16 投機 [t'óu-chī] : to speculate; speculation, profiteering; speculative

投機份子 [t'óu-chī fèn-tzu] : opportunist, adventurer

— 5 Strokes —

拆

5 拆台 [ch'āi-t'ái] : to undercut, to cut out from under

10 拆除 [ch'āi-ch'ú] : to dismantle

12 拆開 [ch'āi-k'āi] : to disassociate from

拆散 [ch'āi-sàn] : to break up (i.e., as to break up Arab unity)

16 拆墻脚 [ch'āi ch'iáng-chiăo] : to undermine

招

3 招工 [chāo-kūng] : to recruit labor

6 招收 **[chāo-shōu]**: to enroll, to accept, to admit, to take in

7 招兵 **[chāo-pīng]**: to raise troops, to recruit soldiers, to enlist soldiers

招兵買馬 **[chāo-pīng mǎi-mǎ]**: to hire men and buy horses, to enlist followers, to gather together a following

8 招呼 **[chāo-hū]**: to greet, to call, to hail, to salute, to look after, to take care of

9 招架 **[chāo-chià]**: to resist, to ward off, to withstand, to stand up to, to defend, to stand one's ground against

招架不住 **[chāo-chià pú-chù]**: unable to resist, not to be able to hold one's own

招待 **[chāo-tài]**: to entertain, to receive, to treat to, to give a reception for; reception, hospitality

10 招致 **[chāo-chìh]**: to incur, to give rise to, to cause

12 招牌 **[chāo-p'ái]**: shop sign, sign board (*See* 在…招牌下)

招貼 **[chāo-t'iēh]**: placard, poster, bill

13 招惹 **[chāo-jě]**: to provoke, to arouse, to solicit, to incite

招募 **[chāo-mù]**: to recruit; recruitment

招搖撞騙 **[chāo-yáo chuàng-p'ièn]**: to bluff and deceive, to swindle, to hoax

14 招認 **[chāo-jèn]**: to confess, to admit; confession

抻

8 抻長 **[ch'ēn-ch'áng]**: to protract, to drag out, to stretch

抽

4 抽水機 **[ch'ōu-shǔi-chī]**: pump, water pump

抽水機站 **[ch'ōu-shǔi-chī chàn]**: power pumping station

6 抽考 **[ch'ōu-k'ǎo]**: to take a random sample, to make a spot check

9 抽查 **[ch'ōu-ch'á]**: to take a random sample, to make a spot check

12 抽補 **[ch'ōu-pǔ]**: to repair, to compensate, to make amends for, to set into place

抽稅 **[ch'ōu-shùi]**: to levy taxes, to impose a tax

13 抽象 **[ch'ōu-hsiàng]**: abstraction; abstract

抽象的眞理 **[ch'ōu-hsiàng te chēn-lǐ]**: abstract truth

抽象的同一性 **[ch'ōu-hsiàng te t'úng-ī-hsìng]**: abstract identity

15 抽調 **[ch'ōu-tiào]**: to transfer (to another job)

抽樣 **[ch'ōu-yàng]**: sampling

抽樣法 **[ch'ōu-yàng fǎ]**: sampling method

抽樣複查 **[ch'ōu-yàng fù-ch'á]**: control inspection, sample recheck

抽樣觀察 **[ch'ōu-yàng kuān-ch'á]**: sample observation

抽樣比重 **[ch'ōu-yàng pǐ-chùng]**: relative sample size

抽樣平均數 **[ch'ōu-yàng p'íng-chūn-shù]**: sample mean

抽樣總體 **[ch'ōu-yàng tsǔng-t'ǐ]**: sample population

拒

12 拒絕 **[chù-chüéh]**: to reject, to refuse, to decline, to dismiss, to repudiate, to disclaim; rejection, refusal

拘

10 拘留 **[chū-líu]**: to detain forcibly

11 拘票 **[chū-p'iào]**: warrant for arrest, writ of attachment

13 拘禁 [chū-chìn]: to take into custody, to imprison, to detain; confinement, custody, arrest

拐

10 拐逃 [kuăi-t'áo]: to decoy, to swindle

19 拐騙 [kuăi-p'ièn]: to trick, to swindle, to decoy

拉

1 拉一批，打一批 [lā ì-p'ī, tă ì-p'ī]: get hold of a group of people to attack another group (a phrase used during the Cultural Revolution by the followers of Mao and Lin Piao to describe the method allegedly used by the Liu-Teng faction in sabotaging the Cultural Revolution)

2 拉丁美洲通訊社 [lā-tīng mĕi-chōu t'ūng-hsùn-shè]: Agencia Latina de Noticias

4 拉巴斯 [lā pā-ssū]: La Paz (Bolivia)

拉巴特 [lā-pā-t'è]: Rabat (Morocco)

5 拉布爾 [lā-pù-ĕrh]: Rabaul

拉瓦爾品第 [lā-wă-ĕrh-p'ĭn-tì]: Rawalpindi (Pakistan)

6 拉回老路 [lā-húi lăo-lù]: to drag back, to drag back to the old line

拉各斯 [lā-kò-ssū]: Lagos (Nigeria)

9 拉者 [lā-chĕ]: rajah

拉祜 [lā-hù]: La-hu (minority nationality)

11 拉密堡 [lā-mì păo]: Fort Lamy (Chad)

拉莎 [lā-shā]: Lhasa (Tibet)

拉脫維亞 [lā-t'ō-wéi-yà]: Latvia

14 拉緊 [lā-chĭn]: to tighten, to fasten tighter

18 拉薩 [lā-sà]: Lhasa (Tibet)

拉薩革命造反總部 [lā-sà kó-mìng tsào-făn tsŭng-pù]: Lhasa Revolutionary Rebel General Group (an organization formed during the Cultural Revolution)

19 拉攏 [lā-lŭng]: to ingratiate oneself with, to win over, to recruit, to associate with, to dally, to dawdle

抹

11 抹掉 [mŏ-tiào]: to erase, to wipe away, to obliterate

12 抹煞 [mŏ-shà]: to ignore, to wipe out, to sweep away, to erase, to disregard, to negate, to deny

拔

8 拔河 [pá-hó]: a tug of war

13 拔腿 [pá-t'ŭi]: to escape, to withdraw, to take to one's heels

拜

7 拜見 [pài-chièn]: to visit, to pay a visit

8 拜金主義 [pài-chīn chŭ-ì]: mammonism, worship of mammon, worship of gold

拜物教 [pài-wù chiào]: fetishism

拜亞爾 [pài-yà-ĕrh]: Bayar, Celal (Turkish statesman)

11 拜訪 [pài-făng]: to visit, to call and inquire after

13 拜會 [pài-hùi]: to pay a visit, to make a call

拍

10 拍馬屁 [p'āi mă-p'ì]: to toady to someone, to flatter someone, to fawn on someone, to be a toady, to be obsequious, to be a sycophant; sycophancy

拍馬屁的人 [p'āi mă-p'ì te jén]: toady, flatterer, sycophant, fawner, flunkey

15 拍賣 [p'āi-mài]: to auction; an auction

拌

16 拌嘴[pàn-tsŭi]: to wrangle, to bicker, to squabble, to dispute; altercation

抱

4 抱不平[pào pù-p'íng]: to take up the cudgels for, to take up the cudgels against injustice, to be the champion of the oppressed

6 抱有[pào-yŭ]: to hold, to harbor, to entertain

抱有懷疑[pào-yŭ huái-í]: to entertain suspicions of

抱有幻想[pào-yŭ huàn-hsiăng]: to harbor illusions

7 抱佛脚[pào fó-chiăo]: to clasp the feet of the Buddha, to seek help at a critical moment

9 抱負[pào-fù]: ambition, aspiration

抱怨[pào-yüàn]: to complain, to complain against, to mutter against

13 抱愧[pào-k'uèi]: to feel shame, to be ashamed of one's mistakes

14 抱歉[pào-ch'ièn]: to apologize, to regret, to feel sorry; sorry

披

12 披着 ... 外衣[p'ēi-che . . . wài-ì]: to wear the cloak of, to be clothed in, to be disguised as; under the cloak of

抨

17 抨擊[p'ēng-chī]: to attack, to criticize, to censure, to disparage, to condemn, to find fault with, to denounce

抬

10 抬高[t'ái-kāo]: to elevate

16 抬頭[t'ái-t'óu]: to lift the head

抵

4 抵不住[tĭ-pú-chù]: to be unable to resist, not able to hold out

7 抵抗[tĭ-k'àng]: to resist, to withstand, to strive against, to stand up to; resistance

8 抵制[tĭ-chìh]: to boycott, to oppose, to resist

10 抵消[tĭ-hsiāo]: to cancel, to counterbalance, to offset

12 抵換[tĭ-huàn]: to barter, to exchange

抵補[tĭ-pŭ]: to replace, to offset

15 抵銷[tĭ-hsiāo]: to cancel, to counterbalance, to offset

16 抵賴[tĭ-lài]: to quibble, to deny

20 抵觸[tĭ-ch'ù]: to oppose, to conflict, to contradict, to infringe upon; offence, interference, contradictory

拖

拖[t'ō]: to draw, to tow, to haul, to draw into

2 拖人下水[t'ō-jén hsià-shŭi]: to pull others in, to drag others down, to get someone to share the responsibility for

7 拖車[t'ō-ch'ē]: trailer

拖住 ... 的手[t'ō-chù . . . te shŏu]: to stay the hands of

8 拖長的[t'ō-ch'áng te]: protracted

拖拉機[t'ō-lā-chī]: tractor

拖拉機工作隊[t'ō-lā-chī kūng-tsò tùi]: tractor work team

拖泥帶水[t'ō-ní tài-shŭi]: loathsome, muddled, messy

拖延[t'ō-yén]: to delay, to put off, to draw out, to protract, to play for time; procrastination, stalling; protracted

11 拖船[t'ō-ch'uán]: tugboat

14 拖駁運輸[t'ō-pó yǜn-shū]: tug transport

— 6 Strokes —

按

2 按人口平均計算[àn jén-k'ŏu p'íng-chǖn chì-suàn]: per capita, per head

按人口平均計算的產量[àn jén-k'ŏu p'íng-chǖn chì-suàn te ch'ăn-liàng]: per capita output

4 按比例發展[àn pĭ-lì fā-chăn]: to develop in proportion

5 按可比部分計算[àn k'ŏ-pĭ pù-fēn chì-suàn]: calculated on the basis of comparable sectors

6 按件計酬[àn-chièn chì-ch'óu]: to pay on a piecework basis

按件包工[àn chièn pāo-kūng]: contract by piecework

按行業[àn háng-yèh]: by entire trades (i.e., as transformation of capitalist industry by entire trades into state-private enterprise)

10 按級彙總[àn-chí hùi-tsŭng]: non-centralized data processing

11 按部就班的[àn-pù chìu-pān te]: step by step

12 按勞取酬[àn-láo ch'ǚ-ch'óu]: remuneration according to labor, pay according to work

按勞分配[àn-láo fēn-p'èi]: to each according to his work

13 按照[àn-chào]: according to, in accordance with, in the light of, in line with

按照...意旨[àn-chào . . . ì-chĭh]: under the orders of

按照...的命令[àn-chào . . . te mìng-lìng]: by order of

按照表面價值[àn-chào piăo-mièn chià-chíh]: at one's face value

按照...的比例[àn-chào . . . te pĭ-lì]: in proportion to

14 按需分配[àn-hsǖ fēn-p'èi]: to each according to his needs

按語[àn-yǚ]: commentary, note, remark

拯

11 拯救[chĕng-chìu]: to rescue, to save

指

4 指引[chĭh-yĭn]: to point out, to guide, to lead

5 指出[chĭh-ch'ū]: to point out, to indicate, to denote, to note, to show

指示[chĭh-shìh]: to order, to instruct, to direct; directive, order, direction, instruction, ordinance, injunction

8 指使[chĭh-shĭh]: to instigate, to incite, to prompt; inspired

指定[chĭh-tìng]: to assign, to appoint, to depute, to delegate, to name, to specify

9 指南[chĭh-nán]: guide, compass

指南針[chĭh-nán-chēn]: compass (during the Cultural Revolution, a simile for the Thought of Mao Tse-tung)

11 指責[chĭh-tsé]: to charge, to censure, to denounce, to condemn, to criticize; charge, censure, accusation, condemnation

指望[chĭh-wàng]: to aim at, to look for, to expect, to anticipate, to count on

12 指揮[chĭh-hūi]: to direct, to conduct, to command; guidance, direction, command

指揮位置提前[chĭh-hūi wèi-chìh t'í-ch'ién]: command advancement (a military system whereby a commanding officer or his deputy moves to the next lower level unit headquarters to expedite tactical decisions)

指揮員 **[chĭh-hūi-yüán]**: commander

指爲 **[chĭh-wéi]**: to label as, to brand as, to call, to name as

13 指路明燈 **[chĭh-lù míng-tēng]**: a bright lantern lighting the road (during the Cultural Revolution, a simile for the Thought of Mao Tse-tung)

15 指標 **[chĭh-piāo]**: index, quota, target, aim, mark, indicator

指標落實 **[chĭh-piāo lò-shíh]**: to fix targets in relation to specific measures for their fulfillment

指數 **[chĭh-shù]**: index

指數法 **[chĭh-shù fă]**: index method

指數分析法 **[chĭh-shù fēn-hsī fă]**: index method of analysis

指數化數直 **[chĭh-shù huà-shù chíh]**: index level

指數理論 **[chĭh-shù lĭ-lùn]**: index theory

指數數列 **[chĭh-shù shù-lièh]**: index series

指數體系 **[chĭh-shù t'ĭ-hsì]**: index system

16 指戰員 **[chĭh-chàn-yüán]**: commanders and fighters, officers and men

指導 **[chĭh-tăo]**: to direct, to guide, to pilot, to steer; guidance, lead, direction, steering

指導計劃 **[chĭh-tăo chì-huà]**: master plan

指導思想 **[chĭh-tăo ssū-hsiăng]**: guiding thought, guiding theory, guiding idea

指導委員會 **[chĭh-tăo wĕi-yüán-hùi]**: steering committee

持

3 持久 **[ch'íh-chĭu]**: lasting, enduring, sustained, persistent, protracted

持久戰 **[ch'íh-chĭu chàn]**: protracted war, protracted warfare

持久和平 **[ch'íh-chĭu hó-p'íng]**: durable peace, enduring peace

7 持身 **[ch'íh-shēn]**: to restrain one's emotions

15 持論 **[ch'íh-lùn]**: to argue with, to present one's opinion, to make an assertion

21 持續期間 **[ch'íh-hsù ch'ī-chiēn]**: duration

拳

11 拳術 **[ch'üán-shù]**: pugilism, boxing

拷

5 拷打 **[k'ăo-tă]**: to beat in order to extort a confession, to beat up, to torture

拱

8 拱門 **[kŭng-mén]**: arch

16 拱衞 **[kŭng-wèi]**: to surround, to guard, to protect

拼

8 拼命 **[p'īn-mìng]**: desperate, wild, reckless

拼命主義 **[p'īn-mìng chŭ-ì]**: desperadoism

9 拼音字母 **[p'īn-yīn tzù-mŭ]**: "pinyin" alphabet, phonetic alphabet

11 拼湊 **[p'īn-ts'òu]**: to whip up, to scrape together, to get something together

拴

拴 **[shuān]**: to fasten, to hitch up

挑

3 挑三揀四 **[t'iāo-sān chiĕn-ssù]**: fastidious, difficult to please

10 挑起[t'iăo-ch'ĭ]: to provoke, to stir up, to incite, to instigate, to prompt

挑剔[t'iāo-t'ī]: to find fault with, to weed out; critical, captious, carping

挑剔和夸大缺點[t'iāo-t'ī hó k'uā-tà ch'üēh-tiĕn]: to pick out faults and exaggerate shortcomings

15 挑選[t'iāo-hsüăn]: to select, to choose, to pick out

挑撥[t'iăo-pō]: to sow dissension, to sow discord, to incite discord and dissension

16 挑戰[t'iăo-chàn]: to challenge to battle, to provoke a fight, to challenge, to provoke

25 挑釁[t'iăo-hsìn]: to provoke; provocation, challenge; provocative

挑釁者[t'iăo-hsìn-chĕ]: provocateur

挖

11 挖掘[wā-chüéh]: to dig up, to excavate

挖掘潛力[wā-chüéh ch'ién-lì]: to dig out resources, to bring out latent power, tapping of reserves

15 挖蔣根運動[wā chiăng-kēn yǜn-tùng]: movement to eliminate the ideology of Chiang Kai-shek

挖窮根[wā ch'iúng-kēn]: to dig out the roots of poverty, to uproot poverty

17 挖牆脚[wā ch'iáng-chiăo]: to undermine

— 7 Strokes —

挨

6 挨次[āi-tz'ù]: in order, by turns

10 挨家挨戶[āi-chiā āi-hù]: house to house

14 挨說[āi-shuō]: to be criticized

15 挨德蒙吞[ài-té-méng-t'ūn]: Edmonton

振

7 振作[chèn-tsò]: to hearten, to inspire, to animate, to rouse, to stir up, to stimulate

12 振幅[chèn-fú]: amplitude

16 振奮[chèn-fèn]: to rouse, stimulate

振奮人心[chèn-fèn jén-hsīn]: to cause excitement, to inspire, to stir; exciting, inspiring, encouraging

捐

19 捐贈[chüān-tsèng]: donation, contribution, subscription, offering

捍

16 捍衛[hàn-wèi]: to defend, to protect

捍衛毛澤東思想[hàn-wèi máo tsé-tūng ssū-hsiăng]: defend the thought of Mao Tse-tung (a slogan in the early stages of the Cultural Revolution)

捍禦[hàn-yǜ]: to guard against, to resist an attack, to fend off

挾

9 挾恨[hsiéh-hèn]: to nurse a grievance

13 挾嫌[hsiéh-hsién]: to cherish resentment

捆

7 捆住[k'ŭn-chù]: to tie up

挪

挪[nó]: to move, to shift to one side, to divert, to remove

5 挪用[nó-yùng]: to embezzle, to steal, to misappropriate

9 挪威[nó-wēi]: Norway

挪威王國[nó-wēi wáng-kuó]: Kingdom of Norway

捕

10 捕捉[pŭ-chō]: to seize, to capture

17 捕獲[pŭ-huò]: to capture, to take prisoner

挺

7 挺身[t'ĭng-shēn]: to straighten the body, to put oneself forward, to thrust forward boldly

挺身而出[t'ĭng-shēn érh ch'ū]: to step out

12 挺進[t'ĭng-chìn]: to thrust into, to push on

挺進部隊[t'ĭng-chìn pù-tùi]: spearhead

挺進隊[t'ĭng-chìn-tùi]: raiding party, storm troops

挫

7 挫折[ts'ò-ché]: to rebuff; setback, reverse, rebuff, check

11 挫敗[ts'ò-pài]: to frustrate, to defeat, to baffle, to foil, to thwart, to circumvent, to outwit; frustration, defeat

挽

6 挽回[wăn-húi]: to reverse, to save (a situation), to make good (a mistake)

挽回面子的[wăn-húi mièn-tzu te]: face-saving

10 挽留[wăn-líu]: to detain, to keep, to hold, to retain

11 挽救[wăn-chìu]: to save, to rescue, to deliver, to help, to extricate

— 8 Strokes —

掌

12 掌握[chăng-wò]: to control, to hold, to master, to take over, to assume, to manage, to take charge of

掌握基本環節[chăng-wò chī-pĕn huán-chiéh]: to grasp the key link, to grasp the key to a situation

掌握至高無上的權力[chăng-wò chìh-kāo wú-shàng te ch'üán-lì]: to obtain supreme power, to reign supreme

掌握重點，照顧其他[chăng-wò chùng-tiĕn, chào-kù ch'í-t'ā]: to give priority to the most important aspects and due consideration to the rest

掌握分寸[chăng-wò fēn-ts'ùn]: to handle appropriately

22 掌權[chăng-ch'üán]: to hold power

掙

4 掙扎[chēng-chá]: to struggle, to strive, to tussle; struggle

11 掙脫[chèng-t'ō]: to shake off, to break loose from, to get free, to escape from, to get rid of, to unfetter

接

2 接二連三[chiēh-èrh lién-sān]: one after the other, repeatedly

接力賽跑[chiēh-lì sài-p'ăo]: relay race

4 接木[chiēh-mù]: to graft, to crossbreed

接手[chiēh-shŏu]: to take over; a receiver, an accomplice

5 接收[**chiēh-shōu**] : to take, to receive

7 接見[**chiēh-chièn**] : to interview, to grant an audience; reception

接防 [**chiēh-fáng**] : to relieve a garrison

8 接近 [**chiēh-chìn**] : to draw near, to border on; rapprochement; almost, nearly, approximately

接近末日 [**chiēh-chìn mò-jìh**] : to draw to a close, to draw to an end, to come to a finish, to have one's days numbered

接受 [**chiēh-shòu**] : to accept, to receive, to embrace, to take; acceptance

接受教訓 [**chiēh-shòu chiào-hsùn**] : to learn the lessons of

9 接洽 [**chiēh-ch'ià**] : to come to agreement after negotiations, to meet together

接風 [**chiēh-fēng**] : to welcome back

接待 [**chiēh-tài**] : to receive, to entertain

10 接納 [**chiēh-nà**] : to receive, to accept

接班 [**chiēh-pān**] : to take a turn on duty, to take on a job

接班人 [**chiēh-pān-jén**] : a relief, successor

11 接連 [**chiēh-lién**] : in succession, successively, repeatedly, over and over

12 接着 [**chiēh-che**] : next, subsequent, ensuing, following, afterward, then

接替 [**chiēh-t'ì**] : to take the place of, to take someone's place

14 接管 [**chiēh-kuǎn**] : to take over, to take over administration

16 接頭 [**chiēh-t'óu**] : to meet and discuss, to establish contact

17 接濟 [**chiēh-chì**] : to help, to supply, to support

接應 [**chiēh-yìng**] : to be in reserve, to respond

20 接觸 [**chiēh-ch'ù**] : to contact, to get in touch with, to give access to; contact

接壤 [**chiēh-jǎng**] : to border on

捷

7 捷克 [**chiéh-k'ò**] : Czechoslovakia (abbreviation)

捷克斯洛伐克共和國 [**chiéh-k'ò-ssū-lò-fá-k'ò kùng-hó-kuó**] : Republic of Czechoslovakia

捷克斯洛伐克共和國國民議會 [**chiéh-k'ò-ssū-lò-fá-k'ò kùng-hó-kuó kuó-mín-ì-hùi**] : National Assembly of the Republic of Czechoslovakia

捷克斯洛伐克通訊社 [**chiéh-k'ò-ssū-lò-fá-k'ò t'ūng-hsùn-shè**] : Czechoslovak Telegraph Agency (CTK)

10 捷徑 [**chiéh-chìng**] : short cut

12 捷報 [**chiéh-pào**] : victory message, victory announcement

13 捷電 [**chiéh-tièn**] : telegram reporting success (in work)

掮

9 掮客 [**ch'ién-k'ò**] : broker

捲

2 捲入 [**chüǎn-jù**] : to involve, to draw into, to engulf, to plunge into

3 捲土重來 [**chüǎn-t'ǔ ch'úng-lái**] : to stage a comeback

12 捲揚機 [**chüǎn-yáng-chī**] : winch, hoisting machine

掘

12 掘進手 [**chüéh-chìn-shǒu**] : diggers (i.e., expert coal miners)

14 掘墓人[chüéh-mù jén]: grave digger

17 掘壕[chüéh-háo]: to entrench, to dig a trench

掀

10 掀起[hsiēn-ch'ĭ]: to cause, to bring about, to set going, to incite, to raise, to engender, to kindle

掛

掛[kuà]: to unfurl, to fly, to hoist

4 掛心[kuà-hsīn]: to be worried, to be anxious; anxiety

6 掛名[kuà-míng]: to have the name only; titular, nominal

8 掛念[kuà-nièn]: to worry, to be anxious, to miss, to long for; suspense

9 掛帥[kuà-shuài]: to take the lead, to marshall, to lead, to direct

11 掛彩[kuà-ts'ăi]: to be wounded in battle

12 掛鈎[kuà-kōu]: to link up; suspension hook

掛牌子[kuà p'ái-tzu]: to put up a signboard, to hang up one's shingle

14 掛號[kuà-hào]: to register, to inscribe, to enter

控

7 控告[k'ùng-kào]: to accuse one of, to charge one with, to complain before a court, to file a complaint against, to make a complaint against, to level a charge against someone

8 控制[k'ùng-chìh]: to control, to dominate, to subjugate, to hold in check; domination, grip

控制不住[k'ùng-chìh pú-chù]: to get out of hand, out of control

掠

14 掠奪[lüèh-tó]: to seize, to rob, to loot, to pillage, to plunder, to pilfer, to rifle, to sack; predatory, rapacious

掠奪者[lüèh-tó-chĕ]: plunderer, pillager, looter, ravager

排

排[p'ái]: platoon, a row, a line, a rank; to place in order, to dispose, to push

4 排中律[p'ái-chūng lǜ]: law of the excluded middle

排水[p'ái-shŭi]: to drain, to pump; drainage, draining

排水量[p'ái-shŭi liàng]: displacement

5 排斥[p'ái-ch'ìh]: to reject, to expel, to exclude, to eject, to bar, to ban, to repudiate; tabooed, prohibited, proscribed

排外[p'ái-wài]: anti-foreign

排外主義[p'ái-wài chŭ-ì]: exclusionism, xenophobia, anti-foreign policy

排外性的[p'ái-wài-hsìng te]: exclusive

6 排列[p'ái-lièh]: to rank, to place, to arrange in a line, to arrange in a series, to permute; permutation

排印[p'ái-yìn]: to set type and print, to set up and print from type

10 排除[p'ái-ch'ú]: to preclude, to rule out, to proscribe, to reject, to discard

12 排隊[p'ái-tùi]: to queue up, to form a line, to arrange things in the order of their relative importance

14 排演[p'ái-yĕn]: to rehearse, to arrange staging of a play; rehearsal

15 排澇[p'ái-lào]: to drain water; flood divergency

排澇治碱[p'ái-lào chìh-chiĕn]: to drain

water and treat alkaline soil

17 排擠[p'ái-chǐ]: to squeeze out, to thrust aside, to edge out, to crowd out, to force out, to push aside

21 排灌設備[p'ái-kuàn shè-pèi]: drainage and irrigation equipment

捧

捧[p'ěng]: to eulogize, to praise, to hold in two hands, to offer in two hands

12 捧場[p'ěng-ch'ǎng]: to applaud a performance, to support, to form a claque for; claque, organized applause

捧場的人[p'ěng-ch'ǎng te jén]: claque

捧場文章[p'ěng-ch'ǎng wén-chāng]: write-up

掃

7 掃尾工作[sǎo-wěi kūng-tsò]: tail-sweeping work (i.e., the final stage of a construction project or the finishing touch on a piece of work)

8 掃盲[sǎo-máng]: to eliminate blindness, to wipe out illiteracy

掃盲課程[sǎo-máng k'ò-ch'éng]: literacy courses

掃盲運動[sǎo-máng yǜn-tùng]: literacy campaign, campaign to eliminate illiteracy

10 掃除[sǎo-ch'ú]: to wipe out, to sweep aside, to root out, to uproot, to clear out, to get rid of, to do away with

掃除積垢[sǎo-ch'ú chī-kòu]: to clean up accumulated dirt

掃除文盲[sǎo-ch'ú wén-máng]: to eliminate illiteracy, to wipe out illiteracy

掃除文盲協會[sǎo-ch'ú wén-máng hsiéh-hùi]: wipe out illiteracy association

掃射[sǎo-shè]: to strafe

11 掃清[sǎo-ch'īng]: to wipe out, to clear, to eliminate, to sweep clean

13 掃雷艇[sǎo-léi-t'ǐng]: mine-sweeper

16 掃蕩[sǎo-tàng]: to mop up (i.e., as enemy remnants), to exterminate, to liquidate

授

8 授於[shòu-yǘ]: to award, to entrust, to delegate, to vest

18 授職[shòu-chíh]: to confer official rank; investiture (in office)

22 授權[shòu-ch'üán]: to authorize, to empower

探

3 探子[t'àn-tzu]: spy

5 探出[t'àn-ch'ū]: to ferret out, to explore, to prospect, to probe; exploration

7 探求[t'àn-ch'íu]: to fish for, to pry out of, to wrest from, to seek

10 探馬[t'àn-mǎ]: a scout

探索[t'àn-sǒ]: to grope for

探討[t'àn-t'ǎo]: to examine, to inquire about

13 探照燈[t'àn-chào-tēng]: floodlight, search light

掉

11 掉隊[tiào-tùi]: to straggle, to fall out, to fall out of ranks

掂

14 掂算[tiēn-suàn]: to estimate, to weigh

掂對[tiēn-tùi]: to deliberate

採

5 採用[ts'ăi-yùng]: to employ, to adopt, to introduce, to apply, to use, to put to use; application

8 採取[ts'ăi-ch'ŭ]: to take, to adopt, to pursue, to follow, to embark on

10 採納[ts'ăi-nà]: to accept, to receive

11 採訪[ts'ăi-făng]: to make inquiries, to investigate, to report (as a trial), to cover

13 採煤[ts'ăi-méi]: to excavate coal; coal mining

採煤機[ts'ăi-méi-chī]: coal mining machinery

16 採選[ts'ăi-hsüăn]: to select

17 採購[ts'ăi-kòu]: to purchase, to procure; procurement

採購站[ts'ăi-kòu chàn]: purchasing station

採購供應站[ts'ăi-kòu kūng-yìng chàn]: purchase and supply station

20 採礦設備[ts'ăi-k'uàng shè-pèi]: mining equipment

措

9 措施[ts'ò-shīh]: to publish, to work, to arrange, to execute, to administer; measure, steps

12 措詞[ts'ò-tz'ú]: phrasing, terms, in terms of

13 措置[ts'ò-chìh]: to arrange, to place, to devise ways and means

推

3 推土機[t'ūi-t'ŭ-chī]: bulldozer

6 推行[t'ūi-hsíng]: to carry out, to push ahead, to push on with, to push through

8 推定[t'ūi-tìng]: to presume, to conclude

10 推薦[t'ūi-chièn]: to commend, to endorse, to nominate, to recommend; recommendation, endorsement, nomination

11 推陳出新[t'ūi-ch'én ch'ū-hsīn]: to weed out the old to let the new emerge, to discard what has outlived its time and to develop the new

推理[t'ūi-lĭ]: reasoning

推理法[t'ui-lĭ fă]: deductive method, line of reasoning

推動[t'ūi-tùng]: to propel, to impel, to move, to give impetus to; propulsion

推動人[t'ūi-tùng jén]: a promoter

推動力[t'ūi-tùng-lì]: impetus, propelling force, moving force, motivational force, impelling force

12 推進[t'ūi-chìn]: to drive, to push, to boost, to push ahead with; propulsion

推測[t'ūi-ts'è]: to speculate, to suppose, to deduce, to reckon, to conjecture; speculation, prognosis

14 推敲[t'ūi-ch'iāo]: to perfect, to work out in detail, to elaborate, to polish, to weigh carefully, to seek the mot juste

推算法[t'ūi-suàn fă]: projection method

15 推銷[t'ūi-hsiāo]: to sell, to peddle, to hawk; sales promotion

推廣[t'ūi-kuăng]: to extend, to propagate, to impart, to broaden, to popularize, to spread; popularization

推廣站[t'ūi-kuăng chàn]: instruction center, popularization center

推廣經驗[t'ūi-kuăng chīng-yèn]: to propagate experience (i.e., the sharing of the experience one has gained with others)

推廣典型[t'ūi-kuăng tiĕn-hsíng]: to spread exemplary experience, to popularize exemplary experience (particularly among production units)

推論[t'ūi-lùn]: to infer from, to deduce, to

reason, to draw an inference; conclusions, deductions

推諉[**t'ūi-wěi**]: to shift, to transfer, to back out of, to shirk, to make excuses

18 推翻[**t'ūi-fān**]: to overthrow, to upset, to turn over, to demolish

掩

14 掩蓋[**yěn-kài**]: to cover, to conceal, to hide, to screen

掩飾[**yěn-shìh**]: to cover, to conceal, to hide, to screen, to gloss over

21 掩護[**yěn-hù**]: to cover, to conceal, to hide, to screen; protection, cover; protective, covering

掩護部隊[**yěn-hù pù-tùi**]: covering forces

— 9 Strokes —

插

2 插入[**ch'ā-jù**]: to insert into, to insert between, to interpolate

3 插口[**ch'ā-k'ǒu**]: to interrupt, to meddle by words

4 插手[**ch'ā-shǒu**]: to interpose, to take a hand in, to meddle in, to step in

6 插曲[**ch'ā-ch'ǚ**]: episode, intermezzo

9 插紅旗[**ch'ā húng-ch'í**]: to plant a red flag, to hoist a red flag (i.e., a signal of advance or victory)

插紅旗，拔白旗[**ch'ā húng-ch'í, pá pái-ch'í**]: to take out the white flag and plant the red flag (i.e., of revolution)

10 插班[**ch'ā-pān**]: to place (a student) in the appropriate class; an intermediate class

插秧[**ch'ā-yāng**]: to transplant rice shoots; rice transplanting

12 插進[**ch'ā-chìn**]: to intervene in

13 插話[**ch'ā-huà**]: to interrupt, to interject; episode

15 插標布點[**ch'ā-piāo pù-tiěn**]: to set up targets and designate units (i.e., the setting of targets in political studies, production techniques, and management on the basis of the experience of an advanced production brigade)

揭

5 揭示[**chiēh-shìh**]: to post proclamations, to post a notice, to announce, to publish

9 揭竿[**chiēh-kān**]: to raise a revolt

揭竿而起[**chiēh-kān érh ch'ǐ**]: to raise a rebellion; outbreak of rebellion

10 揭穿[**chiēh-ch'uān**]: to expose, to uncover, to reveal, to divulge

揭破[**chiēh-p'ò**]: to disclose, to lay bare

12 揭發[**chiēh-fā**]: to reveal, to divulge, to unmask, to disclose

揭開[**chiēh-k'āi**]: to lift off the cover, to uncover, to strip off, to open

揭開蓋子[**chiēh-k'āi kài-tzu**]: to take off the cover (i.e., to remove the cover to expose evils or evil-doers, a phrase appearing quite frequently in Red Guard publications and referring to the uncovering of the evils of the "power-holders")

揭短[**chiēh-tuǎn**]: to reveal the failings of another, to pick out other's defects, to find fault

14 揭蓋子[**chiēh kài-tzu**]: to remove the lid, to remove hindrances to progress (*See* 蓋子)

揭幕[**chiēh-mù**]: to raise the curtain, to inaugurate; inauguration

16 揭曉[**chiēh-hsiǎo**]: to publish, to make known, to publish a list of successful examination candidates

21 揭露[**chiēh-lù**]: to uncover, to divulge, to disclose, to expose, to unmask

揭露無餘[chiēh-lù wú-yǘ]: to expose thoroughly, to unmask completely

揀

16 揀選[chiĕn-hsüăn]: to choose, to select, to elect

揀擇[chiĕn-tsé]: to choose, to pick out

揣

8 揣度[ch'uăi-tù]: to consider, to conjecture, to estimate

12 揣測[ch'uăi-ts'è]: to fathom, to measure, to weigh

15 揣靡[ch'uăi-mó]: to reflect on, to consider, to conjecture, to estimate

換

3 換工[huàn-kūng]: labor exchange

換工班[huàn-kūng pān]: labor exchange group

4 換文[huàn-wén]: exchange of notes, exchange of diplomatic notes

6 換成[huàn-ch'éng]: to change into, to alter, to transform, to turn into

7 換防[huàn-fáng]: to relieve the guard

8 換取[huàn-ch'ü̆]: to change, to exchange

10 換班[huàn-pān]: to relieve a shift, to relieve the guard, to relieve someone on duty

11 換貨[huàn-huò]: to barter; barter

換崗[huàn-kāng]: to relieve the guard, to change the guard

14 換算[huàn-suàn]: to convert

17 換樣[huàn-yàng]: to alternate, to take on a new shape

揮

8 揮金如土[hūi chīn jú t'ŭ]: to scatter money like dirt, to spend money freely

12 揮發油[hūi-fā yú]: naphtha

16 揮霍[hūi-huò]: to waste, to spend money freely, to squander, lavish in spending

描

15 描寫[miáo-hsiĕh]: to portray, to sketch, to describe, to represent, to depict, to delineate

揑

11 揑造[niēh-tsào]: to fabricate, to make up, to trump up, to invent; fabrication, false story

搜

9 搜查[sōu-ch'á]: to search, to seek, to look for, to ransack for, to investigate

10 搜捕[sōu-pŭ]: to round up, to capture, to take, to seize, to arrest

搜索[sōu-sŏ]: to hunt for, to make a search for; search, reconnaissance

12 搜集[sōu-chí]: to compile, to collect

搜集情報[sōu-chí ch'íng-pào]: to collect information, to gather intelligence

20 搜羅[sōu-ló]: to gather, to assemble, to call together

提

4 提升[t'í-shēng]: to promote, to advance, to raise prices

5 提出[t'í-ch'ū]: to present, to submit, to bring up, to raise, to propose, to advocate

6 提交[t'í-chiāo]: to deliver, to hand over, to submit to, to refer to

提名[t'í-míng]: to nominate, nomination

提早[t'í-tsăo]: in advance of schedule, ahead of schedule

7 提防[t'í-fáng]: to be on the alert for, to be on one's guard, to be on guard against, to take precautions; wary, watchful, vigilant

8 提供[t'í-kūng]: to provide, to give, to offer, to supply

提供消息人士[t'í-kūng hsiāo-hsí jén-shìh]: informant

提拔[t'í-pá]: to promote, to advance

提到[t'í-tào]: to mention, to refer to, to touch on

9 提前[t'í-ch'ién]: to do ahead of time, to give precedence to; advance (adj.)

提前釋放[t'í-ch'ién shìh-fàng]: to release before sentence expires

提前完成[t'í-ch'ién wán-ch'éng]: to finish ahead of schedule, pre-schedule fulfillment

10 提倡[t'í-ch'àng]: to advocate, to encourage

提級[t'í-chí]: to promote in rank

提高[t'í-kāo]: to raise, to heighten, to enhance, to increase, to grow, to improve; increase, elevation, growth, improvement

提高紀律性[t'í-kāo chì-lü-hsìng]: to heighten one's sense of discipline

提高警惕[t'í-kāo chĭng-t'ì]: to sharpen one's vigilance (against)

提高覺悟性[t'í-kāo chüéh-wù-hsìng]: to raise one's level of political consciousness

12 提都[t'í-tū]: Chita (U.S.S.R.)

13 提煉[t'í-lièn]: to refine, to purify

14 提綱[t'í-kāng]: outline, summary, draft, program, theme

15 提請[t'í-ch'ĭng]: to propose, to request

提請注意[t'í-ch'ĭng chù-ì]: to bring a matter to one's notice, to draw one's attention to

提審[t'í-shĕn]: to bring a case up for trial

20 提議[t'í-ì]: to suggest, to propose, to put forward a proposal; proposal, suggestion, motion, proposition

揍

揍 [tsòu]: to beat, to beat up; a beating

握

4 握手[wò-shŏu]: to shake hands

7 握住[wò-chù]: to catch hold of, to grasp, to have a firm grip on, to hold

揚

7 揚言[yáng-yén]: to clamor, to make a clamor, claim, to proclaim, to bandy about

援

4 援引[yüán-yĭn]: to quote, to cite

援引經典[yüán-yĭn chīng-tiĕn]: to quote from the classics

5 援外[yüán-wài]: foreign aid

7 援助[yüán-chù]: to aid, to assist, to help; aid, assistance, help

援兵[yüán-pīng]: reinforcements, relief troops

8 援例[yüán-lì]: to quote as a precedent

11 援救[yüán-chìu]: to rescue, to relieve

— 10 Strokes —

6 搶收[ch'iăng-shōu]: to rush a harvest

[8] 搶劫[ch'iăng-chiéh]: to rob, to sack, to loot, to grab, to ransack, to pillage

[10] 搶修險工[ch'iăng-hsīu hsiĕn-kūng]: to rush-repair danger points

[11] 搶救[ch'iăng-chìu]: to rush to the rescue of

[14] 搶種[ch'iăng-chùng]: to rush-plant (crops)

[17] 搶購[ch'iăng-kòu]: to rush to buy; shopping rush

搞

搞[kăo]: to do, to handle, to take care of, to carry out, to implement

[4] 搞不清[kăo-pù-ch'īng]: to wonder, to be confused, not to understand, unable to discriminate, perplexed

搞不好[kăo-pù-hăo]: to fail to handle properly

[6] 搞好[kăo-hăo]: to do, to arrange, to make a success

搞好了[kăo-hăo le]: finished

搞好關係[kăo-hăo kuān-hsì]: to foster good relations

搞在一起[kăo tsài ì-ch'ĭ]: to join, to join forces with, to put together, to merge, to amalgamate

[9] 搞垮[kăo-k'uă]: to destroy, to disrupt, to tear down, to upset, to smash, to shatter, to crush, to wreck, to devastate

[11] 搞通[kăo-t'ūng]: to be in agreement, to work out a complete acceptance of Communist ideology by overcoming mental resistance

搞通思想[kăo-t'ūng ssū-hsiăng]: to arrive at a correct perception of, to see the light, to correct one's ideology

[16] 搞糟[kăo-tsāo]: to botch, to bungle, to make a mess of

搬

[10] 搬家[pān-chiā]: to move, to resettle; resettlement

[13] 搬運[pān-yùn]: to transport, to move, to transplant

損

[2] 損人利己[sŭn-jén lì-chĭ]: to reap profit at the expense of others, to injure others in order to benefit oneself, to gain at other's expense; selfish

[5] 損失[sŭn-shīh]: to damage, to lose, to meet with a loss; loss, damage

[10] 損害[sŭn-hài]: to damage, to injure, to infringe on, to stand in the way of; damage, harm, detriment; detrimental

損害主權[sŭn-hài chŭ-ch'üán]: to infringe on one's sovereignty, to encroach upon one's sovereignty

搭

[9] 搭客[tā-k'ò]: passenger, traveler

[10] 搭配[tā-p'èi]: to join as a partner, to be a partner of, to match, to copulate (animals)

[11] 搭救[tā-chìu]: to help, to rescue

[15] 搭夥[tā-hŭo]: to join in partnership, to club together, to join forces, to combine forces

搗

[13] 搗亂[tăo-luàn]: to make trouble, to disturb; trouble-making

搖

[7] 搖尾乞憐[yáo-wĕi ch'ĭ-lién]: to fawn on

[11] 搖動[yáo-tùng]: to waver, to shake, to rock,

to sway; oscillation, vibration

13 搖搖擺擺 **[yáo-yáo pǎi-pǎi]**: to swagger; swagger, swaggering

搖搖欲墜 **[yáo-yáo yǜ-chùi]**: tottering, shaky, crumbling, precarious

14 搖旗吶喊 **[yáo-ch'í nà-hǎn]**: to clamor, to wave the flag and shout

— 11 Strokes —

摘

3 摘下假面具，露出本來面目 **[chāi-hsià chiǎ mièn-chǜ, lòu-ch'ū pěn-lái mièn-mù]**: to tear off the mask and show the true colors underneath

摘下僞善的面具 **[chāi-hsià wěi-shàn te mièn-chǜ]**: to drop one's mask of hypocrisy, to peel off one's hypocritical mask

9 摘要 **[chāi-yào]**: summary, abstract, précis, digest, abridgment; to make extracts

16 摘錄 **[chāi-lù]**: to excerpt, to make extracts from a document; excerpt

摻

18 摻雜 **[ch'ān-tsá]**: to be mixed with

摸

摸 **[mō]**: to feel for, to feel after, to grope, to guess

4 摸不透 **[mō-pú-t'òu]**: to wonder, to be puzzled, to be bewildered, to be lost and perplexed, to be confused

8 摸底 **[mō-tǐ]**: to feel the bottom, to find out what you have (i.e., as a factory manager knowing how many workmen and how much material he has)

10 摸索 **[mō-sǒ]**: to grope for, to feel, to stroke

11 摸清 ... 底細 **[mō-ch'īng . . . tǐ-hsì]**: to see through a person

摩

4 摩天大樓 **[mó-t'iēn tà-lóu]**: skyscraper

5 摩加迪沙 **[mó-chiā-tí-shā]**: Mogadiscio (Somali Republic)

摩卡 **[mó-k'ǎ]**: Mocha (Yemen)

6 摩托化部隊 **[mó-t'ō-huà pù-tùi]**: motorized unit

9 摩洛哥 **[mó-lò-kō]**: Morocco

摩洛哥王國 **[mó-lò-kō wáng-kuó]**: Kingdom of Morocco

10 摩納哥 **[mó-nà-kō]**: Monaco

摩納哥侯國 **[mó-nà-kō hóu-kuó]**: Principality of Monaco

11 摩勒斯比港 **[mó-lè-ssū-pǐ kǎng]**: Port Moresby

19 摩羅開島 **[mó-ló-k'āi tǎo]**: Molokai (Hawaiian Islands)

摧

11 摧族 **[ts'ūi-tsú]**: Ts'ui-hui (minority nationality)

12 摧殘 **[ts'ūi-ts'án]**: to trample underfoot, to tread underfoot, to destroy, to defile, to deny

13 摧毀 **[ts'ūi-hǔi]**: to destroy

— 12 Strokes —

撤

6 撤回 **[ch'è-húi]**: to withdraw

7 撤兵 **[ch'è-pīng]**: to withdraw troops, to pull back troops

10 撤除 **[ch'è-ch'ú]**: to remove

撤退 **[ch'è-t'ùi]**: to retreat, to draw back, to evacuate; evacuation, withdrawal

12 撤換[ch'è-huàn]: to recall and replace with another

15 撤銷[ch'è-hsiāo]: to annul, to revoke, to lift

撤銷職務[ch'è-hsiāo chíh-wù]: to dismiss from, to remove from; removal

18 撤職[ch'è-chíh]: to degrade, to depose, to dismiss, to remove from a post; dismissal, dismissal from a position

撐

13 撐腰[ch'ēng-yāo]: to support, to back

撐腰的[ch'ēng-yāo te]: supporter, backer

撫

9 撫恤[fŭ-hsù]: survivor's pension

撫恤費[fŭ-hsù fèi]: relief fund

15 撫慰[fŭ-wèi]: to placate, to console, to soothe, to relieve, to alleviate, to comfort

撈

1 撈一把[lāo ì-pă]: to reap some profit

撇

12 撇開[p'iēh-k'āi]: to bypass, to side-step, to put aside, to set aside, to sidetrack

撥

5 撥正[pō-chèng]: to correct, to make straight

撥用[pō-yùng]: to appropriate for, to place at the disposal of

12 撥發[pō-fā]: to distribute, to transfer

撥款[pō-k'uăn]: to allot, to allocate, to appropriate; appropriation

撥款監督[pō-k'uăn chiēn-tū]: budgetary allocations supervision

播

10 播送[pō-sùng]: to broadcast, to transmit; broadcast, transmission

12 播散[pō-sàn]: to disseminate

14 播種[pō-chŭng]: to sow

播種機[pō-chŭng-chī]: seeder, seed planting machine

播種面積[pō-chŭng mièn-chī]: sown area

13 撲滅[p'ū-mièh]: to quell, to quench, to stamp out, to exterminate

撒

2 撒丁[sā-tīng]: Sardinia

4 撒手[sā-shŏu]: to let go of, to lose control of, to loosen the hand

撒手不管[sā-shŏu pù-kuăn]: to give up, to relinquish one's hold on, to take no further interest in

5 撒尼[sā-ní]: Sani (minority nationality)

7 撒冷[sā-lĕng]: Salem

8 撒拉[sā-lā]: Salars (minority nationality)

10 撒馬爾汗[sā-mă-ĕrh-hàn]: Samarkand

撕

13 撕毀[ssū-hŭi]: to tear up, to scrap, to tear to shreds, to destroy

撣[shàn]: Shan (minority nationality)

撮

6 撮合[ts'ō-hó] : to unite, to bring together, to bring about a reconciliation

9 撮要[ts'ō-yào] : to extract, to make extracts from; extracts, outlines, abstract, resume

— 13 Strokes —

擊

4 擊中痛處[chī-chùng t'ùng-ch'ù] : to hit one where it hurts

擊中要害[chī-chùng yào-hài] : to hit one in one's vitals, to strike home, to hit the point

10 擊破[chī-p'ò] : to smash

擊退[chī-t'ùi] : to repel, to rebuff, to repulse, to beat back, to drive back

11 擊敗[chī-pài] : to defeat, to triumph over, to overpower, to overcome, to vanquish

13 擊落[chī-lò] : to shoot down

15 擊潰[chī-k'uèi] : to rout, to defeat utterly, to smash, to crush

擊潰戰[chī-k'uèi chàn] : war of annihilation

17 擊斃[chī-pì] : to kill

據

據[chǜ] : according to

2 據了解[chǜ liăo-chiĕh] : it is understood that

9 據信[chǜ hsìn] : it is believed that

據宣佈[chǜ hsüān-pù] : it was announced that

11 據悉[chǜ hsī] : it is reported that, it is learned that, from information received, reportedly

據推測[chǜ t'ūi-ts'è] : it is reported that, it is guessed that, it is thought that

14 據認爲[chǜ jèn-wéi] : it is held that

據說[chǜ shūo] : it is said that, to be alleged to, to be quoted, to be described

17 據點[chǜ-tiĕn] : stronghold, base, bastion, foothold

擅

6 擅自[shàn-tzù] : to take upon oneself, arbitrarily, without permission, on one's own authority

擔

4 擔心[tān-hsīn] : apprehensive, concerned, worried

6 擔任[tān-jèn] : to undertake, to take charge of, to take over

9 擔架[tān-chià] : stretcher, litter

擔負[tān-fù] : to undertake, to bear, to carry

擔保[tān-păo] : to assure, to guarantee, to be responsible for; assurance, guarantee

擔待[tān-tài] : to take responsibility, to put up with, to bear with

擋

7 擋住[tăng-chù] : to block, to hamper, to obstruct, to stop, to prevent, to stand in the way, to bar, to impede, to check

15 擋箭牌[tăng-chièn p'ái] : shield, excuse

操

6 操行[ts'āo-hsíng] : behavior, conduct, deportment

7 操作[ts'āo-tsò] : to operate, to handle, to manipulate, to run, to manage, to dominate

操作法[ts'āo-tsò fă]: method of operation, work procedure

操作規程[ts'āo-tsò kuēi-ch'éng]: work regulations, work specifications, regulations for operations

8 操法[ts'āo-fă]: military training, drill

9 操持[ts'āo-ch'íh]: to manage, to administer, to supply

17 操縱[ts'āo-tsùng]: to control, to manipulate, to steer, to maneuver; manipulation, control, maneuver

擁

6 擁有[yūng-yŭ]: to possess, to have, to own, to hold

8 擁抱[yūng-pào]: to embrace, to hug, to clasp (in one's arms)

9 擁政愛民[yūng-chèng ài-mín]: to support the government and cherish the people

擁軍優屬[yūng-chūn yū-shŭ]: to support the army and give preferential treatment to the families of soldiers

13 擁幹愛民運動[yūng-kàn ài-mín yùn-tùng]: campaign of support for cadres and love of the people

17 擁擠[yūng-chĭ]: to crowd, to jam, to squeeze; crowd, jam, congestion; crowded, congested, pressed together

21 擁護[yūng-hù]: to support, to uphold, to stand up for

擁護者[yūng-hù-chĕ]: champion, supporter, defender, follower, guardian

— 14 Strokes —

擠

4 擠不動[chĭ-pú-tùng]: to be packed in, to be wedged tight in a crowd, to be unable to move

5 擠出[chĭ-ch'ū]: to squeeze out, to pry out, to extract, to wring from

14 擠滿[chĭ-măn]: to be packed to capacity, to be jammed with, to be tightly packed, crowded

擱

11 擱淺[kō-ch'iĕn]: to founder, to run aground

13 擱置[kō-chìh]: to shelve, to put to one side, to waive, to discard

擬

2 擬人觀[nĭ-jén kuān]: anthropomorphism

8 擬定[nĭ-tìng]: to map out, to decide

9 擬訂[nĭ-tìng]: to draw up, to work out, to map out

擯

5 擯斥[pìn-ch'ìh]: to reject, to repudiate

10 擯除[pìn-ch'ú]: to eliminate, to reject

擡

17 擡舉[t'ái-chŭ]: to advance, to recommend, to exalt, to extoll

— 15 Strokes —

擾

13 擾亂[jăo-luàn]: to disturb, to perturb, to agitate, to upset

擴

3 擴大[k'uò-tà]: to enlarge, to expand, to broaden, to widen, to extend, to aggravate, to magnify, to spread; enlargement, expansion

擴大戰果[**k'uò-tà chàn-kuǒ**]: to exploit a victory

擴大會議[**k'uò-tà hùi-ì**]: enlarged session, enlarged meeting, enlarged conference

擴大再生產[**k'uò-tà tsài-shēng-ch'ǎn**]: expanded reproduction

9 擴建 [**k'uò-chièn**]: to build an annex, to expand; expansion, extension

擴軍備戰 [**k'uò-chūn pèi-chàn**]: armaments expansion and war preparations; military expansion and war preparations

擴音器 [**k'uò-yīn-ch'ì**]: amplifier, loud speaker

10 擴展 [**k'uò-chǎn**]: to extend, to expand, to advance, to spread, to raise; extension

11 擴張 [**k'uò-chāng**]: to expand, to amplify, to enlarge upon; expansion, enlargement, extension, increase, augmentation, aggrandizement

擴張政策 [**k'uò-chāng chèng-ts'è**]: expansionist policy

擴張主義 [**k'uò-chāng chǔ-ì**]: expansionism

擴張主義份子 [**k'uò-chāng chǔ-ì fèn-tzu**]: expansionist

擴張軍備 [**k'uò-chāng chūn-pèi**]: arms drive

攆

7 攆走 [**niěn-tsǒu**]: to kick out, to drive out, to expel, to eject, to cast out; expulsion

擺

5 擺正 [**pǎi-chèng**]: to set things right

擺出 [**pǎi-ch'ū**]: to lay out, to exhibit, to present

擺出...樣子 [**pǎi-ch'ū . . . yàng-tzu**] to put on a show, to assume airs of

擺布 [**pǎi-pù**]: to arrange, to exhibit, to manipulate, to do someone injury, to ride roughshod over

7 擺弄 [**pǎi-nùng**]: to play with, to sport with, to meddle with

8 擺事實 [**pǎi shìh-shíh**]: to bring out the facts, to put the facts on the table

擺事實講道理 [**pǎi shìh-shíh chiǎng tào-lǐ**]: to present the facts and explain the reasons

9 擺架子 [**pǎi chià-tzu**]: to put on airs, to make a display, to act important

11 擺脫 [**pǎi-t'ō**]: to throw off, to shake off, to get rid of, to shake free, to be relieved of

擺渡 [**pǎi-tù**]: to ferry, to ferry across, to transfer; a ferry

攀

12 攀登高峰 [**p'ān-tēng kāo-fēng**]: to scale the summit (i.e., to master skills and techniques, particularly in science and technology)

— 17 Strokes —

攔

7 攔住 [**lán-chù**]: to stop, to check, to hold up, to keep away, to hold back

8 攔河閘 [**lán-hó chá**]: regulating dam

— 18 Strokes —

攙

10 攙起 [**ch'ān-ch'ǐ**]: to raise up, to erect

11 攙假 [**ch'ān-chiǎ**]: to adulterate, to mix with substitutes; adulteration

18 攙雜 [**ch'ān-tsá**]: mixed, impure; to mix up, to blend

攜

[4] 攜手 **[hsī-shǒu]**: to lead by the hand; hand in hand

攜手幷進 **[hsī-shǒu pìng-chìn]**: to march forward hand in hand

[11] 攜帶 **[hsī-tài]**: to carry, to bring, to have with one

攝

[15] 攝影場 **[shè-yǐng-ch'ǎng]**: studio

攝影記者 **[shè-yǐng chì-chě]**: cameraman, photographer

攝影術 **[shè-yǐng shù]**: photography

— 19 Strokes —

攤

[11] 攤販 **[t'ān-fàn]**: street vendor, stall trader, stall-keeper and peddler, booth keeper and vendor

[12] 攤牌 **[t'ān-p'ái]**: to lay one's cards on the table, to show one's full hand; showdown

攤牌會議 **[t'ān-p'ái hùi-ì]**: showdown conference

— 20 Strokes —

攪

[8] 攪和 **[chiǎo-huò]**: to stir, to mix

攪拌 **[chiǎo-pàn]**: to stir, to mix

攪拌機 **[chiǎo-pàn-chī]**: mixer

[11] 攪混 **[chiǎo-hùn]**: to cause confusion, to cause unrest, to cause disorder

[15] 攪鬧 **[chiǎo-nào]**: to make noise, to cause excitement

[18] 攪擾 **[chiǎo-jǎo]**: to confuse, to annoy, to cause a disturbance

攫

[8] 攫取 **[chüéh-ch'ǚ]**: to seize and carry off

— RADICAL 支 65 —

支

[5] 支出 **[chīh-ch'ū]**: to disburse; expenditure, expenses

支出總數 **[chīh-ch'ū tsǔng-shù]**: total expenditure

支付 **[chīh-fù]**: to pay, to spend, to settle; payment, settlement

支左不支派 **[chīh tsǒ pù-chīh p'ài]**: support the left but not factions (a slogan indicating that the PLA, in intervening in the Cultural Revolution, should support left wing mass organizations but not factions)

[9] 支前 **[chīh-ch'ién]**: to support the battlefront

支持 **[chīh-ch'íh]**: to support, to back, to uphold; support

支持者 **[chīh-ch'íh-chě]**: supporter, adherent, advocate, backer, partisan

支柱 **[chīh-chù]**: mainstay, brace, buttress, pillar, prop

[10] 支配 **[chīh-p'èi]**: to manage, to direct, to control, to distribute, to allocate; domination rule, control

支配權 **[chīh-p'èi ch'üán]**: power of control over, domination

[11] 支票 **[chīh-p'iào]**: check, draft

支部[**chīh-pù**]: Party branch

支部大會[**chīh-pù tà-hùi**]: general membership meeting of the Party branch

支部委員會[**chīh-pù wěi-yüán-hùi**]: branch committee

12 支隊[**chīh-tùi**]: detachment (i.e., a unit of about regimental size or larger)

支援[**chīh-yüán**]: to aid, to help, to relieve; aid assistance, help, relief

— RADICAL 攴攵 66 —

— 2 Strokes —

收

2 收入[**shōu-jù**]: income

4 收支[**shōu-chīh**]: revenue and expenditure, income and expenses, receipts and payments

6 收回[**shōu-húi**]: to revoke, to retract, to take back, to recover, to recapture, to rescind

7 收兵[**shōu-pīng**]: to call off a battle, to end a campaign

收兵休整[**shōu-pīng hsīu-chěng**]: to retire to rest and consolidate

9 收拾[**shōu-shíh**]: to dispose of, to tidy up, to put in order

10 收效[**shōu-hsiào**]: to have results, to produce results; productive, fruitful

收訊台[**shōu-hsǜn t'ái**]: receiving station

收益[**shōu-ì**]: gain, profits, returns, fruit, benefit, advantage, proceeds

收容[**shōu-júng**]: to accept, to take in, to house

12 收場[**shōu-ch'ăng**]: to end, to bring to an end

收發[**shōu-fā**]: to receive and send; receiving and transmitting

收發室[**shōu-fā shìh**]: message center

收復[**shōu-fù**]: to recapture, to recover, to regain

收割[**shōu-kō**]: to gather in a harvest, to reap

收割機[**shōu-kō-chī**]: harvester, harvesting machine

收買[**shōu-măi**]: to buy over, to bribe, to buy off

15 收編[**shōu-piēn**]: to incorporate

17 收獲[**shōu-huò**]: harvest, crop, yield

收獲量[**shōu-huò liàng**]: harvest yield

收購[**shōu-kòu**]: to buy up, to buy

收購站[**shōu-kòu chàn**]: purchasing station

收購價格[**shōu-kòu chià-kó**]: procurement price, purchasing price

收縮[**shōu-sō**]: shrinkage, contraction, constriction

18 收歸[**shōu-kuēi**]: to revert to

收歸國有[**shōu-kuēi kuó-yŭ**]: to nationalize; nationalization

19 收繳[**shōu-chiăo**]: to take over

— 3 Strokes —

5 改正[**kăi-chèng**]: to correct, to rectify, to amend; correction, rectification, amendment

7 改良[**kăi-liáng**]: to reform, to improve; reform

改良主義[kăi-liáng chŭ-ì]: reformism (i.e., that which is practiced by those who pretend to be revolutionaries, but who, in fact, only make superficial alterations to the status quo)

8 改弦更張[kăi-hsién kēng-chāng]: to change the course, to alter regulations

9 改信[kăi-hsìn]: to be converted to

改革[kăi-kó]: to reform; reform, reformation

改訂[kăi-tìng]: to revise, to rewrite

11 改掉[kăi-tiào]: to change, to get rid of

改造[kăi-tsào]: to rebuild, to remould, to transform; transformation, remoulding

改組[kăi-tsŭ]: to reorganize; reorganization

12 改朝換代[kăi-ch'áo huàn-tài]: change of government, change of dynasty

改進[kăi-chìn]: to improve, to progress, to make progress

改善[kăi-shàn]: to improve, to better, to ameliorate; improvement, betterment

13 改裝[kăi-chuāng]: to re-fit, to re-equip, to provide new equipment; modification, conversion

改過[kăi-kuò]: to reform, to correct mistakes

15 改選[kăi-hsüăn]: to re-elect, to replace; re-election, replacement

改編[kăi-piēn]: to reorganize, to adapt; reorganization

16 改頭換面[kăi-t'óu huàn-mièn]: camouflaged; to change the external appearance, to dissemble

23 改變[kăi-pièn]: to alter, to change

改變主義[kăi-pièn chŭ-ì]: a change of mind

改變顏色[kăi-pièn yén-sè]: to change color (i.e., a deviation from being "red")

攻

3 攻下[kūng-hsià]: to batter down, to capture, to take, to take by storm

5 攻打[kūng-tă]: to attack, to storm

6 攻守同盟[kūng-shŏu t'úng-méng]: offensive and defensive alliance

7 攻克[kūng-k'ò]: to attack and capture, to overcome, to vanquish

10 攻訐[kūng-chiéh]: to attack, to criticize, to bring a charge against

11 攻堅戰術[kūng-chiēn chàn-shù]: the tactics of storming heavily fortified points

13 攻勢[kūng-shìh]: offensive, attack

17 攻擊[kūng-chī]: to attack, to assault, to storm, to besiege

攸

15 攸樂[yū-lò]: Yu-lo (minority nationality)

— 4 Strokes —

放

2 放刁[fàng-tiāo]: to act impudently, to act insolently, to get fresh

3 放下[fàng-hsià]: to lay down, to put aside

放下架子[fàng-hsià chià-tzu]: to discard haughty airs, to get off one's high horse

放下官架子[fàng-hsià kuān-chià-tzu]: to discard bureaucratic airs, to discard pretentious airs and graces

放下包袱[fàng-hsià pāo-fú]: to lay down the burden

放下武器[fàng-hsià wŭ-ch'ì]: to lay down arms

放工[fàng-kūng]: to stop work, to release from work

放大 **[fàng-tà]** : to enlarge

4 放火 **[fàng-huŏ]** : to commit arson, to set on fire, to set fire to

放火者 **[fàng-huŏ-chĕ]** : arsonist

放手 **[fàng-shŏu]** : to let go, to let loose, to give a free rein

放手地做 **[fàng-shŏu tì tsò]** : to do to the fullest extent

6 放行 **[fàng-hsíng]** : to release, to liberate, to let go free, to let pass

放任 **[fàng-jèn]** : to let things take their course, to let alone; laissez-faire

放任主義 **[fàng-jèn chŭ-ì]** : laissez-faire, the laissez-faire principle

放任自流 **[fàng-jèn tzù-líu]** : to let something take its own course

7 放冷箭 **[fàng lĕng-chièn]** : to draw a bow at a venture, to make sarcastic remarks, to injure insidiously, to stab in the back

放走 **[fàng-tsŏu]** : to let go, to set one free, to let someone get off

放言高論 **[fàng-yén kāo-lùn]** : to make high-sounding remarks, to pontificate, to sound off

8 放長綫釣大魚 **[fàng ch'áng-hsièn tiào tà-yű]** : to angle for a fish with a long line, to go after something big with foresight

9 放映 **[fàng-yìng]** : to project, to show

10 放哨 **[fàng-shào]** : to stand guard, to be on watch, to keep watch; sentinel, scout, watch

放射 **[fàng-shè]** : to give off, to radiate; emission, radiation

放射性 **[fàng-shè-hsìng]** : radioactivity; radioactive

放射性化學 **[fàng-shè-hsìng huà-hsüéh]** : radiochemistry

放射性測量 **[fàng-shè-hsìng ts'è-liáng]** : radio-surveying, surveying method using radioactive apparatus

放射性同位素 **[fàng-shè-hsìng t'úng-wèi-sù]** : radioactive isotope

放射性物質 **[fàng-shè-hsìng wù-chíh]** : radioactive substance

放射性原素 **[fàng-shè-hsìng yüán-sù]** : radioactive element

放射醫學研究所 **[fàng-shè ī-hsüéh yén-chìu-sŏ]** : Radiology Institute

放射能 **[fàng-shè-néng]** : radiation

放射生物學 **[fàng-shè shēng-wù-hsüéh]** : radiobiology

放射微粒 **[fàng-shè wēi-lì]** : fallout, radioactive fallout

放送 **[fàng-sùng]** : to send, to transmit (i.e., by radio)

11 放逐 **[fàng-chú]** : to drive away, to banish, to deport, to exile

12 放棄 **[fàng-ch'ì]** : to abandon, to renounce, to relinquish, to renounce, to give up, to back down

13 放過機會 **[fàng-kuò chī-hùi]** : to let a chance go by, to let an opportunity pass

放肆 **[fàng-ssù]** : unbridled, rampant, unscrupulous, unchecked, wanton

14 放槍 **[fàng-ch'iāng]** : to shoot, to fire a gun

15 放寬 **[fàng-k'uān]** : to widen, to broaden, to loosen, to open wide

放寬限制 **[fàng-k'uān hsièn-chìh]** : relaxation of restrictions

16 放蕩 **[fàng-tàng]** : profligate, heedless, reckless, indolent

放閻王賬 **[fàng yén-wáng chàng]** : to charge a high rate of interest; usury

17 放縱 **[fàng-tsùng]** : to indulge in, to let loose, to abandon oneself, to give reins to, to run wild; self-indulgence

18 放鬆 **[fàng-sūng]** : to relax, to slacken, to loosen

放鬆警惕[fàng-sūng chĭng-t'ì]: to lower one's vigilance, to relax one's guard, to be off one's guard

放鬆努力[fàng-sūng nŭ-lì]: to relax one's efforts

— 5 Strokes —

政

7 政局[chèng-chǘ]: political situation

8 政治安全事務部[chèng-chìh ān-ch'üán shìh-wù pù]: Political Security Affairs Department

政治成熟程度[chèng-chìh ch'éng-shóu ch'éng-tù]: a degree of political maturity

政治季刊[chèng-chìh chì-k'ān]: Political Quarterly (British periodical)

政治家[chèng-chìh-chiā]: statesman, politician

政治家長[chèng-chìh chiā-chăng]: political patriarch (indicates an individual who is most advanced in studying the Thought of Mao Tse-tung and who should therefore be regarded as head of his family regardless of age or sex)

政治界綫[chèng-chìh chièh-hsièn]: political demarcation line

政治掮客[chèng-chìh ch'ién-k'ò]: political broker

政治指導員[chèng-chìh chìh-tăo-yüán]: political director

政治經濟學[chèng-chìh chīng-chì hsüéh]: political economy

政治經歷[chèng-chìh chīng-lì]: personal records of political activities

政治局[chèng-chìh chǘ]: Political Bureau, Politburo

政治覺悟[chèng-chìh chüéh-wù]: political awareness, political consciousness, political understanding, political awakening

政治犯[chèng-chìh fàn]: political offender, political detainee

政治嗅覺[chèng-chìh hsìu-chüéh]: political acumen (literally, political sense of smell)

政治掛帥[chèng-chìh kuà-shuài]: politics takes command, with politics in the lead (i.e., all work should pivot upon Party leadership, so that politics commands everybody and everything)

政治力量[chèng-chìh lì-liàng]: political forces

政治理論課[chèng-chìh lĭ-lùn k'ò]: political and theoretical subject, political and theoretical course of study

政治目的[chèng-chìh mù-tì]: political aims, political purposes, political designs

政治報[chèng-chìh pào]: Politika (Yugoslav daily newspaper)

政治閉塞[chèng-chìh pì-sāi]: to be politically uninformed

政治標準[chèng-chìh piāo-chŭn]: political criterion

政治上動搖[chèng-chìh-shàng tùng-yáo]: to waver politically, to be unsteady politically

政治事故[chèng-chìh shìh-kù]: political incident, subversion

政治是靈魂[chèng-chìh shìh líng-hún]: politics is the soul

政治是統帥[chèng-chìh shìh t'ŭng-shuài]: politics is the commander

政治思想[chèng-chìh ssū-hsiăng]: political outlook, political thought

政治特權及豪門勢力[chèng-chìh t'è-ch'üán chí háo-mén shìh-lì]: political prerogatives and the influence of wealth and position

政治資本[chèng-chìh tzū-pĕn]: political stock-in-trade

政治委員[chèng-chìh wĕi-yüán]: political commissar, commissar

政治影響[**chèng-chìh yǐng-hsiǎng**]: political influence

政法工作部[**chèng-fǎ kūng-tsò pù**]: Political and Judicial Work Department

政法辦公室[**chèng-fǎ pàn-kūng-shìh**]: Staff Office for Political and Legal Affairs

政府[**chèng-fǔ**]: government, administration

政府機關[**chèng-fǔ chī-kuān**]: government organ, government administration

政府之間的[**chèng-fǔ chīh chiēn te**]: intergovernmental

政府經營的[**chèng-fǔ chīng-yíng te**]: government operated

政府人士[**chèng-fǔ jén-shìh**]: government circles, members of the government

政協全國委員會[**chèng-hsiéh ch'üán-kuó wěi-yüán-hùi**]: National Committee of the Chinese People's Political Consultative Conference

政社合一[**chèng-shè hó-ī**]: integration of government and commune, to integrate government administration and commune management, to merge government administration with commune management

政委[**chèng-wěi**]: political commissar

9 政界[**chèng-chièh**]: political circles

政客[**chèng-k'ò**]: politician

10 政訓[**chèng-hsǜn**]: political indoctrination

11 政教分裂[**chèng-chiào fēn-lièh**]: to separate church from state; separation of church and state

政務院[**chèng-wù yüàn**]: Government Administrative Council (renamed the 國務院 in 1954)

12 政策[**chèng-ts'è**]: policy, government policy, administrative policy

14 政綱[**chèng-kāng**]: political program, political platform

15 政論家[**chèng-lùn-chiā**]: political commentator, publicist

20 政黨[**chèng-tǎng**]: political party

22 政權[**chèng-ch'üán**]: state power, reigns of government, regime, government

政權機關[**chèng-ch'üán chī-kuān**]: organs of political power

政權建設[**chèng-ch'üán chièn-shè**]: the building of political authority

23 政變[**chèng-pièn**]: coup, coup d'état

政體[**chèng-t'ǐ**]: form of government, system of government, political system

故

3 故土[**kù-t'ǔ**]: place of birth, native place, homeland, home

7 故步自封[**kù-pù tzù-fēng**]: to adhere to traditional forms and customs rigidly

8 故事[**kù-shìh**]: anecdote, story, tale, episode

故事片[**kù-shìh p'ièn**]: feature film, narrative movie

12 故鄉[**kù-hsiāng**]: native village, home, place of birth

14 故障[**kù-chàng**]: breakdown, hindrance, obstruction; out of order, out of gear

— 6 Strokes —

8 效忠於[**hsiào-chūng yǘ**]: to be loyal to, to be faithful to

效果[**hsiào-kuǒ**]: effect, result

10 效能[**hsiào-néng**]: effectiveness, efficiency, efficaciousness, efficacy

11 效率[**hsiào-lǜ**]: efficiency

— 7 Strokes —

教

3 教士[chiào-shih]: missionary

4 教父哲學[chiào-fù ché-hsüéh]: patristic philosophy

教友派[chiào-yŭ p'ài]: Society of Friends, the Quaker sect, Quakers

5 教本[chiào-pĕn]: textbook

7 教材[chiào-ts'ái]: teaching material

8 教長[chiào-chăng]: Imam

教具[chiào-chü]: training aids, teaching apparatus

教法[chiào-fă]: teaching method

教門[chiào-mén]: sect; Mohammedans

教育[chiào-yü]: to educate; education, upbringing; educational

教育機構[chiào-yü chī-kòu]: educational institution

教育家[chiào-yü-chiā]: educator

教育界[chiào-yü chièh]: educational circles, the educational world

教育制度[chiào-yü chìh-tù]: educational system

教育方針[chiào-yü fāng-chēn]: educational policies, guidelines for education

教育費[chiào-yü fèi]: educational expenditures

教育學[chiào-yü-hsüéh]: pedagogy, education

教育部[chiào-yü pù]: Ministry of Education

教育爲政治服務[chiào-yü wèi chèng-chìh fú-wù]: education in the service of politics

教育與生產勞動相結合[chiào-yü yǚ shēng-ch'ăn láo-tùng hsiāng chiéh-hó]: to combine education with productive labor

9 教皇[chiào-huáng]: pope, the Holy Father

教科書[chiào-k'ō-shū]: textbook

教派[chiào-p'ài]: religious sect, denomination or group

教室[chiào-shìh]: classroom

10 教案[chiào-àn]: religious dispute

教訓[chiào-hsün]: to instruct, to inculcate, to teach; teaching, instruction

教師報[chiào-shīh pào]: The Teacher's Journal (a Chinese Communist newspaper appearing twice weekly)

教書[chiào-shū]: to instruct, to teach

教唆[chiào-sō]: to instigate, to goad, to stir up, to excite

教條[chiào-t'iáo]: dogma; doctrinaire, dogmatic

教條主義[chiào-t'iáo chŭ-ì]: dogmatism, doctrinairism

教條主義者[chiào-t'iáo chŭ-ì chĕ]: dogmatist, doctrinaire

教徒[chiào-t'ú]: believer, adherent, member or follower of a religion, member of a religious community

教務[chiào-wù]: education, educational matters

教務處[chiào-wù ch'ù]: educational affairs office, dean's office

教員[chiào-yüán]: teacher

11 教區[chiào-ch'ü]: parish

教授[chiào-shòu]: professor

教授法[chiào-shòu fă]: teaching method

教堂[chiào-t'áng]: church

教研組[**chiào-yén tsŭ**]: teaching and research group (abbreviation of 教學研究組)

12 教程[**chiào-ch'éng**]: course of instruction

教給[**chiào-kĕi**]: to teach, to instruct

13 教會[**chiào-hùi**]: to teach how to do; church, mission

14 教誨[**chiào-hŭi**]: to teach, to instruct, to educate

15 教練[**chiào-lièn**]: to train, to exercise, to drill; training, instruction; trainer, coach

教練機[**chiào-lièn-chī**]: training aircraft

教養[**chiào-yăng**]: to educate and bring up; culture, education and rearing

教養不好[**chiào-yăng pù-hăo**]: ill breeding, bad upbringing

教養院[**chiào-yăng-yüàn**]: reformatory, workhouse

16 教學[**chiào-hsüéh**]: to teach school

教學法[**chiào-hsüéh fă**]: teaching methods

教學內容[**chiào-hsüéh nèi-júng**]: content of instruction

教學大綱[**chiào-hsüéh tà-kāng**]: teaching outline, lecture outline, teaching syllabus

教學研究組[**chiào-hsüéh yén-chìu tsŭ**]: teaching and research group

教導[**chiào-tăo**]: to teach, to instruct

教導員[**chiào-tăo-yüán**]: instructor, instruction officer (PLA political officer)

救

5 救出[**chìu-ch'ū**]: to save, to rescue

7 救災[**chìu-tsāi**]: to provide relief in calamity

8 救命[**chìu-mìng**]: to save a life; Help!

9 救星[**chìu-hsīng**]: savior, deliverer

11 救國[**chìu-kuó**]: to save the state; national salvation

17 救濟[**chìu-chì**]: relief

敘

7 敘利亞[**hsü-lì-yà**]: Syria

9 敘述[**hsü-shù**]: to describe, to narrate, to relate, to recite

敏

13 敏感[**mĭn-kăn**]: sensitiveness, sensitivity, keen feeling; sensitive

15 敏銳[**mĭn-jùi**]: keen, penetrating, pointed, sharp

敗

5 敗仗[**pài-chàng**]: a defeat, a losing battle

8 敗於[**pài-yǘ**]: to lose to, to be defeated by

10 敗家子[**pài-chiā-tzu**]: spendthrift, "black sheep," "prodigal son"

12 敗訴[**pài-sù**]: to lose a case at law

19 敗壞[**pài-huài**]: to harm, to injure, to ruin

敗壞風紀[**pài-huài fēng-chì**]: demoralization

敗類[**pài-lèi**]: degenerate, miscreant, rogue, rascal, scum, dregs, riffraff, outcast

— 8 Strokes —

敢

6 敢死隊[**kăn-ssŭ tùi**]: shock troops, suicide squad

8 敢於鬥爭，敢於勝利[**kăn yǘ tòu-chēng, kăn yǘ shèng-lì**]: to be bold to struggle and seize victory

14 敢說，敢想，敢做 **[kăn-shuō, kăn-hsiăng, kăn-tsò]**: to speak, think, and act with daring and courage

散

7 散佈 **[sàn-pù]**: to sow, to disseminate, to spread, to scatter, to broadcast, to disperse

12 散發 **[sàn-fā]**: to distribute, to circulate, to release, to propagate, to promulgate, to diffuse, to scatter

13 散會 **[sàn-hùi]**: to conclude, to close, to end, to disperse, to adjourn, to break up (a meeting)

14 散漫 **[sàn-màn]**: diffuseness

15 散播 **[sàn-pō]**: to sow, to disseminate, to spread, to scatter, to disperse, to broadcast

敦

9 敦厚 **[tūn-hòu]**: honest, reliable

敦促 **[tūn-ts'ù]**: to urge

13 敦睦 **[tūn-mù]**: cordial, friendly

— 9 Strokes —

敬

6 敬老院 **[chìng-lăo yüàn]**: old age home (i.e., in the commune)

10 敬畏 **[chìng-wèi]**: to stand in awe of, to fear and respect

13 敬愛的 **[chìng-ài te]**: respected and beloved, respected

敬意 **[chìng-ì]**: regards, admiration, esteem, tribute

18 敬禮 **[chìng-lĭ]**: to salute; salute

— 10 Strokes —

敲

10 敲骨吸髓 **[ch'iāo-kŭ hsī-sŭi]**: to suck the life blood

12 敲詐 **[ch'iāo-chà]**: to blackmail, to extort, to swindle, to defraud; blackmail, racket, racketeer

敲詐勒索 **[ch'iāo-chà lè-sŏ]**: to blackmail and impose exactions on, to extort and racketeer

— 11 Strokes —

整

7 整批的 **[chĕng-p'ī te]**: the entire group

整批交易 **[chĕng-p'ī chiāo-ì]**: package deal

8 整社 **[chĕng-shè]**: rectification of the communes, to check up on the communes

9 整軍運動 **[chĕng-chün yün-tùng]**: ideological education movement in the army

整風運動 **[chĕng-fēng yün-tùng]**: rectification campaign, rectification of the work style movement (a campaign first carried out in 1942 by the Party to "enhance the people's consciousness of Communism so as to conform with the requirements for consolidating the Socialist system and further developing production," and using the method of "criticism and self-criticism"; the campaign was first launched among Party members to rectify their working style and test their loyalty to the Party, and resulted in purges)

10 整訓 **[chĕng-hsün]**: training and consolidation, reorganization and training

整個 **[chĕng-kò]**: whole, overall, total, entire, complete

整套設備 **[chĕng-t'ào shè-pèi]**: a complete set of equipment

11 整理 **[chĕng-lĭ]**: to put in order, to adjust, to arrange, to regulate

整理綱要 **[chěng-lǐ kāng-yào]**: processing program, processing schedule

整理表 **[chěng-lǐ piǎo]**: working table, work sheet

整理黨的組織 **[chěng-lǐ tǎng te tsǔ-chīh]**: consolidation of Party organizations

13 整裝待命 **[chěng-chuāng tài-mìng]**: to stand by waiting for orders in full battle array; ready to move at short notice

整頓 **[chěng-tùn]**: to rectify, to put in order, to reorganize, to readjust; readjustment

整頓學風 **[chěng-tùn hsüéh-fēng]**: to rectify an unsound approach to study

整頓，鞏固，充實，提高 **[chěng-tùn, kǔng-kù, ch'ūng-shíh, t'í-kāo]**: readjustment, consolidation, filling up, elevation

整頓黨的作風 **[chěng-tùn tǎng te tsò-fēng]**: to rectify the Party's working style

14 整齊 **[chěng-ch'í]**: in good order, orderly, trim, tidy, neat

整肅 **[chěng-sù]**: to rectify, to purge

15 整編 **[chěng-piēn]**: reorganization, regrouping, reshuffle

整編師 **[chěng-piēn shīh]**: reorganized division

整編黨的隊伍 **[chěng-piēn tǎng te tùi-wǔ]**: to educate and reorganize the ranks of the Party

整編委員會 **[chěng-piēn wěi-yüán-hùi]**: reorganization committee

20 整黨 **[chěng-tǎng]**: Party consolidation

23 整體 **[chěng-t'ǐ]**: the whole, entirety

整體化 **[chěng-t'ǐ-huà]**: to integrate; integration

整體觀念 **[chěng-t'ǐ kuān-nièn]**: the concept of the whole, viewing a situation as a whole (i.e., industrial, organizational, and other planning in which interests of the whole industry, organization, or country are taken into consideration)

敷

5 敷用 **[fū-yùng]**: adequate, sufficient, adequate for the need

9 敷衍 **[fū-yěn]**: to make a display, to act perfunctorily or slovenly

敷衍態度 **[fū-yěn t'ài-tù]**: perfunctory attitude

11 敷設 **[fū-shè]**: to establish, to lay out, to found, to erect

數

2 數十 **[shù-shíh]**: scores, dozens, tens

6 數列 **[shù-lièh]**: series

數字 **[shù-tzù]**: figures, numbers

數字計算機 **[shù-tzù chì-suàn-chī]**: digital computer

12 數量 **[shù-liàng]**: quantity, numerical quantity

13 數達 **[shù-tá]**: to amount to, to reach the sum of, to reach the amount of

16 數學 **[shù-hsüéh]**: mathematics, arithmetic

數學研究所 **[shù-hsüéh yén-chìu-sǒ]**: Mathematics Institute

敵

2 敵人 **[tí-jén]**: enemy, foe, antagonist, adversary, opponent, rival

4 敵不過 **[tí-pú-kuò]**: to be no match for, powerless against, not able to stand off

5 敵占區 **[tí-chàn ch'ū]**: zone of enemy occupation, enemy occupied zone

7 敵我矛盾 **[tí-wǒ máo-tùn]**: contradictions between the enemy and ourselves

11 敵得過 **[tí-té-kuò]**: to be a match for, to rival, to be able to fight against

敵僞 **[tí-wěi]**: the enemy (Japan) and the puppet (government)

12 敵視 **[tí-shìh]**: hostility, enmity; hostile, antagonistic

14 敵對 **[tí-tùi]**: hostility, enmity; antagonistic, hostile, opposite

敵對分子 **[tí-tùi fèn-tzu]**: hostile element

— 13 Strokes —

斂

13 斂跡 **[liěn-chī]**: to cover one's traces, to give up evil ways, to stay at home

— 14 Strokes —

斃

8 斃命 **[pì-mìng]**: to die, to pass away

— RADICAL 文 67 —

文

2 文人詩歌 **[wén-jén shīh-kō]**: intellectual poetry

3 文工團 **[wén-kūng-t'uán]**: ensemble, troupe, cultural work group

4 文化 **[wén-huà]**: 1. culture, 2. Vanhoa (Vietnam)

文化戰綫 **[wén-huà chàn-hsièn]**: the cultural front

文化交流 **[wén-huà chiāo-líu]**: cultural exchange, cultural interchange

文化教育機關 **[wén-huà chiào-yǜ chī-kuān]**: cultural and educational institutions

文化教育工作部 **[wén-huà chiào-yǜ kūng-tsò pù]**: cultural and education work department

文化教育工作委員會 **[wén-huà chiào-yǜ kūng-tsò wěi-yüán-hùi]**: culture and education work committee

文化界 **[wén-huà chièh]**: cultural circles, the cultural sphere

文化界名流 **[wén-huà chièh míng-líu]**: famous cultural figures

文化遺產 **[wén-huà í-ch'ǎn]**: cultural heritage

文化人 **[wén-huà jén]**: cultural worker

文化幹部 **[wén-huà kàn-pù]**: cultural cadre (i.e., political officer at the platoon level in the PLA)

文化革命 **[wén-huà kó-mìng]**: Cultural Revolution (i.e., the Great Proletarian Cultural Revolution)

文化課 **[wén-huà k'ò]**: cultural course, literacy class

文化館 **[wén-huà kuǎn]**: cultural center, cultural hall

文化部 **[wén-huà pù]**: Ministry of Culture

文化生活 **[wén-huà shēng-huó]**: cultural life, intellectual life

文化水平 **[wén-huà shŭi-p'íng]**: cultural level

文化大革命 **[wén-huà tà kó-mìng]**: the Great Cultural Revolution (started in November 1965 as an attack on the play Hai Jui Dismissed from Office, by Wu Han, later involving other writers and artists, and developing in the summer of 1966 into a stormy movement for the purpose of weeding out "those in power who are travelling on the road to capitalism")

文化團體[wén-huà t'uán-t'ǐ]: cultural organization

文化委員會[wén-huà wěi-yüán-hùi]: cultural committee

文化搖籃[wén-huà yáo-lán]: cradle of culture

5 文本[wén-pěn]: version

6 文件[wén-chièn]: document, paper

文字改革[wén-tzù kǎi-kó]: language reform, reform of Chinese characters

7 文告[wén-kào]: statement, proclamation

文攻武衞[wén-kūng wǔ-wèi]: to attack with reasoning and to defend with force (a slogan put forth by Chiang Ch'ing (Mme Mao) in July 1967 signifying that pro-Mao Red Guards were justified in using force against violent attacks from their opponents but that they must use only reasoning in dealing with their ideological enemies)

8 文盲[wén-máng]: illiteracy; illiterate

文盲狀態[wén-máng chuàng-t'ài]: illiteracy condition or situation

文明[wén-míng]: civilization, culture; civilized, cultured, enlightened

文明社會[wén-míng shè-hùi]: civilized community, cultured society

文委會[wén-wěi-hùi]: cultural committee (abbreviation of 文化委員會)

文物[wén-wù]: cultural relics, documents and objects (of cultural or historical significance)

文物古迹[wén-wù kǔ-chī]: cultural and historical relics and places of cultural and historical interest

9 文風[wén-fēng]: literary style, literary tendency

10 文書[wén-shū]: clerk, secretary; official dispatch

文鬥,武鬥[wén-tòu, wǔ-tòu]: struggle by reasoning and struggle by violence

文娛活動[wén-yǘ huó-tùng]: literary recreational activities

11 文章[wén-chāng]: writing, article, essay, literary work

文教[wén-chiào]: culture and education

文教戰綫[wén-chiào chàn-hsièn]: cultural and educational front

文教辦公室[wén-chiào pàn-kūng-shìh]: staff office for culture and education

文教組織[wén-chiào tsǔ-chīh]: UNESCO

文教事業[wén-chiào shìh-yèh]: cultural and educational enterprises or callings

文部省[wén-pù shěng]: Ministry of Education (Japan)

12 文萊[wén-lái]: Brunei (Borneo)

文萊蘇丹國[wén-lái sū-tān-kuó]: Sultanate of Brunei

13 文匯報[wén hùi pào]: Wen Hui Pao (Shanghai newspaper)

16 文學[wén-hsüéh]: literature

文學和藝術服從政治[wén-hsüéh hó ì-shù fú-ts'úng chèng-chìh]: subordination of literature and art to politics

文學藝術[wén-hsüéh ì-shù]: literature and art

文學藝術遺產[wén-hsüéh ì-shù í-ch'ǎn]: literary and artistic heritage

19 文藝界[wén-ì chièh]: literary and artistic circles

文藝創作[wén-ì ch'uàng-tsò]: literary and artistic creation, literary creation, literary works

文藝復興[wén-ì fù-hsīng]: the Renaissance

文藝工作者[wén-ì kūng-tsò-chě]: artists and writers, workers in art and literature

文藝報[wén-ì pào]: Literature and Art Gazette (Chinese Communist weekly periodical)

文藝事務處 **[wén-ì shìh-wù ch'ù]**: office of literary and art affairs

文藝團體 **[wén-ì t'uán-t'ǐ]**: literary and art organization

文藝爲工農兵服務 **[wén-ì wèi-kūng-núng-pīng fú-wù]**: "Literature and art should serve the workers, peasants, and soldiers"

文牘主義 **[wén-tú chǔ-ì]**: documentalism, red-tape-ism (refers to cadres interested only in reading and writing official letters or documents without giving attention to other matters)

20 文獻記錄片 **[wén-hsièn chì-lù-p'ièn]**: documentary film

文鬥 **[wén-tòu]**: to struggle civilly; persuasion; struggle by reasoning

— RADICAL 斗 68 —

— 6 Strokes —

料

3 料子服 **[liào-tzu fú]**: suits of woolen cloth (i.e., in contrast to the coarse cotton coats usually worn in Communist China)

— 9 Strokes —

斟

10 斟酌 **[chēn-chó]**: to deliberate, to consider, to consult

斟酌情況 **[chēn-chó ch'íng-k'uàng]**: considering the special circumstance of the case, in the light of specific circumstances, according to circumstances

— 10 Strokes —

斡

11 斡旋 **[wò-hsüán]**: to mediate, to intercede, to retrieve, to revolve; good offices

— RADICAL 斤 69 —

斤

斤 **[chīn]**: catty

4 斤斤計較 **[chīn-chīn chì-chiào]**: to think about narrow personal gains and losses; minute squaring of accounts

— 1 Stroke —

斥

8 斥革 **[ch'ìh-kó]**: to dismiss, to remove from office

10 斥候 **[ch'ìh-hòu]**: to patrol, to observe the enemy; patrol

斥退 **[ch'ìh-t'ùi]**: to dismiss, to drive away

11 斥責 **[ch'ìh-tsé]**: to blame, to reprimand, to denounce

12 斥爲 **[ch'ìh wéi]**: to dismiss as

— 4 Strokes —

3 斧山 **[fǔ-shān]**: Pusan (Korea)

— 7 Strokes —

斬

[9] 斬首 **[chăn-shŏu]**: to behead, to execute

[18] 斬斷魔爪 **[chăn-tuàn mó-chăo]**: to cut off the Devil's claws, to trim the claws of

— 8 Strokes —

斯

[3] 斯大林 **[ssū-tà-lín]**: Stalin, Josef (Russian political leader; 1879–1953)

斯大林格勒 **[ssū-tà-lín-kó-lè]**: Stalingrad

[4] 斯巴克 **[ssū-pā-k'ò]**: Spaak, Paul Henri (Belgian lawyer and statesman)

[6] 斯多噶學派 **[ssū-tō-kó hsüéh-p'ài]**: Stoicism

[8] 斯坦萊 **[ssū-t'ăn-lái]**: Stanley (Falkland Islands)

[9] 斯洛伐克 **[ssū-lò-fā-k'ò]**: Slovakia

斯泰哈諾夫運動 **[ssū-t'ài-hā-nò-fū yŭn-tùng]**: Stakhanov movement

斯威士蘭 **[ssū-wēi-shìh-lán]**: Swaziland

[10] 斯特拉斯堡 **[ssū-t'è-lā-ssū-păo]**: Strasbourg (France)

[12] 斯堪的納維亞半島 **[ssū-k'ān-tì-nà-wéi-yà pàn tăo]**: Scandinavia

[15] 斯摩稜斯克 **[ssū-mó-léng-ssū-k'ò]**: Smolensk

斯賓塞 **[ssū-pīn-sè]**: Spencer, Herbert (1820–1903)

斯賓諾沙 **[ssū-pīn-nò-shā]**: Spinoza, Benedict (1632–1677)

斯德哥爾摩 **[ssū-té-kō-ĕrh-mó]**: Stockholm (Sweden)

— 9 Strokes —

新

新 **[hsīn]**: 1. new, neo-; 2. Sinkiang (abbreviation of 新疆)

[2] 新几內亞 **[hsīn chī-nèi-yà]**: New Guinea

新人 **[hsīn-jén]**: a new man, new people (i.e., people who are making a fresh start in life)

新人新事 **[hsīn-jén hsīn-shìh]**: new people and new things

新人輩出 **[hsīn-jén pèi-ch'ū]**: mass emergence of new people

新人文主義 **[hsīn jén-wén chŭ-ì]**: New Humanism (of the second half of the eighteenth century in Germany)

[3] 新三民主義 **[hsīn sān-mín chŭ-ì]**: New Sun Yat-sen-ism

[4] 新不列顛島 **[hsīn pú-lièh-tiēn tăo]**: New Britain Island

新手 **[hsīn-shŏu]**: newcomer, novice

新文化 **[hsīn wén-huà]**: new culture (an objective of the Proletarian Cultural Revolution and one of the 四新, q.v.)

新五篇 **[hsīn wŭ-p'iēn]**: the "new five articles" (five articles written by Mao Tse-tung and first mentioned in a declaration of the Peking Secondary School Red Guard Congress of March 28, 1967: 1) On the Rectification of Erroneous Thought in the Party [December 1929]; 2) To Oppose Liberalism [September 1937]; 3) Directives on the Reaffirmation of the "Three Main Rules of Discipline and Eight Points for Attention" [October 1947]; 4) On the Rectification of the Party Style [February 1942]; 5) The Work Methods of the Party Committee [March 1949])

[5] 新加坡 **[hsīn-chiā-p'ō]**: Singapore

新加坡自治邦 **[hsīn-chiā-p'ō tzù-chìh-pāng]**: State of Singapore

新古典主義[**hsīn kŭ-tiĕn chŭ-ì**]: neo-classicism

新民主主義[**hsīn mín-chŭ chŭ-ì**]: new democracy, new democratic

新民主主義青年團 [**hsīn mín-chŭ chŭ-ì ch'īng-nién-t'uán**]: New Democracy Youth Corps; China New Democratic Youth League

新民主主義革命[**hsīn mín-chŭ chŭ-ì kó-mìng**]: new democratic revolution

新民主主義論 [**hsīn mín-chŭ chŭ-ì lùn**]: On New Democracy (a treatise by Mao, 1940)

新生[**hsīn-shēng**]: rebirth, rejuvenation, resurrection; new-born

新生力量[**hsīn-shēng lì-liàng**]: new-born forces, new forces, new rising forces

新生報[**hsīn shēng pào**]: Hsin Sheng Pao (Taiwan daily newspaper)

新四軍[**hsīn ssù-chūn**]: New Fourth Army

新安徽報[**hsīn ān-hūi pào**]: New Anhui Daily (newspaper)

新西蘭[**hsīn hsī-lán**]: New Zealand

新西蘭自治領 [**hsīn hsī-lán tzù-chìh-lĭng**]: Dominion of New Zealand

新共和[**hsīn kùng-hó**]: New Republic (American weekly periodical)

新共和國聯盟 [**hsīn kùng-hó-kuó lién-méng**]: Union for the New Republic (France)

新式富農[**hsīn-shìh fù-núng**]: new-type rich peasant

新式農具[**hsīn-shìh núng-chù**]: new style farm implements, improved farm implements

7 新罕布什爾[**hsīn hăn-pù-shíh-ĕrh**]: New Hampshire

新兵[**hsīn-pīng**]: recruit

8 新近獨立的[**hsīn-chìn tú-lì te**]: newly independent

新金山[**hsīn-chīn-shān**]: Melbourne

新法[**hsīn-fă**]: innovation, recent methods, improved processes

新門羅主義[**hsīn mén-ló chŭ-ì**]: New Monroe Doctrine (i.e., in reference to American policy after the Second World War)

新事物[**hsīn shìh-wù**]: new phenomena

新亞書院[**hsīn-yà shū-yüàn**]: New Asia College (Hong Kong)

9 新政[**hsīn-chèng**]: New Deal

新政治家和民族[**hsīn chèng-chìh-chiā hó mín-tsú**]: New Statesman and Nation (British periodical)

新建設[**hsīn chièn-shè**]: 1. reconstruction; 2. New Construction (Chinese Communist monthly periodical)

新飛躍[**hsīn fēi-yüèh**]: New Flying Leap (an expression that first appeared in 1968 and that has been used to describe intentions and achievements in particular sections of the economy; it apparently does not embrace the same scope as the Great Leap Forward)

新風氣[**hsīn fēng-ch'ì**]: new atmosphere, new prevailing practice

新風俗[**hsīn fēng-sú**]: new customs (an objective of the Cultural Revolution and one of the 四新, q.v.)

新型[**hsīn-hsíng**]: new pattern, new type, new model

新美[**hsīn-mĕi**]: Tanmy (Vietnam)

新面貌[**hsīn mièn-mào**]: new look, new appearance

新品質[**hsīn p'ĭn-chíh**]: new trait, new characteristic, new character

新思想[**hsīn ssū-hsiăng**]: new thought, new

ideology (an objective of the Cultural Revolution and one of the 四新, q.v.)

新英雄主義[**hsīn yīng-hsiúng chŭ-ì**]: new heroism

10 新城[**hsīn-ch'éng**]: Kota Bharu

新高打[**hsīn kāo-tă**]: Kota Bharu

新浪漫主義[**hsīn làng-màn chŭ-ì**]: neo-romanticism

新時代[**hsīn shíh-tài**]: 1. new era, new epoch, new age; 2. Novoe Vremya (Russian periodical)

新原始主義[**hsīn yüán-shĭh chŭ-ì**]: neo-primitivism

11 新習慣[**hsīn hsí-kuàn**]: new habits (an objective of the Proletarian Cultural Revolution and one of the 四新, q.v.)

新現實主義[**hsīn hsièn-shíh chŭ-ì**]: neo-realism

新修正主義[**hsīn hsīu-chèng chŭ-ì**]: neo-revisionism

新康德主義[**hsīn k'āng-té chŭ-ì**]: neo-Kantism

12 新殖民主義[**hsīn chíh-mín chŭ-ì**]: neo-colonialism

新華半月刊[**hsīn-huá pàn-yüèh-k'ān**]: Hsin Hua Journal (Chinese Communist semi-monthly periodical)

新華社[**hsīn-huá shè**]: Hsinhua News Agency (official Chinese Communist news agency), New China News Agency

新華通訊社[**hsīn-huá t'ūng-hsǜn shè**]: Hsinhua News Agency (same as 新華社)

新喀里多尼亞島[**hsīn k'à-lĭ-tō-ní-yà tăo**]: New Caledonia Island

新港[**hsīn-kăng**]: Newport

新報[**hsīn pào**]: Sin Po (an Indonesian daily newspaper with English and Chinese editions)

13 新愛國主義[**hsīn ài-kuó chŭ-ì**]: New Patriotism

新奧爾良[**hsīn ào-ĕrh-liáng**]: New Orleans

新愚公[**hsīn yǘ-kūng**]: a new Yü-kung (i.e., a new Foolish Old Man, a reference to 愚公移山, q.v.)

14 新嘉坡[**hsīn-chiā-p'ō**]: Singapore

新閩日報[**hsīn-mĭn jìh-pào**]: Fookien Times (a Manila Chinese language newspaper)

新聞紀錄片[**hsīn-wén chì-lù p'ièn**]: newsreel

新聞記事報[**hsīn-wén chì-shìh pào**]: News Chronicle (British newspaper)

新聞週報[**hsīn-wén chōu-pào**]: Newsweek (American weekly periodical)

新聞發布官[**hsīn-wén fā-pù-kuān**]: press officer

新聞封鎖[**hsīn-wén fēng-sŏ**]: news blackout

新聞學[**hsīn-wén-hsüéh**]: journalism

新聞工作者[**hsīn-wén kūng-tsò-chĕ**]: journalist

新聞聯合社[**hsīn-wén lién-hó shè**]: Associated Press

新聞報[**hsīn-wén pào**]: La Presse (Canadian daily newspaper)

新聞事業[**hsīn-wén shìh-yèh**]: journalism, journalistic enterprise

新聞司[**hsīn-wén ssū**]: Department of Information, news division

新聞參贊[**hsīn-wén ts'ān-tsàn**]: press attache, press counselor

15 新潟[**hsīn-hsì**]: Niigata (Japan)

新興力量運動會[**hsīn-hsīng lì-liàng yǜn-tùng-hùi**]: Games of the New Emerging Forces (GANEFO)

新興事業[**hsīn-hsīng shìh-yèh**]: new undertakings, newly established undertakings

新墨西哥[**hsīn mò-hsī-kō**]: New Mexico

新德里 **[hsīn té-lǐ]** : New Delhi (India)

新德意志報 **[hsīn té-ì-chìh pào]** : Neues Deutschland (East German daily newspaper)

新增的生產能力 **[hsīn-tsēng te shēng-ch'ǎn néng-lì]** : newly added productive capacity

16 新學 **[hsīn hsüéh]** : new learning (i.e., Western learning pursued by Chinese after 1840)

新澤西 **[hsīn tsé-hsī]** : New Jersey

25 新觀察 **[hsīn kuān-ch'á]** : New Observer (Chinese Communist semi-monthly periodical)

— 14 Strokes —

6 斷交 **[tuàn-chiāo]** : to break off relations, to break off a friendship

7 斷言 **[tuàn-yén]** : to assert, to affirm, to maintain

8 斷定 **[tuàn-tìng]** : to assert, to state with conviction, to judge, to determine

10 斷案 **[tuàn-àn]** : to settle a case at law

斷根 **[tuàn-kēn]** : to cure thoroughly, to cure completely, to sever the roots

11 斷章取義 **[tuàn-chāng ch'ǚ-ì]** : to distort, to make a deliberate misinterpretation out of context

12 斷絕 **[tuàn-chüéh]** : to break off, to interrupt, to stop

斷絕關係 **[tuàn-chüéh kuān-hsì]** : to break off relations, to sever relations, to sever connections

斷然 **[tuàn-ján]** : utter, unequivocal, positive; categorically, flatly

14 斷斷續續 **[tuàn-tuàn hsǜ-hsǜ]** : intermittent, recurrent, alternating, periodic, at intervals

斷語 **[tuàn-yǚ]** : judgment, verdict

— RADICAL 方 70 —

方

3 方寸 **[fāng-ts'ùn]** : a square inch

4 方尺 **[fāng-ch'ǐh]** : a square foot

6 方向 **[fāng-hsiàng]** : trend, direction, tendency, orientation

7 方式 **[fāng-shìh]** : method, way, fashion, mode

方位 **[fāng-wèi]** : location, bearing, position

方言 **[fāng-yén]** : dialect

8 方法 **[fāng-fǎ]** : procedure, method, device, process, approach, ways and means

方法論 **[fāng-fǎ-lùn]** : methodology

9 方面 **[fāng-mièn]** : phase, aspect, sides, sector, section, field

方便 **[fāng-pièn]** : expediency, convenience, facility, expedient, convenient

10 方案 **[fāng-àn]** : program, formula, proposal, suggestion

方針 **[fāng-chēn]** : policy, direction, course, guideline, guiding principles

方針政策 **[fāng-chēn chèng-ts'è]** : general and specific policies

12 方程式 **[fāng-ch'éng shìh]** : equation

15 方興未艾的 **[fāng-hsīng wèi-ài te]** : rising, in the ascendant, on the upgrade

— 4 Strokes —

於

9 於是 [yǘ-shìh]: therefore, accordingly, consequently, thereupon, whereupon

— 5 Strokes —

施

3 施工 [shīh-kūng]: to labor, to employ labor; building, construction

施工程序 [shīh-kūng ch'éng-hsǜ]: order of construction

5 施加古 [shīh-chiā-kŭ]: Chicago

施加壓力 [shīh-chiā yā-lì]: to bring pressure, to exert pressure, to put pressure on

8 施肥 [shīh-féi]: application of fertilizer

10 施展 [shīh-chăn]: to expand, to display

施展軟工夫 [shīh-chăn juăn kūng-fū]: to use finesse, to apply clever and patient tactics, to maneuver

施恩 [shīh-ēn]: to bestow a favor, to show favor

15 施暴行 [shīh pào-hsíng]: to commit atrocities

— 6 Strokes —

旅

旅 [lǚ]: 1. brigade; 2. Port Arthur (abbreviation of 旅順)

6 旅行 [lǚ-hsíng]: to travel, to tour, to go on a tour; travel, trip, journey, excursion

8 旅委 [lǚ-wĕi]: brigade Party committee

9 旅客 [lǚ-k'ò]: passenger, tourist, traveller

17 旅館 [lǚ-kuăn]: hotel, inn, guest house

旁

19 旁證 [p'áng-chèng]: circumstantial evidence

22 旁聽席 [p'áng-t'īng hsí]: visitors' seats

旁聽生 [p'áng-t'īng-shēng]: listener, auditor

25 旁觀者 [p'áng-kuān-chĕ]: Spectator (British weekly periodical); a spectator

— 7 Strokes —

旋

9 旋風 [hsüàn-fēng]: whirlwind

旋律 [hsüán-lǜ]: rhythm, melody, cadence

12 旋渦 [hsüàn-wō]: vortex, whirlpool, eddy

18 旋轉 [hsüán-chuàn]: to revolve, to spin, to circle, to rotate

旋轉乾坤 [hsüán-chuăn ch'ién-k'ūn]: to change the universe, to change nature

— 10 Strokes —

旗

旗 [ch'í]: banner (i.e., Mongol or Manchu banners)

13 旗鼓相當 [ch'í-kŭ hsiāng-tāng]: well-matched

15 旗幟 [ch'í-chìh]: flag, banner, standard, streamer, pennant

20 旗艦 [ch'í-chièn]: flagship

— RADICAL 无旡 71 —

— 7 Strokes —

旣

6 旣成事實 **[chì-ch'éng shìh-shíh]**: since it has become an established fact or a fait accompli

8 旣定目標 **[chì-tìng mù-piāo]**: since the target is set; the set target, the set goal

旣往 **[chì-wăng]**: the bygone, the past, what is gone or done, former standing, former condition

旣往不咎 **[chì-wăng pú-chiù]**: not to punish for past misdeeds, to let bygones be bygones

11 旣得利益 **[chì-té lì-ì]**: vested interests

12 旣然 **[chì-ján]**: since, as

旣然如此 **[chì-ján jú-tz'ŭ]**: such being the case, since it is so

— RADICAL 日 72 —

日

4 日內 **[jìh-nèi]**: at an early date, in a few days, very soon, shortly

日內瓦 **[jìh-nèi-wă]**: Geneva (Switzerland)

日內瓦公約 **[jìh-nèi-wă kūng-yüēh]**: Geneva Convention

5 日立 **[jìh-lì]**: Hitachi (Japan)

日本 **[jìh-pĕn]**: Japan

日本國會 **[jìh-pĕn kuó-hùi]**: Japanese National Diet

日本社會黨訪華親善使節團 **[jìh-pĕn shè-hùi-tăng făng-huá ch'īn-shàn shĭh-chiéh-t'úan]**: Goodwill Mission of the Japanese Socialist Party to China

日用品 **[jìh-yùng p'ĭn]**: daily necessities, articles of daily use

9 日食 **[jìh-shíh]**: solar eclipse

10 日益 **[jìh-ì]**: day by day, more and more, progressively, increasingly

11 日常 **[jìh-ch'áng]**: usual, ordinary, daily, day-to-day, routine, everyday

日常眞理 **[jìh-ch'áng chēn-lĭ]**: everyday truth, plain truth

日常需要 **[jìh-ch'áng hsü-yào]**: the needs of daily life, daily necessities

12 日程 **[jìh-ch'éng]**: daily agenda, itinerary

日程表 **[jìh-ch'éng-piăo]**: order of the day, schedule of the day, agenda for the day, time-table for the day, itinerary chart

日喀則 **[jìh-k'à-tsé]**: Shigatse (Tibet)

日報 **[jìh-pào]**: daily news, daily report, daily reporting; daily, daily paper, daily journal

日惹 **[jìh-jĕ]**: Jogjakarta (Indonesia)

— 2 Strokes —

6 旨在 **[chĭh-tsài]**: to aim at, to intend, to aspire to, with the object of

4 旭日 **[hsü-jìh]**: rising sun

旭日初昇[hsü-jìh ch'ū-shēng]: the newly risen morning sun

旭日東昇[hsü-jìh tūng-shēng]: the morning sun rising in the eastern sky

旬

4 旬日[hsún-jìh]: ten-day period

12 旬報[hsún-pào]: reporting at ten-day intervals; a newspaper published at ten-day intervals

早

3 早已破產的[tsǎo-ǐ p'ò-ch'ǎn te]: long-bankrupt

6 早在[tsǎo-tsài]: as early as, as far back as

15 早熟作物[tsǎo-shóu tsò-wù]: early crops, early ripening crops

— 3 Strokes —

旱

6 旱地[hàn-tì]: dry land, non-irrigated land, non-irrigated fields

7 旱災[hàn-tsāi]: drought

10 旱荒[hàn-huāng]: drought

15 旱澇不收[hàn-lào pù-shōu]: a bad harvest as a result of drought and flood

— 4 Strokes —

昂

12 昂然[áng-ján]: dignified, exalted

昂揚[áng-yáng]: elation; enthusiastic

14 昂維斯[áng-wéi-ssū]: Antwerp (Belgium)

昌

8 昌明[ch'āng-míng]: magnificent, glorious, shining

12 昌盛[ch'āng-shèng]: prosperous, flourishing, abundant, ample

昏

7 昏君[hūn-chün]: a libertine, a despot, a stupid ruler

12 昏黑[hūn-hēi]: dark, somber

13 昏暗[hūn-àn]: dark, somber

14 昏亂[hūn-luàn]: confused, stupid

昏睡[hūn-shùi]: lethargy

易

6 易如反掌[ì jú fǎn-chǎng]: as easy as turning one's hand

8 易於[ì yü]: easy to, to be apt to, to be prone to, easily

昆

昆[k'ūn]: Kunming (abbreviation of 昆明)

18 昆蟲研究所[k'ūn-ch'úng yén-chìu-sǒ]: Entomology Institute

明

5 明目張膽[míng-mù chāng-tǎn]: flagrant, open, undisguised, naked, in a flagrant way; to speak out openly

明尼蘇達[míng-ní-sū-tá]: Minnesota

明白[míng-pái]: to understand, to know, to

be aware of, to perceive, to comprehend; plain, clear, explicit

明白無誤的[míng-pái wú-wù te]: unmistakable, clear-cut

8 明知故犯[míng-chīh kù-fàn]: to transgress or offend deliberately

9 明信片[míng-hsìn p'ièn]: postcard

12 明報[míng pào]: Ming Pao (Hong Kong newspaper)

16 明確[míng-ch'üèh]: correct, precise, specific, exact, clear-cut

23 明顯[míng-hsiěn]: evident, obvious, apparent, manifest, overt, clear, outstanding, striking

旺

11 旺盛生命力[wàng-shèng shēng-mìng-lì]: full of vigor and vitality

— 5 Strokes —

春

3 春川[ch'ūn-ch'uān]: Chunchon (Korea)

6 春安[ch'ūn-ān]: Xuanyen (Vietnam)

10 春耕[ch'ūn-kēng]: spring cultivation

15 春節[ch'ūn-chiéh]: Spring Festival, New Year's Day (on the old calendar)

星

5 星加坡[hsīng-chiā-p'ō]: Singapore

9 星洲[hsīng-chōu]: Singapore

星洲日報[hsīng-chōu jìh-pào]: Sin Chew Jit Poh (Singapore Chinese language newspaper)

星星之火，可以燎原[hsīng-hsīng chīh huŏ, k'ŏ-ĭ liáo yüán]: a tiny spark can start a prairie fire

10 星島[hsīng-tăo]: Singapore

星島日報[hsīng-tăo jìh-pào]: Sing Tao Jih Pao (Hong Kong newspaper)

星座[hsīng-tsò]: constellation

12 星雲[hsīng-yün]: nebula

14 星際[hsīng-chì]: interstellar, interplanetary

星際飛船[hsīng-chì fēi-ch'uán]: space ship

星際飛行[hsīng-chì fēi-hsíng]: interplanetary flight

星際空間[hsīng-chì k'ūng-chiēn]: interplanetary space

星際旅行[hsīng-chì lü̆-hsíng]: space travel, interplanetary travel

是

8 是非[shìh-fēi]: right and wrong, principle, fuss, trouble

是非曲直[shìh-fēi ch'ū̆-chíh]: merits and demerits, rights and wrongs

是非問題[shìh-fēi wèn-t'í]: a question of right and wrong, a problem of right and wrong

— 6 Strokes —

晉[chìn]: Shansi (abbreviation for 山西)

6 晉州[chìn-choū]: Chinju (Korea)

晃

[16] 晃蕩[huàng-tàng]: to waver, to vacillate, to totter, to shake; shaky, tottery

時

[5] 時代[shíh-tài]: 1. era, age, epoch, period, time; 2. Time (American weekly periodical)

時代的錯誤[shíh-tài te ts'ò-wù]: anachronism; mistakes or errors of an era or epoch

[7] 時局[shíh-chü]: current situation

時作時輟 [shíh-tsò shíh-ch'ò]: to do something by fits and starts

[8] 時事[shíh-shìh]: current events or affairs

時事通訊社[shíh-shìh t'ūng-hsün-shè]: Jiji News Agency (Japan)

[10] 時起時伏[shíh-ch'ĭ shíh-fú]: to vary in intensity from time to time; to rise and fall intermittently

[11] 時常[shíh-ch'áng]: frequent, from time to time, often

[12] 時期[shíh-ch'í]: period, stage, phase

時間[shíh-chiēn]: time

時間表[shíh-chiēn piăo]: time-table, schedule

[16] 時機[shíh-chī]: time, moment, juncture, contingency, opportunity

— 7 Strokes —

晨

[6] 晨光[ch'én-kuāng]: daybreak, daylight

晦

[11] 晦氣[hùi-ch'ì]: misfortune, bad luck

晚

[12] 晚報[wăn-pào]: evening newspaper

[13] 晚會[wăn-hùi]: evening meeting, evening party or reception

— 8 Strokes —

智

[7] 智利[chìh-lì]: Chile

智利共和國[chìh-lì kùng-hó-kuó]: Republic of Chile

[8] 智取威虎山[chìh-ch'ŭ wēi-hŭ shān]: Taking the Bandits' Stronghold (a "reformed" play)

智育[chìh-yü]: culture, mental training, intellectual education

[17] 智慧[chìh-hùi]: wisdom

景

[6] 景色[chĭng-sè]: landscape, scenery, scene, skyline, picture

[10] 景氣[chĭng-ch'ì]: business conditions, market conditions, condition of affairs, boom, prosperity

[14] 景頗[chĭng-p'ō]: Ching-po (minority nationality)

[17] 景邁[chĭng-mài]: Chiengmai (Thailand)

普

[4] 普及[p'ŭ-chí]: to popularize, to universalize, to extend, to disseminate, to make widely available; popularization; universal

普及教育[p'ŭ-chí chiào-yü]: universal education, education for all

普及和提高[p'ŭ-chí hó t'í-kāo]: popularization and elevation

[7] 普那卡 [p'ŭ-nà-k'ă]: Punaka (winter capital of Bhutan)

[9] 普洛塔哥拉斯 [p'ŭ-lò-t'ă-kō-lā-ssū]: Protagoras

普洛提諾斯 [p'ŭ-lò-t'í-nò-ssū]: Plotinus

[10] 普查 [p'ŭ-ch'á]: census, enumeration, general investigation

普查詳查 [p'ŭ-ch'á hsiáng-ch'á]: general and detailed investigation

普查表 [p'ŭ-ch'á piăo]: census form, enumeration form

普通 [p'ŭ-t'ūng]: ordinary, common

普通照會 [p'ŭ-t'ūng chào-hùi]: verbal note, common notification

普通中學 [p'ŭ-t'ūng chūng-hsüéh]: general course middle school

普通話 [p'ŭ-t'ūng hùa]: the vernacular, current speech, the common language

普通人 [p'ŭ-t'ūng jén]: the average man, the ordinary man, the man in the street

普通民兵 [p'ŭ-t'ūng mín-pīng]: ordinary militiaman, ordinary militia

[12] 普遍 [p'ŭ-pièn]: universal, general, widespread, world-wide

普遍眞理 [p'ŭ-pièn chēn-lĭ]: universal truth, universally applicable truth

普遍性 [p'ŭ-pièn-hsìng]: universality

普遍意義 [p'ŭ-pièn i-i]: universal significance

普遍深入的 [p'ŭ-pièn shēn-jù te]: extensive and thoroughgoing

普遍裁軍 [p'ŭ-pièn ts'ái-chün]: universal disarmament

[16] 普選 [p'ŭ-hsüăn]: general election

普選制度 [p'ŭ-hsüăn chìh-tù]: universal franchise, universal suffrage

— 9 Strokes —

暗

[4] 暗中 [àn-chūng]: underhandedly, clandestinely

暗中支持 [àn-chūng chīh-ch'íh]: disguised support, support under cover

暗中反對 [àn-chūng făn-tùi]: veiled resistance

暗中摸索 [àn-chūng mō-sŏ]: to grope in the dark

[5] 暗示 [àn-shìh]: to hint, to hint at, to intimate; hint

[6] 暗合 [àn-hó]: unintentional agreement, agreement without prior consultation

暗地 [àn-tì]: secretly, behind the back, quietly, clandestinely

[9] 暗指 [àn-chĭh]: to allude to, to imply

[10] 暗害 [àn-hài]: to sabotage, to hurt others by secret means; sabotage

暗笑 [àn-hsiào]: to laugh up one's sleeve

暗殺 [àn-shā]: to assassinate; assassination

[11] 暗淡 [àn-tàn]: dim, gloomy, somber, dismal

[12] 暗號 [àn-hào]: signal, password, secret sign

[13] 暗想 [àn-hsiăng]: to reflect, to think to oneself

[14] 暗箭 [àn-chièn]: secret arrow, covert attack

暗算 [àn-suàn]: to plot in secret

[18] 暗藏的反革命份子 [àn-ts'áng te făn-kó-mìng fèn-tzu]: hidden counter-revolutionaries

暑

[11] 暑假 [shŭ-chià]: summer vacation

— 10 Strokes —

暢

25 暢觀樓事件[**ch'àng-kuān-lóu shìh-chièn**]: the Changkuanlou incident (refers to an alleged plot engineered by P'eng Chen in 1961 to overthrow Mao Tse-tung; so called because the plotters met at the Changkuanlou in the Peking Zoo)

— 11 Strokes —

暫

6 暫行[**chàn-hsíng**]: temporary, provisional

暫行條例[**chàn-hsíng t'iáo-lì**]: provisional regulation, provisional measure

暫存的[**chàn-ts'ún te**]: transitory, transient, impermanent, ephemeral

8 暫定議程[**chàn-tìng ì-ch'éng**]: tentative agenda

10 暫時[**chàn-shíh**]: temporary, transient, provisional; for the present, for the time being

暫時利益服從長遠利益[**chàn-shíh lì-ì fú-ts'úng ch'áng-yüǎn lì-ì**]: to subordinate temporary interests to long-range interests

暫時的局部的缺點 [**chàn-shíh te chǘ-pù te ch'üēh-tiěn**]: transient and local shortcomings

暫時因素[**chàn-shíh yīn-sù**]: transient factor, temporary factor

11 暫停[**chàn-t'íng**]: stop-over, temporary halt, temporary cessation, temporary suspension, lull, pause; to pause

暮

10 暮氣[**mù-ch'ì**]: apathetic airs; listless, spiritless, indifferent, gloomy, depressed, downcast

暴

2 暴力[**pào-lì**]: violence, force

6 暴行[**pào-hsíng**]: savage conduct, atrocity

7 暴君[**pào-chūn**]: tyrant

暴利[**pào-lì**]: usurious profit

9 暴政[**pào-chèng**]: despotism, tyranny

10 暴徒[**pào-t'ú**]: mob, one who opposes law with force

11 暴動[**pào-tùng**]: riot, insurrection, rebellion, uprising

12 暴跌[**pào-tiéh**]: a sudden drop in prices

13 暴發戶[**pào-fā hù**]: suddenly wealthy persons, newly rich, *nouveau riche*

— 12 Strokes —

暨

9 暨南大學[**chì-nán tà-hsüéh**]: Chi Nan University (Shanghai)

曆

8 曆來[**lì-lái**]: all along, hitherto; consistent, long-continued

— 13 Strokes —

9 曖昧[**ài-mèi**]: ambiguity, obscurity; ambiguous, obscure, vague, indefinite, equivocal

— 14 Strokes —

曙

6 曙光[**shǔ-kuāng**]: dawn, dawn light, hopeful conditions

— RADICAL 曰 73 —

— 2 Strokes —

3 曲子 **[ch'ŭ-tzu]**: tune, song, musical piece, melody

7 曲折 **[ch'ū-ché]**: winding, tortuous, intricate, devious, circuitous

曲里島 **[ch'ū-lĭ-tăo]**: Honlon (Vietnam)

13 曲解 **[ch'ū-chiĕh]**: to distort, to twist, to misinterpret

14 曲綫 **[ch'ū-hsièn]**: curve, curved line, curvature

曲綫救國 **[ch'ū-hsièn chìu-kuó]**: to save the nation by a devious path

15 曲調 **[ch'ŭ-tiào]**: song tunes, melody

19 曲藝 **[ch'ŭ-ì]**: ballad singing and story telling, variety show

曳

4 曳引機 **[yèh-yĭn-chī]**: tractor

— 3 Strokes —

更 **[kèng]**: more, still

4 更不用說 **[kèng pú-yùng shuō]**: there is less need to say, to let alone, to say nothing of

5 更正 **[kēng-chèng]**: to reform, to correct, to amend, to alter, to rectify

更生 **[kēng-shēng]**: to be reborn, to be resurrected; rebirth

6 更改 **[kēng-kăi]**: to alter, to change

8 更其 **[kèng ch'í]**: all the more, even more (so)

12 更換 **[kēng-huàn]**: to replace, to substitute; replacement, removal, supercession

更替 **[kēng-t'ì]**: to exchange, to alternate, to interchange, to replace

13 更新 **[kēng-hsīn]**: to renew, to renovate, to improve, to reform, to make a fresh start

— 6 Strokes —

5 書刊 **[shū-k'ān]**: books, publications

書刊租賃處 **[shū-k'ān tsū-lìn ch'ù]**: lending library

書本知識 **[shū-pĕn chīh-shíh]**: book knowledge, bookish knowledge

9 書面 **[shū-mièn]**: in writing, in written form

書面聲明 **[shū-mièn shēng-míng]**: a written statement

書面的談判 **[shū-mièn te t'án-p'àn]**: negotiations by exchange of notes

10 書記 **[shū-chì]**: secretary, clerk

書記職位 **[shū-chì chíh-wèi]**: secretaryship

書記處 **[shū-chì-ch'ù]**: secretariat

書記掛帥，層層負責 **[shū-chì kuà-shuài, ts'éng-ts'éng fù-tsé]**: the Party secretary takes the lead, at each and every level someone must be in charge

— 7 Strokes —

曼

5 曼尼 **[màn-ní]**: Mani (Tibet)

7 曼谷 **[màn-kŭ]**: Bangkok (Thailand)

9 曼南 **[màn-nán]**: Mangnang (Tibet)

[10] 曼納馬 **[màn-nà-mă]** : Manamah (Bahrein)

[15] 曼徹斯特衛報 **[màn-ch'è-ssū-t'è wèi-pào]** : Manchester Guardian (British daily newspaper)

曼德禮 **[màn-té-lĭ]** : Mandalay (Burma)

曼德禮專區 **[màn-té-lĭ chuān-ch'ü]** : Mandalay Division (Burma)

— 8 Strokes —

替

[13] 替罪羊 **[t'ì-tsùi-yáng]** : scapegoat

最

[3] 最小 **[tsùi-hsiăo]** : smallest, minimum

最大 **[tsùi-tà]** : maximum, greatest

最大限度 **[tsùi-tà hsièn-tù]** : maximum or utmost limit or extent

[4] 最反動 **[tsùi făn-tùng]** : ultra-reactionary, arch-reactionary

[6] 最兇惡的敵人 **[tsùi hsiūng-ò te tí-jén]** : the most vicious enemy

[7] 最初 **[tsùi-ch'ū]** : initial, original, at the very beginning

最低 **[tsùi-tī]** : minimum

最低限度 **[tsùi-tī hsièn-tù]** : the minimum or least extent or limit

[9] 最前綫 **[tsùi ch'ién-hsièn]** : forefront

最後掙扎 **[tsùi-hòu chēng-chá]** : final struggle, death throes; to fight a last ditch battle

最後決定權 **[tsùi-hòu chüéh-tìng ch'üán]** : final say, final decision

最後目的 **[tsùi-hòu mù-tì]** : ultimate goal, ultimate objective

最後堡壘 **[tsùi-hòu păo-lĕi]** : last fortress

最後勝利 **[tsùi-hòu shèng-lì]** : final victory, ultimate triumph

最後手段 **[tsùi-hòu shŏu-tuàn]** : last resort, the last card up one's sleeve

最後通牒 **[tsùi-hòu t'ūng-tiéh]** : ultimatum

最後武器 **[tsùi-hòu wŭ-ch'ì]** : ultimate weapon

[10] 最高 **[tsùi-kāo]** : supreme, highest

最高級 **[tsùi-kāo-chí]** : highest level

最高級會議 **[tsùi-kāo-chí hùi-ì]** : summit conference

最高權力 **[tsùi-kāo ch'üán-lì]** : supreme power, highest authority

最高決策機關 **[tsùi-kāo chüéh-ts'è chī-kuān]** : highest policy making organ

最高峰 **[tsùi-kāo fēng]** : summit, peak

最高限度 **[tsùi-kāo hsièn-tù]** : maximum or peak, limit or extent

最高人民檢察署 **[tsùi-kāo jén-mín chiĕn-ch'á shŭ]** : Supreme People's Criminal Court

最高人民檢察院 **[tsùi-kāo jén-mín chiĕn-ch'á yüàn]** : Supreme People's Procuratorate

最高人民法院 **[tsùi-kāo jén-mín fă-yüàn]** : Supreme People's Court

最高人民會議 **[tsùi-kāo jén-mín hùi-ì]** : Supreme People's Assembly (Korean People's Democratic Republic)

最高國家權力機關 **[tsùi-kāo kuó-chiā ch'üán-lì chī-kuān]** : highest state authority, highest organ of state authority

最高國務會議 **[tsùi-kāo kuó-wù hùi-ì]** : Supreme State Conference

最高流量 **[tsùi-kāo líu-liàng]** : peak flow, crest flow

最高司法會議 **[tsùi-kāo ssū-fă hùi-ì]** : Supreme Council of Justice

最高蘇維埃[**tsùi-kāo sū-wéi-āi**]: Supreme Soviet (U.S.S.R.)

最高點[**tsùi-kāo tiĕn**]: peak, zenith, highest point

11 最崇高的模範[**tsùi ch'úng-kāo te mó-fàn**]: the most exalted model (i.e., Mao Tse-tung)

12 最終[**tsùi-chūng**]: final, ultimate

最喜愛的[**tsùi hsĭ-ài te**]: most favorite

最惠國待遇[**tsùi hùi-kuó tài-yǜ**]: most-favored-nation treatment

15 最廣泛的民主 [**tsùi kuăng-fàn te mín-chŭ**]: democracy in the widest sense

最廣大的人民 [**tsùi kuăng-tà te jén-mín**]: the broadest masses of the people

— 9 Strokes —

4 會心[**hùi-hsīn**]: to understand, to understand the meaning

6 會合[**hùi-hó**]: to gather, to collect, to meet

會考[**hùi-k'ăo**]: examination (particularly in imperial China)

會同[**hùi-t'úng**]: to act in concert; joint action; in conjunction with, jointly

9 會春[**hùi-ch'ūn**]: Hoixuan (Vietnam)

會客[**hùi-k'ò**]: to receive a guest

會客室[**hùi-k'ò-shìh**]: reception room, reception hall

會計[**k'uài-chì**]: bookkeeping, record keeping

會計檢查院[**k'uài-chì chiĕn-ch'á yüàn**]: Board of Audit

會計年度[**k'uài-chì nién-tù**]: fiscal year

會計師[**k'uài-chì shīh**]: accountant, bookkeeper

會計員[**k'uài-chì yüán**]: accountant, bookkeeper

10 會師[**hùi-shīh**]: to join forces, to muster troops, to mobilize

會員[**hùi-yüán**]: member of a society or association

11 會商[**hùi-shāng**]: to consult, to consult together

會通 [**hùi-t'ūng**]: to understand thoroughly, to be versed in

12 會場 [**hùi-ch'ăng**]: meeting place, meeting room

會集[**hùi-chí**]: to gather, to collect

會費[**hùi-fèi**]: membership dues, dues of a society or association

13 會意[**hùi-ì**]: to understand the implications, to take a hint

會道門 [**hùi-tào-mén**]: religious sect

14 會聚[**hùi-chǜ**]: to assemble, to bring together, to gather together; convergence

會演[**hùi-yĕn**]: festival

15 會審[**hùi-shĕn**]: to interrogate; joint interrogation, joint investigation

會談[**hùi-t'án**]: negotiation, talks, conversation, discussion, parley, conference, meeting

20 會議[**hùi-ì**]: meeting, convention, conference, parley, council, congress

— RADICAL 月 74 —

月

5 月刊 [**yüèh-k'ān**] : monthly, monthly periodical

月台 [**yüèh-t'ái**] : platform

9 月計表 [**yüèh-chì piăo**] : monthly statement

11 月球 [**yüèh-ch'íu**] : the moon; lunar

月球火箭 [**yüèh-ch'íu huŏ-chièn**] : Lunik; moon rocket

— 2 Strokes —

有

2 有力 [**yŭ-lì**] : powerful, potent, vigorous, mighty, energetic, forceful

3 有才能 [**yŭ ts'ái-néng**] : talented, gifted, capable, able, proficient

4 有仇 [**yŭ-ch'óu**] : to be enemies, to have a grudge, to be on bad terms with; hostility, rancor; hostile

有反必肅，有錯必糾 [**yŭ făn pì sù, yŭ ts'ò pì chīu**] : counter-revolutionaries must be suppressed whenever they are found; mistakes must be corrected whenever they are discovered

5 有正義感 [**yŭ chèng-ì kăn**] : having a righteous feeling

有出息的 [**yŭ ch'ū-hsí te**] : promising

有功 [**yŭ-kūng**] : to perform meritorious service, to render distinguished service, meritorious service, distinguished service; meritorious

有目的地 [**yŭ mù-tì tì**] : purposefully, with intent; to have a destination

有生氣 [**yŭ shēng-ch'ì**] : vitality, vigor; vigorous

有生力量 [**yŭ-shēng lì-liàng**] : effective strength

有失身分 [**yŭ shīh shēn-fèn**] : beneath one's dignity

有失無得 [**yŭ shīh wú té**] : no gain but only loss

有史以來 [**yŭ shĭh ĭ-lái**] : since the beginning of history

6 有名 [**yŭ-míng**] : famous, well-known, celebrated, eminent, prominent

有名人物 [**yŭ-míng jén-wù**] : celebrity, famous personage

有名無實 [**yŭ-míng wú-shíh**] : nominal, titular, symbolic, ceremonial, to be a figurehead

有色金屬 [**yŭ-sè chīn-shŭ**] : non-ferrous metals, non-ferrous

有色金屬工業 [**yŭ-sè chīn-shŭ kūng-yèh**] : non-ferrous industry

有色冶金 [**yŭ-sè yĕh-chīn**] : non-ferrous metallurgy

有自由 [**yŭ tzù-yú**] : to have freedom, to be at liberty to, to have a free hand in

7 有成績 [**yŭ ch'éng-chī**] : to achieve, to get credit for achievement or result, to be credited with an achievement or a result

有志氣的 [**yŭ chìh-ch'ì te**] : having noble aspirations

有助於 [**yŭ-chù yü**] : helpful to, beneficial to

有希望 [**yŭ hsī-wàng**] : hopeful, promising, favorable, auspicious, propitious

有系統的 [**yŭ hsì-t'ŭng te**] : systematic

有利形勢 [**yŭ-lì hsíng-shìh**] : favorable situation

有利可圖 [**yŭ lì k'ŏ-t'ú**] : there is profit to

be derived, there is something in it

有利條件 **[yŭ-lì t'iáo-chièn]**: favorable or advantageous condition

有利因素 **[yŭ-lì yīn-sù]**: favorable factor

有利於 **[yŭ-lì yű]**: beneficial to, advantageous to, favorable to

有利於國計民生 **[yŭ-lì yű kuó-chì mín-shēng]**: beneficial to national welfare and the people's livelihood

有步驟地 **[yŭ pù-tsòu tì]**: methodically, step by step

8 有知識的 **[yŭ chīh-shíh te]**: intellectual, learned, well-read, erudite, well-educated

有事和群衆商量 **[yŭ-shìh hó ch'ǘn-chùng shāng-liáng]**: to consult the masses whenever problems arise

有所不爲而後可以有爲 **[yŭ sŏ pù-wéi érh hòu k'ŏ-ĭ yŭ wéi]**: you must be able to refrain from doing some things in order to be able to do others; you must be able to restrain yourself in order to accomplish

有的放矢 **[yŭ-tì fàng-shĭh]**: to shoot an arrow at a target; purposive; with a definite object in view

有毒的 **[yŭ-tú te]**: poisonous, venomous

9 有計劃地 **[yŭ chì-huà tì]**: in a planned way, according to plan

有紀律的 **[yŭ chì-lǜ te]**: disciplined, orderly

有神論 **[yŭ-shén-lùn]**: theism

有待 **[yŭ-tài]**: to have still to, to have yet to, to remain to be seen

有待於 **[yŭ-tài yű]**: to be dependent on, to be contingent on

有則改之，無則加勉 **[yŭ tsé kăi chīh, wú tsé chiā miĕn]**: to correct mistakes if you have made them and avoid them if you have not

有約束性的 **[yŭ yüēh-shù-hsìng te]**: binding, obligatory

10 有記載的歷史 **[yŭ chì-tsăi te lì-shĭh]**: recorded history

有害的 **[yŭ-hài te]**: harmful, detrimental, injurious, deleterious, destructive

有效 **[yŭ-hsiào]**: effective, efficient, efficacious, valid, effectual

有益於 **[yŭ-ì yű]**: helpful, beneficial, useful, advantageous to

有時 **[yŭ-shíh]**: sometimes, at times, occasionally, now and then, from time to time

11 有產階級 **[yŭ-ch'ăn chiēh-chí]**: the capitalist class, the propertied class, the bourgeoisie

有理，有利，有節 **[yŭ-lĭ, yŭ-lì, yŭ-chiéh]**: with reason, with advantage, and with restraint

有理由 **[yŭ lĭ-yú]**: reasonable, justifiable, rational, justified; there is good reason for

有條件的 **[yŭ t'iáo-chièn te]**: conditional, conditioned, qualified, contingent on

有條不紊 **[yŭ-t'iáo pú-wèn]**: systematic, methodical, with regularity and thoroughness

有組織地 **[yŭ tsŭ-chīh tì]**: in an organized way

有眼光 **[yŭ yĕn-kuāng]**: far-seeing, far-sighted, with insight into

12 有期徒刑 **[yŭ-ch'í t'ú-hsíng]**: a definite term of penal servitude, a fixed prison term (i.e., a prison term other than life imprisonment)

13 有準備 **[yŭ chŭn-pèi]**: prepared, with preparations made

有意 **[yŭ-ì]**: intentional, intended, deliberate, by design, knowingly; to have a mind to

有意義的 **[yŭ ì-ì te]**: significant, meaningful

有意識 **[yŭ ì-shìh]**: consciously

有勢力的[yŭ shìh-lì te]: influential, potent, powerful

有資格的[yŭ tzū-kó te]: qualified, competent, eligible, entitled

14 有綫廣播[yŭ-hsièn kuăng-pō]: wire broadcasting

有綫電話[yŭ-hsièn tièn-huà]: wire telephone

有綫電報[yŭ-hsièn tièn-pào]: wire telegraph, wire telegraphy

有領導的[yŭ lĭng-tăo te]: guided, with leadership

有實際意義的創舉[yŭ shíh-chì ì-ì te ch'uàng-chŭ]: practical initiation

有罪[yŭ-tsùi]: to be guilty, at fault, deserving blame, reprehensible

有團結有鬥爭，以鬥爭求團結[yŭ t'uán-chiéh yŭ tòu-chēng, ĭ tòu-chēng ch'íu t'uán-chiéh]: unity, struggle, and unity through struggle

15 有價值的[yŭ-chià-chíh te]: worthwhile, valuable

有影響[yŭ yĭng-hsiăng]: influential, to have an influence on

16 有機肥料[yŭ-chī féi-liào]: organic fertilizer, manure

有機合成化學[yŭ-chī hó-ch'éng huà-hsüéh]: organic synthetic chemistry

有機化學[yŭ-chī huà-hsüéh]: organic chemistry

有機化學研究所[yŭ-chī huà-hsüéh yén-chìu-sŏ]: Organic Chemistry Institute

有機物[yŭ-chī wù]: organic matter

有賴於[yŭ-lài yü]: to depend on, to rely on, to be contingent on

有辦法[yŭ pàn-fă]: to be able to manage; resourceful, ingenious, inventive, skillful, adroit, proficient, efficient, competent

17 有點過分[yŭ-tiĕn kuò-fèn]: a bit too much, a little overdone, slightly excessive

18 有職無權[yŭ-chíh wú-ch'üán]: to hold a position without the authority that goes with it, to have a nominal position

有職有權[yŭ-chíh yŭ-ch'üán]: to exercise the functions and powers that go with a post, to have an office and the authority that goes with it

有關[yŭ-kuān]: concerned, interested, related, pertinent to, affiliated

— 4 Strokes —

服

2 服人[fú-jén]: to submit to another, to cause one to submit

5 服用[fú-yùng]: to take (medicine)

6 服刑[fú-hsíng]: to serve a sentence

7 服兵役[fú pīng-ì]: to do military service, to serve in the army

8 服侍[fú-shìh]: to serve, to wait on

10 服務[fú-wù]: to serve, to render service, to do one's duty; service

服務站[fú-wù chàn]: public service station

服務性行業[fú-wù-hsìng háng-yèh]: service trades

服務員[fú-wù-yüán]: attendant, waiter, steward

11 服氣[fú-ch'ì]: to admit defeat, to see the point, to be convinced

服從[fú-ts'úng]: to obey, to submit, to comply with, to defer to; obedience, submission; obedient, submissive

16 服輸[fú-shū]: to admit defeat

19 服藥[fú-yào]: to take medicine, to take medication

— 7 Strokes —

望

9 望風 [wàng-fēng] : looking for fame, looking for reputation, ambitious

望風披靡[wàng-fēng p'ī-mí] : to flee in disorder

14 望遠鏡和顯微鏡 [wàng-yüăn-chìng hó hsiĕn-wēi-chìng] : telescope and microscope (during the Cultural Revolution, similes for the "thought of Mao Tse-tung")

— 8 Strokes —

朝

3 朝三暮四[chāo-sān mù-ssù] : caprice; capricious, changeable, fickle, opportunist

4 朝日新聞[chāo-jìh hsīn-wén] : Asahi Shimbun (Japanese daily newspaper)

5 朝代 [ch'áo-tài] : dynasty

10 朝氣[chāo-ch'ì] : vigor, animation, vitality, life

朝氣蓬勃 [chāo-ch'ì p'éng-pó] : full of vigor and vitality, teeming with life and vitality

17 朝鮮 [ch'áo-hsiēn] : Korea

朝鮮軍事停戰委員會 [ch'áo-hsiēn chūn-shìh t'íng-chàn wĕi-yüán-hùi] : Korean Military Armistice Committee

朝鮮民主主義人民共和國 [ch'áo-hsiēn mín-chŭ chŭ-ì jén-mín kùng-hó-kuó] : The Democratic People's Republic of Korea

朝鮮民主主義人民共和國最高人民會議 [ch'áo-hsiēn mín-chŭ chŭ-ì jén-mín kùng-hó-kuó tsùi-kāo jén-mín hùi-ì] : Supreme People's Assembly of the Korean Democratic People's Republic

朝鮮停戰協定 [ch'áo-hsiēn t'íng-chàn hsiéh-tìng] : Korean Military Armistice Agreement (July 27, 1953)

期

期 [chī] : a year, a full year

期 [ch'í] : an issue, a number (i.e., of a periodical); a period, a date, a period of time, a limit of time; one hundred years

9 期待 [ch'í-tài] : to expect

11 期貨 [ch'í-huò] : forwards, futures; dealing in futures

期貨市場[ch'í-huò shìh-ch'ăng] : option market

期滿 [ch'í-măn] : to expire, to run out; expiration

期票 [ch'í-p'iào] : promissory note

期望 [ch'í-wàng] : to hope, to look forward to

期間 [ch'í-chiēn] : period, term, time, course

— RADICAL 木 75 —

7 木材 **[mù-ts′ái]**: lumber, timber, wood

木材加工工業 **[mù-ts′ái chiā-kūng kūng-yèh]**: wood-working industry, lumber industry

木材工業 **[mù-ts′ái kūng-yèh]**: lumber industry, timber industry

9 木星 **[mù-hsīng]**: Jupiter

木炭 **[mù-t′àn]**: charcoal

木偶戲 **[mù-ŏu hsì]**: puppet show, puppet play

15 木廠 **[mù-ch′ăng]**: lumber yard, timber mill

— 1 Stroke —

13 札幌 **[chá-huăng]**: Sapporo (Japan)

末

4 末日可數 **[mò-jìh k′ŏ-shŭ]**: one's days are numbered

12 末期 **[mò-ch′í]**: last stage, final stage, closing stage, ultimate stage

15 末節 **[mò-chiéh]**: fine details, insignificant details

未

5 未加工的 **[wèi chiā-kūng te]**: crude, raw, unfinished, in a rough state

未必有的 **[wèi pì-yŭ te]**: improbable, doubtful, not necessarily true

未用去的 **[wèi yùng-ch′ǜ te]**: unspent, unused

7 未成熟的 **[wèi ch′éng-shóu te]**: premature, inopportune, unripe, raw, immature

8 未來 **[wèi-lái]**: the future; forthcoming, coming, future, upcoming

未來主義 **[wèi-lái chŭ-ì]**: future-ism, Marinetti-ism

11 未被證實的消息 **[wèi pèi-chèng-shíh te hsīao-hsí]**: unconfirmed news or report

12 未發表姓名的 **[wèi fā-piăo hsìng-míng te]**: unnamed, unidentified

未開發的 **[wèi k′āi-fā te]**: underdeveloped

19 未證明身分的 **[wèi chèng-míng shēn-fèn te]**: unidentified

本

3 本年 **[pĕn-nién]**: the present year, the current year

本年度支出 **[pĕn nién-tù chīh-ch′ū]**: current annual expenditure

本年度收入 **[pĕn nién-tù shōu-jù]**: current annual revenue

本土 **[pĕn-t′ŭ]**: native, proper

4 本分 **[pĕn-fèn]**: a person's duty or obligations

本文 **[pĕn-wén]**: original text

5 本古里昂 **[pĕn-kŭ-lĭ-áng]**: Ben-Gurion, David (Israeli statesman)

本末 **[pĕn-mò]**: first and last, essential and non-essential, beginning and end; an event in its entirety

本本主義 **[pĕn-pĕn chŭ-ì]**: bookism

6 本州 **[pĕn-chōu]**: Honshu (Japan)

本色 **[pĕn-sè]**: natural color, basic color

本地 **[pĕn-tì]**: local, native

本地幹部[pĕn-tì kàn-pù]: local cadres

本有觀念[pĕn-yŭ kuān-nièn]: innate ideas

7 本利[pĕn-lì]: principal and interest or profit

本身[pĕn-shēn]: per se, in itself

本身具有[pĕn-shēn chǜ-yŭ]: to possess in itself

本身包含[pĕn-shēn pāo-hán]: to contain in itself

本位主義[pĕn-wèi chŭ-ì]: departmentalism, particularism, group egoism (i.e., to consider one's own unit more important than other units or to place departmental interests over higher interests)

8 本金[pĕn-chīn]: capital, invested capital

本性[pĕn-hsìng]: innate nature, nature, essence, character, natural inclination

本來[pĕn-lái]: originally; the fact (is), as a matter of fact

本來面目[pĕn-lái mièn-mù]: one's true colors, what one is

9 本科[pĕn-k'ō]: undergraduate course

10 本息[pĕn-hsī]: principal and interest

本能[pĕn-néng]: instinct, instinctive capacity

12 本着[pĕn-che]: according to, in line with

本着…的精神[pĕn-che ... te chīng-shén]: in the spirit of . . .

13 本義[pĕn-ì]: original meaning, basic meaning, literal sense

本意[pĕn-ì]: original idea, actual intention, initial idea

本當[pĕn-tāng]: should, ought to

本源[pĕn-yüán]: cause, origin, source

14 本領[pĕn-lĭng]: ability, proficiency, skill, flair

15 本質[pĕn-chìh]: essence, substance; essential

本質上[pĕn-chìh-shàng]: by nature, in essence, substantially

16 本錢[pĕn-ch'ién]: capital, assets, principal

23 本體[pĕn-t'ĭ]: noumenon, the thing-in-itself

本體論[pĕn-t'ĭ-lùn]: ontology; ontological

— 2 Strokes —

朱

16 朱篤[chū-tŭ]: Chaudoc (Vietnam)

— 3 Strokes —

李

8 李承晚[lĭ ch'éng-wăn]: Rhee, Syngman (Korean statesman)

12 李普門[lĭ-p'ŭ-mén]: Lippmann, Walter (American journalist)

束

4 束手[shù-shŏu]: to tie one's hands (figuratively)

束手束脚[shù-shŏu shù-chiăo]: undue caution, overcautiousness

16 束縛[shù-fù]: to bind, to tie; yoke, shackles, chains, fetters, restraint, bondage

束縛性的[shù-fù-hsìng te]: binding, restraining, restricting, constraining, confining

材

10 材料[ts'ái-liào]: materials, stuff

材料部[ts'ái-liào pù]: Ministry of Materials

村

村 [ts'ūn] : rural village

8 村長 [ts'ūn-chăng] : village headman

杜

5 杜布曼 [tù-pù-mán] : Tubman, William (Liberian lawyer and statesman)

8 杜林 [tù-lín] : Dühring, Eugen (1833–1921)

12 杜絕 [tù-chüéh] : to put an end to, to put a stop to

杜開姆 [tù-k'āi-mŭ] : Durkheim, Emile (1838–1917)

14 杜爾 [tù-ĕrh] : Touré, Sékou (Guinean trade unionist and statesman)

15 杜撰 [tù-chuàn] : to trump up, to fabricate

杜撰的 [tù-chuàn te] : fabricated, invented, trumped up, fictitious

杜魯門 [tù-lŭ-mén] : Truman, Harry

杜魯門主義 [tù-lŭ-mén chŭ-ì] : Trumanism, Truman Doctrine

— 4 Strokes —

枕

4 枕戈待旦 [chĕn-kō tài-tàn] : in fighting trim, in battle array, ready for battle

枕木 [chĕn-mù] : railway tie

枝

15 枝節問題 [chīh-chiéh wèn-t'í] : a minor problem

杭

杭 [háng] : Hangchow (abbreviation of 杭州)

果

7 果決 [kuŏ-chüéh] : to resolve, to decide with determination; determination

12 果然 [kuŏ-ján] : indeed, true enough, as was expected, as it turned out

果敢 [kuŏ-kăn] : intrepid, undaunted, determined and bold, stout-hearted

14 果實 [kuŏ-shíh] : fruit

18 果斷 [kuŏ-tuàn] : decided, firmly determined; determination

果斷的人 [kuŏ-tuàn te jén] : man of determined character, man of decision

林

4 林木 [lín-mù] : forest, wood, grove of trees

13 林業 [lín-yèh] : forestry

林業部 [lín-yèh pù] : Ministry of Forestry

林業土壤研究所 [lín-yèh t'ŭ-jăng yén-chiù-sŏ] : Forestry and Pedology Institute

板

8 板門店 [păn-mén-tièn] : Panmunjon (Korea)

12 板報 [păn-pào] : wall newspaper

14 板滯 [păn-chìh] : stagnant, uninventive, formal

杯

4 杯水主義 **[pēi-shŭi chŭ-ì]** : free love (literally, cup-of-water-ism)

松

4 松巴 **[sūng-pā]** : Zomba (Malawi)

松巴哇 **[sūng-pā-wā]** : Sumbawa (Indonesia)

8 松花江 **[sūng-hūa chiāng]** : Sungari River (Manchuria)

東

3 東山再起 **[tūng-shān tsài-ch'ĭ]** : to stage a comeback

4 東化 **[tūng-huà]** : Donghoa (Vietnam)

5 東正教會 **[tūng-chèng chiào-hùi]** : Greek Orthodox Church

東半球 **[tūng pàn-ch'íu]** : Eastern Hemisphere

8 東京 **[tūng-chīng]** : Tokyo (Japan)

東京灣 **[tūng-chīng wān]** : 1. Tokyo Bay; 2. Tonkin Gulf

東波 **[tūng-pō]** : Tuksum (Tibet)

9 東春 **[tūng-ch'ūn]** : Dongxuan (Vietnam)

東風壓倒西風 **[tūng-fēng yā-tăo hsī-fēng]** : "the East wind prevails over the West wind" (i.e., the forces of socialism prevail over the forces of imperialism; originally a remark by Lin Tai-yü in the Dream of the Red Chamber, quoted by Mao in a talk to Chinese students in Moscow on November 17, 1957)

東南亞 **[tūng-nán-yà]** : Southeast Asia

東南亞集體防務條約 **[tūng-nán-yà chí-t'ĭ fáng-wù t'iáo-yüēh]** : Southeast Asia Collective Defense Treaty

東南亞集體防務條約組織 **[tūng-nán-yà chí-t'ĭ fáng-wù t'iáo-yüēh tsŭ-chīh]** : Southeast Asia Collective Defense Treaty Organization (SEATO)

東南亞條約組織 **[tūng-nán-yà t'iáo-yüēh tsŭ-chīh]** : Southeast Asia Treaty Organization (SEATO)

12 東鄉族 **[tūng-hsiāng tsú]** : Tunghsiang (a minority nationality in Kansu)

13 東會 **[tūng-hùi]** : Donghoi (Vietnam)

15 東潮 **[tūng-ch'áo]** : Dongtrieu (Vietnam)

枉

12 枉費心機 **[wăng-fèi hsīn-chī]** : to waste one's efforts; fruitless efforts

— 5 Strokes —

3 查三問四 **[ch'á-sān wèn-ssù]** : to investigate thoroughly

7 查希爾 **[ch'á-hsī-ĕrh]** : Mohammed, Zahir Shah (King of Afghanistan)

查抄 **[ch'á-ch'āo]** : to confiscate

8 查明 **[ch'á-míng]** : to examine, to search into, to clarify by investigation

查定 **[ch'á-tìng]** : to determine by investigation

查夜 **[ch'á-yèh]** : to stand night watch

9 查封 **[ch'á-fēng]** : to confiscate, to take into custody, to sequester; confiscation

10 查案 **[ch'á-àn]** : to examine a case

75

查核[ch'á-hó]: to determine, to test, to investigate

查根問底[ch'á-kēn wèn-tǐ]: to investigate thoroughly

查哨[ch'á-shào]: to make a round of guard posts; a patrol

11 查問[ch'á-wèn]: to investigate, to make inquiries, to inquire, to gather information; examination

14 查對[ch'á-tùi]: to check

15 查賬[ch'á-chàng]: to audit the accounts

16 查辦[ch'á-pàn]: to examine into and deal with accordingly

查點[ch'á-tiěn]: to check things against a list, to make inventory

23 查驗[ch'á-yèn]: to test, to verify

柴

8 柴油[ch'ái-yú]: diesel oil, unrefined oil

柴油機[ch'ái-yú chī]: diesel motor, diesel engine

架

3 架工[chià-kūng]: metal construction worker

架子[chià-tzu]: frame, stand, scaffold, haughty behavior

6 架次[chià-tz'ù]: flight number, serial order, sortie

8 架空[chià-k'ūng]: hovering in the air, unrealistic

16 架橋[chià-ch'iáo]: to build a bridge

枷

18 枷鎖[chiā-sǒ]: yoke, shackle, cangue, fetters, chains, irons

柬

10 柬埔寨[chiěn-pǔ-chài]: Cambodia

柬埔寨王國[chiěn-pǔ-chài wáng-kuó]: Kingdom of Cambodia

染

6 染色[jǎn-sè]: to dye; dye

9 染指[jǎn-chǐh]: to dye the fingers, to have a finger in the pie, to come in for a share, to get one's cut, to receive bribes

10 染料[jǎn-liào]: dye, dyestuffs

7 柔佛[jóu-fó]: Johore (Malaya)

12 柔順[jóu-shùn]: complaisance, affability; meek, submissive, pliant, agreeable, yielding

柯

6 柯西金[k'ō-hsī-chīn]: Kosygin, Alexei Nikolaevich (Russian statesman)

10 柯倫[k'ō-lún]: Cologne

14 柯爾克斯[k'ō-ěrh-k'ò-ssū]: Kirghiz (minority nationality)

柯爾克孜[k'ō-ěrh-k'ò-tzū]: Kirghiz

柯爾克滋[k'o-erh-k'o-tzū]: Kirghiz

某

7 某些[mǒu-hsiēh]: certain, some, a few, a number of, an amount of

柄

9 柄政[pǐng-chèng]: to have governing authority, to hold political power

柏

[7] 柏克利[pó-k'ò-lì]: Berkeley (proper name)

[8] 柏林[pó-lín]: Berlin

柏林晨報[pó-lín ch'én-pào]: Berliner Morgenpost (a West German daily newspaper)

柏林日報 [pó-lín jìh-pào]: Berliner Zeitung (an East German daily newspaper)

柏油[păi-yú]; also pron. [pó-yú]: asphalt, pitch

[10] 柏格森[pó-kó-sēn]: Bergson, Henri

[11] 柏第耶夫[pó-tì-yēh-fū]: Berdaiev, Nikolai

栃

[4] 栃木[tochi-mù]: Tochigi (Japan) (*Note:* the first character in this compound is a Japanese invention and does not occur in Chinese)

柞

[24] 柞蠶[tsò-ts'án]: tussah (i.e., a kind of Asiatic silkworm)

柞蠶絲[tsò-ts'án ssū]: tussah, tussah silk, wild silk

— 6 Strokes —

案

[3] 案子[àn-tzu]: a case at law; a table

[6] 案件[àn-chièn]: a case, a trial

[11] 案情[àn-ch'íng]: the facts of a case

案卷[àn-chüăn]: records of a case, files, archives, official documents

校

[5] 校正[chiào-chèng]: to revise

[9] 校訂[chiào-tìng]: to collate, to edit

[11] 校勘[chiào-k'ān]: to collate, to edit

[12] 校量[chiào-liàng]: to compare

[13] 校園[hsiào-yüán]: campus, school compound

[14] 校對[chiào-tùi]: to proof read, to check and correct; proof-reading, checking

桎

[11] 桎梏[chìh-kù]: shackles, fetters, yoke

核

[3] 核子[hó-tzŭ]: nucleus, atomic nucleus

核子輻射[hó-tzŭ fú-shè]: nuclear radiation

核子化學[hó-tzŭ huà-hsüéh]: nuclear chemistry

核子物理學[hó-tzŭ wù-lĭ-hsüéh]: nuclear physics

[4] 核反應[hó făn-yìng]: nuclear reaction

核反應堆[hó făn-yìng tūi]: nuclear reactor

核分裂[hó fēn-lièh]: nuclear fission

核心[hó-hsīn]: core, nucleus, center, heart, focus, kernel

核心小組[hó-hsīn hsiăo-tsŭ]: central team (a revolutionary governing group in Shansi in January 1967)

[8] 核定資金[hó-tìng tzū-chīn]: fixed capital

[9] 核武器 [hó wŭ-ch'ì]: nuclear weapon

[10] 核能 [hó-néng]: nuclear energy

核原料[hó yüán-liào]: nuclear raw material

11 核連鎖反應[hó lién-sŏ făn-yìng]: nuclear chain reaction

12 核裂產物[hó-lièh ch'ăn-wù]: nuclear fission product

14 核實[hó-shíh]: to verify; verification

核算[hó-suàn]: to audit, to check over

核算制度[hó-suàn chìh-tù]: computation system, auditing system

核對[hó-tùi]: to check, to go over, to confirm

15 核彈頭[hó tàn-t'óu]: nuclear warhead, nuclear charge

16 核戰鬥[hó chàn-tòu]: nuclear warfare

核燃料[hó ján-liào]: nuclear fuel

根

5 根本[kēn-pĕn]: fundamental, essential, ultimate

根本性質的變化[kēn-pĕn hsìng-chíh te pièn-huà]: a change of fundamental character, fundamental change, basic change

根本不[kēn-pĕn pù]: basically not, fundamentally not

8 根治水患[kēn-chìh shŭi-huàn]: permanent flood control

9 根底[kēn-tĭ]: foundation

10 根除[kēn-ch'ú]: to root out, to weed out, to uproot, to sweep away, to eradicate

12 根絕[kēn-chüéh]: to root out thoroughly

13 根源[kēn-yüán]: origin, source, starting point

16 根據[kēn-chǜ]: according to, in accordance with, in the terms of

根據地[kēn-chǜ tì]: base (military)

格

5 格外[kó-wài]: exceptional, unusual, extraordinary; all the more

格外分明[kó-wài fēn-míng]: crystal clear, exceptionally clear

7 格式[kó-shìh]: form

格言[kó-yén]: maxim, saying, adage

8 格拉斯哥[kó-lā-ssū-kō]: Glasgow (Scotland)

格林蘭[kó-lín-lán]: Greenland

格林維支[kó-lín-wéi-chīh]: Greenwich

10 格格不入[kó-kó pú-jù]: repulsive, contrary, incongruous, alien to

格朗[kó-lăng]: Ko-lang (minority nationality)

格殺打撲[kó-shā-tă-p'ū]: Gestapo

11 格陵蘭[kó-líng-lán]: Greenland

19 格羅米科[kó-ló-mĭ-k'ō]: Gromyko, Andrei (Russian diplomat)

格羅斯忒[kó-ló-ssū-t'è]: Gloucester

格羅提渥[kó-ló-t'í-wò]: Grotewohl, Otto (East German political leader)

21 格蘭姆[kó-lán-mŭ]: gram

框

10 框框[k'uàng-k'uang]: frame, restriction, rut, standards, "shackles"

桂

桂[kuèi]: 1. Kwangsi (abbreviation for 廣西); 2. Kweilin (abbreviation of 桂林)

3 桂山[kuèi-shān]: Queson (Vietnam)

7 桂系[kuèi-hsì]: Kwangsi Clique

12 桑給巴爾[sāng-chĭ-pā-ěrh]: Zanzibar

桃

13 桃園經驗[t'áo-yüán chīng-yèn]: Peach Garden Experience (a work by Wang Kuang-mei (Mme. Liu Shao-ch'i) suggesting that lower level cadres should go through a cleansing process)

栽

11 栽培[tsāi-p'éi]: to cultivate, to foster, to tend

— 7 Strokes —

梵

4 梵文[fàn-wén]: Sanskrit

13 梵蒂岡[fàn-tì-kāng]: Vatican

梵蒂岡教廷[fàn-tì-kāng chiào-t'íng]: Papal State of the Vatican

桿

12 桿菌[kăn-chŭn]: bacterium

梗

16 梗概[kĕng-kài]: outline, in outline, on the whole, generally speaking

梅

8 梅林[méi-lín]: Mehring, Franz (1846–1919)

梯

5 梯田[t'ī-t'ién]: terraced field

條

條[t'iáo]: item, clause, section, branch, twig

4 條文[t'iáo-wén]: article, text

6 條件[t'iáo-chièn]: condition, term, conditional, conditioned, qualified

條件成熟[t'iáo-chièn ch'éng-shóu]: conditions are ripe

條件反射[t'iáo-chièn făn-shè]: conditioned reflex

8 條例[t'iáo-lì]: regulation, ordinance, statute

9 條約[t'iáo-yüēh]: treaty, pact

條約港[t'iáo-yüēh kăng]: treaty port

12 條款[t'iáo-k'uăn]: clause, section of a treaty or pact

— 8 Strokes —

8 棧房[chàn-fáng]: warehouse, storehouse, depot

極

2 極力[chí-lì]: with all one's strength

3 極大[chí-tà]: tremendous, enormous, huge, immense

4 極少數[chí shăo-shù]: a handful, a few, a small number

5 極目[chí-mù]: as far as the eye can see

6 極刑[chí-hsíng]: death penalty

8 極其[chí-ch'í]: very, exceedingly, extremely

極其明確[chí-ch'í míng-ch'üèh]: with striking clarity, extremely clear

極度[chí-tù]: utmost, extremely, to the highest degree

極度憤慨[chí-tù fèn-k'ăi]: extreme indignation

9 極致[chí-chìh]: the acme of achievement, the acme of perfection

極限[chí-hsièn]: farthest border, utmost limit

極星[chí-hsīng]: pole star, North star

極品[chí-p'ĭn]: best quality, highest rank

11 極圈[chí-ch'üān]: arctic circle, antarctic circle

極頂[chí-tĭng]: summit, peak

12 極量[chí-liàng]: the maximum, maximum dose, fullest measure

14 極盡[chí-chìn]: to the extreme, to the utmost

極端[chí-tuān]: extreme, utmost, to the greatest degree, extremely, ultra-

極端仇視[chí-tuān ch'óu-shìh]: extremely hostile, violently hostile

極端民主的[chí-tuān mín-chŭ te]: ultra-democratic

極端貧困[chí-tuān p'ín-k'ùn]: utmost poverty, extreme poverty

16 極機密[chí chī-mì]: extremely secret, top secret

17 極點[chí-tiĕn]: apex, zenith, climax, summit, peak, terminal point

22 極權的[chí-ch'üán te]: totalitarian, dictatorial

極權主義[chí-ch'üán chŭ-ì]: totalitarianism; totalitarian

棘

4 棘手[chí-shŏu]: to prick the hands; thorny, prickly, touchy, baffling, difficult, perplexing, distressing, troublesome

17 棘鍼[chí-chēn]: thorn, spur, spike

棄

12 棄絕[ch'ì-chüéh]: to forsake, to abandon, to desert, to renounce

17 棄嬰[ch'ì-yīng]: foundling

22 棄權[ch'ì-ch'üán]: to abstain, to abstain from voting, to relinquish, to waive; abstention

植

8 植物[chíh-wù]: vegetable, plant, flora

植物分類研究所[chíh-wù fēn-lèi yén-chìu-sŏ]: Institute of Systematic Botany

植物學[chíh-wù-hsüéh]: botany

植物保護[chíh-wù păo-hù]: plant protection

植物保護研究所[chíh-wù păo-hù yén-chìu-sŏ]: Institute of Plant Protection

植物生理研究所[chíh-wù shēng-lĭ yén-chìu-sŏ]: Institute of Plant Physiology

植物研究所[chíh-wù yén-chìu-sŏ]: Botany Institute

植物油[chíh-wù yú]: vegetable oil

16 植樹[chíh-shù]: to plant trees; forestation

棺

4 棺木[kuān-mù]: coffin

[7] 棺材[kuān-ts'ái]: coffin

棉

[5] 棉布[mién-pù]: cotton cloth, cotton textiles, cotton piece goods

[8] 棉花[mién-huā]: cotton, raw cotton

棉花研究所[mién-huā yén-chiù-sŏ]: Cotton Institute

[9] 棉姥[mién-lăo]: Mindanao (Philippines)

[10] 棉紡織廠[mién făng-chīh ch'ăng]: cotton textile mill

棉紗[mién-shā]: cotton yarn

[19] 棉織廠[mién-chīh ch'ăng]: cotton textile mill

棉織品[mién-chīh-p'ĭn]: cotton fabrics, woven cottons

森

[8] 森林經營所[sēn-lín chīng-yíng sŏ]: forestry management office

森林工業[sēn-lín kūng-yèh]: timber industry, lumber industry

— 9 Strokes —

楚

楚[ch'ŭ]: Hupeh (abbreviation for 湖北); Ch'u (minority nationality)

楔

[2] 楔入[hsiēh-jù]: to wedge, to drive a wedge between

椰

[3] 椰子[yēh-tzu]: coconut

業

[5] 業主[yèh-chŭ]: proprietor, owner

[11] 業務[yèh-wù]: profession, work, business, occupation, task, function, job; functional, operational, occupational, professional, vocational

業務部門[yèh-wù pù-mén]: operational departments

[15] 業餘[yèh-yǘ]: spare-time

業餘愛好者[yèh-yǘ ài-hào chĕ]: amateur

業餘初等學校[yèh-yǘ ch'ū-tĕng hsüéh-hsiào]: spare-time elementary school

業餘劇團[yèh-yǘ chǜ-t'uán]: amateur troup

業餘學校[yèh-yǘ hsüéh-hsiào]: spare-time school

業餘黨校[yèh-yǘ tăng-hsiào]: spare-time Party school

業餘文藝[yèh-yǘ wén-ì]: amateur literature

楡

楡[yǘ]: Shanhaikuan (abbreviation for 山海關)

— 10 Strokes —

榨

[5] 榨出[chà-ch'ū]: to extract, to wring from, to squeeze out, to press out

槍

[11] 槍桿詩[ch'iāng-kăn shīh]: gun-stock poetry (i.e., poetry composed by soldiers and carved or pasted on the stocks of their guns)

18 槍斃 **[ch'iāng-pì]**: to shoot, to execute by shooting

榕

榕 **[júng]**: Foochow (abbreviation for 福州)

榮

8 榮幸 **[júng-hsìng]**: to have the honor of; honored

21 榮譽 **[júng-yǜ]**: honor; honorary

榮譽稱號 **[júng-yǜ ch'ēng-hào]**: title of honor

榮譽軍人 **[júng-yǜ chūn-jén]**: disabled veteran, disabled ex-serviceman, disabled soldier

構

6 構成 **[kòu-ch'éng]**: to constitute, to complete

11 構陷 **[kòu-hsièn]**: to hatch plots, to implicate another

構造 **[kòu-tsào]**: to make, to produce, to shape, to build; a frame, a structure

14 構圖 **[kòu-t'ú]**: to design, to draw, to plan

榴

15 榴彈炮 **[líu-tàn p'ào]**: howitzer

榜

5 榜示 **[păng-shìh]**: to make public by means of a list, to announce, to make a public notification

14 榜樣 **[păng-yàng]**: model, pattern, example

— 11 Strokes —

概

8 概念 **[kài-nièn]**: concept, idea, conception, notion

概念化 **[kài-nièn-huà]**: to conceptualize; abstract generalization, conceptualization

概念論 **[kài-nièn-lùn]**: conceptualism

9 概括 **[kài-k'uò]**: outline, abstract, generalization

概要 **[kài-yào]**: essentials

11 概略 **[kài-lüèh]**: summary, in general, generally speaking

14 概算 **[kài-suàn]**: to estimate; general estimate, a rough estimate

15 概論 **[kài-lùn]**: generalization, outline, summary, abstract

25 概觀 **[kài-kuān]**: general idea, concept

樂

13 樂意 **[lè-ì]**: to be willing to, to be agreeable to; willingness, readiness

樂園 **[lè-yüán]**: paradise, garden of Eden, Elysium

25 樂觀 **[lè-kuān]**: optimism, optimistic

樂觀主義 **[lè-kuān chŭ-ì]**: optimism

模

6 模仿 **[mó-făng]**: to emulate, to imitate, to copy, to model after; imitation

9 模型 **[mó-hsíng]**: model, matrix, mould

13 模稜兩可的 **[mó-léng liăng-k'ŏ te]**: equivocal, ambiguous, dubious

[15] 模範 [mó-fàn]: model, example, ideal, standard, pattern

模範農場 [mó-fàn núng-ch'ăng]: model farm

模糊 [mó-hú]: vague, nebulous, obscure, indistinct, indefinite, unintelligible

標

[5] 標本 [piāo-pĕn]: specimen, sample, demonstration piece, showpiece

[7] 標兵 [piāo-pīng]: standard bearer, pacesetter, model soldier, one who sets an example

[8] 標定 [piāo-tìng]: to fix, to standardize

[9] 標竿 [piāo-kān]: beacon, semaphore

[13] 標準 [piāo-chŭn]: criterion, measure, standard

標準軌 [piāo-chŭn kuĕi]: standard gauge

[14] 標誌 [piāo-chìh]: to mark, to symbolize; symbol, mark, gauge

標榜 [piāo-păng]: to advertise, to brag about (originally, to list the names of successful candidates in the examinations)

標語 [piāo-yŭ]: slogan, notice, poster

標語牌 [piāo-yŭ p'ái]: placard, poster

[15] 標賣 [piāo-mài]: to sell at a fixed price

[17] 標點 [piāo-tiĕn]: to punctuate; punctuation

[18] 標題 [piāo-t'í]: to headline; heading, headline, caption

[19] 標簽 [piāo-ch'iēn]: label, mark

樞

[10] 樞紐 [shū-nĭu]: axis, pivot, key position, key point

樞紐工程 [shū-nĭu kūng-ch'éng]: pivotal project, multi-purpose project

樣

[3] 樣子 [yàng-tzu]: shape, form, manner, figure, feature, fashion

[5] 樣本 [yàng-pĕn]: sample, specimen copy

[6] 樣式 [yàng-shìh]: shape, form, manner, figure, feature, fashion

[8] 樣板 [yàng-păn]: model, template

樣板戲 [yàng-păn hsì]: exemplary plays (Peking operas and ballets remodelled or recommended by Chiang Ch'ing as examples of "revolutionary plays"–these plays include The White-Haired Girl, Shachiapang, Raid on the White Tiger Regiment, The Red Detachment of Women, The Red Lantern, Pinghsing Pass, and Taking the Bandit's Stronghold)

樣板田 [yàng-păn t'ién]: demonstration field (i.e., an experimental plot for the purpose of demonstrating the superiority of a new technique)

[9] 樣品 [yàng-p'ĭn]: specimen, sample

— 12 Strokes —

機

[3] 機工 [chī-kūng]: mechanical engineering; textile worker

[5] 機巧 [chī-ch'iăo]: skilful, ingenious, cunning

[6] 機匠 [chī-chiàng]: mechanic

機件 [chī-chièn]: machine part, accessory

機帆船 [chī-fān ch'uán]: motor boat, motorized junk

機米 [chī-mĭ]: polished rice

7 機車[chī-ch'ē]: locomotive

機車廠[chī-ch'ē ch'ăng]: locomotive works

機車車輛廠[chī-ch'ē ch'ē-liàng ch'ăng]: locomotive and rolling stock works

機車載重量[chī-ch'ē tsài-chùng liàng]: hauling capacity of a locomotive

機床[chī-ch'uáng]: machine tool

機床廠[chī-ch'uáng ch'ăng]: machine tool plant

機床製造業[chī-ch'uáng chìh-tsào yèh]: machine tool making industry

8 機宜[chī-í]: instruction, assignment, policy, line of action

9 機要[chī-yào]: secret, confidential

機要祕書[chī-yào mì-shū]: confidential secretary

10 機耕[chī-kēng]: machine cultivated; mechanized farming

機耕農場[chī-kēng núng-ch'ăng]: mechanized farm

機庫[chī-k'ù]: hangar

機敏[chī-mĭn]: quick, supple, skilful, clever, shrewd, ingenious

機能[chī-néng]: function, effectiveness, ability

機師[chī-shīh]: pilot, engineer

機務[chī-wù]: technical matters, mechanical matters, important affairs

11 機械[chī-hsièh]: machine, machinery; mechanical, mechanized

機械廠[chī-hsièh ch'ăng]: machinery plant

機械化[chī-hsièh-huà]: to mechanize; mechanization; mechanized

機械化耕作[chī-hsièh-huà kēng-tsò]: mechanized farming

機械耕作[chī-hsièh kēng-tsò]: mechanized cultivation, mechanized farming

機械工業[chī-hsièh kūng-yèh]: machine industry, engineering industry

機械工業部[chī-hsièh kūng-yèh pù]: Ministry of Machine Industry

機械論[chī-hsièh lùn]: mechanicalism, theory of mechanism, mechanistic theory

機械師[chī-hsièh shīh]: mechanic

機械電機研究所[chī-hsièh tièn-chī yén-chìu-sŏ]: Mechanical and Electrical Engineering Institute

機械唯物論[chī-hsièh wéi-wù lùn]: mechanistic materialism

機械五金廠[chī-hsièh wŭ-chīn ch'ăng]: machinery and metals plant

機械研究所[chī-hsièh yén-chìu-sŏ]: Machinery Institute

機率[chī-lǜ]: probability

機率論[chī-lǜ lùn]: probability theory

機密[chī-mì]: secret, confidential, in confidence

機動車[chī-tùng ch'ē]: motorized vehicle

機動性[chī-tùng-hsìng]: flexibility

機動糧[chī-tùng liáng]: flexible grain, emergency grain (i.e., grain reserves kept by local authorities at various levels)

機動靈活[chī-tùng líng-huó]: operationally flexible

機動兵力[chī-tùng pīng-lì]: striking force

機動作戰[chī-tùng tsò-chàn]: mobile warfare, mobile operations

12 機智[chī-chìh]: skilful, ingenious, clever, tactful, resourceful

13 機會[chī-hùi]: chance, opportunity, occasion, opening, break

機會主義[chī-hùi chŭ-ì]: opportunism; opportunist (adj.)

機會主義者[chī-hùi chŭ-ì-chĕ]: opportunist

機會均等 [chī-hùi chūn-těng]: equal opportunity, the principle of equal opportunity for all

14 機場 [chī-ch'ǎng]: airport, airfield

機槍 [chī-ch'iāng]: machine gun

機槍手 [chī-ch'iāng shǒu]: machine gunner

機構 [chī-kòu]: institution, machine, machinery, mechanism, structure, set-up

機構臃腫 [chī-kòu yūng-chǔng]: inflated departments, unwieldly organizations, overexpansion of organizations

機構臃腫，層次重疊 [chī-kòu yūng-chǔng, ts'éng-tz'ù ch'úng-tiéh]: unwieldly and overlapping organizations, overstaffed and divided into many overlapping levels

16 機器 [chī-ch'ì]: machine, machinery

機器廠 [chī-ch'ì ch'ǎng]: machinery plant

機器脚踏車 [chī-ch'ì chiǎo-t'à ch'ē]: motorcycle

機器製造工人 [chī-ch'ì chìh-tsào kūng-jén]: machinist, machine building worker

機器製造工業 [chī-ch'ì chìh-tsào kūng-yèh]: machine building industry, machine tool industry

機器彙總 [chī-ch'ì hùi-tsǔng]: machine data processing

機謀 [chī-móu]: tactics, trick, post

18 機關 [chī-kuān]: government office, government institution, organ, organization

機關鎗 [chī-kuān-ch'iāng]: machine gun

機關刊物 [chī-kuān k'ān-wù]: organ publication

機關報 [chī-kuān pào]: organ newspaper

20 機警 [chī-chǐng]: vigilant, alert, sharp

23 機變 [chī-pièn]: opportunism, versatility, astuteness, trick

機體 [chī-t'ǐ]: fuselage; organism

橋

11 橋梁 [ch'iáo-liáng]: bridge, girders of a bridge

橋梁作用 [ch'iáo-liáng tsò-yùng]: to serve as a link

15 橋墩 [ch'iáo-tūn]: abutment, foundation piers, pier

16 橋頭 [ch'iáo-t'óu]: approach of a bridge, approach to a bridge

橋頭堡 [ch'iáo-t'óu pǎo]: bridgehead

橫

5 橫加梗阻 [héng-chiā kěng-tsǔ]: to obstruct willfully

6 橫行 [héng-hsíng]: to be infested with, to be overrun with, to act against the law; unreasonable conduct, outrageous behavior, perversity

橫行霸道 [héng-hsíng pà-tào]: to act contrary to reason, to act in a tyrannous manner, to act violently, to lord it over, to run wild; lawlessness, gun law, gangsterism

8 橫征暴斂 [héng-chēng pào-liěn]: to extort taxes and levies

12 橫幅標語 [héng-fú piāo-yǚ]: streamer, banner

橫須賀 [héng-hsū-hò]: Yokosuka (Japan)

橫越 [héng-yüèh]: spanning, across, through, trans-; to stretch across

14 橫暴 [hèng-pào]: brutal violence; to commit atrocities; violent, rampant, savage, wild, raging, inhuman

17 橫濱 [héng-pīn]: Yokohama (Japan)

25 橫蠻 [hèng-mán]: rebellious, ruthless, stubborn, rough, barbaric

樺

[4] 樺太 **[huà-t'ài]** : Sakhalin (Japan)

樸

[10] 樸素 **[p'ú-sù]** : plain, simple, unaffected

— 13 Strokes —

檢

[8] 檢波器 **[chiĕn-pō ch'ì]** : detector

檢定 **[chiĕn-tìng]** : to authorize, to weigh; official sanction

[9] 檢查 **[chiĕn-ch'á]** : to check, to test, to inspect, to review; check-up, test, inspection, review, censorship

檢查站 **[chiĕn-ch'á chàn]** : inspection station, check point

檢查官 **[chiĕn-ch'á kuān]** : procurator, prosecutor, an inspecting official

檢修 **[chiĕn-hsīu]** : to overhaul

[14] 檢察 **[chiĕn-ch'á]** : to inspect

檢察機關 **[chiĕn-ch'á chī-kuān]** : procuratory organ, prosecution organ

檢察官 **[chiĕn-ch'á kuān]** : procurator, prosecuting attorney, public procurator

檢察員 **[chiĕn-ch'á yüán]** : procurators

[15] 檢閱 **[chiĕn-yüèh]** : to review, to inspect

[17] 檢舉 **[chiĕn-chŭ]** : to accuse, to charge, to indict

檢點 **[chiĕn-tiĕn]** : to sort, to check, to count over

[23] 檢驗 **[chiĕn-yèn]** : to examine, to inspect

檔

[10] 檔案 **[tàng-àn]** : files, documents, archives, dossier

— 18 Strokes —

權

[2] 權力 **[ch'üán-lì]** : power, authority

權力機關 **[ch'üán-lì chī-kuān]** : organs of state power

[7] 權利 **[ch'üán-lì]** : right, claim, rights and privileges

權位 **[ch'üán-wèi]** : official position

[8] 權宜 **[ch'üán-í]** : to deal with in an expedient way; expediency

權宜之計 **[ch'üán-í chīh chì]** : stop-gap measure, temporary expedient, make-shift device, expedient measure

[9] 權限 **[ch'üán-hsièn]** : limits of authority, extent of authority, jurisdiction, terms of reference

權威 **[ch'üán-wēi]** : authority

權威人士 **[ch'üán-wēi jén-shìh]** : authoritative individuals or people

— RADICAL 欠 76 —

— 2 Strokes —

4 次日**[tzʼù-jìh]**: the following day, the next day, on the second day

6 次序**[tzʼù-hsǜ]**: order, sequence

9 次品**[tzʼù-pʼǐn]**: second-rate goods, goods of inferior quality

次要**[tzʼù-yào]**: of secondary importance

11 次貨**[tzʼù-huò]**: low quality goods, inferior goods

12 次等**[tzʼù-těng]**: second rate, low grade

15 次數**[tzʼù-shù]**: frequency

— 4 Strokes —

8 欣欣向榮**[hsīn-hsīn hsiàng-júng]**: prospering, prosperous, thriving,

12 欣然同意**[hsīn-ján tʼúng-ì]**: to agree readily

— 7 Strokes —

欲

11 欲望**[yǜ-wàng]**: desire, longing, appetite

14 欲蓋彌彰**[yǜ-kài mí-chāng]**: the more (they) try to hide, the more (they) are exposed

— 8 Strokes —

10 欺神滅道**[chʼī-shén mièh-tào]**: to abuse the gods and destroy religion

11 欺軟怕强**[chʼī-juǎn pʼà-chʼiáng]**: to browbeat the weak but fear the strong, to be a bully

12 欺詐取勝**[chʼī-chà chʼǚ-shèng]**: to circumvent, to delude, to gain advantage by deception, to blackmail, to extort, to despoil

19 欺騙**[chʼī-pʼièn]**: to cheat, to deceive, to swindle, to defraud, to trick; deception, a swindle, a bluff; deceptive

欽

8 欽佩**[chʼīn-pʼèi]**: to admire, to hold in great esteem; admiration

10 欽差大臣**[chʼīn-chʼai tà-chʼén]**: imperial envoy, viceroy, special envoy

款

12 款項**[kʼuǎn-hsiàng]**: sum of money, funds

— 10 Strokes —

歌

5 歌功頌德**[kō-kūng sùng-té]**: to flatter or praise exaggeratedly

11 歌唱**[kō-chʼàng]**: to sing, to chant

13 歌頌**[kō-sùng]**: to sing praises, to eulogize, to extol

14 歌舞團**[kō-wǔ tʼuán]**: song and dance troupe, song and dance team

15 歌劇**[kō-chǜ]**: opera, operetta

— 11 Strokes —

4 歐文**[ōu-wén]**: Owen, Robert (1771–1858)

[9] 歐洲經濟共同體[ōu-chōu chīng-chì kùng-t′úng-t′ĭ]: European Economic Community

歐洲經濟聯盟 [ōu-chōu chīng-chì lién-méng]: European Economic Community

歐洲核裁軍大會[ōu-chōu hó-ts′ái-chŭn tà-hùi]: European Congress for Nuclear Disarmament

歐洲共同市場 [ōu-chōu kùng-t′úng shìh-ch′ăng]: European Common Market

歐洲聯盟[ōu-chōu lién-méng]: European Community

歐洲煤鋼聯盟 [ōu-chōu méi-kāng lién-méng]: European Coal and Steel Community (ECSC)

歐洲委員會[ōu-chōu wĕi-yüán-hùi]: Council of Europe

歐洲原子能聯盟 [ōu-chōu yüán-tzŭ-néng lién-méng]: European Atomic Energy Community (Euratom)

歐洲原子能聯營組織 [ōu-chōu yüán-tzŭ-néng lién-yíng tsŭ-chīh]: European Atomic Energy Community (Euratom)

— 18 Strokes —

歡

[8] 歡呼 [huān-hū]: to cheer, to acclaim, to give an ovation; ovation, cheer, applause

歡迎 [huān-yíng]: to welcome, to greet, to hail, to meet, to approve; welcome, greeting, approval

[10] 歡送 [huān-sùng]: to see off, to bid farewell, to send off

[12] 歡喜 [huān-hsĭ]: pleased, delighted, happy, joyful, gay

[15] 歡樂 [huān-lè]: gladness, delight, joy, happiness

— RADICAL 止 77 —

止

[7] 止住 [chĭh-chù]: to stop, to cease, to hold back

[14] 止境 [chĭh-chìng]: limit, stopping place

— 1 Stroke —

正

[6] 正名 [chèng-míng]: rectification of names; to rectify names

正式 [chèng-shìh]: formal, official

正式聲明[chèng-shìh shēng-míng]: to declare officially or formally; official statement

正式黨員[chèng-shìh tăng-yüán]: full Party member

正式委員[chèng-shìh wĕi-yüán]: full member of a committee

[8] 正直 [chèng-chíh]: fair-minded, just-minded, upright, honest

正直無私[chèng-chíh wú-ssū]: upright, impartial, just, honest

[9] 正相反[chèng hsiāng-făn]: diametrically opposite, the direct opposite

正軌 [chèng-kuĕi]: right track; regular

正軌教育[chèng-kuĕi chiào-yǜ]: regular education, proper education

正面 [chèng-mièn]: the positive side, the right side; positive, correct

正面戰場[chèng-mièn chàn-ch′ăng]: front-line battlefield

正面教育[chèng-mièn chiào-yǜ]: positive education (i.e., teaching by positive example to show desirable consequences arising from good behavior, etc.)

正面人物 **[chèng-mièn jén-wù]**: positive personality, positive character, positive people

正派 **[chèng-p'ài]**: orthodox party; orthodox

10 正氣 **[chèng-ch'ì]**: uprightness, integrity, probity, honor, rectitude

11 正常化 **[chèng-ch'áng-huà]**: to normalize, to make sound, to put on a proper foundation; normalization

正教 **[chèng-chiào]**: orthodox religion, orthodox church

12 正視 **[chèng-shìh]**: to envisage, to face squarely, to look in the face

正稅 **[chèng-shùi]**: regular tax

正統 **[chèng-t'ŭng]**: orthodox

正統馬克思主義 **[chèng-t'ŭng mă-k'ò-ssū chŭ-ì]**: Kautsky-Marxism

正統派 **[chèng-t'ŭng p'ài]**: orthodox party or faction

13 正義 **[chèng-ì]**: justice, righteousness; just, right, righteous

正義戰爭 **[chèng-ì chàn-chēng]**: just war

正義人道 **[chèng-ì jén-tào]**: justice and humanity

正義感 **[chèng-ì kăn]**: sense of righteousness, a sense of what is right

正當 **[chèng-tàng]**: proper, rightful

16 正確 **[chèng-ch'üèh]**: correct, right, accurate

正確處理人民內部矛盾 **[chèng-ch'üèh ch'ŭ-lĭ jén-mín nèi-pù máo-tùn]**: On the Correct Handling of Contradictions Among the People (Mao)

正確的退却 **[chèng-ch'üèh te t'ùi-ch'üèh]**: appropriate retreat, a retreat at the proper time

正題 **[chèng-t'í]**: thesis

— 2 Strokes —

此

5 此令 **[tz'ŭ-lìng]**: so ordered (a standard phrase for closing a government order)

此外 **[tz'ŭ-wài]**: in addition, moreover, besides, furthermore

9 此後 **[tz'ŭ-hòu]**: thereafter, hereafter, henceforth

— 3 Strokes —

步

6 步伐 **[pù-fá]**: steps, stride, pace

步行 **[pù-hsíng]**: to walk; on foot

7 步兵 **[pù-pīng]**: foot soldier, infantryman, infantry

步兵炮 **[pù-pīng p'ào]**: infantry artillery

10 步哨 **[pù-shào]**: sentry, sentinel, guard

24 步驟 **[pù-tsòu]**: steps, procedure, measure, course

— 4 Strokes —

11 歧視 **[ch'í-shìh]**: to discriminate against; discrimination, prejudice

歪

6 歪曲 **[wāi-ch'ū]**: to distort, to twist, to misrepresent; distortion

9 歪風 **[wāi-fēng]**: ill wind, perverted tendency

武

武 **[wŭ]**: Wuchang (abbreviation of 武昌); martial

2 武力解決[**wŭ-lì chiĕh-chüéh**]: settlement by force

4 武文牡[**wŭ wén mŭ**]: U Win Maung (Burmese statesman)

8 武官[**wŭ-kuān**]: military attaché

10 武訓傳[**wŭ hsǜn chuàn**]: The Life of Wu Hsün (title of a moving picture that fell under communist criticism)

12 武裝[**wŭ-chuāng**]: to arm; armament; armed

武裝基幹民兵[**wŭ-chuāng chī-kàn mín-pīng**]: armed backbone militia

武裝起義[**wŭ-chuāng ch'ĭ-ì**]: armed uprising

武裝衝突[**wŭ-chuāng ch'ūng-t'ù**]: armed conflict, armed clash

武裝干涉[**wŭ-chuāng kān-shè**]: armed intervention

武裝工作隊[**wŭ-chuāng kūng-tsò tùi**]: armed working team, militia work team

武裝工作委員會[**wŭ-chuāng kūng-tsò wĕi-yüán-hùi**]: militia work committee

武裝保衛部[**wŭ-chuāng păo-wèi pù**]: armed militia department

武裝鬥爭[**wŭ-chuāng tòu-chēng**]: armed struggle

13 武漢微生物研究室[**wŭ-hàn wēi-shēng-wù yén-chìu-shìh**]: Wuhan Microbiology Research Laboratory

16 武器[**wŭ-ch'ì**]: weapon, arms (during the Cultural Revolution, used as a simile for the Thought of Mao Tse-tung)

武器彈藥[**wŭ-ch'ì tàn-yào**]: arms and ammunition

18 武斷[**wŭ-tuàn**]: arbitrary decision; arbitrary, dogmatic

20 武鬥[**wŭ-tòu**]: to struggle militantly; coercion by force

— 9 Strokes —

歲

2 歲入[**sùi-jù**]: annual revenue

5 歲出[**sùi-ch'ū**]: annual expenditure

— 12 Strokes —

5 歷史[**lì-shĭh**]: history, chronicles, annals; historical

歷史潮流[**lì-shĭh ch'áo-líu**]: historical trend, tide of history, trend of historical development

歷史車輪[**lì-shĭh ch'ē-lún**]: the wheel of history

歷史性[**lì-shĭh-hsìng**]: historical nature

歷史任務[**lì-shĭh jèn-wù**]: historic task

歷史博物館[**lì-shĭh pó-wù-kuăn**]: historical museum

歷史上的[**lì-shĭh-shàng te**]: historical

歷史唯物論[**lì-shĭh wéi-wù lùn**]: historical materialism

歷史舞台[**lì-shĭh wŭ-t'ái**]: the stage of history

歷史研究所第二所[**lì-shĭh yén-chìu-sŏ tì-èrh sŏ**]: Second History Institute

歷史研究所第一所[**lì-shĭh yén-chìu-sŏ tì-ī sŏ**]: First History Institute

歷史研究所第三所[**lì-shĭh yén-chìu-sŏ tì-sān sŏ**]: Third History Institute

6 歷次[**lì-tz'ù**]: repeatedly, successively; successive

8 歷來[**lì-lái**]: to date, so far, up to now, hitherto, until now

— 14 Strokes —

歸

5 歸功於[kuēi-kūng yǘ]: to attribute merit to, to credit with

6 歸因於[kuēi-yīn yǘ]: to attribute the reason to

8 歸咎[kuēi-chìu]: to blame, to reproach, to blame something on someone

歸於[kuēi-yǘ]: to be ascribed to, to be attributed to, to be imputed to, to belong to

10 歸案[kuēi-àn]: to bring to court

歸案法辦[kuēi-àn fă-pàn]: to bring to trial and settle according to law

歸根結蒂[kuēi-kēn chiéh-tì]: in the end, in the final analysis, to get to the root of the problem

歸納[kuēi-nà]: induction; inductive

歸納成以下幾點[kuēi-nà ch′éng ĭ-hsìa chĭ-tiĕn]: to sum up as follows, to summarize under the following points

歸納法[kuēi-nà fă]: inductive method, induction

11 歸國[kuēi-kuó]: to return home, to return to one's native country, to repatriate

12 歸結[kuēi-chiéh]: to conclude, to summarize, to terminate, to wind up

歸順[kuēi-shùn]: to submit, to surrender, to give in, to subordinate oneself

歸隊[kuēi-tùi]: to resume one's assigned work

歸爲[kuēi-wéi]: to fall under (i.e., as categories)

歸罪[kuēi-tsùi]: to blame, to reproach

歸罪於[kuēi-tsùi yü]: to place the blame with, to blame

16 歸檔[kuēi-tăng]: to file away

17 歸還[kuēi-huán]: to give back, to return, to reimburse

歸總[kuēi-tsŭng]: to unite, to put together, to summarize

19 歸攏[kuēi-lŭng]: to put together, to summarize

— RADICAL 歹 歺 78 —

歹

4 歹心[tăi-hsīn]: evil intent

10 歹毒[tăi-tú]: malicious

歹徒[tăi-t′ú]: vicious element, bad element, undesirable element

— 2 Strokes —

死

3 死亡[ssŭ-wáng]: to die; death, dissolution, fatalities

死亡率[ssŭ-wáng lǜ]: death rate, mortality rate

6 死刑[ssŭ-hsíng]: death penalty, capital sentence

死守[ssŭ-shŏu]: to defend to the last

8 死板[ssŭ-păn]: stodgy, dull, punctilious, stick-in-the-mud

死板的教條[ssŭ-păn te chiào-t′iáo]: rigid dogma

10 死記 [ssŭ-chì]: to learn by rote

12 死硬 [ssŭ-yìng]: intransigent, irreconcilable, uncompromising, stubborn, stiff and unbending

死硬派 [ssŭ-yìng p'ài]: diehards; diehard clique

14 死對頭 [ssŭ tùi-t'óu]: deadly enemy, determined antagonist

15 死胡同 [ssŭ hú-t'ùng]: blind alley

死敵 [ssŭ-tí]: deadly enemy, sworn enemy

19 死難 [ssŭ-nàn]: to die for one's country, to die for a noble cause

— 6 Strokes —

殉

11 殉國 [hsǜn-kuó]: to die for one's country

— 8 Strokes —

殖

5 殖民 [chíh-mín]: to colonize; colonial

殖民枷鎖 [chíh-mín chiā-sŏ]: colonial yoke

殖民主義 [chíh-mín chŭ-ì]: colonialism

殖民主義者 [chíh-mín chŭ-ì chĕ]: colonialist

殖民主義國家 [chíh-mín chŭ-ì kuó-chīa]: colonial power

殖民主義的奴役 [chíh-mín chŭ-ì te nú-i]: colonial enslavement

殖民主義的災害 [chíh-mín chŭ-ì te tsāi-hài]: the scourge of colonialism

殖民擴張 [chíh-mín k'uò-chāng]: colonial aggrandizement

殖民地 [chíh-mín-tì]: colony, settlement

殖民地化 [chíh-mín-tì-huà]: colonization

殖民地國家 [chíh-mín-tì kuó-chiā]: colonial country

殖民地部 [chíh-mín-tì pù]: Colonial Office

殖民統治 [chíh-mín t'ŭng-chìh]: colonial rule

殘

6 殘存 [ts'án-ts'ún]: to survive, to be left over; remnant

殘存者 [ts'án-ts'ún-chĕ]: survivors, survivals

殘存物 [ts'án-ts'ún wù]: survivals, survivors

7 殘忍 [ts'án-jĕn]: cruel, brutal, bloodthirsty, savage, barbarous, inhuman

10 殘缺 [ts'án-ch'üēh]: deficient, broken, incomplete

殘害 [ts'án-hài]: to kill, to destroy, to injure

殘害人民 [ts'án-hài jén-mín]: to trample the people underfoot

12 殘毀 [ts'án-hŭi]: to destroy, to ruin

14 殘廢 [ts'án-fèi]: to deform, to mutilate, to maim, to cripple, to injure; deformation

殘廢者 [ts'án-fèi chĕ]: invalid, cripple

殘廢軍人 [ts'án-fèi chūn-jén]: disabled ex-serviceman, disabled veteran

殘酷 [ts'án-k'ù]: ruthless, cruel, brutal, merciless, vicious, savage; brutality, ruthlessness, savagery

15 殘暴 [ts'án-pào]: atrocity; brutal, bloodthirsty, savage, barbarous, inhuman

16 殘餘 [ts'án-yǘ]: survivors, survivals, remnant, left-over

殘餘勢力 [ts'án-yǘ shìh-lì]: remnant forces

— 17 Strokes —

殲

13 殲滅 [chiēn-mièh]: to exterminate; annihilation, extermination

殲滅戰 [chiēn-mièh chàn]: war of annihilation

— RADICAL 殳 79 —

— 6 Strokes —

殺

殺 [shā]: to kill, to slaughter, to destroy, to murder

2 殺人放火 [shā-jén fàng-huǒ]: killing and burning

12 殺菌劑 [shā-chǜn-chì]: fungicide, germicide, bactericide

15 殺價 [shā-chià]: to force prices down, to slash prices

殺戮 [shā-lù]: to kill, to slaughter

18 殺蟲藥劑 [shā-ch'úng yào-chì]: insecticide

殷

13 殷勤 [yīn-ch'ín]: attentiveness, diligence; attentively, with great concern

殷勤招待 [yīn-ch'ín chāo-tài]: to receive attentively, to usher hospitably

— 9 Strokes —

毀

13 毀滅 [hŭi-mièh]: to annihilate, to destroy, to lay waste, to demolish, to exterminate, to extinguish; destruction, annihilation

毀傷 [hŭi-shāng]: to wound, to injure, to mutilate

毀損 [hŭi-sŭn]: to damage, to wound

17 毀謗 [hŭi-pàng]: to vilify, to slander, to defame; defamation, slander, vilification; slanderous, libelous, defamatory

19 毀壞 [hŭi-huài]: to destroy, to ruin; ruin, destruction

— 11 Strokes —

毅

2 毅力 [ì-lì]: persistence, perseverance

— RADICAL 毋 80 —

— 2 Strokes —

每

每 **[mĕi]**: each, every, per

4 每日先驅報**[mĕi-jìh hsiēn-ch'ū pào]**: Daily Herald (British daily newspaper)

每日新聞**[mĕi-jìh hsīn-wén]**: Mainichi Shimbun (Japanese daily newspaper)

每日快報**[mĕi-jìh k'uài-pào]**: Daily Express (British daily newspaper)

每日郵報**[mĕi-jìh yú-pào]**: Daily Mail (British daily newspaper)

6 每年 **[mĕi-nién]**: annual, every year, per year

— 4 Strokes —

4 毒手 **[tú-shŏu]**: a malicious person

9 毒計 **[tú-chì]**: evil plans, a malicious scheme

10 毒氣 **[tú-ch'ì]**: poison gas

毒氣室**[tú-ch'ì shìh]**: gas chamber, lethal chamber

毒氣彈 **[tú-ch'ì tàn]**: gas shell, gas projectile

毒害 **[tú-hài]**: to poison, to infect, to corrupt; venemous

毒素 **[tú-sù]**: toxin

毒草 **[tú-ts'ăo]**: poisonous weeds (i.e., literary or artistic works that are harmful to the communist cause and that are not in accordance with the Party line or the thoughts of Mao)

11 毒蛇 **[tú-shé]**: poisonous snakes (during the Cultural Revolution, an epithet for anti-Mao elements)

13 毒辣 **[tú-là]**: raw, ruthless, brutal

— RADICAL 匕匕 81 —

比

比 **[pĭ]**: to compare; comparison; in comparison with, as against

4 比之於**[pĭ-chīh yǘ]**: to liken to, to compare to

5 比以前**[pĭ ĭ-ch'ién]**: compared with before, than ever

6 比先進**[pĭ hsiēn-chìn]**: to emulate the advanced (*See* 比學趕幫)

比先進，趕先進，學先進 **[pĭ hsiēn-chìn, kăn hsiēn-chìn, hsüéh hsiēn-chìn]**: emulate the advanced, overtake the advanced, and learn from the advanced (*See* 比學趕幫)

7 比利牛斯山脈**[pĭ-lì-níu-ssū shān-mò]**: Pyrenees Mountains

比利時**[pĭ-lì-shíh]**: Belgium

比利時王國**[pĭ-lì-shíh wáng-kuó]**: Kingdom of Belgium

8 比例 **[pĭ-lì]**: proportion, ratio

比例代表制**[pĭ-lì tài-piăo chìh]**: proportional representation

比例尺度**[pĭ-lì ch'ĭh-tù]**: scale (as on a map), size

比度 **[pĭ-tù]**: scale, size

[10] 比率[pǐ-lǜ]: proportional rate, ratio

[11] 比基島[pǐ-chī tǎo]: Bikini Island

比國[pǐ-kuó]: Belgium

比紹[pǐ-shào]: Bissau (Portuguese Guinea)

比得上[pǐ-té-shàng]: to match, to be equal to; comparable with

比勒陀利亞[pǐ-lè-t'ó-lì-yà]: Pretoria (South Africa)

[12] 比斯開灣[pǐ-ssū-k'āi wān]: Bay of Biscay

比斯他[pǐ-ssū-t'ā]: piaster

比喻[pǐ-yǜ]: metaphor, allegory, comparison, simile, parable, fable

[13] 比較[pǐ-chiào]: to compare; comparative, relative

比劃[pǐ-huà]: to communicate through sign language, to inform by means of hand signals

[16] 比學趕幫[pǐ-hsüéh-kǎn-pāng]: compare (oneself with the advanced), learn from (the advanced), overtake (the advanced), and help (the backward) (a campaign for production increase and economy in industry that began in 1964)

比學趕幫超運動[pǐ-hsüéh-kǎn-pāng-ch'āo yǜn-tùng]: campaign to compare with, learn from, and overtake (the advanced), to help (the backward), and surpass (the advanced) (the campaign began with the first four characters, as in the entry above; the fifth character was added by P'eng Chen)

[17] 比擬[pǐ-nǐ]: to compare

比賽[pǐ-sài]: competition, contest, match, tournament

— RADICAL 毛 82 —

毛

[5] 毛主席語錄[máo chǔ-hsí yǔ-lù]: Sayings of Chairman Mao (i.e., the "little red book" of quotations from Mao)

毛皮[máo-p'í]: fur

[7] 毛里求斯島[máo-lǐ-ch'íu-ssū tǎo]: Mauritius

毛里塔尼亞伊斯蘭共和國[máo-lǐ-t'ǎ-ní-yà ī-ssū-lán kùng-hó-kuó]: Islamic Republic of Mauritania

毛利[máo-lì]: gross profit

[9] 毛重[máo-chùng]: gross weight

[10] 毛紡織廠[máo fǎng-chīh ch'ǎng]: woolen textile mill, wool mill

[11] 毛產[máo-ch'ǎn]: gross output

毛淡棉縣[máo-tàn-mién hsièn]: Moulmein (Burma)

[14] 毛綫[máo-hsièn]: knitting wool

[16] 毛澤東主義[máo tsé-tūng chǔ-ì]: Maoism

毛澤東時代[máo tsé-tūng shíh-tài]: The Age of Mao Tse-tung

毛澤東思想[máo tsé-tūng ssū-hsiǎng]: The thought of Mao Tse-tung

毛澤東思想掛帥[máo tsé-tūng ssū-hsiǎng kuà-shuài]: the thought of Mao Tse-tung takes command (a slogan of the Cultural Revolution)

毛澤東思想偉大紅旗[máo tsé-tūng ssū-hsiǎng wěi-tà húng-ch'í]: the great red banner of Mao Tse-tung's thought (a slogan from the Cultural Revolution)

[18] 毛織廠[máo-chīh ch'ǎng]: woolen textile mill

毛織品[máo-chīh p'ǐn]: woolen fabrics, woolen textiles

[19] 毛難[máo-nán]: Mao-nan (a minority nationality)

— 7 Strokes —

毫

[4] 毫不**[háo-pù]**: not in the least, not a bit, in no way, by no means, in no respect

毫不知恥的**[háo-pù chīh-ch'ĭh te]**: to have the impudence to; impudent; absolutely, shamelessly

毫不含糊的**[háo-pù hán-hú te]**: very clear-cut, clear, or well-defined, unambiguous, unequivocal; quite clearly

毫不懷疑**[háo-pù huái-í]**: to have no doubt at all

毫不悔改**[háo-pù hŭi-kăi]**: to fail to show any sign of repentance

毫不調和的**[háo-pù t'iáo-hó te]**: uncompromising

毫不在乎**[háo-pú tsài-hú]**: not to care about in the least

[12] 毫無權利**[háo-wú ch'üán-lì]**: to have no rights at all; utter lack of rights

毫無希望**[háo-wú hsī-wàng]**: with no hope at all, quite hopeless; quite hopelessly

毫無信義**[háo-wú hsìn-ì]**: utterly faithless

毫無疑問**[háo-wú í-wèn]**: there is no doubt about, thěre is no room for doubt that

毫無骨氣**[háo-wú kŭ-ch'ì]**: utterly spineless

毫無例外**[háo-wú lì-wài]**: without exception

毫無道理**[háo-wú tào-lĭ]**: not to be justified in any way, entirely without reason

毫無隱晦**[háo-wú yĭn-hùi]**: with great candor

毫無用處**[háo-wú yùng-ch'ù]**: to serve no useful purpose, utterly useless

— RADICAL 氏 83 —

— 1 Stroke —

[3] 民工**[mín-kūng]**: corvee workers

民工大隊**[mín-kūng tà-tùi]**: service troops, civilian labor unit

[5] 民主**[mín-chŭ]**: democracy; democratic

民主基礎上集中，集中指導下的民主 **[mín-chŭ chī-ch'ŭ-shàng chí-chūng, chí-chūng chĭh-tăo-hsià te mín-chŭ]**: centralism on the basis of democracy and democracy under centralized leadership

民主集中制**[mín-chŭ chí-chūng chìh]**: system of democratic centralism

民主主義青年團**[mín-chŭ chŭ-ì ch'īng-nién-t'uán]**: Democratic Youth League

民主憲政**[mín-chŭ hsièn-chèng]**: democratic constitutionalism

民主化**[mín-chŭ-huà]**: democratization

民主人士**[mín-chŭ jén-shìh]**: democratic personages, democratic elements

民主改革**[mín-chŭ kăi-kó]**: democratic reform

民主個人主義**[mín-chŭ kò-jén chŭ-ì]**: democratic individualism

民主個人主義者**[mín-chŭ kò-jén chŭ-ì chĕ]**: democratic individualist

民主革命**[mín-chŭ kó-mìng]**: democratic revolution

民主評定**[mín-chŭ p'íng-tìng]**: democratic assessment

民主黨派**[mín-chŭ tăng-p'ài]**: democratic

parties (i.e., political parties formed during the war against Japan and which joined the Communists against the Nationalist government)

民生主義[mín-shēng chŭ-ì]: the principle of national livelihood, people's livelihood (*See* 三民主義)

民用 [mín-yùng]: for the use of the people, for civilian use; civilian, civil

民用航空[mín-yùng háng-k'ūng]: civil aviation

7 民兵[mín-pīng]: militia, People's Militia

8 民法[mín-fă]: civil law, civil code

民事[mín-shìh]: civil case, civil suit

民事審判庭[mín-shìh shĕn-p'àn t'íng]: civil court

9 民政工作委員會[mín-chèng kūng-tsò wĕi-yüán-hùi]: civil affairs work committee

民建[mín-chièn]: China Democratic National Construction Association (abbreviation of 中國民主建國會)

民革[mín-kó]: Revolutionary Committee of the Kuomintang (abbreviation of 中國國民黨革命委員會)

10 民家[mín-chiā]: Pai (a minority nationality of aborigines in Yunnan)

民航部[mín-háng pù]: Ministry of Civil Aviation

11 民族[mín-tsú]: 1. nation, race, peoples, nationality; national, racial; 2. The Nation (American weekly periodical); 3. the principle of nationalism; people's race (*See* 三民主義)

民族教育[mín-tsú chiào-yü]: education for nationalities

民族解放運動[mín-tsú chiĕh-fàng yǜn-tùng]: national liberation movement

民族主義[mín-tsú chŭ-ì]: nationalism, the principle of nationalism (*See* 三民主義)

民族主義國家[mín-tsú chŭ-ì kuó-chiā]: nationalist state

民族區域自治[mín-tsú ch'ū-yü tzù-chìh]: regional autonomy for nationalities

民族分裂主義[mín-tsú fēn-lièh chŭ-ì]: national secessionism

民族形式[mín-tsú hsíng-shìh]: national form

民族虛無主義者[mín-tsú hsū-wú chŭ-ì chĕ]: national nihilist

民族遺產[mín-tsú í-ch'ăn]: national heritage, national legacy

民族議會[mín-tsú ì-hùi]: National Council (Czechoslovakia)

民族感情[mín-tsú kăn-ch'íng]: national sentiments, national feeling

民族革命戰爭的大衆文學[mín-tsú kó-mìng chàn-chēng te tà-chùng wén-hsüéh]: Popular Literature of the National Revolutionary War (a slogan used by Lu Hsün in the 1930s and which by 1966 had come to be praised as opposed to 國防文學, q.v.)

民族工商業[mín-tsú kūng-shāng-yèh]: the industry and commerce of the national bourgeoisie

民族工商業者[mín-tsú kūng-shāng-yèh chĕ]: national bourgeois industrialists and merchants

民族色彩[mín-tsú sè-ts'ăi]: national color, national flavor, national characteristics

民族事務委員會[mín-tsú shìh-wù wĕi-yüán-hùi]: Nationalities Affairs Commission

民族大家庭[mín-tsú tà chiā-t'íng]: the great family of nationalities

民族大義[mín-tsú tà-ì]: noble national cause

民族團結[mín-tsú t'uán-chiéh]: national unity, national solidarity

民族統一戰綫[mín-tsú t'ŭng-ī chàn-hsièn]:

national united front

民族資產階級[mín-tsú tzū-ch'ăn chiēh-chí]: national bourgeoisie

民族自治[mín-tsú tzù-chìh]: national autonomy

民族自決[mín-tsú tzù-chüéh]: national self-dermination

民族委員會[mín-tsú wĕi-yüán-hùi]: Nationalities Committee

民族亞洲主義[mín-tsú yà-chōu chŭ-ì]: Asian nationalism

民族研究所[mín-tsú yén-chìu-sŏ]: Ethnology Institute

民族英雄[mín-tsú yīng-hsiúng]: national hero

12 民間[mín-chiēn]: among the people, civil, folk-

民間傳說[mín-chiēn ch'uán-shuō]: folklore

民間藝術[mín-chiēn ì-shù]: popular art, folk art

民間故事[mín-chiēn kù-shìh]: folk tale, folklore

民間舞蹈[mín-chiēn wŭ-tào]: folk dance

民間音樂[mín-chiēn yīn-yüèh]: folk music

民衆[mín-chùng]: the masses

13 民意[mín-ì]: popular opinion, will of the people

民意機關[mín-ì chī-kuān]: organs of public opinion

民意測驗[mín-ì ts'è-yèn]: public opinion poll

民盟[mín-méng]: China Democratic League (abbreviation for 中國民主同盟會)

14 民監[mín-chiēn]: People's Supervisory Committee (abbreviation for 人民監察委員會)

民歌[mín-kō]: ballad, folk song

16 民選[mín-hsüăn]: by popular election

民辦[mín-pàn]: managed by the people

民辦中學[mín-pàn chūng-hsüéh]: a middle school managed by the people

17 民憤[mín-fèn]: people's indignation

22 民權主義[mín-ch'üán chŭ-ì]: the principle of democracy; people's rights (*See* 三民主義)

民權集中制[mín-ch'üán chí-chūng chìh]: system of democratic centralism

— RADICAL 气 84 —

— 4 Strokes —

13 氛圍[fēn-wéi]: atmosphere, mood, humor, morale

— 6 Strokes —

8 氣氛[ch'ì-fēn]: atmosphere, air, mood, character

氣味[ch'ì-wèi]: flavor, taste, savor, smell, odor

9 氣派[ch'ì-p'ài]: attitude, temperament, spirit, frame of mind, bearing

10 氣候[ch'ì-hòu]: climate, weather conditions

氣候預報[ch'ì-hòu yü-pào]: weather forecast, meteorological forecast

11 氣球[ch'ì-ch'íu]: balloon

12 氣象站[ch'ì-hsiàng chàn]: weather station

氣象記載[ch'ì-hsiàng chì-tsăi]: meteorological data

氣象學[ch'ì-hsiàng-hsüéh]: meteorology

氣象台[ch'ì-hsiàng t'ái]: weather station

14 氣槍[ch'ì-ch'iāng]: air gun, air rifle

15 氣質[ch'ì-chíh]: aptitude, character, natural tendency, disposition, temperament, physique

氣概[ch'ì-kài]: bearing, manner

氣魄[ch'ì-p'ò]: spirit, courage, daring, boldness, force, strength, vitality, character

— 7 Strokes —

8 氫武器[ch'īng wŭ-ch'ì]: hydrogen weapons

15 氫彈[ch'īng-tàn]: hydrogen bomb

— 8 Strokes —

10 氰氨化鈣廠[ch'īng-ān-huà-kài ch'ăng]: calcium cyanamide plant

氯

14 氯酸鉀工廠[lǜ-suān-chiă kūng-ch'ăng]: potassium chlorate plant

氮

8 氮肥[tàn-féi]: nitrogenous fertilizer, nitrate fertilizer

氮肥廠[tàn-féi ch'ăng]: nitrogenous fertilizer plant

10 氮氣[tàn-ch'ì]: nitrogen

— RADICAL 水氵85 —

水

水[shŭi]: 1. river; 2. irrigation (one of the characters of the 八字憲法, q.v.); 3. water

2 水力[shŭi-lì]: hydraulic

水力發電[shŭi-lì fā-tièn]: hydroelectric power, hydroelectricity

水力發電站[shŭi-lì fā-tièn chàn]: hydroelectric station

水力發電廠[shŭi-lì fā-tièn ch'ăng]: hydroelectric power plant

水力採煤[shŭi-lì ts'ăi-méi]: hydraulic mining

3 水下[shŭi-hsià]: submarine, underwater (adj.)

水土[shŭi-t'ŭ]: climate, water and soil

水土流失[shŭi-t'ŭ líu-shīh]: soil erosion, water loss and soil erosion

水土保持[shŭi-t'ŭ păo-ch'íh]: water and soil conservancy, conservation of water and soil

4 水戶[shŭi-hù]: Mito (Japan)

水文站[shŭi-wén chàn]: hydrological station, hydrographic station

水文學[shŭi-wén-hsüéh]: hydrology

水文工作者[shŭi-wén kūng-tsò chĕ]: hydrologist

5 水平[shŭi-p'íng]: level, standard

水生生物研究所[shŭi-shēng shēng-wù yén-chiù-sŏ]: Hydrobiology Institute

水田[shŭi-t'ién]: paddy fields, irrigated fields, wet rice field

7 水車[shŭi-ch'ē]: water wheel, water mill

85

水系[shŭi-hsì]: river system

水利[shŭi-lì]: water conservancy

水利系[shŭi-lì hsì]: hydraulic engineering department

水利科學研究所[shŭi-lì k'ō-hsüéh yén-chìu-sŏ]: Hydraulic Research Institute

水利工程[shŭi-lì kūng-ch'éng]: water conservancy project

水利部[shŭi-lì pù]: Ministry of Water Conservancy

水利樞紐[shŭi-lì shū-nĭu]: hydro-juncture

水利電力部[shŭi-lì tièn-lì pù]: Ministry of Water Conservancy and Electric Power

水利資源[shŭi-lì tzū-yüán]: water resources

水兵[shŭi-pīng]: seaman, sailor

水災[shŭi-tsāi]: flood, inundation

水位[shŭi-wèi]: water level

8 水泥[shŭi-ní]: cement

9 水星[shŭi-hsīng]: Mercury

10 水家[shŭi-chiā]: Shui-chia (minority nationality)

水庫[shŭi-k'ù]: reservoir

水原[shŭi-yüán]: Suwon (Korea)

11 水產[shŭi-ch'ăn]: marine products, aquatic products

水產部[shŭi-ch'ăn pù]: Ministry of Aquatic Products

水產業[shŭi-ch'ăn yèh]: aquatic products industry

水陸兩棲[shŭi-lù liăng-ch'ī]: amphibious

水陸兩棲部隊[shŭi-lù liăng-ch'ī pù-tùi]: amphibious detachment

水彩畫[shŭi-ts'ăi huà]: water-color painting

13 水閘[shŭi-chá]: sluice gate, lock, water gate, mill, dam

水雷[shŭi-léi]: sea mine

水雷密布[shŭi-léi mì-pù]: heavily mined

15 水稻[shŭi-tào]: paddy rice, wet rice

24 水壩[shŭi-pà]: dam

— 1 Stroke —

冰

3 冰川期[pīng-ch'uān ch'í]: ice age, glacial epoch

冰山[pīng-shān]: iceberg

4 冰片[pīng-p'ièn]: camphor

10 冰島[pīng-tăo]: Iceland

冰島共和國[pīng-tăo kùng-hó-kuó]: Republic of Iceland

3 永久[yŭng-chĭu]: permanent, eternal, everlasting, lasting, enduring

永久的主題[yŭng-chĭu te chŭ-t'í]: eternal theme

4 永不枯竭 [yŭng pù-k'ū-chiéh]: never failing, inexhaustible

6 永安[yŭng-ān]: 1. Vinh Yen (Vietnam); 2. Yungan Hsien (China)

永州[yŭng-chōu]: Vinhchau (Vietnam)

8 永垂不朽[yŭng ch'úi-pù-hsĭu]: undying, immortal

9 永恒[yŭng-héng]: permanent, lasting

永恒報[yŭng-héng pào]: Abadi (Indonesian daily newspaper)

11 永盛不衰[yŭng-shèng pù-shuāi]: to blos-

som forever, to be forever green, to be ever flourishing

14 永遠 **[yŭng-yüăn]**: permanent, eternal, everlasting, lasting, enduring

16 永龍 **[yŭng-lúng]**: Vinhlong (Vietnam)

— 2 Strokes —

求 **[ch'íu]**: to ask, to ask for, to request, to petition, to implore, to entreat

6 求同存異 **[ch'íu-t'úng ts'ún-ì]**: to seek common ground while reserving differences

8 求和 **[ch'íu-hó]**: to sue for peace, to find the sum; summation

9 求降 **[ch'íu-hsiáng]**: to surrender, to capitulate

19 求穩怕亂 **[ch'íu-wĕn p'à-luàn]**: to seek security and fear trouble, to be overcautious

氾

17 氾濫 **[fàn-làn]**: to flood; inundation, flood

氾濫成災 **[fàn-làn ch'éng-tsāi]**: inundation that becomes a disaster

— 3 Strokes —

江

3 江山 **[chiāng-shān]**: rivers and hills, land, landscape, scenery, country, the state

5 江北 **[chiāng-pĕi]**: north of the Yangtze

江右 **[chiāng-yù]**: Kiangsi

6 江西 **[chiāng-hsī]**: Kiangsi Province

8 江東 **[chiāng-tūng]**: Kiangsu; the region of the lower reaches of the Yangtze

9 江南 **[chiāng-nán]**: Kiangsu and Anhwei

10 江浙 **[chiāng-chè]**: Kiangsu and Chekiang

江海關 **[chiāng hăi-kuān]**: The Shanghai Custom House

11 江淮 **[chiāng-huái]**: the region between the Yangtze and Huai Rivers; Kiangsu and Anhwei

12 江湖 **[chiāng-hú]**: rivers and lakes; to travel, to roam around; unreliable; seasoned

14 江漢關 **[chiāng-hàn kuān]**: Hankow Custom House

20 江蘇 **[chiāng-sū]**: Kiangsu Province

池

5 池田勇 **[ch'íh-t'ién yŭng]**: Ikeda, Hayato (Japanese statesman)

汎

9 汎神論 **[fàn-shén lùn]**: pantheism

11 汎理論 **[fàn-lĭ lùn]**: panlogism

汛

12 汛期 **[hsùn-ch'í]**: high water season, flood season

汕

汕 **[shàn]**: Swatow (abbreviation for 汕頭)

16 汕頭 **[shàn-t'óu]**: Swatow

污

8 污毒 **[wū-tú]**: filth and poison

15 污蔑 **[wū-mièh]**: to slander, to smear, to malign, to vilify, to libel; calumny; defamatory, scurrilous

— 4 Strokes —

沈

6 沈住了氣 **[ch'én-chù-le ch'ì]**: to be able to master oneself, to hold oneself in check

7 沈沒 **[ch'én-mò]**: to immerse, to sink, to perish

9 沈重 **[ch'én-chùng]**: heavy, weighty, grave, important

沈思 **[ch'én-ssū]**: to contemplate, to meditate, to reflect deeply

10 沈痾 **[ch'én-k'ō]**: chronic illness

沈迷 **[ch'én-mí]**: to wallow in, to indulge in, to be addicted to a vice

11 沈寂 **[ch'én-chí]**: silent, quieted down, subsided

沈寂下去 **[ch'én-chí hsià-ch'ǜ]**: to subside

16 沈靜 **[ch'én-chìng]**: quiet, well-behaved, with a quiet demeanor

沈默 **[ch'én-mò]**: silence; silent

汽

7 汽車 **[ch'ì-ch'ē]**: automobile, motor vehicle

汽車製造廠 **[ch'ì-ch'ē chìh-tsào ch'ǎng]**: automobile plant, motor vehicle plant

汽車製造業 **[ch'ì-ch'ē chìh-tsào yèh]**: automobile industry

汽車附件廠 **[ch'ì-ch'ē fù-chièn ch'ǎng]**: automobile accessory plant

汽車修理廠 **[ch'ì-ch'ē hsīu-lǐ ch'ǎng]**: motor repair shop, automobile repair shop

汽車材料製造廠 **[ch'ì-ch'ē ts'ái-liào chìh-tsào ch'ǎng]**: automobile supplies factory

汽車隊 **[ch'ì-ch'ē tùi]**: motorcade, convoy

8 汽油 **[ch'ì-yú]**: gasoline

汽油機車 **[ch'ì-yú chī-ch'ē]**: gasoline locomotive

汽油彈 **[ch'ì-yú tàn]**: gasoline bomb, napalm

9 汽缸 **[ch'ì-kāng]**: cylinder

11 汽船 **[ch'ì-ch'uán]**: motor boat, motor vessel

13 汽艇 **[ch'ì-t'ǐng]**: launch, steamboat

15 汽輪機 **[ch'ì-lún-chī]**: steam turbine

汽輪機廠 **[ch'ì-lún-chī ch'ǎng]**: steam turbine plant

17 汽壓 **[ch'ì-yā]**: steam pressure

19 沖繩 **[ch'ūng-shéng]**: Okinawa

3 決口 **[chüéh-k'ǒu]**: breach, gap, crack

4 決心 **[chüéh-hsīn]**: to be determined to, to be resolved to, to make up one's mind, to resolve to; resolution, decisiveness, determination, resolve

決不 **[chüéh-pù]**: in no way, in no case, by no means, on no account, never, under no circumstance

6 決死戰 **[chüéh-ssŭ chàn]**: desperate fight, fight to the death

決死鬥爭 **[chüéh-ssŭ tòu-chēng]**: life and death struggle

8 決定 **[chüéh-tìng]**: to decide, to resolve, to determine, to come to a decision; decision

決定性的 **[chüéh-tìng-hsìng te]**: decisive, crucial, critical

決定因素 **[chüéh-tìng yīn-sù]**: deciding factor, determining factor, deciding element, determining element

決定於 **[chüéh-tìng yǘ]**: to depend on, to

hinge on, to be contingent upon

[12] 決裂 **[chüéh-lièh]**: to break with, to break apart; rupture, breach

決雌雄 **[chüéh tz'ú-hsiúng]**: to fight it out

[14] 決算 **[chüéh-suàn]**: settlement, balance sheet, financial report, final account

[20] 決議 **[chüéh-ì]**: resolution, decision

決議草案 **[chüéh-ì ts'ǎo-àn]**: draft resolution

決鬥 **[chüéh-tòu]**: duel, struggle

沒

[6] 沒收 **[mò-shōu]**: to confiscate, to expropriate, to forfeit, to impound, to appropriate, to dispossess, to commandeer; confiscation, expropriation

沒有 **[méi-yǔ]**: not to have, there is not

沒有誠意 **[méi-yǔ ch'éng-ì]**: insincere, hollow, faithless

沒有結果 **[méi-yǔ chiéh-kuǒ]**: with no result, with no good end, to come to nothing, to yield no result

沒有前例的 **[méi-yǔ ch'ién-lì te]**: unprecedented, with no precedent

沒有止境 **[méi-yǔ chǐh-chìng]**: there is no limit to, there is no stop to

沒有出路 **[méi-yǔ ch'ū-lù]**: to be in a blind alley; without a way out

沒有充分利用的 **[méi-yǔ ch'ūng-fên lì-yùng te]**: not yet adequately utilized

沒有系統的 **[méi-yǔ hsì-t'ǔng te]**: desultory, unsystematic

沒有改變 **[méi-yǔ kǎi-pièn]**: unchanged, unaltered, unvaried

沒有根據 **[méi-yǔ kēn-chǜ]**: without basis; groundless, unfounded

沒有理由 **[méi-yǔ lǐ-yú]**: without reason, irrational, unreasonable, unjustifiable

沒有把握 **[méi-yǔ pǎ-wò]**: without grasp or control, not sure of, uncertain, doubtful, dubious, undecided

沒有保證的 **[méi-yǔ pǎo-chèng te]**: without any guarantee, unwarranted, undue, unjustified, unsanctioned, unentitled

沒有被否認 **[méi-yǔ pèi fǒu-jèn]**: unchallenged, to pass without denial

沒有偏見的 **[méi-yǔ p'iēn-chièn te]**: unbiased, unprejudiced, impartial

沒有道理 **[méi-yǔ tào-lǐ]**: uncalled for, irrational, unreasonable, unjustifiable

沒有資格 **[méi-yǔ tzū-kó]**: to have no competency to, not to be competent to, not qualified to

沒有用 **[méi-yǔ yùng]**: of no avail, of no use, useless, futile, unavailing, ineffectual

沒有預料的 **[méi-yǔ yǜ-liào te]**: unforeseen, unexpected, unanticipated

沒有原則的 **[méi-yǔ yüán-tsé te]**: unprincipled, not according to principle

[13] 沒落 **[mò-lò]**: to decline, to fall, to decay, to sink; decline; decadent, declining, on the decline, in declining circumstances

[14] 沒精打采 **[méi-chīng tǎ-ts'ǎi]**: listless, spiritless, inattentive, indifferent, absent-minded

[3] 汶山 **[wèn-shān]**: Munsan (Korea)

汴 **[pièn]**: Kaifeng (abbreviation for 開封)

[2] 沙人 **[shā-jén]**: Shajen (minority nationality in Yunnan)

4 沙文主義[shā-wén chŭ-ì]: chauvinism

6 沙地阿拉伯[shā-tì ā-lā-pò]: Saudi Arabia

9 沙皇[shā-huáng]: tsar

沙皇制度[shā-huáng chìh-tù]: tsarism

沙皇主義[shā-huáng chŭ-ì]: tsarism

沙特阿拉伯[shā-t'è à-lā-pó]: Saudi Arabia

沙特阿拉伯王國[shā-t'è à-lā-pó wáng-kuó]: Kingdom of Saudi Arabia

10 沙納尼康[shā-nà-ní-k'āng]: Sananikane, Thao Phoui (Laotian statesman)

14 沙爾[shā-ĕrh]: tsar

沙漠[shā-mò]: desert

15 沙撈越[shā-lāo-yüèh]: Sarawak

22 沙灘[shā-t'ān]: sand bank, sandbar, beach

— 5 Strokes —

沾

8 沾沾自喜[chān-chān tzù-hsĭ]: self-complacent, pleased with oneself

9 沾染[chān-jăn]: to contaminate

沼

10 沼氣[chăo-ch'ì]: marsh gas, fire-damp, methane gas

16 沼澤[chăo-tsé]: bog, swamp, marsh, morass, quagmire

治

5 治本工程[chìh-pĕn kūng-ch'éng]: permanent control project (i.e., river control)

治外法權[chìh-wài fă-ch'üán]: extraterritoriality

6 治安[chìh-ān]: public order, order, public security

治安工作委員會[chìh-ān kūng-tsò wĕi-yüán-hùi]: local security work committee

9 治洪[chìh-húng]: flood control

10 治病救人[chìh-pìng chìu-jén]: to treat illness in order to save people (in a political sense, the correct attitude to take in treating such ideological "diseases" as subjectivism, sectarianism, and formalism)

12 治喪委員會[chìh-sāng wĕi-yüán-hùi]: funeral committee, memorial committee

17 治療[chìh-liáo]: to treat, to heal; remedy, cure

注

2 注入[chù-jù]: to instill, to imbue, to impart, to infuse, to implant, to introduce into, to put into

8 注定[chù-tìng]: to be doomed, to be destined to, to be fated to; predetermined

10 注射[chù-shè]: to inoculate, to inject; inoculation, injection

11 注視[chù-shìh]: to stare at, to gaze; to watch closely

13 注意[chù-ì]: to pay attention to, to be attentive to, to take note of, to keep in mind, to be mindful of, to heed; attention

沮

12 沮喪[chŭ-sàng]: depression (i.e., in morale); downcast, low-spirited

法

5 法令[fă-lìng]: decree, order, ordinance, statute, edict

6 法西斯[fă-hsī-ssŭ]: fascist

法西斯主義[fă-hsī-ssū chŭ-ì]: fascism

8 法治[fă-chìh]: the rule of law

法制[fă-chìh]: legal system

法制局[fă-chĭh chǘ]: Bureau of Legal Affairs (國務院); The Legislative Bureau

法制委員會[fă-chĭh wĕi-yüán-hùi]: Codification Committee

法典[fă-tiĕn]: code, law code, canon

法定[fă-tìng]: determined by law, provided by law, prescribed by law; legal

法定人數[fă-tìng jén-shù]: quorum

9 法律[fă-lǜ]: law; legal

法律制裁[fă-lü chĭh-ts'ái]: legal sanction

法律系[fă-lü hsì]: legal department, law department

法律工作者[fă-lǜ kūng-tsò chĕ]: jurist

法律上[fă-lü-shàng]: legal, legally, de jure, according to the law

法則[fă-tsé]: rule, pattern, law

10 法案[fă-àn]: bill, act

法案委員會[fă-àn wĕi-yüán-hùi]: Bills Committee

法郎[fă-láng]: franc

法庭[fă-t'īng]: court room, court of law

法庭庭長[fă-t'īng t'īng-chăng]: president of the court

法庭審判長[fă-t'īng shĕn-pàn chăng]: chief judge of a court of law

法院[fă-yüàn]: court, law court

11 法規[fă-kuēi]: laws and regulations

法國[fà-kuó]: France

法國新聞社[fà-kuó hsīn-wén-shè]: Agence France Presse (French news agency)

12 法場[fă-ch'ăng]: execution grounds

法統[fă-t'ŭng]: legally constituted authority, system of justice

13 法新社[fà-hsīn-shè]: Agence France Presse (AFP)

16 法學[fă-hsüéh]: law (as a branch of study), jurisprudence

法學家[fă-hsüéh-chiā]: jurist

法辦[fă-pàn]: to deal with by legal processes, to settle according to the law

19 法寶[fă-păo]: sutra, mysterious thing; magic weapon (during the Cultural Revolution, a simile for the thought of Mao Tse-tung)

21 法蘭西共和國[fà-lán-hsī kùng-hó-kuó]: Republic of France

法蘭西共和國參議院[fà-lán-hsī kùng-hó-kuó ts'ān-ì-yüàn]: Council of the Republic (of France)

法蘭西晚報[fà-lán-hsī wăn-pào]: France Soir (French daily newspaper)

法蘭克福[fà-lán-k'ò-fú]: Frankfurt (Germany)

法蘭克福匯報[fà-lán-k'ò-fù hùi-pào]: Frankfurter Allgemeine (West German daily newspaper)

法屬西印度群島[fà-shŭ hsī-yìn-tù ch'ǘn-tăo]: Guadeloupe and Dependencies

法屬圭亞那[fà-shŭ kuēi-yà-nà]: French Guiana

法屬索馬里[fà-shŭ sŏ-mă-lĭ]: French Somaliland

22 法權[fă-ch'üán]: jurisdiction, judical power

泛

泛[fàn]: pan- (prefix)

4 泛日耳曼主義[fàn jìh-ĕrh-mán chŭ-ì]: Pan-Germanism

6 泛回教主義[fàn húi-chiào chŭ-ì]: Pan-Moslemism

8 泛泛地[fàn-fàn ti]: in general terms, generally

泛亞社[fàn-yà shè]: Pan-Asia News Agency (PANA)

9 泛美主義[fàn-mĕi chŭ-ì] : Pan-Americanism

17 泛濫[fàn-làn] : to flood, to inundate, to overflow; inundation

沸

沸點[fèi-tiĕn] : boiling point

20 沸騰[fèi-t′éng] : to boil, to bubble

河

4 河內[hó-nèi] : Hanoi (capital of the Vietnamese Democratic Republic)

7 河床[hó-ch′uáng] : river bed

河身[hó-shēn] : river bed, volume of current in a river

8 河岸[hó-àn] : river bank

9 河南[hó-nán] : Honan

10 河流[hó-líu] : current, flow

12 河堤[hó-t′í] : river dyke

13 河道[hó-tào] : the channel of a river

24 河壩[hó-pà] : river dam

泄

7 泄私憤[hsièh ssū-fèn] : to vent personal grievances, to work off one's spleen

10 泄氣[hsièh-ch′ì] : to vent anger, to let off steam, to exhaust, to fizzle out; disappointing, annoying, crushing

20 泄露[hsièh-lù] : to divulge, to leak, to let out, to betray, to reveal, to expose; revelation

泥

7 泥坑[ní-k′ēng] : muddy pit

波

3 波士頓[pō-shìh-tùn] : Boston

4 波及[pō-chí] : to involve

6 波多黎各[pō-tō lí-kò] : Puerto Rico

波多諾伏[pō-tō nò-fú] : Porto Novo (Dahomey)

7 波折[pō-ché] : to encounter obstacles; difficulty, complication

波希米亞 [pō-hsī-mĭ-yà] : Bohemia

波坎[pō-k′ăn] : Bokham (Indochina)

波利維亞[pō-lí-wéi-yà] : Bolivia

8 波長[pō-ch′áng] : wave length

波河[pō hó] : Po River

波的尼亞灣[pō-tí-ní-yà wān] : Gulf of Bothnia

10 波恩[pō-ēn] : Bonn (West Germany)

波哥大[pō-kō-tà] : Bogota (Colombia)

波浪[pō-làng] : wave

波浪式起伏[pō-làng-shìh ch′ĭ-fú] : undulating movement

波浪式前進[pō-làng-shìh ch′íen-chìn] : to move ahead like waves

波倫亞[pō-lún-yà] : Bologna

波特蘭[pō-t′è-lán] : Portland

波茨坦協定[pō-tz′ú-t′ăn hsiéh-tìng] : Potsdam Agreement (August 3, 1945)

11 波動[pō-tùng] : fluctuation, wave movement, unrest

12 波斯[pō-ssū] : Persia

波斯尼亞[pō-ssū-ní-yà] : Bosnia

波斯灣[pō-ssū wān] : Persian Gulf

14 波爾多[pō-ĕrh-tō] : Bordeaux

15 波璃絲[pō-lí ssū] : glass fiber

19 波羅的海[pō-ló-tì hăi] : Baltic Sea

20 波瀾[pō-lán] : wave, billow, anticlimax

21 波蘭[pō-lán] : Poland

波蘭人民共和國[pō-lán jén-mín kùng-hó-kuó] : People's Republic of Poland

波蘭人民共和國國民議會[pō-lán jén-mín kùng-hó-kuó kuó-mín ì-hùi] : Sjem of the People's Republic of Poland

波蘭通訊社[pō-lán t'ūng-hsün-shè] : Polish Press Agency (PAP)

泗

4 泗水[ssù-shŭi] : Soerabaja

泰

8 泰姆士[t'ài-mŭ-shìh] : Thames

11 泰國[t'ài-kuó] : Thailand, Siam

泰晤士報[t'ài-wù-shìh pào] : The Times (British daily newspaper)

12 泰然自若[t'ài-ján tzù-jò] : imperturbable, cool and collected, sang-froid

沿

10 沿海的[yén-hăi te] : coastal, off-shore, along the coast

沿海貿易船[yén-hăi mào-ì ch'uán] : coaster

沿海漁場[yén-hăi yü-ch'ăng] : in-shore fishery, off-shore fishery

11 沿習[yén-hsí] : to follow old customs, to follow old habits

油

5 油田[yú-t'ién] : oil field

9 油氈廠[yú-chān ch'ăng] : tar paper plant

10 油料作物[yú-liào tsò-wù] : oil-bearing crops

11 油船[yú-ch'uán] : tanker, oiler

12 油腔滑調[yú-ch'iāng huá-tiào] : unctuous, glib, facile, with tongue in cheek

油畫[yú-huà] : oil painting

油菜子[yú-ts'ài-tzu] : rapeseed

14 油漆[yú-ch'ī] : paint; to apply paint

油漆廠[yú-ch'ī ch'ăng] : paint plant

油管[yú-kuăn] : pipeline

15 油層[yú-ts'éng] : oil zone, oil pool, oil reservoir

— 6 Strokes —

津[chīn] : Tientsin (abbreviation for 天津)

9 津津有味的[chīn-chīn yŭ-wèi te] : tasteful, delicious

12 津貼[chīn-t'iēh] : allowance, subsidy, grant

洲

洲[chōu] : continent

14 洲際的[chōu-chì te] : intercontinental

洲際導彈[chōu-chì tăo-tàn] : intercontinental ballistic missile

洗

4 洗手不幹[hsĭ-shŏu pú-kàn] : to wash one's

hands of, to be through with; to reform one's ways, to go straight

8 洗刷 [hsǐ-shūa]: to wash, to cleanse, to rinse, to be cleared of, to whitewash

17 洗臉擦黑運動 [hsǐ-liěn ts'ā-hēi yün-tùng]: the "wash the face and rub off the black" movement (i.e., a movement for the purpose of correcting one's own faults and disclosing the shortcomings of others)

洩

20 洩露 [hsièh-lù]: to leak

洶

12 洶湧[hsiūng-yǔng]: the dashing of waves, the rush of a torrent, surging, sweeping and surging

洪

4 洪水 [húng-shŭi]: flood, deluge

洪水位 [húng-shŭi wèi]: high water mark

8 洪泛區 [húng-fàn ch'ū]: flood stricken area

9 洪亮 [húng-liàng]: high, clear, loud

10 洪峰 [húng-fēng]: flood crest, flood peak

12 洪都拉斯[húng-tū-lā-ssū]: Honduras

洪都拉斯共和國[húng-tū-lā-ssū kùng-hó-kuó]: Republic of Honduras

20 洪爐 [húng-lú]: furnace, smelting furnace

活

2 活力 [huó-lì]: vitality, vigor, dynamic energy, vital energy

5 活生生的[huó-shēng-shēng te]: lively, vivid, living, vital, dynamic

6 活材料 [huó ts'ái-liào]: living material, living data

7 活佛 [huó-fó]: living Buddha

8 活門 [huó-mén]: valve

9 活計 [huó-chì]: livelihood, occupation

10 活捉 [huó-chō]: to take prisoner, to capture alive

11 活動 [huó-tùng]: activity, action, operation, function, work, play; to be active

活動站 [huó-tùng chàn]: activity station (i.e., for the benefit of young people whose parents both work)

活動家 [huó-tùng-chiā]: activist, political activist

活動餘地 [huó-tùng yǘ-tì]: leeway

12 活報劇 [huó-pào chǜ]: poster drama, politically current play

活期存款[huó-chí ts'ún-k'uǎn]: current deposit

13 活話 [huó-huà]: inaccurate statement, uncertain promise

活路 [huó-lù]: thoroughfare, way out, outlet

活塞 [huó-sāi]: piston

活愚公 [huó yǘ-kūng]: a living Yü Kung, a model of faith and perseverance (*See* 愚公精神)

15 活潑 [huó-p'ō]: 1. lively; 2. activeness (i.e., two of the eight characters of the 三八作風, q.v.)

16 活學活用 [huó-hsüéh huó-yùng]: to creatively study and apply, to learn and apply with full vigor (in reference particularly to the works of Mao)

21 活躍 [huó-yüèh]: animation; lively, animated, active, smart, gay, vivacious, bright, brisk

洛

洛 [lò]: Loyang (abbreviation for 洛陽)

3 洛山磯 [lò-shān-chī]: Los Angeles

7 洛克 [lò-k'ò] : Locke, John (1632–1704)

8 洛奇 [lò-ch'í] : Lodge (proper name)

9 洛美 [lò-měi] : Lomé (Republic of Togo)

10 洛倫索馬貴斯 [lò-lún-sō mǎ-kuèi-ssū] : Lourenço Marques (Mozambique)

洛基非勒 [lò-chī-fēi-lè] : Rockefeller (proper name)

派

5 派出所 [p'ài-ch'ū-sǒ] : substation, police station, precinct station

派生 [p'ài-shēng] : derivative (adj. and noun)

派生國語 [p'ài-shēng kuó-yǔ] : daughter language

7 派系 [p'ài-hsì] : clique, faction, bloc, caucus, junto, cabal, branch, line of descent; factional

派別 [p'ài-pién] : faction, clique

派別活動 [p'ài-pién huó-tùng] : factionalism, factionism

14 派遣 [p'ài-ch'iěn] : to send, to dispatch, to delegate, to detach, to expedite

派遣勤務 [p'ài-ch'iěn ch'ín-wù] : detached duty

派遣軍 [p'ài-ch'iěn chūn] : expeditionary forces, detachment, detached party

洞

洞 [tùng] : 1. cave, tunnel, hole; 2. Tong (Korean village)

10 洞庭湖 [tùng-t'íng hú] : Tungting Lake (Hunan Province)

14 洞察 [tùng-ch'á] : to examine thoroughly, to observe, to perceive; judgment, penetrating insight

洋

8 洋法 [yáng-fǎ] : modern method, foreign method

9 洋洋大觀 [yáng-yáng tà-kuān] : spectacular, impressive, grand, imposing

10 洋框框 [yáng k'uàng-k'uang] : foreign frames (i.e., foreign models, foreign influences)

洋鬼子 [yáng kuěi-tzu] : foreign devil, foreigner

洋財東 [yáng ts'ái-tūng] : foreign rich proprietors

11 洋裡洋氣 [yáng-lǐ yáng-ch'ì] : exotic flavor, foreign flavor, outlandish

— 7 Strokes —

浙 [chè] : Chekiang (abbreviation for 浙江)

6 浙江日報 [chè-chiāng jìh-pào] : Chekiang Daily (newspaper)

浸

2 浸入 [chìn-jù] : to immerse, to plunge into, to submerge, to put under (water)

14 浸種 [chìn-chǔng] : to soak seeds, soaking of seeds

18 浸禮會 [chìn-lǐ hùi] : Baptist Church

2 浮力 [fú-lì] : buoyancy

6 浮名 [fú-míng] : an empty name

8 浮泛 [fú-fàn] : floating about, superficial

9 浮面 [fú-mièn] : floating on the surface

10 浮財 [fú-ts'ái] : moveable property, moveable assets

12 浮報[fú-pào]: to give an exaggerated account

13 浮誇[fú-k'uā]: to exaggerate, to brag, to vaunt; exaggeration, pompous boasting, bragging

15 浮標[fú-piāo]: buoy

16 浮橋[fú-ch'iáo]: pontoon bridge

浮頭[fú-t'óu]: surface

20 浮躁[fú-tsào]: lighthearted, lightheaded, fickle minded, unstable

海

3 海上的[hăi-shàng te]: oceanic, maritime, marine, at sea

4 海牙[hăi-yá]: The Hague

海牙會議[hăi-yá hùi-ì]: The Hague Conference

海牙公約[hăi-yá kūng-yüēh]: The Hague Convention

5 海外[hăi-wài]: overseas, abroad

海外部[hăi-wài pù]: Ministry for Overseas Affairs

6 海地[hăi-tì]: Haiti

海地共和國[hăi-tì kùng-hó-kuó]: Republic of Haiti

7 海防部隊[hăi-fáng pù-tùi]: coastguard

海里[hăi-lĭ]: nautical mile, knot

8 海岸[hăi-àn]: seacoast, seashore

海岸綫[hăi-àn hsièn]: coast line

海岸砲兵[hăi-àn p'ào-pīng]: coast artillery, coast battery

海拉爾[hăi-lā-ĕrh]: Hailar (Inner Mongolia)

海拔[hăi-pá]: height above sea level, above sea level

9 海軍[hăi-chūn]: navy; naval

海軍陸戰隊[hăi-chūn lù-chàn tùi]: marine corps, marines

海軍部[hăi-chūn pù]: Admiralty, Department of the Navy

海軍司令部[hăi-chūn ssū-lìng-pù]: Navy Headquarters

海軍元帥[hăi-chūn yüán-shuài]: Admiral of the Navy (Russian Navy)

海南[hăi-nán]: Haenam (Korea); Hainan (China)

海洋性氣候[hăi-yáng-hsìng ch'ì-hòu]: marine climate

海洋研究所[hăi-yáng yén-chìu-sŏ]: Oceanography Institute

10 海峽[hăi-hsiá]: strait

11 海陸空聯合作戰[hăi-lù-k'ūng lién-hó tsò-chàn]: aero-amphibious warfare

海帶[hăi-tài]: algae, kelp

12 海港[hăi-kăng]: seaport; Sea Harbor (name of a play)

海港停工事件[hăi-kăng t'íng-kūng shìh-chièn]: seaport work stoppage incident (January 8, 1967, when workers in Shanghai walked off their jobs)

海報[hăi-pào]: theater announcement, announcement of theater plays

海盜[hăi-tào]: pirate, corsair, buccaneer

13 海瑞罷官[hăi jùi pà-kuān]: Hai Jui Dismissed From Office (title of a play by Wu Han about an official who was unjustly dismissed from office and in which Hai Jui was said to stand for P'eng Te-huai, the former Minister of Defense, who was dismissed in 1959; the attack on this play signaled the beginning of the Cultural Revolution)

17 海濱[hăi-pīn]: beach

19 海關[hăi-kuān]: custom's office, customs

海關總署[hăi-kuān tsŭng-shŭ]: Bureau of

Customs Affairs

海邊[hăi-piēn]: seaside, shore, coast

浩

7 浩劫[hào-chiéh]: great disaster or calamity, cataclysm

16 浩蕩[hào-tàng]: great and vast, grand and magnificent

消

3 消亡[hsiāo-wáng]: to wither away, to die out

5 消失[hsiāo-shīh]: to disappear, to cease to exist, to fade away, to dissolve, to vanish, to die out, to pass away

9 消弭[hsiāo-mĭ]: to end, to remove, to dispel

10 消除[hsiāo-ch'ú]: to eliminate, to liquidate, to remove, to delete

消除異己[hsiāo-ch'ú ì-chĭ]: to liquidate those not of one's own ilk

消耗[hsiāo-hào]: to waste, to exhaust, to drain, to eat up

消耗戰[hsiāo-hào chàn]: war of attrition

消息[hsiāo-hsí]: news, report, dispatch, communication, information

消息靈通人士[hsiāo-hsí líng-t'ūng jén-shìh]: well informed circles, well informed sources

消息報[hsiāo-hsí pào]: Izvestia (Russian daily newspaper)

11 消逝[hsiāo-shìh]: to wither away, to fade, to pass away, to elapse

12 消極[hsiāo-chí]: passivity, inactivity; negative; passive, inactive, inert

消極份子[hsiāo-chí fèn-tzu]: passive elements

消極平衡論[hsiāo-chí p'íng-héng lùn]: theory of negative balancing

消極態度[hsiāo-chí t'ài-tù]: negative attitude, passive attitude

消極等待和觀望態度[hsiāo-chí tĕng-tài hó kuān-wàng t'ài-tù]: a passive wait-and-see attitude

消費[hsiāo-fèi]: consumption, expenditure, expense; to consume, to expend

消費者[hsiāo-fèi chĕ]: consumer

消費合作社[hsiāo-fèi hó-tsò-shè]: Consumer's Co-operative

消費性固定資產[hsiāo-fèi-hsìng kù-tìng tzū-ch'ăn]: consumable fixed assets

消費品[hsiāo-fèi p'ĭn]: consumer goods, consumable goods

消費稅[hsiāo-fèi shùi]: excise tax

消費地區[hsiāo-fèi tì-ch'ū]: consumption areas

消費資料[hsiāo-fèi tzū-liào]: consumption supplies, consumer goods

消散[hsiāo-sàn]: to disperse, to scatter, to diffuse

13 消滅[hsiāo-mièh]: to eliminate, to eradicate, to abolish, to extirpate, to annihilate, to wipe out; annihilation, extermination, extirpation

浪

12 浪費[làng-fèi]: to squander, to waste; extravagant; squander, extravagance, reckless spending (also, one of the targets of the 三反, q.v.)

15 浪潮[làng-ch'áo]: wave, tide

浪漫主義[làng-màn chŭ-ì]: romanticism

浬

浬[lĭ]: nautical mile (abbreviation for 海里)

流

2 流入[líu-jù]: to flow into

3 流亡[líu-wáng]: to exile; exile

4 流水[líu-shŭi]: flowing stream, running water

流水作業法[líu-shŭi tsò-yèh-fă]: streamlined method of work, streamlined production, streamlined coordination conveyer system, conveyer system, streamlined method (an assembly line method in which each worker does a part of the work, the process going on without interruption)

6 流行[líu-hsíng]: to prevail, to circulate; prevalence; prevalent, common, popular

流行病[líu-hsíng pìng]: epidemic

流行病學研究所[líu-hsíng pìng-hsüéh yén-chìu-sŏ]: Epidemiology Institute

流行病學與微生物學研究所[líu-hsíng pìng-hsüéh yü wēi-shēng-wù-hsüéh yén-chìu-sŏ]: Epidemiology and Microbiology Institute

流血[líu-hsüĕh]: to shed blood, to bleed; bloodshed; bloody, sanguinary

7 流利[líu-lì]: fluent, lively, glibly, smoothly, flippantly, fluently, flowingly

流沙[líu-shā]: shifting sands

8 流放[líu-fàng]: to banish; banishment

流氓[líu-máng]: vagrant, loafer, hooligan, ruffian, tramp, vagabond, riff-raff

流氓無產階級[líu-máng wú-ch'ăn chiēh-chí]: vagrant proletariat, Lumpenproletariat

9 流星[líu-hsīng]: meteor

10 流浪[líu-làng]: floating about drifting

11 流產[líu-ch'ăn]: to miscarry; miscarriage

流動資產[líu-tùng tzū-ch'ăn]: liquid assets, floating assets, current assets

流動資金[líu-tùng tzū-chīn]: working capital, circulating funds, current capital

流動資本[líu-tùng tzū-pĕn]: floating capital, working capital

流通[líu-t'ūng]: to circulate; circulation

流域[líu-yǜ]: valley, basin, river reaches, river valley

12 流量[líu-liàng]: volume of flow, amount of flow, flux

13 流傳[líu-ch'uán]: to spread, to be made known extensively, to hand down

14 流綫型[líu-hsièn-hsíng]: streamline; streamlined

15 流彈[líu-tàn]: stray bullet

19 流離失所[líu-lí shīh-sŏ]: destitute and homeless

浦

浦[p'ŭ]: Pukow (abbreviation for 浦口)

4 涉及[shè-chí]: to involve, to concern, to range over, to cover

11 涌現[yŭng-hsièn]: to gush forth and appear

— 8 Strokes —

淺

17 淺薄[ch'iĕn-pó]: superficial

清

1 清一色[ch'īng-í-sè]: monochromatic, all of

the same color, all of one suit (in mahjong counts as three doubles)

4 清化[ch'īng-huà]: Thanhhoa (Vietnam)

清水[ch'īng-shŭi]: Shimizu (Japan)

6 清州[ch'īng-chōu]: Chongju (Korea)

9 清查[ch'īng-ch'á]: to check thoroughly, to investigate clearly, to inquire thoroughly, to examine carefully

清洗[ch'īng-hsĭ]: to cleanse thoroughly, to purge; purge, thorough cleansing

10 清眞寺[ch'īng-chēn ssù]: mosque

清除[ch'īng-ch'ú]: to remove completely, to clean out thoroughly, to weed out carefully

清除廢料[ch'īng-ch'ú fèi-liào]: to clean out rubbish (a phrase meaning to get rid of proven renegades, enemy agents, absolutely unrepentant persons in power taking the capitalist road, degenerates, and alien-class elements from the Party–from an editorial in Red Flag of October 15, 1968)

清高[ch'īng-kāo]: lofty and pure

清宮祕史[ch'īng-kūng mì-shĭh]: Inside Story of the Ch'ing Court (a film produced in Hong Kong in 1949 and shown in mainland China from about 1950 in which the Ch'ing court was portrayed favorably and the Boxers unfavorably, for which reason it was criticized during the Cultural Revolution)

清規戒律[ch'īng-kuēi chièh-lǜ]: taboos and commandments, interdictions and taboos, taboos, doctrinairism

清理[ch'īng-lĭ]: to liquidate, to clear up

清理階級隊伍[ch'īng-lĭ chiēh-chí tùi-wŭ]: to cleanse the class ranks (the purging of those who do not follow closely Chairman Mao's revolutionary line among the mass organizations)

12 清華大學[ch'īng-huá tà-hsüéh]: Tsinghua University

13 清剿[ch'īng-chiăo]: to exterminate

14 清算[ch'īng-suàn]: to liquidate, to settle accounts, to settle scores, to settle old debts; liquidation

清算鬥爭[ch'īng-suàn tòu-chēng]: a liquidation struggle, a struggle to settle accounts

15 清潔[ch'īng-chiéh]: clean, pure, unsullied

清潔隊[ch'īng-chiéh tùi]: cleaning squad, clean-up party

清樣[ch'īng-yàng]: final proof, clean proof, foundry proof

16 清靜[ch'īng-chìng]: secluded, nice and quiet, calm, free of evil thoughts

清醒[ch'īng-hsĭng]: wide awake, alert, sober, sane

17 清償[ch'īng-ch'áng]: to compensate in full, to repay fully, to settle debts in full

清邁[ch'īng-mài]: Chingmei (Thailand)

清點物資[ch'īng-tiĕn wù-tzū]: to take an inventory, to make a list

20 清黨[ch'īng-tăng]: to purge a party; a party purge

清黨運動[ch'īng-tăng yùn-tùng]: campaign to purge the Party

9 涵洞[hán-tùng]: sluice, culvert

13 涵閘[hán-chá]: sluice gate, floodgate

14 涵管[hán-kuăn]: drainage pipe

淮

淮[huái]: Huai River

10 淮海戰役[huái-hăi chàn-ì]: the battle of Huaihai (in 1948, during the Civil War)

2 混入[hùn-jù]: to sneak in, to creep in

[6] 混充 **[hùn-ch'ūng]**: to palm off, to deceive, to pass oneself off for

混合 **[hùn-hó]**: to mix, to mix with, to mingle, to blend, to merge; mixed

混血 **[hùn-hsüěh]**: half-breed, hybrid

[9] 混爲一談 **[hùn-wéi ī-t'án]**: to confuse the issue, to confuse unidentical things as if they were identical, to lump together arbitrarily

[11] 混帳 **[hùn-chàng]**: scoundrel, rascal; damn! the damn...

混淆 **[hùn-yáo]**: to confuse, to mix up, to confuse one with another

混淆是非 **[hùn-yáo shìh-fēi]**: to confuse right and wrong

混淆視聽 **[hùn-yáo shìh-t'īng]**: to confuse the public, to confuse public opinion

混淆敵我 **[hùn-yáo tí-wǒ]**: to confuse friend with foe

[12] 混進 **[hùn-chìn]**: to sneak into, to get into under cover

[13] 混亂 **[hùn-luàn]**: chaos, panic, flurry, confusion, disorder, turmoil; chaotic, confused, disorderly

[16] 混戰 **[hùn-chàn]**: savage battle

混凝土 **[hùn-níng t'ǔ]**: concrete

混凝土工廠 **[hùn-níng t'ǔ kūng-ch'ǎng]**: concrete plant

深

[2] 深入 **[shēn-jù]**: to penetrate deeply into

深入群衆 **[shēn-jù ch'ǘn-chùng]**: to penetrate deeply the masses

[4] 深切 **[shēn-ch'ièh]**: deep, profound, intense

[8] 深刻 **[shēn-k'ò]**: penetrating, profound, thorough

[9] 深重 **[shēn-chùng]**: grave

深厚 **[shēn-hòu]**: profound; on very good terms with, intimate; inexhaustible

[10] 深耕 **[shēn-kēng]**: deep plowing

深耕細作 **[shēn-kēng hsì-tsò]**: deep plowing and careful cultivation

[14] 深遠 **[shēn-yüǎn]**: profound and far-reaching

涮

[9] 涮洗 **[shuàn-hsǐ]**: to wash, to cleanse, to clean, to scrub, to rinse

涮洗罪名 **[shuàn-hsǐ tsùi-míng]**: to wash away charges, to erase charges, to obliterate charges

淡

[4] 淡水 **[tàn-shǔi]**: fresh water; Tamsui (Taiwan)

[8] 淡季 **[tàn-chì]**: off season, slack season (i.e., for business)

[16] 淡薄 **[tàn-páo]**: moderate, insipid, tasteless, poor

添

[8] 添油加醋 **[t'iēn-yú chiā-ts'ù]**: to misrepresent by overstating, to enlarge beyond bounds or truth

液

[23] 液體 **[yèh-t'ǐ]**: fluid; liquid

液體燃料 **[yèh-t'ǐ ján-liào]**: liquid fuel

液體有機肥料 **[yèh-t'ǐ yǔ-chī féi-liào]**: liquid organic fertilizer

淵

[12] 淵博 **[yüān-pó]**: deep and broad, comprehensive

— 9 Strokes —

渣

[13] 渣滓 [chā-tzǔ] : dregs, scum, sediment

減

[4] 減少 [chiěn-shǎo] : to reduce, to decrease, to drop, to fall, to diminish, to lessen, to cut down, to abate; decrease, reduction

[5] 減去 [chiěn-ch'ü] : to diminish, to take off, to subtract, to deduct

減半 [chiěn-pàn] : to cut in half, to halve, to reduce by one half

[6] 減色 [chiěn-sè] : to dim, to obscure, to overshadow, to damage, to detract from

減刑 [chiěn-hsíng] : to commute a sentence, to reduce punishment; commutation of sentence, reduction of sentence

[7] 減低 [chiěn-tī] : to reduce, to lower

[8] 減法 [chiěn-fǎ] : subtraction

減免 [chiěn-miěn] : to reduce

[9] 減省 [chiěn-shěng] : to diminish, to retrench, to save; frugal, economical

[10] 減弱 [chiěn-jò] : to diminish, to reduce, to weaken

減料 [chiěn-liào] : cheating on materials, skimping on materials—a target of the 五反 campaign (See 五反)

減租 [chiěn-tsū] : to reduce rent

減租減息 [chiěn-tsū chiěn-hsī] : to reduce rent and rate of interest; reduction in rent and interest

減租退押 [chiěn-tsū t'ùi-yā] : to reduce rents and refund land rent deposits

[11] 減產 [chiěn-ch'ǎn] : to decrease production or output; decrease in output, drop in production

[13] 減損 [chiěn-sǔn] : to reduce, to diminish; hurt, injury

[14] 減輕 [chiěn-ch'īng] : to lighten, to reduce, to mitigate, to allay, to alleviate, to ease, to relieve

[15] 減價 [chiěn-chià] : to reduce the price; price reduction, price cut

減緩 [chiěn-huǎn] : to retard, to slow down, to slacken

渠

[13] 渠道 [ch'ü-tào] : irrigation canal, canal, drain, sewer, channel, gutter, ditch

湘

湘 [hsiāng] : Hunan (abbreviation for 湖南)

渙

[12] 渙散 [huàn-sàn] : disorganization, disunity, disunion, disruption, disintegration, dispersal; dispersed, scattered

渾

[4] 渾天儀 [hún-t'iēn-í] : armillary sphere, celestial globe

[7] 渾身是膽 [hún-shēn shìh-tǎn] : foolhardy, thoroughly bold or daring

[12] 渾然 [hún-ján] : completely, totally, through and through

[13] 渾圓 [hún-yúan] : spherical, completely rounded-out

[21] 渾鐵 [hún-t'iěh] : crude iron, iron-ore, pig iron

港

[3] 港口 [kǎng-k'ǒu] : port, harbor

25 港灣 [kăng-wān] : bay

渴

11 渴望 [k'ŏ-wàng] : to long for eagerly, to hope earnestly, to aspire earnestly to

湄

4 湄公河 [méi-kūng hó] : Mekong River (Burma)

渺

9 渺茫 [miăo-máng] : vague, indistinct, dim and remote, hazy

渤

10 渤海 [pó-hăi] : Gulf of Chihli

測

8 測度 [ts'ê-tò] : to calculate, to measure, to estimate

10 測候 [ts'ê-hòu] : to make meteorological observations, to make astronomical observations

12 測量 [ts'ê-liáng] : to measure, to survey; measurement, mensuration

測量及地球物理研究所 [ts'ê-liáng chí tì-ch'íu wù-lĭ yén-chìu-sŏ] : Geodesy and Geophysics Institute

測量製圖研究所 [ts'ê-liáng chìh-t'ú yén-chìu-sŏ] : Geodesy and Cartography Institute

23 測驗 [ts'ê-yèn] : to test; test

湊

4 湊手 [ts'òu-shŏu] : convenient to the hand, ready to hand

6 湊成 [ts'òu-ch'éng] : to add up to, to make in all

湊合 [ts'òu-hó] : to collect, to assemble, to amass, to converge

8 湊近 [ts'òu-chìn] : to get near

渡

3 渡口 [tù-k'ŏu] : ford, crossing

11 渡船 [tù-ch'uán] : ferryboat

13 渡過 [tù-kuò] : to ferry, to cross over, to get through, to get over, to tide over

16 渡頭 [tù-t'óu] : river crossing, ford, ferry

溫

7 溫床 [wēn-ch'uáng] : hotbed

8 溫和 [wēn-hó] : moderate, gentle, mild, soft, lenient, temperate, not extreme

溫和派 [wēn-hó p'ài] : moderates, moderate party

9 溫室 [wēn-shìh] : hothouse

10 溫哥華太陽報 [wēn-kō-huá t'ài-yáng pào] : Vancouver Sun (Canadian daily newspaper)

溫情主義 [wēn-ch'íng chŭ-ì] : bonhomie-ism (good treatment of workers by capitalists)

溫得和克 [wēn-té-hó-k'ò] : Windhoek (Southwest Africa)

渦

15 渦輪機 [wō-lún-chī] : turbine

渥

4 渥太華 [wò-t'ài-huá] : Ottawa (Canada)

渥太華日報 [wò-t'ài-huá jìh-pào] : Ottawa

Journal (Canadian daily newspaper)

游

5 游民 **[yú-mín]**: vagabonds, wanderers, vagrants, homeless people

游民無產者 **[yú-mín wú-ch'ăn-chĕ]**: member of the Lumpenproletariat

游民無產階級 **[yú-mín wú-ch'ăn chiēh-chí]**: Lumpenproletariat

6 游行 **[yú-hsíng]**: to parade, to demonstrate; procession, parade, demonstration

游行示威 **[yú-hsíng shìh-wēi]**: to parade; parade, demonstration, procession

游行自由 **[yú-hsíng tzù-yú]**: freedom of demonstration, freedom to hold processions or parades

9 游客 **[yú-k'ò]**: traveller, tourist, visitor

13 游艇 **[yú-t'ĭng]**: yacht, motor boat

游資 **[yú-tzū]**: idle capital, idle money, idle funds

游園會 **[yú-yüán-hùi]**: garden party

16 游歷 **[yú-lì]**: to travel; travel, tour, excursion, tourism

17 游擊戰 **[yú-chī chàn]**: guerrilla warfare, partisan warfare

游擊主義 **[yú-chī chŭ-ì]**: guerrilla-ism

游擊隊 **[yú-chī tùi]**: guerrilla forces, guerrilla unit

21 游覽 **[yú-lăn]**: to go sightseeing, to go on an excursion; sightseeing, excursion

游覽地 **[yú-lăn tì]**: popular resort, center for excursions

湧

5 湧出 **[yŭng-ch'ū]**: to gush or spurt forth, to burst out; outpouring

11 湧現 **[yŭng-hsièn]**: to gush forth and appear

— 10 Strokes —

準

12 準備 **[chŭn-pèi]**: to prepare, to get ready; preparation, preparedness, readiness

16 準確 **[chŭn-ch'üèh]**: accuracy, exactness, precision; accurate, precise, exact

溪

5 溪布 **[hsī-pù]**: Khebo (Vietnam)

滑 **[huá]**: to slide, to slip, to glide; slippery, smooth, polished

7 滑車 **[huá-ch'ē]**: pulley

12 滑翔 **[huá-hsiáng]**: to glide

滑翔機 **[huá-hsiáng chī]**: glider

13 滑溜 **[huá-líu]**: to slip, to slide; slippery, cunning

15 滑稽 **[huá-chī]**: funny, farcical, ridiculous, humorous; farce, humor; fawning, plausible

滑潤油 **[huá-jùn yú]**: grease, lubricating oil

滑輪 **[huá-lún]**: pulley, windlass

16 滑劑 **[huá-chì]**: grease, lubricant

滑頭 **[huá-t'óu]**: scoundrel, crook, hypocrite, a slippery customer; cunning, roguish, mendacious, false, hypocritical

滙

5 滙付 **[hùi-fù]**: to pay to, to pay out

6 滙合 **[hùi-hó]**: to converge, to flow together, to meet, to coincide, to assemble; confluence, meeting, coincidence, assembly

[7] 匯兌[hùi-tùi]: to transmit money; remittance

匯兌網[hùi-tùi wǎng]: remittance network

[11] 匯票[hùi-p'iào]: money order, draft, letter of credit, bill of exchange

[12] 匯款[hùi-k'uǎn]: to remit money; remittance, draft

匯報[hùi-pào]: to report, to give an account of; briefing, comprehensive report, compiled report

[15] 匯編[hùi-piēn]: collection, compilation

溢

[9] 溢洪道[ì-húng tào]: flood diversion channel, spillway

溢洪堰[ì-húng yěn]: storage dam, overflow spillway

溶

[13] 溶解[júng-chiěh]: to thaw, to melt, to dissolve, to disintegrate, to soften

溝

溝[kōu]: ditch, gutter, groove, flume, gully, channel

[11] 溝渠[kōu-ch'ǘ]: ditch, channel, gutter

滅

[3] 滅亡[mièh-wáng]: to extirpate, to exterminate, to destroy; extermination, elimination, annihilation

[4] 滅火[mièh-huǒ]: extirpation, to extinguish or quench, to put out a fire

[12] 滅絕[mièh-chüéh]: to exterminate, to extirpate, to annihilate; extermination, elimination, annihilation

溥

[14] 溥瑪[p'ǔ-mǎ]: Prince Phouma, S. (Laotian political leader)

滔

[4] 滔天[t'āo-t'iēn]: to reach to the heavens; extremely great; dreadful

滔天罪行[t'āo-t'iēn tsùi-hsìng]: towering crimes, monstrous crimes, atrocities

滇

滇[tiēn]: Yunnan (abbreviation for 雲南)

[15] 滇緬公路[tiēn-miěn kūng-lù]: Burma Road

滋

[5] 滋生[tzū-shēng]: to sprout, to spring up, to multiply

[8] 滋長[tzū-chǎng]: to spring up, to grow

滋味[tzū-wèi]: flavor, taste

[15] 滋養[tzū-yǎng]: nourishment; nutritious, nourishing

源

[9] 源泉[yüán-ch'üán]: source, origin, mainspring

—11 Strokes—

漲

[4] 漲水季節[chǎng-shǔi chì-chiéh]: high water season

[9] 漲風[chǎng-fēng]: upward trend, rising tendency

15 漲潮[chăng-ch'áo] : rising tide

漲價[chăng-chià] : rise in price

漸

6 漸次[chièn-tz'ù]: one after the other, in order, gradual

12 漸進[chièn-chìn]: to develop gradually; gradual advance, gradual progress

14 漸漸推進[chièn-chièn t'ūi-chìn]: to inch forward, to advance by small degrees

滯

10 滯留[chìh-líu] : to hold up, to obstruct, to impede, to hinder, to stop, to defer, to detain, to retain

滯納金[chìh-nà chīn]: fine for delayed payment

漢

漢[hàn]: Hankow (abbreviation for 漢口)

2 漢人[hàn-jén]: the men of Han, the Han people, the Chinese

6 漢江[hàn chiāng] : Han River (Korea)

漢奸[hàn-chiēn] : traitor to China, traitor

漢字簡化方案[hàn-tzù chiĕn-huà fāng-àn]: Program for the Simplification of the Chinese Language

9 漢城[hàn-ch'éng] : Seoul (Korea)

12 漢堡[hàn-păo] : Hamburg

14 漢語[hàn-yŭ] : the Chinese language

漢語規範化[hàn-yŭ kuēi-fàn-huà]: standardization of the Chinese language

漢語拼音方案[hàn-yŭ p'īn-yīn fāng-àn]: Program for the Phonetic Spelling of the Chinese Language

漢語拼音符號[hàn-yŭ p'īn-yīn fú-hào]: Chinese phonetic alphabet; phonetic transcription of Chinese characters

16 漢學家[hàn-hsüéh-chiā] : sinologist

滬

滬[hù]: Shanghai (abbreviation for 上海)

15 滬劇[hù-chü] : Shanghai Opera

滾

5 滾出[kŭn-ch'ū] : to get out, scram

10 滾珠軸承廠[kŭn-chū chóu-ch'éng ch'ăng]: ball bearing plant

漏

9 漏洞[lòu-tùng] : hole, gap, loophole

11 漏掉[lòu-tiào] : to overlook, to leave out

滿

滿[măn] : Manchus

7 滿足[măn-tsú]: to satisfy, to fulfil, to gratify; satisfied, content

9 滿洲[măn-chōu] : Manchuria

10 滿座[măn-tsò] : full house, packed house

12 滿期[măn-ch'ī] : to mature, to reach the end of a term, to expire, to run out, to fall due; expiration, reaching, maturity

13 滿意[măn-ì]: to be satisfied, to be content with; satisfaction, satisfactory

滿載超軸運動[măn-tsài ch'āo-chóu yùn-tùng]: movement for capacity loads and bigger haulage

漫

8 漫長 **[màn-ch'áng]**: lengthy, extensive, far reaching

漫長曲折的 **[màn-ch'áng ch'ǖ-ché te]**: long and tortuous

12 漫畫 **[màn-huà]**: caricature, cartoon

漫畫家 **[màn-huà-chiā]**: cartoonist

漠

4 漠不關心 **[mò pù-kuān-hsīn]**: indifference, unconcern; apathetic, indifferent, cold, unconcerned, half-hearted

漂

9 漂亮 **[p'iào-liàng]**: brilliant, fresh, smart, bright, suave, sleek and glossy, neat and attractive, pretty

滲

2 滲入 **[shèn-jù]**: to infiltrate, to penetrate, infiltration, penetration

11 滲透 **[shèn-t'òu]**: to permeate; percolation, osmosis

滴

14 滴滴涕 **[tī-tī-t'ì]**: DDT (i.e., insecticide)

演

4 演化 **[yěn-huà]**: to evolve; evolution

5 演出 **[yěn-ch'ū]**: to perform, to stage; performance, presentation

演出人 **[yěn-ch'ū jén]**: producer (i.e., of movies, plays, etc.)

10 演員 **[yěn-yüán]**: actor, actress, player, performer

11 演習 **[yěn-hsí]**: to practice, to learn; drill, practice, maneuvers, exercises

17 演講 **[yěn-chiǎng]**: to make a speech, to lecture, to address; speech, address, lecture

19 演繹 **[yěn-ì]**: to deduce; deduction; deductive

演繹法 **[yěn-ì fǎ]**: deductive method

漁

5 漁民 **[yǘ-mín]**: fishermen, fishing population

8 漁具 **[yǘ-chǜ]**: fishing gear, fishing tackle

11 漁船 **[yǘ-ch'uán]**: fishing boat, trawler

13 漁業 **[yǘ-yèh]**: fishery, fishing industry

— 12 Strokes —

潮

4 潮升 **[ch'áo-shēng]**: to rise like a tide

潮水 **[ch'áo-shuǐ]**: the tide

潮水戰術 **[ch'áo-shuǐ chàn-shù]**: infiltration tactics

10 潮流 **[ch'áo-líu]**: tide, current, trend

13 潮落 **[ch'áo-lò]**: to ebb like a tide

澆

17 澆薄 **[chiāo-pó]**: indecent, unreliable, disloyal, bad, ungrateful

潔

3 潔己奉公 **[chiéh-chǐ fèng-kūng]**: incorruptible, honest, loyal in service

7 潔身自好[chiéh-shēn tzǔ-hǎo]: to remain incorruptible

11 潔淨[chiéh-chìng]: pure, clear, chaste, clean

潛

2 潛力[ch'ién-lì]: potential strength, latent force

4 潛水艇[ch'ién-shuǐ-t'ǐng]: submarine

10 潛能[ch'ién-néng]: latent force, potentiality

13 潛意識[ch'ién ì-shìh]: the subconscious

潤

6 潤色[jùn-sè]: to color, to embellish, to polish, to give the final polish to, to put the finishing touches on

13 潤滑油[jùn-huá yú]: lubricating oil, lubricating grease, lubricant

潰

4 潰不成軍[k'uèi pù-ch'éng chūn]: to be utterly routed

21 潰爛[k'uèi-làn]: to ulcerate; ulceration; ulcerative

潘

8 潘迪特夫人[p'ān-tí-t'è fū-jén]: Pandit, Mrs. Vijaya Lakshmi (Indian stateswoman)

澎

12 澎湃[p'éng-p'ài]: to surge; surging, rising, boom, sound of breaking waves

澄

11 澄清[tèng-ch'īng]: to clarify

— 13 Strokes —

澳

3 澳大利亞[ào-tà-lì-yà]: Australia

澳大利亞聯邦[ào-tà-lì-yà lién-pāng]: Commonwealth of Australia

8 澳門[ào-mén]: Macao

9 澳洲[ào-chōu]: Australia

激

8 激昂[chī-áng]: to stimulate to a high degree of excitement; excitement; excited, moved

9 激怒[chī-nù]: to irritate, to anger, to provoke, to enrage, to infuriate

10 激起[chī-ch'ǐ]: to arouse, to stir up, to incite, to excite, to stimulate; incitement

激烈[chī-lièh]: violent, fierce, acute, sharp, keen, intense, drastic

激流[chī-líu]: torrent, violent stream

11 激動[chī-tùng]: to excite, to inspire, to stimulate

12 激進主義[chī-chìn chǔ-ì]: radicalism, maximalism

激進派民主人士[chī-chìn-p'ài mín-chǔ jén-shìh]: democrat of the radical type

激發[chī-fā]: to arouse, to spur on

16 激戰[chī-chàn]: fierce battle, pitched battle, intense fighting

23 激變[chī-pièn]: to revolt, to incite to rebellion, to incite to mutiny

— 14 Strokes —

濟

濟[chǐ]: Tsinan (abbreviation for 濟南)

6 濟州島 [chì-chōu tăo] : Cheju Island (Korea)

9 濟急 [chì-chí] : to help someone in need

濫

5 濫用 [làn-yùng] : to abuse, to misuse, to use indiscriminately; extravagant, lavish, wanton

6 濫伐林木 [làn-fā lín-mù] : unregulated cutting of timber

— 15 Strokes —

21 瀏覽 [líu-lăn] : to glance, to go over

— 16 Strokes —

10 瀟灑 [hsiāo-să] : light-hearted, unconventional, lifted above the sordid bustle of life

瀕

17 瀕臨 [pīn-lín] : to get near, to approach; near, close to, on the verge of, just about to

— 18 Strokes —

灌

9 灌音 [kuàn-yīn] : to record on tape; tape recording

13 灌溉 [kuàn-kài] : to irrigate, to water

灌溉渠 [kuàn-kài ch'ǘ] : irrigation canal

灌溉面積 [kuàn-kài mièn-chī] : irrigated area

16 灌輸 [kuàn-shū] : to introduce, to teach, to pour into; indoctrination, inculcation

— 19 Strokes —

灘 [t'ān] : sand bank, rapid

— 22 Strokes —

13 灣路 [wān-lù] : winding road, detour

— RADICAL 火 灬 丶 86 —

火

2 火力 [huŏ-lì] : firepower

火力發電廠 [huŏ-lì fā-tièn ch'ăng] : thermal power plant

火力發電設備 [huŏ-lì fā-tièn shè-pèi] : thermo-electric power generating equipment

火力電站 [huŏ-lì tièn-chàn] : thermo-electric power station

3 火山 [huŏ-shān] : volcano

火山口 [huŏ-shān k'ŏu] : volcanic crater

火上加油 [huŏ-shàng chiā-yú] : to add fuel to the flames, to pour oil over the flames, to stir things up

7 火車 [huŏ-ch'ē] : train

火車車廂 [huŏ-ch'ē ch'ē-hsiāng] : carriage, car, coach (i.e., of train)

火車道 [huŏ-ch'ē tào] : railroad line, railroad track

火車頭 [huŏ-ch'ē t'óu] : a locomotive (during the Cultural Revolution, a simile for the thought of Mao)

8 火花 [huŏ-huā] : spark

火油 [huŏ-yú] : kerosene

9 火炬 [huŏ-chǜ] : torch, torchlight

火星 [huŏ-hsīng] : Mars; sparks

火星報 [huŏ-hsīng pào] : Iskra (a Russian newspaper published by Lenin)

10 火柴 [huŏ-ch'ái] : match (for producing fire)

火海戰鬥團[huŏ-hăi chàn-tòu t'uán] : Sea of Flames Fighting Troop (a non-genuine Revolutionary Rebel Group in Heilungchiang during the Cultural Revolution)

11 火速 [huŏ-sù] : quickly, at express speed, posthaste

12 火焰 [huŏ-yèn] : flame, blaze of a fire

13 火傷 [huŏ-shāng] : burn, burn wound

火葬 [huŏ-tsàng] : cremation; to cremate

14 火暴性子[huŏ-pào hsìng-tzu] : hothead, hot temper, fiery temperament; hotheaded, irascible, easily angered

火網 [huŏ-wăng] : cross fire, barrage, belt of fire, fire net

15 火箭 [huŏ-chièn] : rocket

火箭發射臺[huŏ-chièn fā-shè-t'ái] : rocket launch pad, rocket firing ramp

火箭砲 [huŏ-chièn p'ào] : rocket launcher, rocket gun, bazooka

火箭筒 [huŏ-chièn t'ŭng] : rocket launcher, bazooka

火線 [huŏ-hsièn] : front, firing line, line of fire

火熱 [huŏ-jè] : passionate, enthusiastic, ardent, fervent

火輪 [huŏ-lún] : steamer, steamship

16 火器 [huŏ-ch'ì] : firearm

19 火警 [huŏ-chĭng] : fire alarm

火藥 [huŏ-yào] : gunpowder

— 2 Strokes —

灰

4 灰心 [hūi-hsīn] : to be disheartened, to despair; dejection, depression; discouraged, depressed

5 灰白 [hūi-pái] : pale, ashen

6 灰色人生觀[hūi-sè jén-shēng-kuān] : a pessimistic philosophy of life, a pessimistic attitude toward life

8 灰泥 [hūi-ní] : mortar, plaster

— 3 Strokes —

5 災民 [tsāi-mín] : disaster victims, victims of natural calamities

10 災害 [tsāi-hài] : disaster, calamity

災荒 [tsāi-huāng] : famine

19 災難 [tsāi-nàn] : disaster, calamity, adversity, catastrophe

災難深重[tsāi-nàn shēn-chùng] : great calamities, grave disasters; woe-stricken, heavily laden with calamities

— 5 Strokes —

炸

10 炸破 [chà-p'ò] : to blast, to explode open

13 炸燬 [chà-hŭi] : to blow up, to dynamite

15 炸彈 [chà-tàn] : bomb

19 炸藥 [chà-yào] : dynamite, explosive

炫

20 炫耀 [hsüàn-yào] : to boast, to show off

炫耀武力[hsüàn-yào wŭ-lì] : to show one's force

炮

4 炮手[p'ào-shŏu] : gunner, artillery man

5 炮台[p'ào-t'ái] : fortress, fort, fortification, battery, emplacement

6 炮灰[p'ào-hūi] : cannon fodder

7 炮兵[p'ào-pīng] : artillery

12 炮隊[p'ào-tùi] : battery, gun detachment

15 炮樓[p'ào-lóu] : gun turret

17 炮擊[p'ào-chī] : to bombard; bombardment

20 炮艦[p'ào-chièn] : gunboat

炮艦政策[p'ào-chièn chèng-ts'è] : gunboat policy

— 6 Strokes —

烈

3 烈士[lièh-shìh] : martyr

21 烈屬[lièh-shŭ] : family of a martyr, dependents of war dead

烏

3 烏干達[wū-kān-tá] : Uganda

4 烏什[wū-shìh] : Uch Turfan (Sinkiang)

5 烏市[wū-shìh] : Urumchi; Tihua

6 烏合之衆[wū-hó chīh chùng] : mob, rabble

烏托邦[wū-t'ō pāng] : Utopia; utopian

8 烏拉圭[wū-lā-kuēi] : Uruguay

烏拉圭共和國[wū-lā-kuēi kùng-hó-kuó] : Republic of Uruguay

烏松布拉[wū-sūng-pù-lā] : Usumbura (Burundi)

10 烏玆白克[wū-tzū-pó-k'ò] : Uzbek (minority nationality)

烏玆貝克[wū-tzū-pèi-k'ò] : Uzbek (minority nationality)

烏玆別克[wū-tzū-piéh-k'ò] : Uzbek (minority nationality)

烏烟瘴氣[wū-yēn chàng-ch'ì] : foul atmosphere; murky, noisome, fetid

12 烏斯庫達[wū-ssū-k'ù-tá] : Uskudar (Turkey)

13 烏路圭[wū-lù-kuēi] : Uruguay

21 烏蘭夫[wū-lán-fū] : Ulanfu (Mongolian political leader)

烏蘭牧騎[wū-lán mù-ch'í] : Ulanmuchi; red cultural team (a form of team formed by artists and writers of Inner Mongolia who travel about the country serving the herdsmen–the term has been broadened to mean a travelling cultural group performing for villagers)

烏蘭巴托[wū-lán pā-t'ō] : Ulan Bator (Outer Mongolia)

烟

10 烟草[yēn-ts'ăo] : tobacco

13 烟煤[yēn-méi] : bituminous coal, soft coal

烟葉[yēn-yèh] : leaf tobacco

14 烟幕[yēn-mù] : smokescreen

— 7 Strokes —

焊

焊[hàn] : welding, weld

3 焊工[hàn-kūng] : welder

— 8 Strokes —

焦

3 焦土[chiāo-t'ŭ] : charred soil, scorched earth

焦土政策[chiāo-t'ǔ chèng-ts'è]: "scorched earth" policy

9 焦急[chiāo-chí]: vexed, worried, grieved

焦炭[chiāo-t'àn]: coke

10 焦砟[chiāo-chă]: coke slag

13 焦煤[chiāo-méi]: coke, coking coal

15 焦慮[chiāo-lǜ]: anxiety, concern; anxious, worried

17 焦點[chiāo-tiĕn]: focus, focal point

無

1 無一漏網[wú-ī lòu-wăng]: none escape from the net

2 無人的[wú-jén te]: deserted, empty, uninhabited, unoccupied

3 無上的[wú-shàng te]: insuperable, unsurpassable, topmost, highest, culminating, crowning, supreme

4 無中不能生有 [wú-chūng pù-néng shēng-yǔ]: "From nothing, nothing comes"

無中生有[wú-chūng shēng-yǔ]: sheer fabrication; to create out of clean air; out of a clear sky, groundless, fictitious, invented, fabricated, unfounded, trumped up

無孔不入[wú-k'ŭng pú-jù]: to lose no chance, to have a finger in every pie, always trying to penetrate into; all-pervasive

無比的[wú-pĭ te]: incomparable, inimitable, unique, peerless, unrivalled, matchless, unequalled, beyond comparison

無文化[wú-wén-huà]: uncultured

5 無出路[wú ch'ū-lù]: no way out

無可爭辯的[wú-k'ŏ chēng-pièn te]: incontestable, indisputable, unimpeachable, irrefutable, unquestionable

無可諱言[wú-k'ŏ hùi-yén]: undeniable, past dispute, beyond all question

無可無不可[wú-k'ŏ wú pù-k'ŏ]: indecisive, uncertain, without any preconceived ideas, not something which one must or must not do

無用的[wú-yùng te]: futile, useless, inefficacious, unavailing, ineffectual, unserviceable

6 無共同之處[wú kùng-t'úng chīh ch'ù]: to have nothing in common with

無名小卒[wú-míng hsiăo-tsú]: a nobody, a cypher, a nameless member of the crowd

7 無利可圖[wú-lì k'ŏ-t'ú]: unprofitable, no profit to seek

無私的[wú-ssū te]: selfless, self-denying, self-sacrificing, disinterested, unselfish, altruistic

無私援助[wú-ssū yüán-chù]: selfless aid (i.e., refers to Soviet aid during the period of dependence on the Soviet Union)

8 無法[wú-fă]: no way, no means of, no means to; lawless

無法解脫[wú-fă chiĕh-t'ō]: inextricable

無法無天[wú-fă wú-t'ïen]: lawless, reckless, unruly, bold, shameless, immoral

無非是[wú fēi-shìh]: merely, nothing but, nothing more than

無依無靠[wú-ī wú-k'ào]: to have no dependents and no one to depend upon, to have no family

無怪[wú-kuài]: it is not to be wondered that, it is not surprising that, no wonder that

無例外地[wú lì-wài tì]: without exception

無事生非[wú-shìh shēng-fēi]: to create something out of nothing

無時無刻[wú-shíh wú-k'ò]: constantly, at all times, without a moment's pause

無所不[wú-sŏ pù]: nothing which is not, nothing (he, etc.) won't . . .

無所不至[wú-sŏ pú-chìh]: to go to all lengths, by every possible means, capable of anything, reckless

無所顧忌[wú-sŏ kù-chì]: unscrupulous, fearless

無底洞[wú-tĭ tùng]: a bottomless hole

無的放矢[wú-tì fàng-shĭh]: to shoot when there is no target, to let fly at nothing; aimless shooting

9 無政府[wú chèng-fŭ]: anarchy

無政府主義[wú chèng-fŭ chŭ-ì]: anarchism

無政府狀態[wú chèng-fŭ chuàng-t'ài]: anarchical condition, chaotic condition

無紀律[wú chì-lǜ]: undisciplined, disorderly

無限[wú-hsièn]: infinite, indefinite, boundless, unlimited, limitless

無限期[wú hsièn-ch'í]: for an indefinite period of time, unlimited time; indefinitely

無限忠心[wú-hsièn chūng-hsīn]: boundless loyalty

無限關懷[wú-hsièn kuān-huái]: boundless concern

無限上綱[wú-hsièn shàng-kāng]: building up crimes (a slang expression of North China meaning to inflate small matters into serious offences in order to incriminate a person or a group of persons, and which, during the Cultural Revolution, was often used by Red Guard factions in accusing each other)

無故[wú-kù]: without reason, without cause, for no reason

無保留的[wú pǎo-líu te]: unreserved, unconditional; without reservation

無保留地支持[wú pǎo-líu tì chīh-ch'íh]: to support unreservedly, to support unconditionally; unconditional support, all-out support

無神論[wú-shén lùn]: atheism

10 無記名投票[wú chì-míng t'óu-p'iào]: secret ballot

無恥[wú-ch'ĭh]: blatant, barefaced, brazen, shameless; unabashed effrontery

無恥到極點[wú-ch'ĭh tào chí-tièn]: brazen in the extreme

無害的[wú-hài te]: harmless, inoffensive, innocuous

無效[wú-hsiào]: invalid, ineffective, futile, inoperative, null and void

無效果[wú hsiào-kuŏ]: fruitless, unproductive; of no effect

無容身之地[wú júng-shēn chīh tì]: with no place to hide, nowhere to lay one's head

無根據的[wú kēn-chǜ te]: groundless, unsound, unfounded, false, fallacious, erroneous, without foundation

無能[wú-néng]: impotence, inability, incompetence; impotent, unable, incapable, incompetent

無能爲力[wú-néng wéi-lì]: powerless, unable, impotent, incapable

無病呻吟[wú-pìng shēn-yín]: groaning when not really in pain, making a fuss about nothing

無原則的[wú yüán-tsé te]: unprincipled, not based on any principle

無原子武器區[wú yüán-tzŭ wŭ-ch'ì ch'ū]: atom free zone, non-atomic zone, atomic weapon free zone

11 無產階級[wú-ch'ăn chiēh-chí]: proletariat; proletarian

無產階級專政[wú-ch'ăn chiēh-chí chuān-chèng]: dictatorship of the proletariat

無產階級革命[wú-ch'ăn chiēh-chí kó-mìng]: proletarian revolution

無產階級革命接班人[wú-ch'ăn chiēh-chí kó-mìng chiēh-pān-jén]: proletarian revolutionary successor

無產階級革命接班人的五個條件[wú-ch'ăn chiēh-chí kó-mìng chiēh-pān-jén te wŭ-kò t'iáo-chièn]: the five conditions for being a proletarian revolutionary successor (*See* 五個條件)

無產階級革命路綫[**wú-ch'ăn chiēh-chí kó-mìng lù-hsièn**]: proletarian revolutionary line (i.e., the ideology and policies of Mao Tse-tung)

無產階級國際主義原則[**wú-ch'ăn chiēh-chí kuó-chì chŭ-ì yüán-tsé**]: the principle of proletarian internationalism

無產階級文化大革命[**wú-ch'ăn chiēh-chí wén-huà tà kó-mìng**]: the Great Proletarian Cultural Revolution

無情[**wú-ch'íng**]: merciless, unfeeling, cruel

無情打擊[**wú-ch'íng tă-chī**]: merciless blow, pitiless blow

無異[**wú-ì**]: to differ in no way from, to be tantamount to, not different

無理[**wú-lĭ**]: unreasonable

無理取鬧[**wú-lĭ ch'ŭ-nào**]: unreasonable altercation, unprovoked quarrel

無理由地[**wú lĭ-yú ti**]: unreasonably, gratuitously, unprovoked, unwarrantedly, unjustifiably

無聊[**wú-liáo**]: ennui, nonsense; purposeless, silly, boring

無條件[**wú t'iáo-chièn**]: unconditioned, unconditional, unqualified, unreserved; unconditionally

無動於中[**wú-tùng yü chūng**]: aloof and indifferent, untouched, unmoved, insensible, unconcerned

12 無期徒刑[**wú-ch'í t'ú-hsíng**]: to be sentenced for life; life imprisonment

無結果[**wú chiéh-kuŏ**]: without result, to achieve nothing

無辜[**wú-kū**]: innocent, guiltless

無辜者[**wú-kū-chĕ**]: an innocent person, an innocent victim

無視[**wú-shìh**]: to ignore, to disregard, in defiance of

13 無意[**wú-ì**]: unintentional, inadvertent

無意中[**wú-ì chūng**]: casually, unintentionally, without design, by chance, unwittingly, inadvertently, accidentally

無意義的[**wú ì-ì te**]: meaningless, void of meaning, senseless, with no sense

無意識的[**wú ì-shìh te**]: unconscious

無端[**wú-tuān**]: unprovoked, without provocation, without cause or reason, for no reason

無微不至[**wú-wēi pú-chìh**]: meticulous

14 無精打彩[**wú-chīng tă-ts'ăi**]: listless, dejected, disheartened, apathetic

無綫電技術研究所[**wú-hsièn-tièn chì-shù yén-chìu-sŏ**]: Radio Technology Institute (Shanghai)

無綫電傳眞[**wú-hsièn-tièn ch'uán-chēn**]: radio facsimile

無綫電控制[**wú-hsièn-tièn k'ùng-chìh**]: radio control

無綫電電子學[**wú-hsièn-tièn tièn-tzŭ-hsüéh**]: radio electronics

無需[**wú-hsǖ**]: to have no need of, to dispense with, to go without, to do without; not necessary

無疑[**wú-í**]: without doubt, beyond a doubt, doubtless, there is no question that

15 無稽之談[**wú-chī chīh t'án**]: unfounded remarks, fiction, fabrication

無價之寶[**wú-chià chīh păo**]: priceless treasure, invaluable asset

無窮[**wú-ch'iúng**]: endless, unending, infinite, inexhaustible, interminable

無衝突論[**wú ch'ūng-t'ù lùn**]: no-conflict theory

無賴[**wú-lài**]: to be without means of support, good-for-nothing, worthless fellow, hooligan, rascal, scoundrel

無賴子 **[wú-lài-tzu]** : a good-for-nothing

無論 **[wú-lùn]** : regardless, no matter, whatever, however

無論如何 **[wú-lùn jú-hó]** : in any event, in any case, under any circumstances, no matter what happens

無數 **[wú-shù]** : innumerable, countless, numberless, incalculable, immeasurable, myriad

無敵於天下 **[wú-tí yü t'iēn-hsià]** : with no equal in the world, invincible

無影無踪 **[wú-yǐng wú-tsūng]** : not a trace remaining, to have disappeared without a trace

無緣無故 **[wú-yüán wú-kù]** : without rhyme or reason, for no reason at all

16 無懈可擊 **[wú-hsièh k'ŏ-chī]** : invulnerable, unassailable, impregnable

17 無濟於事的 **[wú-chì yü-shìh te]** : of no help, of no use, of no avail

18 無關 **[wú-kuān]** : unrelated, no connection with, to have nothing to do with

20 無黨派人物 **[wú tăng-p'ài jén-wù]** : public figures without party affiliation

無黨派民主人士 **[wú tăng-p'ài mín-chŭ jén-shìh]** : democratic figures without party affiliation

21 無顧忌的批評 **[wú kù-chì te p'ī-p'íng]** : fearless criticism, unshrinking criticism

22 無權過問 **[wú-ch'üán kuò-wèn]** : to have no right to question, not within one's jurisdiction to question

焰

4 焰火 **[yèn-huŏ]** : fireworks, pyrotechnic display

— 9 Strokes —

照

4 照片 **[chào-p'ièn]** : photograph, picture

5 照出 **[chào-ch'ū]** : to break forth, to emit rays of light, to give light, to shine on, to light up

7 照抄 **[chào-ch'āo]** : to copy verbatim; mechanical copying of an original text

照抄照搬 **[chào-ch'āo chào-pān]** : uncritical duplication and appropriation (i.e., of old or foreign things)

照妖鏡 **[chào-yāo chìng]** : demon-exposing mirror (a magic instrument or device that uncovers Mao's opponents)

8 照例 **[chào-lì]** : routine, as usual

照明 **[chào-míng]** : to light, to light up, to illumine, to illuminate; lighting, illumination

照明彈 **[chào-míng-tàn]** : illuminating shell, flare, flare bomb

13 照會 **[chào-hùi]** : to inform officially; diplomatic note

14 照管 **[chào-kuăn]** : to look after, to take care of, to give due consideration to

15 照様做 **[chào-yàng tsò]** : to follow suit, to do the same

21 照顧 **[chào-kù]** : to look after, to take care of, to give due consideration to

照顧大局 **[chào-kù tà-chǘ]** : to be mindful of the whole situation

煎

4 煎心 **[chiēn-hsīn]** : anxious, worried

15 煎熬 **[chiēn-áo]** : to cook, to fry in fat, to suffer; tormented, worried, tortured

煩

[7] 煩言[fán-yén]: quarreling, wrangling; quarrel

[11] 煩惱[fán-nǎo]: to annoy; annoyance; annoyed, vexed, irked

[14] 煩瑣[fán-sǒ]: troublesome, annoying with petty details

[18] 煩擾[fán-jǎo]: to disturb, to trouble, to bother, to annoy

煩雜[fán-tsá]: confused, unclear, without clear order

熙

[3] 熙川[hsī-ch'uān]: Huichon (Korea)

煥

[12] 煥發[huàn-fā]: shining, radiating; to shine, to radiate

煥然一新[huàn-ján ì-hsīn]: to take on an altogether new aspect, done over like new

煉

[8] 煉金術[lièn-chīn shù]: alchemy

煉油廠[lièn-yú ch'ǎng]: oil refinery

[12] 煉焦[lièn-chiāo]: coking

煉焦廠[lièn-chiāo ch'ǎng]: coke oven plant

煉焦爐[lièn-chiāo lú]: coke oven

煉焦煤[lièn-chiāo méi]: coking coal

[16] 煉鋼[lièn-kāng]: steel refining, steel smelting, founding

煉鋼廠[lièn-kāng ch'ǎng]: steel refinery, steel plant, steel works, steel foundry

煉鋼工人[lièn-kāng kūng-jén]: steelworker, steel-maker

煉鋼爐[lièn-kāng lú]: smelting furnace, blast furnace

[21] 煉鐵[lièn-t'iěh]: iron-smelting

煉鐵廠[lièn-t'iěh ch'ǎng]: blast furnace plant

煤

[4] 煤斗車[méi-tǒu ch'ē]: hopper car

[5] 煤田[méi-t'ién]: coal field

[7] 煤坑[méi-k'ēng]: coal pit

[8] 煤油[méi-yú]: kerosene

[9] 煤炭工業[méi-t'àn kūng-yèh]: coal industry

煤炭工業部[méi-t'àn kūng-yèh pù]: Ministry of Coal Industry

[10] 煤氣[méi-ch'ì]: coal gas

[12] 煤焦油[méi-chiāo yú]: coal tar

[15] 煤層[méi-ts'éng]: coal seam, coal layer

[20] 煤礦[méi-k'uàng]: coal mine, colliery

煤礦藏[méi k'uàng-tsàng]: coal deposit, coal reserve

煅

[3] 煅工[tuàn-kūng]: smith

[12] 煅煉[tuàn-lièn]: to forge iron, to refine, to steel

[21] 煅鐵[tuàn-t'iěh]: to hammer hot iron; wrought iron

— 10 Strokes —

熄

13 熄滅 **[hsī-mièh]**: to extinguish, to put out, to go out

態

5 態本 **[hsiúng-pĕn]**: Kumamoto (Japan)

熔

21 熔鐵 **[júng-t'iĕh]**: to smelt iron

熔鐵爐 **[júng-t'iĕh lú]**: iron-smelting furnace, blast furnace

24 熔爐 **[júng-lú]**: blast furnace, mubble furnace

煽

10 煽起 **[shān-ch'ĭ]**: to stir up, to excite

11 煽動 **[shān-tùng]**: to incite, to foment, to instigate, to stir up, to arouse

煽動者 **[shān-tùng-chĕ]**: agitator, instigator, provocateur

煽動性的 **[shān-tùng-hsìng te]**: provocative

12 煽惑 **[shān-huò]**: to mislead, to deceive

— 11 Strokes —

熬

8 熬夜 **[áo-yèh]**: to work at night

13 熬煎 **[áo-chiēn]**: to harass, to worry

熱

熱 **[jè]**: Jehol (abbreviation for 熱河); hot, thermal

4 熱心 **[jè-hsīn]**: ardor, zeal, enthusiasm; earnest, ardent, enthusiastic, zealous

熱心人 **[jè-hsīn jén]**: zealot, enthusiast, an enthusiastic person

8 熱河 **[jè-hó]**: Jehol

10 熱核 **[jè-hó]**: thermonuclear

熱核反應 **[jè-hó făn-yìng]**: thermonuclear reaction

熱烈 **[jè-lièh]**: warm, ardent, passionate, fervent, fiery

11 熱情 **[jè-ch'íng]**: fervor, passion, zeal, enthusiasm, warmth; fervent, enthusiastic

熱望 **[jè-wàng]**: aspiration, fervent hope

12 熱量單位 **[jè-liàng tān-wèi]**: thermal unit, caloric unit, calorie

13 熱愛 **[jè-ài]**: to love ardently, to be enthusiastic about

熱電站 **[jè-tièn chàn]**: thermoelectric plant, thermoelectric power station

熱誠 **[jè-ch'éng]**: earnestness, sincerity, enthusiasm, dedication; earnest, enthusiastic, warm, sincere

16 熱諷 **[jè-fèng]**: burning satire

熟

10 熟荒地 **[shóu-huāng tì]**: disused land, abandoned land, long fallow land

11 熟悉 **[shú-hsī]**: to be familiar with, to be well acquainted with; familiarity

12 熟視無睹 **[shóu-shìh wú-tŭ]**: to turn a blind eye to, to fail to notice, to ignore

15 熟練工人 **[shóu-lièn kūng-jén]**: skilled worker, experienced worker

— 12 Strokes —

燃 **[ján]**: to burn, to kindle, to set fire, to

ignite, to light

8 燃放 **[ján-fàng]** : to ignite, to touch off, to set off

10 燃料 **[ján-liào]** : fuel

燃料工業部 **[ján-liào kūng-yèh pù]** : Ministry of Fuel Industry

燈

4 燈火管制 **[tēng-huŏ kuăn-chìh]** : restriction of illumination, black-out

8 燈油戰術 **[tēng-yú chàn-shù]** : lamp-oil tactics (i.e., tactics of false economy in which inadequate numbers of men and amounts of material are used and consequently lost)

12 燈塔 **[tēng-t'ă]** : lighthouse (during the Cultural Revolution, a simile for the thought of Mao)

燕

11 燕麥 **[yèn-mài]** : oats

— 13 Strokes —

營 **[yíng]** : battalion; to manage, to plan

11 營造 **[yíng-tsào]** : to build, to construct, to lay out, to erect

13 營業 **[yíng-yèh]** : business, commerce, trade, commercial enterprise

營業收入 **[yíng-yèh shōu-jù]** : revenue from services and sales

營業稅 **[yíng-yèh shùi]** : business tax

15 營養 **[yíng-yăng]** : nutrition, nutriment, nourishment

營養食堂 **[yíng-yăng shíh-t'áng]** : nutrition canteen

— 15 Strokes —

爆

6 爆竹 **[pào-chú]** : fireworks, firecracker

9 爆炸 **[pào-chà]** : to explode, to burst; explosion

10 爆破 **[pào-p'ò]** : to burst, to explode, to fly into the air

爆破筒 **[pào-p'ò t'ŭng]** : primer

12 爆發性 **[pào-fā-hsìng]** : explosive capacity

— 17 Strokes —

爛 **[làn]** : rotten, soft, soggy, pulpy, overripe, broken, smashed, ragged

3 爛下去 **[làn-hsià-ch'ü]** : to rot, to decay, to putrify, to corrode, to become more and more dilapidated

22 爛攤子 **[làn t'ān-tzu]** : a broken-down stall, a rotten legacy, an awful mess, a dreadful mess

— RADICAL 爪 爫 87 —

4 爪瓦 [chăo-wă] : Java

爪牙 [chăo-yá] : tooth and nail, claws and teeth; lackey, flunkey, henchman, servant, agent

9 爪哇 [chăo-wā] : Java

— 4 Strokes —

6 爭名奪利 [chēng-míng tó-lì] : to strive for fame and wealth

爭先 [chēng-hsiēn] : to contend for first place, to compete to be the first to

7 爭吵 [chēng-ch'ăo] : to quarrel, to dispute, to bicker; quarrel, squabble

8 爭取 [chēng-ch'ŭ] : to fight for, to strive for, to struggle for

10 爭氣 [chēng-ch'ì] : to put forth effort, to compete to surpass, to squabble; determination

11 爭執 [chēng-chíh] : to dispute, to argue; dispute, argument, controversy, disagreement; controversial

爭執點 [chēng-chíh tiĕn] : point of dispute, bone of contention

13 爭端 [chēng-tuān] : dispute, strife, cause of debate

14 爭奪 [chēng-tó] : to contend, to compete for, to seize, to fasten upon

15 爭論 [chēng-lùn] : to contend, to dispute, to argue, to debate; controversy, contention

爭論中心 [chēng-lùn chūng-hsīn] : the center of a controversy or dispute

21 爭辯 [chēng-pièn] : to dispute

22 爭權奪利 [chēng-ch'üán tó-lì] : to fight for power and profit

3 爬山隊 [p'á-shān tùi] : mountaineering team, mountain climbing team

— 8 Strokes —

2 爲人民服務 [wèi jén-mín fú-wù] : To Serve the People (Mao, September 8, 1944; one of the 老三篇, q.v.)

爲人所不齒 [wéi jén sŏ pù-ch'ĭh] : unmentionable, disreputable, infamous, beneath contempt, spoken only to one's shame

爲了 [wèi-le] : for, as to, so that, for the purpose of, in order to, with the intent of, for the sake of

爲了酬答 [wèi-le ch'óu-tá] : for purposes of reward or compensation

爲了.... 事業 [wèi-le . . . shìh-yèh] : for the sake of the . . . undertaking or enterprise

3 爲工人階級政治服務 [wèi kūng-jén chiēh-chí chèng-chìh fú-wù] : to serve working class politics

爲工農兵服務 [wèi kūng-núng-pīng fú-wù] : to serve the workers, peasants, and soldiers

5 爲主 [wéi-chŭ] : to predominate, to prevail, to be the main thing; dominating, outweighing, prevalent; with. . . as the key, with. . . playing the leading role

6 爲虎作倀 [wèi-hŭ tsò-ch'āng] : to act as a cat's paw

8 爲非作歹 [wéi-fēi tsò-tăi] : to commit evil deeds, to do evil things, to be evil and wicked

9 爲首 **[wéi-shŏu]** : to serve as the main thing, to stand at the head of, to act as leader; headed by, led by, in the foreground

10 爲時過早的 **[wéi-shíh kuò-tsăo te]** : too early, premature, inopportune

11 爲教育而教育 **[wèi chiào-yü érh chiào-yü]** : education for its own sake

19 爲難 **[wéi-nán]** : to make trouble, to embarrass, to encumber, to put obstacles in the way, to be in a quandary, at a loss, in a dilemma

— 14 Strokes —

3 爵士 **[chüéh-shìh]** : lord, noble, nobleman, peer; jazz music

— RADICAL 父 88 —

— RADICAL 爻 89 —

— 7 Strokes —

7 爽快 **[shuăng-k'uài]** : refreshing, cheerful, genial, pleasant, free, open, invigorating

— RADICAL 爿 90 —

— 13 Strokes —

牆

12 牆畫 **[ch'iáng-huà]** : mural painting

牆報 **[ch'iáng-pào]** : wall newspaper

— RADICAL 片 91 —

片

9 片面 **[p'ièn-mièn]** : one-sided, unilateral, arbitrary

片面眞理 **[p'ièn-mièn chēn-lĭ]** : one-sided truth

片面性 **[p'ièn-mièn-hsìng]** : one-sidedness

18 片斷 **[p'ièn-tuàn]** : fragmentary; fragments

— 4 Strokes —

版

5 版本 **[păn-pĕn]** : edition

14 版圖 **[păn-t'ú]** : plan, map; population and territory

20 版權 **[păn-ch'üán]** : copyright, publication rights

— 8 Strokes —

牌

3 牌子 **[p'ái-tzu]** : brand, label, trademark

— RADICAL 牙 92 —

牙

6 牙庄 **[yă-chuāng]** : Nhatrang (Vietnam)

— RADICAL 牛 93 —

牛

9 牛津大學 **[níu-chīn tà-hsüéh]** : Oxford University

10 牛鬼蛇神 **[níu-kueĭ shé-shén]** : monsters and freaks, demons and monsters (literally, cow-devils and snake-gods, a term of vilification used during the Cultural Revolution against bourgeois-minded elements and anti-Mao elements)

12 牛痘 **[níu-tòu]** : smallpox vaccine

13 牛頓 **[níu-tùn]** : Newton (proper name)

14 牛鼻子 **[níu pí-tzu]** : the nose of the ox (i.e., the key point of a problem by which it can easily be resolved)

— 2 Strokes —

牟

7 牟利 **[móu-lì]** : to profiteer

— 3 Strokes —

牢

4 牢不可破的 **[láo pù-k'ŏ p'ò]** : unbreakable, indestructible

8 牢固 **[láo-kù]** : solid, firm, secure

— 4 Strokes —

牧

2 牧人 **[mù-jén]** : herdsman, shepherd

5 牧民 **[mù-mín]** : herdsman, shepherd

9 牧師 **[mù-shīh]** : clergyman, pastor, priest, Christian minister, Reverend

10 牧畜 **[mù-hsǜ]** : stock raising, livestock breeding

牧草 **[mù-ts'ăo]** : fodder, fodder grass, pasture grass

牧草地 **[mù-ts'ăo tì]** : livestock farm, pasture land, grazing field

11 牧區 **[mù-ch'ǖ]** : pasture area

12 牧場 **[mù-ch'ăng]** : livestock farm, pasture land, pasture, grazing field

牧童 **[mù-t'úng]** : cowherd

物

6 物自體 **[wù-tzù-t'ĭ]** : thing-in-itself

[9] 物美價廉[**wù-mĕi chià-lién**]: high grade and inexpensive, good quality and modestly priced

[11] 物理學[**wù-lĭ-hsüéh**]: physics

物理學家[**wù-lĭ-hsüéh-chiā**]: physicist

特理研究所[**wù-lĭ yén-chìu-sŏ**]: Physics Institute

[13] 物資[**wù-tzū**]: material, goods, commodity

物資交流[**wù-tzū chiāo-líu**]: interflow of commodities

物資交流會[**wù-tzū chiāo-líu hùi**]: commodity exchange conference

物資交流大會[**wù-tzū chiāo-líu tà-hùi**]: trade exhibition (a gathering for the sale and interchange of commodities)

物資儲備[**wù-tzū ch'ú-pèi**]: material reserve, stock

[15] 物價[**wù-chià**]: commodity price

物價指數[**wù-chià chĭh-shù**]: price index

物價波動[**wù-chià pō-tùng**]: fluctuation of commodity prices, price fluctuations

物質[**wù-chíh**]: matter; material, physical

物質基礎[**wù-chíh chī-ch'ŭ**]: material basis

物質利益[**wù-chíh lì-ì**]: material well-being, material interests

物質力量[**wù-chíh lì-liàng**]: material force

物質生活[**wù-chíh shēng-huó**]: material life, physical life, material well-being

物質財富[**wù-chíh ts'ái-fù**]: material wealth, material values

物質文明[**wù-chíh wén-míng**]: material culture

[19] 物證[**wù-chèng**]: material evidence

— 5 Strokes —

牲

[10] 牲畜[**shēng-ch'ù**]: cattle, livestock, domestic animals

— 6 Strokes —

特

[5] 特古西加爾巴[**t'è-kŭ-hsī-chiā-ĕrh-pā**]: Tegucigalpa (Honduras)

[6] 特色[**t'è-sè**]: special features, characteristics, peculiarities

特有[**t'è-yŭ**]: to possess or own exclusively, peculiar to, specific

[7] 特快消息[**t'è-k'uài hsiāo-hsí**]: scoop, beat, tip (i.e., in reference to news)

特利波利斯[**t'è-lì-pō-lì-ssū**]: Tripoli

特別[**t'è-piéh**]: specific, especial, particular; especially, specifically, particularly

[8] 特性[**t'è-hsìng**]: special characteristic, specialty, property, nature, feature

特拉華[**t'è-lā-huá**]: Delaware

特命[**t'è-mìng**]: special appointment, special order, special assignment

特命全權公使[**t'è-mìng ch'üán-ch'üán kūng-shĭh**]: envoy extraordinary and minister plenipotentiary

特命全權大使[**t'è-mìng ch'üán-ch'üán tà-shĭh**]: ambassador extraordinary and plenipotentiary

特使[**t'è-shĭh**]: special envoy

特定[**t'è-tìng**]: specific, specified, specifically designated

[9] 特派代表[**t'è-p'ài tài-piăo**]: special representative

[10] 特殊[**t'è-shū**]: special, distinctive

特殊風[t'è-shū fēng]: a special air (i.e., an air of privilege and importance)

11 特產[t'è-ch'ǎn]: special product, local specialty, indigenous product, key product

特產品[t'è-ch'ǎn p'ǐn]: special product, specialty

特許[t'è-hsǚ]: concession, grant, license, special permit, patent, franchise monopoly; chartered, exclusive

特赦[t'è-shè]: special pardon; amnesty, pardon

特務[t'è-wù]: secret agent, agent, spy, intelligence agent

特務份子[t'è-wù fèn-tzu]: special agent

特務組織[t'è-wù tsǔ-chīh]: espionage organization, secret service, special service

12 特惠關稅制[t'è-hùi kuān-shùi chìh]: preferential tariff system

14 特種戶口[t'è-chǔng hù-k'ǒu]: special family (i.e., a family under suspicion)

特種兵團[t'è-chǔng pīng-t'uán]: special army group

特種部隊[t'è-chǔng pù-tùi]: special troops

15 特徵[t'è-chēng]: feature, characteristic, specific feature, trait; to be characterized by

特寫[t'è-hsiěh]: feature article, special article

特魯希略城[t'è-lǔ-hsī-lüèh ch'éng]: Ciudad Trujillo (Dominican Republic)

17 特邀代表[t'è-yāo tài-piǎo]: representative by special invitation

19 特羅伊[t'è-ló-ī]: Troy; Troja

22 特權[t'è-ch'üán]: special right, immunity, concession, prerogative

特權階級[t'è-ch'üán chiēh-chí]: the privileged class, privileged classes

— 7 Strokes —

4 牽牛戰術[ch'iēn-níu chàn-shù]: "ox-leading tactics" (i.e., tactics of drawing the enemy out from a strong position)

7 牽扯[ch'iēn-ch'ě]: to involve, to implicate

8 牽制[ch'iēn-chìh]: to impede

犁[lí]: plow

— 16 Strokes —

犧

9 犧牲[hsī-shēng]: to sacrifice, to be martyred, to become a martyr; sacrifice

犧牲品[hsī-shēng-p'ǐn]: sacrificial offering, scapegoat, victim, prey

犧牲生命[hsī-shēng shēng-mìng]: to sacrifice one's life, to lay down one's life

— RADICAL 犬 犭 94 —

犬

16 犬儒學派 **[ch'üăn-jú hsüéh-p'ài]** : cynics

— 2 Strokes —

犯

2 犯人 **[fàn-jén]** : criminal, prisoner, felon, convict, those serving sentences, the guilty, the accused

8 犯法 **[fàn-fă]** : to violate the law

犯法者 **[fàn-fă-chĕ]** : transgressor, law breaker, law-breaking element

13 犯罪 **[fàn-tsùi]** : to commit a crime; crime

16 犯錯誤 **[fàn ts'ò-wù]** : to make a mistake, to commit an error

— 4 Strokes —

狀

14 狀態 **[chuàng-t'ài]** : condition, situation, state of affairs

狂

2 狂人 **[k'uáng-jén]** : maniac, madman, lunatic, insane person

6 狂妄 **[k'uáng-wàng]** : frenzied, frantic, rabid, arrogant, wild, fantastic

狂妄的計劃 **[k'uáng-wàng te chì-huà]** : wild scheme

狂妄自大 **[k'uáng-wàng tzù-tà]** : conceit; conceited, haughty, arrogant, pompous, vainglorious

13 狂想曲 **[k'uáng-hsiăng ch'ŭ]** : fantasy, rhapsody

15 狂熱 **[k'uáng-jè]** : blind passion, mad enthusiasm, bigoted zeal; rabid, frantic, frenzied, feverish, insane, mad, demented

22 狂歡 **[k'uáng-huān]** : wild cheers, lively celebrations

狄

6 狄托 **[tí-t'ō]** : Tito, Josif Broz (Yugoslav political leader)

— 5 Strokes —

17 狙擊 **[chū-chī]** : ambush, snipe

狙擊射手 **[chū-chī shè-shŏu]** : sniper, sharpshooter

狐

11 狐假虎威 **[hú chiă hŭ-wēi]** : a fox in the role of a tiger, the fox borrows the terror of the tiger, to pretend to power, to boast of strange powers, to presume to the rights of others

13 狐群狗黨 **[hú-ch'ün kŏu-tăng]** : a band of scoundrels, bad company

14 狐疑 **[hú-í]** : suspicious, distrustful

狐疑不決 **[hú-í pù-chüéh]** : undecided, undetermined

狗

8 狗命 **[kŏu-mìng]** : a dog's life, a lowly and miserable existence

13 狗腿子 **[kŏu t'ŭi-tzu]** : lackey, toady, flunkey

— 6 Strokes —

狡

[7] 狡兔三窟[chiăo-t'ù sān-k'ū]: a sly rabbit has three exits to its burrow; crafty foresight, cunning foresight

[12] 狡詐[chiăo-chà]: deceptive, cunning

[13] 狡猾[chiăo-huá]: deceitful, crafty, wily, tricky, artful

[16] 狡賴[chiăo-lài]: to prevaricate, to shuffle, to make cunning excuses

[18] 狡黠[chiăo-hsiá]: crafty, sly, cunning

[21] 狡辯[chiăo-pièn]: to quibble, to equivocate; crafty argument, sophistry, equivocation

狠

[4] 狠心[hĕn-hsīn]: cruel, savage, hardhearted; to have a hard heart

[9] 狠毒[hĕn-tú]: cruel, malicious

— 7 Strokes —

狹

[13] 狹隘[hsiá-ài]: bottleneck; narrow, contracted

狹隘觀點[hsiá-ài kuān-tiĕn]: narrow view, narrow-minded idea

狼

[3] 狼子野心[láng-tzu yĕh-hsīn]: the aggressive designs of wolves; brutal, ferocious

[10] 狼狽[láng-pèi]: distressed, embarrassed; helplessly dependent, helter-skelter

狼狽處境[láng-pèi ch'ŭ-chìng]: quandary, predicament, plight, dilemma, impasse

狼狽爲奸[láng-pèi wéi-chiēn]: to collude for ignoble or seditious purposes

— 8 Strokes —

猖

[7] 猖狂[ch'āng-k'uáng]: frenzied, wild, violent, raging, insubordinate, seditious, unruly

[15] 猖獗[ch'āng-chüéh]: wild, violent, raging, unbridled, rampant

猙

[17] 猙獰[chēng-níng]: repulsive, repellent, hideous, frightful, gruesome

猙獰面貌[chēng-níng mièn-mào]: grim visage, forbidding countenance, hideous looks

猛

[7] 猛攻[mĕng-kūng]: heavy attack, fierce attack, onslaught

[10] 猛烈[mĕng-lièh]: fierce, vehement, intense, tough, violent, furious, severe, sharp

[12] 猛街[mĕng-chiēh]: Moncay (Vietnam)

[14] 猛漲[mĕng-chàng]: to skyrocket, to shoot up, to soar; steep rise

猜

猜[ts'āi]: to guess, to conjecture, to speculate, to surmise

[7] 猜忌[ts'āi-chì]: to envy; envy; envious

[8] 猜度[ts'āi-tò]: to estimate, to guess

[12] 猜測[ts'āi-ts'è]: to guess, to conjecture

[14] 猜疑[ts'āi-í]: to suspect, to doubt

— 9 Strokes —

猶

[4] 猶太復國主義者[yú-t'ài fù-kuó chŭ-ì

chĕ] : Zionist

猶太人[yú-t'ài jén] : Jew

16 猶豫[yú-yü] : to hesitate, to vacillate, to falter; uncertain, doubtful

— 10 Strokes —

獃

8 獃板[tāi-păn] : a failure, a wooden person; mechanical, inflexible

— 13 Strokes —

獨

4 獨夫民賊[tú-fū mín-tséi] : autocrat and traitor to the people

5 獨占[tú-chàn] : to monopolize, to gain sole control; monopoly

獨占資本[tú-chàn tzū-pĕn] : monopoly capital

獨立[tú-lì] : to be independent; independence; independent

獨立宣言[tú-lì hsüān-yén] : proclamation of independence, declaration of independence

獨立勞動者[tú-lì láo-tùng chĕ] : independent craftsman

獨立自治[tú-lì tzù-chìh] : self-government

獨立自主[tú-lì tzù-chŭ] : independent

獨立王國[tú-lì wáng-kuó] : independent kingdom (i.e., any area or field of work under the authority of any high-placed Communist who runs it according to his own will and for his own interests in disregard of the central government)

獨立運動[tú-lì yǜn-tùng] : independence movement

獨白[tú-pái] : monologue

6 獨自[tú-tzù] : all by oneself, alone, solely, singly, single-handed

10 獨特的[tú-t'è te] : specific, peculiar, particular, unique, original, especial, exceptional, exclusive, singular

11 獨裁[tú-ts'ái] : dictatorial, arbitrary; to act dictatorially or arbitrarily

獨裁者[tú-ts'ái-chĕ] : dictator

獨裁、內戰、和賣國三位一體 [tú-ts'ái, nèi-chàn, hó mài-kuó sān-wèi ì t'ı] : trinity of dictatorship, civil war, and selling out one's country

16 獨龍[tú-lúng] : Tulung (a minority nationality)

18 獨斷論[tú-tuàn lùn] : dogmatism

獨斷獨行[tú-tuàn tú-hsíng] : to take an arbitrary action, to act arbitrarily

20 獨霸[tú-pà] : to monopolize, to dominate, to bring everthing under one's control

— 14 Strokes —

獲

7 獲利[huò-lì] : to make profit, to profit from

11 獲得[huò-té] : to obtain, to get, to attain, to achieve

13 獲罪[huò-tsùi] : to sin against, to incur punishment

— 15 Strokes —

獸

2 獸力車[shòu-lì ch'ē] : animal-drawn cart

18 獸醫[shòu-ī] : veterinarian

— 16 Strokes —

獻

獻[hsièn] : to present, to give, to donate, to

bestow, to confer, to contribute

5 獻出 **[hsièn-ch'ū]** : to present, to offer, to contribute

獻出生命 **[hsièn-ch'ū shēng-mìng]** : to offer one's life

7 獻身於 **[hsièn-shēn yǘ]** : to offer oneself to, to be dedicated to

8 獻花圈 **[hsièn huā-ch'üān]** : to present a wreath

9 獻計 **[hsièn-chì]** : to present plans, to offer plans

10 獻殷勤 **[hsièn yīn-ch'ín]** : to offer one's attentiveness, to curry favor with, to pay one's court to, to be at someone's beck and call

— RADICAL 玄 95 —

— 6 Strokes —

率 **[lǜ]** : rate; **[shuài]** : to lead; frank, candid, outspoken

8 率直 **[shuài-chíh]** : frank, candid, outspoken, open, unreserved, blunt, direct, straight, straight forward, ingenuous

14 率領 **[shuài-lǐng]** : to lead, to head

— RADICAL 玉 王 96 —

王

3 王子 **[wáng-tzŭ]** : prince

7 王位 **[wáng-wèi]** : throne, crown

8 王明路綫 **[wáng míng lù-hsièn]** : the Wang Ming line (i.e., a "bourgeois ideology" in the Party and one of the objects of Mao's rectification campaign begun in 1942)

9 王室 **[wáng-shìh]** : royal house, royal family

10 王島 **[wáng tăo]** : King Island (Burma)

11 王國 **[wáng-kuó]** : kingdom

12 王朝 **[wáng-ch'áo]** : dynasty, royal house

王傑 **[wáng chiéh]** : Wang Chieh (a model soldier who threw himself on exploding dynamite to save 12 others)

王牌 **[wáng-p'ái]** : trump, trump card

— 1 Stroke —

玉

5 玉石 **[yǜ-shíh]** : jade, gem, precious stone

6 玉米 **[yǜ-mĭ]** : maize, Indian corn

13 玉蜀黍 **[yǜ shŭ-shŭ]** : maize, Indian corn

— 4 Strokes —

玩

4 玩火 **[wán-huŏ]** : to play with fire

7 玩弄 **[wán-nùng]** : to play with, to flirt with, to amuse oneself with

玩弄詞句 **[wán-nùng tz'ú-chǜ]** : to bandy words with

8 玩具 **[wán-chǜ]** : plaything, toy

— 5 Strokes —

珍

10 珍珠港[chēn-chū kăng] : Pearl Harbor

珍島[chēn-tăo] : Chindo (Korea)

12 珍視[chēn-shìh] : to prize, to cherish, to treasure, to esteem, to attach great value to

玻

7 玻利維亞[pō-lì-wéi-yà] : Bolivia

玻利維亞共和國[pō-lì-wéi-yà kùng-hó-kuó] : Republic of Bolivia

玻里內西亞[pō-lĭ-nèi-hsī-yà] : Polynesia

12 玻斯尼亞[pō-ssū-ní-yà] : Bosnia

15 玻璃市[pō-lí-shìh] : Perlis (Malaya)

玷

7 玷汚[tièn-wū] : to disgrace, to dishonor, to desecrate

— 6 Strokes —

珞

4 珞巴[lò-pā] : the Luppa (a Tibetan nationality near Lhasa declared a separate nationality by Peking in September 1965)

班

班[pān] : squad, class, company

5 班加西[pān-chiā-hsī] : Benghazi (Libya)

6 班吉[pān-chí] : Bangui (Central African Republic)

8 班長[pān-chăng] : squad leader, group leader, class leader

班房子[pān-fáng-tzu] : jail

班門弄斧[pān-mén nùng-fŭ] : conceited, vain, eager for recognition

13 班達拉乃克[pān-tá-lā-năi-k'ò] : Bandaranaike, Mrs. Sirimano (Ceylonese political leader)

14 班資[pān-tzū] : Bunche, Ralph (American political figure)

16 班禪喇嘛[pān-ch'án lā-má] : Panchen Lama

班機[pān-chī] : scheduled airliner, airplane on a regular schedule

— 7 Strokes —

現

4 現今[hsièn-chīn] : now, at present, at the moment, for the time being

5 現出[hsièn-ch'ū] : to show, to manifest, to demonstrate, to reveal, to make apparent; manifestation

現代[hsièn-tài] : the present generation; modern, up-to-date

現代劇[hsièn-tài chü] : modern play, contemporary drama

現代修正主義[hsièn-tài hsīu-chèng chŭ-ì] : modern revisionism

現代化[hsièn-tài-huà] : to modernize, to streamline, to make up-to-date; modernization

6 現行反革命份子[hsièn-hsíng făn-kó-mìng fèn-tzu] : active counterrevolutionary

現在[hsièn-tsài] : now, at present, at the moment, for the time being, right now, right away, current, present, existing, prevailing, prevalent, actual

現存的 **[hsièn-ts'ún te]** : existing

現有的 **[hsièn-yŭ te]** : available, existing, on hand

現有的人力 **[hsièn-yŭ te jén-lì]** : available manpower

7 現成的 **[hsièn-ch'éng te]** : ready-made

現役 **[hsièn-ì]** : active service, active duty, on active service

現役軍人 **[hsièn-ì chŭn-jén]** : military personnel on active duty

8 現金 **[hsièn-chīn]** : cash

現金交易 **[hsièn-chīn chiāo-ì]** : cash payment

現狀 **[hsièn-chuàng]** : status quo, the present state of affairs

10 現時的 **[hsièn-shíh te]** : current

現原形 **[hsièn yüán-hsíng]** : to show one's original colors

11 現貨 **[hsièn-huò]** : regular stock, stock on hand, spot goods

現貨交易 **[hsièn-huò chiāo-ì]** : over-the-counter trading, spot transaction

12 現場 **[hsièn-ch'ăng]** : on-the-spot

現場會議 **[hsièn-ch'ăng hùi-ì]** : on-the-spot conference, on-the-spot meeting

現象 **[hsièn-hsiàng]** : phenomenon

現象學 **[hsièn-hsiàng-hsüéh]** : phenomenology

現象論 **[hsièn-hsiàng-lùn]** : phenomenalism

15 現實 **[hsièn-shíh]** : reality, actuality; realistic

現實主義 **[hsièn-shíh chŭ-ì]** : realism

現實性 **[hsièn-shíh-hsìng]** : actuality

現實條件 **[hsièn-shíh t'iáo-chièn]** : actual conditions

理

3 理工 **[lĭ-kūng]** : science and engineering

5 理由 **[lĭ-yú]** : reason, ground, justification, cause, occasion, rational motive, argument

8 理性 **[lĭ-hsìng]** : reason, sense; rational

理事 **[lĭ-shìh]** : to transact business; manager, council member

理事會 **[lĭ-shìh-hùi]** : council, administrative committee, board of governors

理所當然 **[lĭ sŏ tāng-ján]** : both natural and right, matter of course, as it should be

12 理智 **[lĭ-chìh]** : intellect, intelligence; rational, intellectual

13 理解 **[lĭ-chiĕh]** : to perceive, to comprehend, to understand; understanding, comprehension

理想 **[lĭ-hsiăng]** : ideal, aspiration

理想型 **[lĭ-hsiăng hsíng]** : ideal type

理想化 **[lĭ-hsiăng-huà]** : to idealize

理會 **[lĭ-hùi]** : to understand, to comprehend, to perceive; understanding, comprehension

理睬 **[lĭ-ts'ăi]** : to take notice of, to regard with care, to pay attention to, to notice, to heed, to regard

15 理論 **[lĭ-lùn]** : theory; theoretical

理論宣傳事務處 **[lĭ-lùn hsüān-ch'uán shìh-wù ch'ù]** : Office of Theoretical and Propaganda Affairs

理論聯系實際 **[lĭ-lùn lién-hsì shíh-chì]** : to unite theory and reality; integration of theory and reality

理論脫離實際 **[lĭ-lùn t'ō-lí shíh-chì]** : theory divorced from reality, discrepancy between theory and reality

理論與實踐 **[lĭ-lùn yŭ shíh-chièn]** : theory and practice

琉

11 琉球 **[líu-ch'íu]** : Ryukyu Islands

— 9 Strokes —

瑞

3 瑞山 **[jùi-shān]** : Sosan (Korea)

瑞士 **[jùi-shìh]** : Switzerland

瑞士聯邦 **[jùi-shìh lién-pāng]** : Swiss Confederation

8 瑞典 **[jùi-tiěn]** : Sweden

瑞典王國 **[jùi-tiěn wáng-kuó]** : Kingdom of Sweden

11 瑞國 **[jùi-kuó]** : Sweden

12 瑞敦 **[jùi-tūn]** : Sweden

— 10 Strokes —

瑣

8 瑣事 **[sŏ-shìh]** : a trifling affair, trifles

— 13 Strokes —

環

8 環抱 **[huán-pào]** : to embrace, to encompass

13 環節 **[huán-chiéh]** : link part, sector, point

14 環境 **[huán-chìng]** : circumstances, surroundings, environment, conditions

18 環繞 **[huán-jào]** : to encircle, to surround, to go around

— RADICAL 瓜 97 —

瓜

4 瓜分 **[kuā-fēn]** : to carve up, to partition, to dismember, to divide up; division, partition

5 瓜代 **[kuā-tài]** : to relieve another official, one official relieving another

— RADICAL 瓦 98 —

瓦

瓦 **[wă]** : watt

5 瓦加杜古 **[wă-chiā-tù-kŭ]** : Ouagadougou (Republic of Upper Volta)

7 瓦杜玆 **[wă-tù-tzū]** : Vaduz (Principality of Liechtenstein)

12 瓦萊塔 **[wă-lái-t'ă]** : Valetta (British Malta)

13 瓦解 **[wă-chiěh]** : to disintegrate, to break up, to gragmentize, to dissolve, to fall apart; disintegration, collapse, fragmentation, disorganization

瓦稜西亞 **[wă-léng-hsī-yà]** : Valencia

17 瓦薩 **[wă-sà]** : Warsaw

— 3 Strokes —

瓩

瓩 **[wă]** : kilowatt

— 11 Strokes —

甌

10 甌海關[ōu hăi-kuān]: Wenchow Custom House

— RADICAL 甘 99 —

甘

甘 [kān] : Kansu (abbreviation of 甘肅)

4 甘心 [kān-hsīn] : to be reconciled to, to be content to, to be complacent about; pleased, contented, willing

6 甘托克 [kān-t'ō-k'ò] : Gangtok (Sikkim)

8 甘居中游[kān-chū̆ chūng-yú]: content to be mediocre (refers to cadres who neither wish to forge ahead to become advanced elements nor dare to remain backward)

甘居下游[kān-chū̆ hsià-yú]: to be content with lagging behind

9 甘迺迪 [kān-năi-tí]: Kennedy (proper name)

14 甘蔗 [kān-chè] : sugar cane

18 甘薯 [kān-shŭ] : sweet potato

20 甘露 [kān-lù] : Camlo (Vietnam)

— 6 Strokes —

7 甜言蜜語[t'ién-yén mì-yŭ]: sweet words and honeyed phrases, flattery

12 甜菜 [t'ién-ts'ài] : sugar beet

— RADICAL 生 100 —

生

2 生力軍 [shēng-lì chū̆n]: reinforcements, fresh troops

6 生成 [shēng-ch'éng] : innate, second nature; to grow to

生死不明[shēng-ssŭ pù-míng]: missing, whereabouts unknown

生死攸關[shēng-ssŭ yū-kuān]: a matter of life and death

生存 [shēng-ts'ún] : to exist; existence, life, survival, subsistence

8 生長 [shēng-chăng] : to grow

生命 [shēng-mìng] : life

生命綫 [shēng-mìng hsièn] : life line, breath of life, lifeblood

生命力 [shēng-mìng lì] : life force, vitality, Lebenskraft

生事 [shēng-shìh] : to create trouble, to make trouble

生物製品 [shēng-wù chìh-p'ĭn] : biologicals, biological products

生物製品研究所 [shēng-wù chìh-p'ĭn yén-chìu-sŏ] : Biological Products Institute

生物學 [shēng-wù-hsüéh] : biology; biological

生物化學研究所 [shēng-wù huà-hsüéh

yén-chìu-sŏ] : Biochemistry Institute

生物物理研究所 **[shēng-wù wù-lĭ yén-chìu-sŏ]** : Biophysics Institute

9 生計 **[shēng-chì]** : livelihood, life, living

生活 **[shēng-huó]** : 1. life, living, livelihood; 2. Life (American weekly periodical)

生活集體化 **[shēng-huó chí-t'ĭ-huà]** : collectivization of life; to live collectively (one of the 三化, q.v.)

生活指數 **[shēng-huó chĭh-shù]** : living index

生活指導 **[shēng-huó chĭh-tăo]** : life guidance (a program for elementary school pupils set forth by the Ministry of Education in the early 1950s which involved specific rules for training in hygenic habits, organizational discipline, courtesy, and politics and ideology)

生活費用 **[shēng-huó fèi-yùng]** : cost of living, living expenses

生活必需品 **[shēng-huó pì-hsū p'ĭn]** : daily needs, daily necessities

生活實際 **[shēng-huó shíh-chì]** : the realities of life, the actuality of life

生活水平 **[shēng-huó shŭi-p'íng]** : standard of living, living standards

生活資料 **[shēng-huó tzū-liào]** : means of subsistence, means of livelihood

10 生效 **[shēng-hsiào]** : to take effect, to go into effect, to come into force

生效期 **[shēng-hsiào ch'í]** : period of validity, period during which something is in effect

生荒地 **[shēng-huāng-tì]** : virgin soil, virgin land

生根 **[shēng-kēn]** : to take root in, to strike roots

11 生產 **[shēng-ch'ăn]** : to produce, to manufacture, to make; production

生產按人口計算 **[shēng-ch'ăn àn jén-k'ŏu chì-suàn]** : per capita production

生產者 **[shēng-ch'ăn-chĕ]** : producer

生產成本 **[shēng-ch'ăn ch'éng-pĕn]** : production costs, costs of production

生產積極性 **[shēng-ch'ăn chī-chí-hsìng]** : enthusiasm for production, activist attitude toward production

生產計劃 **[shēng-ch'ăn chì-huà]** : production plans

生產潛力 **[shēng-ch'ăn ch'ién-lì]** : latent productive capacity, potential for production

生產指標 **[shēng-ch'ăn chĭh-piāo]** : production quota, production target, production norm, output target

生產競賽 **[shēng-ch'ăn chìng-sài]** : production drive, production emulation (campaign)

生產中隊 **[shēng-ch'ăn chūng-tùi]** : intermediate production team

生產方式 **[shēng-ch'ăn fāng-shìh]** : mode of production

生產費用基金 **[shēng-ch'ăn fèi-yùng chī-chīn]** : production expenditure share fund

生產合作工作委員會 **[shēng-ch'ăn hó-tsò kūng-tsò wĕi-yüán-hùi]** : Production and Cooperative Work Committee

生產效率 **[shēng-ch'ăn hsiào-lǜ]** : production efficiency

生產關係 **[shēng-ch'ăn kuān-hsì]** : relations of production

生產管理 **[shēng-ch'ăn kuăn-lĭ]** : production management, production control

生產工具 **[shēng-ch'ăn kūng-chǜ]** : means of production

生產勞動 **[shēng-ch'ăn láo-tùng]** : productive labor

生產力 **[shēng-ch'ăn lì]** : productive capacity, productive power

生產量 **[shēng-ch'ăn liàng]** : productive capacity, output

生產率 [shēng-ch'ăn lǜ]: rate of productivity

生產能力 [shēng-ch'ăn néng-lì]: productive capacity, productive power

生產大隊 [shēng-ch'ăn tà-tùi]: production brigade

生產定額 [shēng-ch'ăn tìng-ó]: production target, output target

生產停頓 [shēng-ch'ăn t'íng-tùn]: halt in production

生產鬥爭 [shēng-ch'ăn tòu-chēng]: struggle for production

生產責任制 [shēng-ch'ăn tsé-jèn chìh]: system of fixed individual responsibility in production

生產突擊隊 [shēng-ch'ăn t'ù-chī tùi]: frontline production brigade

生產隊 [shēng-ch'ăn tùi]: production team, work brigade

生產資料 [shēng-ch'ăn tzū-liào]: means of production, capital goods

生理學 [shēng-lĭ-hsüéh]: physiology

生理研究所 [shēng-lĭ yén-chìu-sŏ]: Physiology Institute

生動的 [shēng-tùng te]: vivid, lively, impressive, dramatic, alive, life-like

12 生疏 [shēng-shū]: to be a stranger to; unfamiliar

生硬 [shēng-yìng]: rigid, stern, stiff, rigorous, harsh, hard and fast, peremptory

13 生意 [shēng-ì]: business, trade, livelihood; vitality, desires

16 生機論 [shēng-chī lùn]: vitalism

生擒 [shēng-ch'ín]: to capture alive

21 生鐵 [shēng-t'iĕh]: pig iron

— 6 Strokes —

產

5 產生 [ch'ăn-shēng]: to give birth to, to engender, to be the cause of, to produce, to bring forth

6 產地 [ch'ăn-tì]: place of origin

8 產物 [ch'ăn-wù]: product

9 產品 [ch'ăn-p'ĭn]: product

產品交換 [ch'ăn-p'ĭn chiāo-huàn]: exchange of products

產品範圍 [ch'ăn-p'ĭn fàn-wéi]: range of products

產品設計革命 [ch'ăn-p'ĭn shè-chì kó-mìng]: products designing revolution

產品設計工作 [ch'ăn-p'ĭn shè-chì kūng-tsò]: product designing

10 產值 [ch'ăn-chíh]: value of production, value of output

11 產假 [ch'ăn-chià]: maternity leave

產婆 [ch'ăn-p'ó]: midwife

12 產量 [ch'ăn-liàng]: volume of production, production, output, yield

13 產業 [ch'ăn-yèh]: property, possessions

產業界 [ch'ăn-yèh chièh]: industrial circles, business circles

產業革命 [ch'ăn-yèh kó-mìng]: Industrial Revolution

產業工會 [ch'ăn-yèh kūng-hùi]: industrial trade union, industrial union

產業稅 [ch'ăn-yèh shùi]: property tax

15 產銷 [ch'ăn-hsiāo]: production and marketing

產銷平衡 [ch'ăn-hsiāo p'íng-héng]: coordination of production and marketing, balance between production and marketing

產銷稅 [ch'ăn-hsiāo shùi] : excise tax, tax on production at point of sale

19 產額 [ch'ăn-ó] : rate of production, quantity of production, output

20 產權 [ch'ăn-ch'üán] : property right

— 9 Strokes —

16 甦醒 [sū-hsĭng] : to revive, to arouse, to rouse, to awaken, to recover consciousness, to reanimate, to resuscitate

— RADICAL 用 101 —

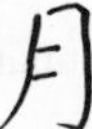

用 [yùng] : to use, to resort to; by means of; use

8 用非所學 [yùng fēi sŏ hsüéh] : failure to use one's specialty

9 用計脫逃 [yùng-chì t'ō-t'áo] : to wriggle out of, to slip away by tricky means

11 用途 [yùng-t'ú] : use, usage

13 用意可疑 [yùng-ì k'ŏ-í] : dubious intentions, suspicious aims

14 用盡 [yùng-chìn] : to deplete, to exhaust, to use up, to drain the resources of

— 2 Strokes —

甬 [yŭng] : Ningpo (abbreviation for 寧波)

— RADICAL 田 102 —

田

12 田間管理 [t'ién-chiēn kuăn-lĭ] : farm management

田間勞動 [t'ién-chiēn láo-tùng] : field labor, farm labor

甲

7 甲板 [chiă-păn] : deck

甲兵 [chiă-pīng] : military equipment; armored soldiers

8 甲府 [chiă-fŭ] : Kofu (Japan)

9 甲冑 [chiă-chòu] : armor

— 1 Stroke —

5 申斥 [shēn-ch'ìh] : to reproach, to censure, to denounce, to reprimand, to reprove, to admonish, to rebuke, to scold

8 申明 [shēn-míng] : to explain clearly, to elucidate

9 申述 [shēn-shù] : elaboration

12 申訴 [shēn-sù] : to appeal, to complain, to address an appeal

15 申請 [shēn-ch'ĭng] : to request, to apply for; application, request

由

4 由少到多[yú shăo tào tō]: from few to many, from small to large numbers

7 由低到高[yú tī tào kāo]: from the elementary to the more advanced

8 由來已久[yú-lái ĭ-chĭu]: deep-seated, deep-rooted

由於[yú-yǘ]: owing to, due to, as a result of, because of, in consequence of

9 由衷的[yú-chūng te]: heartfelt, from the heart

由表及裡[yú piăo chí lĭ]: from the outside to the inside, from the exterior to the interior

11 由淺入深[yú ch′iĕn jù shēn]: from the shallow to the profound

13 由感想出發[yú kăn-hsiăng ch′ū-fā]: on the basis of (mere) impressions

— 2 Strokes —

男

3 男女平等[nán-nŭ p′íng-tĕng]: equality between men and women, equality between the sexes

5 男主角[nán-chŭ-chiăo]: chief actor, male title role, hero

14 男演員[nán-yĕn-yüán]: actor

18 男爵[nán-chüéh]: baron

— 4 Strokes —

界

9 界限[chièh-hsièn]: demarcation line, limit, bounds, dividing line, boundary, border, limitation

15 界樁[chièh-chuāng]: boundary marker, boundary stone

畏

17 畏縮[wèi-sō]: to flinch, to shrink, to shirk, to hang back; timid, faint-hearted

— 5 Strokes —

畜

2 畜力[ch′ù-lì]: animal power, animal traction

8 畜肥[ch′ù-féi]: animal manure

畜牧區[hsǜ-mù ch′ǖ]: pastoral area

畜牧部[hsǜ-mù pù]: animal husbandry department

畜牧業[hsǜ-mù yèh]: animal husbandry

畜牧研究所[hsǜ-mù yén-chìu-sŏ]: Animal Husbandry Institute

11 畜產品[hsǜ-ch′ăn p′ĭn]: animal products

留

3 留下[líu-hsià]: to leave behind, to put aside, to remain

留下後果[líu-hsià hòu-kuŏ]: to entail consequences

6 留有餘地[líu-yŭ yǘ-tì]: to leave ground for, to make allowances for

7 留言[líu-yén]: to leave word

10 留神[líu-shén]: to give heed; wary, watchful, careful, vigilant, attentive

15 留學生[líu-hsüéh-shēng]: returned student, a student who has studied abroad

17 留聲機[líu-shēng-chī]: phonograph

25 留戀[líu-lièn]: to long for, to yearn for, to be loath to part with, to hold on to

畝

畝[mǔ]: mou (i.e., one-sixth of an English acre)

11 畝產量[mǔ ch'ǎn-liàng]: yield per mou, per mou yield

— 6 Strokes —

3 異己份子[ì-chǐ fèn-tzu]: alien element, heretical element

異口同聲[ì-k'ǒu t'úng-shēng]: different people sing the same tune, different people join in the chorus

13 異想天開[ì-hsiǎng t'iēn-k'āi]: to indulge in the wildest fantasy

20 異議[ì-ì]: to dissent, to disagree, to differ; dissension, disagreement

異黨[ì-tǎng]: alien party, heretical party

略

5 略去[lüèh-ch'ǜ]: to omit, to leave out, to neglect

9 略述[lüèh-shù]: to outline, to sketch, to summarize, to brief; outline, sketch, summary

畢

5 畢生[pì-shēng]: lifetime, whole life, lifelong

8 畢奈[pì-nài]: Pinay, Antoine (French industrialist and statesman)

13 畢塔哥拉斯[pì-t'ǎ-kō-lā-ssū]: Pythagoras (532 B.C.–497 B.C.)

畢業[pì-yèh]: to graduate

畢業證書[pì-yèh chèng-shū]: diploma, certificate of graduation

畢業論文[pì-yèh lùn-wén]: dissertation, thesis

畢業設計[pì-yèh shè-chì]: to plan for graduation; plan for graduation

畢業生[pì-yèh-shēng]: graduate

— 7 Strokes —

畫[huà]: painting, stroke; to draw, to make a stroke

5 畫皮[huà-p'í]: painted skin (i.e., a term for a counterrevolutionary masquerading as one of the people)

8 畫供[huà-kūng]: to sign a statement made under oath

10 畫家[huà-chiā]: painter, artist

11 畫蛇添足[huà-shé t'iēn-tsú]: to paint a snake and add feet to it, to do something superfluous, to gild the lily

12 畫報[huà-pào]: illustrated magazine, pictorial journal

畫策[huà-ts'è]: to make plans, to make stratagems, to intrigue

13 畫廊[huà-láng]: gallery

14 畫圖[huà-t'ú]: to draw a plan, to illustrate, to draw; drawing, painting

畬[yǘ]: Yü (a minority nationality)

— 8 Strokes —

畸

7 畸形[chī-hsíng]: deformation, abnormality, disfiguration

畸形現象[chī-hsíng hsièn-hsiàng]: abnormal state of affairs

13 畸零[chī-líng]: bits, refuse, odds and ends, surplus, fraction

14 畸輕畸重[chī-ch'īng chī-chùng]: unbalanced, out of proportion, prejudiced

當

4 當心[tāng-hsīn]: to take care; take care!

5 當代[tāng-tài]: the present age, the current generation; contemporary, contemporaneous, of the time

6 當地[tāng-tì]: local, on the spot

7 當局[tāng-chǘ]: authorities, government, present government, administration, regime

當兵[tāng-pīng]: to be a soldier

8 當事人[tāng-shìh jén]: the person concerned, manager

9 當政[tāng-chèng]: to be in power, to come into power, to be in political office

當家[tāng-chiā]: to manage a household, head of a household

當家作主[tāng-chiā tsò-chǔ]: to be the master of one's own affairs, to be master in one's own house

當前[tāng-ch'ién]: now, present, present-day, current, existing, at present, for the time being

當面[tāng-mièn]: face to face, in the face of, in the presence of

10 當時[tāng-shíh]: at that time, then

當做[tàng-tsò]: to take as, to look on as, to treat as

12 當場[tāng-ch'ǎng]: on-the-spot, then and there

當然支配者[tāng-ján chīh-p'èi-chě]: predestined master

16 當選[tāng-hsüǎn]: to be elected, to be selected, to be chosen

當頭一棍[tāng-t'óu í-kùn]: telling blow

22 當權[tāng-ch'üán]: to be in power, to come to power, to be in office, to take over power

當權派[tāng-ch'üán p'ài]: the clique in authority, the faction in power, (during the Cultural Revolution, referred specifically to Liu Shao-ch'i, Teng Hsiao-p'ing, and their followers)

— 14 Strokes —

疆

3 疆土[chiāng-t'ǔ]: territory, territory of a state

9 疆界[chiāng-chièh]: frontier, border, boundary, bounds, limits

11 疆域[chiāng-yǜ]: border, frontier, limit

14 疆場[chiāng-ch'ǎng]: battlefield

— RADICAL 疋 103 —

疋

疋 [p'ĭ] : bolt (textiles)

— 7 Strokes —

疏

8 疏忽 [shū-hū] : to neglect, to overlook; negligence; negligent, unmindful

14 疏遠 [shū-yüăn] : to estrange, to alienate; estrangement, alienation

17 疏濬 [shū-chǜn] : to dredge

— 9 Strokes —

疑

4 疑心 [í-hsīn] : to mistrust, to distrust, to doubt, to suspect; mistrust, distrust, doubt

12 疑惑 [í-hùo] : to suspect, to doubt; misgiving, apprehension, qualm

疑問 [í-wèn] : query, question, doubt

— RADICAL 疒 104 —

— 3 Strokes —

疙

疙瘩 [kō-tá] : pimple, pustule, lump

— 5 Strokes —

症

8 症狀 [chèng-chuàng] : symptom

疾

9 疾苦 [chí-k'ŭ] : suffering, suffering under oppressive government

疾首 [chí-shŏu] : extremely angry, furious

10 疾病 [chí-pìng] : sickness, ailment, illness, disease

疲

8 疲沓 [p'í-t'à] : inertia

10 疲倦 [p'í-chüàn] : tired, weary, exhausted

病

2 病人 [pìng-jén] : patient, sick man, invalid, the sick

病入膏肓 [pìng-jù kāo-huāng] : to have no hope of recovery, to be incurably sick

8 病毒 [pìng-tú] : virus

病毒學研究所 [pìng-tú-hsüéh yén-chìu-sŏ] : Virology Institute

10 病害 [pìng-hài] : injury, harm

11 病假 [pìng-chià] : sick leave

病情公報 [pìng-ch'íng kūng-pào] : medical bulletin

12 病菌 [pìng-chǜn] : germ, bacteria

16 病歷 [pìng-lì] : medical history

痁

痁 [tièn] : malaria

— 6 Strokes —

痕

13 痕 跡 **[hén-chī]** : trace, vestige, trail, track, footprint, imprint

— 7 Strokes —

痢

10 痢 疾 **[lì-chí]** : dysentery

痘

痘 **[tòu]** : smallpox

9 痘 苗 **[tòu-miáo]** : smallpox vaccine

痛

3 痛 下 決 心 **[t'ùng-hsià chüéh-hsīn]** : to decide with determination, to make a final decision

4 痛 心 **[t'ùng-hsīn]** : pained in heart, heart-broken

5 痛 斥 **[t'ùng-ch'ìh]** : to rebuke, to denounce severely, to rebut vigorously

9 痛 苦 **[t'ùng-k'ŭ]** : pain, bitterness, grief; bitter

— 9 Strokes —

瘋

2 瘋 人 **[fēng-jén]** : maniac, lunatic, madman

7 瘋 狂 **[fēng-k'uáng]** : wild, mad, crazy, insane

24 瘋 癲 **[fēng-tiēn]** : mad, insane, crazy, wild

— 10 Strokes —

9 瘡 疤 **[ch'uāng-pā]** : scar, scab

— 12 Strokes —

療

8 療 法 **[liáo-fă]** : method of cure, therapeutics

15 療 養 地 **[liáo-yăng tì]** : convalescence resort, recuperation center

療 養 院 **[liáo-yăng yüàn]** : sanitarium, convalescence home

癌

癌 **[yén]** : cancer

— 14 Strokes —

癡

4 癡 心 妄 想 **[ch'īh-hsīn wàng-hsiăng]** : to build castles in the air, to engage in wishful thinking, to daydream; wishful thinking, daydream

13 癡 想 **[ch'īh-hsiăng]** : to indulge in wishful thinking, to daydream; wishful thinking, daydream

— 19 Strokes —

癱

14 癱 瘓 **[t'ān-huàn]** : paralysis, palsy; paralytic

癲

14 癲 瘋 **[tiēn-fēng]** : madness, insanity; insane

16 癲 癇 **[tiēn-hsién]** : epilepsy

— RADICAL 癶 105 —

— 7 Strokes —

發

4 發水 **[fā-shŭi]** : to flood

5 發生 **[fā-shēng]** : to occur, to come about, to happen, to take place

發生，發展，和滅亡的過程 **[fā-shēng, fā-chăn, hó mièh-wáng te kuò-ch'éng]** : the course of emergence, development, and extinction; conception, growth, and destruction

發生效力 **[fā-shēng hsiào-lì]** : to take effect, to come into effect, to become effective

發生生理研究室 **[fā-shēng shēng-lĭ yén-chìu-shìh]** : Developmental Physiology Laboratory

發生影響 **[fā-shēng yĭng-hsiăng]** : to exert influence on, to have the effect of, to influence, to affect

7 發牢騷 **[fā láo-sāo]** : to complain, to grumble, to let off steam

發狂的 **[fā-k'uáng te]** : rabid, mad, crazy, insane

發佈 **[fā-pù]** : to promulgate, to decree

發抖 **[fā-tŏu]** : to shake, to shudder, to tremble, to shiver

發作 **[fā-tsò]** : to break out, to flare up, to explode, to become, to develop into

發言 **[fā-yén]** : to talk, to make a speech

發言權 **[fā-yén ch'üán]** : right of free speech

發言人 **[fā-yén jén]** : spokesman

8 發放 **[fā-fàng]** : to discharge, to distribute, to dole out

發明 **[fā-míng]** : to invent; invention

發明家 **[fā-míng-chiā]** : inventor

發明才能 **[fā-míng ts'ái-néng]** : inventiveness, creativeness

發表 **[fā-piăo]** : to publish, to issue, to declare, to make public, to express, to announce, to publicize

發芽 **[fā-yá]** : to bud, to germinate; germination, sprouting

發炎 **[fā-yén]** : to inflame; inflammation

發育 **[fā-yù]** : to grow up, to mature, to thrive; growth

9 發洩 **[fā-hsièh]** : to give vent to, to vent

10 發展 **[fā-chăn]** : to develop, to advance, to further, to promote, to extend; development, growth, progress

發展成為 **[fā-chăn ch'éng-wéi]** : to evolve into, to develop into, to grow into

發展速度 **[fā-chăn sù-tù]** : rate of growth or development

發展的規律 **[fā-chăn te kuēi-lǜ]** : laws of development

發起 **[fā-ch'ĭ]** : to initiate, to start, to promote, to sponsor

發起者 **[fā-ch'ĭ-chĕ]** : sponsor, initiator, proponent

發射 **[fā-shè]** : to fire, to shoot, to discharge, to launch

發射場 **[fā-shè ch'ăng]** : launching site

發射台 **[fā-shè t'ái]** : launching platform

發射地點 **[fā-shè tì-tiĕn]** : launching site

發財 **[fā-ts'ái]** : to get rich, to amass wealth, to amass a fortune; profit-making

發財致富 **[fā-ts'ái chìh-fù]** : to enrich

11 發現 **[fā-hsièn]** : to discover, to find out, to uncover, to detect

發票 **[fā-p'iào]** : invoice

發動[fā-tùng]: to rouse, to mobilize, to initiate, to launch, to unlease, to set in motion

發動戰爭[fā-tùng chàn-chēng]: to launch a war

發動機[fā-tùng chī]: motor

發動群衆[fā-tùng ch'ǘn-chùng]: to mobilize the masses, to arouse the masses

12 發揮[fā-hūi]: to exert, to give play to, to give free scope to, to develop, to manifest

發揮作用[fā-hūi tsò-yùng]: to play a role in, to come into play, to do one's part

發給[fā-kĕi]: to give out, to distribute, to issue

發脾氣[fā p'í-ch'ì]: to lose one's temper, to become angry

發揚[fā-yáng]: to bring to light, to develop, to extend, to glorify

發揚正氣[fā-yáng chèng-ch'ì]: to foster a spirit of righteousness

13 發慌[fā-huāng]: to lose presence of mind; uneasy, agitated

發達[fā-tá]: to develop, to prosper, to flourish

發電[fā-tièn]: to generate electricity

發電站[fā-tièn chàn]: power station

發電廠[fā-tièn ch'ăng]: power plant, electric power house

發電機[fā-tièn-chī]: generator, power generator, electric generator

發電量[fā-tièn liàng]: electric output

發電能力[fā-tièn néng-lì]: power generating capacity

發電設備[fā-tièn shè-pèi]: power generating equipment

發源[fā-yüán]: to originate

14 發爾巴來索[fā-ĕrh-pā-lái-sŏ]: Valparaiso (Chile)

發瘋[fā-fēng]: to run amuck, to go crazy, to become insane

16 發奮圖强[fā-fèn t'ú-ch'iáng]: to strive for strength with great vigor (a phrase in frequent use after the Soviet pullout in 1960)

發憤[fā-fèn]: to make an effort, to try hard, to strive

發憤圖强[fā-fèn t'ú-ch'iáng]: to strive for strength with great vigor (*See* 發奮圖强)

17 發還[fā-huán]: to return, to give back

19 發覺[fā-chüéh]: to come to light, to discover, to find out, to unearth

登

7 登位[tēng-wèi]: to ascend the throne

10 登記[tēng-chì]: to register, to enroll, to make an entry

登記單位[tēng-chì tān-wèi]: unit of account

登記員[tēng-chì-yüán]: registration personnel, accountant

11 登基[tēng-chī]: to be enthroned, to ascend the throne

登陸[tēng-lù]: to land, to debark, to disembark

登陸艇[tēng-lù t'ĭng]: landing ship, landing craft, landing barge

12 登報[tēng-pào]: to publish in the newspaper

13 登載[tēng-tsăi]: to publish in a magazine or newspaper

— RADICAL 白 106 —

白

4 白毛女[**pái-máo nǚ**]: The White-Haired Girl (title of a ballet and moving picture)

5 白令海[**pó-lìng hǎi**]: Bering Sea

白皮書[**pái-p'í shū**]: white paper (i.e., the U.S. white paper on Sino-American relations)

6 白衣戰士[**pái-ī chàn-shìh**]: battlefield nurses

白色恐怖[**pái-sè k'ǔng-pù**]: white terror (i.e., reactionary oppression)

白色時代[**pái-sè shíh-tài**]: "white period" (i.e., the period before the success of the revolution)

7 白求恩[**pái-ch'íu-ēn**]: Bethune, Dr. Norman (Canadian surgeon)

8 白金[**pái-chīn**]: platinum

9 白軍[**pái-chǖn**]: White Army (i.e., Nationalist troops)

白俄[**pái-ó**]: White Russian; White Russia

白俄羅斯[**pái ó-ló-ssū**]: White Russia

10 白宮[**pái-kūng**]: The White House (Washington, D. C.)

白朗[**pái-lǎng**]: Pailang (a minority nationality)

11 白區[**pái-ch'ǖ**]: white district (i.e., an area under Nationalist control during the Civil War of 1927–1936)

白眼[**pái-yěn**]: disdain, scorn

12 白費[**pái-fèi**]: to expend in vain

白喉[**pái-hóu**]: diphtheria

13 白搭[**pái-tā**]: in vain

14 白旗[**pái-ch'í**]: white flag, flag of truce

白種人[**pái-chǔng jén**]: Caucasian

16 白衛份子[**pái-wèi fèn-tzu**]: "White Guardists"

20 白黨[**pái-tǎng**]: "White Guardists"

— 1 Stroke —

百

3 百萬富翁[**pǎi-wàn fù-wēng**]: millionaire

4 百分比[**pǎi-fēn-pǐ**]: percentage, proportion

百分率[**pǎi-fēn-lǜ**]: percentage

百日咳[**pǎi-jìh k'ó**]: whooping cough

6 百年大計[**pǎi-nién tà-chì**]: long-range plan

7 百折不撓[**pǎi-ché pù-náo**]: unflinching, unbending, unafraid, unmoved by a hundred difficulties

8 百花爭艷[**pǎi-huā chēng-yèn**]: "Let a hundred flowers compete with each other in the splendor of their blossoms"

百花齊放，百家爭鳴[**pǎi-huā ch'í-fàng, pǎi-chiā chēng-míng**]: "Let a hundred flowers bloom and a hundred schools of thought contend"

百花齊放推陳出新[**pǎi-huā ch'í-fàng t'ūi-ch'én ch'ū-hsīn**]: "Let a hundred flowers bloom and create the new through the evolution of the old"

9 百科全書[**pǎi-k'ō ch'üán-shū**]: encyclopedia

10 百般[**pǎi-pān**]: all sorts, every kind, various

12 百發百中[**pǎi-fā pǎi-chùng**]: to hit the mark every time, to be successful every time

16 百戰百勝[**pǎi-chàn pǎi-shèng**]: to win every battle; ever-victorious

22 百囊奔[**pó-náng-pēn**]: Pnom-Penh (Cambodia)

— 3 Strokes —

的

[7] 的里雅斯德[**tì-lǐ-yǎ-ssū-té**] : Trieste

[11] 的勒尼安海[**tì-lē-ní-ān hǎi**] : Tyrrhenian Sea

[13] 的當[**tí-tàng**] : careful, proper, correct, accurate, exact

[14] 的黎波里[**tì-lí-pō-lǐ**] : Tripoli (Libya)

[16] 的確[**tí-ch'üèh**] : true; surely, indeed, certainly, in fact

— 4 Strokes —

皇

[4] 皇太后[**huáng-t'ài-hòu**] : Empress-dowager

皇太子[**huáng-t'ài-tzǔ**] : the heir-apparent, crown prince

[6] 皇后[**huáng-hòu**] : empress

[9] 皇城[**huáng-ch'éng**] : imperial city

皇帝[**huáng-tì**] : emperor

[10] 皇家的[**huáng-chiā te**] : royal, imperial, King's, Queen's, His Majesty's, Her Majesty's

皇宮[**huáng-kūng**] : palace, imperial court, imperial palace

皇座[**huáng-tsò**] : throne

[16] 皇曆[**huáng-lì**] : imperial calendar

— 7 Strokes —

皖

皖[**wǎn**] : Anhwei (abbreviation for 安徽)

— RADICAL 皮 107 —

皮

[7] 皮杜爾[**p'í-tù-ěrh**] : Bidault, George (French statesman)

[9] 皮革[**p'í-kó**] : leather, hides

[11] 皮帶[**p'í-tài**] : leather belt, leather girdle

皮帶輪[**p'í-tài lún**] : belt pulley

[12] 皮筏[**p'í-fá**] : raft of inflated skin

皮棉[**p'í-mién**] : ginned cotton

[14] 皮爾遜[**p'í-ěrh-hsùn**] : Pearson, Lester B. (Canadian statesman)

[15] 皮膚性病研究所[**p'í-fū hsìng-pìng yén-chiù-sǒ**] : Dermatology and Venereology Institute

皮影戲[**p'í-yǐng hsì**] : shadow play, puppet shadow show

— RADICAL 皿 108 —

— 4 Strokes —

盆

6 盆地 [p'én-tì] : basin (geographical tèrm)

盈

16 盈餘 [yíng-yǘ] : surplus, overplus

— 6 Strokes —

3 盒子槍 [hó-tzu ch'iāng] : machine pistol

8 盛岡 [shèng-kāng] : Morioka (Japan)

11 盛產 [shèng-ch'ǎn] : to abound in

盛情 [shèng-ch'íng] : great courtesy, hospitality or kindness

— 7 Strokes —

11 盜匪 [tào-fěi] : robbers, bandits

15 盜賣 [tào-mài] : to sell fraudulently, to sell secretly

18 盜騙 [tào-p'ièn] : to steal and swindle

22 盜竊 [tào-ch'ièh] : to plunder, to rob, to steal

— 8 Strokes —

盟

9 盟軍最高司令部 [méng-chǖn tsùi-kāo ssū-lìng-pù] : Supreme Allied Headquarters

— 9 Strokes —

監

3 監工 [chiēn-kūng] : supervisor, foreman, overseer, steward; to supervise work

5 監犯 [chiēn-fàn] : prisoner

7 監牢 [chiēn-láo] : prison, jail

監事會 [chiēn-shìh hùi] : supervisory council, board of comptrollers

11 監理 [chiēn-lǐ] : to supervise, to superintend, to oversee

監造 [chiēn-tsào] : to supervise the manufacture of

12 監視 [chiēn-shìh] : to keep a close watch over, to watch over; surveillance, close supervision

13 監禁 [chiēn-chìn] : to imprison, to jail; imprisonment

監督 [chiēn-tū] : to supervise, to superintend, to oversee, to watch; overseer, supervisor, inspector, dean, chief of curriculum; supervison, surveillance

14 監察 [chiēn-ch'á] : to examine, to inspect

監察人 [chiēn-ch'á jén] : examiners, inspectors

監察部 [chiēn-ch'á pù] : Ministry of Supervision

監察委員會 [chiēn-ch'á wěi-yüán-hùi] : supervisory committee, control commission, committee on people's supervision

監製 [chiēn-chìh] : to supervise the manufacture of

監管 [chiēn-kuǎn] : to superintend, to administer

監獄 [chiēn-yǜ] : prison, jail

21 監護 **[chiēn-hù]** : to guard; guardianship

23 監驗 **[chiēn-yèn]** : to control, to check

盡

1 盡一切辦法 **[chìn í-ch'ièh pàn-fǎ]** : to seek in every way to, by every means

6 盡全力 **[chìn ch'üán-lì]** : to do one's utmost, to do everything in one's power

盡早 **[chìn-tsǎo]** : with the least delay, as soon as possible

8 盡其本分 **[chìn ch'í pěn-fèn]** : to do one's part

14 盡管 **[chìn-kuǎn]** : although, in spite of, notwithstanding, even though, even so, nevertheless, nonetheless

18 盡職 **[chìn-chíh]** : to fulfill one's duties, to do one's duty to the utmost

— 10 Strokes —

盤

7 盤谷 **[p'án-kǔ]** : Bangkok (Thailand)

9 盤查 **[p'án-ch'á]** : to examine, to inquire into

11 盤問 **[p'án-wèn]** : to interrogate, to cross question

盤問口令 **[p'án-wèn k'ǒu-lìng]** : to ask for the password

15 盤踞 **[p'án-chǜ]** : to entrench on, to settle in, to squat over

16 盤據 **[p'án-chǜ]** : to occupy, to hold a place in possession

— 11 Strokes —

盧

8 盧旺達共和國 **[lú-wàng-tá kùng-hó-kuó]** : Republic of Rwanda

11 盧梭 **[lú-sō]** : Rousseau, Jean Jacques

12 盧森堡 **[lú-sēn-pǎo]** : Luxemburg

盧森堡大公國 **[lú-sēn-pǎo tà kūng-kuó]** : Grand Duchy of Luxemburg

18 盧薩卡 **[lú-sà-k'ǎ]** : Luzaka (Northern Rhodesia)

— RADICAL 目 罒 109 —

目

6 目光短淺 **[mù-kuāng tuǎn-ch'iěn]** : short-sighted

目光遠大 **[mù-kuāng yüǎn-tà]** : far-seeing

8 目空一切 **[mù-k'ūng í-ch'ièh]** : to look down on everyone

目的 **[mù-tì]** : purpose, objective, goal, aim, target, end, destination

目的論 **[mù-tì-lùn]** : teleology

目的地 **[mù-tì-tì]** : destination, goal

9 目前 **[mù-ch'ién]** : current, present-day, at present, for the present

15 目標 **[mù-piāo]** : object, target, aim, goal, objective, end, purpose

17 目擊 **[mù-chī]** : to witness, to be an eyewitness

目擊的報告 **[mù-chī te pào-kào]** : on-the-scene report, on-the-spot account, eyewitness account

— 3 Strokes —

4 直升飛機 **[chíh-shēng fēi-chī]** : helicopter

[7] 直系親屬[**chíh-hsì ch′īn-shŭ**]: lineal relations, immediate relations

[11] 直接[**chíh-chiēh**]: first-hand, direct; directly

直接經驗[**chíh-chiēh chīng-yèn**]: direct experience

直接生產人員[**chíh-chiēh shēng-ch′ăn jén-yüán**]: personnel directly engaged in production

直接威脅[**chíh-chiēh wēi-hsiéh**]: direct threat

直率[**chíh-shuài**]: frank, straightforward, forthright, candid, open, outright, plain spoken

[14] 直截了當的[**chíh-chiéh liăo-tāng te**]: point-blank, blunt, pointed, straight, direct

[17] 直轄市[**chíh-hsiá shìh**]: municipality directly under central authority

[19] 直覺[**chíh-chüéh**]: intuition

盲

[5] 盲目[**máng-mù**]: blind, blindly

盲目抄襲[**máng-mù ch′āo-hsí**]: blind imitation, in blind imitation of

盲目崇拜[**máng-mù ch′úng-pài**]: blind worship, blind admiration

盲目發展[**máng-mù fā-chăn**]: blind expansion

盲目性[**máng-mù-hsìng**]: thoughtlessness, blindness

盲目樂觀[**máng-mù lè-kuān**]: blindly optimistic, recklessly optimistic (a phrase intended as a warning to cadres against taking an overly optimistic attitude without reasonable assurance of success)

盲目生產[**máng-mù shēng-ch′ăn**]: blind production (i.e., production without planning)

[11] 盲動主義[**máng-tùng chŭ-ì**]: adventurism, putschism, blind act-ism

— 4 Strokes —

相

[3] 相干[**hsiāng-kān**]: concerned, related, interdependent, interrelated

相干性[**hsiāng-kān-hsìng**]: interrelationship, interdependence

[4] 相反[**hsiāng-făn**]: contrary, antithetical, opposed, counter, adverse to, on the contrary, in contrast to

相反相成[**hsiāng-făn hsiāng-ch′éng**]: to be opposite yet complementary; things opposed to each other but complementing each other

相互的[**hsiāng-hù te**]: reciprocal, mutual

相互關係[**hsiāng-hù kuān-hsì**]: interrelation, interdependence

相匹敵[**hsiāng-p′ĭ-tí**]: equal, peer; an equal match

[6] 相同[**hsiāng-t′úng**]: identical

[7] 相形見絀[**hsiàng-hsíng chièn-ch′ù**]: to throw into the shade; on comparison found to be inferior

相形之下[**hsiàng-hsíng chīh hsià**]: under comparison

相似[**hsiāng-ssù**]: to bear resemblance to, to look like; similar, like

相似處[**hsiāng-ssù ch′ù**]: similarity, resemblance, affinity

[8] 相爭[**hsiāng-chēng**]: to contend with, to compete with, to struggle with each other for

[9] 相持[**hsiāng-ch′íh**]: to wrangle, to quarrel

相持階段[**hsiāng-ch′íh chiēh-tuàn**]: stage of stalemate or standstill

相信[**hsiāng-hsìn**]: to believe in, to have faith in

[10] 相配[**hsiāng-p′èi**]: to match, to go well with

[12] 相結合[hsiāng chiéh-hó]: to combine with, to coordinate with, to go hand in hand with

相提幷論[hsiāng-t'í pìng-lùn]: to put something on a par with, to be mentioned in the same breath, to judge on the same basis

[13] 相當[hsiāng-tāng]: suitable, proportionate; considerably, fairly, comparatively, to a certain extent

[14] 相稱[hsiāng-ch'èn]: to correspond, to match, to suit, to fit, to balance; worth, commensurate

相輔相成[hsiāng-fŭ hsiāng-ch'éng]: mutually supplementary and mutually complementary

相對[hsiāng-tùi]: relative, comparative

相對和絕對[hsiāng-tùi hó chüéh-tùi]: relative and absolute

相對性原理[hsiāng-tùi-hsìng yüán-lĭ]: theory of relativity

相對論[hsiāng-tùi lùn]: relativism

相對的靜止[hsiāng-tùi te chìng-chĭh]: relative immobility

相對多數[hsiāng-tùi tō-shù]: relative majority

[15] 相適應[hsiāng shìh-yìng]: in step (with each other), in proper proportion

相適應又相矛盾[hsiāng shìh-yìng yù hsiāng máo-tùn]: conformity as well as contradiction

[16] 相罵[hsiāng-mà]: bitter exchange, violent abuse, battle of words

[17] 相聲[hsiàng-shēng]: to mimic; mimicry, humorous dialogue, two-man skit, cross-talk

相應[hsiāng-yìng]: to correspond; corresponding, in harmony with, consistent with, in agreement with

[18] 相關[hsiāng-kuān]: mutually affected by, having a sympathetic feeling between, correlated

看

[4] 看中[k'àn-chùng]: to make the right pick, to ascertain

看不起[k'àn-pù-ch'ĭ]: to slight, to despise, to scorn, to disdain, to look down upon, to have contempt for

看不見[k'àn-pú-chièn]: to lose sight of, to be unable to see

[5] 看台[k'àn-t'ái]: reviewing stand

[6] 看守[k'ān-shŏu]: to guard, to watch, to keep a lookout

[8] 看法[k'àn-fă]: view, opinion, belief, sentiment, the way one looks at something

[9] 看待[k'ān-tài]: to regard, to treat

[11] 看淸局勢[k'àn-ch'īng chű-shìh]: to have a correct appraisal of a situation, to size up a situation clearly

看得高[k'àn-té-kāo]: to set one's sights high

看得遠[k'àn-té-yüăn]: to be able to see far, to have a broad view; far-sighted, far-seeing

[14] 看齊[k'àn-ch'í]: to keep abreast of, to keep up with, to follow the example of; to dress (i.e., in close order drill)

盼

[12] 盼望[p'àn-wàng]: to expect, to look forward to, to look at, to long for, to hope for

省

省[shěng]: province; provincial; to reduce, to omit, to be frugal

[2] 省人民代表大會[shěng jén-mín tài-piăo tà-hùi]: Provincial People's Congress

省人民委員會[shěng jén-mín wĕi-yüán-

hùi] : Provincial People's Council

8 省 長**[shěng-chăng]** : provincial governor

省 委**[shěng-wěi]** : provincial Party committee

9 省 城**[shěng-ch'éng]** : capital city of a province

11 省 略**[shěng-lüèh]** : to omit, to leave out; omission

17 省 轄 市**[shěng-hsiá shìh]** : municipality directly controlled by the provincial government

— 5 Strokes —

11 眨 眼**[chă-yěn]** : to wink, to blink

眞

4 眞 心 眞 意 的**[chēn-hsīn chēn-ì te]** : heartfelt, sincere, wholehearted, honest; sincerely, wholeheartedly, honestly

眞 心 善 意**[chēn-hsīn shàn-ì]** : sincere, sincere and with good intentions

5 眞 正 的**[chēn-chèng te]** : true, vital, literal, genuine, real, veritable, authentic

8 眞 空**[chēn-k'ūng]** : vacuum

眞 空 管**[chēn-k'ūng kuăn]** : vacuum tube

9 眞 相**[chēn-hsiàng]** : truth, reality, actuality, actual facts

眞 面 目**[chēn miền-mù]** : true face, true colors, true shape, true form

1 眞 淸**[chēn-ch'īng]** : Chanthanh (Vietnam)

眞 理**[chēn-lĭ]** : truth

眞 理 報**[chēn-lĭ pào]** : Pravda (Russian newspaper)

13 眞 誠**[chēn-ch'éng]** : sincerity; sincere, earnest

14 眞 實**[chēn-shíh]** : factual, real, true, veritable, authentic

眞 實 性**[chēn-shíh-hsìng]** : truthfulness

— 6 Strokes —

衆

9 衆 叛 親 離**[chùng-p'àn ch'īn-lí]** : opposed by the masses and deserted by one's followers

20 衆 議 員**[chùng-ì yüán]** : representative, congressman (U.S.A.)

衆 議 院**[chùng-ì yüàn]** : House of Representatives (U.S.A., Japan); Chamber of Deputies

眼

5 眼 目 中**[yěn-mù chūng]** : in the eyes of, according to a person's way of looking at things

6 眼 光**[yěn-kuāng]** : eyesight, vision, outlook

9 眼 界**[yěn-chièh]** : field of vision, mental view, outlook, horizon

眼 界 挾 窄**[yěn-chièh hsiá-chăi]** : to take a narrow view of things

10 眼 中 釘**[yěn-chūng tīng]** : a nail in the eye, a thorn in the flesh, a thorn in one's side

眼 高 手 低**[yěn-kāo shŏu-tī]** : to have sharp eyes in criticizing others but clumsy hands in doing things oneself

— 7 Strokes —

着

4 着 手**[chó-shŏu]** : to set to work, to proceed with, to set about, to undertake

9 着重說明 **[chó-chùng shuō-míng]**: to emphasize, to stress

着重討論 **[chó-chùng t'ăo-lùn]**: to center discussion on, to discuss. . .as the main topic

— 8 Strokes —

睦

15 睦鄰 **[mù-lín]**: friendly neighbor

睦鄰關係 **[mù-lín kuān-hsì]**: good neighborly relations

督

9 督軍 **[tū-chŭn]**: military governor, warlord, tu-chün

督促 **[tū-ts'ù]**: to urge, to press, to push forward, to spur on

11 督理 **[tū-lĭ]**: to watch over, to lead, to administer, to manage, to direct, a military superintendent

14 督察 **[tū-ch'á]**: to watch over and inspect; inspector

16 督導 **[tū-tăo]**: to watch over and guide

— 9 Strokes —

瞄

13 瞄準 **[miáo-chŭn]**: to take a good or accurate aim

— 11 Strokes —

瞞

瞞 **[mán]**: to deceive, to conceal

— 12 Strokes —

瞭

11 瞭望 **[liào-wàng]**: to observe, to keep a lookout; outlook; overlooking, looking out over

瞭望台 **[liào-wàng t'ái]**: observation post, lookout post

13 瞭解 **[liăo-chiĕh]**: to understand, to inquire (so as to understand)

15 瞭墩 **[liăo-tūn]**: Ledun (Sinkiang)

— 13 Strokes —

瞻

9 瞻前顧後 **[chān-ch'ién kù-hòu]**: to look ahead and to look back, to take into account both past experience and situations that may arise in the future

— RADICAL 矛 110 —

9 矛盾[máo-tùn]: contradiction; contradictory

矛盾尖銳化[máo-tùn chiēn-jùi-huà]: sharpening of contradictions

矛盾律[máo-tùn lǜ]: principle of contradiction

矛盾普遍性[máo-tùn p'ŭ-pièn-hsìng]: universality of contradiction

矛盾特殊性[máo-tùn t'è-shū-hsìng]: particularity of contradiction

矛盾的對立面[máo-tùn te tùi-lì-mièn]: opposites in contradiction

矛盾的統一[máo-tùn te t'ŭng-ī]: unity of contradictions

16 矛頭[máo-t'óu]: spearhead

矛頭針對[máo-t'óu chēn-tùi]: to be spearheaded at

— RADICAL 矢 111 —

— 3 Strokes —

知

3 知己[chīh-chĭ]: intimate friend

4 知心[chīh-hsīn]: intimate friend

知心朋友[chīh-hsīn p'éng-yŭ]: intimate friend

6 知名人士[chīh-míng jén-shìh]: well-known people, famous people, celebrities, outstanding personalities

13 知道[chīh-tào]: to know, to have knowledge of, to be aware of

16 知曉[chīh-hsiăo]: to be cognizant of, to be aware of

18 知禮[chīh-lĭ]: Trile (Vietnam); to know the rules of propriety

19 知識[chīh-shìh]: knowledge, common sense

知識階級[chīh-shìh chiēh-chí]: intellectual class

知識界[chīh-shìh chièh]: intellectual circles

知適青年[chīh-shìh ch'īng-nién]: intellectual youth

知識份子[chīh-shìh fèn-tzu]: intellectual; intelligentsia

知識份子勞動化[chīh-shìh fèn-tzu láo-tùng-huà]: to make the intellectuals become identified with the laboring people

知識化[chīh-shìh-huà]: "to intellectualize," to make knowledgeable

20 知覺[chīh-chüéh]: to perceive; perception

— 7 Strokes —

短

3 短工[tuăn-kūng]: temporary employee, day laborer; piece work, a job

4 短少[tuăn-shăo]: few, insufficient, to be less than, to fall short of

7 短見[tuăn-chièn]: a limited view, limited experience; a wrong idea

短兵相接[tuăn-pīng hsiāng-chiēh]: to fight at close quarters; hand-to-hand fight

8 短長[tuăn-ch'áng]: short and long, defects and excellencies, right and wrong

短波[tuăn-pō]: shortwave

9 短促 [tuǎn-ts'ù] : short, brief, shortness of time, terse

10 短缺 [tuǎn-ch'üēh] : deficiency; deficient

11 短處 [tuǎn-ch'ù] : deficiency, defect, weak point, shortcoming

短途運輸 [tuǎn-t'ú yǜn-shū] : short distance transport (i.e., transport of goods from producing districts to nearby transportation centers)

12 短期 [tuǎn-ch'í] : short-term

短期輪訓 [tuǎn-ch'í lún-hsǜn] : short-term training in rotation

15 短暫 [tuǎn-chàn] : for the moment, temporarily

短篇小說 [tuǎn-p'iēn hsiǎo-shuō] : short story

— 8 Strokes —

矮

2 矮人 [ǎi-jén] : dwarf, pygmy

— 12 Strokes —

矯

5 矯正 [chiǎo-chèng] : to rectify, to correct, to regulate

8 矯枉過正 [chiǎo-wǎng kuò-chèng] : to be overstrict, to go too far in straightening things out

11 矯情 [chiǎo-ch'íng] : to be obstinately unreasonable

12 矯揉造作 [chiǎo-jóu tsào-tsò] : affectation

— RADICAL 石 112 —

石

石 [shíh] : Shihkiachwang (abbreviation of 石家莊)

石 [tàn] : a weight of 120 catties, a picul of 100 catties or 133 1/3 lb.

3 石川 [shíh-ch'uān] : Ishikawa (Japan)

4 石方 [shíh-fāng] : cubic meters of stonework

8 石河 [shíh-hó] : Thachha (Vietnam)

石版畫 [shíh-pǎn huà] : lithograph

石油工業部 [shíh-yú kūng-yèh pù] : Ministry of Petroleum Industry

石油研究所 [shíh-yú yén-chìu-sǒ] : Petroleum Institute

12 石棉廠 [shíh-mién ch'ǎng] : asbestos plant

15 石墨廠 [shíh-mò ch'ǎng] : tannery

— 3 Strokes —

矽

16 矽鋼 [hsì-kāng] : silicon steel

— 4 Strokes —

砍

砍 [k'ǎn] : to chop, to cut down

6 砍伐 [k'ǎn-fā] : to fell, to cut down

砍死 [k'ǎn-ssǔ] : to kill with a sword or axe

— 5 Strokes —

砲

7 砲兵主帥 [p'ào-pīng chǔ-shuài] : Generalissimo of the Artillery (Soviet Army)

破

4 破中有立[p'ò-chūng yŭ-lì]: destroying includes establishing

破天荒[p'ò t'iēn-huāng]: epoch-making, unprecedented, for the first time in history

5 破四舊[p'ò ssù-chìu]: to destroy the four olds (*See* 四舊)

破四舊，立四新[p'ò ssù-chìu, lì ssū-hsīn]: to destroy the four olds and establish the four news (*See* 四舊 and 四新)

6 破冰船[p'ò-pīng ch'uán]: icebreaker, ice cutter

破字當頭[p'ò-tzù tāng-t'óu]: destroying takes first place; destruction first (a phrase in use during the Cultural Revolution)

7 破私立公[p'ò-ssū lì-kūng]: to destroy the self and foster the public (interest) (i.e., to renounce oneself for the sake of the state–a phrase from the Cultural Revolution)

10 破案[p'ò-àn]: to solve a case, to bring a case to book

破除[p'ò-ch'ú]: to dispel, to remove, to eliminate

11 破產[p'ò-ch'ăn]: to go bankrupt; bankruptcy, ruin; bankrupt, insolvent

破產者[p'ò-ch'ăn-chĕ]: a bankrupt or an insolvent person

12 破裂[p'ò-lièh]: to rupture, to break off, to split, to disrupt; rupture, breach, disruption

17 破獲[p'ò-huò]: to unearth, to foil, to uncover, to break (a case), to catch (a culprit)

18 破舊立新[p'ò-chìu lì-hsīn]: to destroy the old and establish the new (*See* 四舊 and 四新)

19 破壞[p'ò-huài]: to ruin, to destroy, to demolish, to disrupt, to wreck, to subvert, to undermine, to sabotage; destruction, ruin

破壞份子[p'ò-huài fèn-tzu]: saboteur elements

破壞活動[p'ò-huài huó-tùng]: sabotage, acts of sabotage, subversive activities

破壞名譽[p'ò-huài míng-yù]: defamation, libel, slander

— 6 Strokes —

研

7 研究[yén-chìu]: to study, to research, to examine, to explore, to go deeply into; research, study

研究分析[yén-chìu fēn-hsī]: study and analysis; to study and analyze

研究生[yén-chìu-shēng]: graduate student

研究生部[yén-chìu-shēng pù]: graduate school, post-graduate department

研究員[yén-chìu-yüán]: research fellow, research worker

研究院[yén-chìu-yüàn]: research institute; graduate school

— 7 Strokes —

硝

4 硝化甘油[hsiāo-huà kān-yú]: nitroglycerine

5 硝石[hsiāo-shíh]: nitre

硬

4 硬分幣[yìng fēn-pì]: coin of small denomination, cent

8 硬性規定[yìng-hsìng kuēi-tìng]: rigid regulations

9 硬是不[yìng-shìh pù]: by no means, in no way, not at all, not in the least

13 硬煤 [yìng-méi] : hard coal, anthracite

硬搬和模仿 [yìng-pān hó mó-fǎng] : uncritical approbation and imitation (i.e., particularly of old or foreign models)

15 硬幣 [yìng-pì] : hard currency

— 8 Strokes —

碑

碑 [pēi] : stone tablet, monument

碉

12 碉堡 [tiāo-pǎo] : bunker, blockhouse

— 9 Strokes —

碱

15 碱廠 [chiĕn-ch'ǎng] : soda plant

碰

8 碰到 [p'èng-tào] : to meet with, to come across, to run into, to run up against

13 碰運氣 [p'èng yǜn-ch'ì] : to depend on luck

16 碰壁 [p'èng-pì] : to meet with a rebuff, to be refused, to be blocked, to be repulsed, to run into an obstacle, to fail

碰頭會 [p'èng-t'óu hùi] : "bump heads meeting" (i.e., an informal, brief, business meeting)

碧

14 碧瑤 [pì-yáo] : Baguio (Philippines)

15 碧澗 [pì-chièn] : Pekan (Malaysia)

磁

2 磁力 [tz'ú-lì] : magnetic force

4 磁化 [tz'ú-huà] : to magnetize; magnetization

5 磁石 [tz'ú-shíh] : magnet, lodestone

8 磁极 [tz'ú-chí] : magnetic pole

14 磁場 [tz'ú-ch'ǎng] : magnetic field

磁暴 [tz'ú-pào] : magnetic storm

21 磁鐵 [tz'ú-t'iěh] : magnetic iron, magnet

23 磁體 [tz'ú-t'ǐ] : magnet

— 10 Strokes —

碼

碼 [mǎ] : yard (i.e., measure)

16 碼頭 [mǎ-t'óu] : wharf, dock, pier

碼頭工人 [mǎ-t'óu kūng-jén] : dock hand, stevedore, longshoreman, docker

碾

6 碾米廠 [niěn-mǐ ch'ǎng] : rice-hulling mill, rice-husking mill

磐

5 磐石般的 [p'án-shíh-pān te] : monolithic, rocklike

磋

11 磋商 [ts'ō-shāng] : to consult with, to confer with, to deliberate together; consultation

— 11 Strokes —

確

8 確定[ch'üèh-tìng]: to affirm, to ascertain, to decide; affirmation, ascertainment, authentication; ascertained, affirmed

9 確信[ch'üèh-hsìn]: to be sure of, to be confident, to believe firmly; firm faith, conviction

確保 [ch'üèh-pǎo]: to assure, to make sure, to make certain, to ensure, to secure, to guarantee

14 確實[ch'üèh-shíh]: true, correct, reliable, certain, genuine, authentic

確實性[ch'üèh-shíh-hsìng]: certainty, certitude

7 磨床[mó-ch'uáng]: grinding machine, grinder

13 磨滅[mó-mièh]: to obliterate, to crush

— 12 Strokes —

磷

8 磷肥[lín-féi]: phosphate fertilizer

— 13 Strokes —

鹼[chiěn]: alkali

3 鹼土[chiěn-t'ǔ]: alkaline soil

4 鹼化[chiěn-huà]: to alkalize

6 鹼地[chiěn-tì]: alkaline soil

— 14 Strokes —

礙[ài]: to hinder, to obstruct

4 礙手[ài-shǒu]: to disturb, to trouble, to be in the way

11 礙眼[ài-yěn]: to see what one would wish not to see; an eyesore; unpleasant

— 15 Strokes —

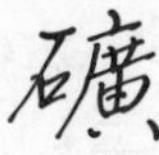

礦[k'uàng]: mineral

3 礦工[k'uàng-kūng]: miner, mine worker

礦山[k'uàng-shān]: mine

7 礦冶研究所[k'uàng-yěh yén-chìu-sŏ]: Mining and Metallurgy Institute

8 礦物[k'uàng-wù]: mineral

礦物肥料[k'uàng-wù féi-liào]: mineral fertilizer

礦物原料研究所[k'uàng-wù yüán-liào yén-chìu-sŏ]: Mineral Raw Materials Institute

9 礦砂[k'uàng-shā]: ore

11 礦產資源[k'uàng-ch'ǎn tzū-yüán]: mineral resources

礦區[k'uàng-ch'ū]: mining area

18 礦藏[k'uàng-ts'áng]: mineral deposit, deposit, mineral reserves

— RADICAL 示 礻 113 —

示

9 示威遊行[**shih-wēi yú-hsíng**] : demonstration, parade

10 示弱[**shih-jò**] : to show weakness

13 示意圖[**shih-ì t'ú**] : drawing, sketch

15 示範[**shih-fàn**] : model, example

示踪原子[**shih-tsūng yüán-tzŭ**] : tracer atom

— 3 Strokes —

社

6 社交[**shè-chiāo**] : social intercourse, social dealing, social activity

社交場合[**shè-chiāo ch'ăng-hó**] : social functions

社交生活[**shè-chiāo shēng-huó**] : social life

8 社長[**shè-chăng**] : commune chief, office chief (newspaper), director (agency)

社來社去[**shè lái shè ch'ǜ**] : from the communes back to the communes (abbreviation of 從公社來，回公社去, which refers generally to the training of commune members in outside schools and returning them to the communes to exercise their skills)

10 社員[**shè-yüán**] : commune member, association or society member

社員大會[**shè-yüán tà-hùi**] : general meeting of commune members

社員代表會議[**shè-yüán tài-piăo hùi-ì**] : Brigade Congress

社員代表大會[**shè-yüán tài-piăo tà-hùi**] : Commune Congress

11 社教[**shè-chiào**] : social studies, social education, social instruction

13 社會[**shè-hùi**] : society, community

社會成份[**shè-hùi ch'éng-fèn**] : social composition

社會集團[**shè-hùi chí-t'uán**] : social group

社會階層[**shè-hùi chiēh-ts'éng**] : social strata

社會制度[**shè-hùi chih-tù**] : social institution, social system

社會進化[**shè-hùi chìn-huà**] : social evolution, progress of society

社會主義[**shè-hùi chŭ-ì**] : socialism; socialist

社會主義者[**shè-hùi chŭ-ì chĕ**] : socialist

社會主義陣營[**shè-hùi chŭ-ì chèn-yíng**] : the socialist camp

社會主義成份[**shè-hùi chŭ-ì ch'éng-fèn**] : socialist sector

社會主義建設[**shè-hùi chŭ-ì chièn-shè**] : socialist construction

社會主義建設事業[**shè-hùi chŭ-ì chièn-shè shih-yèh**] : the work of building socialism, socialist construction enterprises

社會主義競賽[**shè-hùi chŭ-ì chìng-sài**] : socialist emulation (movement)

社會主義覺悟[**shè-hùi chŭ-ì chüéh-wù**] : socialist consciousness

社會主義現實主義[**shè-hùi chŭ-ì hsièn-shíh chŭ-ì**] : socialist realism

社會主義化[**shè-hùi-chŭ-ì-huà**] : to socialize; socialization

社會主義改造[**shè-hùi chŭ-ì kăi-tsào**] : socialist transformation (i.e., change from private ownership of factories or business concerns to collective or government ownership, 1955–1966)

社會主義革命[**shè-hùi chŭ-ì kó-mìng**] : the socialist revolution

社會主義關 **[shè-hùi chŭ-ì kuān]**: the test of socialism

社會主義工業化 **[shè-hùi chŭ-ì kūng-yèh-huà]**: socialist industrialization

社會主義國家共產黨和工人黨代表會議宣言 **[shè-hùi chŭ-ì kuó-chiā kùng-ch'ăn-tăng hó kūng-jén-tăng tài-piăo hùi-ì hsüān-yén]**: Declaration of the Meeting of Representatives of Communist and Workers Parties of Socialist Countries

社會主義國家共產黨和工人黨代表會議聲明 **[shè-hùi chŭ-ì kuó-chiā kùng-ch'ăn-tăng hó kūng-jén-tăng tài-piăo hùi-ì shēng-míng]**: Statement of the Meeting of Representatives of Communist and Workers Parties of Socialist Countries

社會主義所有制 **[shè-hùi chŭ-ì sŏ-yŭ-chìh]**: socialist ownership system

社會主義道德 **[shè-hùi chŭ-ì tào-té]**: socialist morality

社會主義文化大革命 **[shè-hùi chŭ-ì wén-huà tà kó-mìng]**: Great Socialist Cultural Revolution (an earlier term for the Great Proletarian Cultural Revolution)

社會出身 **[shè-hùi ch'ū-shēn]**: social origin

社會風氣 **[shè-hùi fēng-ch'ì]**: social convention

社會賢達 **[shè-hùi hsién-tá]**: enlightened gentry scholars, public personages

社會性 **[shè-hùi-hsìng]**: social nature, social character, sociality

社會形態 **[shè-hùi hsíng-t'ài]**: social form

社會學 **[shè-hùi-hsüéh]**: sociology

社會活動 **[shè-hùi huó-tùng]**: social activity

社會活動家 **[shè-hùi huó-tùng-chiā]**: social activist

社會人士 **[shè-hùi jén-shìh]**: public figures, prominent persons, notables

社會民主黨 **[shè-hùi mín-chŭ-tăng]**: Social Democratic Party (West Germany)

社會名流 **[shè-hùi míng-líu]**: noted public figures, socialite

社會保險 **[shè-hùi păo-hsiĕn]**: social insurance, social security

社會沙文主義 **[shè-hùi shā-wén chŭ-ì]**: social chauvinism (i.e., on the part of Social Democrats who supported World War I)

社會生產力 **[shè-hùi shēng-ch'ăn-lì]**: social productive force

社會事務部 **[shè-hùi shìh-wù pù]**: social affairs department

社會數型 **[shè-hùi shù-hsíng]**: social types

社會黨國際 **[shè-hùi-tăng kuó-chì]**: Socialist International

社會帝國主義 **[shè-hùi tì-kuó chŭ-ì]**: social imperialism, socialist imperialism (a term that first appeared in the People's Daily on August 23, 1968 in reference to modern revisionism, and which the People's Daily on August 30 defined as "imperialism bearing the banner of socialism")

社會輿論 **[shè-hùi yǘ-lùn]**: public opinion

15 社論 **[shè-lùn]**: editorial, lead article

16 社辦 **[shè-pàn]**: commune-run

社辦事業 **[shè-pàn shìh-yèh]**: commune-run undertakings

— 5 Strokes —

12 祝賀 **[chù-hò]**: to congratulate, to greet

14 祝福 **[chù-fú]**: to bless; blessing

神

4 神戶 **[shén-hù]**: Kobe (Japan)

5 神仙會 **[shén-hsiēn hùi]**: Meeting of the Immortals (a meeting at which leading members of the democratic parties made

confessions of their own errors and criticized errors of other participants)

7 神甫[shén-fŭ]: father, priest (Roman Catholic)

8 神奈川[shén-nài-ch'uān]: Kanagawa (Japan)

10 神祕[shén-mì]: mysterious, mystic

神祕主義[shén-mì chŭ-ì]: mysticism

神祕論[shén-mì lùn]: mysticism

12 神智教[shén-chìh-chiào]: theosophy

13 神經戰[shén-chīng chàn]: war of nerves

神經衰弱[shén-chīng shuāi-jò]: nervous breakdown, nervous debility

神話[shén-huà]: myth

神聖[shén-shèng]: sacred, holy

16 神學[shén-hsüéh]: theology

22 神權[shén-ch'üán]: theocratic authority

祖

6 祖先[tsŭ-hsiēn]: forefather, ancestor

11 祖國[tsŭ-kuó]: motherland, fatherland, homeland (refers usually to China)

— 6 Strokes —

6 祥安[hsiáng-ān]: Tuongan (Vietnam)

票

9 票面[p'iào-mièn]: face of a bill

票面價值[p'iào-mièn chià-chíh]: face value, nominal value, face value of a note

16 票據[p'iào-chǜ]: certificate, commercial paper, bill, note

票據交換[p'iào-chǜ chiāo-huàn]: bank clearing

— 8 Strokes —

禁

4 禁止[chìn-chĭh]: to prohibit, to forbid, to ban, to suppress, to outlaw, to proscribe; prohibition, ban, proscription

禁止流通[chìn-chĭh líu-t'ūng]: to forbid circulation

禁止原子彈氫彈世界大會 [chìn-chĭh yüán-tzŭ-tàn ch'īng-tàn shìh-chièh tà-hùi]: World Conference Against Atomic and Hydrogen Bombs

5 禁令[chìn-lìng]: proscription, restriction, prohibition law

11 禁閉[chìn-pì]: to obstruct, to close against

13 禁運[chìn-yǜn]: to prohibit transport, embargo

15 禁慾主義[chìn-yù chŭ-ì]: asceticism

祿

5 祿寧[lù-níng]: Locnin (Vietnam)

祿平[lù-p'íng]: Locbinh (Vietnam)

9 祿南[lù-nán]: Locnam (Vietnam)

稟

8 稟性[pĭng-hsìng]: nature, essence, being, temperament, character

15 稟賦[pĭng-fù]: natural gifts, natural endowment

— 9 Strokes —

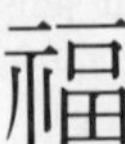

4 福井[fú-chĭng]: Fukui (Japan)

[7] 福克蘭群島 **[fú-k'ò-lán ch'ǘn-tǎo]** : Falkland Islands

福利 **[fú-lì]** : happiness and profit, welfare, well-being

福利金 **[fú-lì chīn]** : welfare fund

福利費 **[fú-lì fèi]** : welfare expenses, a sum paid for welfare facilities

福利設施 **[fú-lì shè-shīh]** : welfare facilities

福利事業 **[fú-lì shìh-yèh]** : welfare, welfare services

[8] 福岡 **[fú-kāng]** : Fukuoka (Japan)

[9] 福建日報 **[fú-chièn jìh-pào]** : Fukien Daily (mainland Chinese daily newspaper)

[10] 福島 **[fú-tǎo]** : Fukushima (Japan)

福特 **[fú-t'è]** : Ford

[11] 福氣 **[fú-ch'ì]** : good luck, happiness

[15] 福興 **[fú-hsīng]** : Thualuu (Vietnam)

福摩薩 **[fú-mó-sà]** : Formosa

禍

[9] 禍首 **[huò-shǒu]** : ringleader, chief actor in a crime, principal criminal

[10] 禍害 **[huò-hài]** : injury, damage, disaster

[14] 禍福 **[huò-fú]** : misfortune and good fortune

— 13 Strokes —

禮

[8] 禮尙往來 **[lǐ-shàng wǎng-lái]** : to give and take; give-and-take

禮物 **[lǐ-wù]** : gift, present

[9] 禮炮 **[lǐ-p'ào]** : gun salute

[11] 禮堂 **[lǐ-t'áng]** : auditorium

[14] 禮賓 **[lǐ-pīn]** : protocol

禮賓司 **[lǐ-pīn ssū]** : office of protocol, protocol department

— RADICAL 内 114 —

— RADICAL 禾 115 —

禾

[9] 禾苗 **[hó-miáo]** : rice seedling

— 2 Strokes —

私

私 **[ssū]** : private, selfish (as opposed to 公, public, the common good)

[2] 私人 **[ssū-jén]** : private person; private, personal

[3] 私下地 **[ssū-hsià tì]** : secretly, privately, not publicly

[4] 私方 **[ssū-fāng]** : private citizens

私方人員 **[ssū-fāng jén-yüán]** : personnel representing the capitalist interest

私心 **[ssū-hsīn]** : selfishness; selfish

[6] 私有制 **[ssū-yǔ chìh]** : private ownership system

私有觀念 **[ssū-yǔ kuān-nièn]** : the concept of private ownership

[8] 私股 **[ssū-kǔ]** : private share

私念 **[ssū-nièn]** : selfish ideas

[15] 私養猪 **[ssū-yǎng chū]** : pigs raised privately

[17] 私營工商業[ssū-yíng kūng-shāng-yèh] : private industry and commerce

[20] 私黨[ssū-tǎng] : clique, exclusive set, one's particular group of followers

— 3 Strokes —

秉

[4] 秉公[pǐng-kūng] : to deal justly

[8] 秉性[pǐng-hsìng] : natural disposition, nature, character

— 4 Strokes —

秋

[5] 秋田[ch'īu-t'ién] : Akita (Japan)

[6] 秋收[ch'īu-shōu] : autumn harvest

秋收起義[ch'īu-shōu ch'ǐ-ì] : Autumn Harvest Uprisings (a series of uprisings in 1927 at the Kiangsi-Hunan-Hubei border under the guidance of Mao Tse-tung)

[9] 秋後算賬[ch'īu-hòu suàn-chàng] : accounts will be reckoned after the autumn harvest; revenge will come after the harvest (a phrase from the Cultural Revolution)

科

[4] 科比[k'ō-pǐ] : kopeck

[6] 科西嘉[k'ō-hsī-chiā] : Corsica

[7] 科克群島[k'ō-k'ò ch'ǘn-tǎo] : Cook Islands

科克海峽[k'ō-k'ò hǎi-hsiá] : Cook Strait

[8] 科林斯灣[k'ō-lín-ssū wān] : Gulf of Corinth

[9] 科威特[k'ō-wēi-t'è] : Kuwait

科威特城[k'ō-wēi-t'è ch'éng] : Al Kuwait (Kuwait)

科威特酋長國[k'ō-wēi-t'è ch'íu-chǎng-kuó] : Sheikdom of Kuwait

[10] 科倫[k'ō-lún] : Colon

科倫坡[k'ō-lún-p'ō] : Colombo (Ceylon)

科倫坡計劃[k'ō-lún-p'ō chì-huà] : Colombo Plan

科納克里[k'ō-nà-k'ò-lǐ] : Conakry (Guinea)

科茲洛夫[k'ō-tzū-lò-fū] : Kozlov, Frol (Russian statesman)

[14] 科爾薩科夫[k'ō-ěrh-sà-k'ō-fū] : Korsakov

[16] 科學[k'ō-hsüéh] : science

科學技術委員會[k'ō-hsüéh chì-shù wěi-yüán-hùi] : Science and Technology Commission

科學獎金委員會[k'ō-hsüéh chiǎng-chīn wěi-yüán-hùi] : Committee on Scientific Prizes

科學性[k'ō-hsüéh-hsìng] : scientific character, imbued with scientific character

科學規劃委員會[k'ō-hsüéh kuēi-huà wěi-yüán-hùi] : Planning Committee for the Development of Science

科學事務處[k'ō-hsüéh shìh-wù ch'ù] : Office of Scientific Affairs

科學院[k'ō-hsüéh-yüàn] : Academy of Sciences, Academia Sinica

[17] 科舉[k'ō-chǚ] : imperial examinations

[19] 科羅拉多[k'ō-ló-lā-tō] : Colorado

— 5 Strokes —

秤

[5] 秤平斗滿[ch'èng-p'íng tǒu-mǎn] : even balance and full measures; fair dealing

秩

[7] 秩序混亂[chìh-hsǜ hùn-luàn] : disorder, confusion, turmoil

秦

8 秦始皇 **[ch'ín shih huáng]**: Ch'in Shih Huang (First Emperor of China and founder of the Ch'in Dynasty in 221 B.C.)

秘

10 祕書 **[mì-shū]**: secretary; secretarial

祕書長 **[mì-shū-chăng]**: Secretary-General

祕書處 **[mì-shū-ch'ù]**: secretariat

11 祕密 **[mì-mì]**: secrecy; secret, private, confidential, classified

祕密投票 **[mì-mì t'óu-p'iào]**: secret ballot

13 祕傳 **[mì-ch'uán]**: secretly handed down, made known secretly; esoteric

15 祕魯 **[pì-lŭ]**: Peru

祕魯共和國 **[pì-lŭ kùng-hó-kuó]**: Republic of Peru

租

5 租用 **[tsū-yùng]**: to lease, to hire, to rent; rented, leased, hired, chartered

9 租界 **[tsū-chièh]**: foreign settlement, leased territory, concession

10 租借法案 **[tsū-chièh fă-àn]**: Lend Lease Act (U.S.)

12 租稅 **[tsū-shùi]**: tax, taxation, rent; to tax

13 租賃 **[tsū-lìn]**: to rent, to lease

秧

秧 **[yāng]**: rice seedling, young rice plant

— 6 Strokes —

移

3 移山倒海 **[í-shān tào-hăi]**: to remove mountains and drain seas

5 移民 **[í-mín]**: to immigrate, to emigrate; emigration, immigration; immigrant, emigrant

移民局 **[í-mín chű]**: immigration office

移民問題 **[í-mín wèn-t'í]**: the migration problem

6 移交 **[í-chiāo]**: to turn over, to hand down, to transfer, to devolve, to hand over, to pass, to transmit

7 移住 **[í-chù]**: to migrate, to resettle; migration, immigration, emigration

9 移風易俗 **[í-fēng ì-sú]**: to change existing customs and habits, to transform customs and habits

11 移情說 **[í-ch'íng shuō]**: theory of seeking a sympathetic understanding

移動 **[í-tùng]**: to move, to shift

12 移植 **[í-chíh]**: to transplant; transplantation

18 移轉 **[í-chuăn]**: to transfer; transfer

— 7 Strokes —

程

6 程序 **[ch'éng-hsǜ]**: order, sequence, sequence of events, procedure, process

程式 **[ch'éng-shìh]**: formula, form, pattern

9 程度 **[ch'éng-tù]**: standard, grade, degree, level, extent

程度不等 **[ch'éng-tù pù-tĕng]**: varying extent, uneven degree

稀

4 稀少的 **[hsī-shăo te]**: rare, scarce, infrequent, uncommon, few and far between

7 稀罕 **[hsī-hăn]**: rare, unusual, uncommon

12 稀疏 **[hsī-shū]**: sparse, scattered, thin

稍

13 稍微 **[shāo-wēi]**: slightly, a little

稅 **[shùi]**: tax, levy, duty, impost

5 稅目 **[shùi-mù]**: tax items

6 稅收 **[shùi-shōu]**: tax revenue

稅收法 **[shùi-shōu fă]**: measures of tax collection

8 稅制 **[shùi-chìh]**: tax system

11 稅率 **[shùi-lǜ]**: tax rate

14 稅種 **[shùi-chŭng]**: categories of taxes

— 8 Strokes —

稠

11 稠密 **[ch'óu-mì]**: congestion; congested, dense, crowded

稗

5 稗史 **[pài-shǐh]**: fictitious histories, novels, romances

— 9 Strokes —

4 稱王稱霸 **[ch'ēng-wáng ch'ēng-pà]**: to declare oneself as king and overlord, to lord over. . .

8 稱呼 **[ch'ēng-hū]**: to style (oneself); title

9 稱爲 **[ch'ēng-wéi]**: to designate, to label as, to brand as, to refer to as; known as

10 稱病 **[ch'ēng-pìng]**: to feign illness, to malinger; malingering

12 稱號 **[ch'ēng-hào]**: to designate; title, designation

13 稱頌 **[ch'ēng-sùng]**: to pay tribute to

稱道 **[ch'ēng-tào]**: to praise, to admire

14 稱說 **[ch'ēng-shuō]**: to relate

18 稱職 **[ch'ēng-chíh]**: competent, up to the requirements of a post, able to fulfil the responsibilities of a post

19 稱贊 **[ch'ēng-tsàn]**: to praise, to commend, to extol, to laud, to show appreciation; appreciation, compliment

種

種 **[chŭng]**: 1. species, kind, seed; 2. good seed strains (one of the eight characters of the 八字憲法, q.v.)

種 **[chùng]**: to plant, to cultivate

3 種子 **[chŭng-tzu]**: seed

11 種族 **[chŭng-tsú]**: clan, race, tribe; racial

種族歧視 **[chŭng-tsú ch'í-shìh]**: racial discrimination

種族主義 **[chŭng-tsú chŭ-ì]**: racism, racialism

種族主義者 **[chŭng-tsú chŭ-ì-chĕ]**: racist, racialist

種族隔離 **[chŭng-tsú kó-lí]**: racial segregation, apartheid

種族上 **[chŭng-tsú-shàng]**: ethnically, racially

12 種植地[chùng-chíh-tì]: plantation

種痘[chùng-tòu]: to vaccinate; vaccination

— 10 Strokes —

稽

8 稽延[chī-yén]: to delay, to hinder, to deter, to postpone

9 稽查[chī-ch'á]: to examine, to investigate

10 稽核[chī-hó]: to examine, to investigate, to test

稽留[chī-líu]: to detain

稿

3 稿子[kǎo-tzu]: manuscript, draft

稼

18 稼穡[chià-sè]: farming, sowing and reaping

穀

3 穀子[kŭ-tzu]: spiked-millet

8 穀物[kŭ-wù]: grain, cereal

10 穀倉[kŭ-ts'āng]: granary

14 穀種[kŭ-chŭng]: seed corn, seed grain

17 穀糠[kŭ-k'āng]: chaff

稻

稻[tào]: unhusked rice

6 稻田[tào-t'ién]: paddy field

— 11 Strokes —

積

4 積分[chī-fēn]: integral calculus, total grades (in course work)

8 積肥[chī-féi]: to stock up manure, to lay in manure

11 積習[chī-hsí]: ingrained habit, long standing practice, old habit

積累[chī-lĕi]: to accumulate, to pile up

積累經驗[chī-lĕi chīng-yèn]: to gather experience; accumulated experience

積累資金[chī-lĕi tzū-chīn]: accumulated capital

12 積極[chī-chí]: active, positive, resolute, energetic, enthusiastic

積極支持[chī-chí chīh-ch'íh]: to support actively, to support enthusiastically, to be squarely behind

積極準備[chī-chí chŭn-pèi]: to make vigorous preparations

積極發揮[chī-chí fā-hūi]: to give full play to

積極份子[chī-chí fèn-tzu]: activist, active element, enthusiast

積極性[chī-chí-hsìng]: positiveness, enthusiasm, fervor, initiative

積極人物[chī-chí jén-wù]: positive personality

積極平衡[chī-chí p'íng-héng]: positive balance

積極參加[chī-chí ts'ān-chiā]: to take an active part in; active participation

積極因素[chī-chí yīn-sù]: positive factor, active factor

14 積聚[chī-chù]: to amass, to accumulate, to collect, to gather; accumulation

積蓄 **[chī-hsü]** : to accumulate, to amass, to build up, to stock up, to store; savings

積穀防荒 **[chī-kŭ fáng-huāng]** : to store up grain reserves against famine

17 積壓 **[chī-yā]** : to be idle, to lie in disuse, to overstock, to hold up

穆

11 穆勒 **[mù-lē]** : Mill (proper name)

12 穆斯林 **[mù-ssū-lín]** : Moslem

— 12 Strokes —

穗 **[sùi]** : Canton (abbreviation for 廣州)

— 14 Strokes —

穩

4 穩扎穩打 **[wĕn-chā wĕn-tă]** : to go ahead steadily and strike sure blows; methodical, slow but sure

7 穩步 **[wĕn-pù]** : steady steps, unfaltering steps; steadily, unfalteringly

穩步前進 **[wĕn-pù ch'ién-chìn]** : to proceed by steady steps; steady advance

8 穩定 **[wĕn-tìng]** : to stabilize, to make firm, to settle; stability, stabilization; stable, steady

11 穩產高產 **[wĕn-ch'ăn kāo-ch'ăn]** : steady production and high yield

穩健 **[wĕn-chièn]** : stable, firm, stable in purpose, firm and steady

— RADICAL 穴 116 —

— 2 Strokes —

究

11 究竟 **[chīu-chìng]** : after all, in the end, finally

— 3 Strokes —

空

4 空中偵察 **[k'ūng-chūng chēn-ch'á]** : air reconnaissance

空中觀察 **[k'ūng-chūng kuān-ch'á]** : aerial observation

空中堡壘 **[k'ūng-chūng păo-lĕi]** : Flying Fortress

5 空白 **[k'ùng-pái]** : blank, blank space

空白點 **[k'ùng-pái tiĕn]** : blank spot, blankness

7 空投 **[k'ūng-t'óu]** : air-drop

空投接濟 **[k'ūng-t'óu chiēh-chì]** : air-dropped supplies

空位 **[k'ūng-wèi]** : vacancy, void, empty space

9 空降 **[k'ūng-chiàng]** : airdrop; airborne

空前 **[k'ūng-ch'ién]** : unprecedented, unparalleled, without precedent

空前絕後 **[k'ūng-ch'ién chüéh-hòu]** : without precedent or follow-up, never before or since

空前的紀錄 **[k'ūng-ch'ién te chì-lù]** : all-time record

空前最高記錄 **[k'ūng-ch'ién tsùi-kāo chì-lù]** : all-time high record

空軍主師 **[k'ūng-chūn chŭ-shuài]** : Generalissimo of the Air Force (Russian Air Force)

空軍部 **[k'ūng-chūn pù]** : Department of Air

Force; Air Ministry

空軍司令部 **[k'ūng-chǖn ssū-lìng-pù]**: Headquarters of the Air Force (China)

空軍元帥 **[k'ūng-chǖn yüán-shuài]**: Marshal of the Air Force (Russian Air Force); Marshal of the Royal Air Force (British Air Force)

空室清野 **[k'ùng-shìh ch'īng-yěh]**: to empty the rooms and clear the fields (i.e., to conceal all possessions against enemy plunder)

空洞的 **[k'ūng-tùng te]**: empty, aimless, obscure, hollow, void, without content

12 空間 **[k'ūng-chiēn]**: space

空閒 **[k'ùng-hsién]**: leisure; idle, unoccupied, not busy, at leisure

空虛 **[k'ūng-hsū]**: depleted, exhausted, drained, empty, devoid of content, devoid of meaning

13 空想 **[k'ūng-hsiǎng]**: to wish for in vain; daydreaming, fantasy, wishful thinking, pipe dream, fancy, reverie; utopian

空想家 **[k'ūng-hsiǎng-chiā]**: dreamer, mere theorist

空想主義 **[k'ūng-hsiǎng chǔ-ì]**: utopianism

空想社會主義 **[k'ūng-hsiǎng shè-hùi chǔ-ì]**: utopian socialism

空話 **[k'ūng-huà]**: idle talk, empty verbiage

空話不做 **[k'ūng-huà pú-tsò]**: to make empty promises, to pay lip service only

15 空談 **[k'ūng-t'án]**: empty talk, idle talk, aimless discussion

空談家 **[k'ūng-t'án-chiā]**: prattler, chatterer, empty talker, windbag

16 空戰 **[k'ūng-chàn]**: air battle, air combat, air fight

空頭 **[k'ùng-t'óu]**: short seller; nominal, titular, empty, hollow, inane

空頭政治家 **[k'ùng-t'óu chèng-chìh-chiā]**: armchair politician

空頭支票 **[k'ùng-t'óu chīh-p'iào]**: bad check, fictitious bill, false check, unhonored bill

22 空襲 **[k'ūng-hsí]**: air attack, air raid

— 4 Strokes —

穿 **[ch'uān]**: to wear, to be clothed, to be dressed in, to put on, to put through, to go through, to thread, to bore

4 穿孔卡 **[ch'uān-k'ǔng k'ǎ]**: punch card

突

5 突出 **[t'ù-ch'ū]**: to protrude, to give prominence to; outstanding, striking, salient, prominent

突出政治 **[t'ù-ch'ū chèng-chìh]**: to give prominence to politics

突尼斯 **[t'ù-ní-ssū]**: Tunisia; Tunis

突尼斯共和國 **[t'ù-ní-ssū kùng-hó-kuó]**: Republic of Tunisia

9 突飛猛進 **[t'ù-fēi měng-chìn]**: to advance by leaps and bounds; rapid development, swift advance, phenomenal progress, a long forward stride

10 突破 **[t'ù-p'ò]**: to break through, to penetrate

12 突然 **[t'ù-ján]**: sudden, abrupt; suddenly, abruptly

突然襲擊 **[t'ù-ján hsí-chī]**: surprise attack, sudden onslaught, raid, shock drive

突圍 **[t'ù-wéi]**: to break through, to break out of encirclement

17 突擊任務 **[t'ù-chī jèn-wù]**: an emergency task (i.e., an especially arduous task for which workers are drafted into or volunteer for "shock brigades"突擊隊)

突擊力量 **[t'ù-chī lì-liàng]**: shock force

突擊隊 **[t'ù-chī tùi]**: shock brigade, assault party, storm troops, shock troops, commandoes (U.S.A.) (refers to workers commandeered or who volunteer for arduous or unpleasant tasks)

— 5 Strokes —

窄

6 窄行播種法 **[chăi-háng pō-chùng fă]**: narrow-row sowing method

9 窄軌鐵路 **[chăi-kuĕi t'iĕh-lù]**: narrow gauge railway

— 6 Strokes —

窒

10 窒息 **[chìh-hsí]**: to stifle, to smother, to suffocate, to choke

— 7 Strokes —

窘

14 窘境 **[chiŭng-chìng]**: dilemma, plight, quandary, predicament, stalemate, impasse, deadlock

— 9 Strokes —

窩

3 窩工 **[wō-kūng]**: to waste the labor supply, to lay up workers; idle workers

窩工待料 **[wō-kūng tài-liào]**: workers lying idle waiting for arrival of raw materials

5 窩尼 **[wō-ní]**: Woni (a minority nationality)

— 10 Strokes —

窮

4 窮凶極惡 **[ch'iúng-hsiūng chí-ò]**: ferocious, atrocious, extreme ferocity, in a vicious and unrestrained way

7 窮困 **[ch'iúng-k'ùn]**: poor, impoverished, in want; poverty, indigence, destitution

窮兵黷武 **[ch'iúng-pīng tú-wŭ]**: militarism, misuse of force; warlike, militaristic

10 窮追 **[ch'iúng-chūi]**: to pressure the enemy by relentless pursuit; unrelenting pursuit, hot pursuit

12 窮棒子精神 **[ch'iúng pàng-tzu chīng-shén]**: pauper's spirit (a spirit of working hard with little means to achieve something)

— 11 Strokes —

窺

5 窺出 **[k'uēi-ch'ū]**: to detect

11 窺探 **[k'uēi-t'àn]**: to detect, to spy, to pry into

— 13 Strokes —

竅

8 竅門 **[ch'iào-mén]**: knack, key, gist, vital point (*See* 找竅門)

竄

6 竄改 **[ts'uàn-kăi]**: to revise, to change, to correct

— RADICAL 立 117 —

立

4 立方 **[lì-fāng]** : cubic, three dimensional

5 立功 **[lì-kūng]** : to demonstrate merit, to render meritorious service, to do a meritorious deed

立功受奬 **[lì-kūng shòu-chiăng]** : to award those who perform meritorious service

立功贖罪 **[lì-kūng shú-tsùi]** : to perform meritorious service to atone for one's crimes

8 立法 **[lì-fă]** : to legislate; legislation, lawmaking; legislative

立法者 **[lì-fă-chĕ]** : legislator, lawmaker, lawgiver, member of a legislative body

立刻 **[lì-k'ò]** : at once, immediate, immediately, promptly, forthwith, instantly, right away

9 立卽 **[lì-chì]** : at once, immediate, immediately, promptly, forthwith, instantly, right away

立竿見影 **[lì-kān chièn-yĭng]** : a pole casts a shadow as soon as it is set up (i.e., a phrase illustrating immediate effect from prompt action)

11 立國際功 **[lì kuó-chì kūng]** : to establish international prestige

立陶宛 **[lì-t'áo-wăn]** : Lithuania

12 立場 **[lì-ch'ăng]** : standpoint, position, stand

16 立憲政體 **[lì-hsièn chèng-t'ĭ]** : constitutional government

— 5 Strokes —

站

4 站不住脚 **[chàn-pú-chù chiăo]** : unable to stand one's ground, untenable, impossible to defend

6 站在前列 **[chàn-tsài ch'ién-lièh]** : to stand in the forefront, to be among the first to

站在一旁說風涼話 **[chàn-tsài ì-p'áng shuō fēng-liáng huà]** : to make irresponsible and carping comments from the sidelines

站在一條戰綫上 **[chàn-tsài ì-t'iáo chàn-hsièn-shàng]** : to line up on the same front

站在人民的立場上 **[chàn-tsài jén-mín te lì-ch'ăng-shàng]** : to have the standpoint of the people

7 站住脚 **[chàn-chù chiăo]** : to be able to stand one's ground; tenable, convincing

11 站崗 **[chàn-kāng]** : to stand sentry, to be on guard, to be sentry

12 站隊 **[chàn-tùi]** : classification

19 站穩立場 **[chàn-wĕn lì-ch'ăng]** : to maintain a firm stand

— 6 Strokes —

12 章程 **[chāng-ch'éng]** : regulations, rules, bylaws

竟

12 竟然 **[chìng-ján]** : after all, even, should, if

— 7 Strokes —

童

13 童話 **[t'úng-huà]** : fairy tale, children's story

— 9 Strokes —

竭

2 竭力 **[chiéh-lì]** : to do the best, to do everything possible, to do one's utmost

[13] 竭誠 **[chiéh-ch'éng]**: absolutely sincere, completely honest

[14] 竭盡 **[chiéh-chìn]**: to exhaust

端

[4] 端午節 **[tuān-wŭ chiéh]**: Dragon Boat Festival (5th day of 5th lunar month)

[5] 端正 **[tuān-chèng]**: correct, respectable, proper, upright

[9] 端倪 **[tuān-ní]**: key, clue

[11] 端莊 **[tuān-chuāng]**: serious, dignified, sober

[12] 端陽 **[tuān-yáng]**: the 5th day of the 5th lunar month, the day of the Dragon Boat Festival

[13] 端詳 **[tuān-hsiáng]**: to look at closely, to consider closely, to scrutinize

— 15 Strokes —

競

[8] 競爭 **[chìng-chēng]**: to compete, to contest, to vie, to rival, to emulate; competition, rivalry, contest

[16] 競選 **[chìng-hsüăn]**: to campaign, to run for, to contest; campaign, contest, election, campaigning

競選伙伴 **[chìng-hsüăn huŏ-pàn]**: running mate

競選綱領 **[chìng-hsüăn kāng-lĭng]**: election program, campaign program

競選旅行 **[chìng-hsüăn lǚ-hsíng]**: election tour, election campaign tour

競選演說 **[chìng-hsüăn yĕn-shuō]**: campaign speech, election speech

競選運動 **[chìng-hsüăn yùn-tùng]**: election campaign

[17] 競賽 **[chìng-sài]**: to compete, to vie; competition, contest, match, rivalry, emulation

— RADICAL 竹 118 —

— 4 Strokes —

笑

[9] 笑面虎 **[hsiào-mièn hŭ]**: tiger with a smiling face

笑柄 **[hsiào-pĭng]**: laughingstock

[16] 笑罵 **[hsiào-mà]**: to ridicule, to revile; invective

笑罵由人 **[hsiào-mà yú-jén]**: let people ridicule and revile

[17] 笑聲 **[hsiào-shēng]**: laughter

— 5 Strokes —

符

[6] 符合 **[fú-hó]**: to suit, to correspond to, to conform to, to be in keeping with, to tally

[13] 符號 **[fú-hào]**: symbol, sign, mark

笨

笨 **[pèn]**: stupid, dull, awkward, clumsy, ungainly

8 笨拙 **[pèn-chō]** : clumsy, awkward, bungling, unskilful

9 笨重勞動 **[pèn-chùng láo-tùng]** : heavy manual labor

笛

5 笛卡兒 **[tí-k'ă-érh]** : Descartes, René (1596–1650)

第

1 第一 **[tì-ī]** : first, first of all, in the first place, primary, at the head

第一機械工業部 **[tì-ī chī-hsièh kūng-yèh pù]** : First Ministry of Machine Building

第一性質 **[tì-ī hsìng-chíh]** : primary quality

第一個五年計劃 **[tì-í-kò wŭ-nién chì-huà]** : the First Five-Year Plan (1953–1957–for the purpose of laying the groundwork for socialist industrialization and for socialist transformation of private property and to be followed by a Second Five-Year Plan, 1958–1962)

第一國際 **[tì-ī kuó-chì]** : First Internationale

第一流 **[tì-ī-líu]** : first class, first-rate

第一手 **[tì-ì-shŏu]** : firsthand

第一次出面 **[tì-í-tz'ù ch'ū-mièn]** : debut, first public appearance, first formal entrance into society

2 第二戰場 **[tì-èrh chàn-ch'ăng]** : the second front

第二機械工業部 **[tì-èrh chī-hsièh kūng-yèh pù]** : Second Ministry of Machine Building

第二防線 **[tì-èrh fáng-hsièn]** : second defense line

第二綫兵力 **[tì-èrh-hsièn pīng-lì]** : second line troops

第二性質 **[tì-èrh hsìng-chíh]** : secondary quality

第二國際 **[tì-èrh kuó-chì]** : Second Internationale

第二次國內革命戰爭時期 **[tì-èrh-tz'ù kuó-nèi kó-mìng chàn-chēng shíh-ch'í]** : The Second Revolutionary Civil War Period (1927–1936)

3 第三機械工業部 **[tì-sān chī-hsièh kūng-yèh pù]** : Third Ministry of Machine Building

第三國際 **[tì-sān kuó-chì]** : Third Internationale

4 第六機械工業部 **[tì-lìu chī-hsièh kūng-yèh pù]** : Sixth Ministry of Machine Building

第五機械工業部 **[tì-wŭ chī-hsièh kūng-yèh pù]** : Fifth Ministry of Machine Building

第五縱隊 **[tì-wŭ tsùng-tùi]** : fifth column

第四機械工業部 **[tì-ssù chī-hsièh kūng-yèh pù]** : Fourth Ministry of Machine Building

— 6 Strokes —

筑

筑 **[chú]** : Kweiyang (abbreviation for 貴陽)

筆

6 筆名 **[pĭ-míng]** : pen name, pseudonym

12 筆鉛 **[pĭ-ch'iēn]** : graphite

答

10 答案 **[tá-àn]** : a reply in writing, answer

12 答復 **[tá-fù]** : to reply, to answer, to respond; reply, answer

[13] 答話 [tá-huà]: to reply, to answer; reply, answer

[14] 答對 [tá-tùi]: to reply, to answer

[17] 答應 [tā-yìng]: to assent to, to answer, to respond, to permit, to allow, to accede to

[21] 答辯 [tá-pièn]: to refute, to rebut; defence, answer, plea

等

[5] 等比級數 [tĕng-pĭ chí-shù]: geometric progression, geometric series

[8] 等於 [tĕng-yú]: equal to, equivalent to; to amount to

[10] 等級 [tĕng-chí]: standards, steps, grade, rank, class, level, degree

等候 [tĕng-hòu]: to wait, to await

[11] 等第 [tĕng-tì]: order, series, rank, class

[12] 等量齊觀 [tĕng-liàng ch'í-kuān]: to match, to draw a parallel between, to place on an equal footing, to equate

[15] 等價交換 [tĕng-chià chiāo-huàn]: to exchange at equal value

策

[11] 策略 [ts'è-lüèh]: tactics, strategy

策動 [ts'è-tùng]: to contrive, to instigate, to incite, to provoke, to goad, to engineer, to maneuver

[13] 策源地 [ts'è-yüán tì]: hotbed, source

[14] 策劃 [ts'è-huà]: to plan, to plot, to contrive, to concoct, to scheme, to design, to conspire

策劃者 [ts'è-huà-chĕ]: planner, originator, designer, plotter, schemer, conspirator

[17] 策勵 [ts'è-lì]: to spur on, to urge on

策應 [ts'è-yìng]: to fight in various places according to a single plan, to relieve

— 8 Strokes —

管

管 [kuăn]: 1. to take care of, to manage, to administer, to supervise; 2. good management, field management (one of the eight characters of the 八字憲法, q.v.); 3. a pipe

[3] 管子 [kuăn-tzu]: pipe, tube

[5] 管用 [kuăn-yùng]: to guarantee

[8] 管制 [kuăn-chìh]: to control

管制份子 [kuăn-chìh fèn-tzu]: controlled person, person under surveillance

管制勞動 [kuăn-chìh láo-tùng]: to work under surveillance, to labor under public surveillance (i.e., refers to landlords, rich peasants, and bad elements who are put to labor under the surveillance of other peasants or commune members)

管事 [kuăn-shìh]: to manage affairs, to take care of; manager, caretaker

管保 [kuăn-păo]: to guarantee

[11] 管教 [kuăn-chiào]: to correct, to teach, to manage, to educate, to discipline

管理 [kuăn-lĭ]: to administer, to control, to manage, to govern, to supervise, to have charge of; administration; administrative

管理制度 [kuăn-lĭ chìh-tù]: system of administration

管理局 [kuăn-lĭ chǘ]: directorate, administration, control bureau

管理區 [kuăn-lĭ ch'ǖ]: control district (Kiangsi only)

管理權 [kuăn-lĭ ch'üán]: administrative authority, legal authority

管理人員 [kuăn-lĭ jén-yüán]: managerial personnel

管理幹部 [kuăn-lĭ kàn-pù]: administrative cadre

管理民主化 **[kuǎn-lǐ mín-chǔ-huà]**: democratization of management

管理體制 **[kuǎn-lǐ t'ǐ-chìh]**: administrative system

管理委員會 **[kuǎn-lǐ wěi-yüán-hùi]**: management committee, administrative committee

管理員 **[kuǎn-lǐ-yüán]**: administrator, supervisor

17 管轄 **[kuǎn-hsiá]**: to have rule over, to govern, to have jurisdiction over; jurisdiction, control

算

3 算三賬 **[suàn sān-chàng]**: to reckon three accounts (i.e., the reckoning of political, economic, and cultural accounts in order that the peasants may see their progress in these fields under the Communist regime)

算上 **[suàn-shàng]**: to take into account, to include in the account, to be brought into the reckoning of

6 算老賬 **[suàn lǎo-chàng]**: to settle old accounts

11 算細賬 **[suàn hsì-chàng]**: to reckon meticulously (1. a slogan used during the land reform to arouse class hatred and indicating a peasant's point-by-point listing of grievances against a landlord; 2. a phrase used in the sense of profit and loss analysis of a sub-norm worker's production as compared with the set quota or target)

算術 **[suàn-shù]**: arithmetic

15 算賬 **[suàn-chàng]**: to settle accounts, to reckon accounts

算數 **[suàn-shù]**: to take as final; in earnest

— 9 Strokes —

節

4 節日 **[chiéh-jìh]**: festival day, feast day; festive

5 節目 **[chiéh-mù]**: section, paragraph, program

節目單 **[chiéh-mù-tān]**: program

節外生枝 **[chiéh-wài shēng-chīh]**: to hit a snag, to run into an unexpected problem, to cause complications

節用 **[chiéh-yùng]**: to economize, to save, frugal, careful use of

6 節衣縮食 **[chiéh-ī sō-shíh]**: to save on food and clothing

8 節制 **[chiéh-chìh]**: to restrict, to control, to limit, to moderate

節制閘 **[chiéh-chìh chá]**: flood regulator, check gate, regulating sluice dam

節制資本 **[chiéh-chìh tzū-pěn]**: to regulate capital

節育 **[chiéh-yǜ]**: birth control

9 節省 **[chiéh-shěng]**: to save, to economize, to practice thrift, to be economical; economy

節奏 **[chiéh-tsòu]**: rhythm

節約 **[chiéh-yüēh]**: to economize, to practice thrift, to be economical; frugality, austerity, economy, retrenchment

10 節骨眼 **[chiéh-kǔ yěn]**: joint, essential point, opportunity

11 節略 **[chiéh-lüèh]**: to summarize; summary, abstract

15 節節勝利 **[chiéh-chiéh shèng-lì]**: to gain victory after victory, to push forward from victory to victory

節儉 **[chiéh-chiĕn]**: frugality; frugal, thrifty

16 節操 **[chiéh-ts'āo]**: moral integrity, high moral principles; fidelity, loyalty; chaste

17 節錄 **[chiéh-lù]**: excerpt, extract, abstract

箭

13 箭靶子 **[chièn-pǎ tzu]**: target

範

5 範本 **[fàn-pĕn]** : sample, model

9 範例 **[fàn-lì]** : model, pattern, example

13 範圍 **[fàn-wéi]** : sphere, jurisdiction, scope, extent, range, context

19 範疇 **[fàn-ch'óu]** : category, domain

— 10 Strokes —

7 篡改 **[ts'uàn-kăi]** : to tamper with, to meddle with

14 篡奪 **[ts'uàn-tó]** : to usurp, to arrogate

— 12 Strokes —

簡

4 簡化 **[chiĕn-huà]** : to simplify, to abbreviate, to reduce, simplification

8 簡直 **[chiĕn-chíh]** : simply, directly

簡易公路 **[chiĕn-ì kūng-lù]** : simple road,

簡明扼要 **[chiĕn-míng è-yào]** : terse and concise

9 簡陋 **[chiĕn-lòu]** : plain and simple, deficient, poor

簡要 **[chiĕn-yào]** : short and concise; brief summary

11 簡略 **[chiĕn-lüèh]** : synopsis, abridgement

12 簡筆字 **[chiĕn-pĭ-tzù]** : simplified writing, simplified characters

簡單 **[chiĕn-tān]** : simple, sketchy, brief

簡單化 **[chiĕn-tān-huà]** : to simplify; simplification

簡單地說 **[chiĕn-tān-tì shuō]** : to put it briefly, briefly, in short, in a word

簡單再生產 **[chiĕn-tān tsài-shēng-ch'ăn]** : simple reproduction

簡短 **[chiĕn-tuăn]** : brief, short

15 簡編 **[chiĕn-piēn]** : outline, summary, abstract, abbreviated addition

18 簡斷截說 **[chiĕn-tuàn chiéh-shuō]** : to speak simply and frankly, to speak without circumlocution

23 簡體字 **[chiĕn-t'ĭ tzù]** : simplified writing, simplified characters

— 13 Strokes —

6 簽名 **[ch'iēn-míng]** : to sign, to endorse; signature, endorsement

19 簽證 **[ch'iēn-chèng]** : visa

—14 Strokes —

籍

11 籍貫 **[chí-kuàn]** : native place, hometown, place of origin

籌

9 籌建 **[ch'óu-chièn]** : to prepare for construction, preparations for construction

10 籌備 **[ch'óu-pèi]** : to prepare, preparatory

籌備處 **[ch'óu-pèi ch'ù]** : preparatory office

籌備委員會 **[ch'óu-pèi wĕi-yüán-hùi]** : preparatory committee

12 籌集 **[ch'óu-chí]** : to accumulate, to raise (i.e., as funds)

籌策 **[ch'óu-ts'è]** : plan, scheme

14 籌劃 **[ch'óu-huà]** : to plan, to project, to engineer, to design, to draft, to frame, to devise

籌劃周密 **[ch'óu-huà chōu-mì]** : well designed

籌劃不周 [ch'óu-huà pù-chōu] : ill-designed, poorly designed

籌算 [ch'óu-suàn] : to calculate, to reckon

16 籌辦 [ch'óu-pàn] : to prepare for, to arrange

— 16 Strokes —

籠

12 籠統 [lúng-t'ǔng] : all together; general

籠統平均數 [lúng-t'ǔng p'íng-chūn-shù] : general average

13 籠罩 [lúng-chào] : to enshroud, to hover over, to blanket, to cover, to close in, to include all

— RADICAL 米 119 —

米

7 米利賓 [mǐ-lì-pīn] : Melbourne (Australia)

10 米高揚 [mǐ-kāo-yáng] : Mikoyan, Anastas (Russian statesman)

21 米蘭 [mǐ-lán] : Milan (Italy)

— 3 Strokes —

籽

12 籽棉 [tzǔ-mién] : raw cotton, unginned cotton

— 4 Strokes —

粉

7 粉身粹骨 [fěn-shēn sùi-kǔ] : to give everything, to give one's all, to give one's life, to perish

8 粉刷 [fěn-shuā] : to whitewash, a whitewash

13 粉粹 [fěn-sùi] : to pulverize, to crush, to smash, to shatter

粉粹枷鎖 [fěn-sùi chiā-sǒ] : to break the shackles, to smash the chains

14 粉飾 [fěn-shìh] : to gild, to gloss over, to slick up, to adorn

— 5 Strokes —

粒

3 粒子加速器 [lì-tzǔ chiā-sù-ch'ì] : particle accelerator

粘

8 粘性 [nién-hsìng] : adhesiveness, stickiness

粗

3 粗大 [ts'ū-tà] : coarse, bulky, rough and large

4 粗心大意 [ts'ū-hsīn tà-ì] : crude and careless, careless

6 粗略 [ts'ū-lüèh] : rough, sketchy

8 粗枝大葉 [ts'ū-chīh tà-yèh] : crude and careless

11 粗淺 [ts'ū-ch'iěn] : superficial, coarse and shallow

粗鹵 [ts'ū-lǔ] : crudity, roughness; crude, rude, rough, boorish, uncouth

13 粗糧 [ts'ū-liáng] : coarse grain, coarse cereal

粗率 [ts'ū-shuài] : rash, imprudent

15 粗暴 [ts'ū-pào] : crude, gross, strong-handed, rough, outrageous, insolent

[17] 粗糙 **[ts'ū-tsāo]**: coarse and rude, crude

— 6 Strokes —

粤

粤 **[yüèh]**: Kwangtung (abbreviation for 廣東)

— 8 Strokes —

精

[2] 精力 **[chīng-lì]**: energy, vigor, spirit

[4] 精心斟酌 **[chīng-hsīn chēn-chó]**: carefully worked out

[5] 精巧 **[chīng-ch'iăo]**: skillful, clever

精打細算 **[chīng-tă hsì-suàn]**: to make a careful and detailed calculation, to count every cent and to make every cent count

[7] 精良 **[chīng-liáng]**: excellent, best, first-rate, superior, skilled, fine

精兵 **[chīng-pīng]**: crack troops

精兵簡政 **[chīng-pīng chiĕn-chèng]**: picked troops and simpler administration, crack troops and efficient government

[8] 精明 **[chīng-míng]**: clever, smart

精明干練 **[chīng-míng kān-lièn]**: sagacious, astute, shrewd, keen and wise

[9] 精神 **[chīng-shén]**: spirit, vitality, energy; spiritual, moral, mental, psychic, psycho-

精神狀態 **[chīng-shén chuàng-t'ài]**: state of mind

精神準備 **[chīng-shén chŭn-pèi]**: mental or psychological preparation, psychologically prepared, mentally prepared

精神反常 **[chīng-shén făn-ch'áng]**: to lose one's mental balance

精神和實質 **[chīng-shén hó shíh-chìh]**: spirit and substance

精神面貌 **[chīng-shén mièn-mào]**: spiritual outlook

精神病 **[chīng-shén pìng]**: insanity, psychosis

精神條件 **[chīng-shén t'iáo-chièn]**: spiritual condition

精神武器 **[chīng-shén wŭ-ch'ì]**: moral weapon

精神原子彈 **[chīng-shén yüán-tzŭ-tàn]**: moral atom bomb

[10] 精耕細作 **[chīng-kēng hsì-tsò]**: careful and intensive cultivation

精疲力盡 **[chīng-p'í lì-chìn]**: exhausted, extremely fatigued, to tire out completely

精通 **[chīng-t'ūng]**: to master, to have a thorough knowledge of; proficiency, mastery; well versed in

[11] 精細 **[chīng-hsì]**: fine (i.e., as material, etc.)

精密機床 **[chīng-mì chī-ch'uáng]**: precision machine tool

精密儀器 **[chīng-mì í-ch'ì]**: precision tools, precision instrument

[12] 精華 **[chīng-huá]**: essence, quintessence, core, extract, the best part

[13] 精煉 **[chīng-lièn]**: refined, finely tempered

精煉廠 **[chīng-lièn ch'ăng]**: refinery

[15] 精銳 **[chīng-jùi]**: picked troops

精銳部隊 **[chīng-jùi pù-tùi]**: crack troops, crack forces, crack units

[16] 精簡 **[chīng-chiĕn]**: to improve efficiency by reduction in force, to improve efficiency by simplification or organization

精簡機關 **[chīng-chiĕn chī-kuān]**: to simplify organizational structure, to simplify an organization, to streamline an organization

精確 **[chīng-ch'üèh]**: accurate, precise, exact; accuracy

[24] 精靈論 **[chīng-líng lùn]**: animism

— 9 Strokes —

糊

3 糊口 **[hú-k'ŏu]** : to make a living

13 糊裏糊塗 **[hú-lĭ hú-tú]** : all mixed up, muddled, with one's mind in a haze

糊塗思想 **[hú-t'ú ssū-hsiăng]** : confused thinking, confused ideas (i.e., ideas contrary to Communist ideology)

糊塗觀點 **[hú-t'ú kuān-tiĕn]** : muddled ideas, muddled views

— 10 Strokes —

糖

6 糖衣 **[t'áng-ī]** : sugar-coated

糖衣炮彈 **[t'áng-ī p'ào-tàn]** : sugar-coated bullets, deceitful propaganda (i.e., methods used to subvert the people from the revolutionary line)

15 糖彈 **[t'áng-tàn]** : sugar bullet

— 11 Strokes —

糞

7 糞坑 **[fèn-k'ēng]** : manure pit, outhouse

8 糞肥 **[fèn-féi]** : manure, fertilizer

糟

11 糟粕 **[tsāo-p'ò]** : dregs

糟得很 **[tsāo-té-hĕn]** : in an awful mess, in very poor shape, terrible

16 糟糕透頂 **[tsāo-kāo t'òu-tĭng]** : rotten to the core, rotten all the way through

17 糟蹋 **[tsāo-t'à]** : to spoil, to waste, to despoil, to ravage

糙

6 糙米 **[tsāo-mĭ]** : coarse rice, unpolished rice

— 12 Strokes —

糧

9 糧食 **[liáng-shíh]** : grain, food, provisions, staple foods

糧食和農業部 **[liáng-shíh hó núng-yèh pù]** : Ministry of Food and Agriculture (India)

糧食供給制 **[liáng-shíh kūng-chĭ chìh]** : food supply system, i.e., communal system of supplying free food (*See* 供給制)

糧食部 **[liáng-shíh pù]** : Ministry of Food

糧食作物 **[liáng-shíh tsò-wù]** : grain crops

10 糧荒 **[liáng-huāng]** : food shortage, grain shortage

— RADICAL 糸糸 120 —

— 1 Stroke —

6 系列 **[hsì-lièh]** : series

12 系統 **[hsì-t'ŭng]** : system; systematic

系統化 **[hsì-t'ŭng-huà]** : to systematize

系統內報表 **[hsì-t'ŭng-nèi pào-piăo]** : intra-departmental reporting

系統外報表 **[hsì-t'ŭng-wài pào-piăo]** : extra-departmental reporting

15 系數 **[hsì-shù]** : coefficient

19 系辭 **[hsì-tz'ú]** : corollary

— 2 Strokes —

糾

5 糾正 **[chīu-chèng]** : to correct, to rectify; rectification

10 糾紛 **[chīu-fēn]** : strife, quarrel, dispute, discord, controversy, contention, bickering

12 糾集 **[chīu-chí]** : to muster, to assemble, to summon together

21 糾纏 **[chīu-ch'án]** : to entangle, to make complicated; entanglement

— 3 Strokes —

紀

4 紀元 **[chì-yüán]** : the beginning of an era, the beginning of a reign

紀元前 **[chì-yüán ch'ién]** : B.C.

紀元後 **[chì-yüán hòu]** : A.D.

6 紀年 **[chì-nién]** : dynasty, reign

8 紀念 **[chì-nièn]** : to remember, to commemorate; commemoration

紀念日 **[chì-nièn jìh]** : commemoration day, memorial day, anniversary

紀念白求恩 **[chì-nièn pái-ch'íu-ēn]** : "In Memory of Bethune" (December 21, 1939; one of the老三篇, q.v.)

紀念碑 **[chì-nièn pēi]** : monument, column, tablet

紀念品 **[chì-nièn p'ĭn]** : memorial, souvenir, memento, keepsake, token, remembrance

紀念堂 **[chì-nièn t'áng]** : memorial hall

紀事 **[chì-shìh]** : to make a memorandum; note, record, memorandum

9 紀律 **[chì-lǜ]** : discipline, written laws; disciplinary

紀律監察委員會 **[chì-lǜ chiēn-ch'á wĕi-yüán-hùi]** : Disciplinary Examination Committee

紀律處分 **[chì-lǜ ch'ŭ-fèn]** : disciplinary action, disciplinary measure

紀律性 **[chì-lǜ-hsìng]** : sense of discipline

17 紀錄 **[chì-lù]** : to place on record, to note down; records, minutes; documentary

紀錄片 **[chì-lù p'ièn]** : documentary film

紅

1 紅一軍團 **[húng-ī chǖn-t'uán]** : First Red Regiment (established in 1931)

2 紅人 **[húng-jén]** : a favorite, a man at the height of his career, a person of good fortune, a person of wide acquaintance, a busy person

紅十字會 **[húng shíh-tzù hùi]** : the Red Cross Society

紅十字國際委員會 **[húng shíh-tzù kuó-chì wĕi-yüán-hùi]** : International Committee of the Red Cross (ICRC)

3 紅三員 **[húng sān yüán]** : the three red personnel (i.e., the young accounting, work-point recording, and storage personnel of the People's Communes)

4 紅心 **[húng-hsīn]** : red heart (i.e., the heart of one who is a total believer in the thought of Mao Tse-tung)

紅太陽 **[húng t'ài-yáng]** : red sun (i.e., a symbol eulogizing Mao, particularly during the Cultural Revolution)

紅五類份子 **[húng wŭ-lèi fèn-tzu]** : the five categories of red elements (i.e., 1) children of workers, 2) poor and lower middle peasants, 3) revolutionary cadres, 4) Liberation Army men, and 5) revolutionary martyrs)

6 紅衣主教 **[húng-ī chŭ-chiào]** : cardinal (i.e., of Catholic Church)

紅色 **[húng-sè]** : red, red color, revolutionary, Communist

紅色接班人 **[húng-sè chiēh-pān-jén]** : Red Successor (i.e., children and Young Pioneers, in particular, who will in time take over the Party and the government from the aged Communists)

紅色專家 **[húng-sè chuān-chiā]** : Red expert (i.e., a person who is technically competent and politically reliable)

紅色新聞 **[húng-sè hsīn-wén]** : Red News (Tibetan newspaper that took over the Tibet Daily on January 10, 1967)

紅色娘子軍 **[húng-sè niáng-tzu chŭn]** : The Red Detachment of Women (name of a ballet)

紅色造反報 **[húng-sè tsào-făn pào]** : Red Rebel Paper (Red Guard newspaper in Lhasa, 1967)

7 紅利 **[húng-lì]** : dividend, bonus

8 紅花 **[húng-huā]** : red flower (i.e., a loyal and conscientious Communist)

9 紅軍 **[húng-chŭn]** : Red Army

紅星報 **[húng hsīng pào]** : Krasnaya Zvezda (i.e., Red Star, Russian daily newspaper)

10 紅哨兵 **[húng shào-pīng]** : Red Sentries (a new method of thought control first invented by the Peking General Knitwear Mill in August 1968 as part of the "Three Loyalties" movement–the Red Sentries worked in teams of two to four persons which changed every few days; their task was to promote Mao's thought and fight against his ideological enemies in factories and enterprises)

紅書 **[húng-shū]** : a red book (i.e., one conforming entirely to Maoist and Party policies)

11 紅專學校 **[húng-chuān hsüéh-hsiào]** : red and expert school (a half-work half-study school combining study and physical labor)

12 紅綫 **[húng-hsièn]** : red line (i.e., the correct, Maoist Party line)

紅透專深 **[húng-t'òu chuān-shēn]** : thoroughly red and highly specialized, thoroughly red and highly qualified

13 紅煤 **[húng-méi]** : best grade anthracite

紅與專 **[húng yŭ chuān]** : Red and expert (to be socialist-minded and professionally qualified; to be both politically and professionally qualified)

14 紅旗 **[húng-ch'í]** : 1. a red flag (symbol of Maoist orthodoxy); 2. Red Flag (journal of the Central Committee of the Chinese Communist Party)

紅旗單位 **[húng-ch'í tān-wèi]** : red flag unit (a commune or factory production team that has excelled in output)

紅旗田 **[húng-ch'í t'ién]** : a red flag field (i.e., a high-yield field)

紅槍會 **[húng-ch'iāng hùi]** : The Red Spears (a secret society in Shantung during the Republican period that served the landed gentry)

紅領巾 [húng lǐng-chīn]: 1. red scarf (insignia of the Young Pioneers); 2. Red Scarf (periodical)

紅榜 [húng-pǎng]: roll of honor

紅銅 [húng-t'úng]: copper

16 紅燈 [húng-tēng]: a red lantern (i.e., an infallible guide, as for example, the works of Mao)

紅燈記 [húng-tēng chì]: The Red Lantern (a reformed play)

紅衛報 [húng wèi pào]: Hung Wei Pao (i.e., Red Guard newspaper, the former 羊城晚報 of Canton)

紅衛兵 [húng-wèi pīng]: Red Guard (organization of militant youths formed in 1966 at the start of the Cultural Revolution)

約

5 約旦 [yüēh-tàn]: Jordan

約旦王國 [yüēh-tàn wáng-kuó]: Hashemite Kingdom of Jordan

7 約束 [yüēh-shù]: to restrain, to bind, to check, to curb; restraint, constraint, curb, check; binding

13 約會 [yüēh-hùi]: appointment, date, engagement

16 約翰遜 [yüēh-hàn-sùn]: Johnson, Lyndon (American political figure)

— 4 Strokes —

級

級 [chí]: level, rank, grade

紙

5 紙包不住火 [chǐh pāo-pú-chù huǒ]: fire cannot be wrapped in paper

6 紙老虎 [chǐh lǎo-hǔ]: paper tiger (a term used principally to categorize the power of American "imperialism," i.e., basically weak although apparently strong)

15 紙幣 [chǐh-pì]: paper currency, paper money, soft money

純

7 純技術觀點 [ch'ún chì-shù kuān-tiěn]: a purely technical viewpoint (i.e., a viewpoint considering only the professional or technical aspects of a matter without regard to the political)

純利 [ch'ún-lì]: pure profit, net profit, net yield

10 純益 [ch'ún-ì]: net profit, net yield, clear profit

11 純淨 [ch'ún-chìng]: pure, clean, unmixed

14 純粹 [ch'ún-ts'ùi]: pure, exclusive, sheer

15 純潔 [ch'ún-chiéh]: to purify; clean, pure, unadulterated

19 純藝術 [ch'ún ì-shù]: pure art

紡

紡織廠 [fǎng-chīh ch'ǎng]: cotton spinning mill

紡織工業 [fǎng-chīh kūng-yèh]: textile industry

紡織工業部 [fǎng-chīh kūng-yèh pù]: Ministry of Textile Industry

紡織品 [fǎng-chīh p'ǐn]: textile fabrics, textiles

紛

8 紛歧 [fēn-ch'í]: in disagreement, disunited

10 紛紛 [fēn-fēn]: in great confusion, highly confused, numerous

13 紛亂 [fēn-luàn]: in confusion, disorderly

18 紛擾 **[fēn-jǎo]** : to disturb the peace, to cause trouble; great confusion

納

2 納入 **[nà-jù]** : to bring into, to organize into, to be subordinated to, to enter into, to fit into

5 納卯 **[nà-mǎo]** : Davao (Philippines)

6 納西 **[nà-hsī]** : Na-hsi (a minority nationality)

12 納稅 **[nà-shùi]** : to pay taxes, to pay duty

13 納塞爾 **[nà-sè-ěrh]** : Nasser, Gamal Abdel (Egyptian political leader)

14 納粹 **[nà-ts'ùi]** : Nazi

納粹主義 **[nà-ts'ùi chǔ-ì]** : Nazism

納粹主義者 **[nà-ts'ùi chǔ-ì-chě]** : Nazi, Hitlerite

紐

5 紐卡斯爾 **[nǐu-k'ǎ-ssū-ěrh]** : Newcastle

6 紐西蘭 **[nǐu hsī-lán]** : New Zealand

8 紐芬蘭 **[nǐu-fēn-lán]** : Newfoundland

9 紐約 **[nǐu-yüēh]** : New York

紐約先驅論壇報 **[nǐu-yüēh hsiēn-ch'ǖ lùn-t'án pào]** : New York Herald-Tribune (U.S. daily newspaper)

紐約世界電訊與太陽報 **[nǐu-yüēh shìh-chièh tièn-hsǜn yǚ t'ài-yáng pào]** : New York World Telegram and Sun (U.S. daily newspaper)

紐約時報 **[nǐu-yüēh shíh-pào]** : The New York Times (U.S. daily newspaper)

15 紗廠 **[shā-ch'ǎng]** : textile mill

索

6 索耳茲伯里 **[sŏ-ěrh-tzū-pó-lǐ]** : Salisbury (Rhodesia)

8 索取 **[sŏ-ch'ǚ]** : to send for, to demand, to obtain, to extort

索非亞 **[sŏ-fēi-yà]** : Sofia (Bulgaria)

10 索格洛夫斯基 **[sŏ-kó-lò-fū-ssū-chī]** : Sokolovsky (Russian military officer)

索倫 **[sŏ-lún]** : Soluns (a minority nationality)

索馬里共和國 **[sŏ-mǎ-lǐ kùng-hó-kuó]** : Somali Republic

— 5 Strokes —

2 終了期 **[chūng-liǎo ch'í]** : the period having ended or expired

4 終止 **[chūng-chǐh]** : to put an end to, to terminate, to end, to conclude; termination, end

6 終年 **[chūng-nién]** : all year long, the whole year

7 終究 **[chūng-chìu]** : after all, finally, in the end, in the long run

終身的 **[chūng-shēn te]** : lifelong

8 終於 **[chūng-yǘ]** : finally, eventually, at last

細

10 細致 **[hsì-chìh]** : thoroughgoing, meticulous, careful, conscientious

12 細菌 **[hsì-chǜn]** : bacterium, germ

細菌戰 **[hsì-chǜn chàn]** : germ warfare, bacteriological warfare

細菌肥料 **[hsì-chǜn féi-liào]** : bacterial fertilizer, bacteriological fertilizer

細菌武器 **[hsì-chǔn wǔ-ch'ì]** : bacteriological weapons

15 細節 **[hsì-chiéh]** : fine details, minutiae

16 細緻 **[hsì-chìh]** : fine, beautiful, careful

累

5 累犯 **[lěi-fàn]** : to commit an offense repeatedly

6 累次 **[lěi-tz'ù]** : repeatedly

12 累進稅 **[lěi-chìn shùi]** : progressive tax

16 累積 **[lěi-chī]** : to accumulate; accumulation

絆

11 絆脚 **[pàn-chiǎo]** : to trip up, to be hindered

絆脚石 **[pàn-chiǎo shíh]** : obstacle, stumbling block

紹

8 紹花 **[shào-huā]** : Thieuhoa (Vietnam)

紳

3 紳士 **[shēn-shìh]** : gentry

組

7 組成 **[tsǔ-ch'éng]** : to organize, to compose, to form, to make up; organization, composition, formation

組成人員 **[tsǔ-ch'éng jén-yüán]** : component members

組成部份 **[tsǔ-ch'éng pù-fèn]** : component part, integral part

12 組距 **[tsǔ-chǜ]** : interval

14 組閣 **[tsǔ-kó]** : to form a cabinet

18 組織 **[tsǔ-chīh]** : to organize; organization

組織照顧 **[tsǔ-chīh chào-kù]** : to receive special care from the organization of which one is a member; special care from one's organization

組織者 **[tsǔ-chīh-chě]** : an organizer

組織處分 **[tsǔ-chīh ch'ǔ-fèn]** : organizational discipline

組織軍事化 **[tsǔ-chīh chǖn-shìh-huà]** : militarization of organization (one of the 三化, q.v.)

組織性 **[tsǔ-chīh-hsìng]** : sense of organization

組織力量 **[tsǔ-chīh lì-liàng]** : organizational strength

組織部 **[tsǔ-chīh pù]** : Ministry of Organization

組織上 **[tsǔ-chīh-shàng]** : organizationally

組織層次 **[tsǔ-chīh ts'éng-tz'ù]** : organizational structure

紫

8 紫金山天文台 **[tzǔ-chīn-shān t'iēn-wén-t'ái]** : Purple Mountain Observatory

13 紫禁城 **[tzǔ-chìn ch'éng]** : Forbidden City (in Peking)

— 6 Strokes —

給

4 給予 **[chǐ-yǔ or kěi-yǔ]** : to give, to accord, to extend, to confer on, to donate, to present, to bestow, to grant, to award, to assign, to contribute, to supply

5 給以致命打擊 **[kěi-ǐ chìh-mìng tǎ-chī]** : to deal a fatal blow

給以首位 **[kěi-ǐ shǒu-wèi]** : to give first place to, to give priority to

給以優先權 **[kěi-ǐ yū-hsiēn-ch'üán]** : to give priority to

13 給與動機 **[kěi-yǔ tùng-chī]** : to motivate

15 給養 **[chĭ-yăng]** : provisions, supplies

絞

6 絞刑 **[chiăo-hsíng]** : death by hanging or strangulation

9 絞架 **[chiăo-chià]** : gallows

10 絞索 **[chiăo-sŏ]** : hangman's rope, noose

11 絞殺 **[chiăo-shā]** : to hang, to strangle

結

3 結子 **[chiēh-tzu]** : knot

6 結成聯盟 **[chiéh-ch'éng lién-méng]** : to enter into alliances, to form a coalition

結交 **[chiéh-chiāo]** : to associate with

結合 **[chiéh-hó]** : to integrate, to unite with, to combine, to connect, to align; combination, connection, bond, conjunction

7 結局 **[chiéh-chű]** : outcome, conclusion, result, finale

結社 **[chiéh-shè]** : to form an association, to form a company

結社、集會、和人身自由 **[chiéh-shè, chí-hùi, hó jén-shēn tzù-yú]** : freedom of association, assembly, and person

結束 **[chiéh-shù]** : to terminate, to end, to conclude, to bring to an end, to be at an end; end, termination

8 結果 **[chiéh-kuŏ]** : outcome, fruit, consequence, result, fruition, effect

10 結案 **[chiéh-àn]** : to close a case, to conclude a case, to wind up a lawsuit

結核病研究所 **[chiéh-hó-pìng yén-chìu-sŏ]** : Tuberculosis Institute

14 結構 **[chiéh-kòu]** : structure, construction; to construct, to build, to compose, to put together; structural

結構和構件 **[chiéh-kòu hó kòu-chièn]** : structure and parts

結構鋼 **[chiéh-kòu kāng]** : structural steel

15 結賬 **[chiéh-chàng]** : to settle accounts, to settle balances; clearing

結論 **[chiéh-lùn]** : conclusion, deduction, interpretation

結實 **[chiēh-shíh]** : strong, tough, enduring, physically fit

16 結餘 **[chiéh-yű]** : surplus, excess, overplus

3 絕大多數 **[chüéh-tà tō-shù]** : overwhelming majority, vast majority, preponderant majority

4 絕不 **[chüéh-pù]** : not at all

6 絕交 **[chüéh-chiāo]** : to break off relations

7 絕技 **[chüéh-chì]** : unique skill, matchless art (indicates a production skill handed down through a family from generation to generation)

11 絕望 **[chüéh-wàng]** : despair, hopelessness, to despair of, to lose all hope of

13 絕路 **[chüéh-lù]** : dead end, predicament, disaster, impasse, catastrophe

14 絕境 **[chüéh-chìng]** : inaccessible place, place of retirement for a recluse, dead end, hopeless situation

絕對 **[chüéh-tùi]** : absolute; absolutely

絕對眞理 **[chüéh-tùi chēn-lĭ]** : absolute truth

絕對民主 **[chüéh-tùi mín-chŭ]** : pure democracy, absolute democracy

絕對命令 **[chüéh-tùi mìng-lìng]** : categorical imperative

絕對平均主義 **[chüéh-tùi p'íng-chűn chŭ-ì]** : absolute equalitarianism

絕對的控制 **[chüéh-tùi te k'ùng-chìh]** : uncontested control, absolute control

絕對的同一性 **[chüéh-tùi te t'úng-í-hsìng]** : absolute identity

絲

11 絲毫 **[ssū-háo]**: in the least, the least bit (negative intensifier)

絲毫不含糊 **[ssū-háo pù-hán-hú]**: in black and white terms, absolutely unambiguous

絲毫不足以 **[ssū-háo pù-tsú ǐ]**: entirely insufficient

18 絲織品 **[ssū-chīh p'ǐn]**: silk fabrics

統

1 統一 **[t'ǔng-ī]**: to unite, to unify; unity, unification, union, integration, identity; united, unified, uniform, standard, standardized

統一安排 **[t'ǔng-ī ān-p'ái]**: overall arrangement, uniform arrangement

統一戰綫 **[t'ǔng-ī chàn-hsièn]**: united front

統一戰綫工作部 **[t'ǔng-ī chàn-hsièn kūng-tsò pù]**: United Front Work Department

統一陣綫 **[t'ǔng-ī chèn-hsièn]**: united front

統一指揮 **[t'ǔng-ī chǐh-hūi]**: single command, unified command

統一經營 **[t'ǔng-ī chīng-yíng]**: centralized management

統一行動 **[t'ǔng-ī hsíng-tùng]**: to act in unison

統一性 **[t'ǔng-ī-hsìng]**: unity

統一規劃 **[t'ǔng-ī kuēi-huà]**: to map out a unified plan

統一國民經濟核算體系 **[t'ǔng-ī kuó-mín chīng-chì hó-suàn t'ǐ-hsì]**: Uniform National Economic Accounting System

統一領導 **[t'ǔng-ī lǐng-tǎo]**: unified leadership

統一領導，全面安排 **[t'ǔng-ī lǐng-tǎo, ch'üán-mièn ān-p'ái]**: centralized leadership and overall arrangement

統一領導，分散經營 **[t'ǔng-ī lǐng-tǎo, fēn-sàn chīng-yíng]**: centralized leadership and decentralized operation

統一平均分配 **[t'ǔng-ī p'íng-chǖn fēn-p'èi]**: equal distribution (among the entire population)

統一社會黨 **[t'ǔng-ī shè-hùi tǎng]**: Socialist Unity Party (East Germany)

統一調度 **[t'ǔng-ī tiào-tù]**: unified distribution

統一祖國 **[t'ǔng-ī tsǔ-kuó]**: unification of the motherland

8 統治 **[t'ǔng-chìh]**: to rule, to reign, to govern, to control; rule, control, sway; ruling

統治階級 **[t'ǔng-chìh chiēh-chí]**: ruling class

統治權 **[t'ǔng-chìh ch'üán]**: sovereignty

9 統計 **[t'ǔng-chì]**: statistics; statistical

統計整理 **[t'ǔng-chì chěng-lǐ]**: processing of statistical data

統計加工 **[t'ǔng-chì chiā-kūng]**: processing of statistical data

統計彙總 **[t'ǔng-chì hùi-tsǔng]**: statistical data processing

統計員 **[t'ǔng-chì-yüán]**: statistician

15 統銷 **[t'ǔng-hsiāo]**: unified marketing

16 統戰部 **[t'ǔng-chàn pù]**: united work front department (abbreviation of 統一戰綫工作部)

17 統購 **[t'ǔng-kòu]**: unified purchasing

統購包銷 **[t'ǔng-kòu pāo-hsiāo]**: planned purchase and contract sale (the purchasing by the state of the output of capitalist enterprises and state distribution of all finished products of a capitalist firm)

統購統銷 **[t'ǔng-kòu t'ǔng-hsiāo]**: planned purchase and distribution; centralized purchase and distribution; unified purchasing and unified marketing

20 統籌 **[t'ŭng-ch'óu]**: to coordinate, to unify; coordination, overall planning

統籌兼顧 **[t'ŭng-ch'óu chiēn-kù]**: unified planning and due consideration of all concerned

— 7 Strokes —

經

3 經久 **[chīng-chiŭ]**: to have gone through a long period of time; durable, prolonged, lasting, enduring

4 經不起 **[chīng-pù-ch'ĭ]**: not able to endure, not able to withstand

經不起考驗 **[chīng-pù-ch'ĭ k'ăo-yèn]**: to be unable to withstand the test of experience, to fail to pass the test

5 經由 **[chīng-yú]**: via, through, by way of

8 經受 **[chīng-shòu]**: to go through, to undergo, to endure, to sustain, to pass through, to survive, to experience

經典 **[chīng-tiĕn]**: classics, scriptures; classical

經典文獻 **[chīng-tiĕn wén-hsièn]**: classical document

9 經紀人 **[chīng-chì jén]**: broker

經度 **[chīng-tù]**: longitude

10 經院哲學 **[chīng-yüàn ché-hsüéh]**: scholasticism

11 經常 **[chīng-ch'áng]**: constant, frequent, regular

經常反復的實踐 **[chīng-ch'áng făn-fù te shíh-chièn]**: recurrent practices

經常開支 **[chīng-ch'áng k'āi-chīh]**: current expenditure, ordinary expenditure

經常觀察 **[chīng-ch'áng kuān-ch'á]**: continuous observation

經常統計 **[chīng-ch'áng t'ŭng-chì]**: current statistics

經理 **[chīng-lĭ]**: to manage, to direct, to oversee, to handle; manager

經得起 **[chīng-té-ch'ĭ]**: to be capable of enduring

經得住考驗 **[chīng-té-chù k'ăo-yèn]**: to be able to stand all tests, to emerge from a test steeled

12 經費 **[chīng-fèi]**: expenses, expenditure, outlay

15 經銷 **[chīng-hsiāo]**: to handle distribution by contract for state enterprises; contract sale, sale on commission

16 經歷 **[chīng-lì]**: to experience, to undergo, to go through, to pass through; experience

17 經濟 **[chīng-chì]**: economics, economy; economic

經濟安定本部 **[chīng-chì ān-tìng pĕn-pù]**: Economic Stabilization Board

經濟成分 **[chīng-chì ch'éng-fèn]**: economic sector

經濟基礎 **[chīng-chì chī-ch'ŭ]**: economic basis, economic base

經濟指數 **[chīng-chì chĭh-shù]**: economic index

經濟主義 **[chīng-chì chŭ-ì]**: economism (the attention given to profit making by certain units; that is, the use of material incentives instead of political consciousness to induce workers and peasants to produce more)

經濟核算制度 **[chīng-chì hó-suàn chìh-tù]**: business accounting system, economic accounting system (a system broader than cost accounting that covers almost the whole field of scientific management)

經濟協作區 **[chīng-chì hsiéh-tsò ch'ü]**: economically coordinated regions

經濟形態 **[chīng-chì hsíng-t'ài]**: economic structure

經濟學家 **[chīng-chì hsüéh-chiā]**: an economist; Economist (British weekly periodical)

經濟會議 [chīng-chì hùi-ì]: Economic Council, economic conference

經濟林 [chīng-chì lín]: economic forest, industrial forest

經濟命脈 [chīng-chì mìng-mài]: economic lifeline, economic arteries, key points of the economy, key branches of the economy

經濟事務部 [chīng-chì shìh-wù pù]: Ministry of Economy Affairs (India)

經濟事務委員會 [chīng-chì shìh-wù wěi-yüán-hùi]: Economic Affairs Commission

經濟作物 [chīng-chì tsò-wù]: economic crop, industrial crop, cash crop

經濟危機 [chīng-chì wéi-chī]: economic crisis

經濟研究所 [chīng-chì yén-chìu-sŏ]: Economics Institute

經營 [chīng-yíng]: to operate, to manage, to run, to deal in; management, operation

經營範圍 [chīng-yíng fàn-wéi]: scope of operations

經營管理 [chīng-yíng kuăn-lĭ]: management

23 經驗 [chīng-yèn]: to verify, to experience; experience; empirical

經驗主義 [chīng-yèn chŭ-ì]: empiricism

經驗論 [chīng-yèn lùn]: empiricism

經驗批判論 [chīng-yèn p'ī-p'àn lùn]: empirical criticism

絹

13 絹絲廠 [chüàn-ssū ch'ăng]: silk mill

綁

9 綁架 [păng-chià]: to kidnap for ransom

11 綁票 [păng-p'iào]: to kidnap, to seize for ransom

綏

13 綏靖 [súi-chìng]: to appease, to pacify, to calm; appeasement, pacification

綏靖政策 [súi-chìng chèng-ts'è]: appeasement policy, pacification policy

— 8 Strokes —

緊

8 緊迫 [chĭn-p'ò]: crisis, panic; pressing

9 緊急 [chĭn-chí]: emergency; urgent, critical

緊急倡議 [chĭn-chí ch'àng-ì]: urgent proposal

緊急建議 [chĭn-chí chièn-ì]: urgent proposal

緊急狀態 [chĭn-chí chuàng-t'ài]: state of emergency

緊急呼籲 [chĭn-chí hū-yǜ]: urgent appeal

緊急會議 [chĭn-chí hùi-ì]: emergency session, emergency meeting, emergency conference

緊急關頭 [chĭn-chí kuān-t'óu]: critical moment, critical situation, crucial juncture

緊急時期 [chĭn-chí shíh-ch'í]: urgent period, critical years, crucial period

緊急通告 [chĭn-chí t'ūng-kào]: urgent notification

緊要 [chĭn-yào]: critical, urgent, important

11 緊張 [chĭn-chāng]: 1. tension, emergency; urgent, tense, critical, strained; 2. earnestness (two of the eight characters of the 三八作風, q.v.)

緊張局勢 [chĭn-chāng chű-shìh]: tense situation, strained situation, critical state

緊張狀態 [chĭn-chāng chuàng-t'ài]: state of emergency

緊密 [chĭn-mì]: secret, close together

12 緊握 **[chĭn-wò]**: to grip firmly; strong grasp, firm grip

17 緊縮 **[chĭn-sō]**: to contract, to shrink, to tighten, to reduce, to cut, to retrench, to economize; compression

緊縮編制 **[chĭn-sō piēn-chìh]**: to reduce staff, to cut down on personnel

綫

10 綫索 **[hsièn-sŏ]**: clue, hint, indication

14 綫圖 **[hsièn-t'ú]**: linear diagram

綱

9 綱要 **[kāng-yào]**: summary, outline, general program

14 綱領 **[kāng-lĭng]**: a principle running through a book, the leading thought, guiding principle, program

綱領性 **[kāng-lĭng-hsìng]**: programmatic

綠

4 綠化 **[lù-huà]**: to afforest, to make green; afforestation, tree planting

8 綠肥 **[lù-féi]**: green fertilizer, green manure

綠肥作物 **[lù-féi tsò-wù]**: green fertilizer crops

10 綠島 **[lù-tăo]**: Greenland

綳

11 綳帶 **[pēng-tài]**: bandage, dressing

17 綳臉 **[pēng-liĕn]**: to assume a serious expression

綜

6 綜合 **[tsūng-hó]**: to gather together, to unite, to synthesize; synthesis; synthetic, general, composite, aggregate, comprehensive

綜合技術的 **[tsūng-hó chì-shù te]**: polytechnical

綜合指標 **[tsūng-hó chĭh-piāo]**: general indicator, aggregate indicator

綜合指數 **[tsūng-hó chĭh-shù]**: aggregate index, composite index

綜合經營 **[tsūng-hó chīng-yíng]**: comprehensive management; diverse economic undertakings

綜合性的 **[tsūng-hó-hsìng te]**: composite, comprehensive

綜合性紅專學校 **[tsūng-hó-hsìng húng-chuān hsüéh-hsiào]**: comprehensive red and expert schools

綜合性工廠 **[tsūng-hó-hsìng kūng-ch'ăng]**: multiple-producing factory

綜合鋼鐵廠 **[tsūng-hó kāng-t'iĕh ch'ăng]**: integral steel plant

綜合考察委員會 **[tsūng-hó k'ăo-ch'á wĕi-yüán-hùi]**: Commission on Comprehensive Expeditions

綜合利用 **[tsūng-hó lì-yùng]**: comprehensive utilization, multi-purpose use

綜合報導 **[tsūng-hó pào-tăo]**: composite report, summing-up report, pooled dispatch

綜合大學 **[tsūng-hó tà-hsüéh]**: comprehensive university (i.e., a university having several departments)

9 綜括 **[tsūng-k'uò]**: to bring together, to generalize, to take a comprehensive view; comprehensive

網

網 **[wăng]**: network, net, web

維

3 維也納 **[wéi-yĕh-nà]**: Vienna (Austria)

[7] 維吾爾 **[wéi-wú-ĕrh]**: Uighurs (minority nationality)

[9] 維持 **[wéi-ch'íh]**: to maintain, to sustain, to support, to shoulder, to shore up; maintenance

維持鎮靜 **[wéi-ch'íh chèn-chìng]**: to keep one's head, to keep cool

維持生活 **[wéi-ch'íh shēng-huó]**: to maintain one's livelihood, to earn a living

[10] 維修 **[wéi-hsīu]**: to maintain and repair; maintenance and overhaul, maintenance and repair

[13] 維新 **[wéi-hsīn]**: to reform, to modernize; reform, modernization

[14] 維爾京群島 **[wéi-ĕrh-chīng ch'ún-tăo]**: Virgin Islands (U.S.)

[21] 維護 **[wéi-hù]**: to safeguard, to uphold, to defend, to protect, to support, to preserve, to maintain; protection, support, preservation

維護者 **[wéi-hù-chĕ]**: defender, guardian, preserver, champion

— 9 Strokes —

緒

[15] 緒論 **[hsù-lùn]**: introduction, preface, foreword, prelude

緩

[4] 緩手 **[huăn-shŏu]**: to delay action

[6] 緩刑 **[huăn-hsíng]**: to reprieve, to suspend a sentence, to put on probation

[7] 緩兵之計 **[huăn-pīng chīh chì]**: delaying tactics, measures to stave off an attack

[8] 緩和 **[huăn-hó]**: to moderate, to ease, to allay, to relieve, to relax, to slacken, to alleviate, to mitigate; slackening, relaxation, thaw

[9] 緩急 **[huăn-chí]**: urgent and not urgent, slow and fast, adverse and prosperous; degree of urgency

[12] 緩期 **[huăn-ch'í]**: to postpone a deadline, to grant a delay

[14] 緩慢 **[huăn-màn]**: slow, sluggish, tardy, delayed, gradual, decelerated; slowness

[15] 緩衝 **[huăn-ch'ūng]**: to roll with the punches, to deaden a punch, to parry a thrust

緩衝國 **[huăn-ch'ūng kuó]**: buffer state

緩衝地帶 **[huăn-ch'ūng tì-tài]**: buffer zone

[16] 緩頰 **[huăn-chiá]**: to intercede for, to put in a good word for someone

緩辦 **[huăn-pàn]**: to postpone action, to delay taking action

緬

[7] 緬甸 **[miĕn-tièn]**: Burma

緬甸聯邦 **[miĕn-tièn lién-pāng]**: Union of Burma

編

[5] 編目 **[piēn-mù]**: to catalog, to compile an index or table of contents

[8] 編者 **[piēn-chĕ]**: editor, compiler

編制 **[piēn-chìh]**: to compile, to work out, to draft, to draw up, to elaborate, to codify; elaboration, organization, composition, table of organization

編制和定員制度 **[piēn-chìh hó tìng-yüán chìh-tù]**: a permanent organization with a fixed number of personnel

[10] 編造 **[piēn-tsào]**: to make, to prepare, to fabricate, to compose

[11] 編排 **[piēn-p'ái]**: 1. to arrange, to arrange in order; setup; 2. to vilify

[12] 編著 **[piēn-chù]**: to compile and edit

編隊 **[piēn-tùi]** : to assign to teams, to assign to units

16 編輯 **[piēn-chí]** : to edit, to arrange, to compile; editor, compiler

編輯部 **[piēn-chí pù]** : editorial department, editorial board

20 編譯 **[piēn-ì]** : translation, editing and translation

編譯出版委員會 **[piēn-ì ch'ū-pǎn wěi-yüán-hùi]** : Commission on Translation and Publications

編纂 **[piēn-tsuǎn]** : to compile, to arrange and edit

締

6 締交 **[tì-chiāo]** : to enter into friendship; closely allied, bound closely

9 締約 **[tì-yüēh]** : to conclude a treaty, to make an alliance

締約國 **[tì-yüēh kuó]** : signatory state (i.e., to a treaty)

12 締結 **[tì-chiéh]** : to establish a bond, to form a union; betrothed, engaged, allied

締結協定 **[tì-chiéh hsiéh-tìng]** : to conclude an agreement

緯

14 緯綫 **[wěi-hsièn]** : latitude

— 10 Strokes —

縣

縣 **[hsièn]** : district, county, hsien

2 縣人民公社 **[hsièn jén-mín kūng-shè]** : County People's Commune

縣人民代表大會 **[hsièn-jén-mín tài-piǎo tà-hùi]** : County People's Congress

8 縣委 **[hsièn-wěi]** : county Party committee, hsien committee

10 縣城 **[hsièn-ch'éng]** : county seat, hsien city

縣級 **[hsièn-chí]** : county level, hsien level

17 縣聯社 **[hsièn-lién-shè]** : county federations of communes

縈

9 縈迴 **[yíng-húi]** : to hover, to flit about

— 11 Strokes —

9 繁重勞動 **[fán-chùng láo-tùng]** : strenuous labor, labor consuming work

12 繁殖 **[fán-chíh]** : to reproduce, to breed, to multiply, to propagate in abundance

繁華 **[fán-huá]** : gaiety, pomp, extravagant display; festive, prosperous, flourishing

14 繁複 **[fán-fù]** : complex, complicated

繁榮 **[fán-júng]** : prosperous, abundant, flourishing, thriving

繁瑣的 **[fán-sǒ te]** : trivial, trifling

18 繁雜 **[fán-tsá]** : complex, intricate, multifarious, confused

縹

13 縹渺 **[p'iǎo-miǎo]** : indistinct, vague, blurred

縮

3 縮小 **[sō-hsiǎo]** : to shrink, to reduce, to lessen, to diminish, to contract, to decrease; reduction, contraction, shrinkage

4 縮手縮脚 **[sō-shǒu sō-chiǎo]** : timid and flinching

12 縮減 **[sō-chiĕn]**: to dwindle, to reduce, to shrink down

縮短 **[sō-tuăn]**: to shorten, to cut down, to curtail, to cut short, to reduce; reduction

縱

4 縱火 **[tsùng-huŏ]**: to set fire to; arson

縱火犯 **[tsùng-huŏ fàn]**: arsonist

10 縱容 **[tsùng-júng]**: to connive at, to pamper, to tolerate, to be indulgent to

12 縱軸 **[tsùng-chóu]**: ordinate, vertical axis

縱隊 **[tsùng-tùi]**: column, brigade

總

3 總工程師 **[tsŭng-kūng ch'éng-shīh]**: chief engineer

4 總之 **[tsŭng-chīh]**: in short, in a word

總支部 **[tsŭng-chīh pù]**: general party branch

5 總平均數 **[tsŭng-p'íng chūn-shù]**: overall average

總司令 **[tsŭng-ssū-lìng]**: commander-in-chief

總司令部 **[tsŭng-ssū-lìng-pù]**: General Headquarters

6 總共 **[tsŭng-kùng]**: gross amount, sum total, total; aggregate, altogether

總收入 **[tsŭng shōu-jù]**: gross income, total income

總危機 **[tsŭng wéi-chī]**: general crisis

8 總和 **[tsŭng-hó]**: total sum

總的 **[tsŭng te]**: overall

9 總前委 **[tsŭng ch'ién-wĕi]**: General Front Committee

總政治部 **[tsŭng chèng-chìh pù]**: general political department

總計 **[tsŭng-chì]**: to amount to, to add up to, to total; sum total

總計劃 **[tsŭng chì-huà]**: overall plan, master plan, general plan

總則 **[tsŭng-tsé]**: general rules, general regulations, general provisions

10 總後勤部 **[tsŭng hòu-ch'ín pù]**: General Logistics Department

總後方勤務部 **[tsŭng hòu-fāng ch'ín-wù pù]**: General Rear Services Department

總訓練部 **[tsŭng hsùn-lièn pù]**: General Training Department

總根源 **[tsŭng kēn-yüán]**: the root cause

總書記 **[tsŭng shū-chì]**: general secretary, secretary general

11 總產值 **[tsŭng ch'ăn-chíh]**: gross value of output, total value of production, value of total output

總產量 **[tsŭng ch'ăn-liàng]**: gross output, total output, gross product, total production

總理 **[tsŭng-lĭ]**: prime minister, premier, chancellor (West Germany)

總理辦公室 **[tsŭng-lĭ pàn-kūng-shìh]**: premier's secretariat

總參謀長 **[tsŭng ts'ān-móu-chăng]**: Chief of the General Staff

總參謀部 **[tsŭng ts'ān-móu pù]**: general staff

總動員 **[tsŭng tùng-yüán]**: general mobilization

總統 **[tsŭng-t'ŭng]**: president; presidential

12 總結 **[tsŭng-chiéh]**: to sum up, to summarize; summary, summing up

總結報告 **[tsŭng-chiéh pào-kào]**: concluding report

總結算 **[tsŭng-chiéh suàn]**: to total up; a general reckoning, a lump sum

13 總幹部管理部 **[tsŭng kàn-pù kuăn-lĭ pù]** : General Personnel Department

總路綫 **[tsŭng-lù-hsièn]** : the general line

總督 **[tsŭng-tū]** : governor general, viceroy

總預備隊 **[tsŭng yǜ-pêi tùi]** : general reserves

14 總監 **[tsŭng-chiēn]** : inspector-general, director-general

總領事 **[tsŭng lĭng-shìh]** : consul-general

總領事館 **[tsŭng lĭng-shìh-kuăn]** : consulate-general

15 總編輯 **[tsŭng piēn-chí]** : chief editor, editor-in-chief

總數 **[tsŭng-shù]** : total sum, grand total, sum total

16 總罷工 **[tsŭng pà-kūng]** : general strike

23 總體 **[tsŭng-t'ĭ]** : entirety; entire, total, overall

總體規劃 **[tsŭng-t'ĭ kuēi-huà]** : overall plan

— 12 Strokes —

織

11 織造品 **[chīh-tsào p'ĭn]** : fabrics, textiles

繞

4 繞月球飛行 **[jào yüèh-ch'íu fēi-hsíng]** : flight around the moon

13 繞過 **[jào-kuò]** : to bypass, to evade, to avoid, to elude, to make a detour around

— 13 Strokes —

繳

6 繳回 **[chiăo-húi]** : to hand back, to give back, to pay back, to turn in

10 繳納 **[chiăo-nà]** : to pay, to pay out

11 繳械 **[chiăo-hsièh]** : to hand over weapons, to disarm

12 繳費 **[chiăo-fèi]** : to pay a fee

繳款 **[chiăo-k'uăn]** : to pay a sum of money

繳稅 **[chiăo-shùi]** : to pay duty, to pay tax

15 繳槍 **[chiăo-ch'iāng]** : to lay one's weapons down, to capitulate, to surrender

17 繳獲 **[chiăo-huò]** : to capture, to take as booty

繭

繭 **[chiĕn]** : cocoon, cocoon of the silkworm

14 繭綢 **[chiĕn-ch'óu]** : natural silk, pongee made from wild silk

繪

14 繪圖 **[hùi-t'ú]** : to sketch, to design, to outline

15 繪影繪聲 **[hùi-yĭng hùi-shēng]** : to illustrate in full detail, to describe vividly

— 14 Strokes —

6 繼任 **[chì-jèn]** : to take someone's place, to succeed, to succeed in office

8 繼承 **[chì-ch'éng]** : to inherit, to succeed to; inheritance, succession

繼承者 **[chì-ch'éng-chĕ]** : successor, heir, inheritor, one who follows, one who succeeds to an office

繼承衣鉢 **[chì-ch'éng ī-pō]** : to step into the shoes of (literally, to inherit the clothes and the alms bowl of [a Buddhist priest])

13 繼電器 **[chì-tièn ch'ì]** : relay equipment

[21] 繼續 **[chì-hsù]**: to continue, to carry on, to connect, to keep on, to resume, to perpetuate, to maintain

繼續不斷 **[chì-hsù pú-tuàn]**: continuously, constantly, consistently, unceasingly, incessantly

繼續說 **[chì-hsù shuō]**: to go on to say, to continue the account or remarks

繼續大躍進 **[chì-hsù tà-yüèh-chìn]**: continued great leap forward

繼續當政 **[chì-hsù tāng-chèng]**: to continue in power

— 15 Strokes —

纏

[14] 纏綿 **[ch'án-mién]**: bound up, involved with something, inseparable, intimate, incessant

— RADICAL 缶 121 —

— 4 Strokes —

缺

[3] 缺口 **[ch'üēh-k'ǒu]**: breach, gap

[4] 缺少 **[ch'üēh-shǎo]**: to lack, to run short of; deficiency, shortage, insufficiency, scarcity

[5] 缺乏 **[ch'üēh-fá]**: to lack, to run short of; deficiency, shortage, insufficiency, scarcity

缺乏實際根據 **[ch'üēh-fá shíh-chì kēn-chù]**: to lack actual basis

[7] 缺材代用 **[ch'üēh-ts'ái tài-yùng]**: to find substitutes for materials in shortage

缺位 **[ch'üēh-wèi]**: vacant post, vacant office, vacancy, unfilled appointment

[10] 缺席 **[ch'üēh-hsí]**: to be absent from a meeting; absence

[13] 缺陷 **[ch'üēh-hsièn]**: defect, shortcoming, flaw, imperfection, inadequacy, insufficiency, deficiency

[17] 缺點 **[ch'üēh-tiěn]**: shortcoming, defect, deficiency, imperfection, weakness

[18] 缺糧戶 **[ch'üēh-liáng hù]**: grain-deficient household

— RADICAL 网 罒 罓 122 —

— 3 Strokes —

罕

[8] 罕事 **[hǎn-shìh]**: rarity

— 6 Strokes —

罣

[8] 罣念 **[kuà-nièn]**: to be worried about, to be anxious about

[16] 罣誤 **[kuà-wù]**: blame for a mistake (made with another person)

[19] 罣礙 **[kuà-ài]**: to hinder, to impede; obstacle, hindrance, restriction, inhibition

— 8 Strokes —

置

[4] 置之不理 **[chìh-chīh pù-lǐ]**: to pay no attention to, to disregard, to ignore

[7] 置身局外 **[chìh-shēn chǘ-wài]**: to keep aloof from, to remain aloof from, not to be drawn into

置身事外 **[chìh-shēn shìh-wài]**: to keep out of trouble

21 置辯 **[chìh-pièn]**: to advance an argument either to defend or refute

罪

罪 **[tsùi]**: offence, crime, misconduct, sin

2 罪人 **[tsùi-jén]**: offender, sinner, culprit, criminal, evildoer

3 罪大惡極 **[tsùi-tà ò-chí]**: to be guilty of terrible crimes, to be criminal and wicked in the extreme; most heinous crimes

5 罪犯 **[tsùi-fàn]**: criminal, delinquent, malefactor

6 罪行 **[tsùi-hsíng]**: criminal conduct, criminal behavior, vicious act, crime, evil deed

罪名 **[tsùi-míng]**: charge, charge against, crime, sentence, penalty, guilt

12 罪惡 **[tsùi-ò]**: evil, sin, wickedness, vice, crime

罪惡昭彰 **[tsùi-ò chāo-chāng]**: flagrant offences, flagrant crimes

14 罪魁 **[tsùi-k′uéi]**: chief criminal, ringleader

— 9 Strokes —

8 罰金 **[fá-chīn]**: a fine

12 罰款 **[fá-k′uǎn]**: to fine; a fine

— 10 Strokes —

罷

3 罷工 **[pà-kūng]**: to strike, to walk out; a strike, a walkout

5 罷市 **[pà-shìh]**: to close (all) shops, to stop doing business; merchants' strike

8 罷免 **[pà-miěn]**: to remove from office, to relieve someone of his office, to recall

15 罷課 **[pà-k′ò]**: students' strike

— 14 Strokes —

羅

6 羅安達 **[ló-ān-tá]**: Luanda (Angola)

8 羅亞 **[ló-yà]**: Roa, Raul (Cuban political leader)

9 羅罔 **[ló-wǎng]**: trammels, net, snare

10 羅馬 **[ló-mǎ]**: Rome (Italy)

羅馬教皇 **[ló-mǎ chiào-huáng]**: Pope

羅馬尼亞 **[ló-mǎ-ní-yà]**: Romania

羅馬尼亞人民共和國 **[ló-mǎ-ní-yà jén-mín kùng-hó-kuó]**: People's Republic of Romania

羅馬尼亞人民共和國大國民議會 **[ló-ma-ní-yà jén-mín kùng-hó-kuó tà kuó-mín i-hùi]**: Grand National Assembly of the People's Republic of Romania

羅馬尼亞通訊社 **[ló-mǎ-ní-yà t′ūng-hsùn-shè]**: AGERPRESS

羅馬天主教 **[ló-mǎ t′iēn-chǔ chiào]**: Roman Catholic Church

羅嗦的 **[ló-sō te]**: verbose, wordy, rambling, not sticking to the point

羅素 **[ló-sù]**: Russell, Bertram (British philosopher)

12 羅斯福 **[ló-ssū-fú]**: Roosevelt (name)

羅斯托夫 **[ló-ssū-t′ō-fū]**: Rostov (Soviet Union)

18 羅羅 **[ló-ló]**: Lolo (minority nationality)

— 19 Strokes —

羈

8 羈押 **[chī-yā]**: to keep in custody

10 羈留 **[chī-líu]**: to keep in custody, to detain

— RADICAL 羊 123 —

羊

5 羊皮 **[yáng-p'í]**: sheep's clothing, sheepskin

10 羊城晚報 **[yáng-ch'éng wăn-pào]**: Yang-ch'eng Evening Paper (Canton)

— 2 Strokes —

羌

羌 **[ch'iāng]**: the Kiang (minority nationality)

— 3 Strokes —

美

4 美化 **[mĕi-huà]**: to beautify, to glorify, to gild, to paint up, to be Americanized; Americanized

5 美以美會 **[mĕi-ĭ-mĕi hùi]**: Methodist Church

7 美孚 **[mĕi-fū]**: Standard Oil Company

美利堅合衆國 **[mĕi-lā-chiēn hó-chùng-kuó]**: United States of America

美妙 **[mĕi-miào]**: beautiful, graceful, fine, good, wonderful, marvellous

8 美和 **[mĕi-hó]**: Myhoa (Vietnam)

美拉諾 **[mĕi-lā-nò]**: Milano

美洲國家組織 **[mĕi-chōu kuó-chiā tsŭ-chīh]**: Organization of American States (OAS)

美帝 **[mĕi-tì]**: U.S. imperialism (abbreviation)

10 美索不達米亞 **[mĕi-sŏ-pù-tá-mĭ-yà]**: Mesopotamia

11 美國 **[mĕi-kuó]**: United States

美國新聞處 **[mĕi-kuó hsīn-wén-ch'ù]**: United States Information Service (USIS)

美國國會 **[mĕi-kuó kuó-hùi]**: Congress of the United States

美國生活方式 **[mĕi-kuó shēng-huó fāng-shìh]**: the American way of life

美國第一主義 **[mĕi-kuó tì-ī chŭ-ì]**: America first-ism

美術 **[mĕi-shù]**: fine arts

美術家 **[mĕi-shù-chiā]**: artist

美術工作者 **[mĕi-shù kūng-tsò-chĕ]**: art worker

美術委員會 **[mĕi-shù wĕi-yüán-hùi]**: Fine Arts Committee

17 美蔣匪幫 **[mĕi-chiăng fĕi-pāng]**: U.S.-Chiang bandit gang

美聯社 **[mĕi-lién-shè]**: Associated Press (AP)

19 美豐銀行 **[mĕi-fēng yín-háng]**: American Oriental Banking Corporation

21 美屬維爾京群島 **[mĕi-shŭ wéi-ĕrh-chīng ch'ŭn-tăo]**: Virgin Islands of the United States

— 5 Strokes —

羞

8 羞怯 **[hsīu-ch'ièh]**: shyness, bashfulness, timidity, diffidence; shy, bashful, timid, diffident

10 羞恥之心 **[hsīu-ch'ĭh chīh hsīn]**: sense of shame

羞辱 **[hsīu-jŭ]**: to insult, to be humbled; shame, disgrace, humiliation; ashamed

— 7 Strokes —

群

[3] 群山 **[ch'ǘn-shān]**: Kunsan (Korea)

[9] 群英會 **[ch'ǘn-yīng-hùi]**: heroes' meeting, pep rally (a meeting held to encourage others to emulate model workers)

群英會診 **[ch'ǘn-yīng-hùi chĕn]**: investigation by a heroes' meeting (i.e., study of a problem not by a single technician but by a group of technicians or specialists)

[10] 群馬 **[ch'ǘn-mă]**: Gumma (Japan)

群島 **[ch'ǘn-tăo]**: islands, island group, archipelago

[12] 群衆 **[ch'ǘn-chùng]**: the masses, the masses of people, rank and file, crowd

群衆積極性 **[ch'ǘn-chùng chī-chí-hsìng]**: mass initiative

群衆創造力 **[ch'ǘn-chùng ch'uàng-tsào-lì]**: creative energies of the masses

群衆呼聲 **[ch'ǘn-chùng hū-shēng]**: voice of the masses

群衆觀點 **[ch'ǘn-chùng kuān-tiĕn]**: mass viewpoint (one of the 四大觀點, q.v.)

群衆工作 **[ch'ǘn-chùng kūng-tsò]**: mass work

群衆路綫 **[ch'ǘn-chùng lù-hsièn]**: mass line (Chinese Communist Party policies, which in theory are formulated on the opinions of the great majority of the people, and which are made known to the masses through propaganda and carried out by them through persuasion)

群衆大會 **[ch'ǘn-chùng tà-hùi]**: rally, mass rally, mass meeting

群衆鬥爭 **[ch'ǘn-chùng tòu-chēng]**: mass struggle

群衆團體 **[ch'ǘn-chùng t'uán-t'ĭ]**: mass organization

群衆運動 **[ch'ǘn-chùng yǜn-tùng]**: mass movement

義

[8] 義和團 **[ì-hó t'uán]**: the Boxers (i.e., of Boxer uprising of 1900)

[9] 義勇兵 **[ì-yŭng pīng]**: a volunteer

義勇隊 **[ì-yŭng tùi]**: volunteers

[11] 義務 **[ì-wù]**: obligation, duty, responsibility, commitment

義務勞動 **[ì-wù láo-tùng]**: voluntary labor (compulsory labor without compensation)

義務兵役制 **[ì-wù pīng-ì chìh]**: conscription system

— RADICAL 羽 124 —

— 5 Strokes —

習

14 習慣 **[hsí-kuàn]**: habit, custom

習慣於 **[hsí-kuàn yǘ]**: to be accustomed to, to be used to, to be in the habit of

— 12 Strokes —

翹

7 翹尾巴 **[ch'iáo wĕi-pā]**: to wag one's tail in the air, to be cocky (over success, etc.)

翻

4 翻天覆地 **[fān-t'iēn fù-tì]**: to overturn the sky and the earth; to turn everything upside down; world-shaking, cataclysmic, drastic

6 翻江倒海 **[fān-chiāng tăo-hăi]**: to overturn the river and drain out the sea; to bring everything into a state of confusion; world-shaking

7 翻身 **[fān-shēn]**: to turn the body over, to turn the tables on, to change the social order, to shake off the feudal yoke; a reversal of position (from inferiority to superiority)

翻身戶 **[fān-shēn hù]**: a family that has turned the tables, a liberated family (i.e., a family that was formerly oppressed but whose condition has changed completely as a result of the new order)

翻身農民 **[fān-shēn núng-mín]**: liberated peasants, peasants who have come into their own, peasants who have overthrown the rule of the landlords

8 翻供 **[fān-kùng]**: to withdraw testimony, to retract testimony

翻版 **[fān-păn]**: to reprint, to reproduce, to pirate; reprint, reproduction

9 翻修 **[fān-hsīu]**: to rebuild

10 翻案 **[fān-àn]**: to reopen a case, to reverse a sentence, to reverse an order, to reverse a decision

11 翻悔 **[fān-hŭi]**: to revoke or retract a statement made previously

12 翻然悔悟 **[fān-ján hŭi-wù]**: to show a change by making a clean break with the past

13 翻新 **[fān-hsīn]**: to renovate

17 翻臉不認人 **[fān-liĕn pú-jèn jén]**: not to recognize someone out of anger, to deny a friend, to turn against a friend

20 翻譯 **[fān-ì]**: to translate, to interpret; translation, interpretation

— 14 Strokes —

8 耀武揚威 **[yào-wŭ yáng-wēi]**: to bluff and bluster, to make a show of one's strength, to brandish one's sword; saber-rattling

— RADICAL 老 125 —

1 老一輩 **[lăo-í-pèi]**: a generation older or more senior

老一套 **[lăo-í-t'ào]**: the same old thing, conventionalism

2 老人家 **[lăo-jén-chiā]**: 1. an aged person (a traditional title of respect for the aged); 2. the grand old man (i.e., Mao Tse-tung; a title that came into use after 1966)

3 老三篇 **[lăo sān-p'iēn]**: the "three old works," the "old three articles" (three short works from the writings of Mao: 1. Serve the People [September 1944]; 2. In Memory of Bethune [December 1939]; and 3. How Yü Kung Removed the Mountains or The Simple Peasant Who Moved the Mountain [June 1945])

老大哥 **[lăo-tà-kō]**: big brother (a term formerly used to designate the U.S.S.R.)

老大難問題 **[lăo-tà-nán wèn-t'í]**: old, great, and difficult problems (i.e., important problems that have remained unsolved for a long time)

4 老五篇 **[lăo wŭ-p'iēn]**: the "old five articles" (this consists of the "old three articles" (老三篇 , q.v.) together with two additional articles also by Mao: On the Recitification of Erroneous Thought in the Party, and To Oppose Liberalism; these were chosen for the Red Guards to read after the "Combat Selfishness and Repudiate Revisionism" campaign was launched in October 1967)

6 老奸巨猾 **[lăo-chiēn chǜ-huá]**: hardened evildoer, an old hand at trickery and deception

老老實實 **[lăo-lăo shíh-shíh]**: unpretentious, unassuming, honest, frank, unostentatious, with sincerity and candor, plain

老百姓 **[lăo-păi-hsìng]**: the common people, the rank and file, the man in the street

7 老作家 **[lăo-tsò-chiā]**: veteran writer

8 老和尚 **[lăo-hó-shàng]**: old monk (a term used to describe high-ranking Communist Party members)

老板 **[lăo-păn]**: boss, owner, manager, master

11 老將 **[lăo-chiàng]**: veteran general

老部下 **[lăo pù-hsià]**: former subordinate

老造反 **[lăo tsào-făn]**: the old rebels (refers to the rowdy youngsters of 1966 during the Cultural Revolution)

12 老街 **[lăo-chiēh]**: Laokay (Vietnam)

老解放地區 **[lăo chiĕh-fàng tì-ch'ü]**: old liberated area

老開 **[lăo-k'āi]**: Laokay (Vietnam)

老牌的賣國賊 **[lăo-p'ái te mài-kuó-tséi]**: a traitor by profession

13 老資格的 **[lăo-tzū-kó te]**: veteran, senior, old hand

15 老調 **[lăo-tiào]**: shopworn tune, hackneyed tune, the same old song

16 老撾 **[lăo-chuā]**: Laos

老撾王國 **[lăo-chuā wáng-kuó]**: Kingdom of Laos

考

5 考古學 **[k'ăo-kŭ-hsüéh]**: archeology; archeological

考古學者 **[k'ăo-kŭ-hsüéh-chĕ]**: archaeologist

考古研究所 **[k'ăo-kŭ yén-chìu-sŏ]**: Archaelogy Institute

10 考茨基 **[k'ăo-tz'ú-chī]**: Kautsky, Karl (German socialist writer, 1854–1938)

13 考試院 **[k'ăo-shìh yüàn]**: Examination Yüan

14 考察 **[k'ăo-ch'á]**: to inspect, to investigate, to search into; investigation, inspection, judicial examination

考察團 **[k'ăo-ch'á t'uán]**: investigating commission, investigation group, inspection group, observation group

15 考慮 **[k'ăo-lǜ]**: to consider thoughtfully, to think over, to deliberate; deliberation

考慮周到的 **[k'ăo-lǜ chōu-tào te]**: well thought out, well deliberated

考慮不周的 **[k'ăo-lǜ pù-chōu te]**: not well thought out, inadequately deliberated

考慮到 **[k'ăo-lǜ tào]**: to deliberate, to bring into careful consideration

考選部 **[k'ăo-hsüăn pù]**: Ministry of Examinations

23 考驗 **[k'ăo-yèn]**: to examine, to test; examination, test

— RADICAL 而 126 —

5 而且 **[érh-ch'iĕh]**: furthermore, moreover, besides, but also

— 2 Strokes —

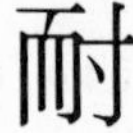

4 耐心 **[nài-hsīn]**: patience, forbearance, endurance

耐心說服教育 **[nài-hsīn shuō-fú chiào-yǜ]**: patient persuasion and education

耐火材料 **[nài-huŏ ts'ái-liào]**: heat-resistant material, refractory material, firebrick

耐水作物 **[nài-shŭi tsò-wù]**: crop resistant to water rot

5 耐用品 **[nài-yùng p'ĭn]**: durable goods, consumer durables

— 3 Strokes —

耍 **[shuă]**: to play, to loaf, to gamble, to trifle

4 耍手腕 **[shuă shŏu-wàn]**: to play politics, to maneuver, to play tricks, to resort to stratagems, to be wily

8 耍花招 **[shuă huā-chāo]**: to play tricks

耍花腔 **[shuă huā-ch'iāng]**: guileful

9 耍威風 **[shuă wēi-fēng]**: to show off authority

12 耍無賴 **[shuă wú-lài]**: to act deliberately dishonestly

— RADICAL 耒 127 —

— 4 Strokes —

耕

耕 **[kēng]**: to cultivate, to plow; cultivation, plowing

5 耕田 **[kēng-t'ién]**: to plow the fields, to plow, to till

耕田隊 **[kēng-t'ién tùi]**: tilling squad (a term used in the early Communist controlled areas in Hunan and Kiangsi Provinces)

6 耕地 **[kēng-tì]**: to plow; land under cultivation

耕地面積 **[kēng-tì mièn-chī]**: cultivated acreage, crop area, cultivated area, area under cultivation

7 耕作時間 **[kēng-tsò shíh-chiēn]**: tillage time

耕作園田化 **[kēng-tsò yüán-t'ién-huà]**: intensive garden style cultivation of farm lands, meticulous garden-like farming

9 耕者有其田 **[kēng-chĕ yŭ ch'í t'ién]**: land to the tillers

10 耕畜 **[kēng-ch'ù]**: plow animal

11 耕種 **[kēng-chùng]**: to engage in agriculture, to engage in farming, to farm, to cultivate and plant

耗

14 耗盡 **[hào-chìn]**: to exhaust, to drain, to wear out

耙

耙 **[p'á]**: rake, harrow

6 耙地 **[p'á-tì]**: to harrow

— RADICAL 耳 128 —

耳

5 耳生 **[ĕrh-shēng]**: strange to the ear

15 耳熟 **[ĕrh-shóu]**: familiar to the ear

23 耳聾 **[ĕrh-lúng]**: deaf

— 3 Strokes —

耶

13 耶路撒冷 **[yēh-lù-sā-lĕng]**: Jerusalem (Israel)

16 耶蘇基督 **[yēh-sū chī-tū]**: Jesus Christ

耶蘇誕辰 **[yēh-sū tàn-ch'én]**: Christmas

— 7 Strokes —

聘

15 聘請 **[p'ìn-ch'ĭng]**: to engage, to call in to appoint

聖

2 聖人 **[shèng-jén]**: saint, sage

4 聖公會 **[shèng-kūng hùi]**: Anglican Church (England); Episcopal Church (U.S.A.)

6 聖伊薩貝爾 **[shèng ī-sà-pèi-ĕrh]**: Santa Isabel (Spanish Guinea)

聖地 **[shèng-tì]**: holy land, place of pilgrimage

聖地亞哥 **[shèng-tì-yà-kō]**: Santiago (Chile)

聖多美 **[shèng tō-mĕi]**: São Tomé (São Tomé and Principe Islands)

聖多美島及普林西比島 **[shèng tō-mĕi tăo chí p'ŭ-lín-hsī-pĭ tăo]**: São Tomé and Principe Islands

[9]聖胡安 **[shèng hú-ān]**: San Juan (Puerto Rico)

聖約翰 **[shèng yüēh-hàn]**: Saint John

聖約瑟 **[shèng yüēh-sè]**: San Jose (Costa Rica)

[10]聖馬力諾 **[shèng mă-lì-nò]**: San Marino

聖馬力諾共和國 **[shèng mă-lì-nò kùng-hó-kuó]**: Republic of San Marino

[13]聖路易 **[shèng-lù-ì]**: Saint Louis

聖路易郵電報 **[shèng-lù-ì yóu-tièn-pào]**: Saint Louis Post Dispatch

[14]聖赫勒拿 **[shèng hò-lè-ná]**: Saint Helena

聖誕節 **[shèng-tàn-chiéh]**: Christmas

[17]聖薩爾瓦多 **[shèng sà-ĕrh-wă-tō]**: San Salvador (El Salvador)

[19]聖羅稜斯 **[shèng ló-léng-ssū]**: Saint Lawrence

— 8 Strokes —

聚

[8]聚居 **[chǜ-chū]**: to live together, to live in compact communities

[12]聚集 **[chǜ-chí]**: to gather, to collect, to flock, to flock together, to assemble, to congregate

[13]聚會 **[chǜ-hùi]**: to assemble, to get together; meeting, gathering

[16]聚積 **[chǜ-chī]**: to amass, to gather, to collect, to accumulate, to pile up

聞

[2]聞人 **[wèn-jén]**: public figures, famous personages, outstanding personalities, people in the news

[6]聞名 **[wén-míng]**: famed, famous, celebrated, well known, renowned

[9]聞香隊 **[wén-hsiāng tùi]**: "sniffing squad," snooping team, block inspection team

— 10 Strokes —

聯

[6]聯合 **[lién-hó]**: to unite, to link up, to join, to associate; joint, combined, united

聯合診所 **[lién-hó chĕn-sŏ]**: clinic

聯合政府 **[lién-hó chèng-fŭ]**: coalition government

聯合會 **[lién-hó-hùi]**: association, federation, joint session

聯合日報 **[lién-hó jìh-pào]**: 1. The United Journal (U.S. Chinese language newspaper; 2. Lien Ho Jih Pao (Taiwan daily newspaper)

聯合國 **[lién-hó kuó]**: United Nations

聯合國安全理事會 **[lién-hó-kuó ān-ch'üán lĭ-shìh-hùi]**: United Nations Security Council

聯合國教育科學文化組織 **[lién-hó-kuó chiào-yǜ k'ō-hsüéh wén-huà tsŭ-chīh]**: United Nations Educational, Scientific, and Cultural Organization (UNESCO)

聯合國緊急軍 **[lién-hó-kuó chĭn-chí chūn]**: United Nations Emergency Force

聯合國兒童基金會 **[lién-hó-kuó érh-t'úng chī-chīn-hùi]**: United Nations Children's Fund

聯合國協會世界聯合會 **[lién-hó-kuó hsiéh-hùi shìh-chièh lién-hó-hùi]**: World Federation of the United Nations Associations (WFUNA)

聯合國憲章 **[lién-hó-kuó hsièn-chāng]**: United Nations Charter

聯合國行政法庭 **[lién-hó-kuó hsíng-chèng fă-t'īng]**: United Nations Administrative Tribunal

聯合國國際兒童緊急救濟基金 **[lién-hó-kuó kuó-chì érh-t'úng chĭn-chí chìu-chì chī-chīn]**: United Nations International Children's Emergency Fund (UNICEF)

聯合國糧食暨農業組織 **[lién-hó-kuó liáng-shíh chì núng-yèh tsŭ-chīh]**: United Nations Food and Agricultural Organization (FAO)

聯合國大會 **[lién-hó-kuó tà-hùi]**: United Nations General Assembly

聯合邦 **[lién-hó-pāng]**: confederation

聯合兵種 **[lién-hó pīng-chŭng]**: combined arms

聯合社 **[lién-hó shè]**: Associated Press (AP)

聯合收割機 **[lién-hó shōu-kō-chī]**: combine harvester

聯共 **[lién-kùng]**: Communist Party of the Soviet Union

聯共黨史 **[lién-kùng tăng-shĭh]**: The History of the Communist Party of the Soviet Union (name of book)

7 聯系 **[lién-hsì]**: to link, to combine with, to have relations with; contact, bond, connection, link

聯系群衆 **[lién-hsì ch'ǘn-chùng]**: to maintain close connections with the masses, to keep close to the masses, to have contact with the masses

聯邦 **[lién-pāng]**: federation, federal union, commonwealth, confederation; federal, confederated

聯邦執行委員會 **[lién-pāng chíh-hsìng wĕi-yüán-hùi]**: Federal Executive Council

聯邦下議院 **[lién-pāng hsià-ì-yüàn]**: Bundestag (West Germany)

聯邦憲法法院 **[lién-pāng hsièn-fă fă-yüàn]**: Federal Constitutional Court

聯邦議會 **[lién-pāng ì-hùi]**: federal parliament; Bundestag (West Germany)

聯邦議院 **[lién-pāng ì-yüàn]**: Bundestag (West Germany)

聯邦參議院 **[lién-pāng ts'ān-ì-yüàn]**: Bundesrat (West Germany)

聯邦總理 **[lién-pāng tsŭng-lĭ]**: Federal Chancellor (West Germany)

聯邦總統 **[lién-pāng tsŭng-t'ŭng]**: Federal President; Bundespräsident (West Germany)

聯邦院 **[lién-pāng yüàn]**: Council of the States (Rajya Sabba) (India)

9 聯席會議 **[lién-hsí hùi-ì]**: joint conference

12 聯絡 **[lién-lò]**: to affiliate, to connect, to maintain contact; liaison, contact

聯盟 **[lién-méng]**: league, union, alliance

聯越 **[lién-yüèh]**: Lienviet (Vietnamese League)

13 聯想 **[lién-hsiăng]**: association of ideas

聯會 **[lién-hùi]**: club, association

聯運 **[lién-yǜn]**: through transport

17 聯賽 **[lién-sài]**: league tournament, league match

22 聯歡 **[lién-huān]**: gathering, party, get-together

聯歡節 **[lién-huān chiéh]**: festival

— 11 Strokes —

聲

6 聲名狼藉 **[shēng-míng láng-chièh]**: discredited, unsavory, notorious, to fall into discredit

7 聲言 **[shēng-yén]**: to proclaim, to say, to express something

8 聲明 **[shēng-míng]**: to state, to declare; statement, declaration, pronouncement, manifesto

11 聲望 **[shēng-wàng]**: fame, reputation, prestige, popularity

聳

2 聳人聽聞 **[sŭng-jén t'īng-wén]**: to cause a sensation, to electrify; sensational, scandalous

— 12 Strokes —

職

3 職工 **[chíh-kūng]**: staff and workers

職工代表大會 **[chíh-kūng tài-piăo tà-hùi]**: workers' congress

職工運動 **[chíh-kūng yǜn-tùng]**: trade union movement

7 職位 **[chíh-wèi]**: official post, position title

10 職員 **[chíh-yüán]**: clerk, functionary, staff, staff member, officer, government worker

13 職業 **[chíh-yèh]**: profession, occupation, trade, vocation, work, job; professional, occupational, vocational

職業學校 **[chíh-yèh hsüéh-hsiào]**: vocational school, technical school

職業病 **[chíh-yèh pìng]**: occupational disease

22 職權 **[chíh-ch'üán]**: authority, authority of office, functions and powers

職權範圍 **[chíh-ch'üán fàn-wéi]**: sphere of one's functions and powers, sphere of authority, terms of reference

— 16 Strokes —

聾

聾 **[lúng]**: deaf

聽

4 聽天命 **[t'ìng t'iēn-mìng]**: to obey the will of Heaven, to submit to fate

聽天由命 **[t'ìng-t'iēn yú-mìng]**: to abide by the will of Heaven, to meet one's fate with resignation

6 聽任 **[t'ìng-jèn]**: to resign oneself to, to allow, to suffer

8 聽其使用 **[t'ìng ch'í shĭh-yùng]**: to make service available to someone, to serve someone at his pleasure

聽其自然的政策 **[t'ìng ch'í tzù-ján te chèng-ts'è]**: laissez-faire policy, drift policy

聽取 **[t'īng-ch'ŭ]**: to give audience to, to hear, to catch

聽取詳細匯報 **[t'īng-ch'ŭ hsiáng-hsì hùi-pào]**: to undergo a detailed briefing

聽取意見 **[t'īng-ch'ŭ ì-chièn]**: to listen to opinions, to conduct hearings on a question

11 聽衆 **[t'īng-chùng]**: audience

聽從 **[t'ìng-ts'úng]**: to listen to, to be obedient to, to obey

— RADICAL 聿 129 —

— 7 Strokes —

肆

12 肆無忌憚 **[ssù wú chì-tàn]**: absolutely unscrupulous, audacious, unprincipled, reckless and unbridled

13 肆意 **[ssù-ì]**: wantonly, recklessly, unscrupulously

肆意侮謾 **[ssù-ì wŭ-màn]**: to resort to unbridled insults and vilification; unscrupulously insulting

— 8 Strokes —

肅

4 肅反 **[sù-făn]**: to clear out counterrevolutionaries; suppression of counterrevolutionaries (abbreviation of 肅清反革命)

10 肅特 **[sù-t'è]**: to clean out (Nationalist) spies

11 肅淸 **[sù-ch'īng]**: to wipe out, to weed out, to root out, to purge, to liquidate, to eliminate, to eradicate

肅淸反革命 **[sù-ch'īng făn-kó-mìng]**: to clear out counterrevolutionaries

肅淸反動勢力 **[sù-ch'īng făn-tùng shìh-lì]**: to clean up reactionary forces

— RADICAL 肉月 130 —

7 肉孜節 **[jòu-tzū-chiéh]**: Bairam (festivals held after Ramadan)

8 肉乳工業 **[jòu-jŭ kūng-yèh]**: meat and dairy industry

11 肉眼 **[jòu-yĕn]**: naked eye

19 肉類 **[jòu-lèi]**: meats

— 3 Strokes —

12 肖象畫 **[hsiào-hsiàng-huà]**: portrait

— 4 Strokes —

6 肩并肩 **[chiēn pìng chiēn]**: shoulder to shoulder; side by side

9 肩負重任 **[chiēn-fù chùng-jèn]**: to shoulder great responsibilities, to bear heavy burdens

肥

肥 **[féi]**: 1. fat, fleshy, fertile, rich; 2. "fertilizer" (one of the eight characters of the 八字憲法, q.v.)

3 肥己 **[féi-chĭ]**: to enrich oneself; egotistical, self-seeking

5 肥田粉 **[féi-t'ién fĕn]**: powdered fertilizer

7 肥沃 **[féi-wò]**: fruitful, fertile

10 肥料 **[féi-liào]**: fertilizer, manure

肯

5 肯尼迪 **[k'ĕn-ní-tí]**: Kennedy, John F.

肯尼亞 **[k'ĕn-ní-yà]**: Kenya

8 肯定 **[k'ĕn-tìng]**: to affirm, to ascertain, to assert; affirmation; assured, certain, affirma-

tive; with certainty, definitely, unquestionably

肯定典型 **[k'ĕn-tìng tiĕn-hsíng]**: affirmative type

股

5 股本 **[kŭ-pĕn]**: share-capital

6 股份 **[kŭ-fèn]**: stock, share

8 股長 **[kŭ-chăng]**: head of a department, subdivision chief

股東 **[kŭ-tūng]**: shareholder, stockholder

10 股息 **[kŭ-hsī]**: dividend

股員 **[kŭ-yüán]**: member of a department, member of a subdivision

11 股票 **[kŭ-p'iào]**: stock, share, share-certificate

股票交易所 **[kŭ-p'iào chiāo-ì-sŏ]**: stock exchange

股票市場 **[kŭ-p'iào shìh-ch'ăng]**: stock market

育

14 育種 **[yù-chŭng]**: seed cultivation

— 5 Strokes —

胡

6 胡同 **[hú-t'ùng]**: alley, lane, side street

7 胡志明 **[hú chìh míng]**: Ho Chi Minh (North Vietnamese political figure)

胡佛 **[hú-fó]**: Hoover, Herbert (American political figure and president)

胡克 **[hú-k'ò]**: Huk

胡克巴拉哈 **[hú-k'ò-pā-lā-hā]**: Hukbalahap

9 胡思亂想 **[hú-ssū luàn-hsiăng]**: to engage in wild flights of fancy

11 胡笙 **[hú-shēng]**: Hussein Ibn Talal (King of Jordan)

13 胡搞 **[hú-kăo]**: to act irresponsibly; recklessness, rashness, imprudence, indiscretion, violence

胡亂 **[hú-luàn]**: confused, disorderly

14 胡鬧 **[hú-nào]**: to do mischief, to cause trouble; reckless quarreling, reckless action

胡說 **[hú-shuō]**: to talk nonsense; to babble; babble, nonsensical talk

23 胡攪 **[hú-chiăo]**: to disturb, to create a disturbance

背

6 背地裡 **[pèi-tì-lĭ]**: underhandedly, clandestinely

9 背信 **[pèi-hsìn]**: to go back on one's word, to break faith; breach of good faith

背信棄義 **[pèi-hsìn ch'ì-ì]**: perfidious, treacherous, dishonest, perfidious and unscrupulous

背後 **[pèi-hòu]**: behind the scenes, in the background, behind the back

背叛 **[pèi-pàn]**: to revolt, to desert, to betray; betrayal

背約 **[pèi-yüēh]**: to violate a contract, to break one's word, to discard treaty obligations

10 背時 **[pèi-shíh]**: unlucky, adverse times

背書 **[pèi-shū]**: to learn by heart, to repeat from memory

11 背棄 **[pèi-ch'ì]**: to go back on, to back out of, to turn one's back on, to abandon

12 背景 **[pèi-chĭng]**: background, backdrop

背道而馳 **[pèi-tào érh ch'íh]**: to run counter to, to be diametrically opposed to, to be foreign to

17 背簍精神 **[pēi-lǒu chīng-shén]**: the basket-on-the-back spirit (the public spirit exemplified by the 背簍商店, q.v.)

背簍商店 **[pēi-lǒu shāng-tièn]**: "basket-on-the-back" stores (refers to salesmen and salesgirls of supply and marketing cooperatives who carry goods in baskets on their backs to sell to villages in remote areas)

18 背謬 **[pèi-mìu]**: falsehood, error

— 6 Strokes —

脅

9 脅迫 **[hsiéh-p'ò]**: to coerce, to compel, to force, to intimidate someone into doing something; intimidation, coercion

11 脅從不問 **[hsiéh-ts'úng pú-wèn]**: not to inquire into the misdeeds of those who were forced to join; not to punish those who were intimidated into joining

胸

4 胸中無數 **[hsiūng-chūng wú shù]**: to have no "figures" in one's head

胸中有數 **[hsiūng-chūng yǔ shù]**: to have a head for "figures"

19 胸襟開闊 **[hsiūng-chīn k'āi-k'uò]**: broad-minded, liberal in outlook

胸懷狹窄 **[hsiūng-huái hsiá-chǎi]**: narrow-mindedness; narrow-minded

能

2 能力 **[néng-lì]**: power, energy, capacity, capability, ability, competence

4 能手 **[néng-shǒu]**: expert, master, master hand, old hand

11 能夠 **[néng-kòu]**: can, to be able to, to be capable of, to be in a position to

脆

10 脆弱的 **[ts'ùi-jò te]**: fragile, frail, weak, vulnerable

— 7 Strokes —

脚

4 脚手架子 **[chiǎo-shǒu chià-tzu]**: scaffolding, building scaffold

5 脚本 **[chiǎo-pěn]**: the libretto of a drama, text

6 脚行 **[chiǎo-háng]**: coolie, porter; Coolie Association

15 脚踏水車 **[chiǎo-t'à shǔi-ch'ē]**: irrigation treadmill

脚踏兩隻船 **[chiǎo-t'à liǎng-chīh ch'uán]**: to straddle two boats, to sit on the fence, to be undecided

脚踏實地 **[chiǎo-t'à shíh-tì]**: to stand on firm ground, to get a solid footing

16 脚錢 **[chiǎo-ch'ién]**: porterage, bearer charge, carrier charge, coolie hire

20 脚鐐 **[chiǎo-liào]**: fetters, shackles, foot-irons

脫

5 脫去 **[t'ō-ch'ù]**: to take off, to remove

9 脫胎換骨 **[t'ō-t'āi huàn-kǔ]**: to get rid of one's mortal frame, to make a radical reformation (used at one time to refer to the reforms that must be made by the intellectuals and bourgeoisie of the old society)

15 脫節 **[t'ō-chiéh]**: to dislocate a joint; lack of coordination, a dislocated joint, a gap, out of gear

脫銷 **[t'ō-hsiāo]**: to run out of supplies; short of supplies, deficient supplies; sold out, unavailable on the market, out of stock

18 脫離 **[t'ō-lí]**: to break away from, to separate from, to divorce from, to get away from, to get out of, to remove from, to depart from, to stay apart from, to lose touch with

脫離政治 **[t'ō-lí chèng-chìh]**: to stand aloof from politics

脫離接觸 **[t'ō-lí chiēh-ch'ù]**: disengagement

脫離群衆 **[t'ō-lí ch'ǘn-chùng]**: to divorce oneself from the masses, to lose touch with the masses, to alienate oneself from the masses, to stay apart from the masses

脫離人民 **[t'ō-lí jén-mín]**: to divorce oneself from the people

脫離生產 **[t'ō-lí shēng-ch'ǎn]**: to be divorced from production, to be diverted from production

脫離實際 **[t'ō-lí shíh-chì]**: to stay apart from practice, to be removed from reality, to be divorced from the realities of life

脫離危險 **[t'ō-lí wéi-hsiěn]**: to extricate oneself from danger, to escape from danger

20 脫黨 **[t'ō-tǎng]**: to withdraw from a party

— 8 Strokes —

腐

4 腐化 **[fǔ-huà]**: to corrupt, to demoralize; corruption, demoralization, decadence; corrupt, demoralized, decadent

腐化份子 **[fǔ-huà fèn-tzu]**: corrupt element, one who tries to injure the cause of a society

7 腐朽 **[fǔ-hsǐu]**: decadent, moribund, rotten, spoiled, corrupted

10 腐敗 **[fǔ-pài]**: to rot, to spoil; rotten, spoiled, debased, dissolute, corrupt

15 腐蝕 **[fǔ-shíh]**: to corrode, to corrupt; erosion, corrosion, etching

21 腐爛 **[fǔ-làn]**: to rot, to decompose, to decay; decay; decayed

腐爛透頂 **[fǔ-làn t'òu-tǐng]**: rotten to the core

— 9 Strokes —

腫

15 腫瘤研究所 **[chǔng-líu yén-chìu-sŏ]**: Oncology Institute (Chinese Academy of Medical Sciences)

腹

9 腹背受敵 **[fù-pèi shòu-tí]**: to be attacked from front and rear, to be under attack from all sides

腦

2 腦力 **[nǎo-lì]**: mental vigor, mental energy; mental

腦力勞動 **[nǎo-lì láo-tùng]**: mental labor, brain work

— 11 Strokes —

膠 **[chiāo]**: Kiaochow (abbreviation for 膠州)

4 膠水 **[chiāo-shǔi]**: liquid glue

5 膠皮 **[chiāo-p'í]**: rubber, india rubber

6 膠合板 **[chiāo-hó pǎn]**: plywood

9 膠柱鼓瑟 **[chiāo-chù kǔ-sè]**: to glue the pegs and then try to play the lute; perverse and stupid, to be unable to act suitably in accordance with the situation

10 膠海關 **[chiāo hǎi-kuān]**: The Chintao Custom House

11 膠着狀態 **[chiāo-chó chuàng-t'ài]**: to be stuck, to be immobilized; condition of being stuck, condition of being immobilized

膠捲 **[chiāo-chüăn]**: film, roll of film

16 膠鞋 **[chiāo-hsiéh]**: sneakers, rubber shoes

膚

6 膚色歧視 **[fū-sè ch'í-shìh]**: racial discrimination

8 膚泛 **[fū-fàn]**: superficial

11 膚淺 **[fū-ch'iĕn]**: skin-deep, shallow, superficial

— 12 Strokes —

膨

14 彭脹 **[p'éng-chàng]**: expansion, rise, inflation, distension

— 13 Strokes —

膽

2 膽力 **[tăn-lì]**: courage, bravery, boldness

11 膽敢 **[tăn-kăn]**: to dare, to have the audacity

12 膽寒 **[tăn-hán]**: to be frightened, afraid or fearful

膽量 **[tăn-liàng]**: courage, daring, boldness

臃

13 臃腫 **[yūng-chŭng]**: swollen, overexpanded, overgrown, bloated, inflated, overstaffed, unwieldy

— RADICAL 臣 131 —

— 11 Strokes —

臨

7 臨別 **[lín-piéh]**: on the point of departure, on the eve of one's departure, just before one's departure

8 臨到 **[lín-tào]**: to approach, to come to, to fall upon, to descend upon

10 臨時 **[lín-shíh]**: provisional, temporary, interim, impromptu, ad hoc

臨時工人 **[lín-shíh kūng-jén]**: casual laborer, temporary worker

臨時代辦 **[lín-shíh tài-pàn]**: chargé d'affaires ad interim, chargé d'affaires ad hoc

臨時應付辦法 **[lín-shíh yìng-fù pàn-fă]**: improvisation; impromptu measures for coping with

— RADICAL 自 132 —

2 自力更生 **[tzù-lì kèng-shēng]**: to rely on one's own efforts to renew one's life, to lead a new life by one's own efforts; to regenerate through one's own efforts; self-reliance (a phrase in use after the Russian pullout of 1960)

3 自下而上 **[tzù hsià érh shàng]**: from bottom to top

自上而下 **[tzù shàng érh hsià]**: from top to bottom

5 自主 **[tzù-chŭ]**: independent

自以爲是 **[tzù ĭ-wéi shìh]**: to consider oneself always in the right, to regard oneself as infallible, to be cocksure

自以爲得計 **[tzù ǐ-wéi té-chì]**: to be pleased with one's own tricks, to think oneself to be clever

自白 **[tzù-pái]**: a personal statement, confession, self-confession

自由 **[tzù-yú]**: freedom, liberty; free, liberal

自由職業 **[tzù-yú chíh-yèh]**: liberal profession

自由競爭 **[tzù-yú chìng-chēng]**: free competition

自由主義 **[tzù-yú chŭ-ì]**: liberalism, freedom, the principle of liberty

自由處理 **[tzù-yú ch'ŭ-lĭ]**: to have a free hand, to be given carte blanche

自由中國 **[tzù-yú chūng-kuó]**: Free China (Taiwan periodical)

自由放任 **[tzù-yú fàng-jèn]**: unrestrained self-indulgence, laissez-faire

自由化 **[tzù-yú-huà]**: to liberalize; liberalization

自由意志 **[tzù-yú ì-chìh]**: free will

自由民主黨 **[tzù-yú mín-chŭ-tăng]**: Liberal Democratic Party (Japan)

自由鳴放 **[tzù-yú míng-fàng]**: to speak out freely, to voice one's views without restraint

自由、平等博愛 **[tzù-yú, p'íng-tĕng, pó-ài]**: "liberty," "equality," "fraternity" (condemned during the Cultural Revolution as a bourgeois slogan and concept)

自由散漫 **[tzù-yú sàn-màn]**: free and aimless, easygoing and desultory

自由詩 **[tzù-yú shīh]**: free verse

自由談 **[tzù-yú t'án]**: Rambler (Taiwan weekly periodical)

自由黨 **[tzù-yú tăng]**: Liberal Party (Canada); National Liberal Party (Great Britain)

自由裁決 **[tzù-yú ts'ái-chüéh]**: to decide as one sees fit, at one's discretion

自由通商口岸 **[tzù-yú t'ūng-shāng k'ŏu-àn]**: an open free port

自由資本 **[tzù-yú tzū-pĕn]**: free capital, non-monopoly capital

6 自行消滅 **[tzù-hsíng hsiāo-mièh]**: self-annihilation

自在的階級 **[tzù-tsài te chiēh-chí]**: a class in itself

自刎 **[tzù-wĕn]**: to cut one's throat, to commit suicide; suicide

7 自助 **[tzù-chù]**: to help oneself; self-help, self-dependence

自吹 **[tzù-ch'ūi]**: to brag about oneself, to blow one's own horn

自決 **[tzù-chüéh]**: self-determination

自告奮勇 **[tzù-kào fèn-yŭng]**: to volunteer one's services for, to offer to take the responsibility upon oneself

自私 **[tzù-ssū]**: selfishness, egotism; selfish, self-seeking, egotistic

自投羅網 **[tzù-t'óu ló-wăng]**: to fall into a trap through one's own fault

自作主張 **[tzù-tsò chŭ-chāng]**: to have one's own way, to decide all by oneself, to follow one's own bent

自走絕路 **[tzù-tsŏu chüéh-lù]**: to lead oneself to a dead end

自我 **[tzù-wŏ]**: ego, self, subjective ego; self-, subjective

自我教育 **[tzù-wŏ chiào-yù]**: self-education

自我解嘲 **[tzù-wŏ chiĕh-ch'áo]**: to console oneself with soothing remarks, to pat oneself on the back because one's feelings have been hurt

自我改造 **[tzù-wŏ kăi-tsào]**: self-remolding, remolding of one's ideology

自我檢討 **[tzù-wŏ chiĕn-t'ăo]**: self-examination

自我革命 **[tzù-wŏ kó-mìng]**: self-revolution

(a term from the Cultural Revolution)

自我批評 **[tzù-wǒ p'ī-p'íng]**: self-criticism

自我陶醉 **[tzù-wǒ t'áo-tsùi]**: self-glorification; to be intoxicated with oneself

8 自知 **[tzù-chīh]**: to know oneself; self-knowledge; self-conscious

自制 **[tzù-chìh]**: to restrain oneself, to control oneself; self-restraint, self-control

自治 **[tzù-chìh]**: self-government, autonomy, self-rule, autonomous rule; autonomous

自治旗 **[tzù-chìh ch'í]**: autonomous banner (hsien level)

自治州 **[tzù-chìh chōu]**: autonomous chou

自治區 **[tzù-chìh ch'ū]**: autonomous region (provincial level); autonomous area (hsien level, Yunnan only)

自治縣 **[tzù-chìh hsièn]**: autonomous hsien

自治的權限 **[tzù-chìh te ch'üán-hsièn]**: autonomous jurisdiction

自治條例 **[tzù-chìh t'iáo-lì]**: statute governing the exercise of autonomy

自居 **[tzù-chū]**: to claim oneself to be, to consider oneself to be

自取滅亡 **[tzù-ch'ǚ mièh-wáng]**: to court one's own ruin, to invite one's own destruction

自命不凡 **[tzù-mìng pù-fán]**: to pride oneself on being out of the ordinary, to consider oneself above the crowd

9 自封 **[tzù-fēng]**: to appoint oneself, to give oneself a title; self-appointed

自相 **[tzù-hsiāng]**: mutual, one another

自相驚擾 **[tzù-hsiāng chīng-jǎo]**: to raise false alarms

自律 **[tzù-lǜ]**: autonomy

自卑 **[tzù-pēi]**: to debase oneself; self-debasement

自卑感 **[tzù-pēi kǎn]**: inferiority complex, feeling of inferiority

自食其果 **[tzù-shíh ch'í-kuǒ]**: to reap what one has sown, to face the consequences of one's actions

自食其力 **[tzù-shíh ch'í-lì]**: to live from one's own toil, to earn one's own living

自恃 **[tzù-shìh]**: to consider oneself right, to swagger; arrogance; arrogant

自首 **[tzù-shǒu]**: to give oneself up; voluntary surrender, voluntary confession

10 自留地 **[tzù-líu tì]**: private plot, household plot, land reserved for private use, land retained as private property

11 自產自銷 **[tzù-ch'ǎn tzù-hsiāo]**: to produce and market on one's own

自掘墳墓 **[tzù-chüéh fén-mù]**: to dig one's own grave

自殺 **[tzù-shā]**: to commit suicide; suicide, suicidal

自動 **[tzù-tùng]**: of one's own accord, of one's own free will, on one's own initiative; automatic, self-moving

自動化 **[tzù-tùng-huà]**: automation

自動化與遠距離操縱研究所 **[tzù-tùng-huà yǚ yüǎn-chǜ-lí ts'āo-tsùng yén-chìu-sǒ]**: Automation and Remote Control Institute

自動化研究所 **[tzù-tùng-huà yén-chìu-sǒ]**: Automation Institute

自動力 **[tzù-tùng-lì]**: automatic power, automatic force, automatism

自動步槍 **[tzù-tùng pù-ch'iāng]**: automatic rifle

12 自給 **[tzù-chǐ]**: self-sufficiency; self-feeding, self-supplying

自給性生產 **[tzù-chǐ-hsìng shēng-ch'ǎn]**: production for one's own consumption

自給戶 **[tzù-chǐ hù]**: self-sufficiency household, self-supporting household

自給自足的 **[tzù-chĭ tzù-tsú te]**: self-reliant, self-supporting, self-contained

自發 **[tzù-fā]**: spontaneous, automatic

自發趨向 **[tzù-fā ch'ü-hsiàng]**: spontaneous tendency

自發趨勢 **[tzù-fā ch'ü-shìh]**: spontaneous tendency (often used in reference to tendencies toward capitalism on the part of the peasants)

自發罷工 **[tzù-fā pà-kūng]**: wildcat strike

自發勢力 **[tzù-fā shìh-lì]**: spontaneous forces

自然 **[tzù-ján]**: nature, naturalness; natural, spontaneous, self-existent; certainly, of course, naturally

自然哲學 **[tzù-ján ché-hsüéh]**: natural philosophy

自然主義 **[tzù-ján chŭ-ì]**: naturalism; naturalistic

自然主義者 **[tzù-ján chŭ-ì chĕ]**: naturalist

自然法則 **[tzù-ján fă-tsé]**: natural laws, laws of nature

自然紅 **[tzù-ján húng]**: naturally red, becoming red naturally (i.e., the incorrect idea held by many young workers and peasants that, having been born into the new society, they are "naturally red" and do not have to go through ideological reform in order to become red)

自然科學 **[tzù-ján k'ō-hsüéh]**: natural science

自然神論 **[tzù-ján shén-lùn]**: deism, natural theology

自然災害 **[tzù-ján tsāi-hài]**: natural calamities

自然村 **[tzù-ján ts'ūn]**: natural village (a village inhabited by a few families and looked after as a unit of an "administrative" village 行政村, q.v.)

自然資源 **[tzù-ján tzū-yüán]**: natural resources, natural wealth

自報公議 **[tzù-pào kūng-ì]**: self-assessment and public discussion

自尊心 **[tzù-tsūn hsīn]**: self-respect, self-pride

自爲的階級 **[tzù-wéi te chiēh-chí]**: a class for itself

13 自愛 **[tzù-ài]**: self-esteem, self-respect

自解 **[tzù-chiĕh]**: to excuse oneself, to justify oneself

自傳 **[tzù-chuàn]**: autobiography

自新 **[tzù-hsīn]**: to renew oneself, to turn over a new leaf, to lead a new life; self-reform

自新之路 **[tzù-hsīn chīh lù]**: the road to self-renewal, the way for self-reform

自滿 **[tzù-măn]**: complacency, smugness, complacence; complacent, self-satisfied

自圓其說 **[tzù-yüán ch'í shuō]**: to make out a good case, to justify one's argument, to justify oneself

14 自稱 **[tzù-ch'ēng]**: to claim, to profess, or to call oneself

自豪 **[tzù-háo]**: to be proud of, to take pride in

自鳴得意 **[tzù-míng té-ì]**: to sing one's own praises

15 自趨滅亡 **[tzù-ch'ü mièh-wáng]**: to head for one's destruction, to destroy oneself

自學 **[tzù-hsüéh]**: self-study

自暴自棄 **[tzù-pào tzù-ch'ì]**: to throw oneself away; reckless, blind to one's own interests

16 自噴油井 **[tzù-p'ēn yú-chĭng]**: flush well

17 自購自銷 **[tzù-kòu tzù-hsiāo]**: to buy and market on one's own

19 自願 **[tzù-yüàn]**: voluntary, of one's own accord

自願互利的政策 **[tzù-yüàn hù-lì te chèng-**

ts'è]: policy of voluntary participation and mutual benefit (in the cooperatives)

20 自覺 **[tzù-chüéh]**: self-conscious, conscious, awakened, aware

自覺性 **[tzù-chüéh-hsìng]**: consciousness, self-awakening

自覺的思想改造 **[tzù-chüéh te ssū-hsiăng kăi-tsào]**: conscious ideological remolding

自覺自願 **[tzù-chüéh tzù-yüàn]**: voluntarily and consciously, voluntarily, of one's own free will

22 自贖 **[tzù-shú]**: to redeem oneself

— 4 Strokes —

臭

6 臭名遠揚的 **[ch'òu-míng yüăn-yáng te]**: notorious, infamous, of bad repute, scandalous

— RADICAL 至 133 —

至

3 至上的 **[chìh-shàng te]**: paramount, supreme, preëminent, foremost

4 至今 **[chìh-chīn]**: up to now, until now, hitherto

至少 **[chìh-shăo]**: at least, minimum

8 至於 **[chìh-yű]**: as for, as to, concerning, with regard to, as regards

9 至是 **[chìh-shìh]**: up to this

11 至理名言 **[chìh-lĭ míng-yén]**: axiom, golden saying

20 至寶 **[chìh-păo]**: treasure

— 3 Strokes —

致

2 致力 **[chìh-lì]**: to devote, to devote one's strength

致力於 **[chìh-lì yű]**: to devote oneself to, to make efforts to, to dedicate oneself to

8 致命的 **[chìh-mìng te]**: fatal, deadly, lethal, mortal

12 致詞 **[chìh-tz'ú]**: to make a speech, to deliver a speech, to speak, to address

13 致敬 **[chìh-chìng]**: to pay tribute to, to pay homage to, to pay respects to, to salute; salutation

致意 **[chìh-ì]**: to give one's compliments to, to extend greetings to

— 8 Strokes —

臺

臺 **[t'ái]**: Taiwan (abbreviation for 臺灣)

3 臺大 **[t'ái-tà]**: Taiwan University (abbreviation for 臺灣大學)

25 臺灣民主自治同盟 **[t'ái-wān mín-chŭ tzù-chìh t'úng-méng]**: Taiwan Democratic Self-Government League

臺灣省立師範大學 **[t'ái-wān shĕng-lì shīh-fàn tà-hsüéh]**: Taiwan Provincial Normal University

臺灣大學 **[t'ái-wān tà-hsüéh]**: Taiwan University

— RADICAL 臼 134 —

臼

[9]臼炮 **[chiù-p'ào]**: mortar

— 6 Strokes —

與

[13]與會國 **[yǜ-hùi kuó]**: participating countries, countries attending a conference

— 9 Strokes —

興

[4]興化 **[hsīng-huà]**: Hunghoa (Vietnam)

[7]興利除弊 **[hsīng-lì ch'ú-pì]**: to promote that which is profitable and abolish that which is evil

興妖作怪 **[hsīng-yāo tsò-kuài]**: to play the devil

[8]興旺 **[hsīng-wàng]**: to prosper, to flourish; prosperous, flourishing

[9]興風作浪 **[hsīng-fēng tsò-làng]**: to fan the flames of disorder, to stir up trouble

[10]興起 **[hsīng-ch'ǐ]**: to rise; growth, ascendancy; on the rise

興修水利 **[hsīng-hsīu shǔi-lì]**: to build irrigation works, to build water conservancy projects

興高采烈 **[hsìng-kāo ts'ǎi-lièh]**: jubilant, exhilarated, buoyant, elated, in high spirits

[12]興無滅資 **[hsīng-wú mièh-tzū]**: to foster proletarian ideology and liquidate bourgeois ideology, to promote proletarian ideas and eliminate bourgeois thoughts

[16]興奮 **[hsīng-fèn]**: to stimulate, to rouse to effort; stimulated, aroused; stimulation, excitement

興辦 **[hsīng-pàn]**: to do, to act, to begin, to begin an enterprise

— 11 Strokes —

舊

[3]舊三民主義 **[chìu sān-mín chǔ-ì]**: Old Sun Yat-sen-ism (i.e., before the First Congress of the Kuomintang)

[4]舊文化 **[chìu wén-huà]**: old culture (one of the 四舊, q.v.)

[6]舊式的 **[chìu-shìh te]**: old-style, old-fashioned

[8]舊制度 **[chìu chìh-tù]**: ancient regime, old system

舊金山 **[chìu chīn-shān]**: San Francisco

舊知識份子 **[chìu chīh-shìh fèn-tzu]**: old-type intellectuals

舊社會 **[chìu shè-hùi]**: the old society (i.e., pre-communist society)

舊事重提 **[chìu-shìh ch'úng-t'í]**: to bring up old matters again; repetition of an old tale

[9]舊風俗 **[chìu fēng-sú]**: old customs (one of the 四舊, q.v.)

舊柔佛 **[chìu-jóu-fú]**: Johore Lama (Malaysia)

舊思想 **[chìu ssū-hsiǎng]**: old thought, old ideology (one of the 四舊, q.v.)

[10]舊病復發 **[chìu-pìng fù-fā]**: to suffer a relapse; relapse, recurrence

舊框框 **[chìu k'ùang-k'uang]**: old frames (i.e., traditional patterns or restrictions)

[11]舊習慣 **[chìu hsí-kuàn]**: old habits, old practices (one of the 四舊, q.v.)

[13]舊傳統 **[chìu ch'uán-t'ǔng]**: age-old tradition

15 舊調重彈 **[chìu-tiào ch'úng-t'án]**: to repeat the same old tunes

16 舊學 **[chìu-hsüéh]**: old learning (i.e., traditional "feudal" Chinese learning)

舊學派 **[chìu-hsüéh p'ài]**: adherents of the old learning

4 舉手表決 **[chǔ-shǒu piǎo-chüéh]**: to vote by a show of hands

5 舉出 **[chǔ-ch'ū]**: to enumerate, to list, to give

舉世注目 **[chǔ-shìh chù-mù]**: to attract world attention

舉世聞名 **[chǔ-shìh wén-míng]**: to be known to all the world, world known

舉世無敵 **[chǔ-shìh wú-tí]**: matchless in the world

6 舉行 **[chǔ-hsíng]**: to carry out, to hold, to conduct, to take place

8 舉例 **[chǔ-lì]**: to give an example, to cite an example

11 舉動 **[chǔ-tùng]**: behavior, conduct, deportment

16 舉辦 **[chǔ-pàn]**: to hold, to conduct, to sponsor, to found

— RADICAL 舌 135 —

— 2 Strokes —

舍

13 舍路 **[shè-lù]**: Seattle

— 6 Strokes —

舒

8 舒服 **[shū-fú]**: comfortable, refreshing, gratifying, giving a sense of comfort; to feel well

— 9 Strokes —

鋪

11 鋪張 **[p'ù-chāng]**: extravagance; extravagant

— RADICAL 舛 136 —

— 8 Strokes —

舞

5 舞台 **[wǔ-t'ái]**: stage, arena

— RADICAL 舟 137 —

— 3 Strokes —

舢

8 舢板 **[shān-pǎn]** : sampan

— 4 Strokes —

航

6 航行 **[háng-hsíng]** : to navigate, to sail; navigation, voyage

8 航空 **[háng-k'ūng]** : aviation, flight, flying; aeronautical, airborne, aerial

航空勘查 **[háng-k'ūng k'ān-ch'á]** : aerial survey

航空母艦 **[háng-k'ūng mǔ-chièn]** : aircraft carrier

航空測量 **[háng-k'ūng ts'è-liàng]** : aerial surveying, aerial photographic survey

11 航郵 **[háng-yú]** : airmail

13 航業 **[háng-yèh]** : shipping business, navigation

航運 **[háng-yǜn]** : to transport by sea, to ship; shipping, navigation

航運公司 **[háng-yǜn kūng-ssū]** : shipping company, shipping line

般

10 般配 **[pān-p'èi]** : equal distribution

— 5 Strokes —

船

7 船身 **[ch'uán-shēn]** : hull

船尾 **[ch'uán-wěi]** : stern

8 船長 **[ch'uán-chǎng]** : captain, skipper

10 船隻 **[ch'uán-chīh]** : vessel, ship, craft

船桅 **[ch'uán-wéi]** : mast

船員 **[ch'uán-yüán]** : crew, sailor, seaman

11 船舶修造廠 **[ch'uán-pó hsīu-tsào ch'ǎng]** : shipyard

13 船塢 **[ch'uán-wù]** : dockyard, drydock, dock

16 船頭 **[ch'uán-t'óu]** : bow

船艙 **[ch'uán-ts'āng]** : hold of a ship, cabin

舶

8 舶來品 **[pó-lái p'ǐn]** : imported goods, imports, foreign goods

舵

3 舵工 **[tò-kūng]** : helmsman

4 舵手 **[tò-shǒu]** : coxswain, pilot, helmsman

15 舵輪 **[tò-lún]** : steering wheel

— 10 Strokes —

3 艙口 **[ts'āng-k'ou]** : ship's hatch, hatchway of a vessel

— 14 Strokes —

艦

艦 **[chièn]** : naval vessel

8 艦長 **[chièn-chǎng]** : captain, naval commander

12 艦隊 **[chièn-tùi]** : fleet, armada, naval squadron

13 艦艇 **[chièn-t'ǐng]** : naval ship

— RADICAL 艮 138 —

— 1 Stroke —

[4] 良心 **[liáng-hsīn]**: conscience, moral goodness

[6] 良好的 **[liáng-hǎo te]**: excellent, good, kind, favorable, benign

[14] 良種 **[liáng-chǔng]**: high quality seeds, picked seeds

— 11 Strokes —

[5] 艱巨任務 **[chiēn-chù jèn-wù]**: formidable task, arduous task, very difficult task

[7] 艱辛 **[chiēn-hsīn]**: grievous, distressing, miserable

[9] 艱苦 **[chiēn-k'ǔ]**: hard and arduous, painstaking, strenuous, intensive, bitter, tough

艱苦戰鬥 **[chiēn-k'ǔ chàn-tòu]**: hard-fought battle, bitter fight

艱苦卓絕 **[chiēn-k'ǔ chō-chüéh]**: to overcome great difficulties with surpassing bravery

艱苦奮鬥 **[chiēn-k'ǔ fèn-tòu]**: to brave hard and bitter struggles, to struggle hard amid difficulties, to work hard and overcome difficulties, to struggle under difficult conditions; a bitter struggle

艱苦奮鬥的作風 **[chiēn-k'ǔ fèn-tòu te tsò-fēng]**: style of plain living and hard struggle

艱苦樸素 **[chiēn-k'ǔ p'ú-sù]**: hard working and plain living

[16] 艱險 **[chiēn-hsiěn]**: difficult and dangerous

[19] 艱難 **[chiēn-nán]**: trouble, distress, difficulty

艱難曲折 **[chiēn-nán ch'ǖ-ché]**: arduous and tortuous; difficulties and setbacks

艱難困苦 **[chiēn-nán k'ùn-k'ǔ]**: hardships and deprivations

— RADICAL 色 139 —

[8] 色盲 **[sè-máng]**: color blindness; color-blind

[11] 色情 **[sè-ch'íng]**: love, sex

色情主義 **[sè-ch'íng chǔ-ì]**: sensualism, eroticism

色彩 **[sè-ts'ǎi]**: color, style (i.e., in art, dress, politics, etc.)

— RADICAL 艸 艹 140 —

— 2 Strokes —

艾

[8] 艾奇遜 **[ài-ch'í-hsǜn]**: Acheson, Dean G. (American statesman)

[10] 艾持里 **[ài-t'è-lĭ]**: Attlee, Clement (British political figure)

[12] 艾森豪威爾 **[ài-sēn-háo-wēi-ĕrh]**: Eisenhower, Dwight (American military and political figure)

艾森豪威爾主義 **[ài-sēn-háo-wēi-ĕrh chŭ-ì]**: The Eisenhower Doctrine

艾登 **[ài-tēng]**: Eden, Sir Anthony (British political figure)

— 3 Strokes —

芒

[6] 芒刺 **[máng-tz'ù]**: barb, spike; barbed

— 4 Strokes —

芝

[5] 芝加哥 **[chīh-chiā-kō]**: Chicago

芝加哥新聞 **[chīh-chiā-kō hsīn-wén]**: Chicago News (U.S. daily newspaper)

芝加哥論壇報 **[chīh-chiā-kō lùn-t'án pào]**: Chicago Tribune (U.S. daily newspaper)

芝加哥太陽時報 **[chīh-chiā-kō t'ài-yáng shíh-pào]**: Chicago Sun-Times (U.S. daily newspaper)

芬

[21] 芬蘭 **[fēn-lán]**: Finland

芬蘭共和國 **[fēn-lán kùng-hó-kuó]**: Republic of Finland

花

[4] 花天酒地 **[huā-t'iēn chiŭ-tì]**: to lead a gay life, to lead a fast life, to indulge in a gay life and debauchery; dissipation

[5] 花布 **[huā-pù]**: cotton prints, printed cloth

花生 **[huā-shēng]**: peanut

[6] 花名册 **[huā-míng ts'è]**: roll of names, list of names, register of names

[7] 花車 **[huā-ch'ē]**: a carriage for festive occasions, a special train for a distinguished person

花言巧語 **[huā-yén ch'iăo-yŭ]**: fine words, honeyed words, luring speech, seductive speech, blandishment, cajolery

[8] 花招 **[huā-chāo]**: disguise

[10] 花砲 **[huā-p'ào]**: fireworks, firecrackers

[11] 花圈 **[huā-ch'üān]**: wreath, floral wreath

花盒子 **[huā-hó-tzu]**: fireworks

[12] 花費 **[huā-fèi]**: expenditure, to spend, disbursement, to expend; expense

花絮 **[huā-hsǜ]**: titbits; miscellaneous items

[15] 花樣 **[huā-yàng]**: pattern, type, trickery

[17] 花臉 **[huā-liĕn]**: a beauty, painted faces (heroic characters in Peking opera)

[25] 花廳 **[huā-t'īng]**: reception hall, reception room

芭

[17] 芭蕾舞 **[pā-léi wŭ]**: ballet

— 5 Strokes —

若

3 若干 **[jò-kān]**: a certain number of, a certain amount

7 若狂 **[jò-k'uáng]**: delirious, frantic, crazy, raving, in a frenzy, beside oneself

11 若望二十三世 **[jò-wàng èrh-shíh-sān shìh]**: Pope John XXIII

苛

10 苛捐雜稅 **[k'ō-chüān tsá-shùi]**: exorbitant taxes and miscellaneous levies

11 苛責 **[k'ō-tsé]**: to castigate, to denounce strongly

苟

5 苟且 **[kǒu-ch'iěh]**: carelessness; careless, improper, lacking foresight

6 苟安 **[kǒu-ān]**: false security, improper ease, fool's paradise

苟全 **[kǒu-ch'üán]**: to maintain a barely viable existence, to live in peace only with the greatest of precautions

9 苟活 **[kǒu-huó]**: to maintain a barely viable existence, to continue living under great oppression, to continue living with great trouble; a careless and dishonorable life

苦

苦 **[k'ŭ]**: bitter, painful, painstaking, hard, harsh, cruel, agonizing, excruciating

3 苦工 **[k'ŭ-kūng]**: hard work, hard labor, drudgery, toil

12 苦惱 **[k'ŭ-nǎo]**: to worry, to torment, to make anxious; trouble, distress, anxiety, annoyance, torment, irritation

苦痛 **[k'ŭ-t'ùng]**: suffering, pain

13 苦幹 **[k'ŭ-kàn]**: to work strenuously

苦幹、實幹、巧幹 **[k'ŭ-kàn, shíh-kàn, ch'iǎo-kàn]**: to work strenuously, perseveringly, and resourcefully

14 苦境 **[k'ŭ-chìng]**: plight, distress, trouble, unfortunate circumstances, mental suffering

16 苦戰 **[k'ŭ-chàn]**: to battle hard for, to wage a hard struggle to; bitter struggle, hard battle

19 苦難 **[k'ŭ-nàn]**: calamity, misery, distress, agony, ordeal, misfortune, disaster, catastrophe

苗

苗 **[miáo]**: Miao (minority nationality)

16 苗頭 **[miáo-t'óu]**: hint, clue, sign, cause

英

3 英寸 **[yīng-ts'ùn]**: inch (British)

4 英尺 **[yīng-ch'ĭh]**: foot (British)

7 英里 **[yīng-lĭ]**: mile (British)

8 英明 **[yīng-míng]**: wise, clear-sighted, discerning, far-seeing, perspicacious

9 英美聯盟 **[yīng-měi lién-méng]**: Anglo-American Alliance

英勇的 **[yīng-yŭng te]**: heroic, brave, valiant, courageous, gallant

10 英畝 **[yīng-mǒu]**: acre (British)

11 英國 **[yīng-kuó]**: England, Britain

英國新聞處 **[yīng-kuó hsīn-wén ch'ù]**: London Press Service (LPS)

12 英雄 **[yīng-hsiúng]**: hero; heroic

英雄主義 **[yīng-hsiúng chŭ-ì]**: heroism

英雄無用武之地 **[yīng-hsiúng wú yùng-wŭ chīh tì]**: to be an able person with no scope for displaying his abilities, a hero with no scope for displaying his heroism

14 英語國家 **[yīng-yŭ kuó-chiā]**: English speaking countries

17 英聯邦 **[yīng-lién pāng]**: British Commonwealth of Nations

英鎊 **[yīng-pàng]**: pound sterling, sterling, pound

英鎊集團 **[yīng-pàng chí-t'uán]**: sterling bloc

21 英屬洪都拉斯 **[yīng-shŭ húng-tū-lā-ssū]**: British Honduras

英屬圭亞那 **[yīng-shŭ kuēi-yà-nà]**: British Guiana

英屬馬耳他 **[yīng-shŭ mă-ĕrh-t'ā]**: British Malta

— 6 Strokes —

茶

8 茶居 **[ch'á-chū̆]**: Tracu (Vietnam)

9 茶美 **[ch'á-mĕi]**: Tramy (Vietnam)

14 茶榮 **[ch'á-júng]**: Travinh (Vietnam)

荒

6 荒年 **[huāng-nién]**: year of a bad harvest, a year of drought

荒地 **[huāng-tì]**: fallow land, uncultivated land

9 荒唐 **[huāng-t'áng]**: wild talk; absurd, fantastic, exaggerated, incoherent, boastful, idle, frivolous

10 荒島 **[huāng-tăo]**: uninhabited island

11 荒涼 **[huāng-liáng]**: uninhabited and deserted, desolate

荒野 **[huāng-yĕh]**: wilderness, desert

12 荒疏 **[huāng-shū]**: out of practice, to have been neglected

荒歉 **[huāng-ch'ièn]**: bad harvest, bad crop

16 荒蕪的 **[huāng-wú te]**: barren, waste, deserted, wild

18 荒謬 **[huāng-mìu]**: absurd, ludicrous, preposterous, fantastic; utter nonsense

荒謬絕倫 **[huāng-mìu chüéh-lún]**: absolutely preposterous

荒誕 **[huāng-tàn]**: unfounded, fictitious

茫

12 茫然 **[máng-ján]**: puzzled, confused, bewildered, at a loss, to look blank

草

5 草包 **[ts'ăo-pāo]**: fodder bag, stupid fellow, good-for-nothing; irascible, coarse, obstinate

草田輪作 **[ts'ăo-t'ién lún-tsò]**: crop rotation in which a grass crop is rotated with a field crop

9 草約 **[ts'ăo-yüēh]**: a draft treaty

10 草案 **[ts'ăo-àn]**: draft, draft resolution

14 草圖 **[ts'ăo-t'ú]**: a preliminary drawing, a sketch

茨

4 茨木 **[tz'ú-mù]**: Ibaraki (Japan)

9 茨城 **[tz'ú-ch'éng]**: Ibaraki (Japan)

— 7 Strokes —

莊

莊 **[chuāng]**: rural village; sober, grave

20 莊嚴 **[chuāng-yén]**: grandeur, dignity,

majesty, splendor, solemnity; solemn, majestic, dignified

荷

4 荷比盧三國 **[hó-pǐ-lú sān-kuó]** : Benelux

9 荷負 **[hò-fù]** : to carry, to bear responsibility, to be competent

21 荷蘭 **[hó-lán]** : Holland

荷蘭王國 **[hó-lán wáng-kuó]** : Kingdom of the Netherlands

荷屬西印度群島 **[hó-shǔ hsī-yìn-tù ch'ǘn-tǎo]** : Netherlands Antilles

荷屬圭亞那 **[hó-shǔ kuēi-yà-nà]** : Netherlands Guiana

莫

3 莫三鼻給 **[mò-sān-pí-kěi]** : Mozambique

6 莫名其妙 **[mò-míng ch'í-miào]** : inexplicable, doubtful, in an incomprehensible manner, peculiar; to be unable to understand, not to know what to make of

8 莫知所措 **[mò-chīh sǒ-ts'ò]** : not to know what to do, not to know what to make of

9 莫洛托夫 **[mò-lò-t'ō-fū]** : Molotov, Vyacheslav (Russian statesman)

11 莫斯科 **[mò-ssū-k'ō]** : Moscow (U.S.S.R.)

莫斯科會議宣言 **[mò-ssū-k'ō hùi-ì hsüān-yén]** : Declaration of the Moscow Meeting

莫斯科會議聲明 **[mò-ssū-k'ō hùi-ì shēng-míng]** : Statement of the Moscow Meeting

— 8 Strokes —

菲

6 菲列得爾菲亞 **[fēi-lièh - té - ěrh - fēi - yà]** : Philadelphia (U.S.A.)

9 菲律賓 **[fēi-lǜ-pīn]** : Philippines

菲律賓共和國 **[fēi-lǜ-pīn kùng-hó-kuó]** : Republic of Philippines

華

5 華北 **[huá-pěi]** : North China

6 華而不實 **[huá érh pù-shíh]** : flashy but without substance, showy without substance

7 華沙 **[huá-shā]** : Warsaw (Poland)

華沙條約 **[huá-shā t'iáo-yüēh]** : Warsaw Pact

華沙條約組織 **[huá-shā t'iáo-yüēh tsǔ-chīh]** : Warsaw Pact Organization

8 華東 **[huá-tūng]** : East China

9 華美 **[huá-měi]** : beautiful, gaudy, magnificent; Sino-American

華美日報 **[huá-měi jìh-pào]** : The China Tribune (U.S. Chinese language newspaper)

11 華商報 **[huá-shāng pào]** : Chinese Commercial Daily (Hong Kong daily newspaper)

華盛頓 **[huá-shèng-tùn]** : Washington (U.S.A.)

華盛頓明星報 **[huá-shèng-tùn míng-hsīng pào]** : Washington Star (U.S. daily newspaper)

華盛頓郵報 **[huá-shèng-tùn yú-pào]** : Washington Post (U.S. daily newspaper)

12 華萊士 **[huá-lái-shìh]** : Wallace, Henry (U.S. political figure)

華越民衆公盟 **[huá-yüèh mín-chùng kūng-méng]** : Sino-Vietnam People's League

華越民衆同盟 **[huá-yüèh mín-chùng t'úng-méng]** : Sino-Vietnam People's League

14 華僑 **[huá-ch'iáo]** : overseas Chinese

華僑日報 **[huá-ch'iáo jìh-pào]** : China Daily News (U.S. Chinese language newspaper)

華僑商報 **[huá-ch'iáo shāng-pào]** : Chinese

Commercial News (Philippine Chinese language newspaper)

華僑事務委員會 **[huá-ch′iáo shìh-wù wěi-yüán-hùi]**: Overseas Chinese Affairs Commission

華爾街 **[huá-ĕrh chiēh]**: Wall Street

華爾街日報 **[huá-ĕrh-chiēh jìh-pào]**: Wall Street Journal

萊

5 萊布尼兹 **[lái-pù-ní-tz′ú]**: Leibniz, Gottfried (1646-1716)

6 萊州 **[lái-chōu]**: Laichao (Vietnam)

萌

8 萌芽 **[méng-yá]**: to sprout, to start, to develop, to bud; early growth, budding sprouts, rudiments; embryonic, rudimentary

萌芽性質 **[méng-yá hsìng-chíh]**: embryonic characteristics

萌芽時期 **[méng-yá shíh-ch′í]**: embryonic age; rudimentary stage

菩

12 菩隆加群島 **[p′ú-lúng-chiā ch′ǘn-tăo]**: Boronga Islands (Burma)

菜

3 菜子 **[ts′ài-tzu]**: rape, rapeseed

8 菜油 **[ts′ài-yú]**: rapeseed oil, colza oil

— 9 Strokes —

著

6 著名的 **[chù-míng te]**: famous, eminent, distinguished, celebrated, noted, renowned

葛

11 葛琅琦 **[kó-láng-ch′í]**: Gronchi, Giovanni (Italian political leader)

12 葛隆奇 **[kó-lúng-ch′í]**: Gronchi, Giovanni (Italian political leader)

19 葛羅米柯 **[kó-ló-mĭ-k′ō]**: Gromyko, Andrei (Russian diplomat)

落

4 落戶 **[lò-hù]**: to resettle, to make a home (refers particularly to educated youth sent to villages and mountainous regions with the idea of having them settle there for life)

6 落地稅 **[lò-tì shùi]**: tax at point of sale

7 落成典禮 **[lò-ch′éng tiĕn-lĭ]**: inauguration

8 落空 **[lò-k′ūng]**: to come to naught, to draw a blank; in vain, to no purpose

9 落後 **[lò-hòu]**: to fall behind; backwardness; backward, underdeveloped

落後份子 **[lò-hòu fèn-tzu]**: backward elements

11 落雪高山實驗室 **[lò-hsüĕh kāo-shān shíh-yèn-shìh]**: Lo-hsüeh High Mountain Laboratory (at Lo-hsüeh, Yunnan Province)

14 落實 **[lò-shíh]**: to put into full effect, to realize, to carry out, to be fully implemented, to boil down to the concrete, to adjust in the light of realities

16 落機山脈 **[lò-chī shān-mò]**: Rocky Mountains

葡

11 葡國 **[p′ú-kuó]**: Portugal

12 葡萄 **[p′ú-t′áo]**: grape

葡萄牙 **[p′ú-t′áo-yá]**: Portugal

葡萄牙共和國 **[p′ú-t′áo-yá kùng-hó-kuó]**: Republic of Portugal

15 葡幣 **[p'ú-pì]**: Pataca (Macao); Escudo (Portugal)

21 葡屬幾內亞 **[p'ú-shŭ chī-nèi-yà]**: Portuguese Guinea

葬

10 葬送 **[tsàng-sùng]**: to ruin

18 葬禮 **[tsàng-lĭ]**: funeral, interment, burial, funeral rites

董

9 董郊 **[tŭng-chiāo]**: Donggiao (Vietnam)

萬

1 萬一 **[wàn-ī]**: in case, if by any chance, if it should happen, in the eventuality of

4 萬不得已 **[wàn pù-té-ĭ]**: by absolute necessity, no alternative, the only thing possible

5 萬古 **[wàn-kŭ]**: antiquity; always, eternally

萬古常青的 **[wàn-kŭ ch'áng-ch'īng te]**: ever new, ever green

萬古不變的 **[wàn-kŭ pú-pièn te]**: eternally immutable, never changing, unchanging,the same for all time

8 萬事大吉 **[wàn-shìh tà-chí]**: everything is in order, everything is auspicious, everything is propitious

10 萬能 **[wàn-néng]**: omnipotent, all-capable, able to do anything

萬能法寶 **[wàn-néng fă-păo]**: omnipotent magic weapon (a simile for the thought of Mao Tse-tung during the Cultural Revolution)

11 萬衆一心 **[wàn-chùng ì-hsīn]**: all of one mind, united as one man

12 萬象 **[wàn-hsiàng]**: Vientiane (Laos)

萬隆會議 **[wàn-lúng hùi-ì]**: Bandung Conference (an Asian-African conference, April 18–24, 1955, at Bandung, Indonesia attended by delegates from 29 Asian and African countries in which Chou En-lai played a leading role which issued a joint communiqué stressing a 10-point principle of peaceful coexistence and friendly cooperation among nations)

萬惡的 **[wàn-ò te]**: outrageously wicked, thoroughly evil

13 萬歲 **[wàn-sùi]**: Long live . . .!

17 萬應良藥 **[wàn-yìng liáng-yào]**: panacea, cure-all

萬應藥 **[wàn-yìng yào]**: panacea, cure-all

— 10 Strokes —

蒸

13 蒸汽 **[chēng-ch'ì]**: steam power, steam, vapor

蒸汽透平 **[chēng-ch'ì t'òu-p'íng]**: steam turbine

蓄

9 蓄洪區 **[hsù-húng ch'ü]**: water dentention basin

蓄洪工程 **[hsù-húng kūng-ch'éng]**: water detention project, flood storage

13 蓄意已久 **[hsù-ì ĭ-chiŭ]**: to hope for a long time, long hoped for

蓉

蓉 **[júng]**: Chengtu (abbreviation for 成都)

蓋

3 蓋子 **[kài-tzu]**: lid (the term "lid" was introduced by intellectuals during the "one-

hundred flowers" period in 1957 as a reference to suppression of freedom of thought and is now used to indicate any hindrance to progress)

5 蓋古多 **[kài-kŭ-tō]** : Dzhekundo (Mongolia)

蒙 **[mĕng]** : Mongolia (abbreviation of 蒙古)

3 蒙大拿 **[méng-tà-ná]** : Montana

5 蒙古 **[mĕng-kŭ]** : Mongolia

蒙古人民共和國 **[mĕng-kŭ jén-mín kùng-hó-kuó]** : People's Republic of Mongolia

蒙古人民共和國人民呼拉爾 **[mĕng-kŭ jén-mín kùng-hó-kuó tà jén-mìn hū-lā-ĕrh]** : Great People's Hural of the People's Republic of Mongolia

7 蒙哥馬利 **[méng-kō-mă-lì]** : Montgomery

9 蒙泰維提俄 **[méng-t'ài-wéi-t'í-ò]** : Montevideo (Uruguay)

10 蒙特卡羅 **[méng-t'è k'ă-ló]** : Monte Carlo

蒙特哥灣 **[méng-t'è-kō wān]** : Montego Bay

蒙特勒 **[méng-t'è-lè]** : Montreux

蒙特利爾 **[méng-t'è-lì-ĕrh]** : Montreal

11 蒙得維的亞 **[méng-té-wéi-tì-yà]** : Montevideo (Uruguay)

15 蒙德勒 **[méng-té-lè]** : Monterrey (Mexico)

16 蒙蔽 **[méng-pì]** : to obscure, to hoodwink, to befuddle, to fool, to delude, to muddle, to mystify, to deceive, to cover

19 蒙藏委員會 **[mĕng-tsàng wĕi-yüán-hùi]** : Mongolian and Tibetan Affairs Commission

20 蒙羅維亞 **[méng-ló-wéi-yà]** : Monrovia (Liberia)

蓖

11 蓖麻 **[pì-má]** : castor-oil plant

蓖麻油 **[pì-má yú]** : castor oil

蒲

14 蒲滿 **[p'ú-măn]** : P'u-man (a minority nationality of Yunnan province)

— 11 Strokes —

蔣

4 蔣介石 **[Chiăng Chièh-shíh]** : Chiang Kai-shek (Nationalist Chinese leader)

蔣介石匪幫 **[Chiăng Chièh-shíh fĕi-pāng]** : the Chiang Kai-shek bandit gang

8 蔓延 **[màn-yén]** : to creep over, to spread out, to sweep over

蔑

12 蔑視 **[mièh-shìh]** : to hold in contempt, to scorn, to disdain, to despise, to look down upon, to deride; contemptuous

蔬

12 蔬菜 **[shū-ts'ài]** : vegetables

— 12 Strokes —

蕎

11 蕎麥 **[ch'iáo-mài]** : buckwheat

蕭

11 蕭條 **[hsiāo-t'iáo]** : lonely and desolate, bleak and deserted; loneliness and desolation, bleakness and desertion

— 13 Strokes —

薦

4 薦引 **[chièn-yǐn]**: to introduce, to recommend

17 薦舉 **[chièn-chǚ]**: to recommend

薪

4 薪水 **[hsīn-shŭi]**: salary

薪水單 **[hsīn-shŭi tān]**: payroll, wage list

8 薪金 **[hsīn-chīn]**: salary

12 薪給標準 **[hsīn-chǐ piāo-chŭn]**: rates of salary payment

13 薪資 **[hsīn-tzū]**: salary

薄

7 薄利多銷 **[pó-lì tō-hsiāo]**: to make a quick turnover by reducing prices, to lower prices in order to increase sales

10 薄弱環節 **[pó-jò huán-chiéh]**: weak link

11 薄情 **[pó-ch'íng]**: destitute of feeling, little sense of gratitude

薄荷油 **[pò-hó yú]**: oil of peppermint

15 薄寮 **[pó-liáo]**: Bac Lieu (Vietnam)

16 薄鋼板 **[páo-kāng pǎn]**: thin steel sheet

薩

6 薩伊德 **[sà-ī-té]**: Port Said

7 薩那 **[sà-nà]**: Sana (Kingdom of Yemen)

8 薩拉曼加 **[sà-lā-màn-chiā]**: Salamanca

9 薩哈連 **[sà-hā-lién]**: Sakhalin

14 薩爾 **[sà-ĕrh]**: Saar

薩爾瓦多 **[sà-ĕrh-wă-tō]**: El Salvador

薩爾瓦多共和國 **[sà-ĕrh-wă-tō kùng-hó-kuó]**: Republic of El Salvador

15 薩摩亞 **[sà-mó-yà]**: Samoa

16 薩噶 **[sā-ká]**: Sakka (Tibet)

— 14 Strokes —

藍

14 藍圖 **[lán-t'ú]**: blue print

藐

12 藐視 **[miăo-shìh]**: to despise, to disdain, to slight, to scorn, to belittle; contempt

薯

18 薯類 **[shŭ-lèi]**: tuber crops, potatoes, yams

藏

藏 **[tsàng]**: Tibet (abbreviation for 西藏)

藏 **[ts'áng]**: to hide, to conceal, to harbor

6 藏奸 **[ts'áng-chiēn]**: to harbor treachery, to provide refuge for traitors

7 藏局 **[tsàng-chǘ]**: Tibetan Bureau

藏私 **[ts'áng-ssū]**: to conceal one's feelings; to be reserved or secretive

11 藏族人民 **[tsàng-tsú jén-mín]**: Tibetans

13 藏幹校 **[tsàng-kàn hsiào]**: Tibetan Cadre School

16 藏頭露尾 **[ts'áng-t'óu lòu-wĕi]**: to secrete the head and leave the tail showing, to give only a partial account of, to wish to conceal without being able to

20 藏籌委 **[tsàng-ch'óu-wĕi]**: Tibet Preparatory Committee

— 15 Strokes —

藩

11 藩屏 **[fān-p'íng]**: to defend, to protect, to guard; a screen, an officer who protects the frontier

18 藩屬 **[fān-shŭ]**: protectorate, vassal, dependency

藝

11 藝術 **[ì-shù]**: art; artistic

藝術家 **[ì-shù-chiā]**: artist

藝術至上主義 **[ì-shù chìh-shàng chŭ-ì]**: the doctrine of art for art's sake

藝術性 **[ì-shù-hsìng]**: artistic quality

藝術科學 **[ì-shù k'ō-hsüéh]**: the science of art

藝術科學的標準 **[ì-shù k'ō-hsüéh te piāo-chŭn]**: criteria of the science of art

藝術妙技 **[ì-shù miào-chì]**: virtuosity, skill, mastery

藝術標準 **[ì-shù piāo-chŭn]**: criterion of art

藝術品 **[ì-shù p'ĭn]**: arts and crafts, art craft

藝術社會主義 **[ì-shù shè-hùi chŭ-ì]**: artistic socialism, Ruskin-ism

藤

7 藤沢 **[t'éng-tsé]**: Fujisawa (Japan)

藥

4 藥方 **[yào-fāng]**: prescription

7 藥材 **[yào-ts'ái]**: materia medica, medicinal herb

8 藥物研究所 **[yào-wù yén-chìu-sŏ]**: Pharmacology Institute

9 藥品 **[yào-p'ĭn]**: medicine, drug, medical drug

11 藥理學 **[yào-lĭ-hsüéh]**: pharmacology

— 16 Strokes —

蘆

13 蘆溝橋 **[lú-kōu ch'iáo]**: Marco Polo Bridge

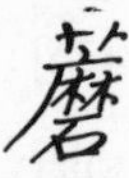

12 蘑菇 **[mó-kū]**: mushroom; fussy (slang term)

蘑菇戰術 **[mó-kū chàn-shù]**: wear and tear tactics

蘇

蘇 **[sū]**: 1. Kiangsu (abbreviation of 江蘇); 2. Soochow (abbreviation of 蘇州)

4 蘇丹 **[sū-tān]**: Sudan

蘇丹共和國 **[sū-tān kùng-hó-kuó]**: Republic of Sudan

蘇丹國 **[sū-tān-kuó]**: sultanate

5 蘇卡諾 **[sū-k'ă-nò]**: Sukarno, Achmed (Indonesian political leader)

蘇必利爾湖 **[sū-pì-lì-ĕrh hú]**: Lake Superior

6 蘇共 **[sū-kùng]**: Soviet Communist Party

8 蘇門答臘 **[sū-mén-tá-là]**: Sumatra

10 蘇修 **[sū-hsīu]**: Soviet revisionism

蘇格拉底 **[sū-kó-lā-tĭ]**: Socrates (469–399 B.C.)

蘇格蘭 **[sū-kó-lán]**: Scotland

蘇班德里約[sū-pān-té-lǐ-yüēh]: Subandrio, Dr. (Indonesian political leader, diplomat, and surgeon)

11 蘇區 [sū-ch'ü]: soviet district (i.e., areas occupied by Communist forces during the war of 1927–1936)

14 蘇維埃社會主義共和國聯盟 [sū-wéi-āi shè-hùi chŭ-ì kùng-hó-kuó lién-méng]: Union of Soviet Socialist Republics (U.S.S.R.)

蘇維埃社會主義共和國聯盟最高蘇維埃 [sū-wéi-āi shè-hùi chŭ-ì kùng-hó-kuó lién-méng tsùi-kāo sū-wéi-āi]: Supreme Soviet of the Union of Soviet Socialist Republics

16 蘇聯 [sū-lién]: Soviet Union

蘇聯聯盟院 [sū-lién lién-méng-yüàn]: Soviet of the Union (of the U.S.S.R.)

蘇聯民族院 [sū-lién mín-tsú-yüàn]: Soviet of the Nationalities (of the U.S.S.R.)

蘇聯部長會議 [sū-lién pù-chăng hùi-ì]: Council of Ministers of the U.S.S.R.

蘇聯最高蘇維埃主席團 [sū-lién tsùi-kāo sū-wéi-āi chŭ-hsí-t'uán]: Presidium of the Supreme Soviet of the U.S.S.R.

蘇聯元帥 [sū-lién yüán-shuài]: Marshal of the Soviet Union

18 蘇彝士運河 [sū-í-shìh yǜn-hó]: Suez Canal

蘊

18 蘊藏 [yǜn-ts'áng]: to hoard, to collect, to lie latent; deposit, reserve

— 17 Strokes —

蘭

蘭 [lán]: Lanchow (abbreviation for 蘭州)

— RADICAL 虍 141 —

— 2 Strokes —

虎

6 虎列拉 [hŭ-lièh-lā]: cholera

8 虎政 [hŭ-chèng]: inhumane government; a cruel, heartless government; maladministration

10 虎倀 [hŭ-ch'āng]: accomplice; assisting an evil man

11 虎視眈眈 [hŭ-shìh tān-tān]: to eye with hostility

16 虎頭蛇尾 [hŭ-t'óu shé-wĕi]: to begin with tigerish energy but peter out at the end; a fine start but a poor finish

— 3 Strokes —

虐

9 虐待 [nüèh-tài]: to maltreat, to ill-treat, to mishandle; maltreatment, ill-treatment

— 5 Strokes —

處

3 處女航 [ch'ŭ-nŭ háng]: maiden voyage

處女地 [ch'ŭ-nŭ tì]: new land, virgin land

4 處方 [ch'ŭ-fāng]: to prescribe for, to write a prescription

處分 [ch'ŭ-fèn]: to punish, to settle, to adjust, to put into execution; punishment, sanction

處心積慮 **[ch'ŭ-hsīn chī-lǜ]**: to brood over a matter for a long time, to deliberate, to concentrate on, to work hard and deliberately at

5 處以絞刑 **[ch'ŭ-ĭ chiăo-hsíng]**: to hang, to hang one by the neck

6 處決 **[ch'ŭ-chüéh]**: to sentence after trial, to execute; execution

處刑 **[ch'ŭ-hsíng]**: to punish, to punish according to the law

處死 **[ch'ŭ-ssŭ]**: to punish by death

8 處事 **[ch'ŭ-shìh]**: to administer, to take care of, to execute

處所 **[ch'ù-sŏ]**: place, location, spot

處於 **[ch'ŭ-yǘ]**: to find oneself in, to stand in

處於險境 **[ch'ŭ-yǘ hsiĕn-chìng]**: to be in a dangerous situation

處於困境 **[ch'ŭ-yǘ k'ùn-chìng]**: to be in difficult circumstances

11 處理 **[ch'ŭ-lĭ]**: to dispose, to handle, to deal with, to dispose of, to manage, to look after, to take charge of; disposition

處處 **[ch'ù-ch'ù]**: everywhere

13 處置 **[ch'ŭ-chìh]**: to manage, to place, to settle, to deal with

14 處境 **[ch'ŭ-chìng]**: circumstances, conditions, state, matter, things, case

處罰 **[ch'ŭ-fá]**: to punish, to punish according to the law; penalty

— 6 Strokes —

虛

6 虛名 **[hsǖ-míng]**: hollow reputation

7 虛位 **[hsǖ-wèi]**: to leave a seat vacant; a vacant seat

11 虛張聲勢 **[hsǖ chāng shēng-shìh]**: to make a pompous but empty show of power

虛僞 **[hsǖ-wĕi]**: false, untrue, insincere; falsity, insincerity, deceit

12 虛虛實實 **[hsǖ-hsǖ shíh-shíh]**: a mixture of truth and deceit

虛報 **[hsǖ-pào]**: false report

虛無主義 **[hsǖ-wú chŭ-ì]**: nihilism

虛無飄渺 **[hsǖ-wú p'iāo-miăo]**: utterly visionary, with no reality whatever

13 虛誇 **[hsǖ-k'uā]**: empty boasting, exaggeration

虛與委蛇 **[hsǖ yǚ wéi-í]**: to pretend interest and sympathy; feigned interest and sympathy

14 虛榮 **[hsǖ-júng]**: vanity, vainglory

虛構 **[hsǖ-kòu]**: to trump up, to concoct; fiction, invention, fabrication; trumped up, sham, imaginary, fictitious

虛構的話 **[hsǖ-kòu te huà]**: tale, story, fabrication

23 虛驚 **[hsǖ-chīng]**: false alarm

— 7 Strokes —

號

5 號召 **[hào-chào]**: to summon, to issue a call, to make a public appeal

8 號呼 **[hào-hū]**: to shout

14 號稱 **[hào-ch'ēng]**: designation, name; to name, to designate; reputedly

— 11 Strokes —

虧

5 虧本 **[k'uēi-pĕn]**: to lose money in business, to lose one's capital

— RADICAL 虫 142 —

— 5 Strokes —

蛋

蛋 **[tàn]**: Tan (minority nationality of South China); egg

10 蛋粉 **[tàn-fěn]**: powdered egg

— 7 Strokes —

蜂

10 蜂起 **[fēng-ch'ǐ]**: to rise, to gather together, to gather, to swarm

14 蜂聚 **[fēng-chǜ]**: to swarm

16 蜂擁 **[fēng-yūng]**: to swarm out; a crowd of people gathering like a swarm of bees

蜂擁而來 **[fēng-yūng érh lái]**: to crowd in, to flock, to swarm, to surge

蜆

12 蜆港 **[hsiěn-kǎng]**: Tourane (Vietnam)

蜀

蜀 **[shǔ]**: Szechwan (abbreviation for 四川)

蛻

4 蛻化 **[shùi-huà]**: to degenerate, to retrogress; degeneration, retrogression

蛻化份子 **[shùi-huà fèn-tzu]**: backslider

— 9 Strokes —

蝗

18 蝗蟲 **[huáng-ch'úng]**: grasshopper, locust

— 10 Strokes —

融

4 融化 **[júng-huà]**: to thaw, to melt, to dissolve, to disintegrate, to soften

6 融合 **[júng-hó]**: to blend, to merge into, to incorporate with, to unite with, to mix, to amalgamate; merger, union

9 融洽 **[júng-hsiá]**: to blend with, to be in unison; mutual understanding, harmony, concord, accord, amity; in harmony with

螢

5 螢石 **[yíng-shíh]**: fluorspar, fluorite

— 12 Strokes —

蟲

7 蟲災 **[ch'úng-tsāi]**: locust plague

— 15 Strokes —

蠢

8 蠢事 **[ch'ǔn-shìh]**: stupid thing or affair, folly

8 蠟板 **[là-pǎn]**: tabula rasa

— 17 Strokes —

蠱

12 蠱惑性宣傳 **[kǔ-huò-hsìng hsüān-ch'uán]**: demagogy; demagogic

蠱惑人心 **[kŭ-huò jén-hsīn]**: to seduce the masses

— 18 Strokes —

蠶

[9] 蠶食 **[ts'án-shíh]**: to nibble up, to feed on; encroachment

[10] 蠶桑業 **[ts'án-sāng yèh]**: sericulture

[12] 蠶絲 **[ts'án-ssū]**: silk

[13] 蠶蛾 **[ts'án-ó]**: silkworm moth

蠶業研究所 **[ts'án-yèh yén-chìu-sŏ]**: Sericulture Institute (under Chinese Academy of Agricultural Sciences

[19] 蠶繭 **[ts'án-chiĕn]**: cocoon of the silkworm

— 19 Strokes —

蠻

[4] 蠻不講理 **[mán pù-chiăng-lĭ]**: violent irrationality, unreasonable atrocity; impervious to reason; to refuse to listen to reason

[16] 蠻橫的 **[mán-hèng te]**: overbearing, high handed, violent, cruel, savage, ruthless, unmerciful

— RADICAL 血 143 —

血

[6] 血汗 **[hsiĕh-hàn]**: blood and sweat

血汗錢 **[hsiĕh-hàn ch'ién]**: wages earned by hard toil

血肉的關係 **[hsüeh-jòu te kuān-hsì]**: flesh and blood relationship, ties of flesh and blood

[8] 血的教訓 **[hsiĕh te chiào-hsǜn]**: bloody lesson

[9] 血洗 **[hsiĕh-hsĭ]**: to slaughter, to massacre; bloodbath, butchery, baptism of blood

[10] 血案 **[hsüèh-àn]**: bloody incident

[13] 血債血來還 **[hsiĕh-chài hsiĕh lái-huán]**: to demand blood for blood, to make someone pay in blood for blood

血腥 **[hsiĕh-hsīng]**: bloody, sanguinary, blood-stained

— RADICAL 行 144 —

行

[4] 行不顧言 **[hsíng pú-kù-yén]**: to act differently from what one says; to say one thing but to do something else

行不通 **[hsíng-pù-t'ūng]**: of no avail; it will not work; it will not do

行市 **[háng-shìh]**: market rate, market price, rate of exchange

[6] 行行出狀元 **[háng-háng ch'ū chuàng-yüán]**: to be able to excel in any occupation; one who can excel in any occupation

[8] 行使 **[hsíng-shĭh]**: to perform, to exercise (i.e., as power, etc.)

行刺 **[hsíng-tz'ù]**: to assassinate, assassination

[9] 行政 **[hsíng-chèng]**: administration, administration of government; administrative

行政區 **[hsíng-chèng ch'ü]**: administrative district

行政區劃 **[hsíng-chèng ch'ü-huà]**: administrative district demarcation (i.e., the area under the jurisdiction of each administrative level)

行政法院 **[hsíng-chèng fă-yüàn]**: administrative court

行政人員 **[hsíng-chèng jén-yüán]**: executive personnel, personnel with administrative duties

行政管理費 **[hsíng-chèng kuăn-lĭ fèi]**: administrative expenses

行政工作人員 **[hsíng-chèng kūng-tsò jén-yüán]**: administrative personnel

行政命令 **[hsíng-chèng mìng-lìng]**: administrative decree, administrative order

行政命令方式 **[hsíng-chèng mìng-lìng fāng-shìh]**: compulsory administrative methods

行政村 **[hsíng-chèng ts'ūn]**: administrative village (a village comprising a large community and having an administrative organ, as contrasted with a "natural village," 自然村, q.v.)

行軍 **[hsíng-chün]**: to march; march

10 行家 **[háng-chiā]**: specialist, expert; business man; profession, trade

行時 **[hsíng-shíh]**: fashionable

11 行情 **[háng-ch'íng]**: market prices, current price, quotation, market conditions

行商 **[hsíng-shāng]**: commercial traveller, travelling trader, peddler, itinerant merchant

行得通 **[hsíng-té-t'ūng]**: it will do

行動 **[hsíng-tùng]**: to act, to move, to do; act, action, deed

行動哲學 **[hsíng-tùng ché-hsüéh]**: philosophy of action

行動指南 **[hsíng-tùng chĭh-nán]**: guide to action

行動方針 **[hsíng-tùng fāng-chēn]**: program of action

行動一致 **[hsíng-tùng í-chìh]**: to act in unison; uniformity of action

行動的號召 **[hsíng-tùng te hào-chào]**: call to action

行動自由 **[hsíng-tùng tzù-yú]**: freedom of movement or action

12 行棧 **[háng-chàn]**: depot, warehouse, storage place

行爲 **[hsíng-wéi]**: to behave; behavior, conduct, deportment, act, action

行爲正値 **[hsíng-wéi chèng-chíh]**: upright behavior, proper conduct

行爲主義 **[hsíng-wéi chŭ-ì]**: behaviorism

13 行會 **[háng-hùi]**: guild, union

行賄 **[hsíng-hùi]**: to bribe; bribery, corruption

行當 **[háng-tàng]**: business, occupation

行業 **[háng-yèh]**: occupation

15 行輩 **[háng-pèi]**: order of seniority, seniority sequence; in the same rank

18 行禮 **[hsíng-lĭ]**: to salute, to perform ceremony

行蹤 **[hsíng-tsūng]**: whereabouts, traces, footsteps, vestiges

— 5 Strokes —

術

14 術語 **[shù-yü]**: technical term, terminology, jargon

術語學 **[shù-yü-hsüéh]**: terminology

— 6 Strokes —

街

4 街市 **[chiēh-shìh]**: streets and markets, market, shopping district

7 街坊 **[chiēh-fāng]**: neighbor, neighborhood

13 街道居民委員會 **[chiēh-tào chū-mín wĕi-yüán-hùi]**: neighborhood administrative station

街道服務站 **[chiēh-tào fú-wù chàn]**: street service station (i.e., stations for repairing and patching work in urban communes)

街道工業 **[chiēh-tào kūng-yèh]**: street industry

15 街談巷議 **[chiēh-t'án hsiàng-ì]**: hearsay, gossip, common talk

18 街壘戰 **[chiēh-lĕi chàn]**: battle at the barricades

— 9 Strokes —

9 衝突 **[ch'ūng-t'ù]**: to clash with, to run counter to; conflict, clash

17 衝擊影響 **[ch'ūng-chī yĭng-hsiăng]**: impact

衞

5 衞生 **[wèi-shēng]**: hygiene, health, sanita-tion; hygienic, sanitary

衞生防疫站 **[wèi-shēng fáng-ì chàn]**: anti-epidemic station

衞生部 **[wèi-shēng pù]**: Ministry of Publi Health

衞生室 **[wèi-shēng shìh]**: health office

衞生所 **[wèi-shēng sŏ]**: clinic, dispensary

6 衞戍 **[wèi-shù]**: garrison

衞戍總司令 **[wèi-shù tsŭng-ssū-lìng]** commander-in-chief of garrison forces

7 衞兵 **[wèi-pīng]**: guard

9 衞星 **[wèi-hsīng]**: satellite, Sputnik

— RADICAL 衣 衤 145 —

— 3 Strokes —

表

5 表示 **[piăo-shìh]**: to indicate, to express, to demonstrate, to represent, to make known, to register, to make public, to show

表示態度 **[piăo-shìh t'ài-tù]**: to make plain one's attitude (i.e., toward a problem)

表册 **[piăo-ts'è]**: a register

7 表決 **[piăo-chüéh]**: to vote, to decide, to put to the vote

表決機器 **[piăo-chüéh chī-ch'i]**: voting machine

表現 **[piăo-hsièn]**: to manifest, to express, to exhibit, to display

表現主義 **[piăo-hsièn chŭ-ì]**: expressionism

表現手法 **[piăo-hsièn shŏu-fă]**: means o expression

表現得好 **[piăo-hsièn-té-hăo]**: to give a good account of oneself

表現在 **[piăo-hsièn tsài]**: to be symbolized in, to be symbolized by

8 表明 **[piăo-míng]**: to reveal, to demonstrate, to show, to prove, to throw light on, to give a demonstration, to manifest, to make clear; manifestation, evidence

9 表面 **[piăo-mièn]**: outward appearance, external expression; superficial, outer, out-ward, apparent, shallow

表面價值 **[piăo-mièn chià-chíh]**: face value

表面化 **[piăo-mièn-huà]**: to externalize

10 表率 **[piăo-shuài]**: model, example, leader to be a model

12 表達 **[piăo-tá]**: to express, to utter, to

pronounce, to give expression to; expression

表揚 **[piăo-yáng]**: to commend, to speak well of, to compliment, to praise, to cite, to mention in a citation; compliment, praise

13 表象 **[piăo-hsiàng]**: expression, presentation

14 表態 **[piăo-t'ài]**: to make plain one's attitude (i.e., toward certain problems)

— 4 Strokes —

衷

4 衷心 **[chūng-hsīn]**: heartfelt, wholehearted

衰

3 衰亡 **[shuāi-wáng]**: to wither away, to die

10 衰退 **[shuāi-t'ùi]**: to decline, to depress, to sink; recession, breakdown, weakening, increasing debility, downturn, slump; declining, decadent

13 衰落 **[shuāi-lò]**: to decline, to fade, to wither away, to go from bad to worse; decayed, failing

— 5 Strokes —

袖

4 袖手旁觀 **[hsìu-shŏu p'áng-kuān]**: to look on with folded arms, to look on with one's hands in one's sleeves, to look on unconcerned, to have nothing to do with a matter

被

7 被告 **[pèi-kào]**: defendant, the accused

8 被拘留的人 **[pèi chū-líu te jén]**: detainee

被屈含冤 **[pèi-ch'ū hán-yüān]**: to be penalized on the basis of a false accusation, to be wrongly punished

被迫 **[pèi-p'ò]**: to be forced to, to be compelled to

被迫亡命 **[pèi-p'ò wáng-mìng]**: to be driven into exile, to be forced into exile

9 被侵略者 **[pèi ch'īn-lüèh-chĕ]**: victims of aggression

被除數 **[pèi-ch'ú-shù]**: dividend

被俘 **[pèi-fú]**: to be taken prisoner

被害 **[pèi-hài]**: to be harmed, to be murdered, to be killed

11 被剝削階級 **[pèi pō-hsüeh chiēh-chí]**: the exploited class

13 被傳出庭 **[pèi-ch'uán ch'ū-t'íng]**: to be summoned to appear in court, to be subpoenaed

被動 **[pèi-tùng]**: state of passivity, a passive position, passive, to maintain a passive attitude; on the defensive

14 被管制份子 **[pèi kuăn-chìh fèn-tzu]**: persons under public surveillance (i.e., persons who have committed minor offenses and who are required to report to the police at regular intervals)

被領導者 **[pèi lĭng-tăo-chĕ]**: people who are led, rank and file

15 被擄 **[pèi-lŭ]**: to be captured, to be taken captive

被徹底粉碎 **[pèi ch'è-tĭ fĕn-sùi]**: to be thoroughly pulverized, to be smashed to bits

17 被選舉權 **[pèi-hsüăn-chŭ ch'üán]**: eligibility to be elected, right to be elected

— 6 Strokes —

裂

17 裂縫 **[lièh-fèng]**: break, rift, cleft, crack, fissure, rent, interstice

裁

7 裁決 **[ts'ái-chüéh]**: to decide, to make a decision; ruling

裁判 **[ts'ái-p'àn]**: to try, to judge, to sentence; judgment

裁判員 **[ts'ái-p'àn yüán]**: umpire, referee

8 裁制 **[ts'ái-chìh]**: to restrict, to restrain, to limit, to apply forceful sanction

裁度 **[ts'ái-tù]**: to decide, to plan, to determine

9 裁軍 **[ts'ái-chün]**: disarmament

裁軍委員會 **[ts'ái-chün wĕi-yüán-hùi]**: Disarmament Commission (United Nations)

12 裁減 **[ts'ái-chiĕn]**: to reduce, to decrease, to limit

14 裁奪 **[ts'ái-tó]**: to plan, to decide

15 裁撤 **[ts'ái-ch'è]**: to do away with, to annul, to cancel

— 7 Strokes —

裝

5 裝甲 **[chuāng-chiă]**: armored

裝甲部隊 **[chuāng-chiă pù-tùi]**: armored force

裝出和平姿態 **[chuāng-ch'ū hó-p'íng tzū-t'ài]**: to assume a posture of peace

7 裝作 **[chuāng-tsò]**: to pretend or pose as

8 裝卸工人 **[chuāng-hsièh kūng-jén]**: docker, longshoreman

10 裝配車間 **[chuāng-p'èi ch'ē-chiēn]**: assembly shop

12 裝備 **[chuāng-pèi]**: to equip, to fit out, to install; equipment, fittings, installation

13 裝飾 **[chuāng-shìh]**: to decorate, to embellish, to adorn; ornament, decoration

裝飾打扮 **[chuāng-shìh tă-pàn]**: to whitewash, to gloss over faults

14 裝置 **[chuāng-chìh]**: to install, to furnish with, to equip with; installation

22 裝聾賣傻 **[chuāng-lúng mài-shă]**: to pretend ignorance, to act the fool, to play the fool

補

5 補白 **[pŭ-pái]**: to fill a gap, to fill a blank, to fill a void

6 補充 **[pŭ-ch'ūng]**: to supplement, to replenish, to resupply, to fill; supplement, addition, replacement; supplementary, subsidiary

7 補助 **[pŭ-chù]**: to assist, to subsidize; auxiliary, subsidiary, supplementary

補助金 **[pŭ-chù-chīn]**: subsidy, allowance, grant, financial aid

補助費 **[pŭ-chù fèi]**: subsidy, stipend, subvention

補考 **[pŭ-k'ăo]**: to take a make-up examination; a make-up examination

補足 **[pŭ-tsú]**: to make up a deficiency, to fill out a deficit

11 補救 **[pŭ-chìu]**: to remedy, to save the situation; a remedy

補缺 **[pŭ-ch'üēh]**: to fill a vacancy

12 補給 **[pŭ-chĭ]**: to replenish, to reinforce

補貼 **[pŭ-t'iēh]**: to support, to help, to supplement, to subsidize, to make up a deficiency

15 補選 **[pŭ-hsüăn]**: by-election

補課 **[pŭ-k'ò]**: to make up for a class or lesson missed

17 補償 **[pŭ-ch'áng]**: to compensate, to indemnify; compensation, indemnification

裕

4 裕仁天皇 **[yù-jén t'iēn-huáng]**: Emperor Hirohito (Emperor of Japan, b. 1901)

8 裕固 **[yǜ-kù]** : Yu-ku (a minority nationality in Kansu Province)

— 8 Strokes —

製

8 製表機 **[chìh-piăo-chī]** : tabulator

11 製造 **[chìh-tsào]** : to manufacture, to make, to produce

製造技術 **[chìh-tsào chì-shù]** : manufacturing technology

製造商 **[chìh-tsào-shāng]** : manufacturer

製造業 **[chìh-tsào yèh]** : manufacturing industry

16 製糖廠 **[chìh-t'áng ch'ăng]** : sugar refinery

19 製藥廠 **[chìh-yào ch'ăng]** : pharmaceutical manufacturing plant

裡

7 裡里 **[lĭ-lĭ]** : Iri (Korea)

10 裡海 **[lĭ-hăi]** : Caspian Sea

7 裹足不前 **[kuŏ-tsú pù-ch'ién]** : to be tied up and unable to advance, to be at a standstill; timidity and hesitancy

10 裹脅 **[kuŏ-hsiéh]** : to coerce, to force to take part

13 裹亂 **[kuŏ-luàn]** : to disturb

14 裹腿 **[kuŏ-t'ŭi]** : gaiters, leggings

裴

6 裴多菲俱樂部 **[p'éi-tō-fēi chǖ-lò-pù]** : Petofi Club (Hungarian literary group associated with the Hungarian uprising in 1956; a term used in accusation of those allegedly intending to launch a counterrevolutionary coup against Mao in the fashion of the Petofi Club)

裨

7 裨助 **[pì-chù]** : to help, to support

12 裨補 **[pì-pŭ]** : to support, to aid, to second, to make up a deficiency

— 9 Strokes —

6 複合 **[fù-hó]** : complex

9 複查 **[fù-ch'á]** : control inspection, spot recheck

14 複種 **[fù-chùng]** : double cropping, multiple cropping

複種指數 **[fù-chùng chĭh-shù]** : multiple crop index

複種面積 **[fù-chùng mièn-chī]** : multiple cropping area, area on which several crops a year are grown

18 複雜 **[fù-tsá]** : complex, complicated, intricate, involved

複雜性 **[fù-tsá-hsìng]** : complexity

複雜化 **[fù-tsá-huà]** : to complicate, to make things complicated

— 10 Strokes —

褫

14 褫奪 **[ch'ĭh-tó]** : to snatch away, to deprive

褫奪公權 **[ch'ĭh-tó kūng-ch'üán]** : to disfranchise

褪

6 褪色 **[t'ùi-sè]** : to shed color (i.e., to lose one's "red" revolutionary quality)

— 16 Strokes —

襲

17 襲擊 **[hsí-chī]**: to attack, to assail, to assault, to make a surprise attack; assault, onslaught, raid

— RADICAL 西 146 —

西

4 西比利亞 **[hsī-pǐ-lì-yà]**: Siberia

5 西弗吉尼亞 **[hsī fú-chí-ní-yà]**: West Virginia

西尼 **[hsī-ní]**: Sydney (Australia)

西尼沙 **[hsī-ní-shā]**: Sendja (Tibet)

西北 **[hsī-pěi]**: northwest; Northwest China

西北農業科學研究所 **[hsī-pěi núng-yèh k'ō-hsüéh yén-chìu-sŏ]**: Northwest Agricultural Research Institute

6 西安事變 **[hsī-ān shìh-pièn]**: the Sian Incident (December 12, 1936, in which Chiang Kai-shek was captured)

西西里 **[hsī-hsī-lǐ]**: Sicily

西印度聯邦 **[hsī yìn-tù lién-pāng]**: The Federation of West Indies

7 西里西亞 **[hsī-lǐ-hsī-yà]**: Silesia

西里伯斯島 **[hsī-lǐ-pó-ssū tăo]**: Celebes

西沙島 **[hsī-shā tăo]**: Paracel Is. (S. China Sea)

8 西明頓 **[hsī-míng-tùn]**: Symington, William Stuart (American political figure)

9 西哈努克 **[hsī-hā-nŭ-k'ò]**: Prince Sihanouk Norodom (Cambodia political figure)

西南非洲 **[hsī-nán fēi-chōu]**: Southwest Africa

10 西宮 **[hsī-kūng]**: Nishinomiya (Japan)

西貢 **[hsī-kùng]**: Saigon (Vietnam)

西姆拉 **[hsī-mŭ-lā]**: Simla

西班牙 **[hsī-pān-yá]**: Spain

西特卡 **[hsī-t'è-k'ă]**: Sitka (Alaska)

西特里 **[hsī-t'è-lǐ]**: Seattle

11 西敏寺 **[hsī-mǐn-ssù]**: Westminster

12 西普魯士 **[hsī p'ŭ-lŭ-shìh]**: West Prussia

西雅圖 **[hsī-yă-t'ú]**: Seattle

14 西寧 **[hsī-níng]**: Tayninh (Vietnam); Sining (China)

15 西歐聯盟 **[hsī-ōu lién-méng]**: Western European Union (WEU)

西德 **[hsī-té]**: West Germany

西德尼 **[hsī-té-ní]**: Sydney (Australia)

17 西薩摩亞 **[hsī sà-mó-yà]**: Western Samoa

西點軍校 **[hsī-tiĕn chūn-hsiào]**: U.S. Military Academy (West Point)

18 西藏日報 **[hsī-tsàng jìh-pào]**: Tibet Daily

21 西屬幾內亞 **[hsī-shŭ chǐ-nèi-yà]**: Spanish Guinea

西屬撒哈拉 **[hsī-shŭ sā-hā-lā]**: Spanish Sahara

— 3 Strokes —

要

6 要求 **[yāo-ch'íu]**: to ask, to request, to demand, to require, to petition, to solicit; request, demand, claim

10 要害 **[yào-hài]**: vital point, key military point, a mortal wound

要素 **[yào-sù]**: essential elements, factors, essence

13 要塞 **[yào-sài]**: stronghold, fortress, bastion

14 要領 **[yāo-lǐng]**: essential element, essentials, the crux of a matter, mainpoint substance

17 要點 **[yào-tiěn]**: main point, important points, essential point, highlight

— RADICAL 見 147 —

見

5 見世面 **[chièn shìh-mièn]**: to have seen the world; experienced; to be thoroughly versed in world affairs; to have experience of the outside world

見外 **[chièn-wài]**: to treat as an outsider, to treat as a stranger

8 見怪 **[chièn-kuài]**: to take offence, to be offended

見物不見人 **[chièn-wù pú-chièn jén]**: to see only things but not human beings

9 見客 **[chièn-k'ò]**: to receive guests

見面 **[chièn-mièn]**: to have an interview with, to meet

10 見笑 **[chièn-hsiào]**: laughable; to be laughed at, to be ridiculed

11 見習 **[chièn-hsí]**: practical experience, practical training, practice

見異思遷 **[chièn-ì ssū-ch'iēn]**: unstable, unfaithful

見責 **[chièn-tsé]**: to be reprimanded

13 見解 **[chièn-chiěh]**: view, opinion, judgment, viewpoint, idea

14 見聞 **[chièn-wén]**: observation, experience, knowledge

15 見機而作 **[chièn-chī érh tsò]**: to act as the occasion serves, to act opportunely

見諒 **[chièn-liàng]**: to excuse, to forgive

17 見縫插針 **[chièn-fèng ch'ā-chēn]**: to insert the needle wherever you see a hole (i.e., turning every spare moment to advantage)

19 見證 **[chièn-chèng]**: to bear witness; witness, eyewitness

見識 **[chièn-shìh]**: experience and knowledge, experience, knowledge, sense

— 4 Strokes —

規

8 規定 **[kuēi-tìng]**: to formulate, to fix, to prescribe, to stipulate, to define, to institute, to provide for; provision, stipulation, determination, formulation

9 規律 **[kuēi-lǜ]**: rule, regulatory law, law

規則 **[kuēi-tsé]**: principle, rule, law, regulation, provision

規約 **[kuēi-yüēh]**: agreement, provisions, governing rules

10 規格 **[kuēi-kó]**: specification, standard, requirement

11 規章 **[kuēi-chāng]**: rule, regulation

規章制度 **[kuēi-chāng chìh-tù]**: codes and conventions

規規矩矩 **[kuēi-kuēi chŭ-chŭ]**: to behave properly

12 規程 **[kuēi-ch'éng]**: rules and regulations, process

14 規劃 **[kuēi-huà]**: to plan, to work out, to map out, to chart, to project, to design, to sketch; a plan, a project, a design

15 規範 **[kuēi-fàn]**: model, standard, example, norm

規範化 **[kuēi-fàn-huà]**: to standardize; standardization, normalization

規範化的 **[kuēi-fàn-huà te]**: standardized

規模 **[kuēi-mó]**: pattern, model, scale, scope, extent, size, proportion

17 規避 **[kuēi-pì]**: to avoid, to shun, to dodge, to parry, to evade, to sidestep, to elude

— 5 Strokes —

視

6 視....而定 **[shìh . . . érh tìng]**: to depend on, to rest on, to be contingent on

14 視察 **[shìh-ch'á]**: to investigate, to look into, to inspect; inspection

— 9 Strokes —

親

親 **[ch'īn]**: pro-, in favor of, adherent to

2 親人 **[ch'īn-jén]**: comrade, compatriot, blood relation

4 親日派 **[ch'īn-jìh p'ài]**: pro-Japanese clique

親王 **[ch'īn-wáng]**: prince

5 親切 **[ch'īn-ch'ièh]**: intimate, sincere, whole-hearted, cordial, warm-hearted, affectionate, friendly

6 親自 **[ch'īn-tzù]**: personally, in person, one's own, oneself

親自出馬 **[ch'īn-tzù ch'ū-mă]**: to come out in person, to come forward oneself; personal appearance

親自出面 **[ch'īn-tzù ch'ū-mièn]**: to appear in person, to come forward oneself; personal appearance

9 親美，恐美，崇美 **[ch'īn-mĕi, k'ŭng-mĕi, ch'úng-mĕi]**: pro-America, fear America, and worship America

11 親戚 **[ch'īn-ch'ī]**: relative, kinsman, relation

親戚關係 **[ch'īn-ch'ī kuān-hsì]**: family ties, kinship relation

親密 **[ch'īn-mì]**: intimate, close

親密戰友 **[ch'īn-mì chàn-yŭ]**: close comrade-in-arms (i.e., a trusted supporter or follower)

12 親筆 **[ch'īn-pĭ]**: personally written

親筆信 **[ch'īn-pĭ hsìn]**: a letter in one's own handwriting

親善 **[ch'īn-shàn]**: to show friendliness; good will, friendship, cordiality, rapprochement; friendly

— 10 Strokes —

覬

16 覬覦 **[chì-yű]**: to have aggressive designs on, to covet, to lust for

— 13 Strokes —

10 覺悟 **[chüéh-wù]**: to realize, to become aware of; consciousness, awareness

覺悟程度 **[chüéh-wù ch'éng-tù]**: level of consciousness

16 覺醒 **[chüéh-hsǐng]** : to wake up; awakening, awareness

— 18 Strokes —

觀

6 觀光 **[kuān-kuāng]** : to travel, to view, to visit; sight-seeing

8 觀念 **[kuān-nièn]** : concept, idea, view, conception

觀念論 **[kuān-nièn lùn]** : idealism

11 觀衆 **[kuān-chùng]** : spectators, audience, attendance

觀衆台 **[kuān-chùng t'ái]** : spectators' stand

觀望 **[kuān-wàng]** : to gaze at, to wait and see, to mark time; looking on, watchful waiting, hesitating

12 觀象台 **[kuān-hsiàng t'ái]** : observatory

觀測 **[kuān-ts'è]** : to observe, to do research

13 觀感 **[kuān-kǎn]** : to be moved by a sight; impression, opinion

14 觀察 **[kuān-ch'á]** : to look into, to observe, to survey; observation

觀察家 **[kuān-ch'á-chiā]** : Observateur (French periodical); observer

觀察家報 **[kuān-ch'á-chiā pào]** : The Observer (British Sunday newspaper)

觀察員 **[kuān-ch'á-yüán]** : observer

15 觀潮派 **[kuān-ch'áo p'ài]** : sceptics, those who stand aside in doubt

觀摩 **[kuān-mó]** : to observe and imitate, to visit (i.e., colleagues to get ideas); exhibition show, festival (for emulation and exchange of experience)

17 觀點 **[kuān-tiěn]** : viewpoint, position, point of view, outlook, standpoint

18 觀禮台 **[kuān-lǐ t'ái]** : rostrum, reviewing stand

— RADICAL 角 148 —

2 角力 **[chüéh-lì]** : to wrestle, to try one's strength

6 角色 **[chüéh-sè]** : part, role, character

9 角柱 **[chiǎo-chù]** : corner beam, corner pillar, corner column

角度 **[chiǎo-tù]** : measurement of an angle, size of an angle

11 角逐 **[chüéh-chú]** : to compete for, to contend for, to strive for mastery

角逐地位 **[chüéh-chú tì-wèi]** : to juggle for position

16 角錐 **[chiǎo-chūi]** : pyramid

角鋼 **[chiǎo-kāng]** : angle steel, angle steel bar

— 6 Strokes —

解

7 解決 **[chiěh-chüéh]** : to settle, to resolve, to solve; settlement, solution

8 解放 **[chiěh-fàng]** : to free, to release, to emancipate, to liberate; liberation, emancipation

解放戰爭 **[chiěh-fàng chàn-chēng]** : The War of Liberation (i.e., the war of 1946–1949 against the Nationalists)

解放前 **[chiěh-fàng ch'ién]** : pre-Liberation days, prior to the Liberation

解放初期 **[chiĕh-fàng ch'ū-ch'í]**: in the early days following the Liberation

解放區 **[chiĕh-fàng ch'ü]**: liberated area

解放入伍 **[chiĕh-fàng jù-wŭ]**: liberated enlistee (i.e., Nationalist soldiers put into the People's Liberation Army)

解放軍 **[chiĕh-fàng-chün]**: Liberation Army

解放軍報 **[chiĕh-fàng-chün pào]**: Liberation Army Daily

解放軍報事件 **[chiĕh-fàng-chün pào shìh-chièn]**: the Liberaton Daily Incident

解放報 **[chiĕh-fàng pào]**: Liberation (French daily newspaper)

解放思想 **[chiĕh-fàng ssū-hsiăng]**: emancipation of minds; to emancipate someone ideologically, to emancipate people's minds

解毒藥 **[chiĕh-tú yào]**: antidote

10 解除 **[chiĕh-ch'ú]**: to dispel, to be freed of, to remove, to relieve, to raise, to expel, to eliminate

解除禁運 **[chiĕh-ch'ú chìn-yǜn]**: to lift an embargo, to raise an embargo

解剖 **[chiĕh-p'ŏu]**: to dissect, to cut open, to explain, to analyze

解剖麻雀 **[chiĕh-p'ŏu má-ch'üèh]**: to dissect sparrows (i.e., scrutinizing a problem by going into minute detail)

解凍 **[chiĕh-tùng]**: to thaw, to defrost

11 解救 **[chiĕh-chìu]**: to relieve, to succor, to aid

解脫 **[chiĕh-t'ō]**: to release, to extricate, to free from, to get rid of, to disengage from

12 解散 **[chiĕh-sàn]**: to dissolve, to break up, to disperse, to disband

解答 **[chiĕh-tá]**: to explain and answer, to answer, to explain

15 解嘲 **[chiĕh-ch'áo]**: to free oneself from ridicule with an explanation

20 解釋 **[chiĕh-shìh]**: to explain, to interpret, to expound, to account for; explanation

23 解體 **[chiĕh-t'ĭ]**: to break up, to disintegrate; disentegration, collapse

— 13 Strokes —

觸

4 觸及 **[ch'ù-chí]**: to touch, to touch on

9 觸怒 **[ch'ù-nù]**: to provoke anger, to offend, to irritate, to affront, to nettle, to enrage

18 觸類旁通 **[ch'ù-lèi p'áng-t'ūng]**: to draw an analogy, to show by analogy

— RADICAL 言 149 —

4 言之過早 **[yén chīh kuò tsăo]**: to make a premature statement

言之無物 **[yén chīh wú-wù]**: empty talk, prattle, speech devoid of substance

言之有理 **[yén chīh yŭ-lĭ]**: to speak with reason; reasonably said

6 言行 **[yén-hsìng]**: words and actions, words and deeds, opinion expressed and action taken

言行不一 **[yén-hsìng pù-ī]**: words and actions fail to correspond; to say one thing and do another

15 言論 **[yén-lùn]**: utterance, words, statement, speech, pronouncement

言論自由 **[yén-lùn tzù-yú]**: freedom of speech

— 2 Strokes —

計

4 計分 **[chì-fēn]** : to record work points

6 計件工資 **[chì-chièn kūng-tzū]** : piecework wages

計件工資制 **[chì-chièn kūng-tzū chìh]** : piecework system, piece wage system, piece rate system, piece rate wage system, piecework wage system

10 計時獎勵工資 **[chì-shíh chiăng-lì kūng-tzū]** : reward system on a time-rate basis

計時工資 **[chì-shíh kūng-tzū]** : time wages, time-rate wages

計時工資制 **[chì-shíh kūng-tzū chìh]** : time-rate wage system, time-work system

12 計量單位 **[chì-liàng tān-wèi]** : unit of measure

13 計較 **[chì-chiăo]** : to consider, to go into a matter, to discuss minutely, to take note of; to be critical of, to find fault with

計較個人名利 **[chì-chiăo kò-jén míng-lì]** : to have concern for personal position and gain

14 計劃 **[chì-huà]** : to plan; plan, planning, program, project, design; planned

計劃指標 **[chì-huà chìh-piāo]** : plan target, planned target

計劃經濟 **[chì-huà chīng-chì]** : planned economy

計劃管理 **[chì-huà kuăn-lĭ]** : planned management

計劃供應 **[chì-huà kūng-yìng]** : planned supply

計劃部 **[chì-huà pù]** : planning department

計劃生產 **[chì-huà shēng-ch'ăn]** : planned production, planned output

計劃收購 **[chì-huà shōu-kòu]** : planned purchase

計劃數字 **[chì-huà shù-tzù]** : plan target, plan quota, plan figure

計算 **[chì-suàn]** : to calculate, to compute; calculation, computation, accounting

計算機 **[chì-suàn-chī]** : calculating machine, computer

計算技術研究所 **[chì-suàn chì-shù yén-chìu-sŏ]** : Computing Technology Institute

計算尺 **[chì-suàn ch'ĭh]** : slide rule

計算員 **[chì-suàn-yüán]** : accountant, a computer

16 計謀 **[chì-móu]** : to plan, to plot; scheme, plan, plot

20 計議 **[chì-ì]** : to debate, to discuss, to deliberate, to weigh

訂

5 訂正 **[tìng-chèng]** : to revise, to edit, to prepare for publication

訂立 **[tìng-lì]** : to conclude, to draw up, to fix on, to enter into (agreement), to contract

6 訂成份 **[tìng ch'éng-fèn]** : to determine class status, to classify as

訂合同 **[tìng hó-t'úng]** : to conclude a contract, to conclude an agreement, to enter into a contract

8 訂制 **[tìng-chìh]** : to determine, to fix, to formulate

訂定 **[tìng-tìng]** : to conclude, to determine, to fix (a date)

10 訂條約 **[tìng t'iáo-yüēh]** : to conclude a treaty

12 訂期 **[tìng-ch'ī]** : to set a time, to fix a date

13 訂盟 **[tìng-méng]** : to conclude an alliance

[17] 訂購 **[tìng-kòu]**: to order, to place an order, to purchase on order

— 3 Strokes —

記

[2] 記入帳內 **[chì-jù chàng-nèi]**: to enter into one's account, to credit to one's account

[3] 記工員 **[chì-kūng-yüán]**: work-recorder, work-point recorder (one of the leading cadre in a production team)

[4] 記仇 **[chì-ch'óu]**: to bear a grudge, to cherish hatred

[5] 記功 **[chì-kūng]**: to record merit, to give a merit

[6] 記名投票 **[chì-míng t'óu-p'iào]**: signed ballot

[7] 記住 **[chì-chù]**: to remember, to keep in mind, to bear in mind

[8] 記取 **[chì-ch'ŭ]**: to remember, to recall something

記性 **[chì-hsìng]**: memory

記事 **[chì-shìh]**: to make a memorandum, to note; notation

[9] 記者 **[chì-chě]**: reporter, newsman, newspaperman, journalist, correspondent

記者招待會 **[chì-chě chāo-tài-hùi]**: press conference, news conference

記述 **[chì-shù]**: to recount something, to describe

[13] 記過 **[chì-kuò]**: to record demerits, to give a demerit

記載 **[chì-tsăi]**: to record, to enter, to inscribe; notation, record

[14] 記號 **[chì-hào]**: sign, trade-mark, mark, symbol, signal

[15] 記賬 **[chì-chàng]**: to charge to an account, to enter into an account

[16] 記憶 **[chì-ì]**: to remember; memory

記憶力 **[chì-ì-lì]**: ability to recall, power of recall, memory

[17] 記錄 **[chì-lù]**: to make a record of, to register, to keep records, to record, to chronicle, to take down; record, chronicle, annals, minutes, minutes of a meeting

記錄片 **[chì-lù p'ièn]**: documentary film

訓

[5] 訓令 **[hsǜn-lìng]**: instruction, injunction, ordinance, order, command

[15] 訓練 **[hsǜn-lièn]**: to train, to drill; training, drill

訕

[10] 訕笑 **[shàn-hsiào]**: to laugh at, to mock; mockery

討

[5] 討平判亂 **[t'ăo-p'íng p'àn-luàn]**: to put down a rebellion

[6] 討伐 **[t'ăo-fā]**: to take punitive action against; punitive campaign, punitive expedition, expeditionary war

討好 **[t'ăo-hăo]**: to ingratiate oneself with, to flatter, to fawn, to toady, to curry favor, to get advantage from

[13] 討債 **[t'ăo-chài]**: to dun, to dun for a debt

[14] 討厭 **[t'ăo-yèn]**: to be disgusted with, to be boring; disagreeable, odious, annoying, detestable, boring

[15] 討價 **[t'ăo-chià]**: to make a price; asking price

討價還價 **[t'ăo-chià huán-chià]**: to bargain, to haggle; bargaining

討論 **[t'ăo-lùn]**: to discuss, to talk over; discussion

討賞 **[t'ăo-shăng]**: to earn a tip

托

14 託管理事會 [t'ō-kuăn lĭ-shìh-hùi] : Trusteeship Council (United Nations)

19 託辭 [t'ō-tz'ú] : to make excuses; excuse, pretext

— 4 Strokes —

訪

9 訪查 [făng-ch'á] : to investigate, to make inquiries

11 訪問 [făng-wèn] : to pay a visit to, to call on, to visit, to make inquiries; interview

訪問團 [făng-wèn t'uán] : visiting mission, visiting delegation

許

5 許可 [hsŭ-k'ŏ] : to allow, to permit, to grant, to sanction; approval, sanction, permission, authorization

許可證 [hsŭ-k'ŏ-chèng] : license, permit, warrant

9 許政 [hsŭ chèng] : Huh Chung (South Korean political leader)

16 許諾 [hsŭ-nò] : to consent, to promise, to give one's word, to commit oneself, to undertake an obligation; consent, promise

訛

12 訛詐 [ó-chà] : to deceive, to cheat, to blackmail; extortion, blackmail

13 訛傳 [ó-ch'uán] : to spread untruths, to spread lies; false stories

設

5 設立 [shè-lì] : to establish, to institute, to set up, to create, to form, to found

6 設在 [shè-tsài] : to be situated

8 設法 [shè-fă] : to devise means, to plan, to try, to endeavor, to attempt, to think of a way

9 設計 [shè-chì] : to plan, to engineer, to scheme, to draw up a plan, to design; plan, project, designing

設計者 [shè-chì-chĕ] : planner, designer, projector

設計能力 [shè-chì néng-lì] : designed capacity

設計院 [shè-chì-yüàn] : designing institute, design and planning institute

設施 [shè-shīh] : plans, methods, programs, arrangements, institutions

12 設備 [shè-pèi] : facilities, installation, equipment

13 設想 [shè-hsiăng] : to conceive, to imagine, to envisage, to presume, to postulate

— 5 Strokes —

詐

19 詐騙 [chà-p'ièn] : to blackmail, to swindle, to extort; blackmail, swindling

詐騙者 [chà-p'ièn-chĕ] : swindler, blackmailer, extortioner

診

8 診所 [chĕn-sŏ] : clinic, polyclinic, doctor's consulting room

18 診斷 [chĕn-tuàn] : to diagnose; diagnosis

詖

15 詖論 [pì-lùn] : paralogism

評

3 評工記分 **[p'íng-kūng chì-fēn]**: evaluation of work and allotment of points

評工記分制度 **[p'íng-kūng chì-fēn chìh-tù]**: system of evaluation of work done and calculation of work points earned

4 評分 **[p'íng-fēn]**: evaluation of work points

評比 **[p'íng-pǐ]**: to compare; comparison, evaluation, competitive judging

5 評功擺好 **[p'íng-kūng pǎi-hǎo]**: to appraise merits and display achievements (i.e., for the instruction and emulation of others)

10 評級 **[p'íng-chí]**: to review one's rank

15 評價 **[p'íng-chià]**: to evaluate, to appraise, to assess; evaluation, appraisal, assessment

評劇 **[p'íng-chǜ]**: Northeast opera (opera originating in Hopeh having female performers)

評論 **[p'íng-lùn]**: to discuss, to comment, to criticize, to review; comment, criticism, review, appraisal, critique

評論家 **[p'íng-lùn-chiā]**: critic, reviewer

評論員 **[p'íng-lùn-yüán]**: commentator

17 評薪 **[p'íng-hsīn]**: to review salary scales; review of salary scales

20 評議 **[p'íng-ì]**: to deliberate; to evaluate; evaluation

評議會 **[p'íng-ì hùi]**: appraisal meeting

訴

9 訴苦 **[sù-k'ŭ]**: to tell one's grievances, to pour out grievances, to air one's grievances, to complain (e.g., the levelling of a charge against a rich landlord by a poor peasant)

11 訴訟 **[sù-sùng]**: lawsuit, case, charges

16 訴諸 **[sù-chū]**: to resort to, to appeal to

詆

13 詆毀 **[tǐ-hŭi]**: to slander, to discredit, to defame

詛

8 詛咒 **[tsŭ-chòu]**: to abuse, to curse, to damn; vituperation, abuse, curse, invective, malediction

詞

20 詞藻 **[tz'ú-tsǎo]**: flowery language

— 6 Strokes —

11 詫異 **[ch'à-ì]**: to be surprised at, amazed

詹

8 詹姆斯敦 **[chān-mŭ-ssū-tūn]**: Jamestown (St. Helena)

誠

13 誠意 **[ch'éng-ì]**: sincerity; unfeigned; with sincerity

17 誠懇 **[ch'éng-k'ěn]**: sincerity, earnestness; sincere, earnest

詰

11 詰問 **[chiéh-wèn]**: to question, to interrogate, to examine

12 詰朝 **[chiéh-chāo]**: tomorrow morning, the next day, the second day

詳

9 詳查 **[hsiáng-ch'á]**: detailed investigation; to investigate in detail

11 詳情 **[hsiáng-ch'íng]**: details, minutiae

詳細說明 **[hsiáng-hsì shuō-míng]**: to explain in detail, to elaborate, to give a detailed account

詳細地 **[hsiáng-hsì tì]**: in detail, carefully, meticulously, scrupulously, conscientiously

14 詳盡的指示 **[hsiáng-chìn te chìh-shìh]**: detailed guidance, detailed instructions

詢

11 詢問 **[hsǖn-wèn]**: to interrogate, to ask, to inquire, to investigate, to question; inquiry, questioning, interrogation, investigation, examination

話

話 **[huà]**: saying, talk, remark

4 話不投機 **[huà pù t'óu-chī]**: uncongenial remarks

9 話柄 **[huà-pǐng]**: topic for conversation, cause for talk, subject for gossip, subject for scandal, something to talk about

話音 **[huà-yīn]**: tone of voice, indication, hint

14 話語 **[huà-yǚ]**: speech, language, words, conversation, phraseology

15 話劇 **[huà-chǜ]**: play, drama

18 話題 **[huà-t'í]**: topic of conversation

該

5 該由 **[kāi-yú]**: up to (i.e., to be up to some one to do something)

14 該管 **[kāi-kuǎn]**: the competent authority, the authorized individual; under the control of, belonging to the jurisdiction of

誇

3 誇口 **[k'uā-k'ǒu]**: to boast, to brag; a boast; boastful

誇大 **[k'uā-tà]**: to exaggerate, to swagger, to boast, to magnify; exaggeration; grandiloquent

5 誇示 **[k'uā-shìh]**: to display; display

13 誇誇其談 **[k'uā-k'uā ch'í t'án]**: big talk; bragging, bombast

20 誇耀 **[k'uā-yào]**: to show off, to boast, to brag; boast; boastful

詭

9 詭計 **[kuěi-chì]**: plot, trick, artful device, maneuver, intrigue, scheme

12 詭詐 **[kuěi-chà]**: tricky, crafty, cunning, treacherous

13 詭詭多端的 **[kuěi-kuěi tō-tuān te]**: crafty, tricky, Machiavellian

21 詭辯 **[kuěi-pièn]**: sophistry, sophism, false reasoning, fallacy

詭辯學派 **[kuěi-pièn hsüéh-p'ài]**: sophists

詬

15 詬罵 **[kòu-mà]**: to curse, to insult, to abuse

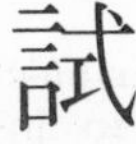

4 試井 **[shìh-chǐng]**: test well

5 試用人員 **[shìh-yùng jén-yüán]**: probationers, persons on probation

6 試行 **[shìh-hsíng]**: to put into operation on

an experimental basis; tentative, experimental, trial

試行生產 **[shih-hsíng shēng-ch'ǎn]**: trial production

8 試制 **[shih-chih]**: trial manufacture

9 試飛 **[shih-fēi]**: test flight

試映 **[shih-ying]**: preview

10 試航 **[shih-háng]**: trial run, test flight

11 試掘 **[shih-chüéh]**: to prospect for; sinking, trial boring

試探 **[shih-t'àn]**: to explore, to sound out, to seek, to test

試探氣球 **[shih-t'àn ch'i-ch'íu]**: trial balloon

14 試製 **[shih-chih]**: to trial-produce, trial manufacture

試圖 **[shih-t'ú]**: to try, to attempt, to intend, to want

23 試驗 **[shih-yèn]**: to test, to experiment; experiment, trial, experimentation, test, examination; experimental

試驗性的 **[shih-yèn-hsìng te]**: tentative, pilot, experimental, trial, test

試驗田 **[shih-yèn t'ién]**: experimental plot, experimental field (i.e., land cultivated by new experimental techniques in order to attain high yields)

— 7 Strokes —

誨

2 誨人不倦 **[hùi-jén pú-chüàn]**: to teach without weariness, to instruct patiently and untiringly

11 誨淫誨盜 **[hùi-yín hùi-tào]**: to debauch people and turn them into gangsters

認

8 認定 **[jèn-tìng]**: to recognize for a certainty

認定為 **[jèn-tìng wéi]**: to identify as, to identify something or somebody

10 認眞 **[jèn-chēn]**: serious, conscientious, painstaking; in earnest, earnestly

認眞對待 **[jèn-chēn tùi-tài]**: to take ... seriously

12 認為 **[jèn-wéi]**: to regard as, to take as, to take the view that, to hold the opinion that, to consider, to think, to maintain

14 認罪 **[jèn-tsùi]**: to confess a crime, to acknowledge guilt, to plead guilty; confession

19 認識 **[jèn-shíh]**: to recognize, to know, to be acquainted with, to be aware of; understanding, awareness, knowledge, cognition

認識論 **[jèn-shíh-lùn]**: theory of knowledge, epistemology

認識模糊 **[jèn-shíh mó-hú]**: lack of clear understanding, vague comprehension

認識水平 **[jèn-shíh shŭi-p'íng]**: level of understanding

誓

7 誓言 **[shih-yén]**: to vow; oath, pledge, vow, word of honor

10 誓師 **[shih-shīh]**: to harangue troops

誓師會議 **[shih-shīh hùi-ì]**: pledge conference

12 誓詞 **[shih-tz'ú]**: oath

說 **[shuō]**: to say, to state, to remark

4 說不盡的 **[shuō-pú-chìn te]**: untold, more than can be said

8 說法 **[shuō-fă]**: way of speaking, version, allegation

說服 **[shuō-fú]**: to persuade, to convince, to induce, to prevail upon; persuasion

說服教育 **[shuō-fú chiào-yǜ]**: education by persuasion

說服工作 **[shuō-fú kūng-tsò]**: persuading, persuasion work

說明 **[shuō-míng]**: to explain, to illustrate, to define, to account for; explanation, illustration, definition; explanatory, expository

說明書 **[shuō-míng-shū]**: synopsis, specifications, operating instructions, instructions

11 說教 **[shuō-chiào]**: to preach; preaching

說理 **[shuō-lĭ]**: reasoning; rational

誕

5 誕生 **[tàn-shēng]**: to be born, to come into being; birth, beginning, inception

誣

7 誣告 **[wū-kào]**: false accusation

誤

2 誤人 **[wù-jén]**: to mislead or misguide people, to lead people astray; misleading

誤入歧途 **[wù-jù ch'í-t'ú]**: to go astray by mistake, to take a wrong path unwittingly

5 誤用 **[wù-yùng]**: to misuse

10 誤差 **[wù-ch'āi]**: to hinder official business

13 誤解 **[wù-chiĕh]**: to misinterpret, to misunderstand; misconception

誤會 **[wù-hùi]**: misunderstanding; to misunderstand

14 誤認爲 **[wù jèn-wéi]**: to mistake for

誘

8 誘拐 **[yù-kuăi]**: to abduct, to kidnap, to entice away

誘使 **[yù-shĭh]**: to induce, to lure, to entice, to tempt, to seduce

語

6 語多乖戾 **[yǚ-tō kuāi-lì]**: most of the remarks are couched in absurd and offensive language

7 語言 **[yǚ-yén]**: language

語言學 **[yǚ-yén-hsüéh]**: linguistics

語言無味 **[yǚ-yén wú-wèi]**: the language is insipid, dull, flat or uninspiring

語言研究所 **[yǚ-yén yén-chìu-sŏ]**: Linguistics and Philology Institute

16 語錄 **[yǚ-lù]**: analects, sayings, aphorisms, discourses, dialogues

— 8 Strokes —

諂

12 諂媚 **[ch'ăn-mèi]**: to flatter, to toady; flattery, sycophancy; flattering

請

6 請求 **[ch'ĭng-ch'íu]**: to ask, to request, to petition, to seek; request, petition

19 請願書 **[ch'ĭng-yüán-shū]**: petition, written petition

誹

[17] 誹謗 **[fĕi-pàng]**: to slander, to defame, to smear, to discredit, to vilify; vilification, slander, defamation

誼

[6] 誼交 **[í-chiāo]**: Ngaigiao (Vietnam)

課

[5] 課外活動 **[k'ò-wài huó-tùng]**: extracurricular activities

[11] 課堂討論 **[k'ò-t'áng t'ăo-lùn]**: seminar; class discussion

[12] 課程 **[k'ò-ch'éng]**: curriculum

諒

[3] 諒山 **[liàng-shān]**: Langson (Vietnam)

[13] 諒解 **[liàng-chiĕh]**: (sympathetic) understanding; to understand

論

[4] 論文 **[lùn-wén]**: essay, thesis, dissertation

[6] 論共產黨員的修養 **[lùn kùng-ch'ăn-tăng-yüán te hsīu-yăng]**: How To Be a Good Communist (title of a booklet by Liu Shao-ch'i)

[9] 論述 **[lùn-shù]**: to elaborate, to deal with, to write in detail, to carry a point in argument

[15] 論壇報 **[lùn-t'án pào]**: Tribune (East German daily newspaper)

[16] 論據 **[lùn-chù]**: argument, basis of argument, contention, data, premise of an argument

[17] 論點 **[lùn-tiĕn]**: point under discussion

[18] 論斷 **[lùn-tuàn]**: to assert, to state, to discuss, to judge, to settle, to conclude

[21] 論辯的 **[lùn-pièn te]**: discursive

談

[4] 談心 **[t'án-hsīn]**: heart-to-heart talk (in particular, "heart-to-heart" talks by the advanced to the less advanced to raise the political understanding of the latter in fighting self-interest and combating revisionist tendencies)

[7] 談判 **[t'án-p'àn]**: to confer, to negotiate; parley, conference, negotiation

[8] 談到 **[t'án-tào]**: to speak of, to talk about, to refer to, to discourse on

[10] 談家史 **[t'án chiā-shĭh]**: to relate family history (e.g., to relate at meetings the family histories of poor peasants and workers in order to arouse class hatred among youth)

調

[3] 調子 **[tiào-tzu]**: tune, tone, air, melody

[5] 調皮 **[t'iáo-p'í]**: sly, cunning, mischievous

調皮搗蛋 **[t'iáo-p'í tăo-tàn]**: to make trouble

[6] 調合 **[t'iáo-hó]**: to mix, to compound, to coordinate

調任 **[tiào-jèn]**: to transfer (e.g., to transfer an official from one post to another)

[7] 調兵遣將 **[tiào-pīng ch'iĕn-chiàng]**: to transfer troops and officers

[8] 調和 **[t'iáo-hó]**: to mix, to blend, to make peace, to placate, to conciliate; conciliation

調和主義 **[t'iáo-hó chŭ-ì]**: "compromise-ism," "adjustism"

調度 **[tiào-tù]**: to calculate, to consider, to arrange; calculation, tactics

[9] 調查 **[tiào-ch'á]**: to examine, to investigate

調查委員會 **[tiào-ch'á wĕi-yüán-hùi]**: investigation committee, investigating committee

調查研究 **[tiào-ch′á yén-chìu]**: investigation and study, investigation and research

調查員 **[tiào-ch′á-yüán]**: inspector, investigator

10 調配 **[tiào-p′èi]**: to allot, to distribute; distribution

11 調動 **[tiào-tùng]**: to move, to transfer

12 調集 **[tiào-chí]**: to assemble

調換 **[tiào-huàn]**: to transpose, to exchange, to change, to alter, to vary, to convert

調開 **[tiào-k′āi]**: to separate, to transfer, to transfer to another post

13 調解 **[t′iáo-chiěh]**: to mediate, to conciliate, to reconcile; mediation, conciliation

調解人 **[t′iáo-chiěh jén]**: mediator, conciliator

調解工作委員會 **[t′iáo-chiěh kūng-tsò wěi-yüán-hùi]**: mediation work committee

調運 **[tiào-yǜn]**: to transport, to ship

15 調整 **[t′iáo-chěng]**: to regulate, to adjust, to tune, to coordinate, to readjust; adjustment, readjustment, regulation, coordination; adjusting, adjusted, regulating

調整價格 **[t′iáo-chěng chià-kó]**: to adjust prices

調整指標 **[t′iáo-chěng chǐh-piāo]**: adjusted targets, adjusted plans

調節 **[t′iáo-chiéh]**: to regulate, to settle

調撥 **[tiào-pō]**: to allot, to distribute, to distribute troops between stations

— 9 Strokes —

15 諫諍 **[chièn-chēng]**: to reprove and warn, to reprimand in a pleasant manner, to reprimand in a friendly manner

諸

13 諸葛亮會 **[chū kó-liàng hùi]**: Chu-ko Liang meeting (i.e., a meeting at which cadres seek the advice of experienced workers and peasants)

諷

9 諷刺 **[fèng-tz′ù]**: to ridicule, to make fun of, to caricature; sarcasm, satire, irony; sarcastic, satiric, ironic

諷刺畫 **[fèng-tz′ù huà]**: caricature, cartoon

諱

7 諱言 **[hùi-yén]**: to conceal, to avoid saying; forbidden talk

10 諱疾忌醫 **[hùi-chí chì-ī]**: to conceal one's sickness and be reluctant to have it cured; to hide a mistake and reject help from others

諱莫如深 **[hùi-mò jú-shēn]**: to conceal, to keep secret

謀

3 謀士 **[móu-shìh]**: counselor, strategist, idea man

5 謀生 **[móu-shēng]**: to make a living, to earn a living, to eke out a living, to earn one's livelihood, to support oneself

7 謀利 **[móu-lì]**: to profit, to turn something to profit, to obtain a return, to make a profit

8 謀取私利 **[móu-ch′ǚ ssū-lì]**: to play one's own game; trying to obtain profit for oneself·

諜

12 諜報 **[tiéh-pào]**: intelligence report, espionage report

諜報員 **[tiéh-pào-yüán]**: spy

諮

13 諮詢 **[tzū-hsǘn]**: to seek advice, to consult, to inquire about

20 諮議委員會 **[tzū-ì wĕi-yüán-hùi]**: advisory committee

諺

14 諺語 **[yèn-yŭ̈]**: proverb, saying, maxim, aphorism, adage

— 10 Strokes —

講

5 講用會 **[chiăng-yùng hùi]**: meeting for discussion and application (i.e., meetings organized during the Cultural Revolution in 1967 for the study of Mao's works and thoughts)

6 講求 **[chiăng-ch'íu]**: to investigate, to search, to seek, to endeavor to do

7 講究 **[chiăng-chìu]**: to investigate, to analyse, to study and perfect carefully, to be particular about; admirable, refined

8 講和 **[chiăng-hó]**: to make peace, to negotiate peace, to discuss the settlement of a dispute

9 講述 **[chiăng-shù]**: to explain, to clarify

10 講師 **[chiăng-shīh]**: lecturer, instructor

講書 **[chiăng-shū]**: to preach, to expound, to explain a text

講座 **[chiăng-tsò]**: professorship, university chair

11 講情 **[chiăng-ch'íng]**: to speak up for someone, to plead for someone, to intercede, to conciliate, to make an appeal

講習 **[chiăng-hsí]**: to explain and discuss, to study; class, lecture

講習班 **[chiăng-hsí pān]**: lecture and study group, study group, class

講理 **[chiăng-lĭ]**: to reason, to appeal to reason, to be reasonable

講授 **[chiăng-shòu]**: to teach, to instruct, to give lectures

講堂 **[chiăng-t'áng]**: classroom, lecture hall, lecture room

13 講解 **[chiăng-chiĕh]**: to explain, to clarify; explanation

講話 **[chiăng-huà]**: to talk, to speak, to address; talk, speech, conversation

講義 **[chiăng-ì]**: lecture syllabus, lecture notes

14 講臺 **[chiăng-t'ái]**: speaker's platform

講演 **[chiăng-yĕn]**: to give a lecture, to speak; lecture, speech

15 講價 **[chiăng-chià]**: to bargain, to haggle

講稿 **[chiăng-kăo]**: manuscript of a lecture, original draft of a speech

講課 **[chiăng-k'ò]**: to instruct, to hold a class, to hold a lecture

16 講學 **[chiăng-hsüéh]**: to devote oneself to learning

講壇 **[chiăng-t'án]**: rostrum, podium, platform, pulpit, tribune

講衞生 **[chiăng wèi-shēng]**: to be careful about hygiene; hygienic

18 講題 **[chiăng-t'í]**: subject of a lecture, topic of a speech

謙

12 謙虛 **[ch'iēn-hsṻ]**: modest, humble, unassuming

謙虛謹慎 **[ch'iēn-hsṻ chĭn-shèn]**: modest and cautious (a personal characteristic of a proletarian revolutionary successor–see the 五個條件, number 5)

謝

8 謝林 **[hsièh-lín]**: Schelling, Friedrich (1775–1854)

14 謝幕 **[hsièh-mù]**: to take bows; curtain call

謝罪 **[hsièh-tsùi]**: to acknowledge a fault, to confess a fault, to apologize

謊

7 謊言 **[huǎng-yén]**: falsehood, fabrication, untruth, distortion

13 謊話 **[huǎng-huà]**: lie, untruth

15 謊價 **[huǎng-chià]**: an overcharge, an exorbitant price

謠

7 謠言 **[yáo-yén]**: rumor, story, gossip

— 11 Strokes —

謹

3 謹小愼微 **[chǐn-hsiǎo shèn-wēi]**: timorous and punctilious, cautious and meticulous

7 謹防 **[chǐn-fáng]**: to guard against, to be heedful, to beware of, to be on one's guard against, to be alert to

13 謹愼 **[chǐn-shèn]**: cautious, discreet, prudent, modest

謾

16 謾罵 **[mân-mà]**: to insult, to abuse

謬

14 謬誤 **[mìu-wù]**: falsehood, error

15 謬論 **[mìu-lùn]**: absurdity, fantastic view, preposterous idea, fallacy, nonsense, false reasoning

謳

14 謳歌 **[ōu-kō]**: to eulogize, to laud; eulogy, panegyric

— 12 Strokes —

證

2 證人 **[chèng-jén]**: witness

6 證件 **[chèng-chièn]**: voucher, certificate

8 證明 **[chèng-míng]**: to certify, to prove, to attest to, to substantiate, to verify, to witness; proof

證明書 **[chèng-míng-shū]**: certificate

11 證章 **[chèng-chāng]**: badge

12 證詞 **[chèng-tz'ú]**: testimony, attestation, declaration

15 證實 **[chèng-shíh]**: to confirm, to verify, to substantiate, to prove, to corroborate, to testify

16 證據 **[chèng-chù]**: proof, evidence, witness, testimony, confirmation, corroboration

譏

8 譏刺 **[chī-tz'ù]**: to ridicule, to deride, to laugh at

10 譏笑 **[chī-hsiào]**: to ridicule, to deride, to jeer at, to laugh at

16 譏諷 **[chī-fèng]**: to satirize; sarcasm, satire, irony; caustic, cutting, stinging

譁

12 譁衆取寵 **[huá-chùng ch'ǚ-ch'ǔng]**: to want to win over the masses by false promises; demagogy

譁然 **[huá-ján]**: noisy, stirred up

22 譁變 **[huá-pièn]**: to mutiny; mutiny

識

6 識字組 **[shíh-tzù tsŭ]**: literacy class

10 識破 **[shíh-p'ò]**: to see through

— 13 Strokes —

警

7 警戒 **[chĭng-chièh]**: to warn, to caution; caution, warning

警戒狀態 **[chĭng-chièh chuàng-t'ài]**: state of alert

警戒綫 **[chĭng-chièh hsièn]**: cordon, warning line

警告 **[chĭng-kào]**: to warn against, to admonish, to give warning, to give the alarm, to warn of danger; warning, admonition

11 警探 **[chĭng-t'àn]**: police spy

警惕 **[chĭng-t'ì]**: to be on the alert; vigilance; alarmed, scared, alert, vigilant

12 警備 **[chĭng-pèi]**: guard, garrison

警備司令 **[chĭng-pèi ssū-lìng]**: garrison commander

警備司令部 **[chĭng-pèi ssū-lìng-pù]**: garrison headquarters

16 警衞 **[chĭng-wèi]**: to guard, to protect, to watch, to stand watch, to stand guard

警衞員 **[chĭng-wèi-yüán]**: bodyguard, guard

20 警覺 **[chĭng-chüéh]**: to arouse from slumber, to stir; vigilance

警覺性 **[chĭng-chüéh-hsìng]**: alertness

譯

4 譯文 **[ì-wén]**: translation, translated text

議

8 議長 **[ì-chăng]**: president (of a parliament); speaker; speaker of the House of Representatives (U.S.); speaker of the House of Commons (Britain)

議定書 **[ì-tìng-shū]**: protocol

議事日程 **[ì-shìh jìh-ch'éng]**: order of the day, agenda

議事規則 **[ì-shìh kuēi-tsé]**: rules of procedure

10 議案 **[ì-àn]**: bill, proposal, recommendation

議員 **[ì-yüán]**: member of parliament, assemblyman, congressman, senator, representative

12 議程 **[ì-ch'éng]**: agenda

13 議會 **[ì-hùi]**: assembly; Parliament (England)

議會領袖 **[ì-hùi lĭng-hsìu]**: parliamentary chief; floor leader (U.S.)

議會黨團 **[ì-hùi tăng-t'uán]**: parliamentary groups

譬

6 譬如 **[p'ì-jú]**: for instance; may be compared with; is like; analagous to

12 譬喻 **[p'ì-yǜ]**: simile, metaphor, allegory, analogy, parable

— 14 Strokes —

譴

11 譴責 **[ch'iĕn-tsé]**: to reprimand, to castigate, to reproach, to rebuke

護

3 護士 **[hù-shìh]**: nurse

8 護岸 **[hù-àn]**: to check bank erosion

護林 **[hù-lín]**: forest protection

10 護航 **[hù-háng]**: escort, convoy

護送 **[hù-sùng]**: to convey, to protect, to escort, to convoy

11 護教論者 **[hù-chiào-lùn-chě]**: apologist

護理 **[hù-lǐ]**: to take care of, to look after a post in the absence of the senior in charge, to act as a locum tenens

12 護堤工程 **[hù-t'í kūng-ch'éng]**: dike strengthening work

護短 **[hù-tuǎn]**: to condone, to excuse someone's faults

13 護照 **[hù-chào]**: passport

16 護衛 **[hù-wèi]**: to protect; protection

— 15 Strokes —

讀

9 讀者 **[tú-chě]**: reader, reading public

10 讀書無用論 **[tú-shū wú-yùng lùn]**: the theory of the futility of studying books (a viewpoint prevailing among Chinese educated youths as a consequence of their disillusionment at being sent to the countryside or remote border areas to be reeducated by the poor and lower middle peasants–a phrase from the Cultural Revolution)

讀書月報 **[tú-shū yüèh-pào]**: The Reader's Monthly (Chinese Communist periodical)

15 讀賣新聞 **[tú-mài hsīn-wén]**: Yomiuri Shimbun (Japanese daily newspaper)

— 16 Strokes —

3 變工 **[pièn-kūng]**: labor exchange; to convert labor power to money

變工隊 **[pièn-kūng tùi]**: labor exchange team, farm work team (mutual assistance work groups in the Communist border regions of Hunan and Kiangsi Provinces)

4 變心 **[pièn-hsīn]**: to alter one's views, to change one's mind

變化 **[pièn-huà]**: to transform, to undergo a change, to change, to metamorphose; change, transformation, metamorphosis, evolution

變天思想 **[pièn-t'iēn ssū-hsiǎng]**: restorationist thought, the hope for the return of the old regime

6 變成 **[pièn-ch'éng]**: to turn into, to change into, to be converted to

變色 **[pièn-sè]**: to change color (i.e., a deviation from being "red" or Communist)

7 變形 **[pièn-hsíng]**: to transform, to change shape; metamorphosis

變更 **[pièn-kēng]**: to change, to transform; change, transformation

8 變例 **[pièn-lì]**: anomaly

9 變相 **[pièn-hsiàng]**: changes, metamorphosis, alteration of outer form; covert, in disguise, under disguised form

變革 **[pièn-kó]**: to reform, to revolutionize; change, reform, reformation

11 變異 **[pièn-ì]**: variation, variance; calamity

變通 **[pièn-t'ūng]**: to accommodate, to fall in with; accommodating

12 變換 **[pièn-huàn]**: to change, to transform

13 變質 **[pièn-chíh]**: to change in quality, to degenerate, to deterioriate

變亂 **[pièn-luàn]**: revolution, rebellion, uprising, mutiny

變電站 **[pièn-tièn chàn]**: transformer station

15 變節 **[pièn-chiéh]**: to alter one's moral principles; to betray, to desert, to become a traitor; apostasy

變節份子 [**piền-chiéh fền-tzu**]: turncoat, apostate, renegade, deserter, backslider

17 變壓器 [**piền-yā ch'ì**]: electric transformer

— 17 Strokes —

讓

7 讓步 [**jàng-pù**]: to yield ground, to give in, to make concessions, to yield a point, to concede; concession

讓步政策 [**jàng-pù chèng-ts'è**]: policy of yielding, policy of concession

讓位於 [**jàng-wèi yǘ**]: to yield place to, to give way to, to abdicate

讕

7 讕言 [**lán-yén**]: slander, defamation, subterfuge, calumny, aspersion, gossip

— 18 Strokes —

讒

7 讒言 [**ch'án-yén**]: slander

17 讒謗 [**ch'án-pàng**]: to slander

— RADICAL 谷 150 —

— 10 Strokes —

豁

3 豁口 [**huō-k'ǒu**]: crack, break

5 豁出去 [**huō-ch'ū-ch'ù**]: to risk, to put everything at stake, to care for nothing

8 豁免 [**huò-miĕn**]: to remit, to exempt from, to free from; immunity from, exemption from

9 豁亮 [**huò-liàng**]: clear, bright

— RADICAL 豆 151 —

豆

16 豆選 [**tòu-hsüăn**]: bean ballots (a method of voting used in rural areas where there is a high percentage of illiteracy whereby the candidates sit with their backs to the voters, there being a dish behind each candidate into which the voter puts a bean to indicate his choice)

— 11 Strokes —

豐

6 豐衣足食 [**fēng-ī tsú-shíh**]: abundant clothing and plentiful food (a slogan used in the land reform to indicate the advantages of the movement)

豐年 [**fēng-nién**]: a plentiful year

豐收 [**fēng-shōu**]: a bumper crop, bumper harvest

11 豐產 [**fēng-ch'ăn**]: rich harvest, abundant production

豐產片 [**fēng-ch'ăn p'ièn**]: a high-yield tract

12 豐富 [**fēng-fù**]: abundant, plentiful, rich

— RADICAL 豕 152 —

— 6 Strokes —

4 象牙海岸共和國 **[hsiàng-yá hăi-àn kùng-hó-kuó]** : Republic of Ivory Coast

15 象徵 **[hsiàng-chēng]** : to symbolize, to signify; symbol, token, emblem; symbolic

象徵主義 **[hsiàng-chēng chŭ-ì]** : symbolism

— 7 Strokes —

7 豪放 **[háo-fàng]** : unrestrained, vigorous

11 豪紳階級 **[háo-shēn chiēh-chí]** : local bully and bad gentry class

豪紳惡霸份子 **[háo-shēn ò-pà fèn-tzu]** : bad gentry and local tyrants

豪爽 **[háo-shuăng]** : magnanimous and straightforward, brave and frank

18 豪舉 **[háo-chŭ]** : heroic deed, heroic plans

— 10 Strokes —

豫 **[yù]** : Honan (abbreviation for 河南)

— RADICAL 豸 153 —

— 3 Strokes —

10 豺狼 **[ch'ái-láng]** : wolf

— RADICAL 貝 154 —

貝

4 貝丹固 **[pèi-tān-kù]** : Betancourt, Romulo (Venezuelan statesman)

11 貝專納 **[pèi-chuān-nà]** : Bechuanaland

14 貝爾格萊德 **[pèi-ĕrh-kó-lái-té]** : Belgrade (Yugoslavia)

15 貝魯特 **[pèi-lŭ-t'è]** : Beirut (Lebanon)

— 2 Strokes —

9 負約 **[fù-yüēh]** : to break an agreement; treaty violation

11 負荷 **[fù-hò]** : to bear the burden on the back, to have the responsibility; load, burden

負責 **[fù-tsé]** : to bear the responsibility, to be responsible

負責人 [fù-tsé jén]: leading member, responsible official, responsible comrade, comrade holding responsible position

13 負債 [fù-chài]: to owe a debt; liabilities, indebtedness

負傷 [fù-shāng]: wounded, injured

16 負擔 [fù-tān]: to bear, to bear a burden; burden, load, care, responsibility

— 3 Strokes —

貢

4 貢什雅 [kùng-shìh-yǎ]: Kungsherya (Tibet)

10 貢紙 [kùng-chǐh]: piaster

16 貢噶 [kùng-ké]: Konka Dzong (Tibet)

20 貢獻 [kùng-hsièn]: to offer, to contribute to, to devote to; offering, contribution

財

2 財力 [ts'ái-lì]: financial strength, power of wealth

5 財主 [ts'ái-chǔ]: wealthy man, capitalist

8 財物 [ts'ái-wù]: property

9 財政 [ts'ái-chèng]: finance, finances, administration of finance; financial, fiscal, monetary

財政後備 [ts'ái-chèng hòu-pèi]: financial reserves

財政貿易工作部 [ts'ái-chèng mào-ì kūng-tsò pù]: Finance and Trade Work Department

財政年度 [ts'ái-chèng nién-tù]: fiscal year

財政撥款 [ts'ái-cheng pō-k'uǎn]: financial allocations

財政部 [ts'ái-chèng pù]: Ministry of Finance

財政部革命造反司令部 [ts'ái-chèng pù kó-mìng tsào-fǎn ssū-lìng-pù]: Ministry of Finance Revolutionary Rebels Headquarters (Cultural Revolution)

財政實力 [ts'ái-chèng shíh-lì]: fiscal solvency, financial solvency

財政收入 [ts'ái-chèng shōu-jù]: financial revenue, state revenue

財政預算 [ts'ái-chèng yǜ-suàn]: budget

10 財迷 [ts'ái-mí]: to be obsessed with the pursuit of wealth; miser

11 財產 [ts'ái-ch'ǎn]: property, assets, possession, treasure, goods and chattels

財貿辦公室 [ts'ái-mào pàn-kūng-shìh]: Staff Office for Finance and Trade

財務管理 [ts'ái-wù kuǎn-lǐ]: financial administration

12 財富 [ts'ái-fù]: wealth, riches, valuables

13 財經 [ts'ái-chīng]: financial and economic

14 財閥 [ts'ái-fá]: plutocrat; Zaibatsu (Japanese term)

18 財糧工作委員會 [ts'ái-liáng kūng-tsò wěi-yüán-hùi]: Finance and Food Work Committee

— 4 Strokes —

販

15 販賣 [fàn-mài]: to sell, to peddle, to traffic in

貨

6 貨色 [huò-sè]: description of goods, varieties of merchandise

7 貨車 [huò-ch'ē]: freight train, freight car, truck

8 貨物 [huò-wù]: goods, freight, cargo, commodity, ware

貨物稅 [huò-wù shùi]: commodity tax, excise tax, goods tax

9 貨品 [huò-p'ǐn] : merchandise, goods

10 貨倉 [huò-ts'āng] : storehouse, silo

11 貨船 [huò-ch'uán] : freighter, cargo vessel

12 貨款 [huò-k'uǎn] : payment for merchandise purchased

貨單 [huò-tān] : manifest, invoice

13 貨源 [huò-yüán] : source of goods supply, commodity supply

14 貨幣 [huò-pì] : coin, currency, medium of exchange

貨幣流通量[huò-pì líu-t'ūng liàng] : amount of currency in circulation

15 貨價 [huò-chià] : price, merchandise price

貫

7 貫串 [kuàn-ch'uàn] : to run through, to go through, to connect

8 貫注 [kuàn-chù] : to concentrate on

9 貫穿 [kuàn-ch'uān] : to go through

11 貫通 [kuàn-t'ūng] : to permeate, to go through, to understand, to have a thorough understanding

15 貫徹 [kuàn-ch'è] : to carry through, to put into effect, to go through with, to carry out thoroughly, to execute, to permeate, to penetrate, to implement

貫徹執行 [kuàn-ch'è chíh-hsíng] : to execute with thoroughness

貫徹方針 [kuàn-ch'è fāng-chēn] : to keep to a policy with thoroughness

貶

貶 [piěn] : to degrade, to demote, to dismiss, to cashier, to censure, to disparage

7 貶抑 [piěn-ì] : to depose, to degrade

貶低 [piěn-tī] : to minimize, to detract from, to degrade, to reduce, to lower, to abuse

10 貶值[piěn-chíh] : to reduce prices, to devaluate, to depreciate; devaluation, depreciation

12 貶爲 [piěn-wéi] : to disparage as, to diminish as

15 貶價 [piěn-chià] : to lower prices, to keep prices down

18 貶謫 [piěn-ché] : to degrade; relegation

貧

5 貧乏 [p'ín-fá] : poor, impoverished, scanty; poverty, impoverishment

貧民 [p'ín-mín] : poor people, poverty-stricken people

貧民窟 [p'ín-mín k'ū] : slum

7 貧困 [p'ín-k'ùn] : privation, poverty, impoverishment, want; poor, in distressed circumstances

13 貧農 [p'ín-núng] : poor peasant

14 貧僱農 [p'ín-kù núng] : poor and landless peasant, poor peasant and hired laborer

貧僱農路綫 [p'ín-kù núng lù-hsièn] : poor peasant-farm laborer line

20 貧礦 [p'ín-k'uàng] : low-grade ore

6 貪多求快 [t'ān-tō ch'íu-k'uài] : to place undue emphasis on quantity and speed

貪多反失 [t'ān-tō fǎn-shīh] : grasp all, lose all

貪污 [t'ān-wū] : corruption, graft (a target of the 三反, q.v.); corrupt

貪污腐化 [t'ān-wū fǔ-huà] : corrupt and degenerate; corruption and degeneration

8 貪官污吏 [t'ān-kuān wū-lì] : corrupt officials

11 貪婪 **[t'ān-lán]**: greedy, ravenous, avaricious, rapacious; greed

責

5 責斥 **[tsé-ch'ìh]**: to reprimand, to rebuke; reprimand, rebuke

責令 **[tsé-lìng]**: to compel

6 責成 **[tsé-ch'éng]**: to lay a charge or responsibility upon, to enjoin, to entrust, to instruct

責任 **[tsé-jèn]**: duty, responsibility, obligation

責任制 **[tsé-jèn chìh]**: responsibility system, system of personal responsibility

責任心 **[tsé-jèn hsīn]**: sense of responsibility

責任事故 **[tsé-jèn shìh-kù]**: accident out of negligence, negligence

12 責備 **[tsé-pèi]**: to reprimand, to rebuke, to scold, to admonish, to reprove, to censure

— 5 Strokes —

費

2 費力 **[fèi-lì]**: to strain oneself, to take pains; effort-consuming, strenuous, laborious, arduous, painstaking

3 費工夫 **[fèi kūng-fū]**: it takes time; time-consuming

5 費用 **[fèi-yùng]**: expenditure, expense, cost, fee, charge, outlay

費加羅報 **[fèi-chiā-ló pào]**: Le Figaro (French daily newspaper)

7 費沙爾 **[fèi-shā-ĕrh]**: Faisal (Crown Prince of Saudi Arabia)

8 費事 **[fèi-shìh]**: vexatious, fussy, troublesome

9 費勁 **[fèi-chìn]**: requiring effort, strenuous

10 費城 **[fèi-ch'éng]**: Philadelphia

13 費瑟 **[fèi-sè]**: Faisal (Crown Prince of Saudi Arabia)

18 費邊主義 **[fèi-piēn chŭ-ì]**: Fabianism

費邊協會 **[fèi-piēn hsiéh-hùi]**: Fabian Society

賀

5 賀功 **[hò-kūng]**: to congratulate someone on his achievement

6 賀年 **[hò-nién]**: new year's greetings

12 賀喜 **[hò-hsĭ]**: to congratulate

賀詞 **[hò-tz'ú]**: congratulatory message, message of greeting

13 賀節 **[hò-chiéh]**: to send greetings on the occasion of a festival

15 賀模 **[hò-mó]**: to congratulate a model worker

貴

9 貴重 **[kuèi-chùng]**: precious, valuable, costly

11 貴族 **[kuèi-tsú]**: the nobility, the aristocracy; noble, aristocratic

14 貴賓 **[kuèi-pīn]**: distinguished guest, guest of honor

15 貴賤之分 **[kuèi-chièn chīh fēn]**: distinction between high and low degree

買

16 買辦 **[mǎi-pàn]**: comprador

買辦階級 **[mǎi-pàn chiēh-chí]**: comprador class

買辦封建制度 **[mǎi-pàn fēng-chièn chìh-tù]**: comprador-feudal system

買辦大資產階級 **[mǎi-pàn tà tzū-ch'ǎn chiēh-chí]**: big comprador bourgeoisie

貿

[8] 貿易 **[mào-ì]**: trade, commerce

貿易議定書 **[mào-ì ì-tìng-shū]**: trade protocol

貿易額 **[mào-ì ó]**: amount of trade

貿易樞紐 **[mào-ì shū-nĭu]**: trade center

貸

[12] 貸款 **[tài-k′uăn]**: to lend, to lend money; loan, credit

— 6 Strokes —

賈

[6] 賈西亞 **[chiă-hsī-yà]**: Garcia, Carlos (Philippine statesman and poet)

[10] 賈桂思想 **[chiă kuèi ssū-hsiăng]**: Chia Kuei's thought (toadyism connected with foreignism, a phrase from the Cultural Revolution)

賄

[13] 賄賂 **[hùi-lù]**: to bribe; bribery

賊

[9] 賊眉鼠眼 **[tséi-méi shŭ-yĕn]**: having an appearance of guilt; to look like a thief

[11] 賊巢 **[tséi-ch′áo]**: robber's den, bandit's lair

[13] 賊贓 **[tséi-tsāng]**: stolen goods, spoils, pillage

[16] 賊頭賊腦 **[tséi-t′óu tséi-năo]**: furtive, villainous looking

資

[4] 資方人員 **[tzū-fāng jén-yüán]**: capitalists and their representatives, those representing capital

[5] 資本 **[tzū-pĕn]**: capital, capital in trade

資本積壓 **[tzū-pĕn chī-yā]**: the tying up of capital

資本家所有制 **[tzū-pĕn-chiā sŏ-yŭ chìh]**: capitalist ownership system

資本主義 **[tzū-pĕn chŭ-ì]**: capitalism; capitalist

資本主義企業 **[tzū-pĕn chŭ-ì ch′ì-yèh]**: capitalist enterprise

資本主義經濟成分 **[tzū-pĕn chŭ-ì chīng-chì ch′éng-fēn]**: capitalist sector of the economy

資本主義復辟 **[tzū-pĕn chŭ-ì fù-pì]**: restoration of capitalism (a phrase particularly current during the Cultural Revolution)

資本主義工商業的社會主義改造 **[tzū-pĕn chŭ-ì kūng-shāng-yèh te shè-hùi chŭ-ì kăi-tsào]**: socialist transformation of capitalist industry and commerce

資本主義社會 **[tzū-pĕn chŭ-ì shè-hùi]**: capitalist society

資本主義所有制 **[tzū-pĕn chŭ-ì sŏ-yŭ chìh]**: capitalist ownership system

資本主義總危機 **[tzū-pĕn chŭ-ì tsŭng wéi-chī]**: general crisis of capitalism

資本主義自發勢力 **[tzū-pĕn chŭ-ì tzù-fā shìh-lì]**: spontaneous tendency toward capitalism

資本累積 **[tzū-pĕn lĕi-chī]**: capital accumulation

資本論 **[tzū-pĕn lùn]**: Das Kapital (Karl Marx)

[7] 資助 **[tzū-chù]**: to finance, to give financial backing to, to contribute funds for

[8] 資金 **[tzū-chīn]**: fund, capital, assets

資金積累 **[tzū-chīn chī-lĕi]**: capital accumulation, accumulation of funds

資金周轉 **[tzū-chīn chōu-chuǎn]**: capital turnover, turnover of capital

10 資格證書 **[tzū-kó chèng-shū]**: credentials

資料 **[tzū-liào]**: data, material

資財 **[tzū-ts'ái]**: wealth, property, valuables, asset

11 資產 **[tzū-ch'ǎn]**: assets, property, estate

資產階級 **[tzū-ch'ǎn chiēh-chí]**: bourgeoisie; bourgeois

資產階級知識份子 **[tzū-ch'ǎn chiēh-chí chīh-shìh fèn-tzu]**: bourgeois intellectuals

資產階級法權 **[tzū-ch'ǎn chiēh-chí fǎ-ch'üán]**: bourgeois rights

資產階級反動路綫 **[tzū-ch'ǎn chiēh-chí fǎn-tùng lù-hsièn]**: bourgeois reactionary line (during the Cultural Revolution, the ideas and policies of Mao's alleged opponents)

資產階級，小資產階級派性 **[tzū-ch'ǎn chiēh-chí, hsiǎo tzū-ch'ǎn chiēh-chí p'ài-hsìng]**: bourgeois and petty bourgeois factionalism (a term used by the press in reference to the self-interest of the various factions involved in the Great Alliance of 1967)

資產階級民主革命 **[tzū-ch'ǎn chiēh-chí mín-chǔ kó-mìng]**: bourgeois democratic revolution

資產階級民族主義 **[tzū-ch'ǎn chiēh-chí mín-tsú chǔ-ì]**: bourgeois nationalism

資產階級民族主義份子 **[tzū-ch'ǎn chiēh-chí mín-tsú chǔ-ì fèn-tzu]**: bourgeois nationalist elements

資產階級思潮 **[tzū-ch'ǎn chiēh-chí ssū-ch'áo]**: a bourgeois trend of thought

資產階級思想 **[tzū-ch'ǎn chiēh-chí ssū-hsiǎng]**: bourgeois ideology

資產階級右派 **[tzū-ch'ǎn chiēh-chí yù-p'ài]**: bourgeois rightists

13 資源 **[tzū-yüán]**: resources

15 資敵 **[tzū-tí]**: to give supplies to the enemy, to support the enemy

— 7 Strokes —

3 賓夕法尼亞 **[pīn-hsī-fǎ-ní-yà]**: Pennsylvania

— 8 Strokes —

6 賤年 **[chièn-nién]**: bad year

9 賤骨頭 **[chièn kǔ-t'óu]**: a loafer, good-for-nothing; a despicable, good-for-nothing fellow

11 賤貨 **[chièn-huò]**: cheap merchandise; a good-for-nothing (i.e., a term of abuse)

15 賤賣 **[chièn-mài]**: to sell cheaply; cheap sale, sale

質

3 質子 **[chíh-tzǔ]**: proton

質子 **[chìh-tzu]**: hostage

質子同步加速器 **[chíh-tzǔ t'úng-pù chiā-sù-ch'ì]**: proton-synchrotron

8 質的 **[chíh-te]**: qualitative

質的飛躍 **[chíh-te fēi-yüèh]**: a qualitative leap, a leap in the quality of (goods, etc.)

11 質問 **[chíh-wèn]**: to question, to inquire into, to cross-examine, to interpolate; interpolation

質問案 **[chíh-wèn àn]**: interpolation

12 質量 **[chíh-liàng]**: mass; quality; qualitative

13 質詢 **[chíh-hsün]**: to question, to inquire into, to cross-examine, to interpolate; interpolation

賦

4 賦予 .... 權力 [**fù-yǘ ... ch'üán-lì**]: to empower, to endow with power, to invest with power, to confer power on

12 賦閑 [**fù-hsién**]: unemployed, out of work, out of office

賢

2 賢人 [**hsién-jén**]: a worthy, a wise man, a man of excellence

8 賢明 [**hsién-míng**]: sagacity, wisdom, intelligence, understanding, enlightenment, discernment; wise

賣

6 賣光 [**mài-kuāng**]: to sell out

7 賣弄 [**mài-nùng**]: to show off, to make a display of

11 賣國 [**mài-kuó**]: to sell out one's country

賣國集團 [**mài-kuó chí-t'uán**]: traitorous clique

賣國條約 [**mài-kuó t'iáo-yüēh**]: treasonable treaty

賣國賊 [**mài-kuó tséi**]: traitor

賠

5 賠本 [**p'éi-pěn**]: to lose one's capital, to run at a loss, to lose one's outlay

14 賠罪 [**p'éi-tsùi**]: to apologize; an apology

17 賠償 [**p'éi-ch'áng**]: to indemnify, to compensate; compensation, indemnity

賠償協定 [**p'éi-ch'áng hsiéh-tìng**]: reparations agreement

賜

13 賜與 [**tz'ù-yǚ**]: to bestow on, to confer on, to grant to

— 9 Strokes —

賴

12 賴着不走 [**lài-ché pù-tsǒu**]: to hang on, refusing to clear out

13 賴債 [**lài-chài**]: to repudiate a debt

賭

8 賭咒 [**tǔ-chòu**]: to take an oath, to vow, to pledge, to swear

11 賭氣 [**tǔ-ch'ì**]: to do something out of rage, to get into a rage and insist on doing something regardless of the consequences

12 賭博 [**tǔ-pó**]: to gamble, to take chances

14 賭誓 [**tǔ-shìh**]: to take an oath, to swear

— 10 Strokes —

賺

11 賺得 [**chuàn-té**]: to earn, to get, to obtain, to acquire, to come by

購

12 購買 [**kòu-mǎi**]: to purchase, to buy

購買力 [**kòu-mǎi lì**]: purchasing power

13 購置 [**kòu-chìh**]: to purchase

16 購辦 [**kòu-pàn**]: to purchase, to acquire, to buy up wholesale

賽

9 賽珍珠 **[sài chēn-chū]**: Pearl Buck (American novelist)

— 12 Strokes —

贊

6 贊成 **[tsàn-ch'éng]**: to approve, to agree to, to endorse, to favor; approval, endorsement, sanction

贊同 **[tsàn-t'úng]**: to join in advocating, to commend, to agree with

7 贊助 **[tsàn-chù]**: to approve, to acquiesce, to assist

12 贊揚 **[tsàn-yáng]**: to praise, to acclaim; commendation, tribute

贈

10 贈送 **[tsèng-sùng]**: to present, to give

12 贈款人 **[tsèng-k'uǎn jén]**: donor

13 贈與 **[tsèng-yǚ]**: to present, to give

— 13 Strokes —

贏

11 贏得 **[yíng-té]**: to win, to obtain, to acquire, to gain

— 15 Strokes —

贖

12 贖買 **[shú-mǎi]**: to redeem, to buy off

贖買金 **[shú-mǎi chīn]**: ransom money

贖買政策 **[shú-mǎi chèng-ts'è]**: redemption policy, buying-out policy (i.e., the policy whereby the Chinese government paid 5 percent annual interest to private shareholders of joint state-private enterprises that were taken from them during the Socialist Transformation of 1955–1956)

14 贖罪 **[shú-tsùi]**: to atone for sin; redemption, atonement

— 17 Strokes —

贛 **[kàn]**: Kiangsi (abbreviation for 江西)

— RADICAL 赤 155 —

赤

3 赤子 **[ch'ìh-tzǔ]**: infant, suckling

4 赤心 **[ch'ìh-hsīn]**: compassionate, sincere, devoted, loyal

赤手空拳 **[ch'ìh-shǒu k'ūng-ch'üán]**: with empty hands, bare-handed, empty-handed, unarmed

6 赤字 **[ch'ìh-tzù]**: deficit figures

11 赤脚教師 **[ch'ìh-chiǎo chiào-shīh]**: barefoot teachers (poor and lower middle peasants who took over control of the schools and the responsibility of teaching the countryside during the Cultural Revolution—People's Daily, October 24, 1968)

赤脚醫生 **[ch'ìh-chiǎo ī-shēng]**: barefoot doctors (young people of the poor and lower middle peasant classes who received elementary medical training in the treatment of common diseases during the Cultural Revolution and who practice in the countryside where qualified doctors are not available)

赤區 **[ch'ìh-ch'ǖ]**: Red areas (i.e., Communist controlled areas)

赤貧 [**ch'ìh-p'ín**]: absolutely poverty stricken, dirt-poor

12 赤痢 [**ch'ìh-lì**]: dysentery

13 赤誠 [**ch'ìh-ch'éng**]: sincere, loyal, honest

赤塔 [**ch'ìh-t'ă**]: Chita

赤道 [**ch'ìh-tào**]: equator; equatorial

赤道上的 [**ch'ìh-tào-shàng te**]: equatorial

14 赤旗日報 [**ch'ìh-ch'í jìh-pào**]: Akahata Nippo (Japanese daily newspaper)

16 赤衞軍 [**ch'ìh-wèi chūn**]: Red Guard

赤衞隊 [**ch'ìh-wèi tùi**]: Red Guard

17 赤膽忠心 [**ch'ìh-tăn chūng-hsīn**]: loyalty, devotion

— 4 Strokes —

赦

赦 [**shè**]: to pardon; pardon

— 7 Strokes —

赫

10 赫哲 [**hò-ché**]: Ho-che (a minority nationality)

14 赫爾辛基 [**hò-ĕrh-hsīn-chī**]: Helsinki (Finland)

赫赫 [**hò-hò**]: awful, fiery, mighty, influential, famous

15 赫魯曉夫 [**hò-lŭ-hsiăo-fū**]: Khrushchev, Nikita S.

赫魯曉夫修正主義集團 [**hò-lŭ-hsiăo-fū hsīu-chèng chŭ-ì chí-t'uán**]: Khrushchev revisionist clique

— RADICAL 走 156 —

走

2 走入歧途 [**tsŏu-jù ch'í-t'ú**]: to go astray, to deviate from the right path, to sidestep, to go off at a tangent

走了一大步 [**tsŏu-le í tà-pù**]: to make a great stride, to make a big step forward

3 走上 [**tsŏu-shàng**]: to travel on, to step onto

走上絕路 [**tsŏu-shàng chüéh-lù**]: to head toward disaster, to head for one's doom

6 走向 [**tsŏu-hsiàng**]: to head towards, to move towards, to step onto

走在前面 [**tsŏu tsài ch'ién-mièn**]: to have the start on, to take the lead, to be in advance of

走在時代的前面 [**tsŏu tsài shíh-tài te ch'ién-mièn**]: to be ahead of the times, to march ahead of the times

7 走私 [**tsŏu-ssū**]: to smuggle; smuggling

走投無路 [**tsŏu-t'óu wú-lù**]: to go down a blind alley, to come to an impasse, to come to a dead end

8 走狗 [**tsŏu-kŏu**]: running dog, lackey, stooge, henchman, hireling

9 走風 [**tsŏu-fēng**]: to let out a secret, to let news leak out

10 走馬看花 [**tsŏu-mă k'àn-huā**]: to take a hurried glance (e.g., to look at wayside flowers from a galloping horse, a phrase used to describe a hasty and superficial investigation of conditions or study of a problem by cadre)

13 走資派 [**tsŏu-tzū p'ài**]: capitalist roaders (those who, in Maoist terms, use or advocate capitalist methods: followers of Liu Shao-ch'i)

16 走鋼絲 **[tsǒu kāng-ssū]**: wire-walking, tight-rope walking

22 走讀生 **[tsǒu-tú-shēng]**: day students, students who live at home

— 2 Strokes —

赴

13 赴會 **[fù-hùi]**: to attend a meeting

15 赴敵 **[fù-tí]**: to go into battle, to plunge into the enemy lines

— 3 Strokes —

起

4 起火 **[ch'ǐ-huǒ]**: to catch fire, to make a fire, to be on fire, to ignite; conflagration

5 起立 **[ch'ǐ-lì]**: to stand up, to rise to one's feet

6 起伏 **[ch'ǐ-fú]**: ups and downs, rising and falling

起因於 **[ch'ǐ-yīn yǘ]**: to result from, to be caused by, to rise from

7 起作用 **[ch'ǐ tsò-yùng]**: to have the function of, to have the effect of, to play a part in

9 起勁 **[ch'ǐ-chìn]**: to be energetic

起飛 **[ch'ǐ-fēi]**: to take off

起哄 **[ch'ǐ-hùng]**: to kick up a fuss over, to disturb, to confuse, to mess up, to railroad (i.e., a vote)

10 起家 **[ch'ǐ-chiā]**: to build up a fortune, to raise the fortunes of one's family

起草 **[ch'ǐ-ts'ǎo]**: to draft, to draw up, to sketch

12 起訴 **[ch'ǐ-sù]**: to sue, to prosecute, to bring a charge against; prosecution, indictment

13 起義 **[ch'ǐ-ì]**: to rebel, to rise in arms; uprising, insurrection, revolt, armed resistance

起義部隊 **[ch'ǐ-ì pù-tùi]**: "insurrection troops" (i.e., Nationalist units that surrendered to the Communists)

起源 **[ch'ǐ-yüán]**: origin

起源於 **[ch'ǐ-yüán yǘ]**: to originate in, to rise from, to take its rise from

15 起碼 **[ch'ǐ-mǎ]**: starting number, opening price; to start from; minimum

17 起點 **[ch'ǐ-tiěn]**: starting point, point of departure

— 5 Strokes —

超

4 超支 **[ch'āo-chīh]**: excess expenditure

超支戶 **[ch'āo-chīh hù]**: deficit household, a household in which expenditures are above income

5 超出 **[ch'āo-ch'ū]**: to stand out, to surpass, to exceed

超包產 **[ch'āo pāo-ch'ǎn]**: to overfulfill a production target

9 超美 **[ch'āo-měi]**: to overtake the United States, to surpass the United States

超帝國主義 **[ch'āo tì-kuó chǔ-ì]**: ultra-imperialism

超音波 **[ch'āo-yīn pō]**: supersonic waves

超音速 **[ch'āo-yīn-sù]**: supersonic speed

超音速飛機 **[ch'āo-yīn-sù fēi-chī]**: supersonic aircraft

超英 **[ch'āo-yīng]**: to overtake England, to surpass England

10 超級炸彈 **[ch'āo-chí chà-tàn]**: superbomb

超高溫 **[ch'āo-kāo wēn]**: super-high temperature

超格 **[ch'āo-kó]**: above average, above standard

超現實主義 **[ch'āo-hsièn-shìh chǔ-ì]**: surrealism

超脫 **[ch'āo-t'ō]**: to transcend, to rise above

超階級 **[ch'āo chiēh-chí]**: to stand above classes; above class, supraclass

超階級的道德觀 **[ch'āo chiēh-chí te tào-té kuān]**: supraclass moral view (i.e., a revisionist, bourgeois point of view)

超絕 **[ch'āo-chüéh]**: surpassing all others; incomparable

超越 **[ch'āo-yüèh]**: to eclipse, to surpass, to excel, to outrival; excelling, surpassing

超越一切的 **[ch'āo-yüèh í-ch'ièh te]**: overriding everything

超經濟的 **[ch'āo chīng-chì te]**: extra-economic

超過 **[ch'āo-kuò]**: to excel, to overtake, to surpass, to pass, to outstrip, to exceed

超聲速導彈 **[ch'āo-shēng-sù tǎo-tàn]**: supersonic guided missile

超額 **[ch'āo-ó]**: to exceed a quota, to overfulfill a norm; overfulfilled quota; above norm, above quota

超額累進工資制 **[ch'āo-ó lěi-chìn kūng-tzū chìh]**: progressive wage system for extra achievement

超額利潤 **[ch'āo-ó lì-jùn]**: surplus profit, above norm profit, super-profit

超額完成 **[ch'āo-ó wán-ch'éng]**: to overfulfill, to surpass, to complete in excess of quota; overfulfillment

趁

趁火打劫 **[ch'èn-huǒ tǎ-chiéh]**: to stir up trouble to one's own advantage, to profit from the misfortune of another

趁空 **[ch'èn-k'ùng]**: to make use of free time, to utilize spare time

9 趁便 **[ch'èn-pièn]**: to take advantage of the opportunity

16 趁機會 **[ch'èn chī-hùi]**: to take advantage of the opportunity

越

5 越出 **[yüèh-ch'ū]**: to exceed, to deviate from, to depart from; departure from principle, aberration

9 越軌 **[yüèh-kuěi]**: to go off the rail or track, to depart from rules, to violate the law; aberrant, improper

越南 **[yüèh-nán]**: Vietnam

越南民主共和國 **[yüèh-nán mín-chǔ kùng-hó-kuó]**: Democratic Republic of Vietnam

越南民主共和國國會 **[yüèh-nán mín-chǔ kùng-hó-kuó kúo-hùi]**: National Assembly of the Democratic Republic of Vietnam

越南通訊社 **[yüèh-nán t'ūng-hsùn-shè]**: Vietnam News Agency (VNA)

13 越獄 **[yüèh-yù]**: to break out of prison, to escape from prison

— 7 Strokes —

趕

3 趕上 **[kǎn-shàng]**: to catch up with, to keep up with

趕上形勢發展 **[kǎn-shàng hsíng-shìh fā-chǎn]**: to keep up with the development of conditions

4 趕不上形勢 **[kǎn-pú-shàng hsíng-shìh]**: to lag behind conditions, not able to keep up with conditions

5 趕出 **[kǎn-ch'ū]**: to expel, to oust, to eject

6 趕先進 **[kǎn hsiēn-chìn]**: to catch up with the advanced (*See* 比學趕幫)

7 趕快 **[kǎn-k'uài]**: to hasten, to hurry up; in a

hurry, rapidly, quickly, hurriedly

趕走 **[kăn-tsŏu]**: to drive out, to expel, to banish, to send away, to cast off

8 趕往 **[kăn-wàng]**: to rush to, to hurry to

13 趕過 **[kăn-kuò]**: to surpass, to overtake

14 趕緊 **[kăn-chĭn]**: speedily, at once; to lose no time

— 10 Strokes —

趨

6 趨向 **[ch'ü-hsiàng]**: to tend to; trend, tendency

13 趨勢 **[ch'ü-shìh]**: to tend to; trend, tendency

— RADICAL 足 157 —

足

12 足跡 **[tsú-chī]**: footprint, trace

足智多謀 **[tsú-chìh tō-móu]**: wise and full of stratagems, wise and resourceful

— 4 Strokes —

趾

10 趾高氣揚的 **[chìh-kāo ch'ì-yáng te]**: cocky, conceited, strutting, swaggering

— 5 Strokes —

距

19 距離 **[chǜ-lí]**: distance, space, interval

距離說 **[chǜ-lí shuō]**: theory of distance

跋

11 跋扈 **[pá-hù]**: domineering

跑

16 跑龍套 **[p'ăo lúng-t'ào]**: to play a minor role; minor post, minor role; utility man; an extra who carries a flag onto stage

跌

14 跌落 **[tiēh-lào]**: to drop, to fall, to descend, to sag

15 跌價 **[tiēh-chià]**: to cut a price; price cut

— 6 Strokes —

跡

12 跡象 **[chī-hsiàng]**: sign, indication, symptom, token

跟

3 跟上 **[kēn-shàng]**: to keep abreast of, to keep pace with, to keep up with

6 跟在後面 **[kēn tsài hòu-mièn]**: to follow on the heels of

12 跟着 **[kēn-che]**: to follow, to come in the wake of

跟着別人學舌 **[kēn-che piéh-jén hsüéh-shé]**: to repeat (mechanically) the words of others, to parrot

15 跟踪 **[kēn-tsūng]**: to follow a clue, to follow a track, to pursue

跨

跨 **[k'uà]**: to span, to extend over, to bestride, to straddle, to surpass, to excel, to pass over

6 跨行業 **[k'uà háng-yèh]**: to permeate the trades; permeation of trades

11 跨部門 **[k'uà pù-mén]**: to permeate departments; permeation of departments

12 跨單位 **[k'uà tān-wèi]**: to permeate the units; permeation of units

路

8 路易斯安那 **[lù-ì-ssū-ān-nà]**: Louisiana

路易斯港 **[lù-ì-ssū kăng]**: Port Louis (Mauritius)

10 路條 **[lù-t'iáo]**: pass, safe-conduct

11 路透社 **[lù-t'òu shè]**: Reuter's Ltd. (British news agency)

14 路綫 **[lù-hsièn]**: course, line, direction

15 路德 **[lù-té]**: Luther, Martin (1483–1546)

路德會 **[lù-té hùi]**: Lutheran Church

跳

8 跳板 **[t'iào-păn]**: springboard (figurative sense); gangway plank, diving board

— 8 Strokes —

踐

9 踐約 **[chièn-yüēh]**: to keep an appointment, to keep an agreement, to fulfill a promise

15 踐踏 **[chièn-t'à]**: to trample, to tread

踏

10 踏脚石 **[t'à-chiăo shíh]**: stepping-stone

踢

5 踢出去 **[t'ī-ch'ū-ch'ù]**: to kick out

踪

13 踪跡 **[tsūng-chī]**: trace, vestige, footprint, track

— 9 Strokes —

蹂

27 蹂躪 **[jóu-lìn]**: to trample down, to crush under one's heel, to ravish, to violate, to ravage; oppressive exactions, the devastations of the military

— 11 Strokes —

蹟

12 蹟象 **[chī-hsiàng]**: sign, indication, symptom, token

蹣

12 蹣跚不前 **[p'án-shān pù-ch'ién]**: to limp along without advancing, to falter, to wobble, to totter

— 12 Strokes —

蹲

17 蹲點 **[tūn-tiĕn]**: (literally) to squat on the spot, to be sent to work in the rural areas to study conditions (i.e., refers to a leading cadre spending a period of time at the grass roots, living and working among the masses

in order to gather experience and then put it to use)

— 13 Strokes —

11 躉貨 **[tŭn-huò]**: to corner the market

15 躉賣 **[tŭn-mài]**: to sell wholesale

— 14 Strokes —

躊

19 躊躇 **[ch'óu-ch'ú]**: to hesitate, to be indecisive; hesitation, vacillation, uncertainty, indecision

躊躇不進 **[ch'óu-ch'ú pú-chìn]**: indecisive; hesitant and not moving forward

躍

12 躍進 **[yüèh-chìn]**: to leap forward; a leap forward

— RADICAL 身 158 —

身

2 身入與深入 **[shēn-jù yǚ shēn-jù]**: to enter physically as well as mentally (e.g., cadres should use brains as well as hands, laboring with the masses but at the same time leading them in revolution

4 身心全面發展的共產主義新人 **[shēn-hsīn ch'üán-mièn fā-chăn te kūng-ch'ăn chŭ-ì hsīn-jén]**: the new Communist man who is well-developed both physically and intellectually

6 身份 **[shēn-fèn]**: status, rank, identity

身份證 **[shēn-fèn chèng]**: identity card, identification card

7 身材 **[shēn-ts'ái]**: figure, build, physique

23 身體好、學習好、工作好 **[shēn-t'ĭ hăo, hsüéh-hsí hăo, kūng-tsò hăo]**: keep healthy, study well, and work well (a phrase coined by Mao Tse-tung in 1955 to exhort students, and which indicates the characteristics of a "three-good student" 三好學生, q.v.)

身體力行 **[shēn-t'ĭ lì-hsíng]**: to put into practice

— 4 Strokes —

躭

15 躭誤 **[tān-wù]**: to delay, to impede, to hinder

17 躭擱 **[tān-kō]**: to hinder, to delay, to loiter, to postpone

— 7 Strokes —

躲

4 躲不開 **[tŏ-pù-k'āi]**: unavoidable, no escape from

16 躲避 **[tŏ-pì]**: to avoid, to withdraw, to hide from

19 躲懶 **[tŏ-lăn]**: to shirk work, to loiter, to be lazy

— 8 Strokes —

躺

10 躺倒不幹 **[t'ăng-tăo pú-kàn]**: to lie low and be inactive

— RADICAL 車 159 —

車

2 車刀 [**ch'ē-tāo**] : lathe tool

3 車工 [**ch'ē-kūng**] : lathe work; lathe operator, machine tool operator

4 車水設備 [**ch'ē-shŭi shè-pèi**] : pumping equipment

7 車床 [**ch'ē-ch'uáng**] : lathe

車身 [**ch'ē-shēn**] : chassis, vehicle body

8 車具 [**ch'ē-chǜ**] : vehicle accessories and parts

9 車架 [**ch'ē-chià**] : chassis, vehicle frame

車軌 [**ch'ē-kuĕi**] : track, rail

12 車間 [**ch'ē-chiēn**] : shop, workshop, machine shop, room

車軸 [**ch'ē-chóu**] : axle

14 車禍 [**ch'ē-huò**] : automobile accident

15 車廠 [**ch'ē-ch'ăng**] : motor pool, vehicle barn

車輛 [**ch'ē-liàng**] : vehicle, car, cart

車輪戰 [**ch'ē-lún chàn**] : many battles in succession with the same opponent (literally, a "cart wheel battle")

— 1 Stroke —

4 軋孔機 [**yà-k'ŭng chī**] : key punch

8 軋花廠 [**yà-huā ch'ăng**] : cotton gin

13 軋碎我字 [**yà-sùi wŏ-tzù**] : to smash the word "I (self)" (i.e., to negate oneself completely, a phrase from the Cultural Revolution)

16 軋鋼廠 [**yà-kāng ch'ăng**] : rolling mill

— 2 Strokes —

軍

軍 [**chūn**] : corps, army

2 軍人 [**chūn-jén**] : serviceman, soldier

軍人家屬 [**chūn-jén chiā-shŭ**] : army dependents, dependents of military personnel

3 軍士長 [**chūn-shìh chăng**] : Master Sergeant (U.S. Army and Air Force); Chief Petty Officer (U.S. Navy)

4 軍分區 [**chūn-fēn ch'ū**] : military subdistrict

軍火 [**chūn-huŏ**] : ammunition, munitions

5 軍民兼顧 [**chūn-mín chiēn-kù**] : to give consideration to both army and people

軍民一致 [**chūn-mín í-chìh**] : with army and people united

8 軍長 [**chūn-chăng**] : corps commander, army commander

軍法 [**chūn-fă**] : military law

軍事 [**chūn-shìh**] : military affairs; military

軍事集團 [**chūn-shìh chí-t'uán**] : military bloc, military group

軍事監察部 [**chūn-shìh chiēn-ch'á pù**] : Inspectorate of the Armed Forces

軍事法庭 [**chūn-shìh fă-t'īng**] : military court, court-martial, provost court (U.S.A.)

軍事學校 [**chūn-shìh hsüéh-hsiào**] : military academy

軍事醫學科學院 [**chūn-shìh ī-hsüéh k'ō-hsüéh-yüàn**] : Academy of Military Medical Sciences (Chinese People's Liberation Army)

軍事管制委員會 [**chūn-shìh kuăn-chìh wĕi-yüán-hùi**] : Military Control Commission

軍事管理[chūn-shìh kuǎn-lǐ]: military administration, military supervision

軍事共產主義 [chūn-shìh kùng-ch'ǎn chǔ-ì]: military communism

軍事工業[chūn-shìh kūng-yèh]: war industries

軍事冒險[chūn-shìh mào-hsiěn]: military adventure, military gamble, military risk

軍事冒險政策 [chūn-shìh mào-hsiěn chèng-ts'è]: military adventurism

軍事委員會[chūn-shìh wěi-yüán-hùi]: Military Affairs Commission

軍事演習[chūn-shìh yěn-hsí]: war exercises, maneuvers, military maneuver

9 軍政一致[chūn-chèng í-chìh]: with army and government united

軍政人員[chūn-chèng jén-yüán]: military and administrative personnel

軍政部 [chūn-chèng pù]: Ministry of War

軍政委員會[chūn-chèng wěi-yüán-hùi]: Military and Administrative Committee

11 軍區[chūn-ch'ū]: military region; military district

軍區司令部[chūn-ch'ū ssū-lìng-pù]: military area command

軍械[chūn-hsièh]: ordnance, military supplies

軍國主義[chūn-kuó chǔ-ì]: militarism

軍部[chūn-pù]: corps headquarters

12 軍備 [chūn-pèi]: armament, arms

軍備競賽[chūn-pèi chìng-sài]: arms race, armaments race

軍備部[chūn-pèi pù]: Ministry of Armaments

軍隊 [chūn-tùi]: troops, military forces

軍隊昇格[chūn-tùi shēng-kó]: advancement of troops status (i.e., from guerrilla to local forces, or from local forces to regular army status)

軍隊地方化[chūn-tùi tì-fāng-huà]: localization of troops (i.e., giving an army a local name based on its geographical location)

14 軍種 [chūn-chǔng]: military branches

軍閥 [chūn-fá]: warlord, militarist

軍閥主義[chūn-fá chǔ-ì]: warlordism, militarism

軍閥作風[chūn-fá tsò-fēng]: warlord style (i.e., refers to the manner of officers who bully enlisted men or soldiers who bully civilians)

軍需人員[chūn-hsū jén-yüán]: supply personnel, quartermaster personnel

軍需品[chūn-hsū p'ǐn]: military supplies, military stores, quartermaster goods

軍團 [chūn-t'uán]: army group, corps

15 軍墾費[chūn-k'ěn fèi]: military land reclamation expenses

軍樂隊 [chūn yüèh-tùi]: military band

18 軍糧 [chūn-liáng]: ration for troops

20 軍艦 [chūn-chièn]: naval vessel, warship

軍齡[chūn-líng]: length of military service (i.e., in the PLA)

軌

11 軌距 [kuěi-chù]: gauge (i.e., of railroad track)

13 軌道 [kuěi-tào]: orbit, track, rail, railway, tramway

15 軌範 [kuěi-fàn]: rule, pattern, sample

— 4 Strokes —

軟

10 軟弱 [juǎn-jò]: weak, feeble

軟弱性 **[juǎn-jò-hsìng]**: flabbiness, softness, weakness, feebleness

12 軟硬兼施 **[juǎn-yìng chiēn-shīh]**: to use persuasion and force together; the "iron fist in the velvet glove"

13 軟禁 **[juǎn-chìn]**: to be under surveillance, to be confined to residence; house arrest, house confinement

19 軟騙硬逼 **[juǎn-p'ièn yìng-pī]**: by menaces and tricks, by blackmail and force

— 5 Strokes —

4 軸心 **[chóu-hsīn]**: axis

軸心國 **[chóu-hsīn kuó]**: the Axis powers

— 6 Strokes —

5 較比 **[chiǎo-pǐ]**: to compare, to test

9 較勁 **[chiǎo-chìn]**: to test one's strength, to compete

12 較著 **[chiǎo-chù]**: to illumine a topic; clear, distinct

較量 **[chiǎo-liàng]**: to compare, to compete, to engage in a match, to engage in a contest; test of strength

載

2 載入 **[tsài-jù]**: to go down on record, to be recorded; inscribed, written down, recorded

8 載波電路 **[tsài-pō tièn-lù]**: carrier wave circuits

9 載重汽車 **[tsài-chùng ch'ì-ch'ē]**: truck

— 7 Strokes —

輕

3 輕工業 **[ch'īng kūng-yèh]**: light industry

輕工業部 **[ch'īng kūng-yèh pù]**: Ministry of Light Industry

7 輕快 **[ch'īng-k'uài]**: light and quick, easy to handle

8 輕易 **[ch'īng-ì]**: to treat with unconcern, recklessly, lightly

9 輕重 **[ch'īng-chùng]**: weight, relative importance

輕重緩急 **[ch'īng-chùng huǎn-chí]**: in order of importance and urgency

輕重倒置 **[ch'īng-chùng tǎo-chìh]**: to lack a sense of proportion

輕信謠言 **[ch'īng-hsìn yáo-yén]**: to give credence to rumors

輕型登陸艇 **[ch'īng-hsíng tēng-lù t'ǐng]**: light landing craft

輕炮 **[ch'īng-p'ào]**: light artillery

輕便 **[ch'īng-pièn]**: light and handy, portable

輕便工作 **[ch'īng-pièn kūng-tsò]**: light work, easy work

輕便鐵道 **[ch'īng-pièn t'iěh-tào]**: light rails, light railway, auxiliary or spur railway

11 輕視 **[ch'īng-shìh]**: to slight, to minimize, to underestimate, to underrate, to be contemptuous of, to depreciate, to disparage, to look down on

輕率 **[ch'īng-shuài]**: careless, rash, hasty, perfunctory, frivolous, disrespectful of; rashness, lack of mature consideration, without sufficient consideration

12 輕勞動 **[ch'īng láo-tùng]**: light work

13 輕傷者 **[ch'īng-shāng-chě]**: the lightly wounded, walking wounded

輕微 [ch'īng-wēi] : slight, light, minor, petty, insignificant, light, feeble, delicate

16 輕機關槍 [ch'īng chī-kuān-ch'iāng] : light machine gun, submachine gun

18 輕騎手 [ch'īng ch'í-shŏu] : light cavalry (i.e., mobile teams of doctors, artists, or technical workers)

輔

7 輔助 [fŭ-chù] : auxiliary

輔助勞動 [fŭ-chù láo-tùng] : auxiliary labor, part-time work

15 輔導 [fŭ-tăo] : assistance and guidance; coach, tutor

輔導員 [fŭ-tăo-yüán] : inspector, director, leader, guide, counsellor

— 8 Strokes —

16 輟學 [ch'ò-hsüéh] : to stop studying, to cease attending school

輪

8 輪作 [lún-tsò] : to rotate crops; crop rotation

輪牧 [lún-mù] : pasture rotation

10 輪流 [lún-líu] : to rotate, to take turns; rotation, shift, in turn

輪班 [lún-pān] : to rotate, to take turns; rotation, shift, in turn

11 輪船 [lún-ch'uán] : steamer, steamship

13 輪廓 [lún-k'ùo] : contour, outline, frame

輝

13 輝煌 [hūi-huáng] : brilliant, glorious, splendid, eminent, illustrious

輥

12 輥軸 [kŭn-chóu] : roller axle

13 輥道 [kŭn-tào] : roller bed

9 輜重 [tzū-chùng] : troop supplies, impedimenta, baggage

— 9 Strokes —

輻

10 輻射 [fú-shè] : radiation

輻射化學 [fú-shè huà-hsüéh] : radiation chemistry

輸

輸 [shū] : to lose, to lose out, to be defeated, to get a beating; to pay, to transport; an offering

2 輸入 [shū-jù] : to import; import, importation

5 輸出 [shū-ch'ū] : to export; exportation

輸出者 [shū-ch'ū-chĕ] : exporter

6 輸血血液病研究所 [shū-hsüeh hsüeh-yèh-pìng yén-chìu-sŏ] : Blood Transfusion and Hematology Institute (Chinese Academy of Medical Sciences)

13 輸電綫 [shū-tièn hsièn] : transmission line

輸電網 [shū-tièn wăng] : transmission network

— 10 Strokes —

輿

15 輿論 [yǜ-lùn] : public opinion

— 11 Strokes —

轉

2 轉入 [chuăn-jù] : to lapse into, to fall into, to get into, to turn into

轉入低潮 [chuăn-jù tī-ch'áo] : to ebb, to subside, to decline, to be on the ebb

轉入地下 [chuăn-jù tì-hsià] : to go underground

4 轉化 [chuăn-huà] : to transform into, to turn into, to change into, to convert to

6 轉交 [chuăn-chiāo] : to hand over to, to turn over to

轉向 [chuăn-hsiàng] : to turn to, to divert to, to change to, to turn towards, to change direction

轉危爲安 [chuăn-wéi wéi-ān] : to turn danger into safety

7 轉折點 [chuăn-ché tiĕn] : turning point

11 轉移 [chuăn-í] : to divert from, to turn away, to shift, to transfer; diversion

12 轉換到 [chuăn-huàn tào] : to switch to, to convert to

13 轉業 [chuăn-yèh] : to change one's occupation; to transfer; conversion, transformation

轉業和復員 [chuăn-yèh hó fù-yüán] : to transfer to civilian work from active service

轉業軍人 [chuăn-yèh chün-jén] : demobilized soldier (i.e., transferred to civilian work)

轉運站 [chuăn-yün chàn] : transfer post, junction, transshipment station

15 轉播 [chuăn-pō] : to relay

20 轉爐 [chuăn-lú] : Bessemer converter

22 轉彎抹角 [chuăn-wān mò-chiăo] : to beat around the bush

23 轉變 [chuăn-pièn] : to convert; transformation, conversion, remolding, modification, alternation

轉變關頭 [chuăn-pièn kuān-t'óu] : turning point, critical moment, critical juncture

— 12 Strokes —

轎

7 轎車 [chiào-ch'ē] : passenger car, sedan

— 14 Strokes —

轟

9 轟炸 [hūng-chà] : to bomb

轟炸機 [hūng-chà-chī] : bomber

11 轟動 [hūng-tùng] : to make a great stir, to be astir with; sensation; sensational, astir, stirring

18 轟擊 [hūng-chī] : to crash, to bombard, to fire on

21 轟轟烈烈 [hūng-hūng lièh-lièh] : with vigor and vitality, enthusiastic, stirring, dynamic, vigorous

— RADICAL 辛 160 —

辛

6 辛亥革命 **[hsīn-hài kó-mìng]**: the Hsin-hai Revolution, the Revolution of 1911

9 辛苦 **[hsīn-k'ŭ]**: hardship, suffering; trying, distressing

辛苦從事 **[hsīn-k'ŭ ts'úng-shìh]**: to labor over, to take great pains over, to take trouble over

辛迪加 **[hsīn-tí-chiā]**: syndicate

13 辛勤的努力 **[hsīn-ch'ín te nŭ-lì]**: devoted labors, assiduous effort

— 5 Strokes —

9 辜負 **[kū-fù]**: to desecrate, to be unworthy of, to let down; ingratitude; ungrateful

— 9 Strokes —

辦

4 辦公 **[pàn-kūng]**: to transact official business

辦公室 **[pàn-kūng-shìh]**: office

6 辦好 **[pàn-hăo]**: to handle well, to manage well; to finish handling or managing

8 辦法 **[pàn-fă]**: means, method, device

辦事 **[pàn-shìh]**: to manage an affair, to handle affairs, to have charge of an affair, to transact business

辦事處 **[pàn-shìh ch'ù]**: administrative area, office

辦事公道 **[pàn-shìh kūng-tào]**: to be fair in handling affairs

13 辦罪 **[pàn-tsùi]**: to punish, to penalize, to sentence

辨

7 辨別 **[pièn-piéh]**: to distinguish, to discriminate, to differentiate

8 辨明 **[pièn-míng]**: to distinguish clearly, to clarify

14 辨認 **[pièn-jèn]**: to recognized, to distinguish, to identify, to perceive

— 12 Strokes —

辭

3 辭工 **[tz'ú-kūng]**: to leave work, to come off duty, to give up work, to resign from work

5 辭去 **[tz'ú-ch'ǜ]**: to resign, to step down

8 辭典 **[tz'ú-tiĕn]**: dictionary, lexicon

10 辭退 **[tz'ú-t'ùi]**: to give up a position, to refuse, to discharge, to dismiss

18 辭職 **[tz'ú-chíh]**: to resign, to resign from office; resignation

— 14 Strokes —

辯

5 辯白 **[pièn-pái]**: to justify, to defend, to explain clearly

10 辯倒 **[pièn-tăo]**: to refute someone's argument, to overturn an argument

12 辯冤 **[pièn-yüān]**: to refute a false accusation, to redress a grievance

14 辯駁 **[pièn-pó]**: to refute, to contest, to argue against

15 辯論 **[pièn-lùn]**: to dispute, to debate, to argue, to contend; debate, debating

辯論會 **[pièn-lùn hùi]**: debating society, debate, forum

19 辯證 **[pièn-chèng]** : dialectical

辯證法 **[pièn-chèng-fǎ]** : dialectics, dialectical method; dialectical

辯證法法則 **[pièn-chèng-fǎ fǎ-tsé]** : law of dialectics

辯證法唯物論 **[pièn-chèng-fǎ wéi-wù-lùn]** : dialectical materialism

辯證發展過程 **[pièn-chèng fā-chǎn kuò-ch'éng]** : dialectical process

辯證唯物主義 **[pièn-chèng wéi-wù chǔ-ì]** : dialectical materialism

辯證唯物主義觀點 **[pièn-chèng wéi-wù chǔ-ì kuān-tiěn]** : viewpoint of dialectical materialism (one of the 四大觀點, q.v.)

21 辯護 **[pièn-hù]** : to defend, to argue for, to apologize for

辯護人 **[pièn-hù-jén]** : barrister, counsel

辯護士 **[pièn-hù-shìh]** : barrister, lawyer, attorney

— RADICAL 辰 161 —

9 辰砂 **[ch'én-shā]** : cinnabar

— 6 Strokes —

震

5 震旦報 **[chèn-tàn pào]** : L'Aurore (French daily newspaper)

農

4 農戶 **[núng-hù]** : peasant household, agricultural household, farming family

5 農民 **[núng-mín]** : peasantry, peasant, farmer

農民翻身大隊 **[núng-mín fān-shēn tà-tùi]** : peasants' corps for effecting the turnover (a term in use during the land reform)

農民協會 **[núng-mín hsiéh-hùi]** : peasants association

農民個體所有制 **[núng-mín kò-t'ǐ sǒ-yǔ chìh]** : system of individual ownership by peasants

農民思想 **[núng-mín ssū-hsiǎng]** : peasant ideology (i.e., narrow-mindedness, shortsightedness)

農民大翻身 **[núng-mín tà fān-shēn]** : the peasants' great turnover (a slogan used during the land reform to arouse class hatred)

農奴 **[núng-nú]** : serf

農奴戟 **[núng-nú chǐ]** : Serf Halberds (Red Guard Fighters in the Tibet Nationality College)

農奴制度 **[núng-nú chìh-tù]** : serfdom

農奴主 **[núng-nú chǔ]** : serf master

農田水利 **[núng-t'ién shǔi-lì]** : irrigation and water conservancy

7 農作物 **[núng tsò-wù]** : crop

農村 **[núng-ts'ūn]** : village, countryside; rural, agrarian, agricultural

農村副業 **[núng-ts'ūn fù-yèh]** : rural subsidiary industry

農村人民公社 **[núng-ts'ūn jén-mín kūng-shè]** : rural people's commune

農村工作部 **[núng-ts'ūn kūng-tsò pù]** : rural work department

農村社會主義教育運動 **[núng-ts'ūn shè-hùi chǔ-ì chiào-yǜ yǜn-tùng]** : farm village socialist education movement

8 農具 **[núng-chǜ]** : farm tool, farm implements

161

農林牧副漁全面發展 **[núng lín mù fù yǘ ch'üán-mièn fā-chǎn]** : all-round development of agriculture, forestry, animal husbandry, side-occupations, and fisheries (a phrase from the Great Leap Forward)

農林牧副漁互相結合的方針 **[núng lín mù fù yǘ hù-hsiāng chiéh-hó te fāng-chēn]** : the policy of combining farming, forestry, animal husbandry, side-occupations, and fisheries

11 農產品 **[núng ch'ǎn-p'ǐn]** : farm goods, farm produce, agricultural products

農產品採購部 **[núng ch'ǎn-p'ǐn ts'ǎi-kòu pù]** : Ministry of Procurements of Agricultural Products

農副業 **[núng fù-yèh]** : subsidiary agricultural production, secondary agricultural production (i.e., meat and vegetables)

農副業產品 **[núng fù-yèh ch'ǎn-p'ǐn]** : subsidiary agricultural products, secondary agricultural products (i.e., meat and vegetables)

12 農場 **[núng-ch'ǎng]** : farmland, farm, plantation, agricultural experiment station

農閑 **[núng-hsién]** : slack farming season

農貸 **[núng-tài]** : agricultural loan, farm loan, government credit for agriculture

13 農會 **[núng-hùi]** : peasant association

農業 **[núng-yèh]** : agriculture; agricultural, farming

農業產業軍 **[núng-yèh ch'ǎn-yèh chǖn]** : industrial army for agriculture

農業機器製造工業 **[núng-yèh chī-ch'ì chìh-tsào kūng-yèh]** : agricultural machine industry

農業機械化 **[núng-yèh chī-hsièh-huà]** : mechanization of agriculture

農業機械化研究所 **[núng-yèh chī-hsièh-huà yén-chìu-sŏ]** : Agricultural Mechanization Institute

農業機械部 **[núng-yèh chī-hsièh pù]** : Ministry of Agricultural Machine Building Industry

農業技術 **[núng-yèh chì-shù]** : agricultural techniques, farming techniques, agrotechniques

農業技術推廣站 **[núng-yèh chì-shù t'ūi-kuǎng chàn]** : agro-technical station

農業技術員 **[núng-yèh chì-shù-yüán]** : agrotechnicians (i.e., graduates of the new schools established after 1968)

農業氣象研究室 **[núng-yèh ch'ì-hsiàng yén-chìu-shìh]** : Agricultural Meteorology Research Laboratory

農業中學 **[núng-yèh chūng-hsüéh]** : agricultural middle school

農業發展綱要 **[núng-yèh fā-chǎn kāng-yào]** : National Program of Agricultural Development

農業副產品 **[núng-yèh fù-ch'ǎn-p'ǐn]** : subsidiary farm product

農業合作化 **[núng-yèh hó-tsò-huà]** : agricultural collectivization

農業現代化 **[núng-yèh hsièn-tài-huà]** : modernization of agriculture

農業信用合作社 **[núng-yèh hsìn-yùng hó-tsò-shè]** : rural credit cooperative, agricultural credit cooperative

農業科學技術 **[núng-yèh k'ō-hsüéh chì-shù]** : scientific agricultural techniques

農業八字憲法 **[núng-yèh pà-tzŭ hsièn-fǎ]** : Eight Point Charter for Agriculture (*See* 八字憲法)

農業部 **[núng-yèh pù]** : Ministry of Agriculture

農業社會主義 **[núng-yèh shè-hùi chǔ-ì]** : agrarian socialism, agricultural socialism (i.e., absolute egalitarianism based on a small farm economy)

農業社會主義改造 **[núng-yèh shè-hùi chǔ-ì kǎi-tsào]** : socialist transformation of agriculture

農業社會化 **[núng-yèh shè-hùi-huà]** : socialization of agriculture

農業生產合作社 **[núng-yèh shēng-ch'ăn hó-tsò-shè]**: agricultural producers' co-operative

農業生產資料 **[núng-yèh shēng-ch'ăn tzū-liào]**: agricultural means of production

農業生物學研究所 **[núng-yèh shēng-wù-hsüéh yén-chìu-sŏ]**: Agrobiology Institute

農業試驗場 **[núng-yèh shìh-yèn ch'ăng]**: experimental farm

農業稅 **[núng-yèh shùi]**: agricultural tax

農業增產競賽 **[núng-yèh tsēng-ch'ăn chìng-sài]**: emulation drive for higher farm output

農業爲基礎 **[núng-yèh wéi chī-ch'ŭ]**: with agriculture as the foundation

14 農漁部 **[núng-yű pù]**: Ministry of Agriculture and Fisheries

15 農學家 **[núng-hsüéh-chiā]**: agronomist, agriculturist

農藝師 **[núng-ì-shīh]**: agro-technician

16 農墾部 **[núng-k'ĕn pù]**: Ministry of State Farms and Land Reclamation

農墾地區 **[núng-k'ĕn tì-ch'ü]**: land reclamation area

農曆 **[núng-lì]**: lunar calendar

19 農藥 **[núng-yào]**: insecticides, agricultural chemicals

— RADICAL 辵 ⻌ 162 —

— 3 Strokes —

迄

4 迄今 **[ch'ì-chīn]**: up to now, until now, so far, as yet, hitherto

迅

11 迅速的 **[hsǜn-sù te]**: swift, fast, quick, rapid, prompt

迂

10 迂迴曲折 **[yū-húi ch'ü-ché]**: twists and turns, ups and downs, tortuous and devious

— 4 Strokes —

近

7 近似 **[chìn-ssù]**: to approach closely; approximation; near, like, similar

8 近來 **[chìn-lái]**: recent; recently, lately, not long ago

9 近郊 **[chìn-chiāo]**: suburb, outskirts

12 近距離 **[chìn chǜ-lí]**: close quarters, at close range

近距離戰鬥 **[chìn chǜ-lí chàn-tòu]**: close quarter fighting

返

3 返工 **[făn-kūng]**: to do over again (i.e., poor work

返工浪費 **[făn-kūng làng-fèi]**: rejection and waste

6 返回 **[făn-húi]**: to revert to, to return, to retrace one's steps

迎

11 迎接 **[yíng-chiēh]**: to meet, to receive (guests), to welcome

16 迎頭 **[yíng-t'óu]**: to run into; faced with

迎頭趕上 **[yíng-t'óu kăn-shàng]**: to catch up with

迎頭痛擊[yíng-t'óu t'ùng-chī]: to deal a telling blow, to deal a severe blow

— 5 Strokes —

迫

4 迫切[p'ò-ch'ièh]: urgent, imminent, instant, pressing

8 迫近[p'ò-chìn]: to draw near, to approach; imminent, close, near

迫使[p'ò-shìh]: to enforce, to force, to coerce, to compel, to drive, to constrain, to oblige

10 迫害[p'ò-hài]: to persecute; persecution, witch-hunting

17 迫擊炮[p'ǎi-chī-p'ào]: trench mortar, mortar

述

14 述說[shù-shuō]: to relate, to narrate, to recount, to give an account of

迪

9 迪拜[tí-pài]: Dibai (Muscat Oman)

— 6 Strokes —

迹

14 迹像[chī-hsiàng]: sign, indication, symptom, token

追

3 追上[chūi-shàng]: to catch up with, to come up to, to draw level with

5 追加支出[chūi-chiā chīh-ch'ū]: additional expenditure, added items of expenditure

追本溯源[chūi-pěn sù-yüán]: to investigate into the origins of, to go into a matter thoroughly, to trace back to the source

6 追求[chūi-ch'íu]: to pursue, to run after, to hunt for, to search

7 追究[chūi-chìu]: to search for, to look into, to investigate

8 追肥[chūi-féi]: additional manure, top-dressing

追述[chūi-shù]: to relate, to recall, to recollect, to review, to trace

9 追查[chūi-ch'á]: to investigate

10 追索[chūi-sǒ]: to search for, to make forcible demands for payment

11 追悼會[chūi-tào hùi]: memorial ceremony, memorial service

13 追溯[chūi-sù]: to trace back, to retrace, to recall

14 追認[chūi-jèn]: to ratify, to acknowledge subsequently; subsequent confirmation

追趕[chūi-kǎn]: to chase, to give chase, to pursue

16 追隨[chūi-súi]: to follow behind, to go after

追隨者[chūi-súi-chě]: follower, attendant

19 追繳[chūi-chiǎo]: to demand repayment

迴

11 迴旋加速器[húi-hsüán chiā-sù-ch'ì]: cyclotron

17 迴避[húi-pì]: to avoid, to stand off, to dodge, to shy away from, to shirk, to retire, to withdraw

迷

迷[mí]: fan (i.e., as a football fan); to confuse, to be infatuated

5 迷失[mí-shīh]: to lose, to mislay

迷失方向[mí-shīh fāng-hsìang]: to lose one's bearings, to lose direction

[9] 迷信[mí-hsìn]: to have blind faith in; to be superstitious; superstition

[12] 迷惑[mí-huò]: to mislead, to puzzle, to confuse, to bewitch, to fascinate, to charm; deception

[13] 迷路[mí-lù]: to lose one's way, not to know where one is; labyrinth; astray, lost

[14] 迷夢[mí-mèng]: pipe dream

迷魂香[mí-hún hsiāng]: soul-deceiving incense (i.e., counterrevolutionary ideas)

逆

[9] 逆差[nì-ch'ā]: deficit, adverse balance, unfavorable balance

[10] 逆流[nì-líu]: to flow in a contrary direction; adverse current, eddy

送

[6] 送行[sùng-hsíng]: to see someone off, to give a send-off

[12] 送進[sùng-chìn]: to throw into, to cast aside into

逃

[3] 逃亡[t'áo-wáng]: to flee, to desert, to run away

逃亡地主[t'áo-wáng tì-chŭ]: runaway landlords

[7] 逃兵[t'áo-pīng]: deserter

逃走[t'áo-tsŏu]: to flee, to desert, to escape, to run away

[11] 逃脫[t'áo-t'ō]: to cast off, to get clear of; evasion

[12] 逃稅[t'áo-shùi]: tax evasion

[17] 逃避[t'áo-pì]: to escape, to avoid, to shun, to shirk, to hide from, to keep out of sight

退

[5] 退出[t'ùi-ch'ū]: to leave, to withdraw from, to quit, to pull out, to get out, to go away

[6] 退伍[t'ùi-wŭ]: to retire from military service, to demobilize, to deactivate; demobilized, deactivated

退伍軍人[t'ùi-wŭ chün-jén]: ex-serviceman, deactivated serviceman

[7] 退却[t'ùi-ch'üèh]: to withdraw, to retreat, to draw back, to back down, to retire

退役[t'ùi-ì]: to be discharged from work or military service

退步[t'ùi-pù]: to regress, to retrograde; regression, retrogression, decline

[13] 退落[t'ùi-lào]: to ebb, to recede, to fall back, to retire

[15] 退潮[t'ùi-ch'áo]: ebb, ebb tide

[18] 退職[t'ùi-chíh]: to retire from work, to withdraw from office; retirement

[20] 退黨[t'ùi-tăng]: to withdraw from a party

[24] 退讓[t'ùi-jàng]: to yield, to give way, to relinquish, to give in, to concede; concession

— 7 Strokes —

逞

[6] 逞兇[ch'ĕng-hsiūng]: to be abusive, to act violently, to act with murderous intent

[9] 逞威風[ch'ĕng wēi-fēng]: to presume on power, to intimidate

[10] 逞能[ch'ĕng-néng]: to show off one's ability; boasting, bragging

[11] 逞强[ch'ĕng-ch'iáng]: to display strength; arrogant, presumptuous

[5] 逐出[chú-ch'ū]: to drive out, to banish, to

deport, to eject from, to expel

6 逐行逐業地**[chú-háng chú-yèh tì]**: trade by trade

逐年**[chú-nién]**: year by year

7 逐步**[chú-pù]**: bit by bit, little by little, step by step, gradual, gradually

逐走**[chú-tsŏu]**: to rid oneself of, to get rid of, to expel, to chase away

10 逐條**[chú-t'iáo]**: item by item, article by article

14 逐漸**[chú-chièn]**: gradual; by steps, step by step, gradually

逍

14 逍遙**[hsiāo-yáo]**: to wander about at leisure, to be at leisure; leisurely, unhurried

逍遙法外**[hsiāo-yáo fă-wài]**: to wander about beyond the reach of law

逍遙學派**[hsiāo-yáo hsüéh-p'ài]**: peripatetic school, the peripatetics

逍遙自在**[hsiāo-yáo tzù-tsài]**: to be at ease, to be at peace with the world and oneself, to be blissfully happy

連

連**[lién]**: company, battery (artillery); to link, to connect, to join

7 連串**[lién-ch'uàn]**: a series, a chain

11 連接判斷**[lién-chiēh p'àn-tuàn]**: conjunctive judgment

12 連結**[lién-chiéh]**: to tie together, to link together, to connect, to join together, to associate, to attach

連隊**[lién-tùi]**: company, unit

14 連綿不斷**[lién-mién pú-tuàn]**: one after another, continuously, uninterruptedly, ceaselessly

18 連鎖反應**[lién-sŏ făn-yìng]**: chain reaction

21 連續**[lién-hsù]**: continuous, serial, consecutive, successive

連續性**[lién-hsù-hsìng]**: continuity

速

6 速成**[sù-ch'éng]**: to accomplish quickly; intensive

速成教學法**[sù-ch'éng chiào-hsüéh fă]**: intensive teaching methods, quick method of teaching

速成中學**[sù-ch'éng chūng-hsüéh]**: accelerated middle school

速成學校**[sù-ch'éng hsüéh-hsiào]**: intensive school

速成識字法**[sù-ch'éng shíh-tzù fă]**: quick method for learning Chinese characters, intensive method of learning to read

速決**[sù-chüéh]**: quick decision

速決戰**[sù-chüéh chàn]**: a quick decisive battle

10 速記**[sù-chì]**: to record quickly; stenography, shorthand

速記員**[sù-chì-yüán]**: stenographer

逗

10 逗留**[tòu-líu]**: to stay, to remain, to linger

透

7 透支**[t'òu-chīh]**: to overdraw, to overpay; overdraft

12 透視**[t'òu-shìh]**: to have an X-ray taken

15 透徹**[t'òu-ch'è]**: thoroughly

20 透露**[t'òu-lù]**: to reveal, to disclose, to bring to light, to come to light; disclosure

透露消息人士[t'òu-lù hsiāo-hsí jén-shìh]: informant

造

4 造反[tsào-fǎn]: to rebel, to revolt, to cause an upset; rebellion

造反派革命委員會[tsào-fǎn-p'ài kó-mìng wěi-yüán-hùi]: Revolutionary Upheaval Committee, Rebels Revolutionary Committee

6 造成[tsào-ch'éng]: to create, to give rise to, to make

造成危機[tsào-ch'éng wéi-chī]: to create a crisis, to precipitate a crisis

8 造林[tsào-lín]: to afforest; afforestation

造林區[tsào-lín ch'ǖ]: afforestation area

造林工作[tsào-lín kūng-tsò]: afforestation work

9 造型藝術[tsào-hsíng ì-shù]: plastic arts

10 造紙工業[tsào-chǐh kūng-yèh]: paper manufacturing industry

12 造船廠[tsào-ch'uán ch'ăng]: shipyard

14 造福於人民[tsào-fú yǘ jén-mín]: to benefit the people

15 造價[tsào-chià]: construction cost

17 造謠[tsào-yáo]: to create rumors, to fabricate rumors; fabrication

造謠生事[tsào-yáo shēng-shìh]: to cause trouble by starting false stories

造謠汚衊[tsào-yáo wū-mièh]: to spread rumors and slanders

途

4 途中[t'ú-chūng]: en route, on the way, along the way

10 途徑[t'ú-chìng]: way, path, road, course

通

2 通力[t'ūng-lì]: a common effort, united strength; cooperative

5 通古斯[t'ūng-kŭ-ssū]: Tungus (minority nationality)

7 通車[t'ūng-ch'ē]: to open to traffic

8 通知[t'ūng-chīh]: to notify, to inform, to communicate, to advise; notice, notification

通知書[t'ūng-chīh-shū]: notification

9 通風[t'ūng-fēng]: to divulge, to communicate; ventilation, air draft

通風報信[t'ūng-fēng pào-hsìn]: to provide someone with information

通信[t'ūng-hsìn]: to correspond, to communicate; correspondence, communication by letters

通信兵[t'ūng-hsìn pīng]: signal corps, signal unit

通信員[t'ūng-hsìn-yüán]: an informer

通俗[t'ūng-sú]: common, popular

通俗化[t'ūng-sú-huà]: popularization

10 通宵[t'ūng-hsiāo]: overnight, through the night, all night

通訊綫路[t'ūng-hsǜn hsièn-lù]: postal and telecommunication line

通訊工具[t'ūng-hsǜn kūng-chǜ]: means of communication

通訊聯絡[t'ūng-hsǜn lién-lò]: signal communications

通訊報導[t'ūng-hsǜn pào-tăo]: reportage

通訊社[t'ūng-hsǜn shè]: news agency, press agency, news service, press service

通訊文學[t'ūng-hsǜn wén-hsüéh]: reportage

通訊員[t'ūng-hsǜn-yüán]: correspondent

11 通常[t'ūng-ch'áng]: ordinary, customary, usual, common

通常可靠人士[t'ūng-ch'áng k'ŏ-k'ào jén-shìh]: usually reliable people

通情達理[t'ūng-ch'íng tá-lĭ]: to be understanding and reasonable

通貨[t'ūng-huò]: currency

通貨膨脹[t'ūng-huò p'éng-chàng]: inflation; inflationary

通貨收縮[t'ūng-huò shōu-sō]: deflation; deflationary

通商口岸[t'ūng-shāng k'ŏu-àn]: treaty port, trading post

12 通報[t'ūng-pào]: to inform, to circularize, to telegraph, to communicate; communication, circular, notification for general information

13 通過[t'ūng-kuò]: to go through, to approve, to carry (as a motion); via, through

通電[t'ūng-tièn]: to circulate a telegram; circular telegram

15 通盤[t'ūng-p'án]: overall, all-round; completely; the whole affair

通盤估計[t'ūng-p'án kū-chì]: overall estimate

— 8 Strokes —

進

1 進一步[chìn í-pù]: to go a step further; further

2 進入[chìn-jù]: to enter, to step into; ingress, intake

3 進口[chìn-k'ŏu]: to import; import

4 進化[chìn-huà]: progress, culture, evolution; evolutionary

進化論[chìn-huà lùn]: theory of evolution

5 進出口平衡[chìn-ch'ū-k'ŏu p'íng-héng]: balance between imports and exports

6 進行[chìn-hsíng]: to conduct, to go on, to proceed, to be underway, to function, to carry on

進行曲[chìn-hsíng ch'ǚ]: marching song, march

進行到底[chìn-hsíng tào-tĭ]: to carry through, to carry through to the end, to carry forward to a conclusion

7 進攻[chìn-kūng]: to attack, to assault; offensive, attack, assault, onslaught

進步[chìn-pù]: to progress, to advance, to make headway; progress, advance; progressive

進步人士[chìn-pù jén-shìh]: progressive people

進步保守黨[chìn-pù păo-shŏu tăng]: Progressive Conservative Party (Canada)

9 進軍[chìn-chǖn]: to advance troops

進修[chìn-hsīu]: to carry out further study

進洪閘[chìn-húng chá]: flood-inlet gate

10 進展[chìn-chăn]: to develop, to advance, to press ahead; development, advance, progress; progressive

逮

10 逮捕[tài-pŭ]: to arrest, to take into custody

— 9 Strokes —

4 過分[kuò-fèn]: to exceed the limit, to go too far; excessive; excessively, unduly

過分講究的[kuò-fèn chiăng-chìu te]: finicky, unduly particular

過戶[kuò-hù]: to transfer, to change owners

過火[**kuò-huŏ**]: extravagance; excessive, intemperate, unbridled, exaggerated

過火現象[**kuò-huŏ hsièn-hsiàng**]: phenomena of excessiveness, excesses

5 過去[**kuò-ch'ǜ**]: the past; to pass away, to pass, to go by, to elapse, to die; earlier, in the past, out of date

過目[**kuò-mù**]: to look over, to go over, to glance over

過失[**kuò-shīh**]: fault, error, mistake

過左傾向[**kuò-tsŏ ch'īng-hsiàng**]: excessive leftist tendency

6 過份集中[**kuò-fèn chí-chūng**]: over-concentration

過早[**kuò-tsăo**]: too early, premature; prematurely, inopportunely, before the time is ripe

7 過低估計[**kuò-tī kū-chì**]: to underestimate

8 過來人[**kuò-lái jén**]: a man of experience, an experienced man

過往[**kuò-wăng**]: to pass by, to visit one another, to have contact with

過於[**kuò-yǘ**]: to exceed; more than, excessive, over

過於强調[**kuò-yǘ ch'iáng-tiào**]: to overemphasize, to lay too much emphasis on

10 過高估計[**kuò-kāo kū-chì**]: to overestimate

過時[**kuò-shíh**]: out-dated, out-moded, old-fashioned, obsolete, out of date

11 過細[**kuò-hsì**]: too minute; to give too close an attention

過堂[**kuò-t'áng**]: to come before the court, to be tried; trial

過得硬[**kuò-té-yìng**]: to live toughly

過渡[**kuò-tù**]: to cross a ferry, to pass over, to go over; transition, shift, conversion, transference; transitional

過渡階段[**kuò-tù chiēh-tuàn**]: transitional stage

過渡狀態[**kuò-tù chuàng-t'ài**]: state of transition

過渡形式[**kuò-tù hsíng-shìh**]: transitional form

過渡時期[**kuò-tù shíh-ch'í**]: transition period

過問[**kuò-wèn**]: to interfere, to explore, to inquire into

12 過程[**kuò-ch'éng**]: process, stage, course

過程中[**kuò-ch'éng chūng**]: in the process of, during the course of

過期[**kuò-ch'í**]: to exceed a deadline, to exceed a time limit; overdue, late, expired

過剩[**kuò-shèng**]: excess, surplus; excessive, superfluous

過硬[**kuò-yìng**]: toughness, resoluteness

13 過路[**kuò-lù**]: to be in transit, to pass through

14 過境[**kuò-chìng**]: to cross the frontier

過境簽證[**kuò-chìng ch'iēn-chèng**]: transit visa

過境貿易[**kuò-chìng mào-ì**]: transit trade

15 過慮[**kuò-lǜ**]: to worry too much; over-anxious

18 過關[**kuò-kuān**]: to pass a test, to go through an ordeal, to pass a barrier (during the land reform, this referred to the liquidation of assets and entry into the ranks of the common people on the part of landlords)

過關證[**kuò-kuān chèng**]: certificate of having passed the barrier (i.e., a document indicating that a landlord had given up his property and joined the masses)

過歸[**kuò-kuēi**]: regression

遏

4 遏止 **[ò-chĭh]**: to stop, to halt, to bring to a standstill

8 遏制 **[ò-chìh]**: to put down, to check

逼

3 逼上梁山 **[pī shàng liáng-shān]**: to be driven to extremes, to be in such straits that there is no way out

8 逼近 **[pī-chìn]**: to draw near, to press onto, to gain on

逼供 **[pī-kùng]**: to extort a confession

逼命 **[pī-mìng]**: to force into suicide, to drive to death

9 逼迫 **[pī-p'ò]**: to force, to drive, to compel, to oblige, to impel; compulsion; pressing

10 逼眞 **[pī-chēn]**: true to life, true, real

達

5 達卡 **[tá-k'ă]**: Dakar (Mali); Dacca (India)

6 達成 **[tá-ch'éng]**: to achieve, to succeed in doing something, to reach (an agreement, etc.)

達成協議 **[tá-ch'éng hsiéh-ì]**: to reach an agreement, to come to an agreement, to agree on

8 達呼爾 **[tá-hū-ĕrh]**: Daghors

達拉第 **[tá-lā-tì]**: Daladier, Edouard (French political leader)

達到 **[tá-tào]**: to accomplish, to achieve, to attain, to reach

11 達荷美共和國 **[tá-hó-mĕi kùng-hó-kuó]**: Republic of Dahomey

達累斯薩拉姆 **[tá-lèi-ssū sà-lā-mŭ]**: Dar es Salaam

達曼 **[tá-mán]**: Daman

12 達喀爾 **[tá-k'ā-ĕrh]**: Dakar (Senegal)

13 達達尼爾 **[tá-tá-ní-ĕrh]**: Dardanelles

14 達爾文 **[tá-ĕrh-wén]**: Darwin, Charles

達爾文主義 **[tá-ĕrh-wén chŭ-ì]**: Darwinism

16 達賴喇嘛 **[tá-lài lă-ma]**: Dalai Lama (Tibetan ruler and religious leader)

道

道 **[tào]**: road, way, path; Taoism; *to* (Korean province)

4 道木 **[tào-mù]**: railroad tie

道比 **[tào-pĭ]**: Dobi, Istvan (Hungarian political leader)

11 道教 **[tào-chiào]**: Taoism

道理 **[tào-lĭ]**: reason, principle, doctrine

12 道賀 **[tào-hò]**: to congratulate; congratulation

13 道義 **[tào-ì]**: reason and right; sense of right and honor; moral

道義上 **[tào-ì-shang]**: moral, morally

道路 **[tào-lù]**: way, road, path, course, line

14 道歉 **[tào-ch'ièn]**: to apologize; apology

16 道德 **[tào-té]**: morality, morals; moral

道德觀 **[tào-té kuān]**: moral view, moral concept

道德品質 **[tào-té p'ĭn-chíh]**: moral character, moral trait, moral qualities

遁

7 遁走 **[tùn-tsŏu]**: to flee, to abscond

10 遁逃 **[tùn-t'áo]**: to flee, to abscond

違

4 違反 **[wéi-fǎn]**: to violate, to defy, to contravene; violation, breach, infringement

8 違法 **[wéi-fǎ]**: unlawful, illegal, lawless, illegitimate, contraband, illicit

違法活動 **[wéi-fǎ huó-tùng]**: illegal activity, illicit activity

違法亂紀 **[wéi-fǎ luàn-chì]**: offenses against law and discipline, violation of laws and discipline

9 違背 **[wéi-pèi]**: to disobey, to act in opposition to, to run counter to, to violate

遇

8 遇到 **[yǜ-tào]**: to encounter, to meet

運

5 運用 **[yǜn-yùng]**: to use, to carry out, to put to use, to apply

8 運河 **[yǜn-hó]**: canal; the Grand Canal

11 運動 **[yǜn-tùng]**: to move, to be in motion, to influence, to exercise; motion, movement, agitation, campaign, drive; mobile

運動戰 **[yǜn-tùng chàn]**: mobile warfare

運動學 **[yǜn-tùng-hsüéh]**: kinetics

13 運載火箭 **[yǜn-tsài huǒ-chièn]**: carrier rocket

16 運輸 **[yǜn-shū]**: to transport, to ship; transport, transportation

運輸和郵電部 **[yǜn-shū hó yú-tièn pù]**: Ministry of Transport and Communications (India)

運輸兵團 **[yǜn-shū pīng-t'uán]**: transportation corps

運輸部 **[yǜn-shū pù]**: Ministry of Transport

運輸業 **[yǜn-shū yèh]**: transport industry, transport trade

20 運籌學 **[yǜn-ch'óu-hsüéh]**: operations research

— 10 Strokes —

遞

5 遞加 **[tì-chiā]**: to add pro rata, to add a certain proportion; progressive increase

10 遞降 **[tì-chiàng]**: progressive decrease

12 遞減 **[tì-chiěn]**: continual decrease, proportionate decrease, progressive decrease, decrease by degrees

遞進 **[tì-chìn]**: progress, advance

遞給 **[tì-kěi]**: to hand to, to hand over, to pass on

15 遞增 **[tì-tsēng]**: progressive increase

遙

11 遙控 **[yáo-k'ùng]**: remote control

遙控測量 **[yáo-k'ùng ts'è-liáng]**: telemetric measurement

14 遙遠 **[yáo-yüǎn]**: remote, distant

遠

3 遠大 **[yüǎn-tà]**: vast and great

遠大理想 **[yüǎn-tà lǐ-hsiǎng]**: great and far-reaching ideal

5 遠古 **[yüǎn-kǔ]**: ancient times, antiquity

6 遠因 **[yüǎn-yīn]**: remote cause

7 遠見 **[yüǎn-chièn]**: farsightedness; farsighted

遠足 **[yüǎn-tsú]**: excursion, trip, picnic, outing

8 遠征[**yüăn-chēng**]: expedition, military expedition

遠征軍[**yüăn-chēng chün**]: expeditionary army, expeditionary forces

遠非[**yüăn-fēi**]: far from, there is much more to it than

9 遠洋[**yüăn-yáng**]: ocean-going

遠洋班船[**yüăn-yáng-pān ch'uán**]: ocean liner

12 遠程火箭[**yüăn-ch'éng huŏ-chièn**]: long-range rocket

遠程射擊[**yüăn-ch'éng shè-chī**]: long-range fire

遠程導彈[**yüăn-ch'éng tăo-tàn**]: long-range guided missile

遠景[**yüăn-chĭng**]: perspective, outlook; long-term

遠距離[**yüăn chü-lí**]: long-distance, long-range

遠距離操縱[**yüăn chü-lí ts'āo-tsùng**]: remote control

遠距離自動操縱[**yüăn chü-lí tzù-tùng ts'āo-tsùng**]: telemechanics

19 遠離[**yüăn-lí**]: to keep away from, to keep at a distance, to stand aloof, to remain at a distance; wide apart, worlds apart

— 11 Strokes —

7 遮住[**chē-chù**]: to cover, to shield

14 遮蓋[**chē-kài**]: to cover, to overcast, to overshadow, to conceal

15 遮遮掩掩地[**chē-chē yĕn-yĕn tì**]: in a disguised manner; dodging and dissembling

16 遮蔽[**chē-pì**]: to shade, to cover, to hide, to conceal

6 遲早[**ch'íh-tsăo**]: sooner or later

8 遲到[**ch'íh-tào**]: to arrive late, to be late

12 遲鈍[**ch'íh-tùn**]: obtuse, ponderous, slow

14 遲疑[**ch'íh-í**]: to hesitate, to vacillate; hesitation, vacillation

遲慢[**ch'íh-màn**]: remiss, late, slow, dilatory, behindhand

15 遲誤[**ch'íh-wù**]: to let an opportunity slip, to spoil a matter by delay

適

5 適用[**shìh-yùng**]: to apply, to apply to, to hold good, to answer the purpose; applicability; applicable

6 適合[**shìh-hó**]: to fit, to suit, to conform with; suited to, suitable, appropriate to, qualified, competent, feasible

10 適時[**shìh-shíh**]: opportune, timely, well-timed, expedient, seasonable

13 適當[**shìh-tàng**]: proper, due, fit, appropriate, suitable, opportune, well-considered

17 適應[**shìh-yìng**]: to adapt to, to correspond to, to adjust to, to accommodate to, to conform to

適應性[**shìh-yìng-hsìng**]: adaptability

20 適齡[**shìh-líng**]: of age

遭

8 遭受[**tsāo-shòu**]: to suffer, to undergo, to be afflicted with, to endure, to be subjected to

遭到[**tsāo-tào**]: to suffer, to come across, to come up against, to encounter, to meet with

遭到挫敗[**tsāo-tào ts'ò-pài**]: to suffer setbacks

9 遭殃[**tsāo-yāng**]: to meet with calamity, to suffer a catastrophe, to suffer

13 遭遇[**tsāo-yǜ**]: to meet, to encounter, to undergo, to suffer; fate, lot, experience

— 12 Strokes —

7 遷延[**ch'iēn-yén**]: to procrastinate, to put off, to postpone, to delay; delay

11 遷徙自由[**ch'iēn-hsǐ tzù-yú**]: freedom of residence, freedom to change one's residence

遷移[**ch'iēn-í**]: to move, to transfer, to shift, to change

12 遷就[**ch'iēn-chìu**]: to appease, to give in to, to meet the demands of, to compromise, to indulge; appeasement; accommodating

暹

9 暹美軍事協定[**hsiēn-mĕi chǖn-shìh hsiéh-tìng**]: Thai–U.S. military alliance

20 暹羅[**hsiēn-ló**]: Thailand; Siam

選

4 選手[**hsüăn-shŏu**]: capable men or contestants chosen

5 選民[**hsüăn-mín**]: electorate, constituency

選民區[**hsüăn-mín ch'ǖ**]: constituency

選民登記[**hsüăn-mín tēng-chì**]: registration of voters

8 選拔[**hsüăn-pá**]: to select and promote

選定[**hsüăn-tìng**]: to designate, to decide on a person (for a certain purpose)

10 選修課[**hsüăn-hsīu k'ō**]: elective course, optional course

12 選集[**hsüăn-chí**]: selected works, anthology

14 選種[**hsüăn-chŭng**]: to select seeds; seed selection

15 選樣[**hsüăn-yàng**]: to sample; sampling

16 選舉[**hsüăn-chǚ**]: to elect; election; electoral

選舉結果[**hsüăn-chǚ chiéh-kuŏ**]: election returns

選舉權[**hsüăn-chǚ ch'üán**]: suffrage, franchise, right to vote

選舉法[**hsüăn-chǚ fă**]: electoral law

選擇[**hsüăn-tsé**]: to choose, to select, to pick; selection, choice

17 選購[**hsüăn-kòu**]: selective purchasing, selective purchase

遺

9 遺毒[**í-tú**]: evil legacy

10 遺留[**í-líu**]: to leave behind, to remain, to bequeath; heritage

11 遺產[**í-ch'ăn**]: heritage, inheritance, legacy

13 遺跡[**í-chī**]: vestige, trace, remains, relic

遺傳[**í-ch'uán**]: to inherit, to remain, to bequeath; tradition, heritage, heredity; hereditary

遺傳學[**í-ch'uán-hsüéh**]: genetics

23 遺體[**í-t'ĭ**]: remains, body, corpse

遼

遼 [**liáo**]: Liaoning (abbreviation of 遼寧)

13 遼寧省農業科學研究所 [**liáo-níng shĕng**

núng-yèh k'ō-hsüéh yén-chìu-sŏ]: Liaoning Province Agricultural Institute

17 遼闊 **[liáo-k'uò]**: broad, spacious, vast, extensive

遵

6 遵守 **[tsūn-shŏu]**: to observe, to follow, to honor, to adhere to

11 遵從 **[tsūn-ts'úng]**: to follow, to obey, to act in accordance with

13 遵照 **[tsūn-chào]**: to comply with, to follow, to obey, to act in accordance with

— 13 Strokes —

邂

10 邂逅 **[hsièh-koù]**: to meet unexpectedly; a chance meeting

還

4 還手 **[huán-shŏu]**: to return a blow, to strike back, to counter

7 還言 **[huán-yén]**: to retort

10 還原 **[huán-yüán]**: to restore, to repair, to return to the original condition

12 還鄉團 **[huán-hsiāng t'uán]**: armed band of returned landowners

還報 **[huán-pào]**: to reply, to answer

13 還債 **[huán-chài]**: to pay a debt

15 還賬 **[huán-chàng]**: to pay a debt

16 還錢 **[huán-ch'ién]**: to pay a debt

避

4 避火梯 **[pì-huŏ t'ī]**: fire escape

6 避孕 **[pì-yùn]**: contraception

8 避免 **[pì-miĕn]**: to avoid, to evade, to abstain from

9 避風 **[pì-fēng]**: to take shelter from the wind, to hide from trouble

12 避開 **[pì-k'āi]**: to parry, to avert, to head off, to steer clear of, to keep away, to dodge, to keep off

15 避彈坑 **[pì-tàn k'ēng]**: trench

19 避難 **[pì-nàn]**: to flee for refuge, to take refuge in

避難權 **[pì-nàn ch'üán]**: the right of asylum

避難所 **[pì-nàn sŏ]**: asylum, sanctuary, place of refuge

邀

15 邀請 **[yāo-ch'ĭng]**: to invite; invitation

— 15 Strokes —

邊

7 邊沁 **[piēn-ch'ìn]**: Bentham, Jeremy (1748–1832)

邊沁主義 **[piēn-ch'ìn chŭ-ì]**: utilitarianism

邊防 **[piēn-fáng]**: frontier defense

8 邊和 **[piēn-hó]**: Bienhoa (Vietnam)

9 邊界 **[piēn-chièh]**: frontier, boundary, border

邊界問題 **[piēn-chièh wèn-t'í]**: boundary question, border question

12 邊區 **[piēn-ch'ū]**: border region, border district (specifically, the regions in which the Chinese Communist people's governments were first established)

14 邊際 **[piēn-chì]**: margin; marginal

邊境 **[piēn-chìng]**: frontier, border

15 邊綫 **[piēn-hsièn]**: boundary line

邊緣[**piēn-yüán**]: verge, brink, fringe

邊緣工會[**piēn-yüán kūng-hùi**]: fringe union

19 邊疆[**piēn-chiāng**]: frontier, frontier region

— 19 Strokes —

邏

16 邏輯[**ló-chí**]: logic; logical

邏輯檢查[**ló-chí chiěn-ch'á**]: logical control, consistent control

邏輯學[**ló-chí-hsüéh**]: logic

— RADICAL 邑阝 163 —

— 4 Strokes —

邪

4 邪不勝正[**hsiéh pú-shèng chèng**]: heresay cannot overthrow the truth

9 邪風[**hsiéh-fēng**]: an erroneous viewpoint, an evil wind

10 邪氣[**hsiéh-ch'ì**]: evil aura, evil emanations, noxious influences, malevolent influences, spirit of reaction

邪氣歪風[**hsiéh-ch'ì wāi-fēng**]: evil influences and bad customs (i.e., pernicious influences spread by bad elements in the villages)

12 邪惡[**hsiéh-ò**]: vicious, evil, wicked, depraved, iniquitous

那

16 那穆陵[**nà-mù-líng**]: Namling (Tibet)

21 那霸[**nà-pà**]: Naha (Okinawa)

邦

6 邦交[**pāng-chiāo**]: intercourse between nations, diplomatic relations

— 5 Strokes —

邱

6 邱吉爾[**ch'īu-chí-ěrh**]: Churchill, Sir Winston

— 6 Strokes —

郊

5 郊外[**chiāo-wài**]: outskirts, environs, edge, suburb; suburban

11 郊區[**chiāo-ch'ū**]: suburb

郊野[**chiāo-yěh**]: countryside

郁

15 郁憤[**yǜ-fèn**]: pent-up fury, suppressed indignation

— 7 Strokes —

9 郎勃拉幫[**láng pò-lā-pāng**]: Luang Prabang (Laos)

163

— 8 Strokes —

部

部 [pù] : ministry, office, section, part

3 部下 [pù-hsià] : subordinate, follower, those under the command

4 部分 [pù-fèn] : part, portion, section, division, group; partial

部分核禁試條約 [pù-fèn hó-chìn-shìh t'iáo-yüēh] : Partial Nuclear Test Ban Treaty

部分利益服從整體利益 [pù-fèn lì-ì fú-ts'úng chěng-t'ǐ lì-ì] : partial interests subordinate to total interests

8 部長 [pù-chăng] : minister, head of a department

部長級的 [pù-chăng-chí te] : ministerial

部長職位 [pù-chăng chíh-wèi] : portfolio

部長會議 [pù-chăng hùi-ì] : Council of Ministers

部長會議主席 [pù-chăng hùi-ì chŭ-hsí] : Chairman of the Council of Ministers

部門 [pù-mén] : department, branch, section, sector, field, division

11 部族 [pù-tsú] : tribe

部族主義 [pù-tsú chŭ-ì] : tribalism

12 部隊 [pù-tùi] : unit, military unit, armed forces

13 部落 [pù-lò] : tribe, aboriginal tribe, tribal settlement

14 部署 [pù-shŭ] : to deploy, to dispose; deployment, disposition

— 9 Strokes —

鄂

鄂 [ò] : Hupeh (abbreviation for 湖北)

4 鄂木斯克 [ò-mù-ssū-k'ò] : Omsk (USSR)

10 鄂倫春 [ò-lún-ch'ūn] : Oronchon (minority nationality of Inner Mongolia and Heilungkiang Province)

16 鄂霍次克海 [ò-huò-tz'ù-k'ò hăi] : Okhotsk Sea

都

5 都市 [tū-shìh] : metropolis, city; urban, municipal, metropolitan

7 都伯林 [tū-pó-lín] : Dublin (Ireland)

11 郵船 [yú-ch'uán] : mail boat

13 郵電 [yú-tièn] : post and telecommunications

郵電部 [yú-tièn pù] : Ministry of Posts and Telecommunications

郵電所 [yú-tièn sŏ] : post and telecommunications center

— 10 Strokes —

鄉

7 鄉村 [hsiāng-ts'ūn] : village; rural

8 鄉社合一 [hsiāng-shè hó-ī] : the township and the commune become one entity; uniting of village and commune

9 鄉政府 [hsiāng chèng-fŭ] : township government

11 鄉郵站 [hsiāng yú-chàn] : rural postal station

— 11 Strokes —

鄙

11 鄙視 [pĭ-shìh] : to despise, to scorn, to belittle, to slight, to disdain, to feel contempt for, to look down on

鄞

鄞 **[yín]** : Ningpo (abbreviation for 寧波)

— 12 Strokes —

鄭 **[chèng]**: Chengchow (abbreviation for 鄭州)

鄰

8 鄰居 **[lín-chǖ]** : neighbor

11 鄰接 **[lín-chiēh]**: contiguous, neighboring, bordering, adjacent to

鄧

9 鄧柯 **[tèng-k'ō]** : Druma Illakong (Sikang)

— RADICAL 酉 164 —

— 2 Strokes —

8 酋長 **[ch'íu-chăng]**: chieftain, ruler, sheik (Kuwait; Bahrein)

酋長國 **[ch'íu-chăng kuó]** : sheikdom

— 3 Strokes —

配

3 配上 **[p'èi-shàng]**: to be harnessed to, to be joined to, to be attached to, to be affixed to

4 配不上 **[p'èi-pú-shàng]**: unworthy, undeserving, unfit, unsuitable

6 配合 **[p'èi-hó]** : to coordinate, to harmonize with; coordination, fit, match

配合得好 **[p'èi-hó-té hăo]**: well-coordinated, well-harmonized

7 配角 **[p'èi-chiăo]**: supporting actor

10 配套 **[p'èi-t'ào]**: to assemble, to fit a book into boards, to bind a book

配套成龍 **[p'èi-t'ào ch'éng-lúng]**: to make up a set to become a dragon (i.e., indicates a complete set of equipment which is useless if one part is missing)

11 配偶 **[p'èi-ŏu]** : to mate, to pair; couple, pair, husband and wife

12 配給 **[p'èi-chĭ]**: to allocate, to furnish, to supply, to ration

配給制度 **[p'èi-chĭ chìh-tù]**: rationing system

13 配電板 **[p'èi-tièn păn]** : switchboard

14 配種 **[p'èi-chŭng]** : artificial insemination, insemination, breeding

配種站 **[p'èi-chŭng chàn]**: breeding station (i.e., for breeding livestock)

— 6 Strokes —

8 酬金 **[ch'óu-chīn]** : a gratuity, compensation, reward money

12 酬報 **[ch'óu-pào]** : to compensate, to requite; honorarium

酬答 **[ch'óu-tá]** : to reciprocate; in reciprocation for, in return for

13 酬資 **[ch'óu-tzū]**: a gratuity, compensation, reward money

— 7 Strokes —

酷

6 酷刑 **[k'ù-hsíng]**: torture, severe punishment, cruel punishment

— 8 Strokes —

醇

9 醇厚 **[ch'ún-hòu]**: pure-minded and honest

醇美 **[ch'ún-měi]**: excellent, pure

17 醇謹 **[ch'ún-chǐn]**: careful, observant

醉

4 醉心於 **[tsùi-hsīn yǘ]**: to be intoxicated with, to be drunk with

14 醉漢 **[tsùi-hàn]**: drunkard, sot

— 9 Strokes —

醒

5 醒目 **[hsǐng-mù]**: to catch the eye, to attract attention

10 醒悟 **[hsǐng-wù]**: to wake, to awake, to come to oneself; awake

— 10 Strokes —

醜

4 醜化 **[ch'ǒu-huà]**: to smear, defame, besmirch, discredit, disgrace, vilify

8 醜事 **[ch'ǒu-shìh]**: scandal

12 醜惡 **[ch'ǒu-ò]**: repulsive, bad, hateful and evil

14 醜態百出 **[ch'ǒu-t'ài pǎi-ch'ū]**: all sorts of ugly behavior

19 醜類 **[ch'ǒu-lèi]**: riffraff, vagabonds and rogues

醞

24 醞釀 **[yǜn-niàng]**: to ferment, to brew, to foment; ferment, brew, preliminary exchange of views in the making; afoot

— 11 Strokes —

醫

5 醫生 **[ī-shēng]**: doctor, physician

8 醫治 **[ī-chìh]**: to cure, to heal; treatment

10 醫院 **[ī-yüàn]**: hospital

11 醫務 **[ī-wù]**: medical affairs; medical

醫務所 **[ī-wù-sǒ]**: clinic, a doctor's office

15 醫學 **[ī-hsüéh]**: medical science; medical

醫學科學院 **[ī-hsüéh k'ō-hsüéh-yüàn]**: Academy of Medical Sciences (i.e., Chinese Academy of Medical Sciences 中國醫學科學院)

醫學院 **[ī-hsüéh-yüàn]**: medical college, medical institute

17 醫療 **[ī-liáo]**: to cure, to heal, to treat; medical treatment, therapy; therapeutic

醫療設施 **[ī-liáo shè-shīh]**: medical service

醫療衛生機構 **[ī-liáo wèi-shēng chī-kòu]**: public health organization

19 醫藥 **[ī-yào]**: healing medicines, drugs

醫藥工業 **[ī-yào kūng-yèh]**: pharmaceutical industry

— RADICAL 釆 165 —

— 13 Strokes —

釋

7 釋免 [**shǐh-miĕn**] : to be acquitted

8 釋放 [**shǐh-fàng**] : to liberate, to free, to set free, to release, to discharge

9 釋迦 [**shǐh-chiā**] : Sakyamuni (Buddha)

14 釋罪 [**shǐh-tsùi**] : to exonerate; exoneration

— RADICAL 里 166 —

里

3 里子 [**lǐ-tzŭ**] : Leeds

5 里加 [**lǐ-chiā**] : Riga (Soviet Union)

8 里昂 [**lǐ-áng**] : Lyons (France)

9 里約熱內盧 [**lǐ-yüēh jò-nèi-lú**] : Rio de Janeiro (Brazil)

12 里斯本 [**lǐ-ssū-pĕn**] : Lisbon (Portugal)

— 2 Strokes —

重

3 重工程工業部 [**chùng kūng-ch'éng kūng-yèh pù**] : Ministry of Heavy Engineering and Industry

重工業 [**chùng kūng-yèh**] : heavy industry

重工業部 [**chùng kūng-yèh pù**] : Ministry of Heavy Industry

重大 [**chùng-tà**] : important, serious, grave

5 重犯 [**chùng-fàn**] : a criminal who has committed a serious offense

重犯 [**ch'úng-fàn**] : to violate again, to offend again

重申 [**ch'úng-shēn**] : to restate, to reaffirm, to reiterate

重用 [**chùng-yùng**] : to put into an important position

9 重建 [**ch'úng-chièn**] : to rebuild, to reconstruct, to reestablish; reconstruction

重型機器製造工業 [**chùng-hsíng chī-ch'ì chǐh-tsào kūng-yèh**] : heavy machine building industry

重型機床 [**chùng-hsíng chī-ch'uáng**] : heavy duty machine tool

重型鋼軌 [**chùng-hsíng kāng-kuĕi**] : heavy rails

重修 [**ch'úng-hsīu**] : to restore, to repair, to rebuild

重要 [**chùng-yào**] : important, significant

重要性 [**chùng-yào-hsìng**] : importance

重要任務 [**chùng-yào jèn-wù**] : an important task, an important mission

重要關頭 [**chùng-yào kuān-t'óu**] : crucial moment, critical time, decisive moment, important juncture

重要問題 [**chùng-yào wèn-t'í**] : important problem, crucial problem

10 重做 [**ch'úng-tsò**] : to repeat, to do again

11 重婚 [**ch'úng-hūn**] : bigamy

重商主義 [**chùng-shāng chŭ-ì**] : mercantilism

12 重復 [**ch'úng-fù**] : to repeat, to duplicate, to overlap; repetition, duplication; again and again, repeatedly, once more

重農主義 [**chùng-núng chŭ-ì**] : physiocratism

重視 [**chùng-shìh**] : to attach importance to, to take seriously

13 重新 [**ch'úng-hsīn**] : again, anew, afresh, once more; re- (i.e., as a prefix)

重新闡明 [**ch'úng-hsīn ch'ǎn-míng**] : to redefine

重新出現 [**ch'úng-hsīn ch'ū-hsièn**] : to reappear; reappearance

重新分配 [**ch'úng-hsīn fēn-p'èi**] : to redistribute; redistribution

重新回到 [**ch'úng-hsīn húi-tào**] : to return anew

重新開放 [**ch'úng-hsīn k'āi-fàng**] : to reopen

重新開始 [**ch'úng-hsīn k'āi-shǐh**] : to resume, to make a fresh start

重新考慮 [**ch'úng-hsīn k'ǎo-lǜ**] : to reconsider, to reopen

重新保證 [**ch'úng-hsīn pǎo-chèng**] : to reassure

重新使用 [**ch'úng-hsīn shǐh-yùng**] : to reactivate

重新調整 [**ch'úng-hsīn t'iáo-chěng**] : to adjust anew; readjustment

重新定居 [**ch'úng-hsīn tìng-chǖ**] : to resettle (i.e., as to resettle in another city)

重新做人 [**ch'úng-hsīn tsò-jén**] : to make a fresh start in life; to turn over a new leaf in life

重新統一 [**ch'úng-hsīn t'ǔng-ī**] : to reunify; reunification

重新武裝 [**ch'úng-hsīn wǔ-chuāng**] : to rearm; rearmament

重新研究 [**ch'úng-hsīn yén-chìu**] : to reexamine

15 重整 [**ch'úng-chěng**] : to repair

重整旗鼓 [**ch'úng-chěng ch'í-kǔ**] : to make a new beginning in spite of setbacks, to take up something again in spite of a setback

17 重慶土壤實驗室 [**ch'úng-ch'ìng t'ǔ-jǎng shíh-yèn-shìh**] : Chungking Pedology Laboratory

重點 [**chùng-tiěn**] : key point, main point, point of emphasis

重點建設 [**chùng-tiěn chièn-shè**] : discriminative construction, priority construction, major construction, key point construction

重點進攻 [**chùng-tiěn chìn-kūng**] : attacks against key sectors

重點防禦 [**chùng-tiěn fáng-yǜ**] : defense of key points

重點觀察 [**chùng-tiěn kuān-ch'á**] : observation of primary mass data

重點工程 [**chùng-tiěn kūng-ch'éng**] : key point project, major project, priority project, key industrial enterprises

重點工業 [**chùng-tiěn kūng-yèh**] : key industries, major industries, priority industries

重點批判 [**chùng-tiěn p'ī-p'àn**] : to criticize a typical example

重點突出，全面安排的方針 [**chùng-tiěn t'ù-ch'ū ch'üán-mièn ān-p'ái te fāng-chēn**] : policy of giving priority to key sectors and making all-round arrangement for the whole

22 重疊 [**ch'úng-t'iéh**] : to pile one thing atop another, to overlap, to duplicate

— 4 Strokes —

4 野心 [**yěh-hsīn**] : mad ambition, unrestrained desire

野心家 [**yěh-hsīn-chiā**] : adventurist, ambitionist, schemer

野心勃勃 [**yěh-hsīn pó-pó**] : to be too ambitious, over ambitious, with mounting ambition

7 野坂參三 [**yěh-pǎn shēn-sān**] : Nozaka, Sanzo (Japanese political figure)

12 野砲[yěh-p'ào] : field gun

16 野戰軍[yěh-chàn chüň] : field army

野戰兵團[yěh-chàn pīng-t'uán] : field army

19 野獸[yěh-shòu] : wild beast

25 野蠻[yěh-mán] : savage, barbaric, barbarous, wild, fierce, ferocious

— 5 Strokes —

量

量[liáng] : to measure

量[liàng] : quantity, volume, amount

8 量具刃具廠[liáng-chǜ jèn-chǜ ch'ăng] : measuring instruments and cutting tools plant

— RADICAL 金 167 —

金

4 金日成[chīn jìh-ch'éng] : Kim Ilsung (North Korean statesman)

金元主義[chīn-yüán chŭ-ì] : dollar imperialism

7 金沢[chīn-tsé] : Kanazawa (Japan)

8 金門[chīn-mén] : Quemoy

9 金泉[chīn-ch'üán] : Kumchon (Korea)

金星[chīn-hsīng] : Venus

金科玉律[chīn-k'ō yǜ-lǜ] : golden rule

10 金浦[chīn-p'ŭ] : Kimpo (Korea)

12 金策[chīn-ts'è] : Kimchaek (Korea)

16 金錢[chīn-ch'ién] : money

金錢關係[chīn-ch'ién kuān-hsì] : cash relations

金融[chīn-júng] : finance, currency, monetary circulation, the money market

金融緊縮政策[chīn-júng chĭn-sō chèng-ts'è] : tight money policy, deflationary policy

金融寡頭[chīn-júng kuă-t'óu] : financial oligarch

金融時報[chīn-júng shíh-pào] : Financial Times (British daily newspaper)

金融投機[chīn-júng t'óu-chī] : monetary speculation

18 金鎊[chīn-pàng] : pound sterling

19 金邊[chīn-piēn] : Pnom Penh (Cambodia)

21 金蘭灣[chīn-lán wān] : Camranh Bay (Vietnam)

金屬[chīn-shŭ] : metal, ore

金屬加工業[chīn-shŭ chiā-kūng yèh] : metal working industry

金屬分幣[chīn-shŭ fēn-pì] : coin, small denomination coin

金屬研究所[chīn-shŭ yén-chìu-sŏ] : Metals Institute

— 2 Strokes —

針

8 針灸研究所[chēn chĭu yén-chìu-sŏ] : Acupuncture and Moxibustion Institute (Chinese Academy of Medical Sciences)

14 針對[chēn-tùi] : to direct against, to point at, to aim at

15 針鋒相對[chēn-fēng hsiāng-tùi] : points of needles pointing at each other; diametrically opposed

針鋒相對，寸土必爭 [chēn-fēng hsiāng-tùi, ts'ùn-t'ǔ pì-chēng] : to take a diametrically opposed position and fight for every inch of land

18 針織廠 [chēn-chīh ch'ǎng] : knit goods mill

針織品 [chēn-chīh p'ǐn] : knit goods

釜

3 釜山 [fú-shān] : Pusan (Korea)

釘

3 釘子 [tīng-tzu] : nail

16 釘錘 [tīng-ch'úi] : hammer

— 4 Strokes —

鈔

11 鈔票 [ch'āo-p'iào] : bank note

鈑

鈑 [pǎn] : steel plate, metal plate

— 5 Strokes —

鉀

鉀 [chiǎ] : potassium

8 鉀肥 [chiǎ-féi] : potassium fertilizer

鉚

3 鉚工 [mǎo-kūng] : riveter; riveting

鉋

7 鉋床 [pào-ch'uáng] : planer, planing machine

鈾

鈾 [yú] : uranium

— 6 Strokes —

銜

10 銜級 [hsién-chí] : title and rank

11 銜接 [hsién-chiēh] : to coordinate and dovetail, to link

銘

10 銘記於心 [míng-chì yǘ-hsīn] : to be engraved in one's heart, to bear in mind; deeply impressed

銅

銅 [t'úng] : copper

銀

6 銀行家 [yín-háng-chiā] : banker

銀行信貸 [yín-háng hsìn-tài] : bank credit, bank loans

— 7 Strokes —

鋤

16 鋤頭 [ch'ú-t'óu] : a hoe

21 鋤殲 [ch'ú-chiēn] : to root out, to liquidate

鋒

7 鋒利 [fēng-lì] : sharp, incisive

鋒芒 [fēng-máng] : edge, spearhead

銷

10 銷案[hsiāo-àn]: to close a case

11 銷售[hsiāo-shòu]: to sell; sale

13 銷毀[hsiāo-hŭi]: to destroy, to ruin, to ravage, to desolate, to devastate

銷路[hsiāo-lù]: sale, circulation, market conditions

銷路不暢[hsiāo-lù pú-ch'àng]: slack market, slack season, poor sale

17 銷聲匿跡[hsiāo-shēng nì-chī]: to draw in one's horns

銳

7 銳利[jùi-lì]: sharp, pointed, keen, acute, penetrating

鋁

鋁[lŭ]: aluminum

鋪

5 鋪平[p'ū-p'íng]: to pave and smooth, to spread out evenly

鋪平道路[p'ū-p'íng tào-lù]: to pave the way, to smooth the way

11 鋪張[p'ū-chāng]: to exaggerate, to splurge; extravagance, layout, display

鋪張浪費[p'ū-chāng làng-fèi]: extravagance and waste

鋪張門面[p'ū-chāng mén-mièn]: to keep up appearances

— 8 Strokes —

錦

錦[chĭn]: Chinchow (abbreviation of 錦州)

6 錦江[chĭn-chiāng]: Kum River (Korea)

鋸

7 鋸床[chǜ-ch'uáng]: sawing machine

錐

3 錐子[chūi-tzu]: awl

錐子會[chūi-tzu hùi]: awl meeting, pricking meeting (a meeting at which workers criticize other's faults and expose their own faults)

錘

3 錘子[ch'úi-tzu]: hammer

13 錘煉[ch'úi-lièn]: to hammer out, to forge, to steel, to temper

錫

6 錫江[hsí-chiāng]: Macassar

7 錫伯[hsí-pó]: Sibo (minority nationality of Sinkiang and Kirin)

8 錫金[hsí-chīn]: Sikkim

9 錫哈諾[hsí-hā-nò]: Prince Norodom Sihanouk (Cambodian statesman)

10 錫茲內羅斯城[hsí-tzū-nèi-ló-ssū ch'éng]: Villaciseñeros (Spanish Sahara)

13 錫箔[hsí-pó]: tinfoil; Hsipaw (Burma)

21 錫蘭[hsí-lán]: Ceylon

錫蘭共和國 **[hsí-lán kùng-hó-kuó]**: Republic of Ceylon

鋼

7 鋼材 **[kāng-ts'ái]**: steel stock, steel products, rolled steel, rolled stock

8 鋼板 **[kāng-păn]**: steel plate

鋼坯 **[kāng-p'ī]**: crude steel, sheetbar

9 鋼軌 **[kāng-kuěi]**: steel rails

10 鋼骨水泥 **[kāng-kŭ shŭi-ní]**: reinforced concrete

鋼料 **[kāng-liào]**: steel materials

12 鋼渣 **[kāng-chā]**: steel slag

鋼筋 **[kāng-chīn]**: reinforced steel bar, corrugated steel bar, reinforced steel girder

鋼筋混凝土 **[kāng-chīn hùn-níng-t'ŭ]**: reinforced concrete

14 鋼種 **[kāng-chŭng]**: aluminum

鋼管 **[kāng-kuăn]**: steel tubes

15 鋼廠 **[kāng-ch'ăng]**: steel mill, steel plant, steelworks

16 鋼錠 **[kāng-tìng]**: steel ingot, steel slab

21 鋼鐵 **[kāng-t'iěh]**: steel

鋼鐵重點企業 **[kāng-t'iěh chùng-tiěn ch'ì-yèh]**: key iron and steel enterprises

鋼鐵工人 **[kāng-t'iěh kūng-jén]**: steel worker, steel maker

鋼鐵聯合企業 **[kāng-t'iěh lién-hó ch'ì-yèh]**: iron and steel complex, integrated iron and steel works

錄

9 錄音 **[lù-yīn]**: to record sounds on tapes

錄音機 **[lù-yīn-chī]**: tape recorder, sound recorder

錄音廣播 **[lù-yīn kuăng-pō]**: to broadcast by electrical transcription; a broadcast from recorded tapes

錳

錳 **[mĕng]**: manganese

錯

13 錯過 **[ts'ò-kuò]**: to miss (the chance), to let slip

錯落 **[ts'ò-lò]**: errors and omissions; confused, disorderly

錯亂 **[ts'ò-luàn]**: mixed up, confused, disorderly

14 錯綜 **[ts'ò-tsùng]**: involved, intricate, complex, entangled

錯綜複雜 **[ts'ò-tsùng fù-tsá]**: complicated

15 錯誤 **[ts'ò-wù]**: to make a mistake; error, mistake, blunder; mistaken, wrong, erroneous, fallacious, incorrect, misguided

錯誤估計 **[ts'ò-wù kū-chì]**: to miscalculate, to misjudge; incorrect appraisal, miscalculation, wrong estimate

20 錯覺 **[ts'ò-chüéh]**: misapprehension, misconception, false impression; misleading

— 9 Strokes —

鍋

20 鍋爐 **[kuō-lú]**: boiler

鍋爐廠 **[kuō-lú ch'ăng]**: boiler plant

鍛

13 鍛煉 **[tuàn-lièn]**: to temper, to steel, to forge, to harden, to refine

— 10 Strokes —

鎮

4 鎮反[**chèn-fǎn**]: to suppress counterrevolutionaries

5 鎮市[**chèn-shìh**]: market town, trading center

8 鎮定[**chèn-tìng**]: to soothe, to calm, to settle down, to allay, to pacify; calm, collected

9 鎮南浦[**chèn-nán-p'ǔ**]: Chinnanpo (Korea)

10 鎮海[**chèn-hǎi**]: Chinhae (Korea)

16 鎮靜[**chèn-chìng**]: to mollify, to calm, to quiet down, to tranquillize, to ease

17 鎮壓[**chèn-yā**]: to suppress, to repress, to stamp out, to quell, to subdue; suppression, repression

鎮壓與寬大相結合 [**chèn-yā yǔ k'uān-tà hsiāng chiéh-hó**]: to combine suppression with leniency

鎊

鎊[**pàng**]: pound sterling (British monetary unit)

鎖

19 鎖鏈[**sŏ-lièn**]: chains, shackles, fetters

— 11 Strokes —

鏟

3 鏟土機[**ch'ǎn-t'ǔ-chī**]: soil scraper

6 鏟式挖泥機[**ch'ǎn-shìh wā-ní-chī**]: dipper dredge

9 鏟除[**ch'ǎn-ch'ú**]: to eradicate, to uproot, to extirpate, to hoe away; eradication, extirpation

鏡

9 鏡城[**chìng-ch'éng**]: Kyongsong (Korea)

鏈

6 鏈式反應[**lièn-shìh fǎn-yìng**]: chain reaction

— 13 Strokes —

鐮

2 鐮刀斧頭[**lién-tāo fǔ-t'óu**]: hammer and sickle

鐵

6 鐵托[**t'iěh-t'ō**]: Tito, Josip Broz (Yugoslav political leader)

8 鐵的事實[**t'iěh te shìh-shíh**]: hard facts, indisputable facts, iron-clad facts

12 鐵道兵[**t'iěh-tào pīng**]: railway corps, railway unit

鐵道部[**t'iěh-tào pù**]: Ministry of Railways

13 鐵路[**t'iěh-lù**]: railway, railroad

鐵路運輸[**t'iěh-lù yùn-shū**]: rail transport, movement by rail

19 鐵證[**t'iěh-chèng**]: iron-clad proofs, strong proof

鐵類金屬工業部[**t'iěh-lèi chīn-shǔ kūng-yèh pù**]: Ministry of ferrous metal industry

— 14 Strokes —

鑒

7 鑒戒[**chièn-chièh**]: a warning example

鑒別[**chièn-piéh**]: to distinguish, to discern, to discriminate; discernment

8 鑒定[**chièn-tìng**]: to appraise, to assay; appraisal

鑒於[**chièn-yǘ**]: in consideration of, in regard to, in view of

15 鑒賞[**chièn-shǎng**]: to enjoy, to appreciate; appreciation

鑄

3 鑄工[**chù-kūng**]: foundry worker

6 鑄件[**chù-chièn**]: casting

11 鑄造[**chù-tsào**]: to cast; casting

— RADICAL 長 镸 168 —

長[**ch'áng**]: Changchun (abbreviation of 長春)

2 長入[**chǎng-jù**]: to grow into

3 長久[**ch'áng-chiǔ**]: a long time; long, protracted, permanent

長工[**ch'áng-kūng**]: regular work; permanent worker (i.e., as opposed to a seasonal worker)

5 長生果[**ch'áng-shēng kuǒ**]: peanut

6 長江[**ch'áng-chiāng**]: Yangtze River

長江大橋[**ch'áng-chiāng tà ch'iáo**]: Yangtze Bridge (at Wuhan)

長老會[**chǎng-lǎo hùi**]: Presbyterian Church

長年互助組[**ch'áng-nién hù-chù tsǔ**]: long-term mutual aid organization

長舌婦[**ch'áng-shé fù**]: a gossipy woman

長自己的志氣 [**chǎng tzù-chí te chìh-ch'ì**]: to heighten one's will (i.e., to fight)

7 長足進展[**ch'áng-tsú chìn-chǎn**]: to make great progress, to make enormous progress

8 長征[**ch'áng-chēng**]: the Long March (1934–1935)

長征幹部[**ch'áng-chēng kàn-pù**]: old-time Communists (i.e., Party members who were on the Long March of 1934–1935)

9 長城[**ch'áng-ch'éng**]: the Great Wall

長春地質實驗室[**ch'áng-ch'ūn tì-chìh shíh-yèn-shìh**]: Changchun Geology Laboratory

10 長眠[**ch'áng-mién**]: the big sleep, death

長時期的[**ch'áng shíh-ch'í te**]: long, of long duration, long-term

11 長崎[**ch'áng-ch'í**]: Nagasaki (Japan)

長假[**ch'áng-chià**]: to leave service; indefinite leave

長處[**ch'áng-ch'ù**]: strong points, merits

長途[**ch'áng-t'ú**]: long distance

長野[**ch'áng-yěh**]: Nagano (Japan)

12 長期[**ch'áng-ch'í**]: long-term, protracted, prolonged

長期共存，互相監督[**ch'áng-ch'í kùng-ts'ún, hù-hsiāng chiēn-tū**]: long-term coexistence and mutual supervision (a promise made to democratic parties during the "Hundred Flowers" campaign)

長期存在的[**ch'áng-ch'í ts'ún-tsài te**]: long-existing, long-standing

13 長遠[**ch'áng-yüǎn**]: long-term, long range

15 長篇謬論[ch'áng-p'iēn miù-lùn]: long-winded tirade

長篇大論[ch'áng-p'iēn tà-lùn]: lengthy speech

長敵人的志氣，滅自己的威風[chăng tí-jén te chìh-ch'ì, mièh tzù-chĭ te wēi-fēng]: to puff up the enemy and lower one's own morale

— RADICAL 門 169 —

門

4 門戶之見[mén-hù chīh chièn]: parochial prejudice

門戶開放[mén-hù k'āi-fàng]: the open door

門戶開放主義[mén-hù k'āi-fàng chŭ-ì]: the Open Door Doctrine

5 門市部[mén-shìh pù]: retail sales department

門司[mén-ssū]: Moji (Japan)

8 門的內哥羅[mén-tì-nèi-kō-ló]: Montenegro (Yugoslavia)

門外漢[mén-wài hàn]: layman, outsider, greenhorn, ignoramus

10 門徑[mén-chìng]: approach to, access to

門徒[mén-t'ú]: adherent, disciple, pupil, follower, apostle

19 門類[mén-lèi]: fields, various branches

門羅主義[mén-ló chŭ-ì]: the Monroe Doctrine

— 2 Strokes —

閃

6 閃光[shăn-kuāng]: to glitter, to sparkle; a flash, a flash of light, glare

11 閃族[shăn-tsú]: Semitic race

13 閃電戰[shăn-tièn chàn]: blitzkrieg

17 閃擊戰[shăn-chī chàn]: blitzkrieg

19 閃爍[shăn-shuò]: to flicker; flicker, scintillation

閃爍其詞[shăn-shuò ch'í-tz'ú]: to dodge or evade issues, to be equivocal

— 3 Strokes —

閉

8 閉門造車[pì-mén tsào-ch'ē]: to draw up plans behind closed doors

13 閉會期間[pì-hùi ch'í-chiēn]: the time when a group is not in session

閉塞[pì-sāi]: to barricade, to stop up

14 閉幕[pì-mù]: to bring down the curtain, to conclude, to close, to adjourn; closing

19 閉關自守[pì-kuān tzù-shŏu]: closed door policy

— 4 Strokes —

間

7 間作密植[chièn-tsò mì-chíh]: intercropping and close cropping

11 間接[chièn-chiēh]: indirect; indirectly

間接經驗[chièn-chiēh chīng-yèn]: indirect experience

間接稅 [chièn-chiēh shùi] : indirect tax

間接語 [chièn-chiēh yǔ] : indirect remarks

13 間隙 [chièn-hsì] : gap, clearance

間隔 [chièn-kó] : to separate; gap, breach, space, distance, interval

14 間歇 [chièn-hsiēh] : pause, interval, intermission, break, recess

16 間諜 [chièn-tiéh] : spy, traitor, agent; espionage

18 間斷 [chièn-tuàn] : to interrupt; interrupted, intermittent, discontinuous, inconsecutive

閑

6 閑地 [hsién-tì] : idle land, fallow land, unutilized land

12 閑散的 [hsién-sǎn te] : idle, loose, disbanded, at ease

13 閑置 [hsién-chǐh] : to keep idle, to leave unused, to let idle

閑置不用 [hsién-chǐh pú-yùng] : to shelve, to lay aside, to put to one side, to put away

15 閑談 [hsién-t'án] : gossip, idle talk, leisurely conversation

閏

6 閏年 [jùn-nién] : leap year, a year with an intercalary month

開

2 開刀 [k'āi-tāo] : to perform surgery; surgical operation

3 開工 [k'āi-kūng] : to begin work, to go into operation, to start operation

開工不足 [k'āi-kūng pù-tsú] : under-capacity operation

4 開支 [k'āi-chīh] : to expend, to spend; outlay, expenditure, expense, spending, disbursement

開火 [k'āi-huǒ] : to open fire

8 開門紅 [k'āi-mén húng] : let the beginning of the year be crowned with achievements

開明 [k'āi-míng] : to list clearly; enlightened

開明紳士 [k'āi-míng shēn-shìh] : enlightened gentry

開始 [k'āi-shǐh] : to start, to begin; beginning

開始期 [k'āi-shǐh ch'í] : initial period, beginning period

開始走上 [k'āi-shǐh tsǒu-shàng] : to take to the path, to begin treading

開拓 [k'āi-t'ò] : to open up

開夜車 [k'āi yèh-ch'ē] : to work at night, to burn the midnight oil

9 開城 [k'āi-ch'éng] : Kaesong (Korea)

10 開展 [k'āi-chǎn] : to develop, to further, to expand

開展城鄉交流 [k'āi-chǎn ch'éng-hsiāng chiāo-líu] : to develop rural-urban trade

開除 [k'āi-ch'ú] : to expel, to dismiss, to discharge, to fire, to oust; expulsion, dismissal, dishonorable discharge from official service

開除黨籍 [k'āi-ch'ú tǎng-chí] : expulsion from the Party

開荒 [k'āi-huāng] : to open up uncultivated land, to develop uncultivated land

開個缺口 [k'āi kò ch'üēh-k'ǒu] : to drive a wedge into, to make a breach in

開倒車 [k'āi-tào ch'ē] : to turn back the clock, to turn back the wheel of history, to go against the times

開庭 [k'āi-t'íng] : to hold court

開庭審理 [k'āi-t'íng shěn-lǐ] : to hold hearings, to try a case, to deal with a case

11 開國 [k'āi-kuó]: to found a state, to establish a new government

開採 [k'āi-ts'ăi]: to mine, to extract, to exploit, to open up

開動 [k'āi-tùng]: to operate, to start, to set into motion, to supply the motivating power

開脫 [k'āi-t'ō]: to get free of

開脫責任 [k'āi-t'ō tsé-jèn]: to absolve someone of responsibility

12 開發 [k'āi-fā]: to exploit, to tap, to prospect, to open up, to develop, to educate; exploitation

開普敦 [k'āi-p'ŭ tūn]: Cape Town (South Africa)

13 開會 [k'āi-hùi]: to hold a meeting, to call a meeting, to attend a meeting, to be in session, to convene a conference

開源節流 [k'āi-yüán chiéh-líu]: to broaden sources of income and economize on expenditures

14 開幕 [k'āi-mù]: to inaugurate, to open, to raise the curtain

開幕式 [k'āi-mù shìh]: opening session

開幕典禮 [k'āi-mù tiĕn-lĭ]: inaugural ceremony

16 開墾 [k'āi-k'ĕn]: to open up waste land, to open, to cultivate, to till

開墾荒地 [k'āi-k'ĕn huāng-tì]: to reclaim waste land, to open up waste land, to bring new land under cultivation, to reclaim land; land reclamation

開辦 [k'āi-pàn]: to set up, to start, to put into operation

開導 [k'āi-tăo]: to enlighten, to teach, to guide

17 開齋 [k'āi-chāi]: to cease from observance of fasting as a rite

開齋節 [k'āi-chāi chiéh]: Bairam (post-Ramadan festival)

開闊 [k'āi-k'uò]: to widen, to broaden

20 開羅 [k'āi-ló]: Cairo (United Arab Republic)

21 開闢 [k'āi-p'ì]: to open up, to break new ground

開闢道路 [k'āi-p'ì tào-lù]: to open up a way, to pave the way, to prepare the way

— 5 Strokes —

鬧

8 鬧事 [nào-shìh]: to create a disturbance, to make trouble; disturbance

— 6 Strokes —

閣

3 閣下 [kó-hsià]: Sir; Your Excellency

閩

閩 [mĭn]: Fukien (abbreviation for 福建)

— 7 Strokes —

閱

7 閱兵 [yüèh-pīng]: to review troops; military review

— 8 Strokes —

閻

4 閻王爺 [yén-wáng yéh]: Yama (Hindu term) the king of Hell (during the Cultural Revolution, an epithet for an influential anti-Mao intellectual leader)

— 9 Strokes —

闊

10 闊氣 [k'uò-ch'ì] : airs of extravagance

— 10 Strokes —

闖

2 闖入 [ch'uăng-jù] : to intrude, to break into, to rush in; intrusion

11 闖將 [ch'uăng-chiàng]: dare-devils (during the Cultural Revolution, refers to the Red Guard members; also a reference to the Ming Dynasty figure Li Tzu-ch'eng)

12 闖過關 [ch'uăng-kuò kuān] : to come triumphantly through an ordeal

— 11 Strokes —

關

3 關口 [kuān-k'ǒu] : pass, Customs station, barrier, Customs barrier

4 關切 [kuān-ch'ièh] : to feel quite concerned

關心 [kuān-hsīn] : to be concerned about, to care for, to pay attention to, to be interested in; concern

關內 [kuān-nèi] : within the passes; south of the Great Wall

5 關卡 [kuān-ch'iă] : customs barrier; a customhouse for receiving the likin

關外 [kuān-wài] : Manchuria; Shansi; outside the suburbs of a city

8 關門主義 [kuān-mén chŭ-ì] : exclusivism, closed-door policy, closed-door sectarianism

關門態度 [kuān-mén t'ài-tù] : closed-door attitude

關於 [kuān-yű] : pertaining to, concerning, respecting, as to, as for, in connection with, in reference to, in matters of

關於正確處理人民內部矛盾的問題 [kuān-yű chèng-ch'üèh ch'ŭ-lĭ jén-mín nèi-pù máo-tùn te wèn-t'í] : On the Correct Handling of Contradictions Among the People (report by Mao Tse-tung, February 27, 1957)

9 關係 [kuān-hsì] : to involve, to relate to, to concern; relationship, connection, consequences, bearing, correlation, reference, association

10 關涉 [kuān-shè] : to concern

關島 [kuān-tăo] : Guam

11 關閉 [kuān-pì] : to close, to shut, to close down, to shut down

12 關進監牢 [kuān-chìn chiēn-láo] : to imprison, to jail

關稅 [kuān-shùi] : tariff, customs tariff, customs duties

關稅同盟 [kuān-shùi t'úng-méng] : tariff union

關稅自主權 [kuān-shùi tzù-chŭ ch'üán] : customs autonomy, tariff autonomy

16 關頭 [kuān-t'óu] : crisis, juncture, crucial moment, turning point

17 關鍵 [kuān-chièn] : key, key to a situation, pivot, pivotal point, crux of a matter; crucial, critical, decisive

關聯 [kuān-lién] : connection, context

19 關懷 [kuān-huái] : to be solicitous, to worry; solicitude, concern; to be concerned with

— 12 Strokes —

闡

8 闡明 [ch'ăn-míng] : to explain, to clarify, to elucidate, to elaborate, to interpret, to define; explanation

9 闡述 [ch'ăn-shù] : to explain, to expound; explanation

— 13 Strokes —

闢

12 闢開 **[p'ì-k'āi]** : to split open, to burst forth, to cleave

17 闢謠 **[p'ì-yáo]** : to repudiate a rumor, to dispel a rumor

— RADICAL 阜阝 170 —

— 4 Strokes —

防

4 防止 **[fáng-chǐh]** : to prevent, to avert, to guard against, to check, to hinder

6 防奸 **[fáng-chiēn]** : to guard against traitors (i.e., to the Communist cause; a slogan of the early 1950s)

防守 **[fáng-shǒu]** : to protect, to defend

7 防沙林 **[fáng-shā lín]** : sand break

8 防空 **[fáng-k'ūng]** : air defense

防空兵司令部 **[fáng-k'ūng-pīng ssū-lìng-pù]** : Air Defense Headquarters

防空部隊 **[fáng-k'ūng pù-tùi]** : antiaircraft forces, antiaircraft troops, air defense units

防空洞 **[fáng-k'ūng tùng]** : air raid shelter; a refuge for undesirable elements

防空演習 **[fáng-k'ūng yěn-hsí]** : air raid drill

9 防風林 **[fáng-fēng lín]** : wind break

防風林帶 **[fáng-fēng lín-tài]** : shelter belt and wind break

防洪 **[fáng-húng]** : flood control, flood prevention

防洪大軍 **[fáng-húng tà-chǖn]** : flood prevention army

防疫 **[fáng-ì]** : prevention of epidemics; quarantine

防疫站 **[fáng-ì chàn]** : epidemic prevention station, quarantine station

11 防患於未然 **[fáng-huàn yǘ wèi-ján]** : to nip troubles in the bud

防微杜漸 **[fáng-wēi tù-chièn]** : to nip troubles in the bud, to prevent growth when a thing is small

防務 **[fáng-wù]** : defense measures or matters

12 防備 **[fáng-pèi]** : to prevent, to be ready for, to watch for, to guard against

防御 **[fáng-yǜ]** : to protect, to guard, to defend

防御性的 **[fáng-yǜ-hsìng te]** : defensive, of a defensive nature

防御工事 **[fáng-yǜ kūng-shìh]** : fortification

防御聯盟 **[fáng-yǜ lién-méng]** : defense alliance, defensive alliance

防御體系 **[fáng-yǜ t'ǐ-hsì]** : defense system, defensive system

15 防範 **[fáng-fàn]** : measures for defense, precautionary measures; to take preventive measures

16 防衛 **[fáng-wèi]** : to protect, to defend

21 防護林 **[fáng-hù lín]** : protective forest

阮

11 阮康[juǎn k'āng]: Nguyen Khan (North Vietnamese government official)

— 5 Strokes —

阿

4 阿比西尼亞[à-pǐ-hsī-ní-yà]: Ethiopia

阿比讓[à-pǐ-jàng]: Abidjan (Ivory Coast)

5 阿卡[à-ch'iǎ]: Akha (a minority group of Yunnan Province)

6 阿西[à-hsī]: Ahsi (minority nationality)

阿批亞[à-p'ī-yà]: Apia (Western Samoa)

7 阿克拉[à-k'ò-lā]: Accra (Ghana)

8 阿昌[à-ch'āng]: Ahchang (minority nationality)

阿肯色[à-k'ěn-sè]: Arkansas (U.S.A.)

阿拉哈巴德[à-lā-hā-pā-té]: Allhabad

阿拉伯[à-lā-pó]: Arabia

阿拉伯叙利亞共和國[à-lā-pó hsǜ-lì-yà kùng-hó-kuó]: Arab Republic of Syria

阿拉伯聯合共和國[à-lā-pó lién-hó kùng-hó-kuó]: United Arab Republic

阿拉伯聯盟[à-lā-pó lién-méng]: Arab League

阿拉斯加[à-lā-ssū-chiā]: Alaska (U.S.A.)

阿姆斯特丹[à-mǔ-ssū-t'è-tān]: Amsterdam (Holland)

阿育布[à-yǜ-pù]: Khan, Mohammad Ayub (Pakistani soldier and statesman)

9 阿飛[à-fēi]: a rowdy or juvenile delinquent (Shanghai dialect)

阿胡島[à-hú tǎo]: Oahu Island (Hawaii)

阿訇[à-húng]: Mohammedan priest; a mullah

阿卑斯[à-pēi-ssū]: Alps

10 阿根廷[à-kēn-t'íng]: Argentina

阿根廷共和國[à-kēn-t'íng kùng-hó-kuó]: Argentine Republic

阿留地安[à-líu-tì-ān]: Aleutian Islands (U.S.A.)

11 阿富汗[à-fù-hàn]: Afghanistan

阿富汗王國[à-fù-hàn wáng-kuó]: Kingdom of Afghanistan

阿勒頗[à-lè-p'ŏ]: Aleppo (Syria)

阿曼[à-màn]: Oman

阿曼伊斯蘭教長會[à-màn ī-ssū-lán chiào-chǎng-kuó]: the Imamate of Oman

12 阿斯特拉罕[à-ssū-t'è-lā-hǎn]: Astrakhan (U.S.S.R.)

阿登諾[à-tēng-nò]: Adenauer, Konrad (German political figure)

14 阿爾及爾[à-ěrh-chí-ěrh]: Algiers (Algeria)

阿爾及利亞[à-ěrh-chí-lì-yà]: Algeria

阿爾及利亞民主人民共和國[à-ěrh-chí-lì-yà mín-chǔ jén-mín kùng-hó-kuó]: Democratic People's Republic of Algeria

阿爾亨格爾斯克 [à-ěrh-hēng-kó-ěrh-ssū-k'ò]: Alkhangelsk

阿爾卑斯 [à-ěrh-pēi-ssū]: Alps

阿爾薩斯[à-ěrh-sā-ssū]: Alsace

阿爾丹河[à-ěrh-tān hó]: Aldan River

阿爾巴尼亞[à-ěrh-pā-ní-yà]: Albania

阿爾巴尼亞人民共和國[à-ěrh-pā-ní-yà jén-mín kùng-hó-kuó]: People's Republic of Albania

阿爾巴尼亞人民共和國人民議會 [à-ěrh-pā-ní-yà jén-mín kùng-hó-kuó jén-mín ì-hùi]:

People's Assembly of the People's Republic of Albania

16 阿諛 **[ō-yǘ]**: to flatter; flattery

阿諛逢迎 **[ō-yǘ féng-yíng]**: to curry favor with, to fawn on, to toady to; toadying, fawning

附

5 附加 **[fù-chiā]**: to attach, to be appended to; insertion, addition, supplement; additional, supplementary

附加稅 **[fù-chiā shùi]**: surtax, an additional tax

6 附件 **[fù-chièn]**: accessory, appendix, appendage, supplement, addendum

8 附近 **[fù-chìn]**: in the neighborhood of, close by

附注 **[fù-chù]**: notes

附和 **[fù-hó]**: to respond to, to acquiesce, to echo, to agree with

9 附則 **[fù-tsé]**: supplementary provision

11 附庸 **[fù-yūng]**: dependency, satellite

附庸國家 **[fù-yūng kuó-chiā]**: satellite country

13 附會 **[fù-hùi]**: to force an interpretation or association

16 附錄 **[fù-lù]**: appendix, supplement

21 附屬 **[fù-shǔ]**: accessory, incidental, secondary, collateral

附屬機構 **[fù-shǔ chī-kòu]**: subordinate organization, affiliated organs

附屬國 **[fù-shǔ kuó]**: dependent country, dependency

附屬國家 **[fù-shǔ kuó-chiā]**: dependent country, vassal state, satellite country

附屬物 **[fù-shǔ wù]**: appendage, adjunct, accessory

附屬於 **[fù-shǔ yǘ]**: adjunct to, affiliated, attached, appended, subsidiary

阻

2 阻力 **[tsǔ-lì]**: resistance

4 阻止 **[tsǔ-chǐh]**: to stop, to hinder, to check, to impede, to obstruct, to block

12 阻援 **[tsǔ-yüán]**: to hold off enemy resistance

15 阻撓 **[tsǔ-náo]**: to impede, to hamper, to obstruct, to hinder; obstruction, obstacle, hindrance, impediment

16 阻擋 **[tsǔ-tǎng]**: to obstruct, to halt, to block, to stop, to hinder, to check, to impede

17 阻擊 **[tsǔ-chī]**: to intercept; interception

阻擊陣地 **[tsǔ-chī chèn-tì]**: blocking position

19 阻礙 **[tsǔ-ài]**: to impede, to hamper, to obstruct, to hinder; obstruction, obstacle, hindrance, impediment

— 6 Strokes —

3 降下 **[chiàng-hsià]**: to drop, to fall, to descend, to go down

5 降生 **[chiàng-shēng]**: to be born

7 降低 **[chiàng-tī]**: to go down, to slump, to decline, to be less; slump, decline

8 降雨量 **[chiàng-yǔ liàng]**: rainfall

降雨地帶 **[chiàng-yǔ tì-tài]**: rain zone

10 降級 **[chiàng-chí]**: to reduce to a lower grade, to degrade, to demote; demotion, demotion in grade

13 降落 **[chiàng-lò]**: to descend, to land, to touch down

降落傘 [chiàng-lò-sǎn] : parachute

14 降旗 [chiàng-ch'í] : to lower a flag

18 降職 [chiàng-chíh] : demotion to a lower position; to demote

限

8 限制 [hsièn-chìh] : to limit, to restrict, to curb, to check, to constrain; limitation, restriction

限制於 [hsièn-chìh yǘ] : to confine to, to restrict to, to be bound to, to be limited to

限度 [hsièn-tù] : standards, restriction, limit, extent

12 限期 [hsièn-ch'í] : time limit, deadline, a set time limit

18 限額 [hsièn-ó] : quota, norm

限額以下的 [hsièn-ó ǐ-hsià te] : below norm

限額以上的 [hsièn-ó ǐ-shàng te] : above norm

— 7 Strokes —

陣

3 陣亡 [chèn-wáng] : to die in battle, to die fighting, to die in action

6 陣地 [chèn-tì] : battlefield, battleground

陣地戰 [chèn-tì chàn] : positional warfare

陣地攻擊戰術 [chèn-tì kūng-chī chàn-shù] : the tactics of positional attack

10 陣容 [chèn-júng] : line-up (i.e., as a party line-up)

12 陣痛 [chèn-t'ùng] : twinge, twitch, spasm, sudden sharp pain

13 陣勢 [chèn-shìh] : battle array, disposition of forces, deployment of forces, position of troops

14 陣綫 [chèn-hsièn] : front

17 陣營 [chèn-yíng] : camp; military

除

2 除了 [ch'ú-le] : except, exclusive of, barring, apart from, besides; to exclude, to get rid of

3 除夕 [ch'ú-hsī] : the last night of the old year, New Year's Eve

5 除去 [ch'ú-ch'ǜ] : to discard, to remove, to get rid of, to throw out, to cast away, to wipe out, to expel

除四害 [ch'ú ssù-hài] : to wipe out the four pests; the elimination of the four pests (*See* 四害)

除...外 [ch'ú . . . wài] : except, exclusive of, barring, apart from, besides; to exclude

6 除名 [ch'ú-míng] : to dismiss, to strike a name from the list, to disenroll, to write someone's name off

7 除災 [ch'ú-tsāi] : to wipe out calamities, to eliminate natural disasters

10 除根 [ch'ú-kēn] : to root out, to exterminate, to clear out, to eradicate

11 除授 [ch'ú-shòu] : to appoint

除掉 [ch'ú-tiào] : to remove, to eliminate, to omit

陝

陝 [shǎn] : Shensi (abbreviation of 陝西)

6 陝西中醫研究所 [shǎn-hsi chūng-ī yén-chìu-sǒ] : Shensi Chinese Traditional Medicine Institute

院

3 院士 [yüàn-shìh] : academician

7 院系 [yüàn-hsì] : university department, schools and departments of a university

院系調整 [yüàn-hsì t'iáo-chěng] : reorganization of colleges and departments of institutions of higher learning

8 院長 [yüàn-chăng]: dean (of a college); superintendent (of a hospital), chief justice (of a law court)

11 院務會議 [yüàn-wù hùi-ì]: academic council meeting

— 8 Strokes —

陳

6 陳列 [ch'én-lièh]: to display, to exhibit, to show, to arrange

陳列館 [ch'én-lièh kuăn]: exhibition hall, museum

9 陳述 [ch'én-shù]: to state, to give an account of, to explain, to set forth

10 陳案 [ch'én-àn]: long-pending cases, shelved cases

11 陳設 [ch'én-shè]: to set out, to display

12 陳腔濫調 [ch'én-ch'iāng làn-tiào]: hackneyed tunes and hackneyed phrases, clichés and stock arguments

14 陳說 [ch'én-shuō]: to explain, to narrate, to state a case

15 陳請 [ch'én-ch'ĭng]: to petition

18 陳舊 [ch'én-chìu]: stale, old-fashioned, outdated, obsolete

陷

2 陷入 [hsièn-jù]: to fall into, to fall into the clutches of, to sink into

陷入僵局 [hsièn-jù chiāng-chŭ]: to reach an impasse

陷入窘境 [hsièn-jù chiŭng-chìng]: to be in a tight corner, to fall into difficult circumstances, to get into an awkward position

陷入圈套 [hsièn-jù ch'üān-t'ào]: to get trapped into, to fall into the clutches of, to fall into a trap

陷入危機 [hsièn-jù wéi-chī]: to be beset with a crisis, to be deep in crisis

7 陷阱 [hsièn-chĭng]: a trap, a snare, a pitfall

陵

13 陵園 [líng-yüán]: imperial mausoleum, tomb

14 陵墓 [líng-mù]: tomb, mausoleum, sepulchre

陪

6 陪同 [p'éi-t'úng]: to accompany, to be in the company of

15 陪審 [p'éi-shĕn]: to assist in trying a case, to act as an assessor in a case; a trial by jury, an assessor

陪審團 [p'éi-shĕn-t'uán]: jury

陪審員 [p'éi-shĕn-yüán]: juryman, juror, member of the jury

陰

13 陰暗面 [yīn-àn mièn]: dark side, seamy side

15 陰謀 [yīn-móu]: to conspire, to plot, to scheme; plot, conspiracy, intrigue; crafty, subtle, designing, contriving

陰謀家 [yīn-móu-chiā]: schemer

陰謀份子 [yīn-móu fèn-tzu]: conspirator, plot-machinator

陰謀活動 [yīn-móu huó-tùng]: conspiratorial activity, subversive activities

陰謀詭計 [yīn-móu kuĕi-chì]: intrigues and plots

16 陰險 [yīn-hsiĕn]: designing, insidious, sinister, malevolent, malicious, deceitful, invidious

170

— 9 Strokes —

階

9 階段 **[chiēh-tuàn]** : stage, step, phase

10 階級 **[chiēh-chí]** : class, step, caste, social class

階級差別 **[chiēh-chí ch'ā-piéh]** : class distinction

階級教育 **[chiēh-chí chiào-yǜ]** : class education (i.e., indoctrination in class struggle and class analysis)

階級制度 **[chiēh-chí chìh-tù]** : class system

階級仇恨 **[chiēh-chí ch'óu-hèn]** : class hatred

階級覺悟 **[chiēh-chí chüéh-wù]** : class consciousness

階級分折 **[chiēh-chí fēn-hsī]** : class analysis

階級分折方法 **[chiēh-chí fēn-hsī fāng-fǎ]** : method of class analysis

階級分化 **[chiēh-chí fēn-huà]** : class differentiation

階級性 **[chiēh-chí-hsìng]** : class character, class nature

階級異已份子 **[chiēh-chí ì-chǐ fèn-tzu]** : alien class element, individuals from alien classes, people of classes different from one's own (i.e., those who do not follow Chairman Mao's revolutionary line)

階級意識 **[chiēh-chí ì-shìh]** : class consciousness

階級關系 **[chiēh-chí kuān-hsì]** : class relationship, relations among the different classes

階級觀點 **[chiēh-chí kuān-tiěn]** : class viewpoint (one of the 四大觀點, q.v.)

階級立場 **[chiēh-chí lì-ch'ǎng]** : class standpoint

階級利害 **[chiēh-chí lì-hài]** : class interests

階級路綫 **[chiēh-chí lù-hsièn]** : class line

階級矛盾 **[chiēh-chí máo-tùn]** : class contradiction

階級報復 **[chiēh-chí pào-fù]** : class revenge (during the Cultural Revolution, revenge taken by the cadre against 地富反壞右, q.v.)

階級本性 **[chiēh-chí pěn-hsìng]** : class character

階級本能 **[chiēh-chí pěn-néng]** : class instinct

階級社會 **[chiēh-chí shè-hùi]** : class society

階級敵人 **[chiēh-chí tí-jén]** : class enemy

階級調和論 **[chiēh-chí t'iáo-hó lùn]** : theory of class harmony

階級鬥爭 **[chiēh-chí tòu-chēng]** : class struggle

階級隊伍 **[chiēh-chí tùi-wǔ]** : class corps (a group made up of poor and lower middle peasants who serve as the activists in any movement and who "supervise" work in the production teams)

15 階層 **[chiēh-ts'éng]** : stratum, layer

隆

9 隆重 **[lúng-chùng]** : solemn, imposing, grand, magnificent, grave, impressive

隆重接待 **[lúng-chùng chiēh-tài]** : grand reception

隊 **[tùi]** : company, band, group, contingent, team, line, rank

6 隊伍 **[tùi-wǔ]** : corps, rank and file, troops, crew

7 隊形 **[tùi-hsíng]** : troop formation

8 隊長 **[tùi-chǎng]** : company leader

隊服 [tùi-fú] : uniform

14 隊旗 [tùi-ch'í] : company guidon, brigade flag

陽

8 陽奉陰違 [yáng-fèng yīn-wéi] : to feign compliance, to pretend compliance; outwardly compliant but inwardly defiant

— 10 Strokes —

隘

12 隘道 [ài-tào] : narrow passage, bottleneck

隔

4 隔手 [kó-shŏu] : through an intermediary; indirect

8 隔岸觀火 [kó-àn kuān-huŏ] : to watch the fire from the other bank of the river; to show unconcern

9 隔音 [kó-yīn] : soundproof

12 隔絕 [kó-chüéh] : to isolate, to seal off

14 隔閡 [kó-hó] : to have nothing in common; barrier, barrier of understanding, lack of understanding, estrangement, alienation; alienated

15 隔膜 [kó-mò] : membrane; lack of mutual understanding; to have no dealings with

18 隔離 [kó-lí] : to set apart, to keep apart, to be separated from one another, to be quarantined

隔斷 [kó-tuàn] : to cut off, to sever

隕

5 隕石 [yŭn-shíh] : meteor

— 11 Strokes —

際

12 際遇 [chì-yǜ] : juncture, crisis, opportunity, destiny

障

19 障礙 [chàng-ài] : to obstruct, to hinder, to check, to impede; obstacle, obstruction, hindrance, barrier, stumbling block

隙

17 隙縫 [hsì-fèng] : cleavage, crack, fissure

— 13 Strokes —

隨

2 隨人俯仰 [súi-jén fŭ-yăng] : to submit to someone's whim and fancy

3 隨大流 [súi tà-líu] : to follow the crowd, to follow the main stream (this refers to the attitude of those who are not enthusiastic followers of Mao's line, but who follow it because it is the general trend)

4 隨心所欲 [súi-hsīn sŏ-yǜ] : at will, at one's will, as one likes, following one's own inclination, at one's own discretion

6 隨行 [súi-hsíng] : to accompany

隨行人員 [súi-hsíng jén-yüán] : entourage, member of one's suite

8 隨其自然發展 [súi ch'í tzù-ján fā-chăn] : to develop according to its natural course

10 隨時準備 [súi-shíh chŭn-pèi] : to be ready at any time

隨員 [súi-yüán] : attaché, entourage

13 隨意 [súi-ì] : at will, at pleasure

隨意處理 [súi-ì ch'ŭ-lĭ] : to deal with something according to one's wishes

[17] 隨聲 **[súi-shēng]** : to agree with everything

隨聲附和 **[súi-shēng fù-hó]** : to echo a line

— 14 Strokes —

隱

[11] 隱晦 **[yǐn-hùi]** : to conceal, to keep secret, to cover up; concealment

[15] 隱瞞 **[yǐn-mán]** : to conceal, to hide; concealment

[16] 隱諱 **[yǐn-hùi]** : to conceal, to keep secret, to cover up

隱蔽活動 **[yǐn-pì huó-tùng]** : to work under cover; underground activity

[18] 隱藏 **[yǐn-ts'áng]** : to secrete, to hide, to conceal, to put out of sight; hidden, latent, dormant

— 15 Strokes —

[15] 隳頹 **[hūi-t'úi]** : destroyed, laid waste

— 16 Strokes —

隴

隴 **[lúng]** : Kansu (abbreviation for 甘肅)

— RADICAL 隶 171 —

— RADICAL 隹 172 —

— 4 Strokes —

集

[3] 集大成 **[chí tà-ch'éng]** : to formulate a complete doctrine or theory based on various ideas gathered

[4] 集中 **[chí-chūng]** : to focus on, to centralize, to concentrate; concentration, centralization; centralized

集中指導 **[chí-chūng chǐh-tǎo]** : centralized guidance

集中經營 **[chí-chūng chīng-yíng]** : centralized management, centralized operation

集中反映 **[chí-chūng fǎn-yìng]** : to embody a concentrated reflection of

集中彙總 **[chí-chūng hùi-tsǔng]** : centralized processing

集中領導 **[chí-chūng lǐng-tǎo]** : centralized leadership

集中領導，分散經營 **[chí-chūng lǐng-tǎo, fēn-sàn chīng-yíng]** : centralized leadership and decentralized management

集中領導和群衆運動相結合 **[chí-chūng lǐng-tǎo hó ch'ǘn-chùng yǜn-tùng hsiāng chiéh-hó]** : to combine centralized leadership with mass movements

集中營 **[chí-chūng yíng]** : concentration camp

集日 **[chí-jìh]** : market day, fair day

集市 **[chí-shìh]** : market, market town

集市貿易 **[chí-shìh mào-ì]** : village fair trade

[6] 集合 **[chí-hó]** : to rally, to collect, to muster, to converge, to congregate, to assemble, to gather

[9] 集思廣益 **[chí-ssū kuǎng-ì]** : to canvass opinions and benefit from them

[10] 集訓 **[chí-hsǜn]** : centralized training

12 集結 **[chí-chiéh]**: grouping, gathering, concentration, build-up

13 集會 **[chí-hùi]**: to assemble, to convene; assembly, gathering, meeting, mass rally, mass meeting

集會自由 **[chí-hùi tzù-yú]**: freedom of assembly

14 集聚 **[chí-chǜ]**: to gather, to collect

集團 **[chí-t'uán]**: bloc, group, clique

集團政策 **[chí-t'uán chèng-ts'è]**: bloc policy

集團軍 **[chí-t'uán chǖn]**: group army, army group

22 集權 **[chí-ch'üán]**: centralization of authority, centralization of government power

23 集體的 **[chí-t'ĭ te]**: collective

集體安全 **[chí-t'ĭ ān-ch'üán]**: collective security

集體經濟 **[chí-t'ĭ chīng-chì]**: collective economy

集體經營 **[chí-t'ĭ chīng-yíng]**: collective management

集體主義 **[chí-t'ĭ chŭ-ì]**: collectivism

集體福利 **[chí-t'ĭ fú-lì]**: collective welfare

集體合同 **[chí-t'ĭ hó-t'úng]**: collective agreement, collective contract

集體化 **[chí-t'ĭ-huà]**: to collectivize; collectivization

集體領導 **[chí-t'ĭ lĭng-tăo]**: collective leadership

集體領導和個人負責相結合的原則 **[chí-t'ĭ lĭng-tăo hó kò-jén fù-tsé hsiāng chiéh-hó te yüán-tsé]**: the principle of combining collective leadership with individual responsibility

集體農場 **[chí-t'ĭ núng-ch'ăng]**: collective farm

集體農民 **[chí-t'ĭ núng-mín]**: collective farmer

集體所有制 **[chí-t'ĭ sŏ-yŭ chì]**: collective ownership system

雄

3 雄才大略 **[hsiúng-ts'ái tà-lüèh]**: outstanding talent and great strategy

4 雄心勃勃 **[hsiúng-hsīn pó-pó]**: ardently ambitious

11 雄偉 **[hsiúng-wĕi]**: brave, strong, capable, imposing, majestic

21 雄辯 **[hsiúng-pièn]**: to debate vigorously; impressive eloquence

僱

5 顧主 **[kù-chŭ]**: employer

顧用 **[kù-yùng]**: to employ, to hire; employment, on hire

13 顧農 **[kù-núng]**: farm laborer, farm hand

顧傭 **[kù-yūng]**: to be employed for wages

顧傭觀點 **[kù-yūng kuān-tiĕn]**: mercenary point of view (the point of view of those who work only when they are paid and who work harder the more they are paid)

顧傭兵 **[kù-yūng pīng]**: mercenary

顧傭思想 **[kù-yūng ssū-hsiăng]**: mercenary thought or ideology (**See** 顧傭觀點)

雅

5 雅加達 **[yă-chiā-tá]**: Djakarta (Indonesia)

8 雅典 **[yă-tiĕn]**: Athens (Greece)

9 雅南 **[yă-nán]**: Nhanam (Vietnam)

10 雅恩德 **[yă-ēn-té]**: Yaounde (Cameroun)

12 雅溫得 **[yă-wēn-té]**: Yaounde (Cameroun)

14 雅爾達協定 **[yă-ĕrh-tá hsiéh-tìng]**: Yalta Agreement

172

雅瑪圖 **[yă-mă-t'ú]**: Yamatugai (Sinkiang)

15 雅魯 **[yă-lŭ]**: Dzhalantun (Mongolia)

雅魯藏布江 **[yă-lŭ-tsàng-pù chiāng]**: Brahmaputra River

— 8 Strokes —

雕

8 雕刻 **[tiāo-k'ò]**: to engrave, to carve; engraving, sculpture

雕刻家 **[tiāo-k'ò-chiā]**: sculptor

雕刻工人 **[tiāo-k'ò kūng-jén]**: engraver

雕板 **[tiāo-păn]**: to cut blocks for printing

14 雕像 **[tiāo-hsiàng]**: statue, bust

— 10 Strokes —

鷄

4 鷄毛蒜皮 **[chī-máo suàn-p'í]**: details, hair-splitting

雛

7 雛形 **[ch'ú-hsíng]**: miniature, prototype

8 雛兒 **[ch'ú-érh]**: young person without experience

雙

4 雙方 **[shuāng-fāng]**: both sides, both parties

雙日 **[shuāng-jìh]**: even date, even day, date with an even number

雙引擎的 **[shuāng yĭn-ch'íng te]**: twin-engined

8 雙任制 **[shuāng-jèn chìh]**: double appointment system (a system whereby cadres hold concurrent posts in both large and small production brigades)

雙季稻 **[shuāng-chì tào]**: double crop paddy rice, double rice crop

9 雙重 **[shuāng-ch'úng]**: dual, twofold, double

雙重國籍 **[shuāng-ch'úng kuó-chí]**: dual nationality

14 雙管齊下 **[shuāng-kuăn ch'í-hsià]**: to work both angles; a pincer drive

18 雙簧 **[shuāng-huáng]**: a two-man act, a two-man performing team, a one-man act accompanied by a hidden singer

19 雙邊的 **[shuāng-piēn te]**: bilateral

雜

4 雜文 **[tsá-wén]**: essays on various topics, essays and sketches, literary miscellany

6 雜色部隊 **[tsá-sè pù-tùi]**: miscellaneous troops

7 雜技 **[tsá-chì]**: acrobatics

雜技團 **[tsá-chì t'uán]**: acrobatic troop

9 雜耍 **[tsá-shuă]**: variety show, vaudeville

10 雜草 **[tsá-ts'ăo]**: weed

12 雜牌軍 **[tsá-p'ái chūn]**: miscellaneous troops, troops of different allegiances

雜稅 **[tsá-shùi]**: sundry tax, tax on sundries

13 雜感 **[tsá-kăn]**: random thoughts

14 雜誌 **[tsá-chìh]**: journal, magazine, periodical

18 雜糧 **[tsá-liáng]**: coarse cereals, miscellaneous grain crops

— 11 Strokes —

離

4 離心傾向 **[lí-hsīn ch'īng-hsiàng]**: separatist tendency, tendency to fall away, tendency to drift away

離心作用 [lí-hsīn tsò-yùng]: centrifugal effects

10 離差 [lí-ch'ā]: deviation

12 離間 [lí-chièn]: to alienate, to sow discord, to drive a wedge, to estrange; estrangement

離開 [lí-k'āi]: to leave, to depart, to fall away from, to be alienated from

18 離職 [lí-chíh]: to resign, to retire from office, to leave one's job

難

5 難以 [nán-ǐ]: difficult to, hard to

難以制服 [nán-ǐ chìh-fú]: difficult to control, unruly, insubordinate, ungovernable, intractable

難以否認 [nán-ǐ fǒu-jèn]: to be difficult to deny; undeniable, irrefutable

難以相信 [nán-ǐ hsiāng-hsìn]: unbelievable, incredible

難以形容 [nán-ǐ hsíng-júng]: to defy description; indescribable, inexpressible, beyond description

難以估計 [nán-ǐ kū-chì]: inestimable, difficult to evaluate

難以比擬 [nán-ǐ pǐ-nǐ]: to hardly match, to hardly equal

難民 [nàn-mín]: refugee, fugitive

7 難局 [nán-chű]: difficult situation, impasse, blind alley

18 難題 [nán-t'í]: difficult problem, difficult subject, baffling problem

— RADICAL 雨 173 —

雨

9 雨後春筍 [yǚ-hòu ch'ūn-sǔn]: bamboo shoots after a spring rain

12 雨量 [yǚ-liàng]: rainfall, precipitation

— 3 Strokes —

雪

4 雪中送炭 [hsüěh-chūng sùng-t'àn]: to offer fuel to a person in snowy weather; timely assistance

8 雪忿 [hsüèh-fèn]: to appease one's anger, to calm one's anger, to avenge

10 雪恥 [hsüèh-ch'ǐh]: to avenge an insult, to wipe out a disgrace

11 雪寃 [hsüèh-yüān]: to clear a person from a false charge

— 5 Strokes —

雷

7 雷克雅未克 [léi-k'ò-yǎ-wèi-k'ò]: Reykjavik (Iceland)

10 雷神式導彈 [léi-shén-shìh tǎo-tàn]: Thor missile

12 雷達 [léi-tá]: radar

雷達螢光板 [léi-tá yíng-kuāng-pǎn]: radar screen

雷提群島 [léi-t'í ch'űn-tǎo]: Leyte (Philippines)

15 雷鋒 [léi fēng]: Lei Feng (a soldier who died on duty and who purportedly left a diary in which he recorded his thoughts and his efforts to learn from the works of Mao, hailed as a model young man for the youth of China to emulate)

雷厲風行 [léi-lì fēng-hsíng]: enforcement in a sweeping manner

16 雷諾新聞 **[léi-nò hsīn-wén]** : Reynold News (British news service)

零

零 **[líng]** : zero, bits, fragments, remains, fraction

3 零工 **[líng-kūng]** : odd-jobber, short term hired labor, casual labor

9 零星 **[líng-hsīng]** : in pieces, in fragments, piecemeal, odds and ends, miscellaneous

11 零售 **[líng-shòu]** : to retail; retail sales; retail

電

2 電力站部 **[tièn-lì-chàn pù]** : Ministry of Power Stations

電力工業部 **[tièn-lì kūng-yèh pù]** : Ministry of Electric Power Industry

3 電工 **[tièn-kūng]** : electrician, electrical technician

電工研究所 **[tièn-kūng yén-chìu-sŏ]** : Electrical Engineering Institute

電子 **[tièn-tzŭ]** : electron

電子計算機 **[tièn-tzŭ chì-suàn-chī]** : electronic computer, electronic calculating machine

電子放映機 **[tièn-tzŭ fàng-yìng-chī]** : electron projector

電子顯微鏡 **[tièn-tzŭ hsiĕn-wēi-chìng]** : electron microscope

電子學 **[tièn-tzŭ-hsüéh]** : electronics

電子迴旋加速器 **[tièn-tzŭ húi-hsüán chiā-sù-ch'ì]** : betatron

電子管 **[tièn-tzŭ kuăn]** : electron tube

電子望遠鏡 **[tièn-tzŭ wàng-yüăn-chìng]** : radio-telescope

電子物理學 **[tièn-tzŭ wù-lĭ-hsüéh]** : electronic physics

電子研究所 **[tièn-tzŭ yén-chìu-sŏ]** : Electronics Institute

4 電木 **[tièn-mù]** : bakelite

5 電石 **[tièn-shíh]** : carbide

6 電池 **[tièn-ch'íh]** : battery, cell

電光 **[tièn-kuāng]** : lightning

7 電位 **[tièn-wèi]** : potential, electrical potential

8 電門 **[tièn-mén]** : switch, electrical switch

9 電信 **[tièn-hsìn]** : telecommunications

10 電站 **[tièn-chàn]** : power station, power plant

電氣 **[tièn-ch'ì]** : electricity

電氣化 **[tièn-ch'ì-huà]** : electrification

電氣工程學 **[tièn-ch'ì kūng-ch'éng-hsüéh]** : electrical engineering

電氣工藝學 **[tièn-ch'ì kūng-ì-hsüéh]** : electrical technology

電氣工業部 **[tièn-ch'ì kūng-yèh pù]** : Ministry of Electrical Industry

電容器 **[tièn-júng-ch'ì]** : capacitor

電流表 **[tièn-líu piăo]** : galvanometer

11 電焊 **[tièn-hàn]** :electric welding

電瓶 **[tièn-p'íng]** : battery

12 電極 **[tièn-chí]** : electrode

電報 **[tièn-pào]** : telegram, wire, cable

電報密碼 **[tièn-pào mì-mă]** : telegraphic code

電視 **[tièn-shìh]** : television

電視廣播 **[tièn-shìh kuăng-pō]** : telecast, television transmission

電梯 **[tièn-t'ī]** : elevator

電筒 **[tièn-t'ŭng]** : flashlight

13 電閘 [tièn-chá] : electric switch, power switch

電解 [tièn-chiĕh] : electrolysis

電傳影 [tièn-ch'uán-yĭng] : radiophoto

電話 [tièn-huà] : telephone

電話交換臺 [tièn-huà chiāo-huàn-t'ái] : telephone exchange

電話綫路 [tièn-huà hsièn-lù] : telephone land line

電話會議 [tièn-huà hùi-ì] : telephone conference

電路 [tièn-lù] : circuit, electric circuit

電業 [tièn-yèh] : electrical industries

14 電滾子 [tièn-kŭn-tzu] : dynamo, motor, generator

電臺 [tièn-t'ái] : radio transmitter, radio station, transmitter, transmitting station

電磁 [tièn-tz'ú] : electromagnetic

15 電熱廠 [tièn-jè ch'ăng] : power and heat plant

電碼 [tièn-mă] : telegraphic code

電影 [tièn-yĭng] : moving picture, film, movie

電影劇本 [tièn-yĭng chù-pĕn] : scenario, screen play

電影放映隊 [tièn-yĭng fàng-yìng tùi] : motion picture projection team

電影部 [tièn-yĭng pù] : Ministry of Cinematography

16 電機廠 [tièn-chī ch'ăng] : electrical machinery plant

電器制造廠 [tièn-ch'ì chìh-tsào ch'ăng] : electrical appliances plant

電鋸 [tièn-chù] : electric saw

電導體 [tièn-tăo-t'ĭ] : electrical conductor

電頭 [tièn-t'óu] : dateline

電鍍 [tièn-tù] : electroplating

電療 [tièn-liáo] : electrotherapy

電壓 [tièn-yā] : voltage

— 6 Strokes —

需

9 需要 [hsū-yào] : to require, to necessitate; requirement, need, necessity, requisite; necessary, essential, imperative

— 7 Strokes —

震

11 震動 [chèn-tùng] : to shake, to rock, to convulse; upheaval, convulsion

— 8 Strokes —

霍

5 霍布士 [huò-pù-shìh] : Hobbes, Thomas (English philosopher, 1588–1679)

14 霍亂 [huò-luàn] : cholera

— 11 Strokes —

霧

霧 [wù] : fog, mist

— 12 Strokes —

露

4 露天開採 [lù-t'iēn k'āi-ts'ăi] : open extraction, open-cut mining, surface mining

露天礦 [lù-t'iēn k'uàng] : open-cut mine

9 露面 **[lù-mièn]**: to appear, to show one's face

10 露骨 **[lù-kŭ]**: barefaced, thinly veiled, crude, transparent, obvious

露原形 **[lù yüán-hsíng]**: to reveal one's true colors

17 露營 **[lù-yíng]**: to bivouac; a bivouac, camp out

— 13 Strokes —

4 霸王 **[pà-wáng]**: tyrant, autocrat, despot, one who rules by force

5 霸占 **[pà-chàn]**: to seize by force, to occupy

22 霸權 **[pà-ch'üán]**: tyranny

— 16 Strokes —

靈

5 靈巧 **[líng-ch'iăo]**: skilful, quick, agile, deft, dexterous, clever; ingeniousness, agility, dexterity

9 靈活 **[líng-huó]**: bright and lively, flexible; liveliness, agility

靈活性 **[líng-huó-hsìng]**: flexibility, agility

11 靈敏 **[líng-mĭn]**: ingenious, clever, sensitive; ingeniousness, cleverness, keenness

13 靈感 **[líng-kăn]**: inspiration; Linhcam (Vietnam)

14 靈魂 **[líng-hún]**: soul

— RADICAL 靑 174 —

靑

靑 **[ch'īng]**: Tsinghai (abbreviation of 靑海); Tsingtao (abbreviation of 靑島)

3 靑山 **[ch'īng-shān]**: Thanhson (Vietnam)

6 靑年節 **[ch'īng-nién chiéh]**: Youth Day (May 4; a holiday in commemoration of the May Fourth movement)

靑年共產黨 **[ch'īng-nién kùng-ch'ăn-tăng]**: Molodoi Kommunist (Russian periodical)

靑年工作委員會 **[ch'īng-nién kūng-tsò wĕi-yüán-huì]**: Youth Work Committee

靑年團 **[ch'īng-nién t'uán]**: Youth Corps

8 靑明 **[ch'īng-míng]**: Thanhminh (Vietnam)

靑委 **[ch'īng-wĕi]**: Youth Commission

9 靑苗 **[ch'īng-miáo]**: young crop, green shoots

12 靑黃不接 **[ch'īng-huáng pù-chiēh]**: between seasons, at the end of spring and the beginning of summer, gap

靑森 **[ch'īng-sēn]**: Aomori (Japan)

13 靑稞 **[ch'īng-k'ò]**: barley

18 靑儲飼料 **[ch'īng-ch'ú ssù-liào]**: silo crops, silage crops, silage

23 靑黴素 **[ch'īng-méi-sù]**: penicillin

— 8 Strokes —

靜

4 靜止 **[chìng-chĭh]**: at rest, quiet, static

8 靜岡 **[chìng-kāng]**: Shizuoka (Japan)

靜物畫 **[chìng-wù huà]**: still life painting

25 靜觀的態度 **[chìng-kuān te t'ài-tù]**: wait-and-see attitude

— RADICAL 非 175 —

非

2 非人 **[fēi-jén]**: deformed person, a cripple; a strange and uncanny thing; inhuman, subhuman

非力所能及 **[fēi lì sŏ néng chí]**: out of one's reach, beyond the reach of one's ability or effort

3 非凡 **[fēi-fán]**: remarkable, extraordinary, uncommon, out of the ordinary

5 非正式 **[fēi chèng-shìh]**: unofficial, informal

非生產 **[fēi shēng-ch'ăn]**: nonproductive

非生產人員 **[fēi shēng-ch'ăn jén-yüán]**: nonproductive personnel

8 非金屬 **[fēi chīn-shŭ]**: nonmetal, nonmetallic

非法 **[fēi-fă]**: illegal, unlawful

非法監禁 **[fēi-fă chiēn-chìn]**: to detain illegally; illegal detention, illegal restraint, illegal confinement, illegal imprisonment

非法報表 **[fēi-fă pào-piăo]**: reports not required by law

非官方的 **[fēi kuān-fāng te]**: unofficial

非美活動委員會 **[fēi-mĕi huó-tùng wĕi-yüán-hùi]**: Committee on Un-American Activities

非定命論 **[fēi tìng-mìng lùn]**: indeterminism

非物質論 **[fēi wù-chíh lùn]**: immaterialism

9 非洲 **[fēi-chōu]**: Africa

非洲解放委員會 **[fēi-chōu chiĕh-fàng wĕi-yüán-hùi]**: African Liberation Committee

非洲國家聯盟 **[fēi-chōu kuó-chiā lién-méng]**: Union of African States

非洲馬爾加什聯盟 **[fēi-chōu-mă-ĕrh-chiā-shíh lién-méng]**: Afro-Malagasy Union

非洲統一組織憲章 **[fēi-chōu t'ŭng-ī tsŭ-chīh hsièn-chāng]**: Charter of the Organization of African Unity

非政府的 **[fēi chèng-fŭ te]**: nongovernmental

非軍事 **[fēi chūn-shìh]**: nonmilitary, civilian

非軍事地區 **[fēi chūn-shìh tì-ch'ü]**: nonmilitary zone

11 非理性的 **[fēi lĭ-hsìng te]**: irrational

非連續的 **[fēi lién-hsù te]**: discontinuous

12 非道德的 **[fēi tào-té te]**: amoral

14 非對抗性的 **[fēi tùi-k'àng-hsìng te]**: nonantagonistic

15 非暴力的反抗 **[fēi pào-lì te făn-k'àng]**: nonviolent resistance

非熟練勞動 **[fēi shóu-lièn láo-tùng]**: unskilled labor

16 非戰鬥人員 **[fēi chàn-tòu jén-yüán]**: noncombatant or civilian personnel

非戰鬥員 **[fēi chàn-tòu yüán]**: a noncombatant

非導體 **[fēi-tăo-t'ĭ]**: nonconductor

19 非難 **[fēi-nán]**: to censure, to criticize

26 非驢非馬 **[fēi-lű fēi-mă]**: neither ass nor horse; to imitate unsuccessfully, to copy another and fail; hybrid

— 7 Strokes —

靠

3 靠山 **[k'ào-shān]**: patron, supporter, protector

6 靠自己 **[k'ào tzù-chĭ]**: to rely on oneself

11 靠剝削人民生活 **[k'ào pō-hsüeh jén-mín shēng-huó]**: to live by exploiting the people

[19] 靠攏[k'ào-lŭng] :to be drawn to, to come close to, to be sympathetic to

靠邊站 [k'ào-piēn chàn]: stand aside (an imperative phrase used frequently during the heyday of the Red Guards ordering cadres or officials to stand aside so as to make way for others to advance and sometimes meaning dismissal of cadres or officials from their posts)

— RADICAL 面 176 —

面

[5] 面目 [mièn-mù]: face, countenance, appearance, social standing

[6] 面向農村 [mièn-hsiàng núng-ts'ūn]: oriented toward the village (i.e., the orientation of industry, commerce, and cultural circles toward the benefit of the villages in support of agricultural production)

[8] 面具 [mièn-chǜ]: mask, countenance

[14] 面貌 [mièn-mào]: visage, look, face, appearance, countenance, features, physiognomy

面貌一新 [mièn-mào ì-hsīn]: to take on a new look, to assume a new appearance

面貌全新 [mièn-mào ch'üán-hsīn]: to change the appearance beyond recognition; a complete change in appearance

面對 [mièn-tùi]: to face, to confront, to encounter

面對面 [mièn tùi mièn]: vis-à-vis, face to face, opposite each other

面對面的領導 [mièn tùi mièn te lĭng-tăo]: face-to-face leadership (i.e., the solving by cadre of local problems and summing up and popularizing the experiences of advanced workers to help the backward)

[17] 面臨 [mièn-lín]: to encounter, to confront, to face

— 7 Strokes —

靦

[15] 靦覥 [mién-t'iĕn]: shy, diffident, bashful; diffidence

— RADICAL 革 177 —

革

[6] 革自己的命 [kó tzù-chĭ te mìng]: to wage revolution against oneself (a phrase from the Cultural Revolution)

[8] 革命 [kó-mìng]: to deprive a ruling dynasty of the divine mandate to rule; revolution, revolt; revolutionary

革命者 [kó-mìng-chĕ]: a revolutionary

革命積極性 [kó-mìng chī-chí-hsìng]: revolutionary potentiality, revolutionary initiative

革命家 [kó-mìng-chiā]: a revolutionary

革命接班人 [kó-mìng chiēh-pān-jén]: revolutionary successor, successor to the revolutionary cause

革命闖將 [kó-mìng ch'uăng-chiàng]: revolutionary storm trooper, dashing revolutionary, revolutionary dare-devil (a phrase used by the Mao-Lin faction during the Cultural Revolution to eulogize the Red Guards)

革命發展階段論 [kó-mìng fā-chăn chiēh-tuàn lùn]: theory of the development of the revolution by stages

革命風暴 [kó-mìng fēng-pào]: revolutionary storm and stress

革命現實主義 [kó-mìng hsièn-shíh chŭ-ì]: revolutionary realism

革命性 [kó-mìng-hsìng]: revolutionary nature, revolutionary character

革命熱情和科學精神相結合 [kó-mìng jè-ch'íng hó k'ō-hsüéh chīng-shén hsiāng chiéh-hó]: combining revolutionary fervor with scientific spirit

革命熔爐 [kó-mìng júng-lú]: revolutionary crucible

革命幹勁 [kó-mìng kàn-chìng]: revolutionary impetus, revolutionary drive, revolutionary enthusiasm

革命鼓動家 [kó-mìng kŭ-tùng-chiā]: revolutionary agitator

革命工人報 [kó-mìng kūng-jén pào]: Revolutionary Workers (Peking Red Guard newspaper during Cultural Revolution)

革命浪漫主義 [kó-mìng làng-màn chŭ-ì]: revolutionary romanticism

革命樂觀主義 [kó-mìng lè-kuān chŭ-ì]: revolutionary optimism

革命派 [kó-mìng p'ài]: revolutionaries (i.e., those loyal to the thought of Mao Tse-tung and who act according to his instructions)

革命本領 [kó-mìng pĕn-lĭng]: revolutionary skills, revolutionary capacity

革命本色 [kó-mìng pĕn-sè]: basic revolutionary color

革命首創精神 [kó-mìng shŏu-ch'uàng chīng-shén]: revolutionary pioneering spirit

革命大聯合 [kó-mìng tà lién-hó]: The Great Revolutionary Alliance (a slogan put out by the Mao-Lin faction when numerous Red Guards were fighting each other in the early summer of 1967)

革命導師 [kó-mìng tăo-shīh]: a teacher of the revolution

革命造反 [kó-mìng tsào-făn]: Revolutionary Rebels (Cultural Revolution)

革命造反派 [kó-mìng tsào-făn p'ài]: revolutionary rebels, revolutionary upheaval group

革命委員會 [kó-mìng wĕi-yüán-hùi]: revolutionary committees (committees set up at all levels as "provisional organs of power" for the period following the overthrow of the Party committees and local government councils until the establishment of new power organs)

革命英雄主義 [kó-mìng yīng-hsiúng chŭ-ì]: revolutionary heroism

9 革面洗心 [kó-mièn hsĭ-hsīn]: to reform (literally, to change the skin of the face and wash the heart)

10 革除 [kó-ch'ú]: to expel, to get rid of, to deduct, to exclude

13 革新 [kó-hsīn]: to innovate, to reform, to renovate; innovations, renovation, reform, change, transformation

18 革職 [kó-chíh]: to dismiss someone from office, to remove, to depose, to displace, to eject

— 4 Strokes —

靶

3 靶子 [pă-tzu]: target

— 6 Strokes —

鞍

3 鞍山鋼 [ān-shān kāng]: Anshan steel

鞏

8 鞏固 [kŭng-kù]: to fortify, to strengthen, to secure, to consolidate; consolidation; well-guarded, secure, firm, consolidated

— 9 Strokes —

鞭

8 鞭長莫及 [piēn-ch'áng mò-chí]: to be out of range; beyond the reach of the law

— 13 Strokes —

韃

[13] 韃靼 [tá-tàn] : Tartar

— RADICAL 韋 178 —

韋

[6] 韋伍德 [wéi-wǔ-té] : Verwoerd, Hendrik (South African political figure)

[9] 韋柏 [wéi-pō] : Weber, Max (1864–1920)

— RADICAL 非 179 —

— RADICAL 音 180 —

音

[15] 音調 [yīn-tiào] : tone, pitch, tune, air, melody

— 13 Strokes —

響

[7] 響尾蛇導彈 [hsiǎng-wěi-shé tǎo-tàn] : sidewinder guided missile

[9] 響亮 [hsiǎng-liàng] : clear-sounding, loud and clear

響亮的呼聲 [hsiǎng-liàng te hū-shēng] : clarion call

[10] 響起 [hsiǎng-ch'ǐ] : to sound, to resound

[15] 響徹雲霄的凱歌 [hsiǎng-ch'è yǘn-hsiāo te k'ǎi-kō] : paean of victory echoing to the skies

[17] 響應 [hsiǎng-yìng] : to respond, to answer, to reply, to react, to echo; echo, reply

— RADICAL 頁 181 —

頁

8 頁岩 **[yèh-yén]**: shale

頁岩油 **[yèh-yén yú]**: shale oil

— 2 Strokes —

頂

8 頂事 **[tǐng-shìh]**: serviceable, useful

9 頂風 **[tǐng-fēng]**: head wind

17 頂點 **[tǐng-tiěn]**: peak, summit, pinnacle, culmination, climax

— 3 Strokes —

項

5 項目 **[hsiàng-mù]**: item

順

4 順化 **[shùn-huà]**: acclimatization; Hue (Vietnam)

7 順利 **[shùn-lì]**: smooth, smoothly, in a workable manner, successfully

9 順便 **[shùn-pièn]**: at one's convenience, as convenient

— 4 Strokes —

頒

5 頒布 **[pān-pù]**: to announce, to publish, to proclaim, to promulgate

6 頒行 **[pān-hsíng]**: to proclaim and put into effect

7 頒佈 **[pān-pù]**: to promulgate

12 頒發 **[pān-fā]**: to make public, to make known, to give out

頌

12 頌詞 **[sùng-tz'ú]**: eulogy, hymn of praise

頌揚 **[sùng-yáng]**: to praise; eulogy

頑

8 頑固 **[wán-kù]**: stubborn, obstinate, obdurate, tenacious, die-hard, inflexible, immovable, unwavering

頑固份子 **[wán-kù fèn-tzu]**: die-hard element, obstinate element, one who insists on retaining his own ideas

頑固堡壘 **[wán-kù pǎo-lěi]**: die-hard fortress

12 頑强 **[wán-ch'iáng]**: staunch, tenacious, strong-willed, unswerving, unyielding

頑强性 **[wán-ch'iáng-hsìng]**: tenacity, staunchness

預

5 預示 **[yǜ-shìh]**: to predict, to foretell, to forebode; prophecy, prediction, foreboding

6 預兆 **[yǜ-chào]**: foreboding, warning, portent

預先 **[yǜ-hsiēn]**: in advance, in anticipation, beforehand, pre-

預先裝配 **[yǜ-hsiēn chuāng-p'èi]**: preassembling, prefabricating; prefabricated

預先斷定 **[yǜ-hsiēn tuàn-tìng]**: to prejudge

預先對付 **[yǜ-hsiēn tùi-fù]**: to forestall

7 預見 **[yǜ-chièn]**: to foresee, to foreknow; foresight, prevision, prescience; prescient

預防 **[yǜ-fáng]**: to prevent; prevention, precaution; preventive, precautionary

預告 **[yǜ-kào]**: to predict, to foretell, to forecast; prophecy, prediction

預告的消息 **[yǜ-kào te hsiāo-hsí]**: tip-off

預言 **[yǜ-yén]**: to foretell, to predict, to forecast; prediction, prophecy

預言家 **[yǜ-yén-chiā]**: prophet

8 預定的 **[yǜ-tìng te]**: scheduled, due, ordered, predetermined, resolved, settled beforehand

10 預料 **[yǜ-liào]**: to expect, to foresee, to anticipate; prospect, prediction

12 預期 **[yǜ-ch'í]**: to expect, to foresee, to anticipate

預報 **[yǜ-pào]**: to forecast; forecast

預備 **[yǜ-pèi]**: to prepare, to make ready; preparation, provision; preparatory

預備期 **[yǜ-pèi ch'í]**: probationary period, period of preparation

預備役 **[yǜ-pèi ì]**: reserve service

預備黨員 **[yǜ-pèi tăng-yüán]**: probationary party member

預備隊 **[yǜ-pèi tùi]**: reserve force

14 預算 **[yǜ-suàn]**: budget; budgetary

預算決算制度 **[yǜ-suàn chüéh-suàn chìh-tù]**: budget and financial statement system

預算收入 **[yǜ-suàn shōu-jù]**: budgetary receipts

預算咨文 **[yǜ-suàn tzū-wén]**: budget message

預算委員會 **[yǜ-suàn wĕi-yüán-hùi]**: budget committee

16 預謀 **[yǜ-móu]**: to premeditate; forethought; premeditated, designed, planned, intended, calculated

— 5 Strokes —

領

3 領土 **[lĭng-t'ŭ]**: territory, land, domain; territorial

領土權 **[lĭng-t'ŭ ch'üán]**: territorial rights, sovereign right over territory

6 領先 **[lĭng-hsiēn]**: to precede, to take precedence over, to be in front of, to take the lead

領空 **[lĭng-k'ūng]**: territorial air, air space

8 領事 **[lĭng-shìh]**: consul

領事館 **[lĭng-shìh kuăn]**: consulate

領事裁判權 **[lĭng-shìh ts'ái-p'àn ch'üán]**: consular jurisdiction, extraterritoriality

領受 **[lĭng-shòu]**: to receive, to accept, to suffer; receptiveness

10 領海 **[lĭng-hăi]**: territorial waters

11 領域 **[lĭng-yǜ]**: domain, field, sphere, realm

12 領進 **[lĭng-chìn]**: to usher in, to introduce into, to lead in

領港員 **[lĭng-kăng-yüán]**: pilot

13 領會 **[lĭng-hùi]**: to grasp, to comprehend, to understand

16 領導 **[lĭng-tăo]**: to lead; leadership; leading cadres, responsible cadres, government officials in leading positions

領導集團 **[lĭng-tăo chí-t'uán]**: leading group

領導權 **[lĭng-tăo ch'üán]**: hegemony

領導方針 **[lĭng-tăo fāng-chēn]**: guiding policy

領導核心 **[lĭng-tăo hó-hsīn]**: nucleus of leadership

領導骨幹 **[lĭng-tăo kŭ-kàn]**: leading cadres, backbone of leadership

領導班子 **[lĭng-tăo pān-tzu]**: leading centers (army supported subprovincial groups for aid in spring plowing in 1967)

領導作用 **[lĭng-tăo tsò-yùng]**: leading role

頗

頗 **[p'ō]**: rather, fairly, somewhat, quite, to a certain degree, to a certain extent

— 6 Strokes —

頤

8 頤和園 **[í-hó yüán]**: Summer Palace

— 7 Strokes —

頻

11 頻率 **[p'ín-lǜ]**: frequency, relative frequency

17 頻繁 **[p'ín-fán]**: incessant, hurried

頭

1 頭一個階段 **[t'óu í-kò chiēh-tuàn]**: initial phase, first stage

3 頭子 **[t'óu-tzu]**: headman, head, chief, boss

5 頭目 **[t'óu-mù]**: chief, headman

8 頭昏眼花的 **[t'óu-hūn yĕn-huā te]**: dizzy, mentally confused, punchdrunk

頭版 **[t'óu-păn]**: front page

12 頭等强國 **[t'óu-tĕng ch'iáng-kuó]**: first-class great power

頭痛醫頭，脚痛醫脚 **[t'óu-t'ùng ī t'óu, chiăo t'ùng ī chiăo]**: to treat the head when the head aches and to treat the foot when the foot aches; to apply stopgap and piecemeal solutions; to use only palliative measures for one's illness; sporadic and piecemeal steps

13 頭腦冷靜 **[t'óu-năo lĕng-chìng]**: sober-minded, clear-headed, cool, calm and collected; cool-headedly

16 頭頭 **[t'óu-t'óu]**: head head (during the Proletarian Cultural Revolution, "Chieftains" of Red Guard factions–a term of contempt)

— 8 Strokes —

顆

11 顆粒狀肥料 **[k'ō-lì-chuàng féi-liào]**: granulated fertilizer

— 9 Strokes —

額

額 **[ó]**: amount, quota

5 額外 **[ó-wài]**: beyond the fixed number, in addition, extra

題

5 題目 **[t'í-mù]**: title, topic, subject, theme

7 題材 **[t'í-ts'ái]**: subject, theme, subject matter

12 題為 **[t'í-wéi]**: entitled, under the title of

— 10 Strokes —

類

類 **[lèi]**: genus, genre

4 類比 **[lèi-pĭ]**: analogy

7 類別 **[lèi-piéh]**: kind, sort, category, class, division, species, variety, type, ilk

類似 **[lèi-ssù]**: to be like, analogous to, similar; kinship, approximation, analogy

9 類型 **[lèi-hsíng]**: type, pattern; typical

顛

13 顛復 **[tiēn-fù]**: to overthrow, to subvert, to undermine; subversion; subversive

19 顛覆 **[tiēn-fù]**: to turn upside down, to overthrow, to subvert; subversion; subversive

顛覆活動 **[tiēn-fù huó-tùng]**: subversive activities

願

11 願望 **[yüàn-wàng]**: to hope, to desire; desire, hope, wish, expectation, aspiration

13 願意 **[yüàn-ì]**: to be desirous, to be willing; willingness, desire

— 12 Strokes —

6 顧全大局 **[kù ch'üán tà chǘ]**: to bear the whole situation in mind, to take the whole situation into consideration, mindful of the whole situation

7 顧忌 **[kù-chì]**: to fear, to avoid, to be apprehensive; worry, apprehension

8 顧念 **[kù-nièn]**: to think of, to care for, to care about

9 顧客 **[kù-k'ò]**: customer, shopper

11 顧問 **[kù-wèn]**: to advise; adviser, counsellor, consultant

15 顧慮 **[kù-lǜ]**: anxiety, misgiving, scruple, apprehension

— 14 Strokes —

顯

5 顯示 **[hsiěn-shìh]**: to manifest, to demonstrate, to display, to show, to reveal; manifestation, revelation

顯示力量 **[hsiěn-shìh lì-liàng]**: to display one's strength, to show one's muscles

6 顯而易見的 **[hsiěn érh ì-chièn te]**: obvious and evident, self-evident, apparent, easy to see, plain and clear

7 顯見 **[hsiěn-chièn]**: obvious, evident

12 顯然 **[hsiěn-ján]**: obviously, apparently, evidently, distinctly, clearly

13 顯著 **[hsiěn-chù]**: remarkable, noteworthy, marked, outstanding, prominent, dominant, pronounced, striking, evident, conspicuous

— RADICAL 風 182 —

2 風力 [fēng-lí]: wind force, wind intensity

3 風土 [fēng-t'ŭ]: climate, local customs

4 風化 [fēng-huà]: influence, example, customs, public morals, to reform by example; to weather; weathering, wind erosion

5 風平浪靜 [fēng-p'íng làng-chìng]: the wind abates and the waves calm down

6 風向 [fēng-hsiàng]: wind direction, tendency

風行 [fēng-hsíng]: to spread or move like a wind

風行一時 [fēng-hsíng ì-shíh]: to be extremely popular for a time; to be the fad

7 風言風語 [fēng-yén fēng-yŭ]: rumor

8 風尙 [fēng-shàng]: custom, style, fashion

風度 [fēng-tù]: appearance and bearing, deportment

9 風紀 [fēng-chì]: discipline

風泵 [fēng-pèng]: wind-powered pump

風俗 [fēng-sú]: customs, usages, practices, public morals

風俗習慣 [fēng-sú hsí-kuàn]: habits and customs, practice, usage

10 風氣 [fēng-ch'ì]: influence, appearance, style, fashion, common practice, atmosphere, taste of the times

風格 [fēng-kó]: style, air, manner, disposition

風馬牛 [fēng mă-níu]: things that have nothing to do with one another

11 風涼話 [fēng-liàng huà]: irresponsible talk

風動工具 [fēng-tùng kūng-chǜ]: pneumatic tool

12 風景 [fēng-chĭng]: view, landscape, scenery

風景畫 [fēng-chĭng huà]: landscape (painting)

風雲 [fēng-yŭn]: wind and clouds, political situation, political climate

風雲人物 [fēng-yŭn jén-wù]: men of the day

13 風傳 [fēng-ch'uán]: according to rumor, as said by everyone, words get around that

風雅 [fēng-yă]: graceful, tasteful, delightful, charming

14 風暴 [fēng-pào]: storm

風蝕 [fēng-shíh]: wind erosion

風聞 [fēng-wén]: according to rumor

15 風潮 [fēng-ch'áo]: wind and tide, unrest, upheaval, agitation

16 風險 [fēng-hsiĕn]: risk, danger

風頭主義 [fēng-t'óu chŭ-ì]: showing offism; craving for popularity

17 風聲 [fēng-shēng]: the sound of the wind, rumors

18 風鎬 [fēng-kăo]: compressed air hammer

25 風鑽 [fēng-tsuàn]: compressed air drill

— 11 Strokes —

12 飄揚 [p'iāo-yáng]: to flutter, to fly

13 飄渺 [p'iăo-miăo]: obscure, misty, dimly seen, unrealistic, impracticable, unattainable, unachievable, unfeasible

— RADICAL 飛 183 —

飛

6 飛行隊形 [fēi-hsíng tùi-hsíng]: flight formation

飛行員 [fēi-hsíng-yüán]: pilot, aviator, airman

7 飛快 [fēi-k'uài]: lightning fast, rapid

8 飛往 [fēi-wàng]: to fly to, to leave by air for

15 飛彈 [fēi-tàn]: missile, buzz bomb

16 飛機 [fēi-chī]: airplane, aircraft

飛機場 [fēi-chī ch'ăng]: airfield, airport, aerodome

飛機制造業 [fēi-chī chìh-tsào yèh]: aircraft industry

飛機出擊 [fēi-chī ch'ū-chī]: sortie

飛機庫 [fēi-chī k'ù]: hangar

20 飛騰 [fēi-t'éng]: to soar

21 飛躍 [fēi-yüèh]: to leap, to leap ahead with great speed

飛躍地 [fēi-yüèh tì]: by leaps and bounds, in flying leaps

— RADICAL 食 184 —

5 食用 [shíh-yùng]: provisions; edible

7 食言 [shíh-yén]: to go back on one's word, to retract a promise

8 食物 [shíh-wù]: foodstuffs, food

9 食品工業 [shíh-p'ĭn kūng-yèh]: food industry

食品工業部 [shíh-p'ĭn kūng-yèh pù]: Ministry of Food Industry

食品工業研究所 [shīh-p'ĭn kūng-yèh yén-chìu-sŏ]: Foodstuffs Industry Institute

11 食堂 [shíh-t'áng]: dining hall, canteen, mess hall

24 食鹽 [shíh-yén]: table-salt

— 4 Strokes —

飭

5 飭令 [ch'ìh-lìng]: to command, to order

9 飭派 [ch'ìh-p'ài]: to dispatch

— 5 Strokes —

飽

8 飽受 [pǎo-shòu]: to have enough of, to suffer enough from

飼

10 飼料 [ssù-liào]: fodder, grain feed

飼料廠 [ssù-liào ch'ăng]: feed factory, fodder mill

飼料穀物 [ssù-liào kŭ-wù]: feed-grain crops

飼料作物 [ssù-liào tsò-wù]: fodder crops

飼草 [ssù-ts'ăo]: hay

15 飼養牲畜 [ssù-yăng shēng-ch'ù]: animal husbandry, livestock breeding

飼養員 [ssù-yăng yüán]: stockman, herdsman, keeper, feeder

— 6 Strokes —

養

6 養成習慣 [**yăng-ch′éng hsí-kuàn**] : to form a habit, to cultivate the habit

養老金 [**yăng-lăo chīn**] : old age pension

8 養兒防修 [**yăng-érh fáng-hsīu**] : raising children to prevent revisionism (a phrase that is adapted from an old Chinese saying 養兒防老 [**yăng-érh fáng-lăo**], meaning "raising children as insurance against old age"; parents were distressed that their children were compelled to go to the countryside to become peasants, and for this reason authorities coined this phrase to remind them that their children are not to be brought up to care for them in their old age, but to carry out Mao's revolutionary line to prevent revisionism–a phrase from the Cultural Revolution)

養育 [**yăng-yù**] : to bring up, to nurture, to foster, to breed, to nurse

12 養猪 [**yăng-chū**] : to raise pigs

養猪業 [**yăng-chū yèh**] : pig breeding

13 養蜂 [**yăng-fēng**] : apiculture, bee-keeping

養蜂場 [**yăng-fēng ch′ăng**] : apiary

養路 [**yăng-lù**] : maintenance of roads, road maintenance

14 養精蓄鋭，以逸待勞 [**yăng-chīng hsù-jùi, ĭ-ì tài-láo**] : to conserve one's strength or store up one's energy and wait at one's ease for the fatigued enemy

24 養蠶 [**yăng-ts′án**] : to raise silkworms; silkworm breeding

養蠶業 [**yăng-ts′án yèh**] : sericulture

— 7 Strokes —

6 餘地 [**yǘ-tì**] : spare ground or room

8 餘波 [**yǘ-pō**] : aftermath, sequel, subsequent events, succeeding events, repercussions

19 餘糧 [**yǘ-liáng**] : surplus grain (i.e., the grain left over after a production team has delivered the "public grain" [公糧, q.v.], sold a set amount of it to the state, and reserved food rations for its own members)

餘糧戶 [**yǘ-liáng hù**] : household with grain reserves, household having surplus grains

— 8 Strokes —

7 餞別 [**chièn-piéh**] : to bid farewell with a dinner, to give a farewell dinner

— 12 Strokes —

5 饑民 [**chī-mín**] : victims of famine

10 饑荒 [**chī-huāng**] : famine, destitution, starvation

12 饑寒交迫 [**chī-hán chiāo-p′ò**] : to suffer from cold and hunger

— RADICAL 首 185 —

首

5 首犯 **[shŏu-fàn]**: arch criminal, chief criminal

6 首先 **[shŏu-hsiēn]**: first of all, first, in the first place, above all, first and foremost

首先考慮 **[shŏu-hsiēn k'ăo-lǜ]**: first consideration, chief consideration, preoccupation

7 首里 **[shŏu-lǐ]**: Shuri (Okinawa)

9 首相 **[shŏu-hsiàng]**: Prime Minister, Premier (England, Japan, etc.)

首要 **[shŏu-yào]**: most important, prime, primary, cardinal, crucial, foremost

首要戰犯 **[shŏu-yào chàn-fàn]**: chief war criminal

10 首倡 **[shŏu-ch'àng]**: to originate, to initiate

首倡精神 **[shŏu-ch'àng chīng-shén]**: initiative

首席 **[shŏu-hsí]**: first place, seat of honor

12 首都 **[shŏu-tū]**: national capital

首都赴藏革命造反總部 **[shŏu-tū fù-tsàng kó-mìng tsào-fǎn tsŭng-pù]**: General Group of Revolutionary Rebels in Tibet from the Capital (Cultural Revolution)

首都紅衞兵第三司令部 **[shŏu-tū húng-wèi-pīng tì-sān ssū-lìng-pù]**: Capital Red Guard Third Headquarters (Cultural Revolution)

13 首腦會議 **[shŏu-năo hùi-ì]**: a summit meeting, a meeting of heads of government

首腦人物 **[shŏu-năo jén-wù]**: leading figures, chief personalities

14 首領 **[shŏu-lǐng]**: chief, boss, leader, chieftain

— RADICAL 香 186 —

3 香川 **[hsiāng-ch'uān]**: Kagawa (Japan)

4 香火 **[hsiāng-huŏ]**: Huonghoa (Vietnam)

8 香花 **[hsiāng-huā]**: fragrant flowers (i.e., writings conducive to the Communist cause and in accordance with the thought of Mao Tse-tung)

香味 **[hsiāng-wèi]**: aroma, scent, fragrance, perfume

9 香風 **[hsiāng-fēng]**: fragrant breeze (i.e., the bourgeois way of life)

10 香料 **[hsiāng-liào]**: spice

12 香港 **[hsiāng-kăng]**: Hong Kong

香港時報 **[hsiāng-kăng shíh-pào]**: Hong Kong Times (Hong Kong daily newspaper)

— RADICAL 馬 187 —

馬

2 馬力[mă-lì]: horsepower

馬丁爐[mă-tīng lú]: Siemens-Martin furnace

3 馬上[mă-shàng]: right away, soon, immediately, instantly

4 馬不停蹄[mă pù-t'íng-t'í]: unceasing, continuous, unceasingly, continuously

5 馬加撒[mă-chiā-sā]: Macassar

馬弗京[mă-fú-chīng]: Mafeking (Botswana)

馬立克[mă-lì-k'ò]: Malik, Charles (Lebanese political figure)

馬尼拉[mă-ní-lā]: Manila (Philippines)

馬尼拉條約[mă-ní-lā t'iáo-yüēh]: Manila Pact (South East Asia Collective Defense Treaty)

6 馬耳他[mă-ĕrh-t'ā]: Malta

馬列[mă-lièh]: Marx and Lenin

馬列主義[mă-lièh chŭ-ì]: Marxism Leninism

馬列主義理論[mă-lièh chŭ-ì lĭ-lùn]: Marxist-Leninist theory

7 馬克思[mă-k'ò-ssū]: Marx, Karl (1818–1883)

馬克思主義[mă-k'ò-ssū chŭ-ì]: Marxism

馬里共和國[mă-lĭ kùng-hó-kuó]: Republic of Mali

馬里蘭[mă-lĭ-lán]: Maryland

馬里亞納群島[mă-lĭ-yă-nà ch'ŭn-tăo]: Mariana Islands

馬利諾夫斯基[mă-lì-nò-fū-ssū-chī]: Malinovsky, Rodion (Russian Army officer)

馬那瓜[mă-nà-kuā]: Managua (Nicaragua)

馬拉加[mă-lā-chiā]: Malaga

馬拉牙[mă-lā-yá]: Malaga

馬來西亞聯邦[mă-lái-hsī-yà lién-pāng]: Malaysia Confederation

馬來亞[mă-lái-yà]: Malaya

馬來亞聯合邦[mă-lái-yà lién-hó-pāng]: Federation of Malaya

9 馬哈[mă-hā]: Mach, Ernst (1838–1916)

馬歇爾[mă-hsiēh-ĕrh]: Marshall, George (American military figure)

馬剌甲[mă-là-chiă]: Malacca

11 馬基阿未利[mă-chī-â-wèi-lì]: Machiavelli, Niccolo (1469–1527)

馬累市[mă-lèi shìh]: Male (Sultanate of Maldive Islands)

馬紹爾群島[mă-shào-ĕrh ch'ŭn-tăo]: Marshall Islands

12 馬斯喀特[mă-ssū-k'ā-t'è]: Muscat (Sultanate of Muscat)

馬斯喀特蘇丹國[mă-ssū-k'ā-t'è sū-tān kuó]: Sultanate of Muscat

馬斯友美黨[mă-ssū-yŭ-mĕi tăng]: Masjumi (Indonesian Moslem Council)

13 馬塞[mă-sāi]: Marseilles (France)

馬塞盧[mă-sāi-lú]: Maseru (Lesotho)

馬達[mă-tá]: motor

14 馬爾加什共和國[mă-ĕrh-chiā-shíh kùng-hó-kuó]: Malagasy Republic

馬爾薩斯[mă-ĕrh-sà-ssū]: Malthus, Thomas (1766–1834)

馬爾代夫蘇丹國[mă-ĕrh-tài-fū sū-tān kuó]: Sultanate of Maldive

15 馬鞍形的[mă-ān-hsíng te]: U-shaped

馬德拉斯 **[mǎ-té-lā-ssū]**: Madras (India)

馬德里 **[mǎ-té-lǐ]**: Madrid (Spain)

17 馬戲 **[mǎ-hsì]**: circus

馬戲團 **[mǎ-hsì t'uán]**: circus troupe

馬薩諸塞 **[mǎ-sà-chū-sāi]**: Massachusetts

— 3 Strokes —

馳

6 馳名 **[ch'íh-míng]**: celebrated, well-known, famous

馴

8 馴服 **[hsǜn-fú]**: to tame, to make obey; docile

馴服工具 **[hsǜn-fú kūng-chǜ]**: docile tool (i.e., of the Party)

— 4 Strokes —

駁

5 駁斥 **[pó-ch'ìh]**: to refute, to repudiate, to repulse; repudiation

6 駁回 **[pó-húi]**: to contradict, to rebut

10 駁倒 **[pó-tǎo]**: to refute, to confound, to defeat in an argument

12 駁殼槍 **[pó-k'ó-ch'iāng]**: heavy pistol

14 駁運 **[pó-yǜn]**: to load, to transport, to tranship

15 駁價 **[pó-chià]**: to bargain, to trade

— 5 Strokes —

駕

12 駕御 **[chià-yǜ]**: to guide, to bridle, to tame, to subjugate, to keep under control

15 駕駛 **[chià-shǐh]**: to drive (a vehicle)

駕駛員 **[chià-shǐh-yüán]**: driver, chauffeur, navigator, pilot, flyer

駐

9 駐軍 **[chù-chǖn]**: to station troops, to billet troops; occupation troops

10 駐紮 **[chù-chā]**: to station; stationing

駛

6 駛向 **[shǐh-hsiàng]**: to sail for

— 8 Strokes —

騎

3 騎士 **[ch'í-shìh]**: knight, cavalier, mounted warrior

6 騎在頭上 **[ch'í-tsài t'óu-shàng]**: to ride roughshod over, to sit on the backs of, to lord it over

7 騎兵 **[ch'í-pīng]**: cavalry, mounted troops

16 騎墻 **[ch'í-ch'iáng]**: to sit on the fence

騎墻派 **[ch'í-ch'iáng p'ài]**: fence sitters

— 9 Strokes —

騙

2 騙人的 **[p'ièn-jén te]**: deceptive, fraudulent, deceitful, false

3 騙子 **[p'ièn-tzu]**: swindler, deceiver, imposter, liar, charlatan, a fraud, a cheat

7 騙局 **[p'ièn-chǘ]**: fraud, double dealing, cheating, trickery, deception, swindle

8 騙取 **[p'ièn-ch'ǚ]**: to gain something by cheating, to cheat out of

— 10 Strokes —

騷

11 騷動 **[sāo-tùng]**: uprising, disorder, riot, insurrection; to riot, to stir up, to excite

13 騷亂 **[sāo-luàn]**: to disturb, to agitate, to harass; harassment, turmoil, turbulence, agitation, ferment, upheaval, disturbance, confusion

18 騷擾 **[sāo-jǎo]**: to disturb, to agitate, to harass; disturbance, harassment, turmoil, turbulence, agitation, ferment, confusion, upheaval

騰

5 騰出來 **[t'éng-ch'ū-lái]**: to empty out (i.e., as a room)

騰出時間 **[t'éng-ch'ū shíh-chiēn]**: to set aside time

騰出地方 **[t'éng-ch'ū tì-fāng]**: to make room for, to clear a space for

— 11 Strokes —

驅

8 驅使 **[ch'ü-shǐh]**: to drive, to whip, to lash, to urge on by force, to dictate, to inspire, to impel

11 驅逐 **[ch'ü-chú]**: to drive out, to expel, to oust, to deport, to eject, to evict

驅逐出境 **[ch'ü-chú ch'ū-chìng]**: to expel from a country; expulsion, deportation

驅逐出境令 **[ch'ü-chú ch'ū-chìng lìng]**: deportation ordinance

12 驅散 **[ch'ü-sàn]**: to scatter, to disperse, to dispel, to drive off, to break up, to dissipate, to dissolve

— 12 Strokes —

驕

12 驕傲 **[chiāo-ào]**: proud, haughty

驕傲自滿 **[chiāo-ào tzù-mǎn]**: conceit and self-complacency; conceited and self-satisfied

驕傲自大 **[chiāo-ào tzù-tà]**: conceited and bragging

驕奢淫逸 **[chiāo-shē yín-ì]**: haughty, luxurious, lewd, and idle; haughty, extravagant, profligate, and idle

16 驕橫 **[chiāo-hèng]**: presumptuous, pretentious, overbearing

驕橫不可一世 **[chiāo-hèng pù-k'ǒ í-shìh]**: insufferably arrogant, extremely overbearing, unbearably conceited

17 驕縱 **[chiāo-tsùng]**: haughty and uninhibited

— 13 Strokes —

驚

2 驚人 **[chīng-jén]**: astonishing, striking, startling, stunning, terrifying, shocking

8 驚奇 **[chīng-ch'í]**: astonished, stunned, astonishment, surprise

11 驚悉 **[chīng-hsī]**: shocked to learn (i.e., a phrase used at the time of receiving bad news

驚動 **[chīng-tùng]**: to startle, to trouble, to disturb, to annoy, to excite, to alarm, to arouse to vigilance

驚訝 **[chīng-yà]**: startled, astonished, stunned; astonishment, surprise

12 驚惶失措 **[chīng-huáng shīh-ts'ò]**: panic, alarm; panic stricken

16 驚險小說 **[chīng-hsiěn hsiǎo-shuō]**: adventure novels (i.e., with emphasis on valor and heroism)

驛

13 驛道 **[ì-tào]**: caravan road, post route

— RADICAL 骨 188 —

骨

2 骨力 **[kŭ-lì]**: strength, firmness; solid, strong, durable, stiff

3 骨子裡頭 **[kŭ-tzŭ lĭ-t'óu]**: underlying, beneath the surface

8 骨肥 **[kŭ-féi]**: bone fertilizer

10 骨氣 **[kŭ-ch'ì]**: moral integrity, moral firmness

骨粉 **[kŭ-fĕn]**: bone meal, bone fertilizer

骨格 **[kŭ-kó]**: skeleton, framework, bone structure

13 骨幹 **[kŭ-kàn]**: backbone, core, mainstay, spine, key men

骨幹份子 **[kŭ-kàn fèn-tzu]**: key elements, backbone elements

15 骨盤 **[kŭ-p'án]**: basin; pelvis

16 骨頭 **[kŭ-t'óu]**: bone

— 13 Strokes —

體

2 體力 **[t'ĭ-lì]**: physical strength, body force; manual, physical

體力勞動 **[t'ĭ-lì láo-tùng]**: manual labor, physical work

7 體系 **[t'ĭ-hsì]**: system

8 體制 **[t'ĭ-chìh]**: system, administrative framework, regulations, fundamental rules

體育 **[t'ĭ-yǜ]**: physical education, physical culture, gymnastics

體育運動委員會 **[t'ĭ-yǜ yǜn-tùng wĕi-yüán-hùi]**: Physical Culture and Sports Commission

9 體面的 **[t'ĭ-mièn te]**: honorable, decent

10 體格 **[t'ĭ-kó]**: physique

體格上的 **[t'ĭ-kó-shàng te]**: physical, corporal

11 體現 **[t'ĭ-hsièn]**: to embody

12 體裁 **[t'ĭ-ts'ái]**: style, literary style, mode of expression; stylistic

13 體會 **[t'ĭ-hùi]**: to appreciate, to experience, to comprehend, to take in, to learn personally, to realize, to realize through personal experience

體會到 **[t'ĭ-hùi tào]**: to understand, to realize

15 體罰 **[t'ĭ-fá]**: corporal punishment

體諒 **[t'ĭ-liàng]**: to allow for, to excuse, to make allowances for

23 體驗 **[t'ĭ-yèn]**: to realize, to learn from experience, to have a personal experience of, to examine oneself thoroughly

— RADICAL 高 189 —

高

2 高人一等[kāo-jén ì-těng]: to tower above others

3 高山[kāo-shān]: Kaoshan (a minority nationality of Taiwan)

4 高手[kāo-shǒu]: skillful person, skilled worker

5 高加索[kāo-chiā-sŏ]: the Caucasus

高出一頭[kāo-ch'ū ī-t'óu]: to stand head and shoulders above others

高平[kāo-p'íng]: Caobang (Vietnam)

6 高地[kāo-tì]: upland, highland, plateau

7 高冷[kāo-lěng]: Caolanh (Vietnam)

高利貸[kāo lì-tài]: usury

高利貸者[kāo lì-tài-chě]: a usurer, a money lender at exorbitant interest rates

8 高空[kāo-k'ūng]: outer space

高空大氣物理研究所 [kāo-k'ūng tà-ch'ì wù-lǐ yén-chìu-sŏ]: Upper Atmospheric Physics Institute

高明[kāo-míng]: wise; lofty and intelligent

高度[kāo-tù]: height, altitude; to a high degree; highly

高度原則性[kāo-tù yüán-tsé-hsìng]: on a high level of principle

9 高昂[kāo-áng]: lofty, ambitious; expensive

高城[kāo-ch'éng]: Kosong (Korea)

高屋建瓴之勢 [kāo-wū chièn-líng chīh shìh]: an irresistibly powerful situation, irresistibly strong

10 高級[kāo-chí]: high class, higher, senior, ranking, high-ranking, leading

高級階段[kāo-chí chiēh-tuàn]: higher phase, higher stage

高級知識份子 [kāo-chí chīh-shìh fèn-tzu]: highly qualified intellectuals

高級中學[kāo-chí chūng-hsüéh]: senior secondary school

高級合作社[kāo-chí hó-tsò-shè]: higher stage cooperative, cooperative of advanced type

高級消費品[kāo-chí hsiāo-fèi-p'ǐn]: luxury consumer goods

高級小學[kāo-chí hsiǎo-hsüéh]: senior primary school

高級幹部[kāo-chí kàn-pù]: high-ranking cadre

高級社 [kāo-chí shè]: high grade cooperative, higher cooperative

高峰[kāo-fēng]: summit, peak, pinnacle

高效利潤[kāo-hsiào lì-jùn]: super-profit

高高在上[kāo-kāo tsài-shàng]: to hold oneself loftily aloof, to consider oneself superior, to ride on one's high horse

高射炮[kāo-shè p'ào]: antiaircraft gun

高射機槍[kāo-shè chī-ch'iāng]: antiaircraft machine gun

高射機關槍[kāo-shè chī-kuān-ch'iāng]: antiaircraft machine gun

高原[kāo-yüán]: plateau

11 高產試驗田[kāo-ch'ǎn shìh-yèn t'ién]: high yield experimental plot

高產作物[kāo-ch'ǎn tsò-wù]: high yield crop

高教部[kāo-chiào pù]: Ministry of Higher Education (abbreviation of 高等教育部)

高深[kāo-shēn]: deep, profound

12 高棉 **[kāo-mién]** : Cambodia

高等 **[kāo-tĕng]** : advanced grade, high class

高等教育 **[kāo-tĕng chiào-yù]** : higher education

高等教育處 **[kāo-tĕng chiào-yù ch'ù]** : Office of Higher Education

高等教育部 **[kāo-tĕng chiào-yù pù]** : Ministry of Higher Education

高等學校 **[kāo-tĕng hsüéh-hsiào]** : institutions of higher education

高等師範教育 **[kāo-tĕng shīh-fàn chiào-yü]** : higher normal education

13 高傲 **[kāo-ào]** : haughty, overbearing, high and mighty

高粱 **[kāo-liáng]** : sorghum, kaoliang

14 高漲 **[kāo-chàng]** : to swell high, to gain momentum; upsurge, upswing; mounting, surging, soaring; on the rise, on the ascendant

15 高潮 **[kāo-ch'áo]** : high tide, upsurge, upswing, surging tide, climax, flood tide; on the upsurge

高價收買 **[kāo-chià shōu-măi]** : to buy at a high price

高踞於人民之上 **[kāo-chù yú jén-mín chīh shàng]** : to remain above the masses

高談闊論 **[kāo-t'án k'uò-lùn]** : high-flown talk, harangue; to talk bombastically

17 高舉 **[kāo-chŭ]** : to hold high, to raise high

高薪 **[kāo-hsīn]** : high salaried, well-paid

高擡物價 **[kāo-t'ái wù-chià]** : to force up the price

高壓 **[kāo-yā]** : high pressure, high voltage

高壓手段 **[kāo-yā shŏu-tuàn]** : steam roller tactics, high-handed measures

高壓輸電綫 **[kāo-yā shū-tièn hsièn]** : high tension power transmission line

高壓電焊 **[kāo-yā tièn-hàn]** : high pressure electric welding

18 高瞻遠矚 **[kāo-chān yüăn-chŭ]** : farsighted

高額 **[kāo-ó]** : high quota

20 高爐 **[kāo-lú]** : blast furnace, iron smelting furnace

— RADICAL 髟 190 —

— 8 Strokes —

6 鬆弛 **[sūng-shĭh]** : to relax, to loosen, to slacken; relaxation, looseness

9 鬆勁泄氣 **[sūng-chìn hsièh-ch'ì]** : slackness and despondency

17 鬆懈 **[sūng-hsièh]** : to relax, to loosen, to slacken, to slacken one's efforts; relaxation; lax

— RADICAL 鬥 191 —

鬥

4 鬥牛式火箭 [tòu-níu-shǐh huŏ-chièn]: Matador (a U.S. ground-to-ground guided missile)

7 鬥志 [tòu-chǐh]: fighting spirit, will to fight

鬥私批修 [tòu-ssū p'ī-hsīu]: combat selfishness and repudiate Revisionism (a slogan put forth by Lin Piao, presumably on Mao's instruction, on October 1, 1967)

8 鬥爭 [tòu-chēng]: to struggle, to combat; fight, struggle, strife, combat

鬥爭性强的 [tòu-chēng hsìng-ch'iáng te]: militant

鬥爭地主 [tòu-chēng tì-chŭ]: to settle scores with the landlords; to struggle against the landlords

10 鬥倒我字 [tòu-tăo wŏ-tzù]: to vanquish the word "I", to negate oneself completely (a phrase from the Cultural Revolution)

12 鬥智 [tòu-chǐh]: war of wits, battle of wits

16 鬥錯 [tòu-ts'ò]: to struggle against mistakenly

— 5 Strokes —

鬧

6 鬧名譽地位 [nào míng-yǘ tì-wèi]: to make a fuss over fame and fortune, to be after fame and fortune

8 鬧事 [nào-shǐh]: to create a disturbance, to make trouble, to stir up a fuss

9 鬧革命 [nào kó-mìng]: to work the revolution

鬧派別 [nào p'ài-piéh]: to be factious, sectarian or cliquish

16 鬧獨立性 [nào tú-lì-hsìng]: to take independent measures, to act independently, to commit acts of autonomism; assertion of independence

— RADICAL 鬯 192 —

— RADICAL 鬲 193 —

— RADICAL 鬼 194 —

鬼

鬼 [kuĕi]: ghost, devil, spirit, phantom, specter, apparition, demon

3 鬼子 [kuĕi-tzu]: devil, foreigner, enemy troops

8 鬼花招 [kuĕi huā-chāo]: ghostly hanky-panky (a phrase from the Cultural Revolution to refer to tricks played by anti-Maoists)

鬼怪 [kuĕi-kuài]: demons (an epithet for anti-Mao elements during the Cultural Revolution

10 鬼鬼祟祟 [kuĕi-kuĕi sùi-sùi]: shifty, evasive; secretly, clandestinely, stealthily, behind one's back

鬼鬼祟祟者 [kuĕi-kuĕi sùi-sùi-chĕ]: a sneak

12 鬼混 [kuĕi-hùn]: to live an idle, slovenly life, to idle away one's time

13 鬼話 [kuĕi-huà]: false words, nonsense;

ghostly language (i.e., a term used during the Cultural Revolution to refer to statements of anti-Mao opinion)

17 鬼臉 **[kuĕi-liĕn]**: devil's face, grimace, mask

— 4 Strokes —

魂

23 魂靈 **[hún-líng]**: soul, spirit

魁

11 魁偉 **[k'uéi-wĕi]**: stalwart, gigantic, majestic, stately, massive, grand, monumental, of great stature

— 5 Strokes —

魄

2 魄力 **[p'ò-lì]**: strength of spirit, spirit, strength, energy, nerve, audacity, physical vigor, courage

— 8 Strokes —

魍

18 魍魎鬼魅 **[wăng-liăng kuĕi-mèi]**: apparitions and specters (epithet for anti-Mao elements during the Cultural Revolution)

— 10 Strokes —

魑

15 魑魅 **[ch'īh-mèi]**: elf, hobgoblin; reactionary; evil person

— 11 Strokes —

魔

8 魔怪 **[mó-kuài]**: monsters (epithet for anti-Mao elements during the Cultural Revolution)

10 魔鬼 **[mó-kuĕi]**: Satan, the Devil; devils (epithet for anti-Mao elements during the Cultural Revolution)

11 魔術 **[mó-shù]**: magic, conjuring, conjuring tricks, juggling

魔術演員 **[mó-shù yĕn-yüán]**: magician, conjurer

— RADICAL 魚 195 —

魚

5 魚目混珠 **[yǘ-mù hùn-chū]**: to pass fish eyes for pearls, to mix the genuine with the fictitious

7 魚肝油 **[yǘ-kān yú]**: cod-liver oil

9 魚苗 **[yǘ-miáo]**: fry, spawn, small fish

12 魚場 **[yǘ-ch'ăng]**: fishery, fishing ground

13 魚雷 **[yǘ-léi]**: torpedo

魚雷艇 **[yǘ-léi t'ĭng]**: torpedo boat

— 4 Strokes —

魯

魯 **[lŭ]**: Shantung (abbreviation for 山東)

12 魯斯 **[lŭ-ssū]**: Luce, Henry (American journalist)

魯斯克 **[lŭ-ssū-k'ò]**: Rusk, Dean (former U.S. Secretary of State, 1961–1969)

— 5 Strokes —

鮑

6 鮑多恩[pào-tō-ēn]: King Baudoin (Belgium)

— 6 Strokes —

鮮

8 鮮明[hsiēn-míng]: vivid, transparent, crystalline, clear, bright

鮮明的對比[hsiēn-míng te tùi-pĭ]: sharp contrast, striking contrast

— 8 Strokes —

鯨

7 鯨吞[chīng-t'ūn]: to annex, to swallow up

— RADICAL 鳥 196 —

鳥

9 鳥取[niăo-ch'ŭ]: Tottori (Japan)

17 鳥瞰[niăo-k'àn]: a bird's eye view

— 3 Strokes —

鳳

5 鳳仙花[fèng-hsiēn huā]: balsam

鳴

8 鳴放[míng-fàng]: contending and blooming; frank airing of views

鳴放辯論[míng-fàng pièn-lùn]: to air one's views and carry on debates; mass airing of views and debates

— 4 Strokes —

鴉

3 鴉片戰爭[yā-p'ièn chàn-chēng]: Opium War (1839–1842)

10 鴉庫次庫[yā-k'ù-tz'ù-k'ù]: Yakutsk (U.S.S.R.)

— 5 Strokes —

鴕

11 鴕鳥[t'ó-niăo]: ostrich

鴕鳥政策[t'ó-niăo chèng-ts'è]: head-in-the-sand policy

鴨

14 鴨綠江[yā-lù chiāng]: Yalu River (Korea)

— 6 Strokes —

鴿

3 鴿子[kō-tzu]: dove

鴻

13 鴻溝[húng-kōu]: a great gap or chasm

— 10 Strokes —

鷄

4 鷄犬不留 **[chī-ch'üăn pù-líu]**: complete extermination, total extermination

鷄毛蒜皮 **[chī-máo suàn-p'í]**: trifles

7 鷄尾酒會 **[chī-wĕi chĭu-hùi]**: cocktail party, cocktail reception

— RADICAL 鹵 197 —

— RADICAL 鹿 198 —

鹿

8 鹿兒島 **[lù-érh-tăo]**: Kagoshima (Japan)

— RADICAL 麥 199 —

麥

4 麥什哈特阿曼 **[mài-shíh-hā-t'è à-màn]**: Muscat Oman

5 麥加 **[mài-chiā]**: Mecca

麥卡帕格 **[mài-k'ă-p'à-kó]**: Macapagal, Diosdado (Philippines political leader)

6 麥地那 **[mài-tì-nà]**: Medina

7 麥克阿瑟 **[mài-k'ò-à-sè]**: MacArthur, Douglas (American military figure)

麥克米倫 **[mài-k'ò-mĭ-lún]**: Macmillan, Harold (British statesman)

15 麥賢得 **[mài hsién-té]**: Mai Hsien-te (a sailor who performed heroically after having been injured by shrapnel and who received the praise of Mao and others)

— RADICAL 麻 200 —

麻

麻 **[má]**: hemp

10 麻紡廠 **[má-făng ch'ăng]**: flax mill

13 麻痹 **[má-pì]**: to numb, to lull; paralysis, lack of initiative; numb, insensitive

麻痹大意 **[má-pì tà-ì]**: to lower one's guard, to be caught off guard; not alert to, lacking vigilance, heedless, careless, insensitive and negligent, benumbed and careless

14 麻瘋 **[má-fēng]**: leprosy

15 麻醉 **[má-tsùi]**: to anesthetize, to stupefy, to numb the feelings

麻醉品 **[má-tsùi p'ĭn]**: anesthetic, narcotic

麻醉藥 **[má-tsùi yào]**: anesthetic

18 麻織品 **[má-chīh p'ĭn]**: linen fabrics, flax goods, ramie goods, hemp goods, jute goods

— 3 Strokes —

麽

7 麽些 **[mō-hsiēh]**: Moso (a minority nationality of Yunnan and Sikang)

— RADICAL 黄 201 —

黃

3 黃土 **[huáng-t'ŭ]**: loess

4 黃牛 **[huáng-níu]**: the common ox of China

6 黃衣國 **[huáng-ī kuó]**: Thailand

黃米 **[huáng-mĭ]**: glutinous millet

黃色 **[huáng-sè]**: yellow, yellow color, decadent, bourgeois

黃色歌曲 **[huáng-sè kō-ch'ŭ]**: decadent songs, bourgeois songs

黃色工會 **[huáng-sè kūng-hùi]**: bourgeois labor union, labor union oriented along bourgeois lines

黃色報刊 **[huáng-sè pào-k'ān]**: yellow journalism, gutter journalism

7 黃豆 **[huáng-tòu]**: soya bean

8 黃金 **[huáng-chīn]**: gold

黃金海岸 **[huáng-chīn hăi-àn]**: Gold Coast (now Ghana)

黃河 **[huáng-hó]**: Yellow River

黃昏 **[huáng-hūn]**: dusk, evening, nightfall

黃油 **[huáng-yú]**: butter

9 黃風 **[huáng-fēng]**: dusty wind

10 黃酒 **[huáng-chĭu]**: rice wine

黃海 **[huáng-hăi]**: Yellow Sea

黃病 **[huáng-pìng]**: jaundice

黃埔 **[huáng-p'ŭ]**: Whampoa

黃埔系 **[huáng-p'ŭ hsì]**: Whampoa Clique

11 黃麻 **[huáng-má]**: jute

黃梅戲 **[huáng-méi hsì]**: Anhui opera

黃梅天 **[huáng-méi t'iēn]**: the rainy season

黃梅雨 **[huáng-méi yŭ]**: rainfall in early summer (lower Yangtze region)

13 黃道 **[huáng-tào]**: zodiac

14 黃銅 **[huáng-t'úng]**: brass

18 黃醬 **[huáng-chiàng]**: soybean sauce

21 黃鐵礦 **[huáng-t'iĕh k'uàng]**: iron pyrite, fool's gold

— RADICAL 黍 202 —

— 3 Strokes —

黎 **[lí]**: Li (a minority nationality of Kuangtung and Hainan)

4 黎巴嫩 **[lí-pā-nèn]**: Lebanon

黎巴嫩共和國 **[lí-pā-nèn kùng-hó-kuó]**: Republic of Lebanon

— RADICAL 黑 203 —

黑

黑 **[hēi]**: black (with the implication of being evil, sinister, or anti-Party); Heilungkiang (abbreviation of 黑龍江)

2 黑人 **[hēi-jén]**: Negro, black

4 黑心 **[hēi-hsīn]**: black-hearted, villainous

黑市 **[hēi-shìh]**: black market

6 黑名單 **[hēi míng-tān]**: black list

黑色冶金業 **[hēi-sè yĕh-chīn yèh]**: ferrous metals industry, iron and steel industry

黑死病 **[hēi-ssŭ pìng]**: the plague, the "black death"

8 黑板 **[hēi-păn]**: blackboard

黑板報 **[hēi-păn pào]**: blackboard bulletin; a bulletin written on a blackboard

黑店 **[hēi-tièn]**: "black inn," i.e., a counter-revolutionary organization, a suspected clandestine organization for plotting against Mao and the Party (a phrase from the Cultural Revolution and a reference to 三家村, q.v.)

9 黑活 **[hēi-huó]**: illicit work

10 黑格爾 **[hēi-kó-ĕrh]**: Hegel (1770–1831)

11 黑船 **[hēi-ch'uán]**: unregistered ship, pirate ship

黑貨 **[hēi-huò]**: smuggled goods, stolen goods; opium

13 黑暗 **[hēi-àn]**: darkness; dark

黑暗時期 **[hēi-àn- shíh-ch'í]**: dark period

黑種 **[hēi-chŭng]**: Negro race, black race

黑會 **[hēi-hùi]**: black meeting, illicit meeting (i.e., during the Cultural Revolution, a meeting of conspiracy against Mao or the Party)

黑話 **[hēi-huà]**: mysterious language, black language (during the Cultural Revolution, statements against Mao)

黑道 **[hēi-tào]**: dark way, wrong road

14 黑旗 **[hēi-ch'í]**: black flag (during the Cultural Revolution, an emblem of Anti-Maoists)

黑幕 **[hēi-mù]**: black screen; what is done under cover

黑榜 **[hēi-păng]**: black list

15 黑綫 **[hēi-hsièn]**: the black line (i.e., the anti-Communist, anti-Socialist, anti-Mao thought; a term from the Cultural Revolution)

16 黑錢 **[hēi-ch'ién]**: illegitimate earnings

黑龍江 **[hēi-lúng-chiāng]**: Heilungkiang (Province); Amur River

17 黑幫 **[hēi-pāng]**: black gang (anti-Party and anti-Mao elements particularly in the fields of literature, culture and propaganda; a term from the Cultural Revolution)

黑穗病 **[hēi-sùi pìng]**: smut

— 4 Strokes —

黔

黔 **[ch'ién]**: Kweichow (abbreviation for 貴州)

默

10 默許 **[mò-hsǔ]**: to acquiesce; tacit consent, tacit acceptance

14 默認 **[mò-jèn]**: to acquiesce; tacit consent, tacit acceptance

— 5 Strokes —

黜

8 黜免 **[ch'ū-miěn]**: to dismiss

10 黜退 **[ch'ū-t'ùi]**: to dismiss

15 黜廢 **[ch'ū-fèi]**: to depose, to degrade

點

4 點火 **[tiěn-huǒ]**: to light a fire, to start trouble

6 點名 **[tiěn-míng]**: to call the roll; roll call

點名批判 **[tiěn-míng p'ī-p'àn]**: to criticize by name (i.e., public humiliation of those believed by the Party to have committed more serious misdeeds)

— 8 Strokes —

黨

2 黨八股 **[tǎng pā-kǔ]**: Party jargon, stereotyped Party writing

4 黨支部 **[tǎng chīh-pù]**: Party branch

黨中央 **[tǎng chūng-yāng]**: Party Central Committee (CCP)

黨內 **[tǎng-nèi]**: within the Party

黨內最大的走資本主義道路的當權派 **[tǎng-nèi tsùi-tà te tsǒu tzū-pěn chǔ-ì tào-lù te tǎng-ch'üán-p'ài]**: "the top Party person in authority taking the capitalist road" (an expression used during the early period of the Cultural Revolution to refer to Liu Shao-ch'i)

黨天下 **[tǎng t'iēn-hsià]**: "Party Kingdom," "Party Empire" (a variation on the old phrase 家天下, the "Empire," as identified with the Emperor's family)

5 黨外民主人士 **[tǎng-wài mín-chǔ jén-shìh]**: non-Party democrats

8 黨性 **[tǎng-hsìng]**: Party spirit, partisanship; party-spirited

黨的基層組織 **[tǎng te chī-ts'éng tsǔ-chīh]**: Party organization at the primary level

黨的核心 **[tǎng te hó-hsīn]**: Party nuclei

黨委 **[tǎng-wěi]**: Party committee

黨委書記 **[tǎng-wěi shū-chì]**: secretary of a Party committee

黨委會 **[tǎng-wěi-hùi]**: Party committee

9 黨政 **[tǎng chèng]**: the Party and the Government

黨紀 **[tǎng-chì]**: Party discipline

黨派 **[tǎng-p'ài]**: political parties, political factions

10 黨校委員會 **[tǎng-hsiào wěi-yüán-hùi]**: Party School Committee

11 黨章 **[tǎng-chāng]**: Party constitution, Party statutes

黨組 **[tǎng-tsǔ]**: Party cell, leading Party member's group

黨組織 **[tǎng tsǔ-chīh]**: Party organization

黨務 **[tǎng-wù]**: Party business

12 黨報委員會 **[tǎng-pào wěi-yüán-hùi]**: Party Press Committee

13 黨群 **[tǎng ch'ǘn]**: the Party and the masses

[14] 黨綱 **[tăng-kāng]**: Party program

黨團員 **[tăng-t'uán-yüán]**: Communist Party and Youth League members

[15] 黨課 **[tăng-k'ò]**: Party training

[20] 黨籍 **[tăng-chí]**: Party membership

黨齡 **[tăng-líng]**: the length of time one has been a Party member

— 15 Strokes —

黷

[8] 黷武主義 **[tú-wŭ chŭ-ì]**: militarism

黷武主義者 **[tú-wŭ chŭ-ì-chĕ]**: militarist, saber-rattler

— RADICAL 黹 204 —

— RADICAL 黽 205 —

— RADICAL 鼎 206 —

— RADICAL 鼓 207 —

鼓

[7] 鼓吹 **[kŭ-ch'ūi]**: to incite, to agitate for, to advocate, to publicize, to air, to speak up for, to encourage

鼓足幹勁 **[kŭ-tsú kàn-chìn]**: to go all out, to exert the utmost effort, to do one's utmost, to summon up one's energy

鼓足幹勁，力爭上游 **[kŭ-tsú kàn-chìn, lì-chēng shàng-yú]**: to go all out and aim high, to put forth the utmost effort and press consistently ahead

鼓足幹勁，力爭上游，多快好省 **[kŭ-tsú kàn-chìn, lì-chēng shàng-yú, tō k'uài hăo shĕng]**: to go all out, aim high, and achieve greater, faster, better, and more economical results

[9] 鼓風機 **[kŭ-fēng chī]**: blower, air blower, blowing engine

鼓風爐 **[kŭ-fēng lú]**: blast furnace

[10] 鼓起 **[kŭ-ch'ĭ]**: to summon up, to stir up

[11] 鼓動 **[kŭ-tùng]**: to agitate, to instigate, to excite, to provoke, to stir up, to fan, to arouse, to incite; incitement, excitement, instigation, provocation

[12] 鼓掌 **[kŭ-chăng]**: to applaud; applause

[15] 鼓勵 **[kŭ-lì]**: to stimulate, to encourage, to prompt, to animate, to inspire, to kindle, to spur, to provide inspiration for

鼓舞 **[kŭ-wŭ]**: to animate, to inspire, to stimulate, to invigorate, to spur on; encouragement, inspiration

鼓舞人心的 **[kŭ-wŭ jén-hsīn te]**: impressive, encouraging, exciting, stirring, inspiring, stimulating, animating, inspiriting

— RADICAL 鼠 208 —

— RADICAL 鼻 209 —

— RADICAL 齊 210 —

齊

4 齊心協力 **[ch'í-hsīn hsiéh-lì]**: of one mind and with united effort

7 齊步前進 **[ch'í-pù ch'ién-chìn]**: to march forward together

16 齊頭幷進 **[ch'í-t'óu pìng-chìn]**: to advance together, to do many things at once, to have many irons in the fire

— 3 Strokes —

齋

7 齋戒節 **[chāi-chièh chiéh]**: Ramadan, the fast of Ramadan

12 齋期 **[chāi-ch'í]**: fast days, period of fasting

— RADICAL 齒 211 —

齒

7 齒冷 **[ch'ǐh-lěng]**: to deride, to scorn

15 齒輪 **[ch'ǐh-lún]**: cogwheel

— 5 Strokes —

齟

22 齟齬 **[chǔ-yǔ]**: discord, quarrel, gap, dispute, strife, dissension; irregular, uneven, friction

— RADICAL 龍 212 —

龍

10 龍套 **[lúng-t'ào]**: dragon coat (i.e., refers to either the costume or those who wear the costume in classical Chinese theater; either guards of nobles or soldiers)

— 3 Strokes —

龐

3 龐大的 **[p'áng-tà te]**: tremendous, enormous, huge, gigantic

— RADICAL 龜 213 —

— RADICAL 龠 214 —